Criminology
A Sociological Understanding

Fifth Edition

Steven E. Barkan

University of Maine

Prentice Hall

Boston   Columbus   Indianapolis   New York   San Francisco   Upper Saddle River
Amsterdam   Cape Town   Dubai   London   Madrid   Milan   Munich   Paris   Montreal   Toronto
Delhi   Mexico City   São Paulo   Sydney   Hong Kong   Seoul   Singapore   Taipei   Tokyo

Editorial Director: *Vernon Anthony*
Acquisitions Editor: *Eric Krassow*
Assistant Editor: *Megan Heintz*
Editorial Assistant: *Lynda Cramer*
Director of Marketing: *David Gesell*
Marketing Manager: *Adam Kloza*
Senior Marketing Coordinator: *Alicia Wozniak*
Marketing Assistant: *Les Roberts*
Senior Managing Editor: *JoEllen Gohr*
Project Manager: *Jessica H. Sykes*
Senior Operations Supervisor: *Pat Tonneman*

Senior Art Director: *Diane Ernsberger*
Text and Cover Designer: *Mike Fruhbeis*
Cover Art: *Image Bank*
Media Editor: *Michelle Churma*
Lead Media Project Manager: *Karen Bretz*
Full-Service Project Management:
Ashley Schneider, S4Carlisle Publishing Services
Composition: *S4Carlisle Publishing Services*
Printer/Binder: *R.R. Donnelley/Willard*
Cover Printer: *Lehigh-Phoenix Color/Hagerstown*
Text Font: *Melior*

Library of Congress Cataloging-in-Publication Data
Barkan, Steven E.
    Criminology : a sociological understanding / Steven E. Barkan. — 5th ed.
        p. cm.
    Includes bibliographical references and index.
    ISBN-13: 978-0-13-510979-3 (alk. paper)
    ISBN-10: 0-13-510979-5 (alk. paper)
    1. Crime—Sociological aspects.   2. Criminology.   I. Title.
    HV6025.B278 2012
    364—dc22

                                                                    2010047572

10 9 8 7 6 5 4 3 2 1

Prentice Hall
is an imprint of

Casebound:
ISBN 10:   0-13-510979-5
ISBN 13: 978-0-13-510979-3

Loose leaf:
ISBN 10:   0-13-270558-3
ISBN 13: 978-0-13-270558-5

Dedication

To Barb,

Dave,

and Joe,

and in memory of my parents

Brief Contents

Contents

PART 2   EXPLAINING CRIME

PART 3   CRIMINAL BEHAVIORS

New to This Edition

This fifth edition has been thoroughly revised. It includes the latest crime and criminal justice statistics available as the book went to press, and it discusses the latest research on crime and criminal justice issues that had appeared by that time, with more than 160 recent references added and some older ones deleted. To have a more streamlined book even more readable than before, material that was deemed somewhat tangential has also been removed from each chapter. This edition continues the popular features of the previous one, including the chapter-opening *Crime in the News* vignettes ripped from the headlines (almost all from 2010) that engage students' attention and demonstrate the text's relevance for real-life events and issues; the *Crime and Controversy* and *International Focus* boxes, several of them new for this edition, that respectively highlight crime and justice issues within the United States and abroad; and the *What Would You Do?* feature at the end of each chapter that presents hypothetical scenarios on real-world situations faced by criminal justice professionals and average citizens alike.

Changes or additions to specific chapters include the following:

Chapter 1. Criminology and the Sociological Perspective. Recent Texas case involving a claimed use of self-defense; discussion of random assignment experiment by California Youth Authority.

Chapter 2. Public Opinion, the News Media, and the Crime Problem. New material on views on police use of force and on attitudes of Alaska Natives and American Indians about police; new International Focus box; updating where appropriate.

Chapter 3. The Measurement and Patterning of Criminal Behavior. New material on aspects of the African-American experience that reduce African-American criminality; updating where appropriate.

Chapter 4. Victims and Victimization. New material on indirect victimization and neighbors; new material on crime victims' views of crime and justice; updating where appropriate.

Chapter 5. Classical and Neoclassical Perspectives. New chapter, including new *Crime and Controversy* and *International Focus* boxes.

Chapter 6. Biological and Sociological Explanations. New material on molecular genetics research on aggression; expanded discussion of the biosocial perspective; updating where appropriate.

Chapter 7. Sociological Theories: Emphasis on Social Structure. Discussion of new research supporting differential opportunity theory; updating where appropriate.

Chapter 8. Sociological Theories: Emphasis on Social Process. New *Crime and Controversy* box; updating where appropriate.

Chapter 9. Sociological Theories: Critical Perspectives. Updating where appropriate.

Chapter 10. Violent Crime: Homicide, Assault, and Robbery. New section on violence against children; updating where appropriate.

Chapter 11. Violence Against Women. Child abuse material from this chapter moved to Chapter 10 to allow violence against women to be highlighted; new *International Focus* box; updating where appropriate.

Chapter 12. Property Crime and Fraud. New material on residential burglary victimization; new material on consumer sentiment and property crime; new material on situational prevention and expanded discussion of target hardening; revised discussion of identity theft; updating where appropriate.

Chapter 13. White-Collar and Organized Crime. New material on suspected fraud in the financial crisis of 2008 and 2009; new material on financial fraud by Bernard Madoff; expanded Crime and Controversy box; new material on suspected deception by Toyota motor company regarding reports of sudden acceleration; new material on suspected safety violations in BP oil spill; other updating where appropriate.

Chapter 14. Political Crime. Updating where appropriate.

Chapter 15. Consensual Crime. New material on drinking by high school students; expanded Crime and Controversy box; updating where appropriate.

Chapter 16. Policing: Dilemmas of Crime Control in a Democratic Society. Expanded Crime and Controversy box; revised discussion of directed police patrol and of zero-tolerance policing; new material on community policing (problem-oriented policing); updating where appropriate.

Chapter 17. Prosecution and Punishment. Revised discussion of the impact of race and ethnicity; new material on gross incapacitation; updating where appropriate.

Chapter 18. Conclusion: How Can We Reduce Crime? Updating where appropriate.

Preface

Welcome to this sociological introduction to the field of criminology! This book emphasizes the need to understand the social causes of criminal behavior in order to be able to significantly reduce crime. This approach is similar to the approach followed in the field of public health. In the case of a disease such as cancer, we naturally try to determine what causes it so that we can prevent people from contracting it. Although it is obviously important to treat people who already have cancer, there will always be more cancer patients unless we discover its causes and then do something about these causes. The analogy to crime is clear: Unless we discover the causes of crime and do something about them, there will always be more criminals.

Unfortunately, this is not the approach the United States has taken during the past few decades. Instead, it has relied on a "get tough" approach to the crime problem that relies on more aggressive policing, longer and more certain prison terms, and the building of more and more prisons. The nation's prison and jail population has soared and has reached about 2.3 million. Many criminologists warn that the surge in prisoners is setting the stage for a crime increase down the line, given that almost all of these prisoners will one day be returned to their communities, many of them penniless, without jobs, and embittered by their incarceration.

In offering a sociological understanding of crime, this book suggests that the "get tough" approach is short-sighted because it ignores the roots of crime in the social structure and social inequality of society. To reduce crime, we must address these structural conditions and appreciate the role that factors such as race and ethnicity, gender, and social class play in criminal behavior. Students in criminology courses in sociology departments will especially benefit from the sociological understanding that this book offers. But this understanding is also important for students in courses in criminal justice or criminology departments. If crime cannot be fully understood without appreciating its structural context, then students in all these departments who do not develop this appreciation have only an incomplete understanding of the reasons for crime and of the most effective strategies to reduce it.

Although street crime has declined since the early 1990s, it remains a national problem, as the residents of high-crime communities know all too well. Meanwhile, white-collar crime continues to cost tens of billions of dollars and thousands of lives annually, even as it receives far less attention than mass murder, terrorism, and everyday violent and property crime.

In presenting a sociological perspective on crime and criminal justice, this book highlights issues of race and ethnicity, gender, and social class in every chapter and emphasizes the criminogenic effects of the social and physical features of urban neighborhoods. This fifth edition features a new chapter on classical and neoclassical perspectives and continues to include certain chapters that remain uncommon in other criminology texts, including Chapter 2: Public Opinion, the News Media, and the Crime Problem; Chapter 14: Political Crime; and Chapter 18: Conclusion: How Can We Reduce Crime? In addition, the book's criminal justice chapters, Chapter 16 (Policing: Dilemmas of Crime Control in a Democratic Society) and Chapter 17 (Prosecution and Punishment), continue to address two central themes in the sociological understanding of crime and criminal justice: (1) the degree to which race and ethnicity, gender, and social class affect the operation of the criminal justice system; and (2) the extent to which reliance on the criminal justice system can reduce the amount of crime. These two themes, in turn, reflect two more general sociological issues: the degree to which inequality affects the dynamics of social institutions and the extent to which formal sanctions affect human behavior.

Supplements

INSTRUCTOR SUPPLEMENTS

The instructor supplements available for the fifth edition include:

- Instructor's Manual with Test Bank
- PowerPoint presentations
- MyTest computerized test bank
- Test item file for WebCT
- Test item file for Blackboard/Course Compass

To access supplementary materials online, instructors need to request an instructor access code. Go to **www.pearsonhighered.com/irc** to register for an instructor access code. Within 48 hours of registering, you will receive a confirming e-mail including an instructor access code. Once you have received your code, locate your text in the online catalog and click on the Instructor Resources button on the left side of the catalog product page. Select a supplement, and a login page will appear. Once you have logged in, you can access instructor material for all Prentice Hall textbooks. If you have any difficulties accessing the site or downloading a supplement, please contact Customer Service at http://247.prenhall.com.

ALTERNATIVE BOOK VERSIONS

Alternatives to traditional printed textbooks, such as our "Student Value Editions" and e-book versions of the text in the "CourseSmart" platform, will be offered.

CourseSmart is an exciting new choice for students looking to save money. As an alternative to purchasing the printed textbook, students can purchase an electronic version of the same content. With a CourseSmart eTextbook, students can search the text, make notes online, print out reading assignments that incorporate lecture notes, and bookmark important passages for later review. For more information, or to purchase access to the CourseSmart eTextbook, visit www.coursesmart.com

Acknowledgments

The first edition of this book stated my personal and intellectual debt to Norman Miller and Forrest Dill, and I continue to acknowledge how much I owe them. Norman Miller was my first undergraduate sociology professor and quickly helped me fall in love with the discipline. He forced me to ask questions about society that I probably still haven't answered. I and the many other students he influenced can offer only an inadequate "thank you" for caring so much about us and, to paraphrase a verse from a great book, for training us in the way we should go. Forrest Dill was my mentor in graduate school and introduced me to criminology and the sociology of law and to the craft of scholarship. His untimely death almost three decades ago continues to leave a deep void.

My professional home since graduate school has been the Sociology Department at the University of Maine. I continue to owe my colleagues there an intellectual debt for sharing and reaffirming my sense of the importance of social structure and social inequality to an understanding of crime and other contemporary issues. They continue to provide a warm, supportive working environment that often seems all too rare in academia.

I also wish to thank the editorial, production, and marketing staff at Prentice Hall for their help on all aspects of the book's revision. In particular, the assistance of development editor Elisa Rogers on this edition was indispensable, as was Eric Krassow's and Tim Peyton's faith in the vision underlying the book. In addition, thanks go to Jessica Sykes for her help and patience in the final stages of the book's production.

I also wish to thank the reviewers who read the fifth edition and provided very helpful comments and criticism. Any errors that remain, of course, are mine alone. These reviewers are: Brian Colwell, University of Missouri; Corey Colyer, West Virginia University; Sheryl J. Grana, University of Minnesota-Duluth; Allison Ann Payne, Villanova University; and Lisa Anne Zilney, Montclair State University.

Finally, as in my first four editions, I acknowledge with heartfelt gratitude the love and support that my wife, Barbara Tennent, and my sons, Dave and Joe, bring to my life. They put up with my need to write, my quirks, and my reactions to the success and failure of our favorite sports teams more than any husband and father has a right to expect.

The fifth edition of this book is again dedicated to my late parents, Morry and Sylvia Barkan, who instilled in me respect for learning and sympathy for those less fortunate than I. As I continue to think about them after so many years, I can only hope that somewhere they are smiling with pride over this latest evidence of their legacy.

About the Author

Steven E. Barkan is professor of sociology at the University of Maine, where he has taught since 1979. His teaching and research interests include criminology, sociology of law, and social movements. He was the 2008–2009 president of the Society for the Study of Social Problems and had previously served as a member of the SSSP Board of Directors, as chair of its Law and Society Division and Editorial and Publications Committee, and as an advisory editor of its journal, *Social Problems*. He is currently a member of the council of the Sociology of Law Section of the American Sociological Association and previously served on its student paper award committee as well as that of the ASA Crime, Law, and Deviance Section.

Professor Barkan has written many journal articles dealing with topics such as racial prejudice and death-penalty attitudes, views on police brutality, political trials, and feminist activism. These articles have appeared in the *American Sociological Review, Journal for the Scientific Study of Religion, Journal of Crime and Justice, Journal of Research in Crime and Delinquency, Justice Quarterly, Social Forces, Social Problems, Sociological Forum, Sociological Inquiry,* and other journals. He has also authored another text, *Law and Society: An Introduction*, with Prentice Hall.

Professor Barkan welcomes comments from students and faculty about this book. They may e-mail him at BARKAN@MAINE.EDU or send regular mail to Department of Sociology, 5728 Fernald Hall, University of Maine, Orono, Maine 04469–5728.

CHAPTER

one

Criminology and
the Sociological
Perspective

Crime in the News

ust before and after Easter in the spring of 2010, a series of shootings around the nation captured headlines and forced friends and relatives to mourn. In Alhambra, California, a city with a population of 93,000 just a few miles northeast of Los Angeles, a 25-year-old man fatally shot his pregnant girlfriend and their infant son before killing himself. A friend of the family said the man was unemployed and had recently become very depressed. In the nation's heartland, two Kansas City residents were found dead in separate gunshot incidents. One was a 25-year-old woman, the other a 20-year-old man. Witnesses saw one man fleeing in a car after the first shooting and two men fleeing in a minivan after the second shooting.

Back east, three people were shot to death in Boston in separate incidents. One of the victims, an auto mechanic with three children, was found in a church parking lot. A local minister lamented, "This murder occurred on church property during Holy Week, which is the holiest week in the Christian calendar." The victim's sister said she could not fathom why anyone would have wanted to kill him, and she added that "the coping is not easy, because he was my brother."

Sources: Andersen 2010; Becker 2010; McIntire 2010; Vaughn 2010.

These many deaths remind us that violence and other street crime continue to trouble people across the nation. Although the U.S. crime rate has actually declined since the early 1990s, the prison and jail population has almost doubled since then, to more than 2.3 million, the highest rate of incarceration in the Western world. The criminal justice system costs about $215 billion annually, compared to only $36 billion in the early 1980s. Why do we have so much violence and other crime? What can we do to reduce our crime rate? What difference do police and prisons make? Could our dollars be spent more wisely? How serious is white-collar crime? Is the war on drugs working? What role do race and ethnicity, social class, and gender play in criminal behavior and in the response of the criminal justice system to such behavior? These are just a few of the questions this book tries to answer.

The rationale for the book is simple. Crime is one of our most important social problems and also one of the least understood. Most of our knowledge about crime comes from what we read in newspapers or see on TV or the Internet. From these sources, we get a distorted picture of crime and hear about solutions to the crime problem that ultimately will do little to reduce it. These are harsh accusations, to be sure, but they are ones with which most criminologists probably agree.

A major reason crime is so misunderstood is that the popular sources of our knowledge about crime say little about its social roots. Crime is not only an individual phenomenon but also a social one. Individuals commit crime, but their social backgrounds profoundly shape their likelihood of doing so. In this sense, crime is no different from other behaviors sociologists study. This basic sociological understanding of crime has an important social policy implication: if crime is rooted in the way our society is organized, then crime-reduction efforts will succeed only to the extent that they address the structural roots of criminality.

This book presents a sociological understanding of crime and criminal justice, an approach commonly called **sociological criminology.** As we will see later, for most of its history virtually all criminology was sociological criminology, and this two-word term would have been redundant. This view of criminology gave explicit attention to issues of poverty and race and ethnicity, as well as to the structure of communities and social relationships. As John Hagan (1994), a former president of the American Society of Criminology, once observed, a sociological criminology is thus a *structural* criminology. It takes into account the social and physical characteristics of communities and the profound influence of race and ethnicity, social class, and gender.

In the past few decades, criminology has moved away from this structural focus toward individualistic explanations, and sociologists worry that sociology and criminology are becoming isolated from each other (Short 2007). The fields of biology and psychology are vying with sociology for prominence in the study of crime. These fields enliven the discipline and have expanded criminology's interdisciplinary focus. However, they ultimately fail to answer three of the most central questions in criminology: (1) Why do crime rates differ across locations and over time? (2) Why do crime rates differ according to the key dimensions of structured social inequality: race and ethnicity, social class, and gender? (3) How and why is the legal response to crime shaped by race and ethnicity, social class, and gender and by other extralegal variables? Only a sociological criminology can begin to answer these questions, which must be answered if we are to have any hope of seriously reducing crime and of achieving a just legal system.

A sociological criminology is not only a structural criminology. To be true to the sociological perspective, it should also be a criminology that debunks incorrect perceptions about crime and false claims about the effectiveness of various crime-control strategies (Currie 2010). In addition, it should expose possible injustice in the application of the criminal label.

These several themes are addressed throughout the book. Part 1, Understanding Crime and Victimization, introduces the sociological perspective and discusses public beliefs about crime and criminal justice. It also discusses what is known about the amount and social patterning of crime and victimization. Part 2, Explaining Crime, critically reviews the major explanations of crime and criminality and discusses their implications for crime reduction. These explanations are integrated into the chapters contained in Part 3, Criminal Behaviors. These chapters discuss the major forms of crime and ways of reducing them. The fourth and final part of the book, Controlling and Preventing Crime, explores among other things two important issues for a sociological understanding of the criminal justice system: (1) To what degree do race and ethnicity, class, and gender unjustly affect the chances of arrest, conviction, and imprisonment? (2) To what degree do arrest and punishment reduce criminal behavior? The concluding chapter of the book presents a sociological prescription for crime reduction.

Our sociological journey into crime and criminal justice begins by reviewing the sociological perspective and discussing the mutual relevance of sociology and criminology. We look briefly at the development of sociological criminology and at its approaches to crime and criminal justice and review some key legal terms and concepts.

The Sociological Perspective

Above all else, the **sociological perspective** stresses that people are *social beings* more than individuals. This means that society profoundly shapes their behavior, attitudes, and life chances. People growing up in societies with different cultures tend to act and think differently from one another. People within a given society growing up in various locations and under diverse socioeconomic circumstances also tend to act and think differently. We cannot understand why people think and behave as they do without understanding their many social backgrounds.

This perspective derives from the work of Émile Durkheim (1858–1917), a French sociologist and a founder of the discipline. Durkheim stressed that social forces influence our behavior and attitudes. In perhaps his most famous study, he found that even suicide, normally regarded as the most individualistic act possible, has social roots (Durkheim 1952 [1897]). Examining data in France and elsewhere, Durkheim found that suicide rates varied across locations and across different kinds of people. Protestants, for example, had higher suicide rates than Catholics. He explained these differences by focusing on structural characteristics, in particular the level of social integration, of the locations and people he studied. People in groups with high social integration, or strong bonds to others within their group, have lower suicide rates. We return to Durkheim's work on suicide in Chapter 6, but for now we simply cite it as a powerful sociological analysis that emphasizes the influence of social structure on an individual behavior such as suicide.

The sociological perspective emphasizes that people are social beings more than individuals. This means that society shapes our behavior, attitudes, and life chances.

What exactly is **social structure?** Briefly, social structure refers to how a society is organized in terms of social relationships and social

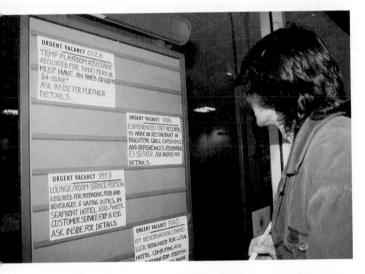

A job-seeker consults a bulletin board listing some employment possibilities. C. Wright Mills considered unemployment a public issue that results from structural problems in society.

interaction. It is both *horizontal* and *vertical*. Horizontal social structure refers to the social and physical characteristics of communities and the networks of social relationships to which an individual belongs. Vertical social structure is more commonly called **social inequality** and refers to how a society ranks different groups of people. In U.S. society, social class, race and ethnicity, and gender are key characteristics that help determine where people rank and whether some are "more equal" than others.

Sociologist C. Wright Mills (1959) emphasized that social structure lies at the root of **private troubles.** If only a few individuals, he wrote, are unemployed, then their private troubles are their own fault. But if masses of individuals are unemployed, structural forces must account for their bad fortune. What people may define as private troubles are thus more accurately described as **public issues,** wrote Mills. Their personal troubles result from the intersection of their personal biography with historical and social conditions. Mills referred to the ability to understand the structural and historical basis for personal troubles as the **sociological imagination.** Once people acquire a sociological imagination, they are better able both to understand and to change the social forces underlying their private troubles.

As Mills's comments suggest, sociology's emphasis on the structural basis for individual behavior and personal troubles often leads it to challenge conventional wisdom. Max Weber (1864–1920), another founder of sociology, echoed this theme when he noted that one of sociology's most important goals was to uncover "inconvenient facts" (Gerth and Mills 1946). As Peter Berger (1963) observed in his classic book, *Invitation to Sociology*, the "first wisdom" of sociology is that things are not always what they seem; research often exposes false claims about reality and taken-for-granted assumptions about social life and social institutions. Berger referred to this sociological tendency as the **debunking motif** and added that one of its implications is that sociologists often study so-called unrespectable elements of social life. Not surprisingly, U.S. sociologists have often studied the poor and the deviants among us, especially in urban communities, and the problems they face.

Review and Discuss

What do we mean by the *sociological perspective*? How does this perspective help us to understand the origins of crime and possible ways of reducing crime?

MUTUAL RELEVANCE OF SOCIOLOGY AND CRIMINOLOGY

With this brief discussion of the sociological perspective in mind, the continuing relevance of sociology for criminology immediately becomes clear (Short 2007). Perhaps most important, crime, victimization, and criminal justice cannot be fully understood without appreciating their structural context. Using Mills's terminology, crime and victimization are public issues rather than private troubles. They are rooted in the social and physical characteristics of communities, in the network of relationships in which people interact, and in the structured social inequalities of race and ethnicity, social class, and gender. Reflecting this point, many of criminology's important concepts, including anomie, relative deprivation, and social conflict, draw from concepts originally developed in the larger body of sociology. Moreover, research methodology originating in sociology provides the basis for much criminological research.

Criminology is just as relevant for its parent field of sociology because of the structural basis for criminality. If crime and victimization derive from community characteristics, social relationships, and inequality, criminological insights both reinforce and advance sociological understanding of all these areas. Crime, victimization, and legal punishment are certainly important negative life chances for people at the bottom of the socioeconomic ladder. More than most other subfields in sociology, criminology shows us how and why social inequality is, as Elliott Currie (1985:160) once put it, "enormously destructive of human personality and of social order." By the same token, positions at the top of the socioeconomic ladder contribute to a greater probability of white-collar crime that results in little or no punishment. Again, perhaps more than most other sociological subfields, criminology illuminates the privileges of those at the top of the social hierarchy.

Another major dimension of inequality, gender, also has important consequences for criminality and victimization and, perhaps, legal punishment. Criminological findings have contributed to the larger body of sociological knowledge about the importance of gender (Renzetti 2011). More generally, the study of crime has furthered understanding of many standard sociological concepts, such as alienation, community, inequality, organization, and social control (Short 2007).

Review and Discuss

In what ways are the disciplines of sociology and criminology relevant for each other?

RISE OF SOCIOLOGICAL CRIMINOLOGY

Many of the themes just outlined shaped the rise of sociological criminology in the United States during the twentieth century. Because Part 2 discusses the development of criminological theory in greater detail, here we simply sketch this history to underscore the intellectual connection between criminology and sociology. Before we do so, it will be helpful to review some basic concepts.

All societies have social **norms,** or standards of behavior. Behavior that violates these norms and arouses negative social reactions is called **deviance.** In most traditional societies studied by anthropologists, the norms remain unwritten and informal and are called **customs.** These customs are enforced through informal **social control** (society's restraint of norm-violating behavior) such as ostracism and ridicule. People obey customs because they believe in them and because they fear the society's informal sanctions. In larger, more modern societies, informal norms and sanctions have less power over individual behavior. Norms tend to be more formal, meaning that they tend to be written, or codified. These formal norms are called **laws.** Social control is also more formal and takes the form of specialized groups of people (legislators, police officers, judges, and corrections officials) who create laws, interpret them, and apprehend and punish law violators. With these concepts in mind, we now trace the rise of sociological criminology.

For much of recorded history, people attributed crime and deviance to religious forces. Individuals were said to commit these behaviors because God or, in polytheistic societies, the gods were punishing or testing them. During the Middle Ages, deviance was blamed on the devil. In the eighteenth century, the *classical school* of criminology stressed that criminals rationally choose to commit crime after deciding that the potential rewards outweigh the risks. In view of this, said classical scholars, legal punishment needed to be severe enough only to deter potential criminals from breaking the law.

During the nineteenth century, scholars began to investigate the causes of criminal behavior through scientific investigation. Perhaps the first such criminologist was Adolphe Quetelet (1796–1874), a Belgian astronomer and mathematician who gathered and analyzed crime data in France. Crime rates there, he found, remained fairly stable over time and, further, were higher for young adults than for older ones and higher among men and the poor than among women and the nonpoor.

Later in the century, Émile Durkheim began providing his major contributions. He stressed the primacy of social structure over the individual and thus established the sociological paradigm. He also observed that deviance will always exist because social norms are never strong enough to prevent *all* rule breaking. Even in a "society of saints," he said, such as a monastery, rules will be broken and negative social reactions aroused. Because Durkheim thought deviance was inevitable, he considered it a *normal* part of every healthy society and stressed its functions for social stability (Durkheim 1962 [1895]). The punishment of deviance, he said, clarifies social norms and reinforces social ties among those doing or watching the punishing. Durkheim further argued that deviance is necessary for social change to take place. A society without deviance, he said, would be one with no freedom of thought; hence, social change would not be possible. A society thus cannot have social change without also having deviance.

Quetelet's and Durkheim's interest in the social roots of crime gave way to interest in its biological roots, as physicians and other researchers began to investigate the biological basis for criminal behavior. Although their methodology was seriously flawed and many of their views were racist, their perspective influenced public and scholarly thinking on crime. The recent rise of biological explanations of crime indicates their continuing popularity for understanding criminal behavior.

At the end of the nineteenth century, famed African-American scholar W. E. B. DuBois disputed a biological basis for crime in his renowned book *The Philadelphia Negro* (DuBois 1899), in which he attributed the relatively high crime rates of African-Americans to negative social conditions rather than to biological problems. His analysis of crime in Philadelphia is today regarded as an early classic of sociological criminology (Gabbidon 2007). DuBois was also one of the first social scientists to write about possible racial discrimination in arrest and sentencing. Another African-American scholar, Ida B. Wells-Barnett, documented perhaps the most extreme use of law in this regard in an 1892 pamphlet titled *Southern Horrors*, an indictment of lynch law (Wells-Barnett 2002). Wells-Barnett wrote the pamphlet after three of her friends were lynched in Memphis, Tennessee, where Wells-Barnett co-owned a newspaper named *Free Speech*. After she editorialized against these and other lynchings, whites threatened to lynch her and other *Free Speech* staff and forced the newspaper to shut down.

The sociological study of crime advanced further at the University of Chicago after the turn of the twentieth century (Short 2007). Scholars there noticed that high crime rates in Chicago's inner-city neighborhoods stayed stable from one year to the next, even as certain immigrant groups moved out and others moved in. They attributed these crime rates to certain social and physical conditions of the neighborhoods, including their stark poverty and residential instability, that reflected a breakdown in conventional social institutions.

One student of the Chicago sociologists was Edwin Sutherland, who soon became a towering figure in the development of sociological criminology. Sensitive to the

criminogenic (crime-causing) conditions of urban neighborhoods, Sutherland was especially interested in how and why these conditions promote criminality and emphasized the importance of peer influences in his famous *differential association theory*. Sutherland also criticized biological explanations of crime, which were still popular in the 1930s and 1940s. He further developed the concept of *white-collar crime* and was sharply critical of the illegal and harmful practices of the nation's biggest corporations. At the heart of his sociological criminology was a concern for issues of race, poverty, and political and economic power.

At about the same time, Robert K. Merton, a Columbia University sociologist, developed his *anomie theory* of deviance. Borrowing heavily from Durkheim, Merton attributed deviance to the poor's inability to achieve economic success in a society that highly values it. His theory was perhaps the most "macro"

Chicago was the site of important sociological research that was carried out by scholars at the University of Chicago in the early twentieth century.

of all the early structural theories of crime and remains influential today. During the 1970s, a new *social control* or *social bonding theory* of criminal behavior rose to prominence. Drawing on Durkheim, this theory emphasized the criminogenic effects of weak bonds to social institutions. Although this theory focused on social relationships, it was less of a macro-structural theory than its social disorganization and anomie forebears.

The 1960s and early 1970s were also a turbulent era marked by intellectual upheaval in several academic disciplines, perhaps most of all sociology. Some sociologists asserted that society was rooted in conflict between the "haves" and "have-nots" in society. In the study of crime and deviance, *labeling* and *conflict theories* emphasized bias and discrimination in the application of criminal labels and in the development of criminal laws. Shortly thereafter, new feminist understandings of gender and society began to make their way into criminology, as feminists criticized the male bias of traditional criminological theories and called attention to the gendered nature of crime and victimization.

Today all of these sociological approaches inform the study of crime and criminal justice. As this textbook will indicate, sociological criminology's emphasis on the structural origins of crime and on the impact of race/ethnicity and poverty continues to guide much contemporary theory and research. To aid your understanding of sociological perspectives on crime, we now discuss some important concepts in the study of crime and deviance.

In this famous photo, a woman reacts in horror after a student is slain by National Guard troops at Kent State University in Ohio on May 4, 1970. The 1960s and early 1970s were a turbulent era that sparked the use of labeling and conflict theories in the study of crime and deviance.

Crime, Deviance, and Criminal Law

Edwin Sutherland (1947) defined **criminology** as the study of the making of laws, of the breaking of laws, and of society's reaction to the breaking of laws. Put another way, criminology is the scientific study of the creation of criminal law, of the causes and dynamics of criminal behavior, and of society's attempt through the criminal justice system and other efforts to punish, control, and prevent crime. Note that criminology as a social science differs from crime-scene investigation, or *forensic science*, featured in *CSI* and other TV shows.

The term *crime* has already appeared many times in this chapter, but what actually is crime? Most simply, **crime** is behavior that is considered so harmful that it is banned by a criminal law. Though straightforward, this definition begs some important questions. For example, how harmful must a behavior be before it is banned by a criminal law? Is it possible for a behavior to be harmful but not banned? Is it possible for a behavior to be banned but not very harmful? Who decides what is or is not harmful? What factors affect such decisions?

As these questions indicate, the definition of crime is not all that straightforward after all. Instead, it is problematic. In sociology, this view of crime derives from the larger study of deviant behavior, of which crime is obviously one very important type. Recall that deviance is behavior that violates social norms and arouses negative social reactions. Durkheim's monastery example, given earlier, raises an interesting point. Behavior considered deviant in a monastery, such as talking, would be perfectly acceptable elsewhere. This illustrates that deviance is a *relative* concept: whether a given behavior is judged deviant depends not on the behavior itself but on the circumstances under which it occurs. Consider murder, the most serious of interpersonal crimes. As a behavior, murder involves killing someone. We consider this act so horrible that sometimes we execute people for it. Yet if soldiers kill someone in wartime, they are doing their job, and if they kill several people in a particularly heroic fashion, they may receive a medal. The behavior itself, killing, is the same, but the circumstances surrounding it determine whether we punish the killer or award a medal.

Whether a given behavior is considered deviant also depends on where it occurs, as the monastery example reminds us. What is considered deviant in one society may be considered acceptable in another. Another way of saying this is that deviance is *relative in space*. As just one example, anthropologists have found that sexual acts condemned in some societies are often practiced in others (Goode 2008a).

Killing in wartime is considered necessary and even heroic, but killing in most other circumstances is considered a crime (homicide).

Deviance is also *relative in time*: within the same society, what is considered deviant in one time period may not be considered deviant in a later period, and vice versa. For example, the use of cocaine, marijuana, and opium was very common (and legal) in the United States just over a century ago, even though all three drugs are illegal today. Many over-the-counter medicines contained opium for such problems as depression, insomnia, and various aches and pains. Marijuana was used to relieve migraines, menstrual cramps, and toothaches. Many over-the-counter products, including Coca-Cola, contained cocaine. Coke was popular when it hit the market in 1894 because it made people feel so good when they drank it (Goode 2008b).

By saying that deviance is a relative concept, we emphasize that deviance is not a quality of a behavior itself but, rather, the result of what other people think about the behavior. This was a central insight of sociologist Howard S. Becker (1963), who famously wrote that "deviance is not a quality of the act the person commits, but rather a consequence of the application by others of rules or sanctions to an 'offender.' The deviant is one to whom that label has been successfully applied; deviant behavior is behavior that people so label."

Becker's observation alerts us to two possibilities. First, some harmful behaviors, such as white-collar crime (see Chapter 12), may not be considered deviant, either because "respectable" people do them, because they occur secretly, or because people know about them but do not deem them harmful. Second, some less harmful behaviors, such as prostitution, may still be considered deviant because people are morally opposed to them or do not like the kinds of people (poor, nonwhite, etc.) who are doing them.

CONSENSUS AND CONFLICT IN THE CREATION OF CRIMINAL LAW

The previous discussion raises two related questions about criminal laws: (1) Why do criminal laws get established? (2) Whom do criminal laws benefit? In criminology, consensus and conflict theories of crime, law, and society try to answer these questions. These views derive from related perspectives in the larger field of sociology (Ritzer 2008).

When Coca-Cola was first manufactured in 1894, it contained cocaine, contributing in no small measure to its instant popularity.

Consensus theory originates in Durkheim's work. It assumes a consensus among people from all walks of life on what the social norms of behavior are and should be. Formal norms, or laws, represent the interests of all segments of the public. People obey laws not because they fear being punished but because they have internalized the norms and regard them as appropriate to obey. When crime and deviance occur, they violate these widely accepted norms, and punishment of the behavior is necessary to ensure continuing social stability.

Conflict theory (discussed further in Chapter 9) derives from the work of Karl Marx and Friedrich Engels and is generally the opposite of consensus theory. It assumes that members of the public disagree on many of society's norms, with their disagreement reflecting their disparate positions based on their inequality of wealth and power. Laws represent the views of the powerful, not the powerless, and help them stay at the top of society's hierarchy and keep the powerless at the bottom. Behavior labeled criminal by laws is conduct by the poor that threatens the interests of the powerful. The powerful may commit very harmful behaviors, but because they determine which laws are created, their behaviors are often legal, or at least not harshly punished even if they are illegal.

These two theories have important implications for how we define and understand crime. In consensus theory, crime is defined simply, if somewhat tautologically, as any behavior that violates a criminal law, to recall our earlier straightforward definition. Criminal law in turn is thought to both represent and protect the interests of all members of society. In conflict theory, the definition of crime is more problematic: it is just as important to consider why some behaviors *do not become* illegal as to consider why others *are* illegal. A conflict view of crime, law, and society thus defines crime more broadly than does a consensus view. In particular, it is willing to consider behaviors as crimes in the larger sense of the word if they are harmful, even if they are not illegal.

Both theories have their merits. The greatest support for consensus theory comes from criminal laws banning the criminal behaviors we call *street crime,* which all segments of society condemn and which victimizes the poor more than the wealthy. Although the historical roots of some of these laws lie in the conflict between rich and poor, today they cannot be said to exist for the protection of the wealthy and powerful. The greatest evidence for conflict theory perhaps comes from corporate misconduct, which is arguably more socially harmful than street crime but is less severely punished. Both kinds of behavior are discussed in the chapters ahead.

GOALS OF CRIMINAL LAW

Criminal law in the United States and other Western democracies ideally tries to achieve several goals. Because criminal law is obviously an essential component of the criminal justice system, perhaps its most important goal is to *help keep the public safe from crime and criminals or,* to put it another way, *to prevent and control crime and criminal behavior.*

A second goal of criminal law is to *articulate our society's moral values and concerns*, a goal that consensus theory emphasizes. Ideally, criminal law bans behaviors that our society considers immoral or wrong for other reasons. Murder is an obvious example here. More controversially, criminal law also bans the use of certain drugs, prostitution, and some other behaviors that people voluntarily commit and for which there may be no unwilling victims. We call these behaviors *consensual* or *victimless* crimes, and critics say that society's effort to ban them amounts to "legislating morality" and may in fact do more harm than good (Meier and Geis 2007).

A third goal of criminal law and the larger criminal justice system is to *protect the rights and freedoms of the nation's citizenry* by protecting it from potential governmental abuses of power. This is what is meant by the *rule of law* that is so fundamental to a democracy and is lacking in authoritarian nations where police and other government agents take away their citizens' freedom and otherwise abuse them. This consideration helps us to understand why reports of torture and abuse by U.S. personnel of persons captured in the Iraq War aroused so much concern during the past decade: the alleged abuse was committed by personnel of a democratic nation and violated the rules of international law governing the treatment of military prisoners and detainees (Cole 2009).

Reports of abuse and torture of Iraqi detainees by U.S. personnel aroused much controversy, in part because critics said these incidents violated international law.

AN OVERVIEW OF CRIMINAL LAW

We turn now from this basic understanding of criminal law to its origins and current dimensions. Law in the United States has its origins in English **common law,** which began during the reign of Henry II in the twelfth century. Over the centuries, England developed a complex system of law that specified the types of illegal behaviors, the punishment for these behaviors, and the elements that had to be proved before someone could be found guilty of a crime. English judges had great powers to interpret the law and in effect to make new *case law.* As a result, much of English law derived from judges' rulings rather than from legislatures' statutes, as in most continental European nations.

During this time the jury was developed to replace ordeals as the chief way to determine a defendant's guilt or innocence. However, the jury's power was limited because jurors could be punished if they found a defendant innocent. Its power and importance grew considerably in 1670 after William Penn was arrested and tried for preaching about Quakerism. When the jurors refused to convict him, the judge imprisoned and starved them. In response, an English court ruled that juries could not be punished for their verdicts. This ruling allowed juries to acquit defendants with impunity and strengthened their historic role as protectors of defendants against arbitrary state power (Barkan 1983).

When English colonists came to the New World beginning with the Pilgrims, they naturally brought with them English common law. Several of their grievances that led to the Revolutionary War centered on England's denial of jury trials for colonial defendants, its search and seizure of colonial homes and property, and its arbitrary use of legal punishment. After the Revolution, the new nation's leaders wrote protections from these and other legal abuses into the Constitution and the Bill of Rights.

Legal Distinctions in Types of Crime

Most U.S. jurisdictions still retain common law concepts of the types of crime and the elements of criminal law violation that must be proved before a defendant can be found guilty. One distinction is made between ***mala in se*** crimes and ***mala prohibita*** crimes, with the former considered more serious than the latter. *Mala in se* (evil in themselves) crimes refer to behaviors that violate traditional norms and moral codes. This category includes the violent and property crimes that most concern the public. *Mala prohibita* (wrong only because prohibited by law) crimes refer to behaviors that violate contemporary standards only; examples include illegal drug use and many white-collar crimes (Davenport 2006).

Another distinction is between felonies and misdemeanors. **Felonies** are crimes punishable by more than one year in prison, and **misdemeanors** are crimes punishable by less than one year. Most people convicted of felonies and then incarcerated are sent to state prisons (or, if convicted of a federal crime, to federal prisons), whereas most people convicted of misdemeanors and then incarcerated serve their sentences in local jails, which also hold people awaiting trial.

Criminal Intent

For a defendant to be found guilty, the key elements that must be proved are ***actus reus*** and ***mens rea.*** *Actus reus* (actual act) refers to the actual criminal act of which the defendant is accused. For a defendant to be found guilty, the evidence must indicate beyond a reasonable doubt that he or she committed a criminal act. *Mens rea* (guilty mind) refers to **criminal intent.** This means that the state must show that the defendant intended to commit the act. Although the concept of criminal intent is complex, it generally means that the defendant committed a criminal act knowingly. If the defendant is too young or mentally incapable of understanding the nature and consequences of the crime, criminal intent is difficult to prove. By the same token, the defendant must have also broken the law willingly. This generally means that the defendant was not in fear of her or his life or safety at the time of the crime. If someone holds a gun to your head and forces you to shoplift (admittedly an unlikely scenario), you do not have criminal intent.

The concept of *mens rea* also covers behaviors in which someone acts recklessly or negligently and injures someone else, even though he or she did not intend the injury to happen. If you accidentally leave an infant inside a car on a hot day and the infant becomes ill or dies, you can be found guilty of a crime even though you did not intend the infant to suffer. If you try to injure someone but end up accidentally hurting someone else instead, you can still be found guilty of a crime even though you did not intend to hurt that person.

Legal Defenses to Criminal Liability

Defendants may offer several types of excuses or justifications as defenses against criminal accusations (Davenport 2006).

ACCIDENT OR MISTAKE

One possible defense is that the defendant committed the act by *accident* or *mistake*. If you are driving a car in the winter at a safe speed but skid on the ice and hit a pedestrian, your act is tragic but probably not criminal. If, however, you were driving too fast for the icy conditions and then skid and hit a pedestrian, you might very well be held responsible.

IGNORANCE

Another defense is that the defendant committed a criminal act out of *ignorance*. Here it is generally true, as the popular slogan says, that "ignorance of the law is no excuse," because people are assumed to be aware of the law generally. However, the law does exempt *mistakes of fact* that occur when someone engages in an illegal activity without being aware it is illegal. If someone gives you a package to mail that, unknown to you, contains illegal drugs or stolen merchandise, you commit a mistake of fact when you mail the package and are not criminally liable.

DURESS

Another defense to criminal prosecution is **duress,** which is usually narrowly defined to mean fear for one's life or safety. During the Vietnam War, several antiwar protesters arrested for civil disobedience claimed in their trials that they were acting under duress of their consciences. However, judges almost always excluded this defense from the jury's consideration (Barkan 1983).

SELF-DEFENSE

A common defense to prosecution is **self-defense** to prevent an offender from harming you or someone nearby. However, if you injure your would-be attacker more than legitimate self-defense would reasonably have required, you may be held liable. How much force someone is allowed to use in self-defense remains a controversial issue, as was seen in a recent Texas case. In March 2008, two teenaged boys walked across the yard of W. C. Frosch, age 74, on their way to a nearby party. When Frosch saw them through his window, he was afraid they were burglars. He retrieved his handgun and shot and slightly wounded one of the boys. Although the shooting alarmed some citizens, police initially speculated that it was not a crime under a state law that permits the use of deadly force to protect a homeowner's property. However, a grand jury indicted Frosch three months later for committing aggravated assault with a deadly weapon (Goldstein and Abshire 2008).

The issue of self-defense has also arisen in cases of battered women who kill their husbands or other male partners (Schneider et al. 2008). Often, such a killing occurs when the husband or partner is sleeping, turned the other way, or otherwise not threatening the woman at that instant. Several women who killed their batterers in this manner have claimed they were acting out of self-defense, even though they were not afraid for their lives at the moment they committed the homicide. Traditionally, the law of self-defense does not apply to this situation, and many judges still refuse to permit this defense. However, some courts have expanded the self-defense concept to cover these circumstances.

ENTRAPMENT

Another possible defense is *entrapment*, which generally refers to a situation in which someone commits a crime only because law enforcement agents induced the offender to do so. For example, suppose you are living in a dormitory and have never used marijuana. A new resident of the dorm offers you a joint, but you turn him down. Over the next couple of weeks, he repeatedly tries to get you to smoke marijuana and finally you give in and take a joint. As you begin to smoke it, your friend, who in fact is an undercover narcotics officer, stuns you by arresting you for illegal drug use. Because you had no history of marijuana use and agreed to try some only after repeated pleas by the undercover officer, you may have a good chance of winning your case, assuming a prosecutor goes forward with it, with an entrapment defense.

INSANITY

A final, very controversial defense is the *insanity* defense. Despite the attention it receives, few criminal defendants plead insanity, diminished capacity, or related mental and emotional states, and abolition of the insanity defense would not affect the operation or effectiveness of the criminal justice system (Walker 2011). This issue aside, if a defendant does not have the capacity (e.g., knowing right from wrong) to have criminal intent at the time he or she commits a criminal act, the person is not assumed to have the necessary *mens rea*, or guilty mind, for criminal liability.

Review and Discuss

What are any three legal defenses to criminal liability? Do you think these defenses should exist, or do you think they have been exploited by criminal defendants?

Research Methods in Criminology

Theory and research lie at the heart of any natural, physical, or social science. Theories and hypotheses must be developed and then tested. Durkheim tested his theory of social integration and suicide by gathering and analyzing suicide-rate data in France and elsewhere. The fact that several kinds of data all supported his theory gave it considerable power. Although research methodology and data analysis in sociology and criminology have advanced considerably since Durkheim's day, his study of suicide remains a classic application of the sociological perspective to an important social problem.

Research is certainly a fundamental part of criminology. As is true of research in sociology and the other social and natural sciences, criminological research often asks whether one variable (e.g., attachment to one's parents) influences another variable (e.g., delinquency). The variable that does the influencing is called the **independent variable,** and the variable that is influenced is called the **dependent variable.** Research typically tests whether the independent variable is associated with the dependent variable, that is, whether the degree of adolescents' attachment to their parents is related to the extent of their delinquency. This book discusses the latest criminological research findings in every chapter. To help understand how crime is studied, this section briefly reviews the major types of research in criminology.

Telephone surveys have become very common in criminology and other social sciences.

SURVEYS

One of the most important types of research in criminology (and sociology) is survey research. A **survey** involves the administration of a questionnaire to some group of respondents who are interviewed either face-to-face in their homes or another location, by telephone, through the mail, or online. However a survey is conducted, it enables a researcher to gather a good deal of information about the respondents, although this information is often relatively superficial.

Often the group of respondents interviewed is a random sample of an entire population of a particular location, either the whole nation, a state, a city, or perhaps a campus. The process of selecting a random sample is very complex but is functionally equivalent to flipping a coin or rolling two dice to determine who is in, and not in, the sample. The familiar Gallup poll is a random sample of the adult population of the United States. Even if the size of a national random sample like this poll might be as small as 400, its results will accurately reflect the opinions and behaviors of the entire U.S. adult population, if we could ever measure them. This means we can **generalize** the results of a random sample to the entire population.

Other surveys are carried out with nonrandom samples. For example, a researcher might hand out a questionnaire to a class of high school seniors or first-year college students. Although we cannot safely generalize from these results to the population, some very well-known studies in criminology rely on such *convenience* or *captive audience* surveys.

In criminology, surveys are used primarily to gather three kinds of information. The first kind involves public opinion on crime and the criminal justice system. Depending on the survey, respondents may be asked about their views on several issues, including the death penalty, spending to reduce crime, their satisfaction with the police in their area, or the reasons they believe people commit crime. Chapter 2 discusses the results of public opinion surveys at greater length. The second kind of information gathered involves self-report data, primarily from adolescents, on crime and delinquency. Respondents are asked to indicate, among other things, how many times in the past they have committed various kinds of offenses. Chapter 3 discusses self-report studies in further detail. The third kind of information concerns criminal victimization. Respondents are asked whether they have been victimized by various crimes and, if so, are further asked about certain details about their victimization. Chapters 3 and 4 further discuss the results of victimization surveys.

Review and Discuss

What three kinds of information do criminological surveys gather?

EXPERIMENTS

Experiments are very common in psychology, but less so in criminology and sociology. Subjects typically are assigned randomly either to an experimental group, which is subjected to an experimental condition, or to a control group for comparison. Many experiments take place in the laboratory. A common laboratory experiment with criminological implications concerns the effects of violent pornography (Ferguson and Hartley 2009). An experimental group of subjects may watch violent pornographic films, while a control group watches nonviolent films. Researchers test both groups before and after the experiment to see whether the subjects in the experimental group became more violent in their attitudes toward women than those in the control group. If they find such evidence, they can reasonably conclude that watching the pornographic films prompted this shift in attitudes.

Certain problems exist with the conclusions drawn from such laboratory experiments. First, even if an experimental effect is found, it might be only a short-term effect rather than a long-term effect. Second, an effect found in the artificial setting of a laboratory will not necessarily be found in a real-world setting. Third, most subjects in laboratory experiments conducted by social scientists are college students, typically in lower-level classes. College students are younger than most people not in college and obviously differ in many ways, and experimental effects found among college students may not necessarily pertain to other people.

Some experiments, called *randomized field experiments* or *randomized field trials,* occur outside a laboratory. Such experiments in criminology go back to the 1950s, and there is growing interest in what has been called "experimental criminology" (Sherman 2011). Randomized field experiments have been used to test the effectiveness of various treatment and prevention programs, and they have also been used to help understand the causes of crime. As one example, the California Youth Authority randomly assigned almost 2,000 parolees to either be tested or not tested for drug use after their release from detention. At the end of one month after their release, youths who were assigned to drug testing were more likely than those assigned to no testing to be employed and/or in school. Because random assignment was used, a reasonable conclusion from this experiment is that drug testing made a positive difference (Kilmer 2008).

Qualitative Research: Observing and Intensive Interviewing

Many classic studies have resulted from researchers spending much time and effort observing various groups. These observational studies are also called *field studies* or *ethnographies.* Two of the most famous such accounts in sociology are the late Elliott Liebow's *Tally's Corner* (1967), a study of urban African-American men, and *Tell Them Who I Am: The Lives of Homeless Women* (1993), which provides a rich account of urban women living on the streets. Classic field studies in criminology and deviance include William Foote Whyte's *Street Corner Society* (1943), a study of leadership in a Chicago gang, and Laud Humphreys's *Tearoom Trade* (1975), a study of male homosexual sex in public bathrooms.

Criminologists have also observed the police. Typically, trained researchers ride in police cars and observe the police as they deal with suspects, victims, witnesses, and other people (Weidner and Terrill 2005). These studies illuminate police behavior and provide important data on several issues, including why police decide to arrest or not to arrest suspects and the extent to which they engage in police brutality. One potential problem with these and other observational studies is that the people being observed—in this case, the police—may change their normal behavior when they know they are being watched.

Another type of qualitative research in criminology involves intensive interviewing of criminal offenders. Some studies interview convicted offenders who are either still imprisoned or on probation or parole. In a recent example, Heith Copes and Lynne M. Vieraitis (2009) interviewed 59 federal prison inmates, 23 men and 36 women, convicted of identity theft. Among other questions, they asked the inmates to discuss how they obtained the identity information they stole. According to the inmates, their most common methods involved stealing it from mailboxes or trash cans or buying it from another individual; very few had used "phishing," "hacking," or other computer techniques. In another example, Candace Kruttschnitt and Kristin Carbone-Lopez (2006) interviewed 66 women prisoners who reported having committed 106 violent crimes. The interviews generally lasted between two and eight hours each and involved a variety of topics. One topic involved the women's reasons for committing their acts of violence; the three most common reasons they reported were perceived disrespect, jealousy, and self-defense.

Other interview studies involve offenders who are still on the streets. As you might expect, this type of study poses several difficulties. Active criminals might not want to cooperate because they fear the interviewer could be an undercover police officer or might report what is heard to the police; interviewers may also face a legal or ethical obligation to report serious crimes. Some offenders may also pose a danger to the interviewer. Nonetheless, criminologists have recently published several fascinating studies of active robbers, burglars, female and male gang members, carjackers, young men in bar brawls, and other types of offenders (Jacobs and Wright 2006; Miller 2001; Mullins, Wright, and Jacobs 2004; Steffensmeier and Ulmer 2005; Valdez and Sifaneck 2004).

Increasingly, intensive interviewing has been combined with surveying in **longitudinal studies,** in which the same people are studied over time. Criminology has a growing number of investigations in which researchers interview children or teenagers and their parents and then reinterview them periodically for one or two decades or even longer. Juvenile and criminal police and court records are often also consulted. Major longitudinal studies are being conducted in cities such as Chicago, Philadelphia, Pittsburgh, and Rochester, New York (McGloin and Piquero 2010; Thornberry 2009). The federal government also sponsors national longitudinal studies that focus on delinquency or that focus on education, health, or other issues but include measures of delinquency; these studies, too, have been important sources of information for criminological research (Anderson and Hughes 2009; McGloin 2009). Longitudinal studies have greatly contributed to the understanding of crime over the life course (see Chapter 8) and are invaluable for the testing of many theories of crime and delinquency.

If criminal offenders have been interviewed at great length, so have criminal victims. Heart-rending accounts of the experiences of women survivors of rape, sexual assault, and domestic violence helped bring these crimes to public attention beginning in the 1970s. Since that time, victims of these and other types of crimes have been interviewed at length (Brabeck and Guzmán 2008; Campbell, Adams, and Wasco 2009; Melton 2007). In a related type of study, interviews of urban residents have helped to illuminate their complex concerns about crime and incivility and have yielded a poignant picture of how the threat of crime and the prospect of being arrested affect their daily lives (Carvalho and Lewis 2003; Goffman 2009).

Qualitative research, whether in the form of observation or intensive interviewing, cannot readily be generalized to other segments of the population, but it has nonetheless provided richer accounts of the motivation, lives, and behavior of criminals than any other research method has yielded. Several ethnographic studies of urban areas, such as Elijah Anderson's (1999) sensitive account of inner-city culture, do not touch on crime directly, but still provide important perspectives that help us understand why street crime is so common in these areas.

Research Using Existing Data

Criminologists often gather and analyze data that have been recorded or gathered by government agencies and other sources. For example, they may code data from the case files of criminal defendants to determine whether defendants' race or ethnicity, social class, or gender affects their likelihood of conviction and imprisonment. They also often combine U.S. Census data with government-produced crime and victimization statistics (see Chapter 3) to assess how the social characteristics of neighborhoods, cities, and counties affect crime and victimization (Cancino, Martinez, and Stowell 2009); some studies also use U.S. Census data to determine how the social characteristics of states affect imprisonment rates, the number of executions, and other criminal justice responses to crime (Jacobs and Kent 2007).

Comparative and Historical Research

Two final types of research that combine several of the kinds already mentioned are comparative and historical research. Comparative research usually means cross-cultural or international research. Different nations' varying rates of crime and imprisonment reflect differences in the nations' social structure and culture (Antonaccio and Tittle 2007; Pridemore 2008). By examining other nations' experiences, we can better understand our own situation. International Focus boxes throughout this book highlight the comparative approach.

Historical research is also important. Much of the work of the three key founders of sociology—Émile Durkheim, Max Weber, and Karl Marx—was historical. Societies change over time, as do their rates of criminal and other behavior. For example, murder rates in Western nations were much higher a few centuries ago than they are now (see Chapter 10). By looking at crime in history, we can better understand our own situation today and the possibilities for change. Most chapters in this book discuss historical research.

Conclusion

Viewed from a sociological perspective, crime is a public issue rooted in the way society is organized, not a private trouble rooted in the personal failures of individuals. Accordingly, a sociological criminology highlights the role played by social structure, broadly defined, in criminal behavior, victimization, and the legal response to crime. It emphasizes the criminogenic social and physical conditions of communities and stresses the impact of social inequalities based on race and ethnicity, social class, and gender. It also challenges commonsense perceptions of crime and the legal order and offers prescriptions for dealing with crime that address its structural roots.

This book's primary aim is to develop your sociological imagination, to allow you to perceive, perhaps a little more than you do right now, the structural basis for crime, victimization, and criminal justice. As you develop your sociological imagination, it is hoped that you will understand yourself, or at least your friends and loved ones, a little better than you do now. As C. Wright Mills (1959:5) observed some fifty years ago, the idea that individuals can understand their own experience only by first understanding the structural and historical forces affecting them is "in many ways a terrible lesson (and) in many ways a magnificent one." It is terrible because it makes us realize that forces affecting our behavior and life chances are often beyond our control; it is magnificent because it enables us to recognize what these forces are, and perhaps, therefore, to change them.

Welcome to the world of sociological criminology. Enjoy the journey you are about to make!

Summary

1. The popular sources of our knowledge about crime say little about its social roots. A sociological understanding of crime and criminal justice emphasizes the need to address the structural roots of crime for crime-reduction efforts to succeed.

2. The sociological perspective states that our social backgrounds influence our attitudes, behaviors, and life chances. Sociologist C. Wright Mills stressed that people's private troubles are rooted in the social structure. A sociological approach often challenges conventional wisdom by exposing false claims about reality and taken-for-granted assumptions about social life and social institutions.

3. Criminology and sociology are mutually relevant. Criminology grew largely out of sociology, and today each discipline addresses concepts and theories and uses methodology that are all relevant for the other discipline.

4. Sociological criminology arose from the writings of Émile Durkheim in France in the late nineteenth century and then from the work of social scientists at the University of Chicago in the early twentieth century. Somewhat later in that century, the pioneering efforts of Edwin Sutherland contributed further to the prominence of sociological criminology. Today several sociological theories of crime vie for scholarly popularity.

5. A sociological approach suggests that the definition of crime is problematic because some behaviors may be harmful but not criminal, and others may be criminal but not very harmful. This view of crime derives from the larger study of deviant behavior, which sociologists consider relative in time and space, given that whether a behavior is considered deviant depends on the circumstances under which it occurs.

6. Consensus and conflict theories of criminal law try to answer two related questions: (1) Why do criminal laws get established? and (2) Whom do criminal laws benefit? Consensus theory assumes that laws represent the interests of all segments of the public, whereas conflict theory assumes that laws represent the views of the powerful and help them stay at the top of society's hierarchy and keep the powerless at the bottom.

7. For a defendant to be found guilty of a crime, criminal intent, among other things, must be proved. This means that the defendant must have committed a criminal behavior knowingly and willingly. Legal defenses to criminal liability include accident or mistake, ignorance, duress, self-defense, entrapment, and insanity.

8. Research methods in criminology include surveys, experiments, observing and intensive interviewing, the use of existing data, and comparative and historical research.

Key Terms

actus reus 13	debunking motif 6	*mala in se* 13	social inequality 6
common law 12	dependent variable 15	*mala prohibita* 13	social structure 5
conflict 11	deviance 7	*mens rea* 13	sociological criminology 4
consensus 11	duress 14	misdemeanor 13	sociological imagination 6
crime 10	felony 13	norms 7	sociological perspective 5
criminal intent 13	generalize 16	private troubles 6	survey 16
criminogenic 9	independent variable 15	public issues 6	
criminology 10	laws 7	self-defense 14	
customs 7	longitudinal studies 18	social control 7	

What Would You Do?

1. Suppose you are a single parent with two young children and are living in a large city. Like many of those urban residents, you and your neighbors are very concerned about the crime and drug trafficking you see in your neighborhood. Some of your neighbors have moved out of the city, but most have stayed, and some have even joined a neighborhood watch group. You can afford to move out of the city, but it would be a severe financial strain to do so. Do you think you would decide to move out of the city, or would you stay? Explain your response. If you stayed, would you join the neighborhood watch group? Why or why not?

2. Suppose you are the college student described in this chapter who smokes your first marijuana joint only after repeated appeals by another dormitory student who turns out to be an undercover police officer. You know you were entrapped, but you also realize that if you decide not to plead guilty and take the case to trial, your entrapment defense might not work and you will face harsher punishment than if you had pled guilty. Would you plead guilty, or would you plead not guilty and argue that the officer entrapped you? Explain your response.

CHAPTER

two

Public Opinion,
the News Media,
and the Crime Problem

Crime in the News

t was April 2010, and a series of shootings had racked what used to be a quiet neighborhood in Muskegon, Michigan, a city of about 40,000 on the shores of Lake Michigan. In the latest shooting, a neighbor said she saw a man running down the street, shouting, "I've been hit! I've been hit!" before he fell to the ground. The neighbor observed, "Things have changed a lot around here in the past few years." Another neighbor agreed, "This is getting a little scary here." A third resident, who had lived in the area since 1955, said she had noticed more guns and drugs than before. "My kids want me to move out, but for the most part it's quiet here." On a nearby street corner, police had spray-painted a parking spot where a car had been hit by a bullet. Although the car had been removed, shattered glass lay in a pile on the sidewalk.

Source: Travis 2010.

Think about why you are taking this criminology course. If you are like many students, you may be taking it because you needed some credits and this course fit into your schedule. Or you might be interested in becoming a probation officer, a juvenile caseworker, a police officer, a prison guard, or a lawyer. Perhaps you even want an academic career in crime and criminal justice. Some students may be taking the course because they broke the law in the past (hopefully not in the present!). Conversely, some may be crime victims themselves or friends or relatives of crime victims. Still others may simply be interested in and even fascinated by crime and criminals. A final group may consider crime a serious social problem and want to know why crime occurs and what can be done about it.

Now think about why you have taken courses in other subject areas: math, biology, English literature, or even many of the social sciences. It may have been to fulfill general education or major requirements, to prepare you for a career, to help you learn more about an interesting topic, or—be honest—to fill a convenient time slot in your schedule.

It is doubtful that you took these courses because you were concerned about their subject matter or because you were worried about the subject matter somehow affecting you. A criminology course differs in this sense because its subject matter is very real to students. They hear about crime from the **news media** and see many crimes portrayed in TV programs and the movies. They come into their criminology courses with real concerns about crime and even fears that they or their friends and relatives will become crime victims. Like the residents of Muskegon and so many other communities, they worry about being unsafe.

In this respect, students are no different from average citizens, as most of us hold strong opinions about crime and criminal justice. But where do these beliefs come from? How accurate are the sources of our beliefs and, for that matter, our beliefs themselves? What does social science research reveal about these matters? To return to a theme of Chapter 1, how does our location in society affect our beliefs? This chapter attempts to answer these questions and to indicate the major findings on public opinion about crime. Before we do so, though, some historical context is in order.

A Brief Look Back

Although crime is a major concern for many people today, it has been considered a serious problem throughout U.S. history. This fact may be of small comfort to the 34 percent of Americans who reported in 2009 that they were afraid to walk alone in their neighborhoods at night and the 74 percent who said there was more crime in the United States than a year earlier (Pastore and Maguire 2010), but it does remind us that perhaps there never were the good old days in which crime was not a problem. As the President's Commission on Law Enforcement and Administration of Justice reported in 1967, "There has always been too much crime. Virtually every generation since the founding of the Nation and before has felt itself threatened by the spectre of rising crime and violence" (Pepinsky and Jesilow 1984:21).

In the nineteenth century, for example, the major East Coast cities were plagued by repeated mob violence beginning in the 1830s, hastening the development of the modern police force (see Chapter 16). Teenage gangs roamed the streets and attacked innocent bystanders, and newspaper stories about crime were common (Roth 2011).

Moving ahead to the next century, the 1920s were a "crime boom" decade with headlines such as "Cities Helpless in the Grip of Crime" and "The Rising Tide of Crime." An American Bar Association committee declared in 1922, "Since 1890 there has been, and continues, a widening, deepening tide of lawlessness in this country, sometimes momentarily receding, to swell again into greater depth and intensity." A New York newspaper agreed: "Never before has the average person, in his place of business, in his home or on the streets, had cause to feel less secure. Never before has a continuous wave of crime given rise to so general a wave of fear" (Wright 1985).

This brief history reminds us that crime has always been considered a serious problem. Although we worry about it today, Americans have always worried about it, and their anxiety has been fueled by news media coverage. This concern helps drive policy decisions about crime and criminal justice. But what if public concern is at least partly the result of misleading media coverage? We explore this issue in the next section.

Public Opinion and Crime Policy

As you undoubtedly learned before you entered college, the most defining feature of a democracy is that citizens elect their leaders by majority vote. A related feature, say scholars of **democratic theory,** is that policy decisions by public officials should reflect **public opinion** (Dye 2010).

Critics have challenged this view on several grounds. A first criticism is that public officials are influenced more by a small, wealthy, powerful elite than by the general public (Domhoff 2010). To the extent this criticism might be true, public policy development differs from the idealized version of democratic theory.

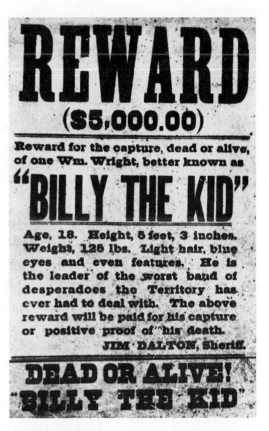

This wanted poster for the notorious outlaw Billy the Kid reminds us that crime has been considered a serious problem throughout U.S. history.

A second criticism is that majority opinion may violate democratic principles of fairness, equality, and justice. Support for slavery before the Civil War is just one of many examples that could be cited from U.S. history. Public opinion that violates democratic principles should not influence **public policy.**

A final challenge to democratic theory is that public opinion is often inaccurate. Europeans used to believe that the earth was flat, but that did not make it flat. In today's world, many people get their information from the news media, but the news media often distort reality (Glassner 2010). Expert opinion may also influence our views, but even expert opinion may be inaccurate. In the late 1800s, some of the most respected U.S. physicians believed that women should not go to college. These "experts" believed that the rigors of higher education would upset women's menstrual cycles and that they would not do well on exams during "that time of the month" (Ehrenreich and English 2005)! Fortunately, we have moved beyond this foolish belief, but the damage it did back then to women's opportunities for higher education was real.

What relevance does all this have for public opinion about crime? People have many concerns and strong opinions about crime and criminal justice. Their views may influence criminal justice policy decisions and, in particular, promote tougher penalties for serious crime. But what if these views are sometimes misinformed? What if public concern about crime stems partly from sensational news media coverage of violent crime and alarmist statements by politicians? Moreover, what if antidemocratic attitudes such as **racial prejudice** affect public views about crime? These possibilities raise some troubling questions about the influence of public opinion on criminal justice policy in a democratic society.

The remainder of this chapter addresses these possibilities. A major goal is to emphasize the problems involved in allowing public opinion on a complex topic such as crime to influence policy without careful evaluation of all available evidence.

Review and Discuss

What are three criticisms or challenges to democratic theory? What is the relevance of these challenges to public opinion about crime?

News Media Coverage of Crime and Criminal Justice

To stimulate your thinking about these issues, complete this minisurvey:

1. What percentage of convicted felony defendants are found guilty by a jury instead of by a judge? Answer: _____

2. How much of the average police officer's time is spent fighting crime (i.e., questioning witnesses, arresting suspects) as opposed to other activities? Answer: _____

3. About how many people die each year from homicides? Answer: _____

4. About how many people die each year from taking illegal drugs? Answer: _____

5. What percentage of all felonies in a given year lead to someone being convicted of a felony and imprisoned? Answer: _____

6. In terms of race and social class, who is the typical criminal in the United States? Answer: _____

If your answers are similar to many of my own students' answers, you would have said the following:

1. Thirty to 60 percent of convicted felons are found guilty at a jury trial.

2. Thirty to 60 percent or more of police officers' time is spent fighting crime.

3. At least 50,000 to 100,000 people die each year from homicides.

4. At least 30,000 to 50,000 people die annually from use of illegal drugs.

5. About 30 or 35 percent of all felonies in a given year lead to someone being imprisoned for committing the felony.

6. The typical criminal, despite many exceptions, is poor and nonwhite.

Now compare your answers to what the best available evidence tells us:

1. Fewer than 10 percent of convicted felons are found guilty at jury trials, with most found guilty as a result of plea bargaining (Robinson 2009).

2. Only about 10 to 20 percent of police officers' time is spent fighting crime; the remainder is spent on directing traffic, responding to traffic accidents, and other relatively mundane matters (Lyman 2010).

3. About 15,000–17,000 people die each year from homicides (Federal Bureau of Investigation 2010).

4. About 17,000 people die each year from the direct or indirect effects of illegal drugs (Mokdad et al. 2004).

5. Well under 10 percent of all felonies in a given year lead to someone being imprisoned for committing the felony (Walker 2011).

6. The profile of the typical criminal, if one includes very common crimes such as employee theft and other kinds of white-collar crime, is certainly not restricted to those who are poor and nonwhite (Rosoff, Pontell, and Tillman 2010).

Despite the importance of juries like the one depicted here, fewer than 10 percent of felony convictions occur as the result of jury trials. Instead, most convictions occur as the result of plea bargaining.

Many students have trouble believing these findings, but each is based on sound evidence that later chapters will discuss. For now, let us assume that these findings are accurate and that public opinion and perceptions on these and other crime and criminal justice matters may sometimes be mistaken. Where do these perceptions come from? Where did you acquire the information that led to your answers? Research suggests that the major source of your information is the news media (Surette 2011). In one poll, 65 percent of respondents named the media as having the greatest influence on their views about crime; only 21 percent mentioned personal experience (Kurtz 1997).

OVERDRAMATIZATION OF CRIME

If so many people rely on the media for their knowledge about crime, it is important that the media depict crime accurately. But how accurate is the media's depiction of crime? To begin our answer to this question, pretend that you are a newspaper editor or a TV news director. Why might it be in your interest to devote a lot of stories to crime and drugs? The answer is obvious: these stories have great potential for capturing readers' or viewers' attention and even increasing their numbers, and thus for advancing your career. Now pretend that you are in charge of nightly programming for one of the TV networks. Recall from the minisurvey which types of events hold the most promise for boosting your network's ratings: jury trials or plea bargains? Violent street crime or white-collar crime? Police chases of violent criminals or traffic citations? The answer is again obvious. Like the news media, the networks' TV schedules will naturally feature the most dramatic kinds of crime and criminal justice activities.

Scholarly investigations of media crime coverage find that the news media do, in fact, **overdramatize** crime. This occurs in several related ways, as we shall now discuss.

Crime Waves

The first way the media overdramatize crime is through **crime waves,** in which a city's news media suddenly devote much attention to a small number of crimes and create a false impression that crime is rampant. In an early study, Felix Frankfurter, a future Justice of the

U.S. Supreme Court, and Roscoe Pound, dean of Harvard Law School, examined the manufacture of a crime wave in Cleveland, Ohio, in January 1919, when the city's Ohio newspapers sharply increased their number of crime stories even though police reports of crime had increased only slightly (Frankfurter and Pound 1922). Frankfurter and Pound criticized the press for alarming the public and for pressuring Cleveland officials to ignore due process rights guaranteed by the U.S. Constitution. In a more recent and widely cited study, Mark Fishman (1978) documented a media crime wave in 1976 by New York City newspapers, which extensively covered a few crimes against the elderly. Although these crimes were not in fact increasing, the media coverage alarmed the public.

Often the media's crime coverage continues to be heavy even though the crime rate may be declining. For example, murder stories on the TV networks' evening newscasts surged, thanks in part to the O. J. Simpson murder case, by 721 percent from 1993 through 1996 (Kurtz 1997). This heavy crime coverage heightened fears that crime was soaring even though the U.S. homicide rate had actually dropped by 20 percent during that time, prompting one TV news reporter to comment, "The myth of rapidly rising crime is so widespread that almost every report(er) believes it's true. I'm as guilty as anyone" (Williams 1994).

In a related phenomenon, the media may devote much attention to very uncommon crimes or even report stories of crimes that never happened. Victor E. Kappeler and Gary W. Potter (2005) describe several such examples. No doubt you have heard of children stricken by poisoned Halloween candy. Such stories surfaced in the mid-1970s when the media reported that several children had died from poisoned candy. However, later investigation confirmed only two deaths, neither involving a stranger giving poisoned candy to a trick-or-treater. In one death, a child died after supposedly eating Halloween candy laced with heroin, but it was later discovered that he had found the drug in his uncle's home. In the other, an 8-year-old boy ate candy laced with cyanide by his father. The truth of both boys' deaths received far less coverage than the initial reports of trusting trick-or-treaters murdered by strangers.

No doubt you have also seen faces of missing children, believed to be kidnapped by strangers, on milk cartons and in heavily publicized news reports. Various government reports indicate that between 1.5 million and 2.5 million children are reported missing each year. However, most missing children are in fact runaways. The relatively few abducted children are usually taken by a parent in a custody battle, and only about 300 are abducted by strangers annually. Although even one child abducted by a stranger is too many, the real number of such children is much smaller than most people think.

Kappeler and Potter (2005) term a final example the "serial killer panic of 1983–85," when many news stories appeared about serial killers who murder people at random. A front-page article in the *New York Times* called serial killing a national epidemic, accounting for roughly 20 percent, or 4,000, of all the yearly U.S. homicides back then (Lindsey 1984). Many other news reports repeated the *Times*'s estimate. However, a later study put the annual number of serial killings at no more than 400 and perhaps as few as 50 (Jenkins 1988). The higher end of the estimate is still only one-tenth the size of the earlier 4,000 figure. Serial killers do exist and must be taken seriously, but they do not appear to be quite the menace the media had us believe.

Despite popular belief, the view that several trick-or-treaters have died from eating poisoned Halloween candy is a myth.

Overreporting of (Violent) Crime

A second way the news media overdramatize crime is simply by reporting so many stories about it. A study of thousands of local TV news stories in 13 U.S. cities found that crime was the most common topic, outpacing weather, accidents and disasters, and human interest stories. Crime stories accounted for four minutes in a typical half-hour local news show, tied with sports and led only by commercials (Public Health Reports 1998).

The media's overreporting tends to focus on violent crime, especially homicide. As the old saying goes, "If it bleeds, it leads." This focus occurs even though most crimes are *not* violent (see Chapter 3). As a result, the media gives the most coverage to the crimes that occur the least. As criminologist Mark Warr put it, "If I were an alien and I came to this planet and I turned on the television, I would think that

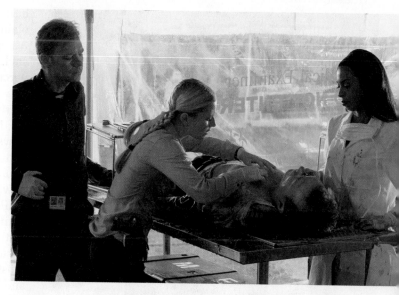

This scene from the television show *CSI; Miami* reminds us that TV news and dramas focus heavily on violent crime, especially homicide.

most crimes were . . . violent crimes, when in fact those are the least common crimes in our society" (Williams 1994). Much research supports this view, with homicide generally accounting for more than one-fourth of all TV and newspaper crime stories, even though it represents less than 1 percent of all crime (Feld 2003).

Review and Discuss

In what ways do the news media overdramatize crime? How and why do crime waves contribute to overdramatization?

CRIME MYTHS

A myth is "a belief or set of beliefs, often unproven or false, that have accrued around a person, phenomenon, or institution" (Random House Webster's College Dictionary 2000). False beliefs about crime are therefore called **crime myths** (Kappeler and Potter 2005). We have just seen that the media contribute to two such myths—that crime is rampant and overly violent—by overdramatizing crime in the ways described. Other aspects of the media's crime coverage generate additional myths.

Racial and Ethnic Minorities

Racial and ethnic minorities have often been the subjects of distorted treatment in media coverage. Several historical examples abound. During the 1870s, whites became concerned about competition from Chinese immigrants for scarce jobs. As a result, labor unions and newspapers began to call attention to the use of opium, then a legal drug, by Chinese immigrants in opium dens. The Chinese were falsely said to be kidnapping white children and turning them into opium addicts. A few decades later, the press began to feature concerns about cocaine, then also a legal drug, saying that its use would make African Americans more cunning, extraordinarily strong, and invulnerable to

Crime stories in TV broadcasts and newspapers pay disproportionate attention to African-American and Latino offenders.

bullets. A few decades after that, press reports claimed that marijuana use would make Mexican-Americans violent (Goode 2008)! We may laugh at such beliefs now, but back then they helped shape perceptions of people of color and helped prompt new laws to ban the use of opium, cocaine, and marijuana.

In modern evidence, TV news broadcasts and newspapers often overrepresent African-American and Latino offenders in their crime stories (Bjornstrom et al. 2010; Surette 2011). In a related problem, the news media often pay disproportionate attention to white crime victims: they feature more articles about white victims than actual crime statistics would justify, and these articles are longer than those about African-American victims. Moreover, even though most violent crime is intraracial (involving offenders and victims of the same race), newspapers tend to include stories with African-American offenders and white victims (Lundman 2003). Finally, African-American and Latino suspects are more likely than white suspects to be portrayed in a menacing context: in the physical custody of police, in a mug shot, or victimizing a stranger (Feld 2003). In all these ways, the media's racially tinged coverage exaggerates the involvement and menacing nature of people of color in crime (especially violence and drugs) and understates their victimization by it (Bing 2010).

Youths

TV news shows and newspapers also disproportionately portray young people as violent offenders. In one study of thousands of news stories on local news broadcasts, 68 percent of the stories about violence focused on youth violence, and 55 percent of the stories about youths focused on their violence (Jackson 1997). In reality, however, only about 14 percent of violent crime is committed by teenagers, and less than 1 percent of all teenagers are arrested annually for violent crime. The news media thus give a distorted picture of youths being heavily involved in violent crime. Perhaps for this reason, respondents in various polls say that teenagers commit most violent crime, which, as just noted, is far from the truth (Dorfman and Schiraldi 2001).

Virtuous Victims

Crime victims come from all walks of life. Many and perhaps most are fine, upright citizens who happened to be in the wrong place at the wrong time, but others are more disreputable and may even have contributed to their own victimization (see Chapter 4). Despite this diversity, the news media tend to give more coverage to crimes whose victims seem to be entirely innocent and even virtuous. These include small children and wealthy white women, even though such women have very low victimization rates. Critics say the media's attention to virtuous victims helps foster even greater public concern about crime (Kappeler and Potter 2005). One media observer put it this way: "Reporters, like vampires, feed on human blood. Tales of tragedy, mayhem, and murder are the daily stuff of front-page headlines and breathless TV newscasts. But journalists rarely restrict their accounts to the sordid, unadorned facts. If the victims of such incidents are sufficiently wealthy, virtuous or beautiful, they are often turned into martyred saints in the epic battle between good and bad" (Cose 1990).

Review and Discuss

What are any four crime myths promoted by news media coverage? How do these myths distort an accurate understanding of crime?

OTHER PROBLEMS IN MEDIA COVERAGE

Several other problems in the news media's crime coverage contribute to the misleading picture it provides (Kappeler and Potter 2005). These include (1) selecting people to be interviewed who support the reporter's point of view, (2) using value-laden language when referring to criminals ("preying on their victims" instead of more neutral terms), (3) presenting data that are misleading (e.g., reporting increases in the number of crimes without noting increases in population size), (4) neglecting various forms of white-collar crime (Mintz 1992), and (5) failing to provide the social and/or historical context for the information presented in a crime story.

A final problem is that the media sometimes deliver a biased or misleading picture of certain aspects of crime, with the possible result that the public misunderstands the crime. For example, the violent crime depicted in the media typically involves strangers, even though most violence is committed by friends or intimates (see Chapter 4). The media also neglect the role of gender in much violent crime. For example, the extensive media coverage of school shootings in Columbine High School and elsewhere in the late 1990s generally failed to indicate that all the offenders were males and a majority of the victims were females (Danner and Carmody 2001).

Media coverage of violence against women (rape and domestic violence) provides another example. Critics say this coverage is biased in several ways. First, the media tend to cover rapes by strangers, even though acquaintances and intimates commit most rapes. Second, reporters sometimes suggest that a woman somehow asked to be raped by emphasizing her "provocative" clothing or "careless" behavior. Third, although men commit the most serious violence against spouses (see Chapter 11), reporters often use vague terms such as a "stormy relationship" that imply either that both spouses were to blame or that no one was to blame. When women do abuse their husbands, these relatively few cases receive disproportionate media attention (Franiuk, Seefelt, and Vandello 2008; Meyers 1996).

EFFECTS OF MEDIA COVERAGE

We have seen that the media provide a misleading picture of crime involving several false beliefs: (1) crime is rampant, (2) crime is overly violent, (3) people of color are more heavily involved in crime and drugs and less likely to be crime victims, (4) teenagers are heavily involved in violent crime, and (5) crime victims are particularly virtuous. Although crime coverage varies among the news media, and in particular depends on whether the news outlet is a quality one or a more popular or tabloid type, one inescapable conclusion is that "images of crime which reach the public through the print [and electronic] media are grossly distorted" (Sheley and Ashkins 1981).

Crime and Controversy

Should the News Media Disclose the Names of Rape Victims?

It is long-standing news-media practice *not* to disclose the name of any woman who tells police she was raped unless, as rarely happens, she agrees to be identified. This practice began in the 1970s when the new women's movement began to emphasize the seriousness of rape. So much shame surrounds this crime, antirape activists said, that media disclosure of rape victims' names would just add to the trauma of the rape itself. In support of this argument, studies of rape victims find that their major concern, and one that outranks fear of sexually transmitted disease, is that their names will become public. Proponents of withholding rape victims' names make at least one additional argument: A woman who thought her name would be known would be less willing to tell the police about her rape, making it more likely that her rapist would never be brought to justice and less likely that rape as a behavior can be deterred.

Although almost all media outlets follow the practice of nondisclosure, it has still been the subject of some debate. Observers who favor identifying rape victims make at least two points. First, if society has the right to know the name of an alleged rapist, they say, then it also has the right to know the name of his or her alleged victim; keeping the name secret might not be fair to the defendant, who has not yet been convicted of any crime. Second, the policy of withholding victims' names ironically reinforces the idea that rape should be considered shameful and embarrassing.

The debate over identifying rape victims intensified after the alleged rape of an exotic dancer in March 2006 by members of the Duke University lacrosse team. Although most mainstream newspapers and news organizations withheld the dancer's name, various Websites soon revealed it. After the charges were dismissed about a year later amid accusations that the dancer had lied about her rape, some mainstream outlets finally revealed her name, while others continued to keep it confidential.

Sources: Ashley 2007; Kristof 2010; Vaden 2007.

Public Ignorance

The media coverage responsible for these images is thought to have several effects (Surette 2011). Perhaps the most important is that "much of the public . . . is ignorant about many aspects of crime and its control" (Cullen, Fisher, and Applegate 2000:3), including the amount of crime, trends in crime rates, and the likelihood of being arrested and imprisoned for committing crime. Media coverage should not bear the total blame for this ignorance, but because it is the public's major source of information on crime and criminal justice, the media shoulder a heavy responsibility.

An example of this effect is that the public exaggerates the number of crimes that occur and may think crime is rising when it is actually falling. As evidence, 67 percent of the respondents in a 2008 Gallup poll said the United States had more crime than a year earlier, even though the crime rate had declined slightly during that period and had been declining since 1993 (Pastore and Magurie 2010). Similarly, public concern about illegal drugs during the mid-1980s soared after the publication of front-page newspaper articles and magazine cover stories on crack cocaine, even though use of this and other illegal drugs actually had been declining since the early 1980s (Beckett 1997).

Public Fear and Concern

A second effect of the media's overreporting of crime is greater public concern about crime, with some research finding that the more people watch local TV news and crime shows, the more they fear crime (Eschholz, Chiricos, and Gertz 2003). Heightened public concern about crime in turn pressures prosecutors to take a hard line in cases involving serious violence and public officials to urge greater spending on crime and the tougher treatment of criminals (Pritchard and Berkowitz 1993). As one media critic put it, "Crime rhetoric has become desperate to the point of it being unthinkable for a candidate for major political office to dare pander to facts instead of fear" (Jackson 1994). Critics say that some public officials add to this problem by making alarmist and racially coded statements about the menace of crime (Beckett and Sasson 2004; Shelden 2010).

Newspaper reports contribute to public concern about crime.

Obscuring Underlying Forces

The media's focus on individual crimes and criminals obscures crime's underlying social and cultural forces, including neighborhood conditions. These forces are the subject of much of the rest of the book, but, as Chapter 1 indicated, they have to be understood and their importance for crime appreciated if the nation is to succeed in reducing the crime rate.

Diversion from White-Collar Crime

Critics say the media's focus on street crime diverts attention from white-collar crime and reinforces negative feelings about poor people (Reiman and Leighton 2010). Although white-collar crime can be very harmful (see Chapter 13), its neglect by the media implies to the public that such crime is not very serious.

Racial and Ethnic Stereotyping

Finally, the media's exaggeration of the violent criminality of African Americans and Latinos and its underplaying of their victimization reinforces negative stereotypes about these groups' violent tendencies (Bjornstrom et al. 2010). For example, whites tend to think they are more likely to be victims of crimes committed by people of color, even though most crimes against whites are committed by other whites (Dorfman and Schiraldi 2001). Similarly, 60 percent of a study's subjects who watched crime stories remembered seeing an offender when in fact one was never shown, and 70 percent of these subjects thought the offender was African American (Gilliam and Iyengar 2000)!

Such stereotyping in turn seems to contribute to white Americans' fear of crime. In an innovative study, Sarah Eschholz (2002) found that watching TV produced greater fear of crime among both African-American and white respondents in a large southeastern city: the more hours spent watching TV, the greater the fear of crime. At the same time, watching programs with higher proportions of African-American offenders produced greater fear of crime among white viewers, but not among African-American viewers.

Although more systematic research is needed, media crime coverage does seem to influence public beliefs and public policy in all the ways just described. To the extent that this is true, this coverage must be as accurate and objective as possible. For this reason, the evidence of the media's misleading portrayal of crime and criminals raises troubling questions for the key beliefs of democratic theory outlined at the start of this chapter.

Review and Discuss

What are any four effects of news media coverage of crime? If you were a newspaper editor or TV news director, how would you want crime covered?

Research on Public Beliefs About Crime and Criminal Justice

We now turn from media coverage to specific public beliefs. A growing body of research addresses the nature and sources of public attitudes about crime and criminal justice. We look first at **fear of crime,** the belief for which there is probably the most research.

FEAR OF CRIME

Take a moment and write down the things you do in your daily life to reduce your chances of becoming a crime victim. If you are like many students, you wrote that you usually lock the doors of your dormitory room, apartment, or house and also of your car (if you have one). You might also have written, especially if you are a woman, that you are careful where you walk alone at night or that you even refuse to walk alone. And you might even have written that you or your family has a gun at home or that you carry a weapon or other means of protection in case you are attacked.

Most of us take some of these precautions, which may be so routine that we do not even think about them. On some lofty intellectual level, we may realize that something like air pollution or price-fixing by large corporations might ultimately pose more danger to us than street crime or cost us more money. But we do not lock our doors to keep out air pollution, and we do not carry a gun or pepper spray to protect ourselves from price-fixing.

We worry about crime because it is so directly and personally threatening. We especially worry about crime by strangers, even though, as Chapter 4 will indicate, we often have more to fear from people we know than from strangers. In addition to the presence of strangers, other situational factors contribute to our fear of crime (Hughes, Marshall, and Sherrill 2003). In particular, we are more afraid if we are in an unfamiliar location, in a setting at night, and alone. We are also more afraid if the people we encounter are young men than if they are women or older people of either sex.

It should not surprise you to learn that many people are afraid of becoming a victim of crime, with some more afraid than others. A standard question included in both the Gallup poll and the General Social Survey (GSS), a random sample of the noninstitutionalized U.S. population that has been conducted regularly since 1972, asks, "Are there any areas around here—that is, within a mile—where you would be afraid to walk alone at night?" In 2009, 34 percent (a figure noted earlier) of Gallup respondents responded yes. More than 45 percent of Gallup respondents also said they worry "frequently" or "occasionally" about having their homes burglarized or their cars stolen or broken into, and 31 percent worried about getting mugged (Pastore and Maguire 2010).

These figures obscure the fact that some people fear crime more than other people. This variation stems from both structural factors and individual characteristics. **Structural factors** concern the social and physical characteristics of the locations in which people live, whereas **individual characteristics** include demographic variables, such as age, gender, and race, and crime-related factors, such as personal victimization and vicarious victimization (knowing someone who has been a crime victim). We now discuss research on both sets of factors.

Fear of crime is generally higher in neighborhoods with dilapidated living conditions.

Structural Factors

Research on structural factors focuses on community characteristics such as the level of social integration (e.g., how well people know their neighbors) of these communities, the quality of the living conditions of respondents' neighborhoods (e.g., whether the neighborhood is filled with abandoned buildings), and the proportion of people of color in respondents' neighborhoods. Fear is generally higher in neighborhoods with lower levels of social integration, more dilapidated living conditions, and higher proportions of nonwhites (Gibson et al. 2002; Lee and Earnest 2003).

As might be expected, population size also matters: the larger the population, the greater the fear of crime. Figure 2.1 indicates this with 2008 GSS data: big-city residents

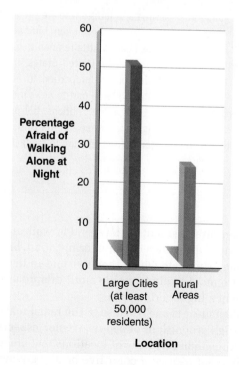

FIGURE 2.1 ▸ Urban/Rural Location and Fear of Crime Source: 2008 General Social Survey.

International Focus

"Headlines Bear So Little Relation to Reality": The Paradox of Fear of Crime in Britain

In the spring of 2010, the British public was very concerned about crime even though crime was down. According to the British Crime Survey, in which residents of England and Wales are asked about their criminal victimization, the British crime rate was down about 45 percent from its highest point in 1995. Yet British residents everywhere were seemingly even more concerned about crime than in years past, naming crime and law and order as one of the most important issues facing their nation. About two-thirds of Britons thought crime was increasing.

Some Britons were so concerned about crime that they simply refused to believe the government statistics. A resident of Redditch, a city of about 80,000 lying about 118 miles northwest of London, said, "I have not suffered from muggings or burglaries, but I know people who have. I would query the figures." Another resident was sure that crime "is going on all around you. Once it used to be on the news, now it's on the streets." Even as they made these claims, crime in Redditch was down 24 percent from four years earlier.

A recent crime had especially alarmed Britons. In northern England, two young boys, ages 9 and 11, were tortured and sexually abused by two other young boys. According to a news report, this crime "seemed to confirm people's perceptions that . . . British society is 'broken,'" a term Britions had begun to use about their society. Even as the nation was alarmed about this hideous crime, however, homicides of children had dropped by almost 50 percent since the mid-1970s.

Britain's prime minister, Gordon Brown, was very aware of the crime decrease throughout Britain but acknowledged that people's fears were real. "Sometimes as damaging as the fear of crime," he declared in a speech, "is the crime of fear."

The public concern in Spring 2010 continued a trend that had begun some years earlier. In 2007, 46 percent of London residents reported feeling unsafe in their neighborhoods at night. A criminal justice professor in London attributed public concern about crime back then to news media coverage: "Media portrayals of crime and justice do seem to be particularly perverse. News stories about soaring crime and judges who are soft on crime and soft in the head are good for circulation, but bad for justice—when the headlines bear so little relation to reality."

Like the United States, then, fear of crime in Britain seems out of proportion to actual trends in crime rates, thanks in large part to news media coverage. Crime is a real problem in both nations, but public concern about crime is heightened when, as the British professor said, "headlines bear so little relation to reality."

Sources: Morris 2008; Ormsby 2010.

are much more likely than rural residents to be afraid to walk alone at night. Several reasons explain this urban–rural difference in fear of crime. First, big-city residents are more likely to perceive a higher crime rate where they live and in their cities as a whole. Second, big-city residents are more likely to reside amid dilapidated conditions, and these conditions suggest to them a higher crime rate.

Third, big-city residents fear crime because of the racial makeup of large cities. Residents of locations with high proportions of people of color, especially African Americans, are more likely to fear crime than residents of locations that are mostly white. Additionally, whites who perceive that people of color live nearby are more afraid of crime than whites who perceive otherwise (Chiricos, McEntire, and Gertz 2001). Because large urban areas typically have higher proportions of people of color, urban residents are more likely to fear crime. Surprisingly, crime rates of communities are only weakly related, if at all, to their residents' fear of crime; when we look at people in communities of similar sizes but with different crime rates, fear of crime does *not* seem to depend on a location's crime rate. This is because people generally do not know the actual crime rate of their place of residence.

Individual Characteristics

Demographic and other characteristics of individuals also influence their fear of crime. Before turning to these, note that one factor surprisingly does not seem to matter very much. If you asked your friends whether crime victims are more likely than nonvictims to fear crime, your friends would probably say yes. However, research results are mixed: some studies find that personal victimization heightens fear of crime, but others find no such effect or only a weak effect (Melde 2009).

Part of the reason for these mixed results is that some of the demographic groups most afraid of crime have relatively low victimization rates. For example, although older people are much less likely than younger people to be crime victims, they feel physically vulnerable to attack and are thus more likely to fear crime (Lichtblau 2000). Similarly, women are more afraid of crime (see Figure 2.2), even though they are less likely than men to be victims of crime other than rape and sexual assault (see Chapter 4). The primary reason for this apparently paradoxical finding is that women, like the elderly, perceive themselves as physically vulnerable to crime, especially rape. Women's high fear of crime thus reflects their fear of rape (Hilinski 2009).

A third demographic variable influencing fear of crime is race/ethnicity, with African Americans and Latinos more fearful than (non-Latino) whites (see Figure 2.3). This difference results largely from the fact that African Americans and Latinos are more likely than whites to live in large cities, which have high crime rates, and to reside in the high-crime areas of these cities. Because of this, they are more likely than whites to see themselves at risk for crime and are thus more fearful. Although fear of crime is highest among the age and gender subgroups *least* likely to be victimized, that pattern does not hold for race/ethnicity. As Chapter 4 discusses, African-Americans' and Latinos' fear of crime does square with harsh reality: they are indeed more likely than whites to be crime victims.

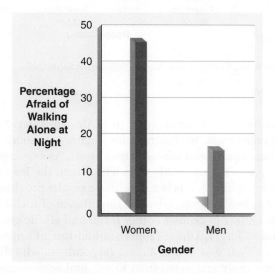

FIGURE 2.2 ▸ **Gender and Fear of Crime** Source: 2008 General Social Survey.

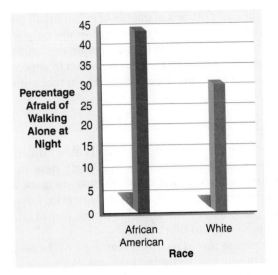

FIGURE 2.3 ▶ **Race and Fear of Crime** Source: 2008 General Social Survey.

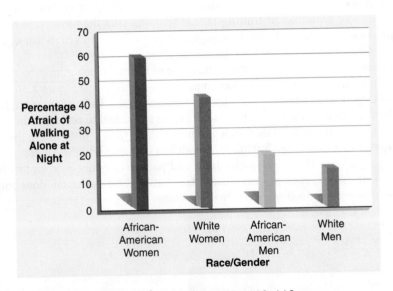

FIGURE 2.4 ▶ **Gender, Race, and Fear of Crime** Source: 2008 General Social Survey.

If gender and race both affect fear of crime, then African-American and Latino women should be especially concerned. To illustrate this, Figure 2.4 reports fear of crime results for African Americans, Latinos, and whites of both sexes. As expected, African-American and Latina women are much more likely than white men, the least afraid group, to fear walking alone in their neighborhoods at night. These results provide striking evidence of the sociological perspective's emphasis on the importance of social backgrounds.

We know less about fear of crime in other racial and ethnic groups. To help fill this gap, Min Sik Lee and Jeffery T. Ulmer (2000) studied fear of crime among 721 Korean Americans in Chicago. Fear was higher among respondents who did not speak English well, who had more recently emigrated from Korea, and who expressed concerns about racial conflict in Chicago and about crime committed by African Americans. These

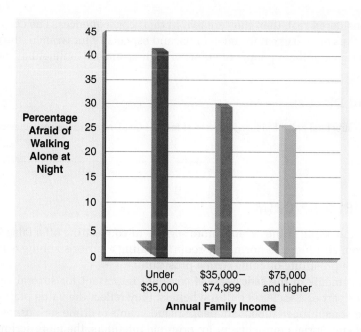

FIGURE 2.5 ▸ **Annual Family Income and Fear of Crime** Source: 2008 General Social Survey.

two latter findings, said the authors, reflected the strained relations between Korean Americans and African Americans in Chicago and other cities. Social class is a final demographic variable linked to fear of crime, with the poor more afraid because they are more apt to live in high-crime areas. If we allow annual family income to be a rough measure of social class, Figure 2.5 portrays the relationship between social class and fear of crime. As expected, the lowest income group in the figure is the most afraid of crime.

Consequences of Fear

What consequences does fear of crime have? Many scholars say that fear of crime weakens social ties within communities, leads to mistrust of others, prompts people to move away from high-crime areas, and threatens the economic viability of whole neighborhoods (Warr 2009). Although we should not exaggerate the effects of fear of crime, we must also not understate them. A large body of research documents how concern about crime affects our daily lives and influences crime policy (Meadows 2010). Concern over crime leads people to take many precautions. A 2007 Gallup poll found that 48 percent of U.S. residents "avoid going to certain places or neighborhoods they might otherwise want to go to," 31 percent "keep a dog for protection," 31 percent "had a burglar alarm installed in their home," and 23 percent "bought a gun for protection of themselves or their home" (Pastore and Maguire 2010). Fear of rape affects women's daily behavior in ways that men never have to experience (Winkler 2002). It has also led to the development of neighborhood watch groups and a burgeoning home security industry involving millions of dollars of products and services (Warr 2009). In the area of criminal justice policy, public concern over crime underlies legislative decisions to increase the penalties for crime and to build new prisons.

In sum, fear of street crime has important consequences. This is true even if this fear is exaggerated by overdramatic media coverage and thus does not always reflect actual levels of crime. To paraphrase William I. Thomas and Dorothy Swaine Thomas (1928), if things are considered real, then they are real in their consequences. The consequences of fear of crime thus are very real for most of us, and especially for women, the elderly, and the residents (most of them people of color) of high-crime urban neighborhoods.

Review and Discuss

> What are the structural and individual correlates of fear of crime? What are the consequences of fear of crime?

SERIOUSNESS OF CRIME

Which of the following crimes seems more serious to you: setting off a false fire alarm or taking $35 from an unlocked dormitory room? Stealing a car or stabbing a stranger with a knife? Being a prostitute or being *with* a prostitute?

Public judgments of the **seriousness of crime** are important for several reasons (Warr 2000). First, as part of a society's cultural beliefs, they reflect the value placed on human life and on personal property. Second, people's judgments of crime seriousness affect their own views of appropriate punishment for criminal offenders; the more serious we regard a specific crime, the more it concerns us and the more harshly we want it punished. Third, and perhaps most important, these judgments influence the penalties stipulated by legislators for violations of criminal laws and the sentences judges give to convicted offenders.

Thorsten Sellin and Marvin Wolfgang (1964) initiated the study of crime seriousness with a survey given to samples of judges, university students, and police officers. Each group was asked to assign a seriousness score to almost 150 offenses (the more serious the crime, the higher the score). Though obviously different in other respects, the three groups assigned similar scores to the various offenses. Wolfgang et al. (1985) later administered a survey of crime seriousness to a random sample of some 60,000 U.S. residents who were asked about more than 200 offenses. Table 2.1 presents the average seriousness scores they assigned to some of the offenses.

These scores demonstrate, among other things, that the public considers selling marijuana more serious than simply smoking it and, perhaps in a bit of sexism, a woman engaging in prostitution slightly more serious than a customer employing her services. Wolfgang and colleagues used the scores to determine why the public judges crimes as more or less serious. Violent crimes were considered more serious than property crimes, crimes against individuals more serious than crimes against businesses, and street crimes more serious than white-collar crimes.

Another important conclusion of this and other research on crime seriousness is that different demographic subgroups—for example, African Americans and whites, women and men, the poor and nonpoor—generally agree on the seriousness of most crimes. This picture is very different from that in the fear-of-crime literature, where these subgroups do differ. Thus, although fear-of-crime research provides strong evidence for the impact of race and ethnicity, class, and gender, research on crime seriousness does not. Instead, its findings are thought to support a consensus view of crime, law, and society (Vogel and Meeker 2001). However, a very different picture emerges from the punitiveness literature, to which we now turn.

PUNITIVENESS

Another public perception concerns judgments of appropriate punishment for convicted criminals, or **punitiveness.** The General Social Survey includes a standard item, "In general do you think the courts in this area deal too harshly or not harshly enough with criminals?"

TABLE 2.1 ▸ **Seriousness Scores for Selected Offenses**

OFFENSE	SCORE
A person plants a bomb in a public building. The bomb explodes and 20 people are killed.	72.1
A man forcibly rapes a woman. As a result of her physical injuries, she dies.	52.8
A man stabs his wife. As a result, she dies.	39.2
A person runs a narcotics ring.	33.8
A person robs a victim of $1,000 at gunpoint. The victim is wounded and requires hospitalization.	21.0
A person breaks into a bank at night and steals $100,000.	15.5
A person steals a locked car and sells it.	10.8
A person sells marijuana to others for resale.	8.5
A person steals $1,000 worth of merchandise from an unlocked car.	6.5
A person turns in a false fire alarm.	3.8
A woman engages in prostitution.	2.1
A person is a customer in a house of prostitution.	1.6
A person smokes marijuana.	1.4
A person under 16 years old plays hookey from school.	0.2

Source: Wolfgang et al. 1985.

In the 2008 GSS, 67 percent of respondents replied "not harshly enough." This figure and other evidence indicate that Americans are punitive regarding crime, even if they also favor rehabilitation and alternatives to imprisonment for certain kinds of crime and criminals (Applegate, Davis, and Cullen 2009; Cullen 2007).

Several punitiveness studies measure public judgments about sentences for people convicted of various kinds of crimes. Like judgments of crime seriousness, public **sentencing preferences** are fairly similar among major demographic subgroups. This similarity again supports consensus perspectives on crime and society and indicates to many scholars that government officials may appropriately consider the high degree of public punitiveness in formulating crime and criminal justice policies (Blumstein and Cohen 1980; Thomas, Cage, and Foster 1976).

However, conclusions of consensus in public sentencing preferences may be premature for at least two reasons. First, although the public is generally punitive, religious fundamentalists, who interpret the Bible literally as the actual word of God, hold especially punitive views (Applegate et al. 2000; Unnever and Cullen 2006). If so, a consensus on punitiveness among people of different religious beliefs cannot be assumed.

Second and more important, significant racial differences exist in certain views on the treatment of criminals. For example, African Americans are somewhat less punitive than whites, partly because they think the criminal justice system is biased (Johnson 2008). This difference is especially strong for the death penalty (Unnever, Cullen, and Jonson 2008); in a 2009 Gallup poll, only 41 percent of African Americans said they believe in the death penalty, versus 69 percent of whites (Pastore and Maguire 2010).

One additional set of findings is relevant, but also very troubling, for crime policy in a democracy: African Americans and whites appear to hold punitive views for very different reasons. In particular, fear of crime motivates African-American support for harsher sentencing, whereas racial prejudice fuels white support (Cohn and Barkan 2004; Unnever and Cullen 2010). (We return to this point next in our discussion of the death penalty.) If racial prejudice does motivate white punitiveness, then sentencing policy based on this support may be misguided. To return to our discussion on democratic theory, to the extent that public support for harsher sentencing is motivated by racial prejudice, it is inappropriate in a democratic society for officials to be influenced by such support.

Death Penalty

A large segment of the punitiveness literature focuses on the death penalty. Because death is the ultimate punishment and because the death penalty is so controversial (see Chapter 16), views on the death penalty are especially important. A large body of research addresses the extent of death-penalty support and reasons for such support (Unnever, Cullen, and Jonson 2008).

Most measures of death-penalty support rely on a single question, such as that used by the General Social Survey: "Do you favor or oppose the death penalty for persons convicted of murder?" Critics say a single question like this does not capture the full complexity of death-penalty opinion and, in particular, artificially inflates support for capital punishment. When people are given an alternative, such as "Do you favor the death penalty for persons convicted of murder, or do you favor life imprisonment without parole?" their support for the death penalty is much lower than when no alternative is given.

This methodological issue aside, the following kinds of people are more likely than their counterparts to support the death penalty: men, whites, older people, those with less education, Southerners, political conservatives, religious fundamentalists, and residents of areas with higher homicide rates and larger proportions of African Americans (Baumer, Messner, and Rosenfeld 2003; Sharp et al. 2007). Echoing the earlier point on harsher sentencing, death-penalty support is also much higher among whites who are racially prejudiced (Unnever and Cullen 2010). This fact prompts Soss, Langbein, and Metelko (2003) to conclude, "White support for the death penalty in the United States has strong ties to antiblack prejudice." This point again raises troubling questions for crime policy in a democracy. It may also have implications for the constitutionality of the death penalty, which, according to the U.S. Supreme Court, rests partly on the fact that public support for capital punishment is so high (Egelko 2002). But if much of this support rests on antiblack prejudice, the Court's reliance on the amount of this support may be inappropriate.

Review and Discuss

Why might conclusions of consensus in public sentencing preferences be premature? Why do the findings on racial prejudice challenge the assumptions of democratic theory regarding public opinion and public policy?

VIEWS ABOUT THE POLICE

Scholars have also studied the public's views about other aspects of the criminal justice system, especially the police (Wu, Sun, and Triplett 2009). In general, satisfaction with the police is lower, as you might expect, among people who have been stopped by the police for traffic violations and other issues; young people of color who have been stopped by police are especially likely to hold negative views of the police (Gau and Brunson 2010).

It is also lower among people living in poor neighborhoods beset by crime and other problems (Reisig and Parks 2000). Certain demographic differences also stand out. Looking first at race and ethnicity, views about the police are more negative among African Americans and Latinos than among whites (Brunson and Weitzer 2009; Weitzer, Tuch, and Skogan 2008). For example, in a 2009 Gallup poll, only 38 percent of African Americans reported a "great deal" or "quite a lot" of confidence in the police, versus 63 percent of whites (Pastore and Maguire 2010). Although very little research exists on the views about police held by members of other racial and ethnic groups, two studies of Alaska Natives and American Indians in parts of Alaska found mixed results. In one study, their views toward police were more positive than whites' views, but in the other study the reverse was true. Methodological differences between these two studies may have accounted for their opposite findings (Giblin and Dillon 2009; Myrstol 2005).

Public satisfaction with the police is lower among people who have been stopped by the police for traffic violations and other problems, and it is lower among people who live in high-crime neighborhoods.

These racial and ethnic differences exist for at least two reasons. First, African Americans and Latinos are more likely than whites to have negative experiences with the police (e.g., being stopped or insulted by police). Second, they are also more likely to live in high-crime neighborhoods where police–citizen relations are contentious (Brunson 2007; Sharp and Johnson 2009; Solis, Portillos, and Brunson 2009). Age and income differences also exist, with younger and poorer people holding more negative views on certain aspects of police performance. For example, 50 percent of young adults (ages 18 to 29) report a "great deal" or "quite a lot" of confidence in the police versus 65 percent of people 65 and older. Similarly, only 50 percent of people with annual incomes under $20,000 express this level of confidence in the police, compared to 70 percent of those with incomes of at least $75,000 (Pastore and Maguire 2010).

A new line of research on views about police involves public approval of police use of force. Studies of this issue yield two related findings (Johnson and Kuhns 2009). First, whites are more likely than African Americans to approve of the use of force by police. Second, racial prejudice partly motivates whites' approval of police use of force. This latter finding echoes a major finding from the punitiveness literature discussed in the previous section.

PERCEPTIONS OF CRIMINAL INJUSTICE

Recent research has begun to focus on the extent and correlates of perceptions of *injustice* in the criminal justice system (Higgins et al. 2009; Matsueda and Drakulich 2009; Unnever 2008). Significant numbers of the public in national polls perceive that such injustice exists in various aspects of the criminal justice system (Pastore and Maguire 2010). For example, about one-third of the public believes that the death penalty is applied unfairly, that the police do only a fair or poor job in treating everyone fairly, and that police brutality occurs in their area. Similarly, about half the public says that racial profiling is "widespread" when police stop motor vehicle drivers, and less than one-third think such profiling is justified.

A key finding by this research is that strong racial and ethnic differences exist in perceptions of injustice in the criminal justice system, with African Americans and, to a smaller degree, Latinos more likely than non-Latino whites to perceive that such injustice exists (Gabbidon and Higgins 2009; Johnson 2008). Because perceptions of criminal injustice may contribute to tension between people of color and police and undermine the former's faith in the criminal justice system and larger society, the strong evidence of racial and ethnic differences in perceptions of criminal injustice presents a troubling portrait.

VIEWS ABOUT CRIME AND CRIMINAL JUSTICE SPENDING

Because such a high amount of government funds, about $215 billion annually, is spent on the criminal justice system, scholars have begun to study public views about government spending priorities on crime and criminal justice. Although this research is still growing, two findings stand out. First, support by whites for greater spending to fight crime is motivated partly by racial prejudice against African Americans (Barkan and Cohn 2005). This result again raises important questions about public opinion and crime policy in a democratic society like the United States. Second, although the public is often said to be punitive toward criminals, and survey evidence does support this conclusion, the public's spending priorities also indicate a strong preference for prevention and treatment measures (Applegate, Davis, and Cullen 2009; Cullen 2007). When survey questions give the public an option between spending on more prisons and spending on prevention of crime and on the treatment of offenders, the public favors prevention and treatment at least as much as more prisons, and sometimes more so. For example, 65 percent of respondents in a 2006 Gallup poll favored trying to lower the crime rate by "attacking the social and economic problems that lead to crime," whereas only 31 percent favored an approach involving "improving law enforcement with more prisons, police, and judges" (Pastore and Maguire 2010). To the extent the public favors prevention and treatment over incarceration, prison construction and other aspects of the "get tough" approach to crime of the last few decades may not reflect public views as much as is commonly thought.

A FINAL WORD ON PUBLIC BELIEFS

There are many public beliefs about crime and criminal justice, and there is much research on them. Our discussion has only begun to summarize all the findings of this research. Nonetheless, one theme stands out: On many beliefs about and reactions to crime, Americans are divided along lines of race and ethnicity, social class, gender, age, and even location. In particular, prejudice against African Americans and Latinos seems to make white Americans both more afraid of crime and more punitive toward it. In general, certain racial and ethnic differences in public beliefs about crime and criminal justice are so strong that it might not be exaggerating to say that racial and ethnic cleavages exist in American society on these beliefs.

This theme brings us back to the discussion in Chapter 1 of the sociological perspective, that our social backgrounds influence our behavior, attitudes, and life chances. Although most of this book is about the behavior we call crime, the discussion of public beliefs demonstrates that our social backgrounds also profoundly influence our attitudes about this behavior and about our nation's reaction to it.

Conclusion

This chapter has now come full circle. It began with a critical discussion of decision making in a democratic society. We saw then that democratic theory neglects the possibilities of elite influence, public views that may violate democratic principles, and inaccurate public beliefs. It next examined distortion in news media coverage about crime and suggested, among other things, that the media often give a false picture of rising crime rates and a false impression of most crime as violent, and that they also exaggerate the involvement of racial and ethnic minorities in crime. Enough evidence exists on the effects of media coverage on public perceptions of crime to call into question the appropriateness of blindly basing criminal justice policy on public opinion.

We next reviewed the major findings on fear of crime and emphasized the effects on fear of dimensions of social inequality and social structure. Fear of crime is a social fact and thus has real and in many ways sad consequences for how people, especially women and the urban poor, live their daily lives.

The vast body of research on public beliefs about and reactions to crime and criminal justice was also reviewed. In a democracy, all these beliefs may have important implications for legislative and judicial policy. The evidence that racial prejudice shapes white Americans' views on the punishment of criminals, including the death penalty, calls into question the appropriateness of basing criminal justice policy on these views (Huddy and Feldman 2009).

A final issue involves measurement problems in assessing public opinion on crime and punishment, as these problems sometimes call into question our ability to gauge public opinion accurately enough for it to be used as a basis for criminal justice policy. In measuring death-penalty opinion, for example, recall that the use of a single question that lacks an alternative, such as life imprisonment without parole, artificially inflates estimates of public support. Yet the U.S. Supreme Court has relied on these inflated estimates in supporting the constitutionality of capital punishment. The Court's conclusion on this issue thus might not be justified. And to the extent that public support for the death penalty rests, as we have seen, partly on racial prejudice, the Court's conclusion may also not be appropriate.

As this chapter has tried to show, public opinion about crime and punishment is often an elusive target. But it is also a fascinating target, precisely because public sentiment about crime and punishment reflects our hopes and fears for society. As a product of our location in society, these hopes and fears further reflect the influence of our race/ethnicity, class, gender, and various aspects of the social structure and organization of the communities in which we live. For better or worse, then, public opinion will continue to affect public policy on crime and criminal justice. If this is true, enlightened policy making demands that social scientists continue their research on the sources and consequences of public opinion and that they continue to improve its measurement. It also requires accurate measures of the nature and incidence of crime itself. Appropriately, Chapter 3 turns to the measurement of crime.

Summary

1. Although crime concerns many Americans today, it has always been perceived as a major problem throughout the nation's history. Repeated mob violence during much of the nineteenth century alarmed the nation.

2. Democratic theory assumes that public opinion should influence the decisions of public officials. However, critics say that elite opinion is sometimes more influential than public opinion and that public opinion may also be mistaken and based on antidemocratic principles.

3. The news media are an important source of information for the public about crime and criminal justice. Yet the media paint a misleading picture of crime by manufacturing crime waves and by overdramatizing crime's more sensational aspects.

4. Crime myths propagated by the media include (1) crime is rampant, (2) crime is overly violent, (3) people of color are more heavily involved in crime and drugs and less likely to be crime victims, (4) teenagers are heavily involved in violent crime, and (5) crime victims are particularly virtuous.

5. Media crime coverage is thought to have several effects. These include public ignorance about crime and criminal justice, greater public concern about crime and hence increased pressure on prosecutors and public officials to take a hard line on crime, diversion of attention from white-collar crime, and reinforcement of racial and ethnic stereotyping.

6. Fear of crime, the subject of extensive criminological research, affects people's daily lives in several ways. It is higher among residents of big cities and of neighborhoods with higher proportions of nonwhites, and it is also higher among big-city residents and among women, the elderly, African Americans, and the poor.

7. Public ratings of the seriousness of crime are important for legislative policy making and judicial decisions on punishment. These ratings reflect a consensus among demographic subgroups.

8. Americans hold a punitive view regarding how harshly criminals should be punished, but African Americans are less punitive than whites, especially regarding the death penalty, and white punitiveness, including support for the death penalty, rests partly on racial prejudice.

9. As with other types of public beliefs on crime and justice, views about the police reflect differences based on race and ethnicity, age, location, and social class.

Key Terms

crime myth 29

crime wave 27

democratic theory 25

fear of crime 34

individual characteristics 35

news media 24

overdramatize 27

public opinion 25

public policy 25

punitiveness 40

racial prejudice 25

sentencing preferences 41

seriousness of crime 40

structural factors 35

What Would You Do?

1. You are the editor of a newspaper in a medium-size city. For most of the past two decades, your newspaper was the only major one in town. Just a year ago, however, another newspaper started up, and it is pretty much of the tabloid variety, with screaming headlines about drugs, robberies, and each of your city's occasional homicides. Your newspaper immediately began losing circulation to this upstart. Your publisher is putting pressure on you to respond with a lot more front-page crime coverage. What do you say to your publisher?

2. Suppose you live in a middle-class suburb of a large city. Almost all the residents of the suburb are white. On your way home from work late one afternoon, you drive by someone walking just a short distance from your home. You did not get a good look at the pedestrian, but you were able to notice that he was a young man with somewhat long hair, a scruffy beard, and a faded baseball cap. He may not have been white, but you are not sure. You cannot help feeling that he looked out of place in your neighborhood, but you realize your fears are probably groundless. Still, your pulse begins racing a bit. What, if anything, do you do?

CHAPTER

three

The Measurement
and Patterning
of Criminal Behavior

Crime in the News

n April 2010, a city audit of crime statistics compiled by the Dallas, Texas, police department found some troubling inaccuracies. These inaccuracies involved the department's decisions to record citizens' reports about crimes as actual, "official" crimes in the reports it regularly submits to the Federal Bureau of Investigation. Although the audit concluded that the department's crime numbers "appear substantially correct," it also found evidence of failures to record citizen crime reports as actual crimes. For example, in a sample of 60 citizen reports that the audit said it randomly selected, 11 should have been categorized as thefts. In another sample of 60 randomly selected citizen reports, 13 should have been categorized as car burglaries. These figures suggested an error rate of 24 out of 120, or 20 percent.

The audit was issued just months after the *Dallas Morning News* found that the police department had failed to count for many years "hundreds and perhaps thousands of offenses" as actual crimes in its reporting to the FBI. For example, the department had recorded reports of attempted burglary as mere vandalism and had failed to count reports of car burglaries. In a one-week sample of cases, the newspaper found that the official burglary rate for that week was 10 percent lower than it would have been had attempted burglaries been counted as such. This general undercount of crime had made Dallas appear to be a safer city than it would have otherwise appeared had the true number of crimes been reported.

Sources: Eiserer and Thompson 2009; Thompson 2010.

This news story from Dallas raises a very interesting and important question: How accurate are crime statistics? When the U.S. Congress investigated the Watergate scandal almost four decades ago that forced President Richard Nixon to resign, Republican Senator Howard Baker of Tennessee asked repeatedly about the president, "What did he know and when did he know it?" The Dallas story suggests that a similar question might be asked of the **measurement** of crime: What do we know and how do we know it? Accurate answers to this question are essential for the creation of fair criminal justice policy and sound criminological theory. For example, we cannot know whether crime is increasing or decreasing unless we first know how much crime occurs now and how much occurred in the past. Similarly, if we want to be able to explain why more crime occurs in urban areas than in rural areas, we first need to know the amount of crime in both kinds of locations.

Unfortunately, crime is very difficult to measure because usually only the offender and victim know about it. Unlike the weather, we cannot observe crime merely by looking out the window. On TV police shows or in crime movies, crimes are always discovered (otherwise there would be no plot). But real life is never that easy: because crime often remains hidden from the police, it is difficult to measure. Thus, we can never know with 100 percent accuracy how much crime there is or what kinds of people or organizations are committing crime and who their victims are.

At best we can measure crime in different ways, with each giving us a piece of the puzzle. When we put all these pieces together, we begin to come up with a more precise picture. Like many jigsaw puzzles lying around, however, some pieces might be missing. We can guess at the picture of crime, sometimes fairly accurately, but we can never know whether our guess is completely correct. Fortunately, the measurement of crime has improved greatly over the past few decades, and we know much more about crime than we used to. This chapter reports the state of our knowledge.

Measuring Crime

UNIFORM CRIME REPORTS

The primary source of U.S. crime statistics is the **Uniform Crime Reports (UCR)** of the Federal Bureau of Investigation (FBI). Begun in the 1930s, the UCR involves massive data collection from almost all the nation's police precincts. Each precinct regularly reports various crimes *known to the police*. The most extensive reporting is done on what are called Part I offenses, which the FBI considers to be the most serious: homicide (murder and non negligent manslaughter), forcible rape, robbery, and aggravated assault, classified as **violent crime**; and burglary, larceny, motor vehicle theft, and arson, classified as **property crime**. The police tell the FBI whether each Part I crime has been *cleared by arrest*. A crime is considered cleared if anyone is arrested for the crime or if the case is closed for another reason, such as the death of the prime suspect. If someone has been arrested, the police report the person's race, gender, and age. The FBI also gathers data from the police on Part II offenses, which include fraud and embezzlement, vandalism, prostitution, gambling, disorderly conduct, and several others (see Figure 3.1).

The FBI classifies the vandalism depicted here as one of many Part II offenses.

Part I Offenses

Criminal Homicide: (a) murder and nonnegligent manslaughter (the willful killing of one human being by another); deaths caused by negligence, attempts to kill, assaults to kill, suicides, accidental deaths, and justifiable homicides are excluded; (b) manslaughter by negligence (the killing of another person through gross negligence; traffic fatalities are excluded)

Forcible Rape: the carnal knowledge of a female forcibly and against her will; includes rapes by force and attempts to rape, but excludes statutory offenses (no force used and victim under age of consent)

Robbery: the taking or attempting to take anything of value from the care, custody, or control of a person or persons by force or threat of force and/or by putting the victim in fear

Aggravated Assault: an unlawful attack by one person upon another to inflict severe bodily injury; usually involves use of a weapon or other means likely to produce death or great bodily harm. Simple assaults are excluded

Burglary: unlawful entry, completed or attempted, of a structure to commit a felony or theft

Larceny-Theft: unlawful taking, completed or attempted, of property from another's possession that does not involve force, threat of force, or fraud; examples include thefts of bicycles or car accessories, shoplifting, pocket-picking

Motor Vehicle Theft: theft or attempted theft of self-propelled motor vehicle that runs on the surface and not on rails; excluded are thefts of boats, construction equipment, airplanes, and farming equipment

Arson: willful burning or attempt to burn a dwelling, public building, personal property, etc.

Part II Offenses

Simple Assaults: assaults and attempted assaults involving no weapon and not resulting in serious injury

Forgery and Counterfeiting: making, altering, uttering, or possessing, with intent to defraud, anything false in the semblance of that which is true

Fraud: fraudulent obtaining of money or property by false pretense; included are confidence games and bad checks

Embezzlement: misappropriation of money or property entrusted to one's care or control

Stolen Property: buying, receiving, and possessing stolen property, including attempts

Vandalism: willful destruction or defacement of public or private property without consent of the owner

Weapons: carrying, possessing, etc. All violations of regulations or statutes controlling the carrying, using, possessing, furnishing, and manufacturing of deadly weapons or silencers. Attempts are included

Prostitution and Commercialized Vice: sex offenses such as prostitution and procuring

Sex Offenses: statutory rape and offenses against common decency, morals, etc.; excludes forcible rape and prostitution and commercial vice

Drug Abuse: unlawful possession, sale, use, growing, and manufacturing of drugs

Gambling

Offenses Against the Family and Children: nonsupport, neglect, desertion, or abuse of family and children

Driving Under the Influence

Liquor Laws: state/local liquor law violations, except drunkenness and driving under the influence

Drunkenness

Disorderly Conduct: breach of the peace

Vagrancy: vagabonding, begging, loitering, etc.

All Other Offenses: all violations of state/local laws, except as above and traffic offenses

Suspicion: no specific offense; suspect released without formal charges being placed

Curfew and Loitering Laws: persons under age 18

Runaways: persons under age 18

FIGURE 3.1 ▸ The Uniform Crime Reports Source: Federal Bureau of Investigation 2007.

In turn, each year the FBI reports to the public the official number of Part I crimes (i.e., the number the FBI hears about from the police) that occurred in the previous year for every state and major city in the United States. (Because of incomplete reporting of arson by police, the total number of arsons is not included in the UCR.) The FBI also reports the number of Part I crimes cleared by arrest and the age, race, and gender distribution of people arrested. This information makes UCR data valuable for understanding the geographical distribution of Part I offenses and the age, race, and gender of the people arrested for them. For Part II offenses, the FBI reports only the number of people arrested. Table 3.1 presents UCR data for Part I crimes. Note that violent crime comprises about 12 percent of all Part I crimes and property crime about 88 percent.

For about three decades after the beginning of the publication of the UCR in the 1930s, the UCR and other official statistics (e.g., arrest records gathered from local police stations) were virtually the only data about U.S. crime. But in the 1960s and 1970s scholars of crime began to question their accuracy. Before reviewing the criticism, let us first see how crimes become known to the police, or official.

How a Crime Becomes Official

A crime typically becomes known to the police only if the victim (or occasionally a witness) reports the crime, usually by calling 911. Yet almost 60 percent of all victims of violent and property crimes do *not* report these crimes. Because the police discover only 3 to 4 percent of all crimes themselves, many crimes remain unknown to the police and do not appear in the UCR count (Lynch and Addington 2007). When the police do hear about a crime, they decide whether to record it. Sometimes they do not believe the victim's account or, even if they do believe it, may not feel that it describes actual criminal conduct. Even if the police believe a crime has occurred, they may be too busy to do the necessary paperwork, particularly if the crime is not very serious. If the police do not record a crime, they do not report it to the FBI, and it does not appear in the UCR crime count. Some evidence suggests that police record only about 65 percent of all calls (Warner and Pierce 1993). For all these reasons, the number of crimes appearing in the UCR is much smaller than the number that actually occurs.

Even when the police do record a crime, an arrest is the exception and not the rule. Unless a victim or witness identifies the offender or the police catch him (or, much less

TABLE 3.1 ▸ Selected UCR Data, 2008

TYPE OF CRIME	NUMBER KNOWN TO POLICE	% CLEARED BY ARREST
Violent crime	1,382,012	45.1
Murder and nonnegligent manslaughter	16,272	63.6
Forcible rape	89,000	40.4
Aggravated assault	834,885	54.9
Robbery	441,855	26.8
Property crime	9,767,915	17.4
Burglary	2,222,196	12.5
Larceny–theft	6,588,873	19.9
Motor vehicle theft	956,846	12.0
Total offenses	11,149,927	20.8

Source: Federal Bureau of Investigation 2009.

often, her) in the act, they probably will fail to make an arrest. Unlike their TV counterparts, police do not have the time to gather evidence and interview witnesses unless the crime is very serious. As Table 3.1 indicates, the proportion of all Part I crimes cleared by arrest is shockingly small. This proportion does vary by the type of crime and is higher for violent crimes. Yet even for homicides, where there is the most evidence (a corpse), fewer than two-thirds are cleared by arrest.

Critique of UCR Data

Increased recognition some thirty years ago of all these problems led to several critiques of the validity of the UCR and other official measures (Catalano 2006c). We discuss each problem briefly.

UNDERESTIMATION OF THE AMOUNT OF CRIME

The UCR seriously underestimates the actual number of crimes committed in the United States and in the individual states and cities every year. We explore the extent of this underestimation later in this chapter.

DIVERSION OF ATTENTION FROM WHITE-COLLAR CRIME

By focusing primarily on Part I crimes, the UCR emphasizes these crimes as the most serious ones facing the nation and diverts attention from white-collar crimes. As a result, the seriousness of the latter is implicitly minimized (Reiman 2007).

MISLEADING DATA ON THE CHARACTERISTICS OF ARRESTEES

UCR data may be more valid indicators of the behavior of the police than that of offenders. If so, the characteristics the UCR presents for the people who get arrested may not accurately reflect those of the vast majority who escape arrest. This possibility is especially likely if police arrest practices discriminate against the kinds of people—typically poor, nonwhite, and male—who are arrested. Chapter 16 explores this issue further, but to the extent that such bias exists, arrest data yield a distorted picture of the typical offender. To compound the problem, because white-collar criminals are even less likely than Part I criminals to get arrested, arrest data again mischaracterize the typical offender and divert attention from white-collar criminals.

CITIZENS' REPORTING OF CRIME

The official number of crimes may change artificially if citizens become more or less likely to report offenses committed against them. For example, if the introduction of the 911 emergency phone number across the United States has had its intended effect, more crime victims may be calling the police. If so, more crimes become known to the police and thus get reported to the FBI, artificially raising the official crime rate. Similarly, increases in UCR rapes since the 1970s probably reflect the greater willingness of rape victims to notify the police (Baumer and Lauritsen 2010).

POLICE RECORDING PRACTICES AND SCANDALS

The official number of crimes may also change artificially because of changes in police behavior. This can happen in two ways. One way is through police crackdowns, involving sweeps of crime-ridden neighborhoods, on prostitution, drug trafficking, and other offenses. The number of crimes known to the police and the number of people arrested for them rise dramatically, artificially increasing the official rate of these crimes, even though the actual level of criminal activity might not have increased.

The second way crime rates reflect police behavior is more ominous: the police can change how often they record offenses reported to them as crimes. They can decide to record more offenses to make it appear that the crime rate is rising, with such "evidence" providing a rationale for increased funding, or they can decide to record fewer offenses to make it appear that the crime rate is falling, with such evidence indicating the local force's effectiveness at fighting crime. Police recording scandals of this nature have rocked several cities during the past two decades; these cities included Atlanta, Baltimore, New York City, and Philadelphia.

The Philadelphia scandal was especially notorious, as that city's police department was found to have downgraded or simply failed to record thousands of rapes and sexual assaults during the early 1980s. Police did not tell the victims they were doing this, and they did not try to capture the rapists (Fazlollah et al. 1999). Two years before this scandal broke, similar crime-reporting problems had forced the FBI to throw out Philadelphia's crime statistics for 1996 and 1997, during which the city's police downgraded many major crimes to minor ones: burglaries and larcenies became "missing" or "lost" property cases, car break-ins became vandalism, and beatings and stabbings were called "hospital cases." This downgrading involved about 10 percent of all serious crime in the city (Matza, McCoy, and Fazlollah 1998). In Atlanta, the city's police department had underreported crimes for several years, in part to help improve the city's image in order to boost tourism. Part of this effort was aimed at helping Atlanta win the right to host the 1996 Summer Olympics. As part of this multiyear effort, thousands of 911 calls were apparently never answered (Hart 2004).

DIFFERENT DEFINITIONS OF CRIMES

Police in various communities may have different understandings and definitions of certain crimes. Police in one area may thus be more likely than police elsewhere to record a given event as a crime. Even when they do record an event, police forces also vary in the degree to which they record the event as a more serious or a less serious crime, as the Dallas story that began this chapter illustrates.

SCHOOL REPORTING PRACTICES

Although not a fault of the UCR per se, crime-reporting practices at collegiate and secondary school campuses have also come into question. Critics say some universities hide evidence of rapes and other crimes in internal judicial proceedings to avoid alarming the public and reducing admissions applications (Shapiro 2010). When university students are victimized just off campus, their crimes are included in the tallies of some campuses, but not in those of others (Chacon 1998).

Victimizations of students just off campus are included in the crime tallies of some universities, but not in those of others. Critics also say that some universities address rape allegations through internal judicial proceedings to avoid alarming the public.

NIBRS and Calls to the Police

One alternative to the UCR as the source of official crime data is being implemented, and another has been suggested and is sometimes used by researchers. The first alternative is the FBI's National Incident-Based Reporting System (NIBRS), which will eventually replace the UCR. Under NIBRS, the police provide the FBI extensive information on each crime incident for the eight Part I crimes and fourteen other Part II crimes, including drug offenses, gambling, prostitution, and weapons violations. The information includes the relationship between offenders and victims and the use of alcohol and other drugs immediately before the offense. Previously, such detailed information had been gathered only for homicides in what are called the Supplementary Homicide Reports (SHR). Although NIBRS will still be subject to the same reporting and recording problems characterizing the UCR, the information it provides on crime incidents promises to greatly increase our understanding of the causes and dynamics of many types of crimes. Accordingly, several recent studies have used NIBRS data (Stolzenberg and D'Alessio 2008; Taylor, Holleran, and Topalli 2009).

As another alternative, some researchers advocate using *calls to police* to indicate the number and nature of crimes in a given community (Warner and Coomer 2003). When crime victims call the police, a dispatcher records their calls. Because these calls do not always find their way into the police records submitted to the FBI, they may provide a more accurate picture of the number and kinds of crimes. One problem is that not every call to the police represents an actual crime. Some callers may describe events that do not fit the definition of any crime, and others may call with falsified reports.

NATIONAL CRIME VICTIMIZATION SURVEY

Another source of crime data is the **National Crime Victimization Survey (NCVS),** begun in the early 1970s under a slightly different name by the U.S. Department of Justice. The Justice Department initiated the NCVS to avoid the UCR problems just noted and to gather information not available from the UCR. This includes the context of crime, such as the time of day and physical setting in which it occurs, and the characteristics of crime victims, including their gender, race, income, extent of injury, and relationship with their offenders. Over the years, the NCVS has provided government officials and social scientists an additional, important source of crime data to determine whether the rates of various crimes are increasing or decreasing and to test various theories of crime.

The NCVS interviews individuals from randomly selected households every six months for a period of three years. During 2008, about 77,852 individuals age 12 and older in 42,093 households were interviewed with a response rate of about 86 percent of eligible residents. Respondents are asked whether they or their household has been a victim in the past half year of any of the following crimes: aggravated and simple assault, rape and sexual assault, robbery, burglary, various kinds of larcenies (including purse snatching and household larceny), and motor vehicle theft. The crimes are described rather than just listed. Notice that these crimes correspond to the Part I crimes included in the UCR, except that the UCR classifies simple assault as a Part II crime. The NCVS excludes the two remaining Part I crimes, homicide and arson (homicide victims obviously cannot be interviewed and too few household arsons occur), and all Part II crimes besides simple assault. The NCVS also does not ask about commercial crimes, such as shoplifting and burglary at a place of business, which the UCR includes. Finally, the NCVS includes sexual assaults short of rape, whereas the UCR excludes them.

The National Crime Victimization Survey collects important information in a large national survey from respondents who have been victims of various kinds of crimes.

For each **victimization,** the NCVS then asks residents additional questions, including the age, race, and gender of the victim and whether the victimization was reported to the police. For crimes such as robbery, assault, and rape in which the victim may have seen the offender, residents are also asked to identify the race and gender they perceived of the offender.

The NCVS estimates that about 21.3 million offenses of the kinds it covers occurred in 2008 (Rand 2009). Table 3.2 reports three kinds of data: (1) NCVS estimates of the number of victimizations for 2006, (2) the percentage of these incidents reported to the police, and (3) the number of corresponding official crimes identified by the UCR for that year. Because of the differences noted earlier in the coverage of the NCVS and the UCR, comparisons between them of crime frequency data are inexact and must be interpreted cautiously.

As you can easily see, many more victimizations occur than the UCR would have us believe, as only a surprisingly small proportion, about 40 percent overall, are reported to the police. The crimes not reported are *hidden* crimes and are often termed the "dark figure of crime" (Biderman and Reiss 1967). If, as most researchers believe, NCVS data are more reliable than UCR data, the NCVS confirms suspicions that the U.S. street crime problem is much worse than official UCR data indicate.

Why do so many crime victims not report their victimizations? Although specific reasons vary by the type of crime, many victims feel that their victimization was not serious enough to justify the time and energy in getting involved with the police. Some also feel that the police would not be able to find the offender anyway. Victims of rape, domestic violence, and other crimes in which they know the offender may also fear further harm if they report what happened, and they may wish to avoid the publicity that would occur if they talked to the police.

Although the number of victimizations reported in Table 3.2 is more than 21 million, the U.S. population is about 304 million. For this reason, the chances of becoming a crime victim should theoretically be fairly low. In some ways this is true for violent crime, because the NCVS estimates that your chances of becoming a victim of a violent

TABLE 3.2 ▸ **Number of Offenses, NCVS and UCR Data, 2008**

TYPE OF CRIME	NCVS	% REPORTED TO POLICE	UCR
Violent crime	4,856,510	47.1	1,382,012
Homicide	—	—	16,272
Forcible rape[a]	203,830	41.4	89,000
Aggravated assault	858,940	62.0	834,885
Simple assault	3,260,920	41.3	—
Robbery	551,830	60.5	441,855
Property crime	16,455,890	40.3	9,767,915
Burglary	3,188,620	56.2	2,222,196
Larceny–theft[b]	12,472,110	33.6	6,588,873
Motor vehicle theft	795,160	79.6	956,894
Total offenses	21,312,400	39.5	11,149,927

Sources: Federal Bureau of Investigation 2009; Rand 2009.
[a]NCVS number for rape includes sexual assaults.
[b]NCVS number for larceny–theft includes NCVS category of personal thefts.

crime in any given year are "only" about 1.9 percent (i.e., the number of violent-crime victimizations is about 19 per 1,000 persons age 12 or older). Your chances of becoming a victim of a property crime, however, are much higher: about 13.5 percent (Rand 2009).

These numbers obscure other figures. First, the risk of victimization varies greatly for the demographic subgroups of the population; depending on your race/ethnicity, social class, gender, and area of residence, you may be much more likely than average (or, if you are lucky, much less likely than average) to become a crime victim in any given year (see Chapter 4). Second, the annual risk of victimization adds up and over the course of a lifetime can become very high. In 1987, for example, the NCVS estimated the following lifetime risks of victimization: violent crime, 83 percent (i.e., 83 percent of the public would one day be a victim of violent crime) and property crime, 99 percent. Specific lifetime risks were as follows: robbery, 30 percent; assault, 74 percent; personal larceny, 99 percent; burglary, 72 percent; household larceny, 90 percent; and motor vehicle theft, 19 percent (Koppel 1987). Although victimization rates have declined since then, these figures indicate that many of us will become a victim of at least one violent or property crime during our lifetime and even of more than one crime.

Evaluating NCVS Data

The NCVS has at least two major advantages over the UCR (Lynch and Addington 2007). First, it yields a much more accurate estimate of the number of crimes. Because it involves a very large random sample of the U.S. population, reliable estimates of the number of victimizations in the population can be made. Second, NCVS information on the characteristics of victims and the context of victimization has furthered the development of theories of victimization (see Chapter 4). As this chapter discusses later, the NCVS also provides (through respondents' reported perceptions) a potentially more accurate portrait than UCR data of the race and gender of offenders.

Certain limitations of NCVS data also exist. A major one is that the NCVS itself underestimates the number of victimizations. Recall that the NCVS excludes commercial crime such as shoplifting and burglary at a business. In two **underreporting** problems, moreover, victims of several crimes may forget about some of them, and some respondents may decline to tell NCVS interviewers about their victimizations even though they remember them. This latter underreporting might be especially high for rape, domestic violence, and other crimes in which victims tend to know their offenders, because they may fear retaliation, wish the event to remain private, or even deem it an unfortunate episode and not a crime. Another reason for potential underestimating is that the NCVS interviews people in households. This means the survey excludes people such as the homeless and teenage runaways who do not live in households and who for various reasons have higher than normal victimization rates. Their exclusion reduces the amount of victimization the NCVS uncovers.

Although the NCVS underestimates some crimes, it might overestimate others (Catalano 2006). Respondents might mistakenly interpret some noncriminal events as crimes. They might also be guilty of *telescoping* by reporting crimes that occurred before the six-month time frame for the NCVS. Further, many of the assaults and larcenies they report are relatively minor in terms of the injury suffered or property taken. Despite possible overestimation, most researchers deem underestimation the more serious problem, and they think NCVS data on robbery, burglary, and motor vehicle theft provide a reasonably accurate picture of the actual number of these crimes in the nation (Lynch and Addington 2007).

One final problem with the NCVS is similar to a problem with the UCR. Because the NCVS solicits information only on street crimes, not on white-collar crimes, it again diverts attention from the seriousness of white-collar crime.

SELF-REPORT STUDIES

A third source of information on crime comes from studies asking respondents about offenses they may have committed in a given time period, usually the past year. Some of these **self-report studies** use interviewers, and others use questionnaires that respondents fill out themselves. Self-report studies can be used to demonstrate the **prevalence** of offending—the proportion of respondents who have committed a particular offense at least once in the time period under study—and the **incidence** of offending—the average number of offenses per person in the study.

Although some self-report studies involve adult inmates of jails and prisons, most involve adolescents, who are asked not only about their offenses but also about various aspects of their families, friends, schooling, and other possible influences on their delinquency. High school students are often studied because they comprise a *convenience sample* (or *captive audience,* as it is also called) that enables researchers to gather much information fairly quickly and cheaply. High school samples also yield a high response rate. (Wouldn't you have wanted to fill out an interesting questionnaire in high school instead of listening to yet another lecture?)

A few notable self-report studies were undertaken beginning in the 1940s, but the impetus for these studies increased as the 1960s approached because of concern, discussed earlier, over the accuracy of official crime and delinquency data. In one of the most influential self-report studies in this early period, James F. Short Jr., and F. Ivan Nye (1957) surveyed a few thousand high school students and a smaller sample of youths in reform schools. They found that a surprising amount of delinquency had been committed by their nondelinquent students and concluded that delinquency was not confined to youths from lower- or working-class backgrounds.

Because of the information it provides on offenders and the influences on their offending, self-report research has permitted major developments in our understanding of delinquent and criminal behavior. One of its most important findings, as the Short and Nye study discovered, is the amount of delinquency that remains hidden from legal officials. Self-report studies thus underscore the extent of the dark figure of crime that the NCVS demonstrates. They remain very common today and often involve local or national longitudinal samples in which the same youths are studied over time and sometimes into adulthood (Cohen, Piquero, and Jennings 2010). Other self-report surveys are *cross-sectional*, meaning their respondents are queried at only one point in time. A very popular self-report survey that involves both a cross-sectional design and a longitudinal follow-up of a sample of its respondents is *Monitoring the Future*, which has been administered to secondary school students and young adults nationwide since 1975. Selected results for the high school senior class of 2008 appear in Figure 3.2. As the results indicate, many high school seniors have broken the law, but far fewer have been arrested.

Self-report surveys of offending are most often given to high school students.

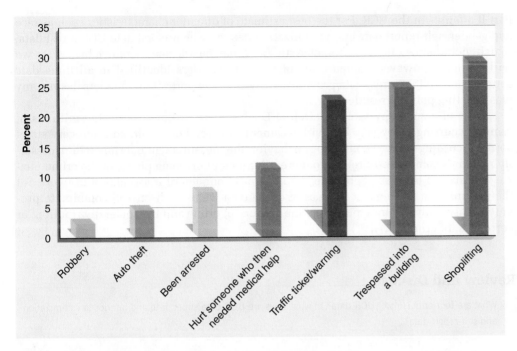

FIGURE 3.2 ▸ **Percentage of High School Seniors (Class of 2008) Reporting Involvement in Selected Activities During Last Twelve Months** Source: Bachman et al. 2008.

Critique of Self-Report Studies

A common criticism of self-report studies is that they focus on minor and trivial offenses: truancy, running away from home, minor drug and alcohol use, and the like. This focus was indeed true of most early self-report research, but recent studies ask their subjects about more serious offenses such as rape and robbery. The inclusion of these offenses has increased self-report research's ability to help us understand the full range of criminal behavior.

A second criticism is that self-report respondents sometimes fib about offenses they have committed. Investigations using lie detectors and police records verify the overall accuracy of respondents' answers (Morris and Slocum 2010), but some research has found that African-American youths are more likely than white youths to underreport their offending. State-of-the-art self-report surveying, using self-administered computer surveys, appears to produce more accurate reports than traditional (paper-and-pencil) surveying, because respondents are presumably more likely to think their answers will remain confidential (Paschall, Ornstein, and Flewelling 2001).

A final criticism is that self-report studies join the UCR and NCVS in ignoring white-collar crime because their subjects—usually adolescents or, occasionally, adult jail and prison inmates—certainly do not commit this type of crime.

EVALUATING THE UCR, THE NCVS, AND SELF-REPORT DATA

None of the three major sources of street-crime data is perfect, but which is the best depends on what one wants to know (Lynch and Addington 2007). For the best estimate of the actual number of crimes, NCVS data are clearly preferable to UCR data. Keep in mind, however, that NCVS data exclude homicide, arson, commercial crimes, and most of the

Part II offenses in the UCR. For the best estimate of offender characteristics such as race and gender, self-report data and victimization data may be preferable to UCR arrest data, which include few offender characteristics and may be affected by police biases. As we will see later, however, comparisons of type of offenders identified in all three data sources suggest that arrest data provide a fairly accurate portrait of offenders despite any bias affecting police arrest decisions.

Short of a superspy satellite circling Earth and recording each of the millions of crimes occurring every year or a video camera in every household and on every street corner recording every second of our behavior, the measurement of crime will necessarily remain incomplete. To return to our earlier metaphor, some pieces of the crime puzzle will always be missing, but we think we have enough of it assembled to figure out the picture. The three major sources of crime data we have discussed combine to provide a reasonably accurate picture of the amount of crime and the social distribution, or correlates, of criminality.

Review and Discuss

What are four criticisms of UCR data? In what ways are UCR data superior to and inferior to victimization and self-report data?

Recent Trends in U.S. Crime Rates

Crime rates rose sharply (UCR rates) during the 1960s and 1970s before declining during the early 1980s and then rising again during the late 1980s. They then began to fall sharply after the early 1990s before declining more slowly during the past several years (see Figures 3.3 and 3.4 for both UCR and NCVS data). Although the UCR and NCVS do not always exhibit the same crime-rate trends because of their different methodologies, the fact that both data sources show declining crime since the early 1990s provides confidence that crime has in fact decreased during this period.

Scholars and other observers have debated why crime fell so dramatically. Some cite changes in police practices and other aspects of the criminal justice system, whereas others cite social factors. The Crime and Controversy box discusses this debate.

Patterning of Criminal Behavior

Crime rates vary according to location, season and climate, and demographic factors such as gender, race, and social class. This section discusses this **patterning.**

GEOGRAPHICAL PATTERNS

International Comparisons

International comparisons of crime data are inexact. (See the International Focus box.) We have already seen that U.S. crime data are not totally reliable. Across the world, different nations have varying definitions and interpretations of criminal behavior and alternative methods of collecting crime data. Although these problems suggest caution in making international comparisons, these comparisons still provide striking evidence of the ways crime is patterned geographically.

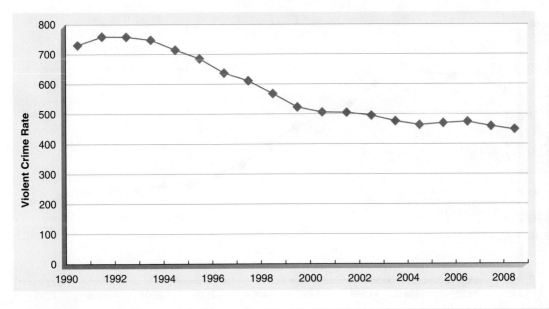

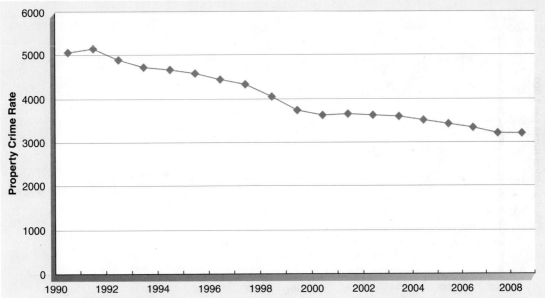

FIGURE 3.3 ▸ **Violent and Property Crime Known to the Police, 1990–2008, UCR (number per 100,000 inhabitants)**
Sources: Federal Bureau of Investigation 2007; Pastore and Maguire 2010.

Simply put, some nations have higher crime rates than others. In this regard, the United States has the highest homicide rate of any Western democratic nation. In the late 1980s it had one of the highest rates of other violent crimes, but by 2000 its violent-crime rate had lowered to about average; its property-crime rate also seems about average (van Dijk 2008). Scholars often attribute nations' crime rates to their cultures. In Japan, for example, one of the most important values is harmony: the Japanese are expected to be peaceable in their relations with each other and respectful of authority. Partly because such a culture inhibits people from committing crimes, Japan's crime rates remain relatively low despite its economic growth since World War II (Johnson 2007).

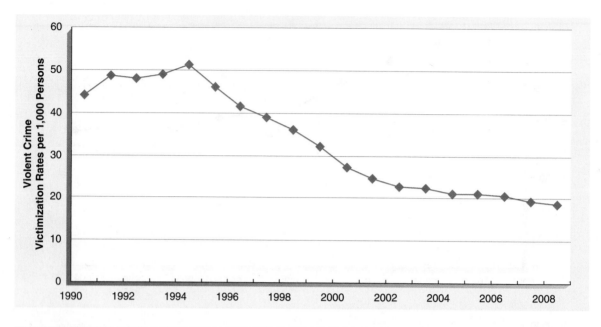

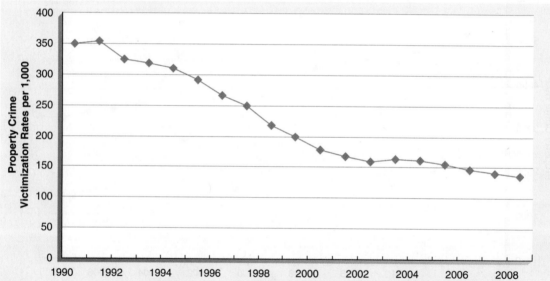

FIGURE 3.4 ▶ **Victimization Rates for Violent and Property Crime, 1993–2005, NCVS (per 1,000 persons 12 or older or 1,000 households)** Source: www.ojp.usdoj.gov/bjs/keytabs.htm.
Note: Because of changes in survey methodology, 2006 estimates for both violent and property crime were not comparable to earlier estimates and thus are omitted.

In contrast to Japan and some other nations, people in the United States are thought to be more individualistic and disrespectful of authority (Messner and Rosenfeld 2007). With the familiar phrase "look out for number one" as a prevailing philosophy, there is less emphasis in the United States on peaceable relations and less sense of social obligation. People do not care as much about offending others and are thus more likely to do so. The United States is also thought to have higher rates of violence than some other industrial nations because of its higher degree of inequality (Chamlin and Cochran 2006). Chapter 7 discusses the inequality–violence linkage further.

Crime and Controversy

Why Did the Crime Rate Fall During the 1990s?

The U.S. crime rate fell dramatically beginning in the early 1990s before leveling off several years ago. Coming after a drastic rise in violent crime beginning in the late 1980s, the 1990s' crime decline was a pleasant surprise for Americans, but also the source of much controversy among criminologists and public officials over why it was occurring. This controversy was no mere intellectual exercise. If the reasons for the decline could be pinpointed, the nation would have gained some valuable information on effective policies and strategies to drive down the crime rate further or at least to keep it from rising again.

Debate over the reasons for the 1990s' crime decline falls into two camps, each centered on a very different set of factors. One side gives the bulk of the credit for the crime decline to the criminal justice system, specifically a get-tough-on-crime approach and smarter policing. According to this view, longer and more certain sentences prompted a rapidly increasing imprisonment rate during the 1990s that kept our streets safer by putting hundreds of thousands of criminals behind bars and by deterring potential offenders from committing crimes in the first place. *Zero-tolerance* policing in New York and other cities rid the streets of panhandlers and other minor offenders who had committed more serious crimes and sent a message of civility to other offenders and the general populace. At the same time, police targeting of neighborhoods rampant with drug crime, prostitution, and other offenses also proved effective.

The other side says that social and demographic factors explain most of the crime-rate decline. According to this view, the thriving economy during the 1990s lessened the motivation to commit crime, and a decline in the number of people in the crime-prone years of adolescence and young adulthood reduced the number of potential offenders. Also, the crack gang wars that fueled the rise in crime during the late 1980s and early 1990s finally subsided as the crack market stabilized. Proponents of this side of the debate also take issue with the arguments of the criminal justice advocates. Crime had risen during the 1980s, these proponents say, even though imprisonment had also risen, casting doubt on a presumed imprisonment–crime decline link during the 1990s. In addition, states that were the toughest on crime during the 1990s often did not experience the greatest crime declines. Although increasing imprisonment might have helped somewhat, they add, it has had harmful collateral consequences for many urban neighborhoods and has cost billions of dollars that could have been better spent on other efforts. Moreover, although new policing strategies might have helped, cities that did not use them also saw their crime rates drop.

Chapters 16 and 17 return to this debate with a more complete discussion of the criminal justice factors that have been credited for the 1990s' crime drop, but the controversy over the reasons continues precisely because of its importance for determining the most effective crime-control strategies. If the first side to the debate is correct, then the United States would be wise to continue to put more and more people behind bars for a greater number of years and to have the police crack down on minor offenses and on the serious offenses that terrorize high-crime neighborhoods. If the second side to the debate is correct, this criminal justice approach does more harm than good, and the dollars it incurs would be better spent on efforts that address the structural and individual factors that underlie crime and that are highlighted in a sociological approach to crime and crime control.

Ironically, it might be possible that neither side has a good explanation for the 1990s' crime decline, because Canada also experienced a significant crime decrease during the 1990s even though its rates of imprisonment and police employment both *decreased* and even though its economy did not fare particularly well. Although Canada, like the United States, did experience a drop in the number of people in their young crime-prone years, this drop was too small in either nation to account for very much of its crime decline. Thus, as Franklin E. Zimring (2006:134), who called attention to the Canadian puzzle, wrote of the two nations' crime declines, "Much of the shared good news of recent history seems to elude easy explanations."

Sources: Blumstein and Wallman 2006; Rosenfeld, Fornango, and Rengifo 2007; Wadsworth 2010; Zimring 2006.

Review and Discuss

Why does the United States have higher crime rates than Japan and several other nations? How do international comparisons of crime rates reflect the sociological perspective?

Comparisons Within the United States

Crime rates within the United States also vary geographically. According to the UCR, the South and West have the highest rates of crime, and the Northeast and Midwest have the lowest rates. Community size also makes a huge difference; crime rates are higher in urban areas than they are in rural areas. Figure 3.5 presents UCR data for crime rates per 100,000 broken down by community size. As you can see, violent- and property-crime rates in our largest cities (MSAs, or metropolitan statistical areas) and other cities are higher than those in rural communities. Chapter 7 will discuss why cities have more crime, but note that urbanization does not automatically mean high crime rates. For example, some of the largest non-U.S. cities (e.g., Toronto, London, and Tokyo) have much lower homicide rates than those in much smaller U.S. cities.

International Focus

Measuring Crime in Other Nations

Although international crime data are gathered by the United Nations and other organizations, the measurement of crime across the world is highly inconsistent. In some countries, such as the United States, Canada, and Great Britain, the government systematically gathers crime data through police reports and victimization surveys. In other nations, especially those that are very poor, crime reporting is haphazard or even virtually nonexistent. Some nations gather and provide arrest and conviction data, whereas others do not. Another problem is that various crimes are defined differently by different nations. For example, what constitutes a rape in some nations may be very different from what constitutes a rape in the United States. Because of its nature, homicide is probably the crime most uniformly defined, and homicide data are believed to be the most consistent international data available about crime. For this reason, many researchers think international comparisons of crime rates should be restricted to homicide.

The three major sources of official international crime data include the International Criminal Police Organization (Interpol), the World Health Organization (WHO), and the United Nations survey. Although these sources differ in the crimes they cover and the definitions of crime they use, they all provide reasonably reliable data about homicide. Interpol and the UN surveys use homicide data collected by appropriate agencies in various nations, whereas WHO uses nations' mortality data that identify homicide as the cause of death. WHO homicide data are considered more accurate than Interpol or UN data and thus tend to be the focus of international homicide research. At the same time, WHO homicide data exist for only about three dozen nations; these nations account for less than 20 percent of the world population, and their homicides account for less than 10 percent of world homicides. On the plus side, WHO data comprise virtually all the wealthy industrialized nations.

Victimization surveys, most of which are conducted in wealthy nations, are another source of international crime data and are becoming more popular (see Chapter 4). Similar to the NCVS, these surveys ask random samples of respondents about the extent and nature of their victimization by a wide variety of offenses. Although social and cultural differences make comparisons of international victimization data somewhat inexact, these data have nonetheless yielded valuable information on international differences in victimization rates.

Sources: Bennett 2009; van Dijk 2008; van Dijk, Kesteren, and Smit 2008.

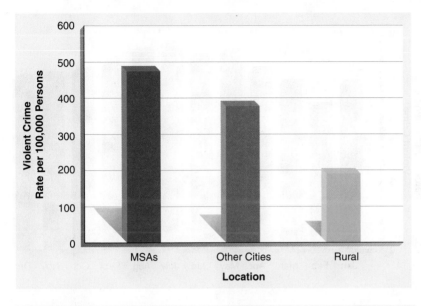

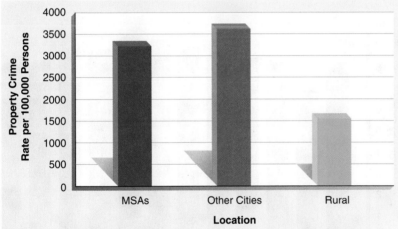

FIGURE 3.5 ▶ **Urbanization and UCR Crime Rates, 2008** Source: Federal Bureau of Investigation 2009.

SEASONAL AND CLIMATOLOGICAL VARIATIONS

Some of the most interesting crime data concern **seasonal** and **climatological** (weather-related) variations (see Figure 3.6). For many people, summer can be very grim because violent crime is generally higher in the warmer months, although robbery remains high through January. Property crime also peaks in the summer.

Explanations for these patterns are speculative but seem to make some sense (Hipp et al. 2004). As you might already realize, the summer heat can cause tempers to flare, perhaps violently. We also tend to interact more when it is warmer, creating opportunities for violent behavior to erupt. In addition, people are outdoors and away from home more often in the summer, creating opportunities for various kinds of thefts. For example, there are more empty homes to attract burglars. Those not on vacation are still more apt to leave windows open to let in fresh air, again making burglary more likely.

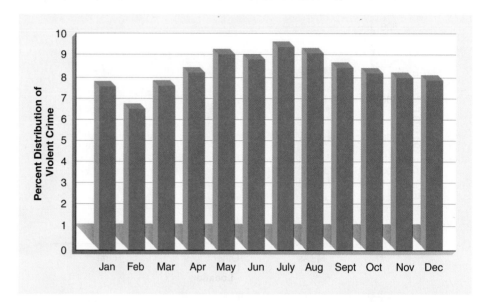

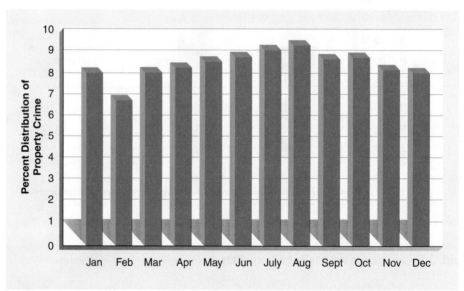

FIGURE 3.6 ▸ **Violent Crime and Property Crime by Month, 2006 (percentage of annual crime that occurs each month)** Source: Federal Bureau of Investigation 2007.

Social Patterns of Criminal Behavior

GENDER AND CRIME

One of the key social correlates of criminal behavior is gender: women's crime rates are much lower than men's. Figure 3.7 displays UCR arrest data broken down by gender. As you can see, men account for about 82 percent of violent-crime arrests and 65 percent of property-crime arrests. It is possible, of course, that police bias may account for the high proportion of male arrests: perhaps the police are less likely to arrest women because they do not think women are very dangerous. However, victimization and self-report data reinforce the UCR's large gender difference. In the NCVS, victims identify men as about 86 percent of all violent offenders (Greenfeld and Snell 1999). Although the gender difference in some self-report studies is smaller than the UCR's, the difference for the most serious self-reported crimes approaches the UCR's. Almost all scholars today acknowledge that women's rates of serious offending are much lower than men's rates, with this gender gap called "one of the few undisputed 'facts' in criminology" (Lauritsen, Heimer, and Lynch 2009).

Explaining Women's Low Crime Rates

In the past, many criminologists ignored female criminality. Some did discuss it, but their explanations emphasized women's biology (Griffin 2010; Klein 1973). For example, one

Crime is generally higher during the summer months, in part because people spend more time together outside their homes, creating greater opportunities for both violent crime and property crime to occur.

of the first scholars of crime, physician Cesare Lombroso, attributed women's low criminality to their natural passivity resulting from the "immobility of the ovule compared with the zoosperm" (Lombroso 1920 [1903]) (see Chapter 6). Followers of the great psychoanalytic thinker Sigmund Freud thought that women commit crime because of *penis envy:* jealous over not having penises, they strive to be more like men by committing crimes (and also by working outside the home). In an interesting twist, Otto Pollak (1950) argued that women's crimes often never show up in official statistics. The reason? Women are naturally deceitful and thus are good at hiding their behavior. The proof of such deceit? Women learn to hide evidence of their menstrual periods and also to fake orgasms!

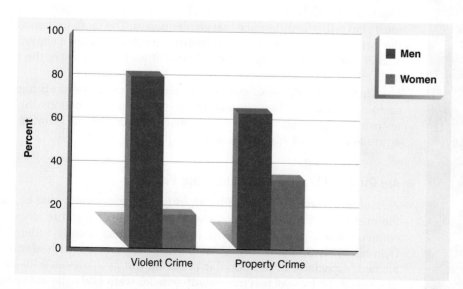

FIGURE 3.7 ▸ **Gender and Arrest, 2008 (percentage of all Part I crime arrests)** Source: Federal Bureau of Investigation 2009.

The field of criminology now considers these early biological explanations outmoded and sexist. In the 1970s, women began to enter the field in greater numbers and, along with some male scholars, began to study the origins and nature of female crime and of crimes such as rape and family violence that especially victimize women. Several factors are now thought to account for women's low crime rates (Van Wormer and Bartollas 2011).

A first explanation concerns the way we socialize girls and boys. Put briefly, we raise boys to be active, assertive, dominant, and to "fight like a man"—in other words, to be masculine. Because these traits are conducive to criminal behavior, especially violence, the way we raise boys increases their odds of becoming criminals. Conversely, we raise girls to be less assertive, less dominant, and more gentle and nurturing (Lindsey 2011). Because these traits are not conducive to criminal behavior, we in effect are raising girls not to be criminals. We will address the *criminogenic* (crime-causing) aspects of masculinity in more depth in Chapters 9 through 11.

A second explanation for the low crime rates of women concerns the different opportunities provided to commit crime. Because of the traditional double standard, parents typically monitor their daughters' behavior more closely than their sons' behavior. Boys thus have more opportunity than girls to commit crime.

A third explanation concerns attachments to families, schools, and other social institutions. Some research indicates that these bonds are stronger for girls than for boys because of socialization. Girls, for example, feel more strongly attached than boys to their parents and thus are more likely to value their parents' norms and values. Girls also place more importance on schooling and are more likely than boys to emphasize obedience to the law. These attachments and beliefs lead to lower rates of female offending.

Yet another reason for girls' lower delinquency is that they have fewer ties than boys have to delinquent peers (McCarthy, Felmlee, and Hagan 2004). Moreover, their greater attachment to parents and schools makes them less vulnerable to the negative influence of any delinquent friends they do have. Conversely, boys' lower attachment makes them more susceptible to the pressure of their peers, most of them boys themselves, to commit delinquency.

Although women certainly commit crime, their crime rates are much lower than men's crime rates.

These basic differences in the way children are raised are key to understanding the origins of crime and how crime might be reduced. Put simply, *we are already doing a good job of raising our girls not to be criminals*. If men's crime rates were as low as women's, crime in the United States would *not* be a major problem. Thus, any effort to reduce criminality must start with the difference that gender makes. The more we know about the origins of both female criminality and law-abiding behavior, the greater our understanding will be of what it will take to lower the rate of male criminality.

These explanations of gender differences in crime rates all highlight sociological factors. Two contemporary biological explanations highlight testosterone differences and evolutionary circumstances favoring male aggression. We will address these in Chapter 6.

Are Girls and Women Becoming More Violent?

Before moving on, let us consider an important controversy that began in the mid-1970s when magazines and scholarly books began to stress that women's arrest rates were rising much faster than men's (Adler 1975; Deming 1977; Simon 1975). This increase was greeted with alarm and blamed, especially in the popular press, on the new women's liberation movement. Because of this movement, females were said to be acting more like males. This blame represented a more general backlash against the women's movement (Faludi 1991). More recent books and popular media articles have also said that girls and women are "catching up" to boys and men in violent behavior (Garbarino 2006).

However, a series of scholarly studies since the 1970s has concluded that this belief is in fact a myth. Although female arrests have risen, that increase reflects an increase in decisions of police to arrest girls and women for violence, rather than an actual increase in their level of violence. Despite the impression conveyed by media reports of "mean girls," female rates of violent crime have been decreasing for many years (see Figure 3.8), and there is no reason to believe that girls and women are catching up to boys and men in criminal behavior (Chesney-Lind and Jones 2010; Males and Chesney-Lind 2010; Schwartz, Steffensmeier, and Feldmeyer 2009).

Review and Discuss

Why do women have lower crime rates than men? To what degree are changes in women's crime rates related to the contemporary women's movement?

RACE, ETHNICITY, AND CRIME

UCR data provide a complex picture of race and criminality in the United States. On the one hand, most criminals are white. In 2008, whites accounted for about 69 percent of all arrests, including 58 percent of violent-crime arrests, 67 percent of property-crime arrests, and at least two-thirds of arrests for forgery and counterfeiting, fraud, vandalism, drug abuse, liquor law offenses and drunkenness, and disorderly conduct (Federal Bureau of Investigation 2009). In terms of sheer numbers, whites commit most crime in the United States, and the typical criminal is white.

On the other hand, African Americans commit a disproportionate amount of crime relative to their numbers in the population. Even though African Americans comprise

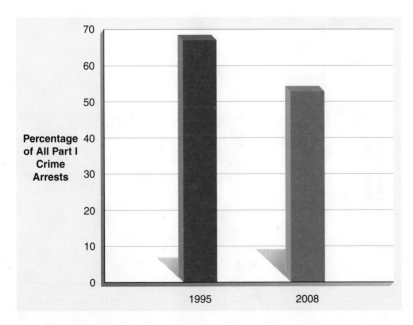

FIGURE 3.8 ▸ Women's Violent Crime Rate (number of violent crime arrests per 100,000 women in population)
Source: Pastore and Maguire 2010.

only about 13 percent of the population, in 2008 they accounted for 28 percent of all arrests, 39 percent of violent-crime arrests (including 50 percent of homicide arrests), and 30 percent of property-crime arrests. Another way of understanding racial differences in arrests is to examine racial arrest rates, or the number of each race arrested for every 100,000 members of that race. Figure 3.9 displays these rates for African Americans and whites. As you see, the African-American arrest rate for violent and property crime is much higher than the white arrest rate. Government statistical analysis estimates that almost one-third of African-American males born in 2001 will one day go to prison, compared to less than 6 percent of white males (Figure 3.10).

The apparent disproportionate involvement of African Americans in street crime is one of the most sensitive but important issues in criminology (Hagan and Peterson 1995;

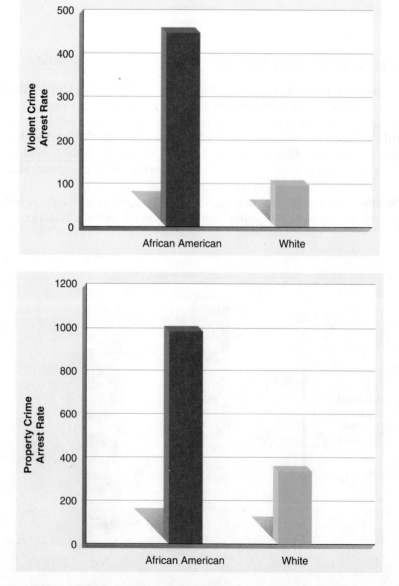

FIGURE 3.9 ▶ **Race and Arrest Rates, 2008 (number of index crime arrests per 100,000 population)**
Sources: U.S. Bureau of the Census 2009; Federal Bureau of Investigation 2009.

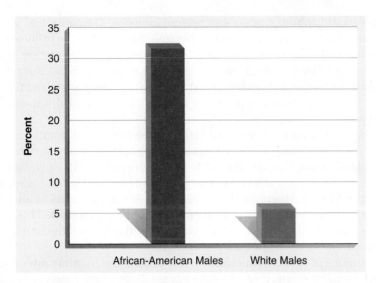

FIGURE 3.10 ▸ **Estimated Lifetime Chances (percentage of all individuals) of Going to Prison for Persons Born in 2008** Source: Bonczar 2003.

Sampson and Wilson 1995). As with gender, all these racial arrest statistics may reflect bias in police arrest practices and in sentencing more than racial differences in actual offending. Once again, however, NCVS data tend to support the UCR portrait of higher African-American crime rates. Recall that NCVS respondents are asked to report the perceived race of offenders for crimes—assault, rape, robbery—in which they saw their offender. Suggesting that African Americans do have higher crime rates, the proportion of offenders identified by NCVS data as African American is similar to the African-American proportion of UCR arrests (Walker, Spohn, and DeLone 2007). Self-report data also find a racial difference in serious offending (Farrington, Loeber, and Stouthamer-Loeber 2003). Notwithstanding possible racial bias in the criminal justice system (see Chapters 16 and 17), then, most scholars today agree that African Americans are indeed more heavily involved in serious street crime (Farrington, Loeber, and Stouthamer-Loeber 2003; Haynie, Weiss, and Piquero 2008; Walker, Spohn, and DeLone 2007). For minor offenses, however, racial differences may be smaller than arrest statistics suggest.

Explaining African-American Crime Rates

If African Americans do commit higher rates of serious street crime, why so? In the early 1900s, racist explanations blamed their supposed biological inferiority (Gabbidon and Greene 2009) (see Chapter 6). Beginning in the 1960s, explanations focusing on a **subculture of violence** (e.g., attitudes approving violence) and on deficiencies in African-American family structure (e.g., absent fathers) became popular (Moynihan 1965; Wolfgang and Ferracuti 1967). Today many scholars consider the evidence for an African-American subculture of violence weak, but others continue to favor this explanation (see Chapter 7). The family structure explanations also remain popular, but evidence that father-absent households produce lawbreaking children is in fact inconsistent (see Chapter 8).

Many criminologists instead cite the negative social conditions in which African Americans and other people of color live. According to this view, "African Americans and other minorities exhibit higher rates of violence than do whites because they are more likely to reside in community contexts with high levels of poverty, unemployment, family disruption, and residential instability. . . . If whites were embedded in similar structural contexts, they would exhibit comparable rates of violence" (McNulty and Bellair 2003a). These structural conditions heighten crime because they weaken the influence of conventional social institutions such as family and schools and create frustration and hopelessness (Gabbidon and Greene 2009; Peterson and Krivo 2005). The racial discrimination felt by African Americans also matters because it is thought to cause anger and frustration that in turn result in criminal behavior (Unnever et al. 2009). Chapter 7 discusses these explanations further.

Before leaving the issue of race and crime, three additional points are worth mentioning. First, race is a *social construction*, something that we make up rather than something real (Gabbidon and Greene 2009; Zatz and Rodriguez 2006). How, for example, do we determine whether someone is African American? In the United States, we usually consider people African American if they have any African ancestry at all, even if most of their ancestry is white. Other countries follow different practices. This ambiguity in measuring race may lead to "faulty conclusions regarding the relationship between race and involvement in crime" (Hawkins 1994).

Second, studies of African-American–white differences in crime rates address street crime, not white-collar crime. If street criminals are disproportionately African American and other people of color, white-collar criminals are typically white. Despite the explanations of African-American criminality stressing a violent subculture, family structure problems, or poor living conditions, whites are quite capable of committing white-collar crime despite growing up in intact families and living in advantaged communities. In this regard, criminologists warn of the myth of the *criminal black man* that depicts a young African-American male as the prototypical serious criminal offender (Russell 2009; Young 2006). This myth, they say, obscures the domination of whites in white-collar crime and ignores the fact that whites, thanks to their large numbers, also account for the majority of street crime.

Third, although certain aspects of the African-American experience contribute to a higher crime rate, recent research finds that other aspects decrease African Americans' criminal behavior (Wright and Younts 2009). These aspects include relatively high levels of religiosity and low levels of alcohol use, strong family ties, and strong belief in the value of education. Sociologists Bradley R. Entner Wright and C. Wesley Younts (2009: 348) say that these "prosocial" aspects have been "virtually ignored in studies of race and crime," and they add that consideration of these aspects "contradicts the stereotypical caricature of African Americans as violent, aggressive, and crime prone."

Fourth, recall from Figure 3.9 that the African-American arrest rate for violent crime in 2008 was 460 per 100,000, and for property crime it was 1,003 per 100,000. Although these numbers exceed those for whites, a more familiar way of understanding them is to say that for every 100 African Americans, about 0.46 are arrested every year for violent crime and 1.00 are arrested for property crime. That means that 99.54 of every 100 African Americans are *not* arrested each year for violent crime, and 99.00 of every 100 African Americans are *not* arrested for property crime. Despite the concern about African-American crime rates, then, the evidence is very clear that virtually all African Americans are not arrested in any given year for Part I crimes.

Regardless, criminology must not shy away from acknowledging and explaining African-American street crime, because even the small absolute rates just cited translate into tens of thousands of crimes nationwide and devastate many urban neighborhoods. As Gary LaFree and Katheryn K. Russell (1993) once put it, "[W]e must face the problem of race and crime directly, forthrightly, and with the most objective evidence we can muster collectively. Ignoring connections between race and crime has not made them go away." It is both possible and important to explain the race–crime connection in a nonracist manner. In this regard, the structural explanations mentioned earlier are especially promising (see Chapters 7 and 10).

Latinos and Other Groups

This section has discussed African Americans because criminology has studied them far more than it has studied other people of color. This focus is understandable for several reasons. First, African Americans historically were America's largest minority and the only one forced to live in slavery. Second, their rates of violent crime have been very high. Third, UCR data record the race of arrestees (white, African American, Native American, Asian, or Pacific Islander), but not their ethnicity. Because Latinos may be of any race, they do not appear as a separate category in UCR arrest data.

As understandable as it may be, criminology's focus on African Americans has translated into neglect of other racial and ethnic groups, and the field knows much less about their criminal behavior and victimization and experiences in the criminal justice system. Now that Latinos are the largest minority group and a growing influence on the cultural and political life of the nation, they are receiving more attention from criminologists, although the lack of adequate arrest data of Latinos continues to be a problem.

That said, the available criminological knowledge does yield a fairly reliable picture of the extent of and reasons for Latino criminality (Haynie and Payne 2006; Martinez and Valenzuela 2006; Miller, Jennings, and Alvarez-Rivera 2009; Vélez 2006). First, Latinos (focusing on adolescents) have higher serious crime and victimization rates than non-Latino whites have, but lower rates than African Americans have. Among Latinos, people of Mexican or Puerto Rican descent have higher rates than those of Cuban descent, who tend to be wealthier. Second, Latinos' crime rates are generally explained by the fact that they tend, like African Americans, to live amid structural criminogenic conditions, including poverty, unemployment, and rundown urban neighborhoods (Rose and McClain 2003). Native American crime rates are also much higher than white rates and for similar structural reasons (Lanier and Huff-Corzine 2006), while Asian-American crime rates appear lower than white rates, perhaps because of Asians' strong family structures and lower use of drugs and alcohol (McNulty and Bellair 2003b).

One interesting question is why Latinos have lower violent-crime rates than African Americans. Scholars cite several reasons for this difference (Vélez 2006). First, Latino neighborhoods and individuals are less poor than their African-American counterparts and have lower rates of other structural problems, including unemployment and single-parent households. Second, Latino communities have higher numbers of immigrants, and immigrants tend to have lower crime rates than U.S.-born residents living in similar socioeconomic circumstances. Third, Latino communities have better relations than African-American communities with the police, local politicians, and bank officials, and these better relations help for many reasons (e.g., the provision of economic and legal resources) to reduce crime rates. Fourth, Latino neighborhoods are less racially segregated than African-American neighborhoods and less physically isolated from white neighborhoods. Latino neighborhoods can thus more easily avoid certain problems created by racial segregation and are also "in a better position to protect themselves from crime because they benefit from the spillover of nearby more affluent and socially organized neighborhoods" (Vélez 2006:101).

Immigrants

The findings that immigrants have relatively low rates of crime, the second reason just noted, merit further discussion here. Contrary to what many Americans might assume, a growing amount of research shows that

Latinos have higher rates of street crime than do non-Latino whites for several reasons, including their greater poverty and greater likelihood of living in rundown neighborhoods.

immigrants have lower rates of crime than nonimmigrants (Ousey and Kubrin 2009; Wadsworth 2010). According to María B. Vélez (2006: 96), at least two factors help explain why "the presence of immigrants in a neighborhood helps to control crime." First, immigrant neighborhoods tend to have high numbers of residents owning or working in the many small businesses (e.g., restaurants) that such neighborhoods need. Second, these neighborhoods also tend to have strong social institutions like churches and schools. For several reasons, the stable employment and strong institutions that thus characterize these neighborhoods help to reduce crime. Other scholars point to the relatively high rates of married households among Latino immigrants as a possible reason for their lower crime rates. Drawing on all this research, some criminologists credit the increased immigration of the 1990s for contributing to the crime rate decline during that decade, and they point out that the evidence of a crime *reducing* effect of immigration "goes against the grain of popular stereotypes" (Sampson 2006).

Interestingly, some research finds that second-generation immigrants commit more crime than new immigrants and that third-generation immigrants commit more crime than second-generation ones (Rumbaut and Ewing 2007; Sampson 2008). Thus, crime among these immigrant families rises the longer they have been in the United States. This may happen for several reasons (Press 2006). First, the children of immigrants may become embittered and abandon their parents' optimism as they experience ethnic discrimination and economic problems. Second, they have time to learn the U.S. culture and in particular two aspects of this culture: (1) its affinity for drugs, flashy possessions, and other temptations that may attract young people into criminal behavior; and (2) its "look out for number one" ideology that is thought more generally to contribute to U.S. crime. In short, as two scholars put it, "The children and grandchildren of many immigrants—as well as many immigrants themselves the longer they live in the United States—become subject to economic and social forces that increase the likelihood of criminal behavior" (Rumbaut and Ewing 2007: 11).

Review and Discuss

Why do African Americans have higher crime rates than whites? Is it racist to claim that this racial difference in crime exists?

SOCIAL CLASS AND CRIME

Most people arrested and imprisoned for street crime are poorly educated with low incomes: about two-thirds of prisoners lack even a high school diploma. Sociologists have long been interested in the association between social class and criminality, and they developed several theories of crime from the 1920s through the 1950s to explain why poor people have higher crime rates (see Chapters 7 and 8).

In the 1960s, many sociologists began to argue that the overrepresentation of the poor in the criminal justice system stemmed more from class bias than from real differences in offending. Several scholars, most notably Tittle, Villemez, and Smith (1978), proclaimed the long-assumed relationship between social class and criminality a myth. While conceding the possibility of class bias, other scholars challenged this new view (Braithwaite 1981; Hindelang, Hirschi, and Weis 1979). Addressing the debate, a president of the American Society of Criminology warned that a failure to recognize the importance of class would leave criminology impoverished (Hagan 1992). Another sociologist wryly observed that "social scientists somehow still knew better than to stroll the streets at night in certain parts of town or even to park there . . . [and they] knew that the parts of town that scared them were not upper-income neighborhoods" (Stark 1987). Supporting these latter views, self-report studies do find that poor youths, especially those whose families live in extreme poverty and chronic unemployment, have higher rates of serious offending (Bjerk 2007; Elliott 1994; Farnworth et al. 1994).

However, if we consider white-collar crime along with street crime, there probably is no relationship between social class and criminality (Rosoff, Pontell, and Tillman 2010). Although very poor individuals have higher rates of serious street crime, middle- and upper-class persons clearly have the monopoly on white-collar crime. Explanations of underclass involvement in street criminality focusing on poverty, unemployment, and related structural conditions cannot account for white-collar criminality.

Review and Discuss

Is the relationship between social class and criminality a myth, or does an actual relationship exist? What is the evidence for and against the existence of an actual relationship?

AGE AND CRIME

As you probably realize by now, criminologists disagree on all sorts of issues involving the measurement and patterning of crime. Age, however, is one area in which there is widespread agreement: "The view that involvement in crime diminishes with age is one of the oldest and most widely accepted in criminology" (Steffensmeier and Allan 2000). Simply put, street crime is disproportionately committed by young people. As Figure 3.11 shows, the 15-to-24 age bracket accounts for only 14.0 percent of the population, but 40.1 percent of all arrests. Crime peaks at ages 17 or 18 and then declines, especially beyond young adulthood. Despite minor variations depending on the type of crime, this pattern holds true whether one looks at UCR arrests, the perceived age of offenders reported to NCVS interviewers, or self-report data (Steffensmeier and Allan 2000). White-collar crime is once again a different matter because older people commit most of it; teenagers and young adults are too young to be in a position to commit such crime.

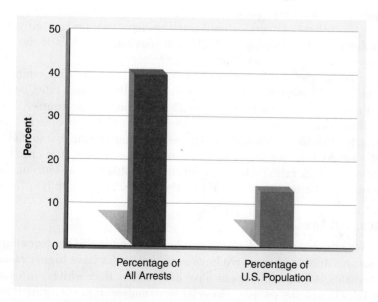

FIGURE 3.11 ▸ **Age and Arrest, 2008 (for ages 15–24)** Source: Federal Bureau of Investigation 2009; U.S. Census Bureau 2009.

Young people commit more street crimes than do older people.

Explaining the Age–Crime Relationship

Why is street crime primarily a young person's phenomenon, and why does it decline after adolescence and young adulthood? Several factors seem to be at work (Steffensmeier and Allan 2000). First, adolescence is a time when peer influences and the desire for friendships are especially strong. To the extent that peers influence one's own delinquent behavior, it is not surprising that adolescence is a peak time for offending. As we move into adulthood, our peer influences diminish, and our peers become more law-abiding than they used to be. As a result, we become more law-abiding as well (Warr 2002).

Second, adolescents, as you well know, have an increasing need for money that part-time jobs or parental allowances may not satisfy. For at least some adolescents, crime provides a means to obtain financial resources. If this is true, one reason crime declines after moving into adulthood might be that our incomes rise as we get full-time jobs; the particularly bleak employment prospects for African Americans is one reason for their higher street-crime rates in young adulthood (Haynie, Weiss, and Piquero 2008). Third, our ties to society strengthen as we become young adults. We acquire full-time jobs, usually get married and have children, and in general start becoming full-fledged members of society. These bonds to society give us an increasing sense of responsibility and stake in conformity and thus reduce our likelihood of committing crime (Laub, Sampson, and Sweeten 2006).

We also become more mature as we leave adolescence; we are no longer the youthful rebels who think everything our parents say and want us to do is ridiculous. We begin to realize that many of the indiscretions of our youth may have been fun and daring but were clearly illegal. What we were ready to excuse back then, we cannot excuse now. "Yes, I did _____ [fill in the blank] when I was a teenager," you might tell your own children, "but I don't want you doing that!" They'll inevitably see this remark as a sign of your hypocrisy; you'll regard it as a sign of your maturity.

An understanding of the age–crime relationship helps us understand shifts in a nation's crime rate. An increased birth rate will, some fifteen years later, begin to lead to an increased number of people in the 15-to-25 crime-prone age group. All other things being equal, the nation's crime rate should rise as the number of people in this age group rises. If the birth rate later declines, then as these young people move into their less crime-prone middle age and are replaced by fewer numbers of youths, the crime rate should decline. One reason U.S. crime rates rose during the 1960s was the entrance of the baby-boom generation born after World War II into the 15-to-25 age group (Ferdinand 1970).

Gender, Race, and Age Combined

In Chapter 2 we saw that race and gender combine to produce higher fear among African-American women. In this chapter we have seen that males have higher rates of serious crime than females, African Americans have higher rates than whites, and young people have higher rates than older people. These patterns suggest that young African-American males should have especially high rates of serious offending and older white women very low rates. Table 3.3 reports homicide arrest rates (per 100,000 persons) for various gender,

TABLE 3.3 ▸ Gender, Race, Age, and Arrest Rates for Homicide, 2005 (per 100,000 persons)

CATEGORY	RATE
Age 18–24	
African-American males	203.3
African-American females	11.8
White males	22.4
White females	2.0
Age 25 and older	
African-American males	41.8
African-American females	4.0
White males	5.5
White females	0.8

Source: http://bjs.ojp.usdoj.gov/content/homicide/ageracesex.cfm.

race, and age combinations. Notice first that the younger age group has higher arrest rates than the older age group for each gender and race combination. Now look just at the 18-to-24 age group. Notice that within each race males have higher arrest rates than females, and within each gender African Americans have higher arrest rates than whites. The same patterns hold true for the older age group. This all works out so that African-American men between the ages of 18 and 24 have the highest rate in the table, 203.3, and white women 25 and older have the lowest rate, 0.8, a huge difference. The patterns displayed in Table 3.3 once again provide powerful evidence of the sociological perspective's emphasis on the importance of social backgrounds for behavior.

Chronic Offenders and Criminal Careers

One of the most important findings of self-report studies, especially those studying the same persons over time, is that roughly 6 percent of adolescents are responsible for most of the serious crimes committed by the entire group of adolescents (Visher 2000). Although many young people break the law, their offenses are usually minor ones. However, a small number commit many offenses each, particularly the more serious offenses, and persist in their offending over time. These **chronic offenders** often continue their offending into adulthood as they enter **criminal careers** (Loeber et al. 2008). Career criminality is more common among those with low education and bleak job prospects, characteristics most common of the urban underclass. Although some scholars feel that offending does not continue long into adulthood and thus dispute the existence of criminal careers, most accept the concept as a valid characterization of a small number of offenders.

Knowledge of the age patterning of crime and of the existence of career criminals has important implications for efforts to reduce crime. The "three strikes and you're out" legislation popular a decade ago required life imprisonment for people convicted of a third felony. Because imprisonment would continue long after the criminality of most offenders would have declined anyway as they aged, critics said this legislation would increase prison overcrowding, but do little to reduce crime (see Chapter 17). Another effort involves identifying youths at risk for becoming career criminals so that they can be targeted for innovative treatment and punishment (Visher 2000). However, the prediction of career criminality can be inaccurate, with many *false positives* (people falsely predicted to be career criminals) resulting. Efforts to target career criminals remain beset by various legal and ethical dilemmas.

Conclusion

This chapter has discussed both the importance and the complexity of measuring crime. Accurate measurement is critical for efforts to understand the origins of crime and how best to reduce it. If we measure crime inaccurately, we may miss important factors that underlie it and thus ways of reducing it.

All the major sources of crime statistics have their advantages and disadvantages. UCR data help us to understand the geographical distribution of crime, but they greatly underestimate the actual number of crimes and are subject to possible police bias. They also tell us relatively little about the social context of crime and victimization and about the characteristics of victims. NCVS data provide the best estimate of the actual number of crimes and provide solid information on the context of victimization and the characteristics of victims, but even they underestimate certain crimes and exclude others. Self-report data provide important information about offenders, including the many influences on their behavior, but are generally limited to adolescents. Inclusion of serious offenses in the most recent self-report studies has made them even more valuable.

Because none of these sources covers white-collar crime, they reinforce impressions that white-collar crime is less serious than street crime. But together they provide a reasonably good picture of street crime in the United States. The picture is of a relatively small number of violent crimes and a much larger number of property crimes. Despite continuing debate, the picture of street crime is also one of offenders who tend to be male, nonwhite, and especially African American, poor, and young. Regarding gender, something about being a female in our society inhibits criminality, and something about being a male promotes it. Continued research on the reasons for this gender difference holds promise for crime reduction. The racial and class distribution of street crime alerts us not only to the effect of race and class on criminality but also to the structural factors accounting for this effect. These factors can and must be explored without resorting to explanations that smack of racial or class prejudice.

Now that we have some idea of the extent of street crime and of the characteristics of offenders in the United States, it is almost time to turn to explanations of such crime. But first we explore further in Chapter 4 the characteristics of crime victims and the theories and consequences of victimization.

3

Summary

1. Accurate measurement of crime is essential to understand geographical and demographic differences in crime rates and gauge whether crime is rising or falling. The nation's sources of crime data provide a good picture of the extent and distribution of crime, but this picture is also necessarily incomplete.

2. The Uniform Crime Reports (UCR) is the nation's official crime source and is based on police reports of crime to the FBI. Problems with the UCR include the fact that (1) many crime victims do not report their victimization to the police; (2) citizens may become more or less likely to report crimes to the police; (3) changes in police behavior, including whether and how they record reported crimes, may affect UCR statistics; and (4) police in different communities may have different definitions and understandings of certain crimes.

3. The National Criminal Victimization Survey (NCVS) measures the nature and extent of victimization. Begun in the early 1970s, it has since provided a valuable source of information on all these issues. Although it does not cover commercial crime and its respondents do not always disclose their victimizations, it provides a more accurate picture than the UCR of the amount of crime.

4. Self-report studies focus mainly on adolescents and measure the extent of their offending. By asking respondents about many aspects of their lives and backgrounds, self-report studies have been invaluable for the development and testing of criminological theory.

5. Crime is patterned geographically, climatologically, and socially. International differences in crime rates reflect aspects of nations' cultures and their degree of inequality. In the United States, crime is higher in cities than in rural areas and generally higher in the South and West than in the East and Midwest. Several types of violent and property crime are more common in warmer months. Despite much debate, serious street-crime rates seem much higher among men than among women, higher among African Americans and Latinos than among non-Latino whites, and higher among the poor than the nonpoor.

6. Chronic offenders, who represent a small percentage of youths, commit the majority of serious offenses committed by all youths. Some chronic offenders continue their criminality past young adulthood. Efforts to predict such career criminals have been inaccurate, making it difficult to identify youths at risk for a career of crime.

Key Terms

chronic offenders 77

climatological 65

criminal careers 77

incidence 58

international comparisons 60

measurement 50

National Crime Victimization Survey (NCVS) 55

patterning 60

prevalence 58

property crime 50

seasonal 65

self-report studies 58

subculture of violence 71

underreporting 57

Uniform Crime Reports (UCR) 50

victimization 56

violent crime 50

What Would You Do?

1. It's a dark, chilly night in October, and you are walking to your car from the mall. In your arms is a box containing a DVD player you bought for a close friend's birthday. Suddenly you are grabbed around your neck from behind. A male voice says, quietly but ominously, "I don't want to hurt you. Just put the box on the ground and move away." Terrified, you comply. As the man picks up the box and runs off, you look in his direction in the darkened parking lot but see only his back. You take out your cell phone to call 911, but as you do so you begin to think the police probably won't be able to catch the robber and reflect that the DVD player cost only $70 anyway. Do you call 911? Why or why not?

2. You are the night manager of a convenience store. Normal closing time is 10:00 P.M., but it has been a slow night and you are pretty tired. It's now 9:50 P.M. The owner has told you it's okay to close a few minutes early when business is slow, so you have just locked the glass door and are cleaning up inside so that you can leave in a few more minutes. You're startled to hear a knock on the door. Looking through the door, you see two young men motioning to let them in. Something about them frightens you, but you don't know what it is. Do you unlock the door for them? Why or why not? Would your response have been different if the two people at the door had been middle-aged women?

CHAPTER

four

Victims and Victimization

Crime in the News

he Victim Support Network in California's Santa Clara County, home to San Jose, holds a ceremony every year to honor "unsung heroes" who help victims of rape, domestic violence, and other crimes. Its luncheon in April 2010 honored fifteen people who had spent many long hours, either as part of their regular jobs or as volunteers, helping crime victims with little fanfare. The honorees came from many walks of life and had helped many types of crime victims. One "unsung hero" was a pediatrician who specializes in child abuse and neglect cases; another was a domestic violence advocate for La Isla Pacifica; and a third was a paralegal in the district attorney's office who worked with rape victims.

The chair of the ceremony, Margaret Petros, executive director of a group called Mothers Against Murder, explained the reason for the event: "It's important to recognize people who work with victims of crime and who don't expect anything in return. The people we're honoring are really exceptional. And we want to re-energize them and show them we appreciate them."

Source: Fernandez 2010.

Before the 1960s, we knew little about crime victims and their families and friends. Criminals monopolized public concern and scholarly research while victims like those helped by these "unsung heroes" in California were forgotten. Crime victims began to attract more attention in the late 1960s as the growing crime rate and urban unrest heightened interest in law and order. The courts, it was said, were giving too many rights to criminals and not enough to their victims. This concern helped put victims on the public agenda. At about the same time, feminists began to address rape as a major crime. One focus of their efforts was the psychological consequences of rape, and another was the experience of rape victims in the criminal justice system after they brought charges. Somewhat later, domestic violence against women began to receive similar attention. The study of victims, or **victimology,** had begun.

The growing interest in victims led to the initiation of the National Crime Survey, now known as the National Crime Victimization Survey (NCVS). As Chapter 3 noted, the NCVS has greatly increased our understanding of victims and **victimization.** Several other victimization surveys in the United States and other nations have added to this understanding, and today the field of victimology is flourishing. This chapter discusses what we know about victims and victimization.

Defining Victims and Studying Victimization

No doubt you and people you know have worried about becoming a victim of a crime such as robbery, burglary, assault, rape, or theft of something from your car or dorm room/apartment. Have you ever worried about becoming a victim of price-fixing or false advertising? Would you even know if you had been a victim? Have you worried about being a victim of air or water pollution? Have you ever worried about eating bacteria-laden poultry or meat, taking unsafe medicine, or driving an unsafe car? If you or someone you know has ever taken ill or been injured in the workplace, did it occur to you that this might constitute crime victimization?

What exactly is a **crime victim?** Presumably one definition is someone who suffers because of a crime. But what if someone or, worse yet, many someones suffer from behavior that does not violate the law and thus is not a crime? To take one example, U.S. pharmaceutical companies routinely send unsafe drugs that are prohibited in the United States to poor nations. Because no U.S. law prohibits the drug companies from sending their products elsewhere, they do not commit any crime. But this noncriminal behavior still causes death and illness, especially in children, every year (Alora and Lumitao 2001).

Another example involving children concerns various corporations that once sent infant formula to poor nations, where it was sold or distributed as free samples to new mothers. Seeing a potential source of great profit, these corporations stressed the ease of formula feeding. Unfortunately, the mothers were often illiterate and could not understand the directions for preparing formula. They mixed it with dirty water that had not been boiled and sterilized and, to save money, often gave their babies less formula than required. Thinking the baby bottle had magical properties, some mothers even let their infants suck on empty bottles. Many infants acquired intestinal ailments, became severely malnourished, or even died. An international protest campaign and boycott began and lasted several years until the companies finally ceased "their lucrative but deadly practices (Viano 1990:xvi)." In the larger sense of the word *victim*, these children were clearly victims, but technically not crime victims, because no crime had been committed.

As this brief discussion suggests, people can be victimized in many ways, but only sometimes are they victims of actual crimes. They can be victims of legal behavior by the kinds of multinational corporations mentioned previously, but this does not make them crime victims. They can also be victims of illegal behavior by corporations. This does make them victims of criminal behavior, but they are not the kinds of victims to whom our hearts go out. We certainly do not usually hear about them in the news media, and they might not even be aware of their victimization. Finally, people can be victims of violations of civil liberties and human rights, including government surveillance, torture, and genocide. If we expand the definition of victims and victimization even further, we may talk about people as victimized by poverty, institutional racism, or institutional sexism. The term *institutional* implies that the very structure of society is one that inherently oppresses, subtly or more overtly, the poor, women, and people of color.

When we move away from individual victims of street crimes to mass victims of white-collar crime, violations of human rights, and the like, we are talking about *collective victimization*, much of it international in scope. Unfortunately, collective victimization is a neglected topic. Because victimology has focused on street crimes, we know far more about victimization by such crimes than we do about victimization by other kinds of crimes and by legal but harmful behaviors.

No universally accepted definition of crime victim exists. Defining victims as people suffering from street crimes or, more broadly, as those hurt by harmful corporate practices, institutional racism, and the like is ultimately a matter of personal preference. As Andrew Karmen (1990: 11) observed, "The key question becomes 'Which suffering people get designated as victims, and which don't, and why?' The answer is important, since it determines whether or not public and private resources will be mobilized to help them out, and end their mistreatment."

Since the beginning of victimology about four decades ago, the answer has been that victims are those people suffering from street crimes. Because street crime is a serious problem, especially in poor urban neighborhoods, the victimization it causes certainly merits scholarly attention. Reflecting the victimology literature, this chapter deals mostly with street crime. But keep in mind that victimization by white-collar crime also deserves the concern of the public, elected officials, and social scientists.

Certain corporations used to market infant formula heavily in poor nations, where it was not used properly. Many infants died or became seriously ill. Because no crime had been committed, these children were not crime victims.

Review and Discuss

Does it make sense to consider people who suffer from the legal behavior of corporations and from poverty to be crime victims? Why or why not?

Patterning of Victimization

According to the NCVS, roughly 14 percent of U.S. households each year experience at least one of the crimes included in NCVS data. (Recall that NCVS violent crime includes aggravated and simple assault, rape and sexual assault, and robbery, but not homicide, and NCVS property crime includes burglary, motor vehicle theft, and other thefts, but not commercial thefts.) More specifically, 3 percent of households experience violent crime, and 12 percent experience property crime (Klaus 2007). These figures obscure the fact that victimization, like the crime rates discussed in Chapter 3, is patterned geographically and socially. Although differences between the NCVS and UCR make comparisons of victimization data to crime data inexact, victimization patterns do resemble those for crime: The locations and people with the highest crime rates usually also have the highest victimization rates.

GEOGRAPHICAL PATTERNS

Victimization rates as measured by the NCVS differ across the United States. Western households have higher victimization rates than other regions. Meanwhile, urban areas have higher victimization rates than suburban or rural areas (see Figure 4.1).

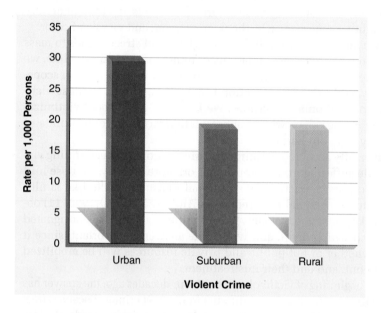

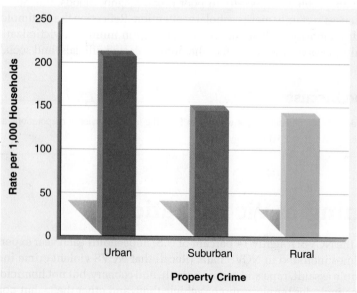

FIGURE 4.1 ▸ **Victimization Rates and Place of Residence, 2004–2005 (number per 1,000 persons age 12 or older or 1,000 households)** Source: Catalano 2006.

SOCIAL PATTERNS

Victimization rates also vary by the demographic characteristics of people. Table 4.1 displays the relevant data for violent crime and property crime. Our discussion centers on these data and also on other information not reported in the table.

Gender, Race, and Ethnicity

For the combined measure of violence reported in Table 4.1, males have a higher victimization rate than females. Males are especially likely to be homicide victims; there are about 3.5 male homicide victims for every 1 female victim. However, women experience almost all the rape victimization reported to NCVS interviewers and almost all the assaults

Cities have higher crime victimization rates than do rural areas.

TABLE 4.1 ▸ **Victimization by Violent Crime and Property Crime, 2009 (victimizations per 1,000 persons age 12 or older for violent crime or per 1,000 households for property crime)**

VARIABLE	VIOLENT CRIME	PROPERTY CRIME
Sex		
Male	18.4	—
Female	15.8	—
Age		
12–15	36.8	—
16–19	30.3	—
20–24	28.1	—
25–34	21.5	—
35–49	16.1	—
50–64	10.7	—
65 or older	3.2	—
Race[a]		
White	15.8	141.9
African American	26.8	170.0
Other race	9.8	129.2
Ethnicity[a]		
Latino	18.1	190.5
Non-Latino	17.0	141.2
Family income[a]		
Less than $7,500	50.7	201.1
$7,500–$14,999	39.0	157.0
$15,000–$24,999	25.9	141.6
$25,000–$34,999	27.5	134.1
$35,000–$49,999	21.7	139.7
$50,000–$74,999	19.8	120.0
$75,000 or more	14.1	124.9

[a]Income data for violent crime are from 2007; race and ethnicity data for property crime are from 2007.
Source: Truman and Rand 2010.

by family members and other intimates (see Chapter 11). Recall from Chapter 3 that the NCVS may produce underestimates of rape and sexual assault and domestic violence. If so, the actual violence victimization rate for women would be higher than the NCVS estimates.

African Americans have somewhat higher violent victimization rates than whites; this racial difference is much greater for homicide, as African Americans are about six times more likely than whites to be homicide victims (see Figure 4.2), Meanwhile, Latinos have somewhat lower violent victimization rates than non-Latinos.

Because Latinos may be of any race, the NCVS compiled average annual victimization rates for violent crime from 1993 to 2000 for Latinos and non-Latino members of the various races (see Figure 4.3). Latinos have slightly higher victimization rates

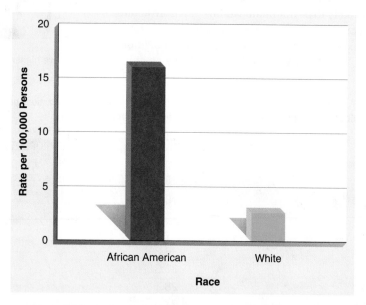

FIGURE 4.2 ▸ **Race and Homicide Victimization, 2009 (per 100,000 persons)** Sources:U.S. Bureau of the Census 2010; Federal Bureau of Investigation 2010.

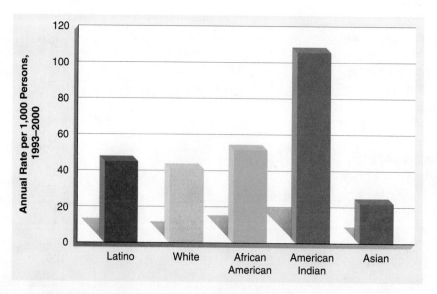

FIGURE 4.3 ▸ **Estimated Average Annual Rate (per 1,000 persons age 12 and older) of Violent Victimization, 1993–2000, Latinos and Race of Non-Latinos** Source: Rennison 2002.

International Focus

The International Crime Victim Survey

Chapter 3 noted that the international crime data apart from homicide are fairly unreliable. For this reason, the initiation of the International Crime Victims Survey (ICVS; http://rechten.uvt.nl/icvs/), sponsored by the United Nations, in the 1980s was an important development for the understanding of international crime and victimization. The aim of the ICVS is to collect international victimization data so that the nations' crime rates and victimization patterns can be compared. Since its inception, the ICVS has become a valuable source of information for crime and victimization in many parts of the world. ICVS data have been collected in six waves: 1988, 1991, 1995, 1999, 2003/04, and 2007/08. Most of the industrialized Western democracies and several developing nations have been included in one or more waves of the survey.

The ICVS asks respondents whether they were the victims during the previous year of any of several different crimes. For reporting purposes, the ICVS divides these crimes into two categories. *Contact crime* includes robbery, sexual offenses (sexual assaults and offensive sexual behavior), and physical assaults and threats. *Property crime* includes theft of cars, theft from cars, vandalism to cars, motorcycle theft, bicycle theft, burglary (completed and attempted), and theft of personal property. The ICVS also combines these two categories into an overall measure of victimization. The ICVS reports both prevalence rates (the percentage of people victimized at least once in the previous year) and incidence rates (the number of crimes experienced by every 100 people).

Although ICVS data have been used to compare nations' victimization rates, questions remain about the validity of such comparisons. These questions stem from the fact that different nations may use different survey and sampling techniques and that the nations' different cultural understandings may affect responses to the identical questions asked in every nation.

With this caveat in mind, the ICVS has revealed some very interesting findings concerning the ranking of the United States relative to that of all thirty industrialized nations in the survey (2003/04 data). For overall victimization, the U.S. prevalence rate was only average, with 17.5 percent of Americans reporting at least one victimization during the previous year. Ireland had the dubious honor of ranking at the top with a prevalence of 21.9 percent, whereas Portugal, Japan, and Northern Ireland tied with the lowest rate, 9.1.

The United States is popularly considered a very violent country, and it does have the highest homicide rate of any industrialized nation. However, it ranks only about average overall for other types of violence. To be more specific, it ranked in the bottom third for robbery, at the top (tied with several other nations) for sexual offenses, and sixth for physical assaults. Northern Ireland ranked first for physical assault, while Japan ranked last.

Despite the different victimization rates and other differences among these nations, the demographic victimization patterns reported for the United States are also found in other countries. For example, higher victimization rates exist for urban residents than for rural residents, for young people than for older people, and for men (excluding rape and domestic violence) than for women. The international similarity of these patterns underscores the impact of urbanism, age, gender, and the like on the risk for victimization.

Source: van Dijk, Kesteren, and Smit 2008.

than non-Latino whites and slightly lower rates than African Americans. Asians have the lowest rate, only about half that of the white rate. But the most striking rate is for American Indians, who are twice as likely as members of any other group to be violent-crime victims.

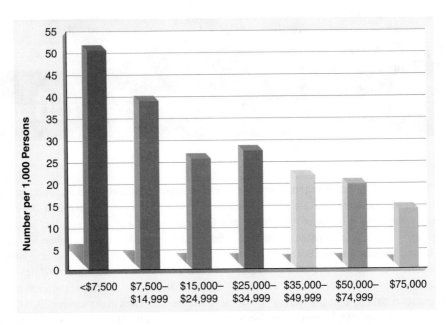

FIGURE 4.4 ▶ **Family Income and Violent Victimization, 2007 (per 1,000 persons age 12 or older)**
Source: Maston 2010.

Family Income

Table 4.1 shows some important differences in violent-crime victimization rates for people with different family incomes. Generally, the lower the income, the higher the rate of victimization. Figure 4.4 displays this trend graphically. For property crime, income is also related to victimization (see Table 4.1) in the same manner: the lower the income, the higher the rate of property-crime victimization.

Age

Figure 4.5 displays the striking difference that age makes in violent victimization. Paralleling age differences in crime rates discussed in Chapter 3, young people are much more likely than older people to be violent-crime victims. In this regard, recall from Chapter 2 that, although people 65 and older are more fearful than younger people of crime, their victimization is much lower.

Race, Gender, and Age Combined

In Chapter 2 we saw how race and gender combine to produce higher fear of crime among African-American women, and in Chapter 3 we saw how race, gender, and age combine to produce higher serious crime rates among young African-American men. In this chapter we have seen that violence victimization rates are higher for men than for women, for African Americans than for whites, and for the young than for the old. Is it possible that gender, race, and age combine to produce especially high victimization rates for African-American men and very low ones for older white women? The answer is yes. To illustrate, Table 4.2 reports homicide victimization rates for various age, race, and gender categories. In each age group, African-American males are the most likely and white females the least likely of the four race–gender categories to be homicide crime victims. The highest rate, 95.5 for African-American

Young people have higher violent-crime victimization rates than do older people.

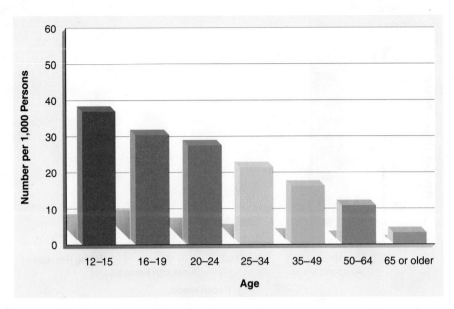

FIGURE 4.5 ▸ **Age and Violent Victimization, 2009 (per 1,000 persons age 12 or older)** Source: Truman and Rand 2010.

TABLE 4.2 ▸ **Age, Race, Gender, and Homicide Victimization, 2005 (per 100,000 persons)**

CATEGORY	RATE
Age 18–24	
African-American males	102.0
African-American females	11.3
White males	12.2
White females	2.5
Age 25 and older	
African-American males	39.9
African-American females	6.2
White males	4.9
White females	1.9

Source: http://bjs.ojp.usdoj.gov/content/homicide/ageracesex.cfm.

men 18 to 24 years old, is about fifty times greater than the lowest rate, 1.9, for white women 25 and older.

To reinforce the impact of race and gender on homicide victimization, Figure 4.6 displays the rates for the 18-to-24 age group. Within each gender, African Americans are much more likely than whites to be killed; within each race, males are much more likely than females to be killed. Race and gender certainly affect our chances of dying a violent death.

Review and Discuss

How do violent victimization rates differ by gender, age, race, and family income? Why do these different rates exist?

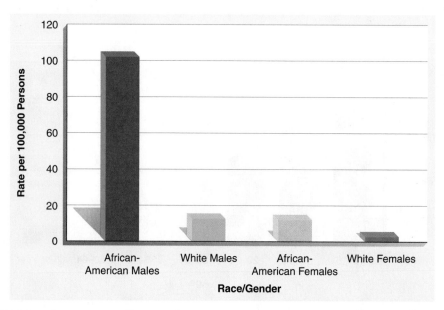

FIGURE 4.6 ▸ **Race, Gender, and Homicide Victimization, Ages 18–24, 2005 (per 100,000 persons)** Source: Fox and Zawitz 2007.

VICTIM–OFFENDER RELATIONSHIP

Strangers Versus Nonstrangers

Recall that the NCVS asks respondents who report aggravated or simple assault, rape or sexual assault, or robbery victimization whether they knew the offender. This information yields a valuable portrait of the **victim–offender relationship.** This might surprise you, but strangers commit *only about 42 percent* of these offenses combined, with the remainder committed by family members, friends, and acquaintances. This 42 percent figure for NCVS violence obscures a striking gender difference (see Table 4.3): Strangers commit 52 percent of men's victimizations but only 31 percent of women's victimizations. Conversely, nonstrangers commit 68 percent of women's victimizations, but only 45 percent of men's victimizations. Women are thus about 2.2 times more likely to be attacked by someone they know than by a stranger. This pattern is no less true of rape and sexual assault: 79 percent of these offenses reported by women to NCVS interviewers

TABLE 4.3 ▸ **Percentage of Violent Victimizations Committed by Strangers, 2009**

TYPE OF CRIME	GENDER OF VICTIM	
	FEMALE	MALE
Aggravated assault	36	52
Simple assault	28	49
Robbery	48	63
Rape or sexual assault	21	—
Total Victimizations	31	52
Source: Truman and Rand 2010.		

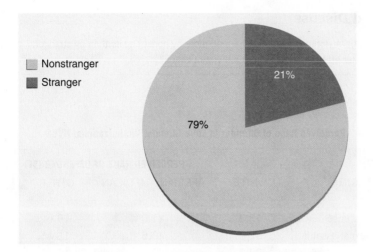

FIGURE 4.7 ▸ **Victim–Offender Relationship for Rape or Sexual Assault 2009 NCVS** Source: Truman and Rand 2010.

were committed by nonstrangers, compared to only 21 percent committed by strangers (see Figure 4.7). Chapter 11 further discusses this harsh reality of rape and sexual assault.

Intimate-Partner Violence

The majority of the nonstrangers who commit violence are friends or acquaintances, but a significant minority are *intimate partners:* spouses, ex-spouses, partners (boyfriends or girlfriends), or ex-partners. *Intimate-partner violence* (IPV) refers to any rape or sexual assault, robbery, or aggravated or simple assault committed by someone with such a relationship to the victim. We discuss IPV further in Chapter 11, but for now comment briefly on what the NCVS and other studies tell us about it. The NCVS estimates that about 655,000 IPV victimizations occurred in 2009, with about 82 percent of these committed against women (Truman and Rand 2010). Women are thus much more likely than men to suffer violence by intimate partners, who commit 26 percent of the violent crimes against women but only 5 percent of the violent crimes against men.

PERCEIVED RACE, GENDER, AND AGE OF OFFENDERS

Chapter 3 noted that NCVS respondents who have been violent-crime victims report that the race, gender, and age distribution of offenders is similar to that found in UCR arrest data: disproportionately young, nonwhite, and male. Table 4.4 includes the relevant NCVS data for race. Although whites account for the majority of all offenses, the proportion of offenders perceived as African American exceeds their proportion (13 percent) in the national population. This is especially true for robbery; African Americans are perceived as committing almost 48 percent of all single-offender robberies.

Many women experience intimate violence from husbands, ex-husbands, boyfriends, or ex-boyfriends.

Review and Discuss

To what extent are victims of violence harmed more by nonstrangers than by strangers? What does this pattern imply for efforts to reduce criminal victimization?

TABLE 4.4 ▸ **Perceived Race of Offender in Lone-Offender Victimizations, NVCS**

TYPE OF CRIME	PERCEIVED RACE OF OFFENDER (%)			
	WHITE	AFRICAN AMERICAN	OTHER	UNKNOWN
All violent crimes	43.3	21.0	9.6	26.0
Rape or sexual assault	32.8	48.5	15.4[a]	3.2[a]
Robbery	27.7	41.2	11.0[a]	20.1
Assault	45.4	17.8	9.2	27.6

Source: Maston 2010.
[a]Estimate is based on about 10 or fewer sample cases.

Again paralleling UCR arrest data, NCVS victims perceive that most offenders (almost 76 percent) in all lone-offender violent crimes combined are male; this figure rises to about 85 percent for the specific crimes of robbery and aggravated assault. Although victims' perceptions of offenders' ages are inexact, they also perceive that most of their offenders are young, once more replicating what UCR arrest data tell us: For all violent crimes involving one offender, more than half are perceived as being under 30 years old.

Some of the most important NCVS data concern the races of the offender and of the victim. A key myth in the public perception of crime is that African-American offenders prey on white victims (see Chapter 2). However, NCVS data reveal a very different pattern; they show that most violent crime is *intraracial*, meaning that it occurs within the same race. Contradicting the myth, about 68 percent of white victims of lone offenders who are able to perceive the offender's race identify it as white, and only about 13 percent identify it as African American. White victims of violence, then, are about five times more likely to be attacked by whites than by African Americans. FBI data confirm this pattern for homicide; about 84 percent of white homicide victims are killed by whites and about 13 percent are killed by African Americans (see Figure 4.8). Robbery is the most *interracial* (i.e., between the races) crime; NCVS data indicate that about one-third of white victims are robbed by African-American offenders.

CRIME CHARACTERISTICS

The NCVS contains much information on various **crime characteristics,** including the use of alcohol and other drugs, the time and place of occurrence of crime, the use of weapons, and the extent of self-protection and resistance by victims (Maston 2010).

Use of Alcohol and Other Drugs

Chapter 15 discusses this topic in greater detail, but it is worth noting here that NCVS crime victims report rather heavy involvement of alcohol and drugs in the commission of violent crimes. Victims report that offenders were under the influence of alcohol or drugs

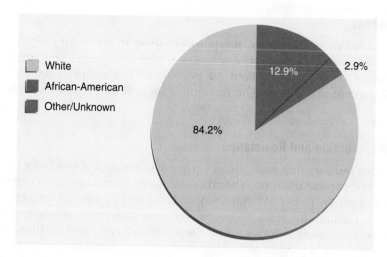

White
African-American
Other/Unknown

12.9%   2.9%

84.2%

FIGURE 4.8 ▸ **Percentage of White Homicide Victims Killed by White Offenders, Black Offenders, and Members of Other Races, 2009 (single-victim/single-offender homicides)** Source: Federal Bureau of Investigation 2010.

in more than half of all the violent crimes in which they could distinguish whether these substances had been used (2007 data).

Time and Place of Occurrence

About 43 percent of violent crimes and also 43 percent of property crimes occur at night (6:00 P.M.–6:00 A.M.). However, some crimes are especially apt to occur at night: 64 percent of all rapes and sexual assaults occur then, as do 61 percent of all motor vehicle thefts. The largest proportions of violent crime occur at or near the victim's home, on school property, and on the street away from the victim's home (see Table 4.5). About 33 percent of all crimes involving nonstrangers occur in the victim's home, compared to only 5 percent of crimes involving strangers.

TABLE 4.5 ▸ **Place of Occurrence for Violent Crime, NCVS (percentage of all incidents)**

PLACE	PERCENTAGE
At victim's home	19
On street away from victim's home	16
School building or property	15
Near home	11
In or near someone else's home	7
Parking lot or garage	7
Other commercial building	6
On street near home	6
Apartment yard, park, field, playground	2
Public transportation	1
Other	6

Source: Maston 2010.

Use of Weapons

According to NCVS respondents, weapons are used in about 20 percent of all violent crimes, including 18 percent of assaults, 6 percent of rapes and sexual assaults, and 47 percent of robberies. About 36 percent of the weapons are firearms, and another 27 percent are knives. The remainder include blunt objects such as a club or rock.

Victim Self-Protection and Resistance

NCVS findings indicate that most violent-crime victims do not passively let the crime occur; almost 60 percent try to stop the crime. Of these, about one-fourth struggle with or threaten the offender, 16 percent run away or hide, and 11 percent try to persuade the offender not to commit the crime. Victims who do use such measures say they helped the situation about two-thirds of the time, hurt the situation 7 percent of the time, both helped and hurt the situation 5 percent of the time, and neither helped nor hurt the situation 12 percent of the time.

Explaining Victimization

These figures provide useful information about crime victims and their victimization, but they do not tell us why people are victimized in the first place. When we attempt to explain crime, we are trying to explain at least two phenomena: Why do some locations have higher crime rates than others, and why are some individuals more likely than others to commit crime? Theories of crime attempt to answer these questions and are presented in several following chapters. When we try to explain victimization, we ask similar questions: Why do some locations have higher victimization rates than others, and why are some individuals more likely than others to become crime victims? In answering these questions, victimologists highlight the opportunities for criminal behavior and victimization.

LIFESTYLE AND ROUTINE ACTIVITIES THEORY

The most popular theory of victimization addresses the lifestyles and routine activities of individuals. This theory stems from two theories, **lifestyle theory** and **routine activities theory,** which developed about the same time in the late 1970s. Although they have somewhat different emphases, they both assume that "the habits, lifestyles, and behavioral patterns of potential crime victims enhance their contact with offenders and thereby increase the chances that crimes will occur" (Miethe and Meier 1990: 244). The theories today are often treated as components of one larger theory.

Lifestyle theory stresses that some lifestyles put people more at risk for becoming crime victims (Fisher, Daigle, and Cullen 2010). These lifestyles include spending much time outside home in places such as bars and nightclubs or just out on the street. This increases the chance of becoming a crime victim: an argument may break out in a bar; a robber may see an easy target. Recognizing that victimization is often committed by nonstrangers, the theory further assumes that people are more apt to become victims if they spend time with people who themselves commit high numbers of crimes. This helps explain why young people have the highest victimization rate for violent crime: They spend much time with other young people, who as a group commit the highest rates of violence, and thus sometimes place themselves in harm's way.

Routine activities theory, which Chapter 5 discusses further, argues that people engage in regular (hence the word *routine*) activities that increase their risk for victimization (Felson and Boba 2010). For victimization to occur, three components must coincide: (1) the presence of an attractive target (property or people), (2) the presence of a likely offender, and (3) the absence of *guardianship* (i.e., people who might observe and stop the crime from being committed). Thus, as more attractive targets emerge over time (e.g., more empty homes because of increased vacation travel or a rise in single-person households), victimization should increase. As more motivated offenders emerge (perhaps because of increasing unemployment), victimization should also increase.

Research testing lifestyle and routine activities theories uses measures such as the average number of nights a week spent walking alone at night or going to bars. This research finds that both theories help explain the occurrence of various types of victimizations against

One reason for the high victimization rate of young people is that they spend time with other young people, who as a group commit relatively high rates of violence.

various kinds of people in various locations (Marcum 2010). Studies of college students are illustrative, as they find that students who eat out and or party more often are more likely to be victims of theft and/or sexual assault (Armstrong, Hamilton, and Sweeney 2006).

Studies like these suggest that some people engage in behavior that puts them at more risk for criminal victimization. By focusing on victims' behavior, lifestyle and routine activities theories might therefore imply that victims to some degree are responsible for their own victimization. The Crime and Controversy box discusses this issue of **victim precipitation** further.

DEVIANT LIFESTYLES AND VICTIMIZATION

A related idea from lifestyle and routine activities theories is that some people increase their chances of becoming crime victims by committing crimes themselves. As Topalli, Wright, and Fornango (2002: 237) observe, "One of criminology's dirty little secrets is that much serious crime, perhaps most, takes place beyond the reach of the criminal law because it is perpetrated against individuals who themselves are involved in lawbreaking." This happens for several reasons. First and not surprisingly, criminals tend to spend time in high-crime areas and with other criminals. Second, their crimes may prompt a victim or the victim's family or friends to retaliate by attacking the offender. Such retaliation is especially likely when victims are criminals themselves because calling the police is not a viable option: If they report the crime, they obviously risk arrest, and they might not be taken seriously anyway. Third, because offenders cannot call the police, other offenders know this and act accordingly. Finally, criminals often have things that other criminals want. As Topalli and colleagues note (2002: 345) for one type of offender, "Drug dealers recognize that their inability to go the police, coupled with their possession of cash and drugs, makes them attractive robbery targets."

Several studies confirm that offending does, in fact, increase victimization. Much of this research focuses on adolescents and finds that those who belong to gangs, who have been arrested for violence or drugs, or who report a history of delinquency are more likely to be victims of homicide or other crimes than youths with no such involvements

(Gibson et al. 2009; Spano, Freilich, and Bolland 2008). Looking beyond adolescents, a study found that homicide victims in Prince George's County, Maryland, were much more likely than nonvictims to have an arrest record, even after taking into account factors such as age, race, and gender. The author concluded that reducing one's own offending would be a "practical method" of reducing the risk of being murdered (Dobrin 2001:169).

Drinking and drug use are also thought to contribute to victimization (Felson and Burchfield 2004). Use of alcohol and other drugs may lead people to provoke other individuals, to engage in other risky behavior, and to be less on guard for potential victimization. It may also make them more attractive targets for potential offenders, who recognize that someone under the influence of alcohol or other drugs might be relatively easy to victimize. The studies of college students mentioned earlier find that students who more often drink and/or use marijuana or cocaine are more likely to become victims of theft and physical and sexual assault.

Review and Discuss

How does routine-activities theory help us understand why criminal victimization occurs? What does this theory imply for efforts to reduce crime?

PHYSICAL PROXIMITY AND VICTIMIZATION

Our individual behavior does matter for victimization, but so does where we live (Xie and McDowall 2008a). Cities have thousands of specific locations or places within them: street corners and intersections, homes and commercial buildings. Because of their social and economic conditions, some areas of cities have higher crime and victimization rates than other areas (see Chapter 7).

Research finds that about 3–5 percent of all a city's locations account for at least 50 percent of the city's crime, and that the vast majority of locations have little or no crime (Sherman, Gartin, and Buerger 1989; Wei-sburd et al. 2004). If people live in or near these high-crime locations, commonly called **hot spots,** they are more likely to be victimized even if they do not have victimization-prone lifestyles (Lauritsen and Schaum 2004). By the same token, people who live in or near hot spots and who have such lifestyles are especially likely to be victimized.

One factor that helps turn locations into hot spots is the presence of bars and taverns (Peterson, Krivo, and Harris 2000; Roncek

The presence of bars and taverns helps turn some urban locations into hot spots for street crime.

⊗ Crime and Controversy

Victim Precipitation

Health care experts urge people not to smoke cigarettes or eat high-fat foods. To the extent that people ignore such advice, it is fair to say that they bear some responsibility and even blame for any health problems that develop.

Are crime victims also to blame for becoming victims? Because lifestyle and routine activities theories explain crime "not in the actions or numbers of motivated offenders, but in the activities and lifestyles of potential victims" (Meier and Miethe 1993: 473), they imply that people would be safer from crime if they changed their behavior. Taken to an extreme, they imply we would all be safer if we never left our homes. By venturing outside, we decrease our guardianship and make ourselves and our homes attractive targets for motivated offenders. People who engage in deviant lifestyles and commit crimes increase their own risk for victimization. It might be possible, of course, for people to change certain risky lifestyles and to cut back on any criminal behavior they might commit. But most of us do not really have anything to change in these areas and thus can do little else to reduce our victimization. We need to go to work every day, and we are not about to stop engaging in leisure activities, including vacations, outside our homes. We cannot just hide under our beds. That said, it *is* true that we could be more careful at times. Leaving the keys in the car might be a mistake. And perhaps some of us could reduce our barhopping.

However, there are *some* crimes in which victims do seem to play an active role in their own victimization. In 1958, Marvin Wolfgang developed the idea of *victim-precipitated* homicide, in which the eventual victim is the one who was the first to use physical force, including a weapon. The person he (men are usually the ones involved) attacks fights back,

perhaps with a weapon, and kills the victim. The victim, in short, precipitates his own death. Although not meant to excuse homicide, the concept of victim-precipitated homicide does point to an element of victim responsibility. In his study of 588 homicides, Wolfgang found that about one-fourth were victim precipitated. Depending on how precipitation is defined, other evidence indicates that some victims also precipitate assaults, robberies, and other crimes. This is especially true when women kill their male partners: Almost half of such killings are precipitated by a physical attack by the man on the woman.

Wolfgang's student, Menachem Amir, applied the victim-precipitated concept to rape not too long after Wolfgang developed it for homicide. Amir defined victim-precipitated rape as any rape that results when a woman engages in sexual relations and then changes her mind or behaves in any way, including accepting a drink, that could be construed as indicating her interest in having sex. Using this definition, Amir concluded that about one-fifth of the rapes he studied in Philadelphia, Pennsylvania, were precipitated by the victim.

As feminists began to study rape in the 1970s, they found Amir's notion of victim-precipitated rape repugnant. It implied that women were at fault for being raped and that rapists simply could not control themselves. It also put the burden for avoiding rape on women and fed common myths about the nature of rape. These myths make it very difficult for a rapist to be convicted if there is any evidence that the woman was wearing attractive clothing, had previously been sexually active, or in any other respect could be construed as somehow consenting to sexual activity (see Chapter 11). It may well be true that some homicide victims start the chain of events leading to their deaths, but it is quite different to say that women precipitate or bear any responsibility for their rapes.

Sources: Smir 1971; Karmen 2010; Meier and Miethe 1993; Wolfgang 1958.

and Maier 1991). Assaults in and outside bars are common because of the use of alcohol. Further, the people going to bars are attractive targets to robbers, as routine activities theory would predict, because they carry credit cards and/or large amounts of money and sometimes make themselves vulnerable by drinking too much.

Review and Discuss

Why do some locations have much higher crime victimization rates than other locations? What does an understanding of location victimization rates imply for efforts to reduce crime?

INDIVIDUAL TRAITS

Routine activities, lifestyle, and proximity explanations are *situational* explanations: They all "stress how the context or situation influences vulnerability to crime" (Schreck, Wright, and Miller 2002: 159). Although lifestyle theory does highlight potential victims' behavior, it says little about *why* certain people are more likely to adopt risky lifestyles or put themselves at increased risk for victimization for other reasons. Recent efforts to address this issue focus on a few individual traits that make some people more likely than others to become crime victims.

Low Self-Control and Lack of Social Relationships

The first two traits are *low self-control* and *lack of social relationships* (Schreck, Stewart, and Fisher 2006; Stewart, Elifson, and Sterk 2004). Low self-control, characterized by impulsiveness and a desire for immediate gratification, leads some people to engage in risky behavior that brings them pleasure in the short run, but negative consequences in the long run. The concept of low self-control was originally developed to explain offending (see Chapter 8), but it also seems useful for explaining victimization. The second trait is a lack of close social relationships. People without family ties may be more inclined and have more opportunity to engage in various types of activities, such as going out to bars, that increase their victimization risk.

Childhood Problems

Another individual factor that increases one's risk for victimization is a history of childhood problems, including behavioral disturbance, sexual abuse, harsh physical punishment, and parental conflict (Rebellon 2005). All these factors predict greater violent victimization during adolescence, in large part because they first lead to violent offending, which then increases the risk for victimization. Childhood problems may also lower self-control and impair social relationships; if so, this would be another reason why they increase victimization.

Mental Disorder

Mental disorder is another individual trait that may increase victimization. Although many stereotypes of the mentally ill exist, it is true that their social relationships "may often become strained as family members and other seek to manage and control" their behavior (Silver 2002: 191). Their social relationships, then, become "conflicted relationships" (p. 193) that lead to violence against the mentally ill.

Puberty

Recent studies have pinpointed the onset of early puberty as a risk factor for adolescent victimization (Haynie and Piquero 2006; Schreck et al. 2007). Puberty is thought to have this effect for at least three reasons. First, it raises the likelihood of offending (see Chapter 6), which, as we have seen, is itself a risk factor for victimization. Second, it prompts adolescents to spend more time with older adolescents away from home and in situations where victimization can and does occur. Third, it leads to emotional distress; teens with such distress act in a way that angers other teens and provokes them to commit violence against the distressed teens.

REPEAT VICTIMIZATION

Sometimes an individual or household that has already been victimized by crime is victimized one or more times again at a later date. The general explanations of victimization outlined earlier help explain why certain individuals and households are more prone to such *repeat victimization*. People who lead more risky lifestyles, including offending themselves, are more likely to be victimized in the first place, but also to be victimized again (Wittebrood and Nieuwbeerta 2000). Individuals and households in or near hot spots are also more likely to be victimized initially and then again.

Repeat victimization is a fairly common occurrence. The NCVS has predicted that almost three-fourths of violent crime victims and almost all property crime victims will be victimized more than once (Koppel 1987). In a study of the National Youth Survey (NYS), a nationwide longitudinal sample of adolescents, 85 percent of respondents reported being victimized more than once, with more than half being victimized by an average of two offenses in any one year. The study concluded that "repeat victimization is the norm, not the exception, in the period from adolescence through early adulthood" (Menard 2000: 571). At the same time, repeat victimization was concentrated in a small proportion of *chronic victims*, 10 percent of all adolescents, who account for more than half of all victimizations and who are disproportionately male and members of ethnic minority groups.

EXPLAINING DEMOGRAPHIC VARIATION IN VICTIMIZATION

Theories of victimization explain the demographic patterns of victimization we have seen. For example, if lifestyles affect victimization, then it is not surprising that young people have much higher rates of victimization than the elderly, because they are much more likely to spend time away from home, especially in bars, nightclubs, and other high-risk areas, and are also more apt to engage in deviant lifestyles. Men are also more likely than women to spend time away from home and to engage in deviant lifestyles. This similarity between young people and men underscores why young males have such particularly high rates of victimization. African Americans and Latinos are more likely than non-Latino whites to live in disadvantaged, high-crime areas and thus more likely to become crime victims. Their higher rate of offending for serious crimes also increases their victimization risk. The same logic applies to people with low family incomes. Given all these factors, it is no surprise that young African-American males have a high victimization rate and that older white females have a low one. Finally, adolescents who become chronic victims likely help secure their fates by having lifestyles and offending rates and patterns that are especially conducive to victimization (Menard 2000).

Lifestyle and routine activities theories are less applicable, however, to violence in the home. Because these theories focus on predatory crime outside the home, they assume that activities outside the home increase the likelihood of such victimization: "Time spent in one's home generally decreases victim risk, while time spent in public settings increases risk" (Meier and Miethe 1993: 466). Because intimate-partner violence often occurs inside the home, however, it cannot be attributed to routine activities or lifestyles conducive to victimization. If this is true, these theories of victimization apply less to women than to men, because a greater proportion of women's victimization is by intimate partners. For obvious reasons, the theories are also irrelevant for physical and sexual abuse of children, because children cannot be considered to engage in lifestyles or routine activities conducive to such abuse. Finally, these theories also do not apply to victimization by most white-collar crime.

Review and Discuss

How do theories of victimization help explain demographic differences in victimization rates? Why are these theories less relevant for family violence than for victimization that occurs outside the home?

VICTIMIZATION OF COLLEGE STUDENTS AND THE HOMELESS

The explanations we have just reviewed will help us to understand some aspects of the criminal victimization of college students and the homeless, even if these two groups have little or nothing else in common.

College Students

We saw earlier that many college students lead lifestyles that increase their chances of becoming crime victims. The NCVS compiled the average annual violent victimization rates (rape or sexual assault, robbery, aggravated or simple assault) of college students from 1995 to 2002 (Baum and Klaus 2005). Table 4.6 presents these rates and shows that about 61 of every 1,000 college students (or 6.1 percent) are victims of violence every year on the average. Because there were about 7.9 million college students in the study's time period, this rate translates to an average annual total of about 479,000 victimizations. Many of these victimizations are simple assaults; if we omit them from the figures, the victimization rate for serious violence (rape or sexual assault, robbery, aggravated assault) drops to 22.3 per 1,000 students, or about 176,000 victimizations, still a very large number.

Male students have a higher victimization rate (in fact twice as high) than female students have (see Table 4.6). The actual gender difference may be smaller than what the NCVS indicates because, as noted earlier, the NCVS may underestimate victimization by rape or sexual assault and by domestic violence. The NCVS college study determined the annual rate of rape or sexual assault victimization for women to be 6.0 per 1,000, but another national study from roughly the same time period determined the rate to be 35 per 1,000, equivalent to 350 rapes annually on a campus with 10,000 women (Fisher, Cullen, and Turner 2000). Because there are now about 6 million full-time college women, these two rates, if still true today, translate to a current annual total of between 36,0000 and 210,000 rapes and sexual assaults on the nation's campuses.

In other figures in Table 4.6, note that the victimization rate for African-American students is slightly lower than that for white students and that both groups' rates are higher than those for students of other races (primarily American Indians and Asians). White students have a very high victimization rate for simple assault. If we omit simple assaults and just consider serious violence, then African-American students emerge with the highest victimization rate (27.5), followed fairly closely by white students (21.6), and those of other races (18.8). Note also that college

Many college students engage in lifestyles, including drinking, that increase their chances of becoming crime victims.

TABLE 4.6 ▸ Average Annual Violent Victimization Rates of College Students and Nonstudents, NCVS, 1995–2002 (per 1,000 persons age 18 to 24)

	COLLEGE STUDENTS	NONSTUDENTS
All individuals	60.7	75.3
Gender		
Male	80.2	79.2
Female	42.7	71.3
Race or ethnicity[a]		
White	64.9	81.2
African American	52.4	83.2
Other	37.2	43.1
Latinos	56.1	55.9

Source: Baum and Klaus 2005.
Note: Rates include rape or sexual assault, robbery, and aggravated or simple assault.
[a]Racial categories do not include Latinos. Other includes Asians, Native Hawaiians, Pacific Islanders, Alaska Natives, and American Indians considered together.

students overall have a lower victimization rate than nonstudents in the 18-to-24 age group. Although many college students have lifestyles that put them at risk for violent victimization, it is evident that nonstudents in the same age bracket have lifestyles or other risk factors, such as proximity to high-crime areas, that make them even more vulnerable to victimization.

The Homeless

Recall from Chapter 3 that the NCVS excludes groups such as the homeless who do not live in households and who have high victimization rates. If the lifestyles of college students puts some of them at risk for crime victimization, homelessness itself might be considered a lifestyle that makes the homeless extremely vulnerable to victimization. They tend to live in high-crime areas and, given their common mental and physical weaknesses, cannot defend themselves and thus lack the guardianship emphasized by routine activities theory.

The little research we have on the homeless does find high rates of victimization. A study of homeless women in Los Angeles found that about one-third had been victims of violence during the preceding year (Wenzel, Leake, and Gelberg 2001). An earlier study of 150 homeless adults in Birmingham, Alabama, found that 35 percent of the sample had been victims of violence or theft in the preceding year (Fitzpatrick, Gory, and Ritchey 1993); this proportion was four times higher than the NCVS's estimate for the general population at the time of the study and three times higher than that for the poorest income bracket.

Another study, of 200 homeless women in New York City, found troubling racial differences in victimization and fear of crime (Coston 1992). The sample included 102 people of color and 98 whites. Sixty percent of the former group had been victimized by crime, usually robbery or assault, while living on the street, compared to only 48 percent of the latter group. People in the former group were also more likely to feel highly vulnerable to future victimization. In terms of victimization and fear of crime, race appears to make a difference in the world of the homeless, just as it does for the vast majority of Americans with a roof over their heads.

Costs and Consequences of Victimization

Crime victims suffer several types of consequences: medical, financial, psychological, and behavioral. Some are injured and require medical attention; some may even have to miss work or other major life activities. Victims of property crime obviously lose money and property. Victims of various crimes may also suffer psychological and/or behavioral problems. We look first at economic and medical costs and consequences and then at psychological and behavioral effects.

ECONOMIC AND MEDICAL COSTS AND CONSEQUENCES

Information on the economic and medical costs of victimization comes from the NCVS, UCR, and other sources. Because these sources use different methodologies and measure different crimes, cost information is inexact but nonetheless indicates the serious impact of crime on victims and their families. The most significant economic and medical costs and consequences are as follows:

- The crimes the NCVS covers (robbery, rape, assault, personal and household theft, burglary, and motor vehicle theft) cost crime victims in 2007 an estimated $18 billion in *direct costs* (Maston 2010). Direct costs means loss to the victim of any money or property stolen or damaged, medical expenses, and any wages lost because of missed work. The average violent crime cost victims $380; the average property crime cost $917. Other estimates that include offenses, such as drunk driving and commercial crime, that the NCVS omits put the annual total of direct costs at more than $100 billion (Miller, Cohen, and Wiersema 1996). *Indirect costs* for victimization (lost productivity, medical care for long-term physical and mental health, police expenses, and victim services) can run into the thousands of dollars for crimes such as rape and robbery. If the quality-of-life cost of consequences such as pain and suffering are taken into account (and not all scholars agree that such costs should be considered or can even be measured), the total cost of victimization may be more than $1 million for homicide, close to $90,000 for rape, and $10,000 for some other crimes, or about $450 billion overall (Miller et al. 1996).

- Only about 18 percent of 2007 NCVS victims who had money or property stolen recovered all of it, and 70 percent recovered none of it.

- About 8 percent of all NCVS violent-crime victims and 6 percent of property-crime victims lost time from work, usually a week or less. More than one-fifth of victims of motor vehicle theft lost time from work.

- Violent victimization during adolescence has long-term income consequences because of its psychological consequences (discussed later). Teens who experience such victimization are more likely by adulthood to have lower educational and occupational achievement and thus lower incomes. Because violent victimization during adolescence is highest for urban males of color, its long-term income consequences are greatest for "individuals already lacking social and economic resources. . . . (E)xposure to criminal violence may play a role in the reproduction of social and economic failure among the disadvantaged" (Macmillan 2000: 575).

- More than one-third of NCVS robbery victims and more than one-fifth of assault victims are physically injured. About half of NCVS violent-crime victims who need medical care obtain it at a hospital, while 12 percent obtain it at a doctor's office and 11 percent at the scene of the crime.

PSYCHOLOGICAL CONSEQUENCES

Before the beginning of victimology, criminologists did not study the **psychological consequences** of criminal victimization. Over the past twenty years, psychologists and other scholars have conducted in-depth interviewing of crime victims to get a picture that goes far beyond the dry economic and medical data just discussed. For some people and for some types of crimes, victimization can be especially traumatic.

In this context, rape has probably been studied more than any other crime, and it has both moderate and serious consequences that can have a lifelong impact (Brown, Testa, and Messman-Moore 2009; DeMaris and Kaukines 2005). We have already seen in Chapter 2 that rape plays a large role in women's high fear of crime. Women victimized by rape often suffer additional psychological effects, including mild depression and loss of self-esteem. These symptoms begin to subside a few months after the rape for most women, but can last much longer for others. Sexual dysfunction, the refusal or inability to engage in sexual relations, is also common. Several studies find that about 20 percent of rape survivors attempt suicide, and 40 to 45 percent consider it. Drug abuse, including alcoholism, is also common, perhaps especially among women victimized as children by rape or other sexual abuse. Many rape survivors may experience *post-traumatic stress disorder* (PTSD), defined as "a persistent reexperiencing of a traumatic event through intrusive memories and dreams and by a variety of anxiety-related symptoms" (Lurigio and Resick 1990: 51), and some also experience depression and other serious psychological disorders.

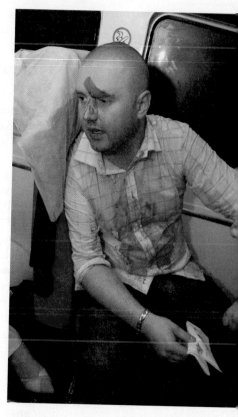

Victims of violent crime may experience various psychological symptoms, including post-traumatic stress disorder.

Studies of victims of other crimes find similar psychological symptoms, although violent crimes appear to have more serious psychological consequences than do property crimes (Menard 2002). Victims of burglary, robbery, and nonsexual assault exhibit higher levels than nonvictims of fear, vulnerability, anxiety, loss of confidence, sleep difficulties, and other similar symptoms. They also can develop PTSD.

An interesting question is whether crimes committed by strangers have more serious psychological consequences than those committed by nonstrangers. Most studies of this issue have examined rape and found that rapes committed by both kinds of offenders generally have the same impact. However, the evidence is again a bit mixed, and some research suggests that rapes are especially traumatic when committed by nonstrangers (Lurigio and Resick 1990).

Recent research has begun to examine *indirect victimization* among relatives and neighbors of crime victims. In general, relatives of homicide victims suffer as least as much grief as that felt by anyone who loses a loved one. These relatives, as well as partners of rape victims, also experience symptoms similar to those of victims of violent crimes, including PTSD (Riggs and Kilpatrick 1990). Neighbors of property-crime victims are more likely to move to another area, while neighbors of violent-crime victims are not more likely to do so, perhaps because the violence they learn about is committed by someone the victim knew and thus is not threatening to the neighbor (Xie and McDowall 2008b).

A final line of research has addressed whether crime victims' views about crime and justice change as a result of being victimized. Somewhat surprisingly, this body of research finds that victims are generally not more likely than nonvictims to hold punitive attitudes toward criminals. Disputing the common saying that "a liberal is someone who has not been mugged," this research also finds that victims are no more likely than non-victims to hold conservative political beliefs (Unnever, Cullen, and Fisher 2007).

SOCIAL AND BEHAVIORAL CONSEQUENCES

Criminal victimization may also have several behavioral consequences. Here criminological attention has focused on higher rates of offending and of drug and alcohol use: Victims of violence at various ages become more likely themselves to commit crime or use drugs, or both, at later ages. This effect is especially strong for physical and sexual abuse during childhood and adolescence (Menard 2002; Siegel and Williams 2003). *Vicarious* physical victimization by one's family members or friends also matters: Adolescents whose family members or friends have been physically victimized become more likely themselves to engage in serious delinquency because of the strain they feel (Agnew 2002).

Although most research on the behavioral consequences of victimization focuses on individuals, some scholars also address the behavioral consequences for neighborhoods where crime and victimization flourish (Hipp 2010; Markowitz et al. 2001). A key consequence involves a neighborhood's cohesion and *informal control* (also called *informal surveillance*), that is, the daily efforts by neighbors to watch out for one another and in this and other ways to ensure a community with high levels of social integration that help keep crime in check. Crime and the fear it generates weaken cohesion and informal control by, among other effects, keeping people inside, reducing their involvement in local voluntary organizations, and even forcing some people to move away. The result is a vicious cycle: Crime and victimization undermine cohesion and informal control, and the weakened cohesion and control increase crime and victimization.

Other research on the consequences of victimization focuses on social relationships. As might be expected, child and adolescent sexual and physical abuse often makes it difficult for an abuse survivor to engage in stable romantic and platonic relationships (Davis and Petretic-Jackson 2000). One study found that low-income women who were abused during childhood or adolescence are less likely, upon reaching adulthood, to be married or otherwise involved in a long-term, stable relationship with a man (Cherlin et al. 2004).

Review and Discuss

What are the major consequences that crime victims suffer? To what extent do these consequences differ by age, gender, social class, and race and ethnicity?

Victims in the Criminal Justice System

A growing body of literature addresses the experiences of victims in the criminal justice system. Much of this literature concerns women who have been raped and who are said to be assaulted a second time in the criminal justice system. The reasons for such a *second victimization* derive from popular myths about rape (see Chapter 11). In the past, many police, prosecutors, and judges believed these myths; and although their attitudes have improved, some criminal justice professionals still greet women's reports of rape with some skepticism (Belknap 2007). In spite of the fact that many states have passed laws to protect women during prosecutions and trials of their offenders, the burden is still on women to prove they did not give consent. Myths about domestic violence also still abound (see Chapter 11), and the criminal justice system has had to adapt to accommodate the needs and concerns of domestic violence victims, most of whom are women.

More generally, scholars and elected and criminal justice officials have begun to recognize that crime victims of all stripes feel shut out of the criminal justice process and otherwise have needs that must be addressed (Karrmen 2010). Several kinds of services and programs for victims have begun across the United States, and some jurisdictions have developed *victim-witness advocate programs* involving court professionals to help steer victims through the morass of the criminal justice system. Many areas have also begun social service and victim restitution programs to help victims deal with the economic and psychological impacts of their victimization.

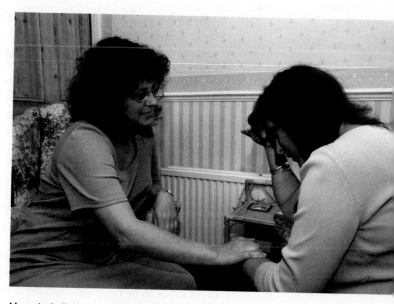

Many jurisdictions have established victim-witness advocate programs to help victims during the various stages of the criminal justice process.

In another innovation, judges have begun to ask victims to submit **victim-impact statements** to consider as the judges decide on the appropriate sentence for convicted offenders. Victim involvement in sentencing is meant to increase victims' satisfaction with the criminal justice process. Evidence indicates that these statements tend to increase victims' satisfaction with how their cases are handled, but that they do not make it more likely that judges will assign harsher sentences to convicted defendants (Roberts 2009). However, some research has found that prison inmates were less likely to be paroled if their files contained victims' letters protesting parole and if their victims attended their parole hearings (Morgan 2005).

A related concept to the victim-impact statement is the *victim-impact panel*. This concept was introduced in 1982 by Mothers Against Drunk Driving to allow people arrested for drunk driving to hear about the harm and trauma suffered by victims of DUI (driving under the influence) traffic accidents. The usual panel consists of four or five victims who each talk for several minutes about how DUI affected their lives. A study in Georgia investigated whether DUI offenders who attended a victim-impact panel were less likely than those who did not (because their DUI occurred before the panels began) to engage in DUI again (Rojek, Coverdill, and Fors 2003). The researchers found that only about 16 percent of the offenders who attended a panel were rearrested for DUI within five years, compared to about one-third (33.5 percent) of those who did not attend a panel.

VICTIMS AND CRIMINAL CASE OUTCOMES

The increasing attention to victims has motivated research on how their behavior and demographic characteristics affect criminal prosecutions and trials by influencing the decisions of prosecutors, judges, and juries. Prosecutors prefer cases with *good victims,* those who, according to a prosecutor of sexual assault cases, "are well-educated and articulate, and are, above all, presentable to a jury" (Bryden and Lengnick 1997: 1247). In contrast, *bad victims* have a prior criminal record or other history of disreputable behavior and have engaged in conduct that may be perceived as provoking the defendant, Because these victims are seen as less credible and their victimization may be considered less serious, prosecutors are less likely to bring their cases to indictment. If their cases do go to trial, they are less likely to end in a conviction (Baumer, Messner, and Felson 2000). Even dead victims—that is, those who were murdered—can be good or bad victims from the prosecutor's perspective. A recent study found that prosecutors are more likely to seek the death penalty in homicide cases when victims are of high social status and in other respects "respectable" (Phillips 2009).

Turning to demographic characteristics, research on the effects of victims' gender and age on case processing and outcomes is inconsistent. However, the race of the victim does seem to matter for homicide and rape cases, in which defendants are treated more harshly in terms of indictment and conviction when victims are white (Baumer et al. 2000).

Other research examines the impact of the victim–offender relationship on the processing of criminal cases, with much of this research focusing on rape and sexual assault (Spohn and Holleran 2001). Two findings from this research stand out. First, rapes and sexual assaults by strangers are more likely than those by nonstrangers to lead to arrest prosecution, and conviction, because the victim's declaration that she did not give consent is more likely to be believed. Second, the impact of victims' behavior and reputation on the likelihood that charges will be filed is higher for cases in which the victim knew the defendant. Because prosecutors fear that the defendant will argue that the victim gave her consent, they are more apt to drop a case if the victim's character or conduct might be called into question.

Victimization by White-Collar Crime

Victimization research focuses on street crime and not on white-collar crime. Because the NCVS does not ask about white-collar crime, its wealth of information on the injuries and economic costs of street-crime victims is lacking for their white-collar-crime counterparts. The inattention to white-collar crime victims is unfortunate because the financial losses, injuries and illnesses, and even deaths that people suffer from white-collar crime are greater than those suffered from street crime (Rosoff, Pontell, and Tillman 2010; see Chapter 13).

A few recent studies have aimed to fill the gap. A national survey found that between 15 and 33 percent of U.S. adults have been victims of one type of white-collar crime, fraud, which costs Americans more than $40 billion yearly (Rebovich and Layne 2000). Yet only one-fifth of fraud victims report their victimization to police, district attorneys, or consumer protection agencies. Another study found that more than half of Tennessee residents had suffered fraud victimization during the preceding five years (Copes et al. 2001).

Some studies document the psychological cost of white-collar crime. One research team interviewed forty-seven people, many of them elderly, who lost funds when a savings and loan company collapsed because of criminal conduct by its officers and employees (Shover, Fox, and Mills 1994: 86–87). Forty percent of the sample lost large sums of money, and many remained angry and/or depressed several years later. One victim said she has thought about it "every day. Every day for eight years. I go to bed with it. I get up with it. I think of it through the day. And my husband . . . I haven't seen my husband smile in eight years. . . . Really, it destroyed our life. We're not happy people anymore." Another victim said, "It's destroying us. It's destroying us. Especially my wife, especially my wife. . . . And I've been the same way, by the way. I've had my ups and downs." Ironically, many victims blamed themselves for what happened as much as they blamed the savings and loan officials. The researchers concluded that "some victims of white-collar crime endure enormous long-term pain and suffering" similar to that experienced by victims of street crime.

Conclusion

Victims of street crime remain a prime subject for social science research and for government action. The social pattern of victimization is disturbingly similar to the pattern for criminality: It is concentrated among the poor, nonwhite, and young sectors of society. Although women are less likely to be victimized than men overall, they face the threat of rape and intimate violence as a daily social fact and generally are more likely than men to be victimized by intimates and other people they know.

The most popular theories of victimization imply that changes in our behavior would reduce our risk for victimization. This is true to an extent, but some behaviors are easier to change than others. We can reduce our visits to bars and taverns, which seem to be special locations for victimization, but we cannot simply shut ourselves in our homes and hide under our beds. These theories further imply that victims are responsible for their victimization. Taken to an extreme, victims might even be said to precipitate their victimization. This may be true for some homicides, but it is an antiquated and even dangerous concept when applied to rape. Unless we want to say that women precipitate their rapes by simply knowing men and spending time with them, an absurd notion, the idea of women's involvement in their rapes must be abandoned.

In looking at public opinion about crime, the extent and patterning of criminal behavior, and the patterning and consequences of criminal victimization in this and the previous two chapters, one theme that emerges is **inequality.** The groups at the bottom of the socioeconomic ladder—the poor, people of color, the young—are most likely to fear crime and have the highest rates of both criminality and victimization. Gender presents somewhat of an exception to this link: Although women, who have less social and economic power than men, are much more likely to fear crime, they have a much lower offending rate and a lower victimization rate. The way we socialize females and males explains much of this pattern. The last three chapters have also stressed the importance of white-collar crime. The focus of media, scholarly, and government attention on street crime is certainly important and well deserved, but the neglect by all three sources of white-collar crime is not.

4

Summary

1. Although there are many kinds of victimizations, the study of victims and victimization in criminology has usually been limited to victimization by street crime. Victimization by white-collar crime has been neglected.

2. Victimization is patterned geographically and sociodemographically, with most of the patterns similar to those for criminality. Victimization rates are lower for whites, women (except for rape and domestic violence), older people, and the nonpoor than for their counterparts. Victimization rates for young African-American males are especially high.

3. NCVS data also show that alcohol and other drugs are involved in much criminal victimization, that weapons are used in about one-fifth of all violent crime, and that most victims try to avoid being victimized by struggling with the offender or trying to run away or hide. NCVS data also show that many nonstrangers commit violent crime and commit the majority of violent crime against women.

4. Lifestyle and routine activities theories emphasize that what people do in their daily lives can increase or decrease their chances of becoming crime victims. These theories help to explain some of the sociodemographic patterns of victimization. College students who spend a lot of time in bars, drink a lot, or misuse other substances increase their chances of victimization.

5. Criminal victimization costs victims nationwide billions of dollars in direct costs every year and perhaps tens of billions of dollars in indirect costs. It also takes a psychological toll, with depression, post-traumatic stress disorder, and other symptoms not uncommon. Behavioral changes may include increased abuse of alcohol and other drugs and increased violent offending. White-collar crime may have consequences similar to those of street crime, but only a few studies have documented these effects.

6. The criminal justice system is increasingly trying to accommodate the needs and desires of crime victims. Victim-witness advocate programs and compensation for victimization are now common throughout the nation. Many judges also ask victims to file victim-impact statements to help the judges decide on the appropriate sentences for convicted offenders.

Key Terms

crime characteristics 92

crime victim 82

hot spots 96

inequality 107

lifestyle theory 94

psychological consequences 103

routine activities theory 94

victim-impact statements 105

victim–offender relationship 106

victim precipitation 95

victimization 82

victimology 82

What Would You Do?

1. A friend from one of your classes confides that over the weekend another student began to attack her sexually. She was able to stop him by threatening to call the police, and he left her room in a fit of anger. Do you advise your friend to call the campus police about this attempted sexual assault? Why or why not?

2. Suppose you are a judge in a case in which the defendant was convicted of aggravated assault. He got into an argument with another man in a bar and beat him so severely that the victim suffered two broken bones in his arm. At your request, the victim files a victim-impact statement that indicates his arm may have suffered some permanent damage. How much, if at all, will the victim's statement affect the sentence you hand out to the defendant? Explain your answer.

CHAPTER

five

Classical and Neoclassical Perspectives

Crime in the News

I n May 2010, a lacrosse player at the University of Virginia allegedly killed his former girlfriend, Yeardley Love, also a lacrosse player, when he slammed her head against her bedroom wall during an argument. In the aftermath of Love's death, reports surfaced that the alleged assailant had allegedly attacked a male student a year earlier for kissing her and had also been put on probation for public intoxication and resisting arrest. The arresting officer in the latter incident said she needed to Taser the young man and that he said he would "kill everyone" at the police station. The officer added, "He was by far the most rude, most hateful and most combative college kid I ever dealt with."

Yeardley Love's death shocked the university and its quiet home town of Charlottesville. Befitting her last name, she was apparently loved by all who knew her. During her funeral service, Love's lacrosse coach recalled her fondly: "She was truly remarkable, not because she tried to be, but because she just was. It came easy for her to be great, to be kind-hearted, welcoming, encouraging and engaging to all who knew her. She was legitimately awesome."

Sources: Macur 2010; Nakamura, Swezey, and Vise 2010; Yanda, Johnson, and Vise 2010.

Why did this terrible crime happen? Why did this particular young man allegedly commit it? What can be done to prevent this type of crime and the many other types of crime that we read or hear about virtually every day?

A central task of criminology is to explain why crime occurs—yet very different explanations of crime exist. Your author once had a student who said the devil caused most crime. Her classmates snickered when they heard this. Undaunted, the student added that the way to reduce crime would be to exorcise the devil from the bodies it possessed. More snickers. I said I respected her religious beliefs, but noted that modern criminological theory does not blame the devil and does not think exorcism would help.

As this story illustrates, assumptions of what causes crime affect what we think should be done to reduce it. If we blame the devil, our crime-reduction efforts will center on removing the devil's influence. If we hold biological or psychological problems in individuals responsible, our efforts will focus on correcting these problems. If we hold poverty and inadequate parenting responsible, our efforts will center on reducing poverty and improving parenting skills. If we instead think criminals are simply depraved and that the criminal justice system is too lenient to keep them from committing crime, our efforts will focus on adding more police, increasing prison terms, and building more prisons. To develop the most effective approach, we must first know why crime occurs.

Contemporary theories of crime differ widely in their assumptions and emphases. In the social and behavioral sciences, sociology has contributed the most to understanding crime, with psychology and economics also making important contributions. Of the remaining sciences, biology has long been interested in crime. This chapter highlights neoclassical explanations, rooted in economic thinking, that emphasize the rationality of crime and criminals, whereas the next chapter discusses biological and psychological explanations. The three subsequent chapters discuss explanations from sociology. After reading these chapters, you should have a good understanding of the reasons for crime that the various disciplines favor, of the strengths and weaknesses of the explanations they offer, and of the possible solutions to crime that these explanations suggest.

Understanding Theories of Crime

Theories of crime try to answer at least one of three questions: (1) Why are some individuals more likely than others to commit crime? (2) Why are some categories or kinds of people more likely than others to commit crime? (3) Why is crime more common in some locations than in other locations? Biological and psychological explanations tend to focus on the first question, whereas neoclassical and sociological explanations tend to focus on the last two questions.

These explanations also differ in other ways. Neoclassical explanations, as we shall soon see, assume that criminals act with free will, whereas the other explanations assume that people are influenced to commit crime by certain internal and external forces. To be more precise, biological and psychological explanations place the causes of crime inside the individual, whereas sociological explanations place these causes in the social environment outside the individual. Put another way, biology and psychology focus on the *micro*, or smaller, picture, and sociology focuses on the *macro*, or larger, picture. This distinction reflects long-standing differences in understanding human behavior. It does not mean that a macro approach is better than a micro approach, and neither does it mean the reverse. The approach you favor depends on whether you think it is more important to understand the smaller picture or the larger one.

Nevertheless, the approaches' different focuses do have different implications for efforts to reduce crime. If the fault for crime lies within the individual, then to reduce crime we must change the individual. If the fault instead lies in the social environment, then we must change this environment. And if neoclassical perspectives are correct, crime can be reduced by measures that convince potential criminals that they are more likely to be arrested and punished severely.

To help understand the distinction between the micro and macro orientations of biology/psychology and sociology respectively, let us leave criminology to consider two related eating disorders, anorexia (undereating or starvation) and bulimia (self-induced regurgitation after eating). What causes these disorders? Psychologists and medical researchers cite problems in the individuals with the disorders. Psychologists emphasize low self-esteem, feelings of inferiority, and lack of control, whereas medical researchers stress possible biochemical imbalances (Friedman and Stancke 2009). These individual-level explanations are valuable, and you may know someone with an eating disorder who was helped by a psychologist or a physician.

A sociological explanation takes a different stance. Recognizing that eating disorders disproportionately affect young women, sociologists say a cultural emphasis on slender female bodies, evidenced by Barbie dolls and photos in women's magazines, leads many women to think they are too heavy and to believe they need to diet. Inevitably, some women will diet to an extreme and perhaps not even eat or else force themselves to regurgitate (Darmon 2009). This type of explanation locates the roots of eating disorders more in society than in individual anorexics or bulimics. No matter how often psychologists and physicians successfully treat such women, other women will always be taking their place as long as the emphasis on female thinness continues. If so, efforts to cure eating disorders may help individual women, but ultimately will do relatively little to reduce the eating disorder problem.

Actress Jamie-Lynn Sigler, who played the daughter in *The Sopranos*, struggled with an eating disorder that began during high school. Whereas psychologists attribute eating disorders to low self-esteem and other psychological problems, sociologists highlight the cultural emphasis on slender female bodies.

Returning to criminology, if the roots of crime are biological and psychological problems inside individuals, then to reduce crime we need to correct these problems. If the roots of crime instead lie more in criminogenic features of the social environment, then new criminals will always be emerging and the crime problem will continue unless we address these features.

That said, it is also true that most people do not commit crime even if they experience a criminogenic social environment, just as most women do not have eating disorders despite the cultural emphasis on thinness. To understand why certain people do commit crime (or why certain women have eating disorders), individual-level explanations are necessary. To reiterate, whether you favor micro or macro explanations of crime (or of eating disorders) depends on whether you think it is more important to understand the smaller picture or the larger one.

It is time now to turn to the many theories of crime. The term *theories* can often make students' eyes glaze over. Perhaps yours just did. That is why this chapter began by stressing the need to understand *why* crime occurs if we want to reduce it. If you recognize this need, you also recognize the importance of theory. As you read about the various theories in the chapters ahead, think about what they imply for successful efforts to reduce crime.

From Theology to Science

Our excursion into the world of theory begins by reviewing the historical change from theology to science in the understanding of crime.

Tens of thousands of women considered to be witches were executed in Europe during the 1400s to the 1700s.

GOD AND DEMONS AS CAUSES OF CRIME AND DEVIANCE

Like many folk societies studied by anthropologists today, Western societies long ago had religious explanations for behavior that violated their norms. People in ancient times were thought to act deviantly for several reasons: (1) God was testing their faith, (2) God was punishing them, (3) God was using their behavior to warn others to follow divine rules, and (4) they were possessed by demons (McCaghy et al. 2008). In the Old Testament, the prophets communicated God's unhappiness to the ancient Hebrews with behavior that today we would call mad and even violent. Yet they, and Jesus after them in the temple, were regarded as divinely inspired. Ancient Greeks and Romans, who believed in multiple gods, had similar explanations for madness.

From ancient times through the Middle Ages, witches—people who supposedly had associated with or been possessed by the devil—were a special focus of attention. The Old Testament mentions witches several times, including the commandment in Exodus (22:18), "Thou shalt not suffer a witch to live." Witches also appear in ancient Greek and Roman literature. Biblical injunctions against witches took an ominous turn in Europe from the 1400s to the 1700s, when some 300,000 "witches," most of them women, were burned at the stake or otherwise executed. Perhaps the most famous witch-hunting victim was Joan of Arc, a military hero for France in its wars with England, whom the English burned at the stake in May 1431. Other witches put to death, often by the Roman Catholic Church that dominated continental Europe, were what today we would call healers, midwives, religious heretics, political protesters, and homosexuals. In short, anyone, and especially any woman, who violated church rules could have been branded a witch (Demos 2008).

As this brief summary suggests, religion was the dominant source of knowledge in the Western world through the Middle Ages. Religion was used to explain norm-violating behavior, but it was also used to explain natural, physical, and social phenomena too numerous to mention. Science was certainly not unknown in the West, but it played a secondary role to religion as people sought to understand the social and physical worlds around them. They widely believed that God controlled all human behavior and that the church's authority was to be accepted without question. Although they learned these basic beliefs from childhood as part of their normal socialization, it is also true that the persecution of alleged witches would have made people afraid to question the primacy of the church. Regardless of the reason, religion was the ruling force during the Middle Ages, and science was hardly even in contention.

THE AGE OF REASON

This fundamental fact of Western life through the Middle Ages began to change during the seventeenth and eighteenth centuries, when religious views began to give way to scientific explanations. This period marked the ripening in Europe of the Age of Reason, or the **Enlightenment**, which developed a new way of thinking about natural and social phenomena that eventually weakened religion's influence. Enlightenment philosophers included such famous figures as René Descartes (1596–1650), Thomas Hobbes (1588–1679), John Locke (1632–1704), and Jean-Jacques Rousseau (1712–1778), all of whom are still read today along with many others. As innumerable works have discussed (e.g., Israel 2010), these political philosophers influenced Western thought in many profound ways, and their ideas are reflected in the Declaration of Independence and other documents crucial to the founding of the United States.

The views of the Enlightenment philosophers differed in several important respects. For example, Rousseau thought that human nature was basically good, Hobbes thought that human nature was basically bad, and Locke thought that it was neither good nor bad as people were born with a "blank slate" and thereafter shaped by their experiences and social environments. Yet as Enlightenment philosophers, they shared certain fundamental assumptions that helped shape the classical school of criminology to be discussed shortly.

One of these assumptions was that God had left people to govern their own affairs through the exercise of free will and reason. In this Enlightenment view, people rationally calculate the rewards and risks of potential actions and adopt behavior promising the greatest pleasure and least pain. To ensure that people not act too emotionally, Enlightenment thinkers stressed the need to acquire an education to develop reasoning ability.

Another assumption centered on the idea of the *social contract*. According to Enlightenment thinkers, individuals as rational actors needed for various reasons to enter into a social contract called the *state*—to form and live in a society characterized by the familiar social institutions of government, education, and the economy. An Enlightenment philosopher's view of the social contract or state as a good thing or bad thing depended heavily on the view held of human nature. For example, because Hobbes thought human nature was so wicked that individuals would normally be perpetually at war without the constraints of society, he thought that the development and existence of the state was both good and necessary. In contrast, because Rousseau and Locke viewed human nature as basically good or neutral, respectively, they feared that the state could corrupt individuals and limit their freedom.

Although these and other Enlightenment views represented significant advances beyond the philosophy of the Middle Ages, this more "enlightened" way of thinking did not extend to the criminal justice system. Europeans suspected of crimes during the Age of Reason were often arrested on flimsy evidence and imprisoned without trial. Torture was commonly used in continental Europe to force people to confess to their alleged crime and to name anyone else involved. In England, the right to jury trials for felonies should have lessened the use of torture. However, English defendants convicted by juries risked losing their land and property to the king. Many defendants thus refused jury trials, only to suffer a form of torture known as *pressing* (finally abolished in 1772), in which a heavy weight was placed on the defendant's body. Some were crushed to death instantly, but others lasted a few days until they either confessed or died. If they managed to die without confessing, their families kept their land and property (Roth 2011).

Although torture was less common in England despite the use of pressing, the death penalty was often used, with more than 200 crimes, including theft, punishable by death. Common citizens could be found guilty of treason for plotting the death of the king, servants for plotting the death of their master, and women for plotting the death of their husband. Execution was a frequent punishment for such "treason," with the "traitors" sometimes disemboweled or dismembered before they were killed.

Justice was severe during this period, but it was also *arbitrary*, as different judges would hand out very different punishments for similar crimes. As Francis T. Cullen and Robert Agnew (2011:22) summarize this problem, "Laws in the 1700s were frequently vague and open to interpretation. Judges, who held great power, would often interpret these laws to suit their own purposes. So the punishment for a particular crime might vary widely, with some people receiving severe penalties and others not being punished at all. Poor people, who could not afford to bribe the judges, were at a special disadvantage."

THE CLASSICAL SCHOOL OF CRIMINOLOGY

Against this frightening backdrop of torture and arbitrary justice, Italian economist and political philosopher Cesare Beccaria (1738–1794) wrote a small, path-breaking book on crime, *Dei Delit ti e Delle Pene (On Crimes and Punishments)*, in 1764 (Beccaria 1819 [1764]). Essentially a plea for justice, Beccaria's treatise helped found what is now called the **classical school** of criminology, also called *utilitarianism* (see Table 5.1). Beccaria was appalled by the horrible conditions in the European criminal justice system at that time. Like other Enlightenment thinkers, he believed that people act rationally and with free will, calculating whether their behavior will cause them more pleasure or more pain; he thought this was true of criminals and noncriminals alike. Influenced by Hobbes, Beccaria also believed that the state needed to ensure that people's natural impulses would stay controlled.

Jeremy Bentham was one of the founders of the classical school of criminology; he felt that the severity of legal punishment should be limited to what was necessary to deter crime.

For this to happen, he wrote, the criminal justice system needed to perform effectively and efficiently. But because people think and act rationally, they will be deterred by a certain degree of punishment, and harsher punishment beyond that is not needed. The criminal justice system thus needed only to be punitive enough to deter people from committing crime, and not more punitive than this level. This reasoning led Beccaria to condemn torture and other treatment of criminals as being much crueler than this more humane standard. He also opposed executions for most crimes and believed that judges should ordinarily hand out similar punishments for similar crimes. To use a contemporary term to describe this latter belief, Beccaria believed that *judicial discretion* should be reduced or eliminated.

As should be clear, Beccaria believed that the primary purpose of the criminal justice system was to deter criminal behavior rather than to avenge the harm that criminals do. He thought that legal punishment is most effective in deterring crime if it is *certain* and *swift*. The criminal justice system thus needs to be efficient in two respects. It needs to ensure that criminals believe they have a strong chance of being arrested and punished, and it needs to ensure that any arrest and punishment happen quickly. In focusing on certainty and swiftness, Beccaria explicitly minimized the importance of the severity of punishment, which he thought far less important than the certainty of punishment for deterring crime. As he put it, "The certainty of a small punishment will make a stronger impression, than the fear of one more severe, if attended with the hopes of escaping" (Beccaria 2006[1764]: 25).

Beccaria is widely regarded as the father of modern criminology, and his treatise is credited with leading to many reforms in the prisons and criminal courts (Bernard, Snipes, and Gerould 2009). However, some critics claim that this credit is at least partly undeserved (Newman and Marongiu 1994). They note that, although Beccaria has been lauded for opposing torture and the death penalty, his treatise actually contains many ambiguous passages about these punishments. Moreover, the criminal justice reforms with which he has been credited were actually already being implemented before he wrote his treatise (Newman and Marongiu 1994). Yet even these critics concede that Beccaria's views greatly influenced legal systems in Europe and affected the thinking of John

TABLE 5.1 ▸ **Classical and Neoclassical Theories in Brief**

THEORY	KEY FIGURE(S)	SYNOPSIS
Classical Theory (Utilitarianism)		
	Cesare Beccaria Jeremy Bentham	People act with free will and calculate whether their behavior will cause them more pleasure or more pain. Legal punishment needs to be severe enough only to deter individuals from committing crime, and not beyond that.
Neoclassical Theories		
Rational Choice Theory	Gary Becker Derek B. Cornish Ronald V. Clarke	Offenders commit crime because of the benefits it brings them. In deciding whether to commit crime, they weigh whether the potential benefits exceed the potential costs. Because offenders do not always have the time or ability to gather and analyze all relevant information relevant for their decision, their decision making is sometimes imperfect.
Deterrence Theory	—	Potential and actual legal punishment can deter crime. General deterrence refers to the deterrence of potential offenders because they fear arrest and/or punishment; specific deterrence refers to the deterrence of convicted offenders because they do not want to experience arrest and/or punishment once again.
Routine Activities Theory	Lawrence E. Cohen Marcus Felson	Crime and victimization are more likely when three factors are simultaneously present: (1) motivated offenders; (2) attractive targets; and (3) an absence of guardianship. Crime trends can be explained by changes in levels of attractive targets and of guardianship.

Adams, Benjamin Franklin, Thomas Jefferson, and the writers of the U.S. Constitution. And it is certainly true that Beccaria's classical belief that "offenders are rational individuals who choose to engage in crime" forms "the foundation of our legal system" today (Cullen and Agnew 2011: 23).

The other great figure of the classical school was English philosopher Jeremy Bentham (1748–1832). Like Beccaria, Bentham felt that people weigh whether their behavior is more apt to cause them pleasure or pain and that the law was far more severe than it needed to be to deter such rational individuals from behaving criminally. His writings inspired changes in the English criminal law in the early 1800s and helped shape the development of the first modern police force in London in 1829. They also influenced the creation of the modern prison. Before the time of Bentham, Beccaria, and other legal reformers, long-term incarceration did not exist; jails were intended only for short-term stays for suspects awaiting trial, torture, or execution. The development of the prison in the early 1800s thus represented a major and still controversial change in the punishment of criminals.

Although the classical school of criminology led to important reforms in the criminal justice system throughout Europe, critics then and now have said that its view of human behavior was too simplistic. Even though individuals sometimes weigh the costs and benefits of their actions, other times they act emotionally. Also, although people often do act to maximize pleasure and to reduce pain, they do not always agree on what is pleasurable. Classical reformers also assumed that the legal system treated all people the same and overlooked the possibility that race or ethnicity, social class, and gender might make a difference.

Review and Discuss

How were criminals treated during the Age of Reason? How may the classical school of criminology be considered a reaction to this treatment?

THE RISE OF POSITIVISM

Notice that we have said nothing about the classical school's views on the causes of crime, other than its belief that some people choose to commit crime when they decide as normal, rational actors that the benefits outweigh the risks. In his famous treatise, Beccaria did not really try to explain why some people are more likely than other people to commit crime, as he focused on the punishment of criminals rather than the reasons for their criminality. But he did acknowledge that a crime like theft results from "misery and despair" among people who are living "but a bare existence." This implied that poor people may reach a different decision than wealthier people in considering the potential risks and rewards of committing theft, and thus that poverty is a cause of this type of crime, but Beccaria did not develop this implication in his book. As Cullen and Agnew (2011: 23) note, then, the explanation of crime beyond the rational calculation of its risks and rewards does "not form a central part of classical theory."

As this observation suggests, classical scholars largely failed to recognize that forces both outside and inside individuals might affect their likelihood of breaking the law. This view was the central insight of a new way of thinking, **positivism,** which came to dominate the nineteenth century and derived from the great discoveries in the physical sciences of Galileo, Newton, and others. These discoveries indicated to social philosophers the potential of using science to understand not only the physical world but also the social world.

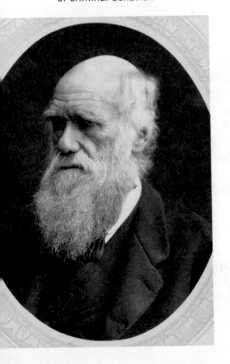

Charles Darwin's theory of evolution established the credibility of science for understanding human behavior and helped usher in scientific explanations of criminal behavior.

French social philosopher Auguste Comte (1798–1857) founded the positive school of philosophy with the publication of his six-volume *Cours de Philosophie Positive (Course in Positive Philosophy)* between 1830 and 1842. Comte argued that human behavior is determined by forces beyond the individual's control. Biologists and psychologists generally locate these forces inside the individual, whereas sociologists find them outside the individual. Research in biology, psychology, and sociology that attempts to explain what causes crime is all positivist in its orientation, even though these disciplines' perspectives differ in many other ways.

The rise of science as a mode of inquiry was cemented in 1859 with the publication of Charles Darwin's *Origin of Species*, in which he outlined his theory of evolution, and in 1871 with the publication of his book on human evolution, *Descent of Man*. The idea that science could explain the origin and development of the human species was revolutionary. It spawned great controversy at the time of Darwin's publications and is still attacked today by people who accept the biblical story of creation. However, Darwin's theory eventually dominated the study of evolution and also established the credibility of science for understanding human behavior and other social and physical phenomena.

Since the time of Comte and Darwin, positivism has guided the study of crime and other human behaviors. Although positivist research has greatly increased our understanding of the origins of crime, critics charge it with several shortcomings (Bernard, Snipes, and Gerould 2009). First, positivism accepts the state's definition of crime by ignoring the possibility (see Chapter 1's discussion of conflict theory) that society's ruling groups define what is criminal. Positivism thus accepts the legitimacy of a social system that may contain serious injustices. Second, in arguing that external and internal forces affect individual criminal behavior, positivism sometimes paints an overly deterministic model of human behavior that denies free will altogether. Third, positivism assumes that criminals are different from the rest of us not only in their behavior, but also in the biological, psychological, and social factors determining their behavior. Noncriminals are thus normal, and criminals are abnormal and even inferior. As self-report studies (see Chapter 3) indicate, however, the line between criminals and noncriminals might be very thin, with "noncriminals" very capable of breaking the law. Despite these criticisms, positivism remains the dominant approach in criminology. This is true for virtually all biologists and psychologists who study crime, but also true, despite notable exceptions, for most sociologists.

Neoclassical Perspectives

We now turn to neoclassical explanations of crime. They are called *neoclassical* because they all ultimately rest on the classical view that criminals are normal, rational individuals who choose to commit crime after calculating the potential risks and rewards of doing so. The three neoclassical explanations we discuss all share this fundamental assumption, even if they differ in other respects. They should thus be viewed as "close cousins" with certain different emphases that ultimately all manifest the classical view just described. As such, they are often said to have revived classical theory.

RATIONAL CHOICE THEORY

Contemporary **rational choice theory** assumes that potential offenders choose whether to commit crime after carefully calculating the possible rewards and risks. An individual commits crime after deciding that the rewards outweigh the risks and does not commit crime after deciding that the risks outweigh the rewards.

As was just stated, the roots of rational choice theory lie in the classical school, but its modern inspiration comes from economic models of rational decision making and more generally from a growing emphasis in sociology and other fields on the rationality of human behavior (McCarthy 2002). In criminology, the introduction of rational choice theory is widely credited to a very influential journal article published more than four decades ago by Gary S. Becker, a famed economist at the University of Chicago (Becker 1968). Becker wrote that choosing whether to commit crime is akin to choosing whether to buy almost any product that consumers purchase. Following what is now termed Becker's *expected utility model*, if individuals decide that the expected utility, or monetary value, of committing a crime exceeds the expected utility of not committing a crime, they decide as rational actors to commit it. Conversely, if they decide that the expected utility of not committing a crime exceeds the expected utility of committing it, they decide not to commit it. In making these decisions, they take into account several factors, including: (1) their possible opportunities for earning money from legitimate occupations; (2) the amount of legitimate money they might earn; (3) the amount of money they might gain from committing crime; (4) the possibility of being arrested for committing crime; and (5) the possibility of being punished if arrested.

In addition to taking into account all these factors, Becker added, people committing crime resemble consumers in at least one other respect. Consumers use whatever information they have to decide how to spend their money. Sometimes they make good decisions, and sometimes they make bad decisions, but whatever decisions they do make are based on a calculation of the relative benefits and costs of the decision. Criminals are no different. They decide whether to commit crime based on whatever information they have; sometimes they make good decisions from their perspective (i.e., they commit a financially beneficial crime and get away with it), and sometimes they make bad decisions (i.e., they get caught).

In likening decisions to commit crime to decisions to purchase a product, Becker explicitly stated that sociological concepts like anomie and differential association (see Chapter 1) are *unimportant* for these decisions. As two scholars have summarized Becker's view on this issue, "As an economic purist, he asserts provocatively that there is little reason for theorizing that treats offenders as if they have a special character that leads them to crime. Becker extends his logic to conclude that the most prominent theories of motivation in criminology are not needed; basic economics addresses their problem sufficiently. Criminal offenders are normal, reasoning economic actors responding to market forces" (Hochstetler and Bouffard 2010: 20–21). However, other economists recognize that concepts from sociology and the other social sciences improve their economic models of criminal behavior (O'Donoghue and Rabin 2001).

As might be expected, Becker's expected utility model of criminal behavior was initially popular but also controversial. Subsequent development of rational choice theory retained Becker's emphasis on the overall rationality of crime, but did not try to reduce decisions to commit crime to a simple matter of economics. Still, most work using a rational choice perspective takes motivation to commit crime as a "given"; that is, it assumes that there will always be people motivated to commit crime and that no special explanation is needed of why some people are more motivated than other people in this regard. Using this assumption of a general motivation to commit crime, the rational choice literature focuses instead on understanding how individuals reach decisions to commit crime and the circumstances that affect their decision making. In doing so, the literature focuses more on decisions to commit a particular crime at a particular time and in a particular place (*event decisions*) than on decisions to commit crime in the first place (*involvement decisions*). Sociological explanations may help understand the latter decisions, many rational choice theorists acknowledge, but rational choice explanations are needed to help understand decisions to commit a specific crime under specific circumstances.

These general assumptions and focus were developed and popularized by two very influential theorists in contemporary rational choice theory, Derek B. Cornish and Ronald V. Clarke (Clarke and Cornish 1985; Clarke and Cornish 2001; Cornish and Clarke 1986). As these authors note, criminology had previously neglected the actual decision-making processes of criminals. In contrast, their rational choice perspective focuses specifically on these processes, as it assumes that offenders choose to commit crime because of the benefits it brings them. Given this assumption, their rational choice perspective "explains the conditions needed for specific crimes to occur, not just why people become involved in crime. It makes little distinction between offenders and nonoffenders and emphasizes the role of crime opportunities in causation" (Clarke and Cornish 2001: 23).

In addition to these elements, Cornish and Clarke emphasized that potential offenders take into account other possible benefits of crime beyond monetary gain, including fun, excitement, and prestige. They also emphasized that offenders do not always have the time or ability

Contemporary rational choice theory assumes that potential offenders take into account other possible benefits of crime beyond monetary gain, including fun, excitement, and prestige.

to gather all information relevant to their decision, and neither do they always have the time and ability to analyze this information completely and accurately. To this extent, criminal offenders are acting with *limited* or *bounded* rationality, as their decision making is often imperfect. Nonetheless, offenders still make decisions that appear rational to them at the time they make them.

Like other rational choice theorists, Cornish and Clarke (2001) distinguish between involvement decisions and event decisions, mentioned just earlier, and focus more on the latter than on the former. Event decisions have at least five stages: (1) preparing to commit a crime; (2) selecting a target; (3) committing the crime; (4) escaping; and (5) aftermath of the crime. Involvement decisions have three stages: (1) committing crime for the first time (*initiation*); (2) continuing to commit crime (*habituation*); and (3) ceasing to commit crime (*desistance*). For a comprehensive understanding of crime, the factors affecting all these decisions must be fully understood.

In this regard, the rational choice perspective has made valuable contributions to understanding event decisions, which criminological theory had previously neglected. In explaining these decisions, the perspective emphasizes two related concepts: (1) *situational factors* (aspects of the immediate physical setting, such as street lighting and the presence or absence of surveillance cameras); and (2) the *opportunities* that exist, or fail to exist, for an offender to commit crime without fear of arrest or other negative consequences. According to Cornish and Clarke, this emphasis in turn leads the rational choice perspective to regard criminals as not very different from noncriminals, as it argues that even normally law-abiding people may turn to crime if the need and temptation are great enough and if the opportunity presents itself.

Evaluating Rational Choice Theory

Rational choice theory has made major contributions to the understanding of criminal behavior by focusing on offenders' decision making. Studies of active (i.e., not incarcerated) robbers, burglars, and other offenders find that they do indeed often plan their crimes by taking into account their chances of being caught and also their chances of being put in danger by victims who resist the crime (Cromwell 1994; McCarthy and Hagan 2005; Wright and Decker 1994; Wright and Decker 1998). Burglars make sure no one is home before they break into a house, and robbers make sure that no police or bystanders are around before they hold someone up (Bernasco and Block 2009; Bernasco and Luykx 2003). White-collar criminals in the world of corporations seem to plan their crimes very carefully (Piquero, Exum, and Simpson 2005). In all these ways, offenders act rationally and proceed only if they perceive that the potential benefits outweigh the potential risks, just as rational choice theory assumes.

The focus of rational choice theory on the criminal event, and especially on the situational factors and opportunities that affect decisions to commit crime, has also made a major contribution. It reminds us that criminals do make choices (Nagin 2007), that criminal behavior is more likely if opportunities for it exist, and that these opportunities must be addressed for crime to be reduced. This focus underlies the work on situational crime prevention that is discussed later in this chapter.

Despite these contributions, rational choice theory has been criticized for exaggerating the rationality of criminal offenders, who often do not think or act as deliberately as rational choice theory implies. Evidence of this problem comes from the studies of active burglars and robbers just mentioned (Shover and Copes 2010). Although, as was noted, many offenders plan their crimes to some degree and try to ensure that they do not get caught, many other offenders actually give very little thought, if any, to this prospect. As one scholar put it, they "simply do not think about the possible legal consequences of their criminal actions before committing crimes" (Tunnell 1990:680). Some offenders also have a fatalistic attitude and go ahead and commit a crime even if they think they might be arrested (Tunnell

International Focus

Mandatory Penalties in International Perspective

A hallmark of the "get tough" approach that has guided U.S. criminal justice policy since the 1970s is the use of mandatory penalties. These include additional prison time for crimes involving the use of guns; long, automatic prison terms for drug crimes and violent crimes; and additional prison time for repeat offenders. These penalties have been intended to deter potential criminal offenders and simply to keep those already convicted locked up for longer durations.

Despite these goals, a large body of research has found that mandatory penalties have had only a small impact, and probably no impact, on the crime rate. This small or nil impact partly reflects the several reasons discussed in the text for why the general deterrent impact of law is usually low or nonexistent. In addition to these reasons, mandatory penalties are not consistently applied. Recognizing that the prison system is already overcrowded, prosecutors often avoid mandatory penalties by charging defendants with lesser crimes. They also reduce the charges because defendants facing long, automatic prison terms have little incentive to forgo jury trials, which are long and expensive. As Samuel Walker (2011:163) notes, "An increase in the severity of the potential punishment creates pressure to avoid its actual application."

The conclusion that mandatory penalties in the United States do not work as intended would be reinforced if it were also found in other nations. However, no other Western nation has enacted mandatory penalties to the extent found in the United States. A few nations do have these penalties to some degree, including Australia, Canada, England and Wales, and South Africa. The effects of mandatory penalties in these nations have been studied, and these studies find that prosecutors and judges find ways to circumvent the harsh penalties. They also find that harsher penalties, including mandatory penalties, do not reduce crime.

For example, the Sentencing Advisory Council in Australia's state of Victoria concluded, "Ultimately, current research in this area indicates that there is a very low likelihood that a mandatory sentencing regime will deliver on its [deterrent] aims." The Canadian Sentencing Commission similarly observed, "Evidence does not support the notion that variations in sanctions . . . affect the deterrent value of sentences. In other words, deterrence cannot be used with empirical justification, to guide the imposition of sentences." The National Research Institute of Policy in Finland concluded, "Can our long prison sentences be defended on the basis of a cost/benefit assessment of their general preventative effect? The answer of the criminological expertise was no."

These international assessments on mandatory penalties and general deterrence reinforce the conclusion from U.S. research that mandatory penalties and other harsher punishments have little or no general deterrent effect. This body of research in the United States and elsewhere leads deterrence expert Michael Tonry (2009:65) to observe, "There is no credible evidence that the enactment or implementation of such sentences has significant deterrent effects."

Sources: Tonry 2009; Walker 2011.

1996). Research on prisoners also finds that about half of all inmates were under the influence of alcohol and/or drugs at the time of their offense (Beck et al. 2000), making it difficult or impossible to think carefully about the possible consequences of their actions. Further, many crimes are obviously violent crimes, and these crimes often tend to be very emotional in nature. People committing them act from strong emotions, such as anger and jealousy, and thus are not able to carefully consider the consequences of their actions as they strike out against someone. For all these reasons, many offenders do not act in the rather careful, deliberate manner that rational choice theory assumes.

DETERRENCE THEORY

Because rational choice theory assumes that criminals weigh the risks of their actions, it implies that they can be deterred from committing crime if the potential risks seem too certain or too severe, as Beccaria argued in his famous treatise. To turn that around, theoretical belief in the law's deterrent impact is based on a rational choice view of potential criminals. As two scholars have observed, "What makes deterrence work is that human beings are both rational and self-interested beings. Persons make rational assessments of the expected costs and benefits of making numerous decisions—buying a house or car, changing jobs, committing a crime—and choose the line of behavior that is most beneficial (profitable) and least costly" (Paternoster and Bachman 2001:14). For obvious reasons, then, rational choice theory is closely aligned with **deterrence theory,** which assumes that potential and actual legal punishment can deter crime. In fact, the two theories are often considered synonymous (Matsueda, Kreager, and Huizinga 2006). Their assumptions underlie the "get tough" approach, involving harsher punishment and more prisons, that the United States has used since the 1970s to fight crime.

TYPES OF DETERRENCE

In addressing the deterrent effect of the law, scholars distinguish several types of deterrence. A first distinction is between absolute deterrence and marginal deterrence. **Absolute deterrence** refers to the effect of having some legal punishment (arrest, incarceration, and so forth) versus the effect of having no legal punishment. The law certainly has a very strong absolute deterrent effect; if the criminal justice system did not exist, crime would be much higher, or so most scholars believe. In the real world, of course, we usually do not have to worry about the criminal justice system disappearing short of a natural or human disaster. Thus, questions of deterrence are actually questions of **marginal deterrence,** which refers to the effect of increasing the severity, certainty, and/or swiftness of legal punishment.

A second distinction is between general and specific deterrence. *General deterrence* occurs when members of the public decide not to break the law because they fear legal punishment. To take a traffic example, we may obey the speed limit because we do not want to get a speeding ticket. **Specific deterrence** (also called *individual deterrence*) occurs when offenders *already punished* for lawbreaking decide not to commit *another* crime because they do not want to face legal consequences again. Remaining with our traffic example, if we have already received a speeding ticket or two and are close to losing our license, we may obey the speed limit because we do not want to suffer further consequences.

A final distinction is between objective and subjective deterrence. **Objective deterrence** refers to the impact of *actual* legal punishment, whereas **subjective deterrence** refers to the impact of people's *perceptions* of the likelihood and severity of legal punishment. Deterrence theory predicts that people are deterred from crime by actual legal punishment that is certain and severe and also by their own perceptions that legal punishment will be certain and severe.

Taking a Closer Look at Deterrence

In considering how much marginal deterrent impact the criminal law might have, it is important to keep in mind several considerations that affect the size of any impact that can be expected.

A first consideration concerns the *type of criminal offense*. Simply put, some types of crime might be more deterrable than other types of crime. A well-known distinction

Violence is expressive behavior. As such, it is relatively difficult to deter by the threat of arrest and punishment.

here is between **instrumental offenses,** those committed for material gain with some degree of planning, and **expressive offenses,** those committed for emotional reasons and with little or no planning. William Chambliss (1967), who popularized this distinction, thought that instrumental crimes are more deterrable than expressive crimes because they are relatively unemotional and planned. Because the people committing expressive crimes are by definition acting emotionally, they often do not take the time to think about the legal consequences of their actions. All things equal, then, marginal deterrence should be higher for instrumental crimes than for expressive crimes, and it might in fact be very low for these latter offenses.

A second consideration, according to Chambliss (1967), is whether offenders have high or low commitment to criminal behavior. Professional criminals such as "cat burglars" are very skilled and also very committed to their way of life; drug addicts are also very committed, because of their addiction, to using illegal drugs. In contrast, amateur criminals such as teenagers who take a car on a joy ride are less committed to criminal behavior. Chambliss said that offenders with higher commitment to their crime are less likely to be deterred by legal punishment.

A final consideration is whether a crime tends to occur in public, such as robbery, or in private, such as domestic violence and some illegal drug use. Public crimes, precisely because they are public and thus potentially more noticeable, are more deterrable by legal punishment, all things equal, than private crimes.

Putting all these considerations together, expressive crimes are less deterrable than instrumental crimes; high-commitment offenders are less deterrable than low-commitment offenders; and public crimes are more deterrable than private crimes. Efforts that try to increase marginal deterrence by making arrest more certain and/or by making punishment harsher are thus likely to have only a relatively small deterrent effect on expressive crimes, on crimes involving high-commitment offenders, and on private offenses. These relatively undeterrable crimes involve many violent and property offenses, and perhaps the bulk of these offenses.

This pessimistic appraisal of the expected size of any marginal deterrent effect becomes even more pessimistic when we recall the studies of active burglars and robbers, discussed earlier, that focus on their decision making. Although these individuals are committing instrumental offenses, recall that many of them do not really think about their chances of getting caught. Others do think about their chances of getting caught but plan their crimes so that they will not be arrested. Still others have a fatalistic attitude and commit a crime with the expectation of being arrested. All these offenders are relatively undeterrable by legal punishment. Also recall that up to half of all offenders are on drugs and/or alcohol at the time of their offense; they, too, are undeterrable by legal punishment. Many offenders, then, do not think or act in the way they must think or act for marginal deterrence to have a relatively large impact (Shover and Copes 2010).

Additional considerations add even further to this pessimistic appraisal (Walker 2011). First, arrest and imprisonment have become so common in the United States, especially among young males in large cities, that scholars think these legal sanctions have lost the stigma they used to have (Hirschfield 2008). Rather, these sanctions have become an expectation, and, if this is true, not a deterrent. Second, arrest and imprisonment have been found to increase the feelings of masculinity of urban youths: they become more "macho" and are more likely to reoffend for that reason (Rios 2009). Third, increased penalties and other deterrence-oriented criminal justice policies are not always implemented as legislators might have expected. For example, prosecutors might not charge an offender with the maximum charge because of prison overcrowding. If these deterrent policies are not fully implemented, then their deterrent impact cannot be expected to be very high.

Fourth, the chances of arrest and imprisonment are so low that it would be surprising if legal sanctions did have a high deterrent impact. Recall from Chapter 3 that victims of violent and property crime report only about 40 percent of their victimizations to the police, and that police make an arrest in only about 20 percent of the crimes known to them. Putting these figures together yields a rough arrest rate of only 8 percent for all violent and property crime. Less than one-fifth of these arrests result in a felony conviction and imprisonment, resulting in a risk of imprisonment of less than 2 percent of all violent and property crime. On TV crime shows, the "perp" usually gets what is coming to him, but in the real world of crime, the perp actually has an incredibly low risk of arrest and punishment. This risk is so low that a strong deterrent effect of the law cannot be expected.

Research on Deterrence

All these considerations suggest that the size of the marginal deterrent effect of legal punishment is likely to be relatively small. Research on deterrence generally confirms this pessimistic expectation. Most research has focused on the **certainty** of punishment (the likelihood of being arrested) and on the **severity** of punishment (whether someone is incarcerated and, if so, for how long).

Early research found that states with high certainty rates, measured as the number of arrests divided by the number of known crimes, had lower crime rates, as deterrence theory would predict. Some early studies also found that states with more severe punishment again had lower crime rates (Gibbs 1968; Tittle 1969). Although these findings indicated a marginal deterrent effect, some scholars challenged this interpretation and instead argued that crime rates affect certainty and severity (Decker and Kohfeld 1985; Pontell 1984). In this way of thinking, called the **system capacity argument,** areas with high levels of crime have lower arrest rates for two reasons: their police are "extra" busy, and their police also realize that too many arrests would overburden the criminal justice system. For these reasons, areas with high crime rates end up with low certainty rates. Similarly, areas with high crime rates also have lower severity of punishment because their prisons are too full to handle their many offenders. Prosecutors and judges both realize this, and prosecutors seek reduced charges and judges impose shorter sentences.

More recent research on deterrence has been much more methodologically sophisticated than the early research, and Chapters 16 and 17 discuss it in further detail. Suffice it to say here that the recent evidence generally finds that arrest and punishment (or, to be more precise, increases in the probability of being arrested and more severely punished) have only a weak general or specific deterrent effect on crime and delinquency, and perhaps no effect at all (Doob and Webster 2003; Pratt et al. 2006; Walker 2011). A recent review concluded that "there is little credible evidence that changes in sanctions affect crime rates" (Tonry 2008:279). To the extent that a deterrent effect does exist, it exists more for the certainty of punishment than for the severity of punishment.

For example, although deterrence theory predicts that higher imprisonment rates should produce lower crime rates, this pattern often does not occur: sometimes crime rates decline when imprisonment rates rise, as deterrence theory would predict, but sometimes crime rates decline only slightly, do not change at all, or even increase. During

Crime and Controversy

Three Strikes Laws Strike Out

Beginning in the 1990s, several states enacted so-called "three strikes" laws in an effort to reduce the crime rate. These laws required life imprisonment or, at the least, a very long prison sentence for offenders convicted of their second or third felony. A major reason given for these laws was that they would send a message to potential offenders and thus deter them from committing their third felony, and perhaps even their first or second felony.

The introduction of these laws provided criminologists an opportunity to test their deterrent impact. Drawing on deterrence theory, they gathered and analyzed various kinds of data to test the hypothesis that three strikes laws would reduce the street crime rate.

A central conclusion that emerges from this body of research is that the three strikes laws have had no discernible deterrent effect on criminal behavior. During the 1990s, violent crime dropped throughout the nation, but it dropped at a greater rate in states that did *not* enact three strikes laws than

in states that did enact them. Moreover, studies of specific states that enacted three strikes laws found that crime did not fall at a greater rate in those states after the laws came into effect. Some studies even find that homicides *increased* after three strikes laws were enacted, perhaps because offenders who are committing their third (or fourth, etc.) felony do not want to risk life imprisonment and thus decide to kill their victim to make it more difficult to arrest and convict them.

If three strikes laws have not reduced crime, they have increased the number of prison inmates serving life sentences or very long terms. Many of these inmates will stay in prison long after they would have "aged out" of crime, imposing a considerable financial cost not only from the cost of keeping them in prison, but also from the geriatric medical care many of them need. Three strikes laws thus provide important evidence against deterrence theory, and they also illustrate the financial costs that the "get tough" policy since the 1970s has incurred.

Sources: Ehlers, Schiraldi, and Ziedenberg 2004; Kovandzic, Sloan, and Vieraitis 2004; Marvell and Moody 2001; Walker 2011.

the late 1980s, U.S. imprisonment rates rose, but so did crime rates. Although crime rates finally declined after the early 1990s as imprisonment rates continued to rise, crime declined less in states with the greatest increase in imprisonment rates than in states with lower increases in imprisonment rates (see the Crime and Controversy box in Chapter 3). Also, deterrence theory predicts that when penalties for certain crimes are made harsher, the rates of these crimes should decline, but once again this often does not happen (Walker 2011).

What about specific deterrence? Although it seems obvious that offenders who are arrested and imprisoned should reoffend less because of their punishment, evidence of this specific deterrent effect is mixed at best. There is even evidence of an opposite effect: that punishment *increases* the chances that offenders will break the law again (Nieuwbeerta, Nagin, and Blokland 2009; Pogarsky and Piquero 2003). A recent review of the literature on this issue concluded that "most studies of the impact of imprisonment on subsequent criminality find [either] no effect or a criminogenic [crime-causing] effect" (Nagin, Cullen, and Jonson 2009:121). The authors added that this conclusion "casts doubt on claims that imprisonment has strong specific deterrent effects" (p. 115).

As was suggested earlier, it should not be very surprising that deterrence research casts doubt on the size of general and specific deterrent effects. For deterrence to occur, criminals must calculate their behavior, as rational choice and deterrence theories assume they do. This assumption is critical for deterrence theory, because if criminals did not weigh the risks of their behavior, then the threat of arrest and punishment could not deter them. Yet, as we have seen, studies of active offenders do not provide much support for this assumption (Shover and Copes 2010). Although some crimes, such as corporate crime, involve careful planning and weighing of all risks, many other crimes typically do not involve such efforts, and many "street crime" offenders do not think and act in the ways that rational choice and deterrence theories assume. Most criminals are smart enough to avoid committing a crime in front of a police station or elsewhere where they might be detected, but in other places many apparently do not worry about being arrested and punished. For this reason, increases in the penalties for crimes do not seem to deter them.

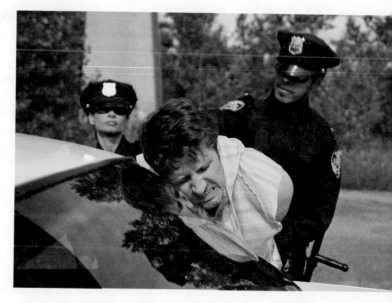

Increases in penalties for crime do not seem to deter criminals, in part because they do not act in the ways that rational choice and deterrence theories assume.

Some research also documents the deterrent effect of internal punishment (e.g., guilt, shame, embarrassment, and conscience) and of informal sanctions such as the disapproval of friends and loved ones (Nagin and Pogarsky 2001). However, such evidence says nothing about the deterrent effect of *legal* punishment (Akers and Sellers 2009).

In sum, deterrence research suggests that the general and specific deterrent effect of legal sanctions is small or nonexistent. Certain policing strategies do seem to deter some types of crime (see Chapter 16), but strategies involving harsher punishment generally do not seem to deter crime. Although deterrence theory might sound appealing at first glance, then, deterrence is more of a dream than a reality in the real world of crime.

ROUTINE ACTIVITIES THEORY

A third and very influential neoclassical perspective is **routine activities theory** (also called *routine activity theory*). This theory was introduced in Chapter 4 as an explanation of criminal victimization patterns. To briefly recall that discussion, routine activities theory assumes that crime is more likely when three factors are simultaneously present: (1) motivated offenders; (2) attractive targets; and (3) an absence of guardianship (such as police, bystanders, and even a dog). Because the theory also assumes that offenders are more likely to decide to commit crime when they have attractive targets and when there are no guardians, it reflects rational choice assumptions of criminal decision making and is considered a neoclassical theory.

Routine activities theory was introduced in 1979 by Lawrence E. Cohen and Marcus Felson (Cohen and Felson 1979) and elaborated in other works (e.g., Felson and Boba 2010). Cohen and Felson wrote that for crime to happen, offenders, targets, and the absence of guardians must all converge at the same time and in the same location. Because routine activities of everyday life affect the likelihood of this convergence, when people's routine activities change, crime rates change as well. Like rational choice theory, routine activities theory further assumes there will always be a supply of motivated offenders, and it does not try to explain why some people are more motivated than others to commit crime, nor why motivation to commit crime might change as other social changes occur. As Cohen and Felson maintain (1979: 604), "The convergence in time and space of suitable targets and the absence of capable guardians can lead to large increases in crime rates without any increase or change in the structural conditions that motivate individuals to engage in crime." As they imply, the theory instead focuses on changes in the supply of attractive targets and in the presence or absence of guardianship as key variables affecting changes in crime rates. Because these variables affect the opportunity for offenders to commit crime, or what Cohen and Felson (1979: 592) call the "criminal opportunity structure," routine activities theory is often considered an *opportunity theory* of crime.

Cohen and Felson reasoned that routine activities inside or near one's home result in less victimization than activities that occur away from home. When people are at home, they are safer from burglary, because they provide guardianship for their home, and they are also safer from robbery and other predatory crimes, because they are not out in public providing attractive targets for motivated offenders. Cohen and Felson also reasoned that as smaller and more expensive consumer items go on the market, people are more likely to have these items in their homes or on their persons when away from home, making them attractive targets for offenders. The authors then used these two sets of reasoning to help understand two important trends in crime and victimization: (1) differences in criminal victimization rates for various categories of people, such as young versus old; and (2) why U.S. crime rates increased during the 1960s even though poverty and unemployment fell and median income and education levels rose during that decade.

For example, they hypothesized that young people should have higher victimization rates than older people because they spend so much more time away from home, and that is exactly what data from national victimization surveys find (see Chapter 4). They also hypothesized that single-person households should suffer higher burglary rates than multiple-person households because they are have less guardianship (i.e., they are more likely to be empty at any one time or to have fewer people at home when someone is there), and that is also what victimization data find.

Turning to the 1960s crime rate increase, Cohen and Felson argued that this increase resulted from the simultaneous increase in suitable targets and decrease of guardianship during that decade. Regarding guardianship, for example, many more women began working outside the home during the 1960s, and many more residences were occupied by only one person. These two facts meant that many more homes began to be empty most of the day as people went to work. Not surprisingly, burglary rates increased dramatically during the 1960s. Regarding target availability, Cohen and Felson found that the sales of consumer goods increased greatly during the 1960s, as did the sale of smaller and more valuable goods (i.e., smaller televisions). These trends provided "more suitable property available for theft" (p. 599), and more such theft occurred.

Cohen and Felson concluded that that crime results in part from the activities that so many people ordinarily enjoy. As they put it, "It is ironic that the very factors which increase the opportunity to enjoy the benefits of life also may increase the opportunity for predatory violations. For example, automobiles provide freedom of movement to offenders as well as average citizens and offer vulnerable targets for theft. . . . Rather than assuming that predatory crime is simply an indicator of social breakdown, one might take it as a byproduct of freedom and prosperity as they manifest themselves in the routine activities of everyday life" (p. 605).

Evaluating Routine Activities Theory

In the more than three decades since its introduction, routine activities theory has proven very popular and has stimulated much research (Marcum 2010). It is popular because it seems to explain important aspects of differences in crime rates among different categories of people and among different locations, and because it also seems to explain important aspects of changes in crime rates over time. For example, crime is ordinarily higher during the summer than other times of the year (see Chapter 3). Routine activities theory provides an explanation for this trend. Homes are more likely to be empty during the summer as people travel, and homes' windows are more likely to be open. These two facts make homes more vulnerable to burglary during the summer. During the summer, people are also more likely to be out in public, increasing their vulnerability to crimes like robbery and assault. To take another example, locations in cities with high numbers of bars and taverns have higher rates of robbery and assault (Roncek and Maier 1991). People visiting these establishments are attractive targets because they tend to carry relatively large sums of money or credit/debit cards, and because they lack personal guardianship once they become inebriated. As routine activities theory would predict, the presence of these establishments contributes to higher rates of crime and victimization.

The popularity of routine activities theory has increased as various works have added to the original insights of Cohen and Felson. Certain studies have deepened understanding of the factors that contribute to target availability and the absence of guardianship. For example, adolescents with strong bonds to their parents reduce their target availability because they are more likely to stay home and not venture out to places where they might encounter motivated offenders (Schreck and Fisher 2004). Other work has extended the theoretical scope of routine activities theory. Although the theory was originally developed to explain victimization, some scholars have used it to explain offending. In their way of thinking, individuals' routine activities can make it more or less likely that they will have the opportunity to offend. When they do have this opportunity, they are more likely to commit crime. For example, adolescents who spend more time away from home and who are not involved in youth activities at school or elsewhere have more opportunity to get in trouble, and so they do (Osgood and Anderson 2004; Osgood et al. 1996).

Situational crime prevention involves efforts in specific locations to reduce the opportunity for criminal behavior. Camera surveillance on city streets is an example of this type of crime prevention.

In one possible problem, routine activities theory has been criticized for ignoring the factors that motivate offenders to commit crime (Akers and Sellers 2009). In their original formulation, Cohen and Felson readily conceded this neglect but argued the importance of considering the factors on which they did focus: target suitability and the absence of guardianship.

Situational Crime Prevention

One of the major contributions of routine activities theory, along with rational choice theory, has been the stimulation of work on **situational crime prevention,** or efforts in specific locations that aim to "reduce exposure to motivated offenders, decrease target suitability, and increase capable guardianship" (Knepper 2009; Marcum 2010: 54; Welsh and Farrington 2009). These efforts try to reduce the opportunities for committing crime by accomplishing all three of these goals. Examples of these efforts include installing or increasing lighting and camera surveillance on city streets or in public parks, and providing and installing better security systems for motor vehicles, commercial buildings, and homes. Another example is *hot-spot policing*, which involves police patrol of high-crime areas (Braga and Bond 2008).

One concern regarding these efforts is that crime might simply be displaced to other locations and to other victims. However, a recent analysis of situational crime-prevention studies concluded that displacement is not a problem (Guerette and Bowers 2009). Sometimes it does occur, but just as often the opposite consequence (*diffusion of benefits*) happens, in which crime is reduced in nearby locations. Moreover, when displacement does occur, the additional crime elsewhere is lower than the crime that was displaced, resulting in a lower crime rate overall. The authors of this analysis concluded that their results "provide continued support for the view that crime does not simply relocate in the aftermath of situational interventions. Instead, crime displacement seems to be the exception rather than the rule, and it is sometimes more likely that diffusion of crime-control benefit will occur. The findings also indicate that when displacement does occur, on average, it tends to be less than the gains achieved by the situational intervention, which means that the initiatives remained worthwhile" (p. 1357).

Conclusion

Classical and neoclassical perspectives all assume that individuals commit crime when they decide that the potential gains outweigh the potential costs. They ultimately attribute crime to the choices offenders make about their own behavior, and they explicitly or implicitly state that increasing the risk of legal punishment should reduce crime. Crime policies based on these views aim to affect offending decisions by making punishment more certain and more severe. However, it is unclear whether the decision making of potential criminals follows the rational choice model, as well as whether increasing the certainty and severity of punishment can reduce crime rates significantly. Moreover, the world of classical and neoclassical perspectives is largely devoid of social inequality. To the extent that inequality helps generate criminality, these perspectives ignore significant sources of crime. At the same time, together they provide an important understanding of crime from the offender's perspective, and they have stimulated contemporary efforts in situational crime prevention that show promise in reducing crime.

Neoclassical perspectives are important for at least one other reason. Their emphasis on the rationality of criminals, belief in the deterrent power of law, and lack of emphasis on the social causes of crime are all reflected in the "get tough" approach that has guided U.S. criminal justice policy since the 1970s. Among other changes, this approach has involved mandatory incarceration and longer prison terms, which most criminologists probably think do little to reduce crime and cause many other problems (see Chapter 17) (Clear 2010). Sound social policy must always be based on good theory, and the neoclassical perspectives are good theories in many ways. But the "get tough" approach is based on assumptions from these perspectives that do not stand up well upon closer inspection. Criminals often do not act as rationally as rational choice theory assumes, and deterrence does not work nearly as well as deterrence theory assumes. Moreover, the advocates of the "get tough" approach tend to minimize or deny the role played by poverty and other structural problems in criminal behavior. Cullen and Agnew (2006:460) say that this denial "ignores the rather substantial body of research showing that inequality and concentrated disadvantage are related to street crime."

Summary

1. To reduce crime most effectively, we must first understand why crime occurs. Biological and psychological explanations place the causes of crime inside the individual, whereas sociological explanations place the causes of crime in the social environment. To reduce crime, biology and psychology thus suggest the need to correct problems inside the individual, whereas sociology suggests the need to correct problems in the social environment.

2. Historically, deviance and crime were first attributed to angry gods and fiendish demons. The Age of Reason eventually led to more scientific explanations, especially those grounded in positivism, which attributes behavior to forces inside and outside the individual. The classical school of criminology arose with the work of writers such as Beccaria and Bentham, who believed that because people act to maximize pleasure and reduce pain, the legal system need only be sufficiently harsh to deter potential criminals from breaking the law.

3. Classical and neoclassical perspectives assume that potential criminals calculate whether lawbreaking will bring them more reward than risk and that increases in the certainty and severity of punishment will thus decrease their likelihood of engaging in crime. However, research finds that most criminals are not as calculating as rational choice theory assumes and that harsher and more certain legal punishment generally has only a weak or inconsistent effect on crime rates, or no effect at all.

Key Terms

absolute deterrence 123

certainty 125

classical school 116

deterrence theory 123

Enlightenment 114

expressive offenses 124

general deterrence 123

instrumental offenses 124

marginal deterrence 123

objective deterrence 123

positivism 118

rational choice theory 119

routine activities theory 127

severity 125

situational crime prevention 129

specific deterrence 123

subjective deterrence 123

system capacity argument 125

What Would You Do?

1. You are a policy advisor to a member of your state legislature. The legislature will soon be voting on a bill that would double the maximum prison term for anyone convicted of armed robbery. Your boss knows that you took a criminology course and has even seen this book proudly displayed on a bookcase in your office. She knows that the bill is very popular with the public, but wonders if it will really do much good and asks you to write a policy recommendation for her to read. What will you recommend to her? What will be the reasons for your recommendation?

2. You are a policy adviser to the mayor of a medium-sized city. A recent spurt of nighttime robberies has alarmed the city's residents and prompted the police to suspend vacation leave until the offenders can be arrested. Based on what you have read in this chapter, what would you advise the mayor to do to reduce the robbery problem in the city?

CHAPTER

six

Biological and Psychological Explanations

Crime in the News

D r. Jim Fallon is a neuroscientist at the University of California–Irvine who studies the biology of human behavior. He has a special interest in violent behavior and has studied the brains and other biological aspects of more than seventy convicted murderers. A few years ago, he gathered brain scans of eight members of his family, including himself, to determine their risk of developing Alzheimer's disease. Then he learned from his mother that his father's ancestry, going back to the colonial period, included eight suspected murderers.

After hearing this, Fallon compared his family members' brain scans and other data to those of the convicted murderers he had studied. Much to his surprise, Fallon found that he had inherited several genes that are thought to be related to violence and aggression. Recalling this discovery, Fallon remarked, "I'm the one who looks most like a serial killer. It's disturbing." He speculated that his happy childhood might have kept him from becoming a violent criminal. "I had a charmed childhood. But if I'd been mistreated as a child, who knows what might have happened."

Yet he kept a sense of humor about his discovery, adding, "These results will cause some problems at the next family party."

Source: Naik 2009.

his news story reminds us that scientists have long been interested in the biological basis of human behavior and perhaps especially of violent behavior. This chapter examines biological and psychological explanations of criminal behavior. As Chapter 5 explained, these two sets of explanations attribute crime primarily to traits inside the individual, whereas sociological explanations attribute crime primarily to aspects of the social environment.

Biological Explanations

As the previous chapter also noted, positivism arose during the nineteenth century as a result of great advances by Darwin and other scientists. When applied to crime, the positivist approach attempts to locate the forces inside and external to individuals that affect whether they will engage in criminal behavior. The first positivist research on crime was primarily biological. Biological explanations enjoy a renewed popularity today, as the news story that begins this chapter illustrates, but remain controversial because of their social policy implications. We will examine older and contemporary biological explanations and then review the controversy. These explanations are summarized in Table 6.1.

TABLE 6.1 ▸ Biological Explanations in Brief

THEORY	KEY FIGURE(S)	SYNOPSIS
Nineteenth-Century Views		
Phrenology	Franz Gall	A specific region of the brain governs criminal behavior. Because this region is largest in criminals, skull dimensions provide good evidence of criminal tendencies.
Atavism	Cesare Lombroso	Criminals are evolutionary accidents who resemble primitive people more than modern people.
Early Nineteenth-Century Views		
Biological Inferiority	Earnest Hooton	Criminals are biologically inferior, and the primary cause of crime is biological inferiority. The government should sterilize or exile criminals.
Body Shapes (Somatology)	William Sheldon	Body shapes affect personalities and thus criminality. Endomorphs are heavy and relatively noncriminal; mesomorphs are muscular and prone to violence; and ectomorphs are thin and introverted.
Contemporary Explanations		
Heredity and Genetics	—	Criminality is inherited. A genetic tendency for criminal behavior is passed from parents to children.
Neurochemical Factors	—	High levels of testosterone contribute to male criminality; premenstrual syndrome contributes to female criminality. Low levels of serotonin contribute to violent behavior.
Diet and Nutrition	—	Among other nutritional problems, high levels of sugar and refined carbohydrates contribute to aggressive behavior.
Pregnancy and Birth Complications	—	Pregnancy and birth complications impair central nervous system functioning and thus produce antisocial behavior.
Early Puberty	—	Adolescents of either sex who experience early puberty are more likely to commit delinquent acts and engage in other antisocial behavior.

Nineteenth-Century Views

PHRENOLOGY

One of earliest biological explanations of crime, **phrenology,** concerned the size and shape of the skull and was popular from the mid-1700s to the mid-1800s (Rafter 2008). An Austrian physician, Franz Gall (1758–1828), was its major proponent. Gall thought that three major regions of the brain govern three types of behavior and personality characteristics: intellectual, moral, and lower. The lower type was associated with criminal behavior and would be largest in criminals. Because phrenologists could not directly measure the three brain regions, they reasoned that the size and shape of the skull corresponded to the brain's size and shape. They thus thought that skull dimensions provided good evidence of criminal tendencies.

Phrenology was popular initially but never really caught on. We now know, of course, that the brain cannot be measured by measuring the skull. But perhaps the most important reason phrenology faded was that its biological determinism clashed with the Enlightenment emphasis on free will, still popular in the early 1800s. The determinism of positivism did not become widely accepted until decades later.

CESARE LOMBROSO: ATAVISM

If Cesare Beccaria was the founder of the classical school of criminology, then Cesare Lombroso (1835–1909), an Italian physician, was the founder of the positivist school of criminology. Influenced by Darwin's work on evolution, Lombroso thought criminals were *atavists*, or throwbacks to an earlier stage of evolution, and said criminal behavior stemmed from **atavism.** In essence, criminals were evolutionary accidents who resembled primitive people more than modern (i.e., nineteenth-century) people. Lombroso's evidence for his theory came from his extensive measurements of the bodies of men in Italian prisons that he compared to his measurements of the bodies of Italian soldiers, his control group. He concluded that the prisoners looked more like primitive men than modern men, because, among other measurements, their arms were abnormally long, their skulls and jaws abnormally large, and their bodies very hairy. Lombroso published his atavist theory in 1876 in his famous book, *L'Uomo Delinquent (The Criminal Man)* (Lombroso 1876).

Cesare Lombroso is considered the founder of the positive school of criminology.

Given the intense interest in evolution from Darwin's work, Lombroso's discovery attracted much attention and his atavist theory of crime became very popular. However, Lombroso's research was methodologically flawed (Bernard, Snipes, and Gerould 2009). Because the Italian criminal justice system then was hardly a fair one, many of the prisoners he measured probably had not actually committed crimes. His control group probably included people who had committed crimes without being imprisoned, as is still true today. Many differences he found between his prisoners and control group subjects were too small to be statistically significant. Lombroso may have also unconsciously measured his subjects in ways that fit his theory. Even if we assume for the sake of argument that his prisoners did look different, it is possible that their imprisonment resulted more from reactions to their unusual appearance than from their criminality. Finally, some of the traits Lombroso described characterize Sicilians, who have long been at the bottom of Italy's socioeconomic ladder. Lombroso's prisoners might have looked like atavists not because his theory made any sense, but because the traits he identified as atavistic happened to be ones belonging to Sicilians.

By the end of his career, Lombroso had modified his view of atavism. Although he continued to think the most serious criminals were atavists, he reasoned that this group comprised only about one-third of all offenders. The remainder were criminals who developed brain problems long after birth and occasional criminals whose behavior stemmed from problems in their social environment. Two of Lombroso's students, Raffaele Garofalo (1852–1934) and Enrico Ferri (1856–1929), carried on his views and made their own contributions to the development of criminology. Garofalo continued to emphasize biological bases for crime, while Ferri stressed that social conditions also play a role. Both scholars attacked the classical view of free will and crime and argued for a more positivist, determinist view of crime causation.

As the founder of modern positive criminology, Lombroso left a lasting legacy; his assumption that criminals are biologically different continues to guide today's biological research on crime. It should come as no surprise, however, that his atavist theory has long been discredited. In 1913, English psychiatrist Charles Goring (1870–1919) published his book *The English Convict*. Goring measured the body dimensions of 3,000 English prisoners and of the members of a large control group. He did not find the differences that Lombroso found and thus found no support for atavism. This latter conclusion prompted Lombroso's theory to fall out of favor.

Lombroso on Women

Chapter 3 noted that few criminologists studied women criminals until fairly recently. Lombroso was one of these few. That is the good news. The bad news is that his explanation of female criminality, reflecting the sexism of his time, rested on antiquated notions of women's biology and physiology. Lombroso published *The Female Offender* in 1895. In it he wrote that women were more likely than men to be atavists and that "even the female criminal is monotonous and uniform compared with her male companion, just as in general woman is inferior to man" (Lombroso 1920 [1903]). He also thought that women "have many traits in common with children," that their "moral sense is deficient," and that "they are revengeful, jealous."

In view of these terrible qualities, how did Lombroso explain why women commit so little crime? He reasoned that women were naturally passive and viewed their "defects (as) neutralized by piety, maternity, want of passion, sexual coldness, weakness and an undeveloped intelligence." A woman who managed to commit crime despite these crime-reducing traits must be, thought Lombroso, "a born criminal more terrible than any man," as her "wickedness must have been enormous before it could triumph over so many obstacles" (Lombroso 1920[1903]: 150–152). Although most modern criminologists consider Lombroso's views hopelessly outdated, his emphasis on women's physiology and supposed biological nature remained influential in the study of women's crime for many years (Chesney-Lind and Jones 2010).

EARLY TWENTIETH-CENTURY VIEWS

Earnest Hooton: Biological Inferiority

After Goring's 1913 refutation of Lombroso's atavism theory, criminologists temporarily abandoned the idea that criminals were physiologically different. Then in 1939, Harvard University anthropologist Earnest Hooton (1887–1954) revived interest in physiological explanations with the publication of two books that reported the results of his measurement of 14,000 male prisoners and 3,200 control group subjects (Hooton 1939a; Hooton 1939b).

Compared to the control group, prisoners tended to have, among other things, low foreheads, crooked noses, narrow jaws, small ears, long necks, and stooped shoulders. Not one to mince words, Hooton labeled criminals "organically inferior" and "low-grade human organisms" and concluded that the "primary cause of crime is biological inferiority. . . . The penitentiaries of our society are built upon the shifting sands and quaking bogs of inferior human organisms" (Hooton 1939b: 130). He further concluded that criminals' body shapes influenced the types of crime they committed. Murderers tended to be tall and thin, for example, whereas rapists were short and heavy. Men with average builds did not specialize in any particular crime because they, like their physical shape, had no specific orientation.

Hooton's belief in the biological inferiority of criminals led him to urge the government to reduce crime by undertaking "the extirpation of the physically, mentally, and morally unfit, or . . . their complete segregation in a socially aseptic environment" (Hooton 1939a: 309). Put more simply, Hooton was advocating that the government sterilize criminals or exile them to reservations (Rafter 2004).

His research suffered from the same methodological flaws as Lombroso's, including the assumptions that all of his prisoners had committed crimes and that all of his control group subjects had not committed crime. It is also doubtful that his control group adequately represented the general population, because a majority were either firefighters or members of the Massachusetts militia. Given their occupations, their physical fitness and size may well have differed from those of the population at large. Because of these and other weaknesses, Hooton's work did not become popular, especially with the onset of World War II and the "extirpation" of the millions of people whom the Nazis considered biologically inferior.

William Sheldon: Body Shapes

Although assumptions of biological inferiority grew less fashionable, interest in physiology and criminality continued. In 1949, William Sheldon (1898–1977) published a book that outlined his theory of **somatology,** which assumes that people's body shapes affect their personalities and hence the crimes they commit (Sheldon 1949). Sheldon identified three such body types, or *somatotypes* (see Figure 6.1). *Endomorphs* are heavy, with short arms and legs; they tend to be relaxed and extroverted and relatively noncriminal. *Mesomorphs* are athletic and muscular; they tend to be aggressive and particularly apt to commit violent

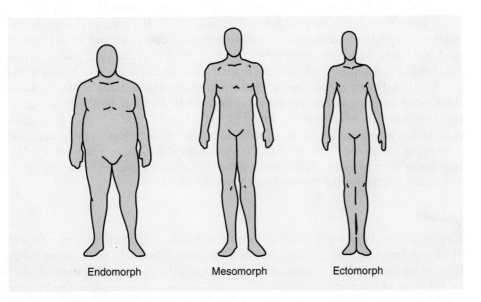

Endomorph   Mesomorph   Ectomorph

FIGURE 6.1 ▸ **William Sheldon's Three Body Shapes** Source: Adapted from Sheldon 1949.

crimes and other crimes requiring strength and speed. Finally, *ectomorphs* are thin, introverted, and overly sensitive. Sheldon compared 200 male delinquents in an institution to a control group of some 4,000 male college students. Compared to the students, the delinquents tended to be mesomorphic, as Sheldon predicted.

Although Sheldon's theory held some appeal, his research suffered from the same methodological flaws that characterized the work of Lombroso, Hooton, and other early biologists (Bernard, Snipes, and Gerould 2009). In addition, even if Sheldon's delinquent subjects were more mesomorphic, he could not rule out the possibility that their muscular, athletic bodies made it more probable that they worried juvenile justice officials and hence were more likely to be institutionalized. These many flaws, coupled with memories of the Holocaust, minimized the popularity of Sheldon's somatological theory of crime (Rafter 2007).

CONTEMPORARY EXPLANATIONS

Although the early biological explanations of crime suffered from methodological and other problems, biological theories are now experiencing a resurgence thanks to developments in molecular genetics (DeLisi et al. 2010; Walsh and Beaver 2009). We discuss some of the major explanations in this section.

Family, Heredity, and Genes

Biologists and medical researchers have long noticed that crime tends to "run in families," and they assume that criminal tendencies are inherited. To these researchers, crime is analogous to disease and illness. Just as many cancers, high cholesterol and heart disease, and other medical problems are often genetically transmitted, so, they say, is criminal behavior and, for that matter, other behavioral problems such as alcoholism and schizophrenia. Work on **heredity,** genes, and crime now occupies a central place in biology and crime research, with much of it using sophisticated techniques from the field of molecular genetics.

EARLY RESEARCH

The first notable study of family transmission of crime was Richard Dugdale's 1877 study of a rural New York family named Jukes (Dugdale 1877). Noticing that six Jukes were behind bars, Dugdale researched their family tree back 200 years and found that about 140 of 1,000 Jukes had been imprisoned. Because he had no control group, however, Dugdale could not determine whether the Jukes's level of criminality was higher than that of other families. Henry H. Goddard's 1912 study of the descendants of Martin Kallikak was somewhat sounder in this regard (Goddard 1912). Kallikak had fathered children through two different women in the late 1700s. Goddard found a higher proportion of crime and other problems in one set of Kallikak's descendants than in the other. Despite the interesting comparison, learning and environmental factors may explain Goddard's findings better than heredity. The "deviant" set of Kallikak's descendants, for example, lived in poverty, whereas the "normal" set lived in wealth.

TWIN STUDIES

The ideal way to study heredity and crime would be to take individuals at birth, clone them genetically, and randomly assign them and their clones to different families across the country living in various kinds of circumstances. You would then monitor the individuals' and clones' behavior for the next forty years or so. At regular intervals throughout this long study, you would determine whether individuals and clones tend to act alike. If crime is inherited, then individuals who commit crime should have clones that also commit crime, and vice versa. For each individual–clone pair, you would thus determine whether (1) both members of the pair commit crime, (2) both members do not commit crime, or (3) one member commits crime and the other does not. When both members of a pair act alike, we have **concordance;** when they don't act alike, we have **discordance.** If crime is inherited, you would find a higher level of concordance than discordance in all individual–clone pairs; if crime is not inherited, you would find similar levels of concordance and discordance.

For better or worse, in the real world we cannot do such an "ideal" study. *Jurassic Park* and other science fiction notwithstanding, we cannot yet clone dinosaurs or humans, despite recent advances in cloning other animals. Even if we could clone humans, we would not be allowed to assign babies and their clones randomly to families across the land. The same holds true for identical twins, who are the genetic equivalent of clones. The closest we can come to

Studies of identical twins suggest that criminal tendencies are genetically transmitted, but other similarities between the twins, including the amount of time they spend together, may account for their similar behaviors.

this ideal study of heredity and crime, then, is to compare identical twins who continue to live with their natural parents with siblings who are not identical twins and thus not genetically the same. We can then determine whether the level of concordance for the identical twins is higher than that for the other siblings. Researchers have performed many such studies and usually find higher concordance among the identical twins than among the other siblings. This evidence is widely interpreted as supporting a strong genetic basis for crime (Arseneault et al. 2003).

However, other reasons may account for the concordance. Compared to other siblings, identical twins spend more time together, tend to have the same friends, are more attached to each other, and tend to think of themselves as alike. They are also more likely than other siblings to be treated the same by their parents, friends, and teachers. All these likenesses produce similar attitudes and behaviors between identical twins, including delinquency and crime (Guo 2005).

ADOPTION STUDIES

To rule out environmental reasons for concordance, some researchers study identical twins separated shortly after birth and raised by different sets of parents. Because the twins do not live together, any concordance must stem from genetic factors. However, identical twins separated at birth are very rare, and too few studies exist to infer a genetic basis for crime. Their results are also mixed: some find a high level of concordance and others do not. Moreover, most of the identical twins in these studies who were reared "separately" were usually raised by parents who were close family members or neighbors. The twins thus lived in roughly the same environments, with many of them even spending a lot of time with each other. Because the twins were not really raised that separately after all, any concordance found may simply reflect their similar environments and not their genetic sameness (Lewontin, Rose, and Kamin 1984).

Other researchers look at non-twin siblings who, through adoption, are raised by different sets of parents. In this kind of study, researchers determine whether natural parents who are criminals tend to have children adopted and raised by other parents who are also criminals, and whether natural parents who are not criminals tend to have adopted children who also are not criminals. These studies usually find that the criminality of natural parents is statistically related to the criminality of their adopted children. For example, a study of about 4,000 adopted Danish males found criminal conviction rates of 24.5 percent among those with natural parents who had been convicted of a crime versus only 14.7 percent among those with natural parents who had not been convicted (Mednick, Gabrielli, and Hutchings 1987).

Although many researchers interpret such evidence as support for a genetic basis for crime, others argue that siblings in adoption studies are often adopted several months after birth and thus experience similar environmental influences before adoption at a critical stage of their development. These influences might thus account for any similarity found later between their behavior and their natural parents' behavior. Another problem is that adoption agencies usually try to find adoptive parents whose socioeconomic status and other characteristics match those of the natural parents. The resulting lack of random assignment in adoption studies creates a bias that may account for the statistical relationships found (Moffitt and Caspi 2006).

MOLECULAR GENETICS

Given the methodological problems in twin and adoption studies, the best evidence for a genetic basis for criminal behavior comes from studies in molecular genetics. Techniques in molecular genetics allow researchers to determine whether individuals possess specific genes and then to determine whether these genes are associated with a greater probability of committing violent and other antisocial behavior. Several studies have identified a number of genes in this regard (DeLisi et al. 2010; Guo, Roettger, and Cai 2008). For example, a mutation in a gene called MAOA has been implicated in high-risk behavior, including criminal behavior. This gene regulates a hormone called serotonin, which normally has a calming effect. Individuals with the mutated version of the gene are less responsive to serotonin and thus more aggressive. A recent study found that boys with the mutated version are more likely to be in juvenile gangs and also more likely to be among the most violent members of the gangs (Beaver et al. 2009).

EVOLUTIONARY BIOLOGY

An essentially genetic explanation of crime comes from the field of *evolutionary biology*, which discusses how evolutionary needs tens of thousands of years ago favored certain behavioral traits that survived through natural selection and thus may account for behavioral tendencies today. If so, these tendencies are genetically based. Several evolutionary explanations of crime exist, but a brief discussion of just one should indicate their general perspective. This explanation assumes that rape provided an evolutionary advantage to some men, called *cads*, because it helped ensure that their genes would be transmitted into future generations (Thornhill and Palmer 2000). These men practiced what is called an *r strategy* by producing many children and then spending little time with them. Men (called *dads*) who practiced a *k strategy* produced fewer children because they were married or otherwise limited themselves to consensual sex. Presumably, cads who committed rapes thousands of years ago transmitted their genetic disposition to rape (and also to commit other antisocial behavior) into some men today. Critics fault this theory for several reasons, including its oversimplification of human history and its implication that rape was evolutionarily advantageous, which gives rape a positive slant (Travis 2003). Recent anthropological evidence also finds that children of rape victims are often killed by their mothers or other individuals, which obviously prevents their father's genes from being transmitted (Begley 2009).

CHROMOSOMAL ABNORMALITIES

Before leaving the world of genetics, we should touch briefly on the issue of abnormal chromosomes. As you might remember from your biology classes in high school and college, each person normally has 23 pairs of chromosomes, or 46 chromosomes altogether. The twenty-third pair determines the sex of the child at the moment of conception. Two X chromosomes (XX) mean the fetus will be female, and one X chromosome and one Y chromosome (XY) mean it will be male. Although sperm usually carry either one X or one Y chromosome, occasionally a sperm will carry two Xs, two Ys, neither an X nor a Y (designated O), or both an X and a Y. The chromosome pattern that results in a fertilized egg will be either XXX, XYY, XO, or XXY, respectively.

The pattern that most interests some criminologists is XYY, which was discovered in 1961 and is found in fewer than one of every 1,000 men. Compared to normal, XY men, XYY men are more likely to be tall with long arms and severe acne and to have low intelligence. The relatively few studies of XYY men find that they are considerably more likely than normal XY men to be arrested or imprisoned, mainly for petty thefts (Carey 1994). Because the XYY abnormality is so rare, however, sample sizes in these studies are very small. Some scholars who view the XYY abnormality as a cause of crime attribute this link to the low intelligence of XYY men. However, other scholars think that the arrests and imprisonment of XYY men are more the result of bias against their unusual and even menacing appearance. In any event, because the XYY abnormality is so rare, at most it explains only a very minuscule fraction of crime.

Neurochemical Factors

The human body is filled with many kinds of substances that act as chemical messengers to help its various parts perform their functions. Because these functions include behavior, biologists have tried to determine the role chemical substances might play in crime. Two substances that have received considerable attention are hormones and neurotransmitters.

A popular biological explanation assumes that higher levels of testosterone make it more likely that males will engage in criminal behavior, especially violent crime.

HORMONES: TESTOSTERONE AND MALE CRIMINALITY

In the human body, endocrine glands secrete hormones into the blood, which then transports them throughout the body. After arriving at their intended organs or tissue, hormones enable certain functions to occur, including growth, metabolism, sex and reproduction, and stress reaction. A popular modern biological explanation of crime centers on **testosterone,** the "male hormone." As Chapter 3 noted, men commit much more crime than women. And as you undoubtedly already know, men also have more testosterone than women. Combining these two basic sex differences, many scholars argue that testosterone, or, to be more precise, variation in the amount of testosterone, is an important cause of male criminality. Testosterone differences explain not only why men commit more crime than women, but also why some men commit more crime than other men.

Ample evidence exists of a correlation between testosterone level and aggression or criminality (Booth et al. 2006). In the animal kingdom, testosterone has often been linked to aggression; among humans, the sex difference both in testosterone and in crime is obvious. Many studies also find that males with records of violent and other offending have higher testosterone than males with no such records (Mazur 2009). A study of 4,462 Vietnam-era male veterans found a testosterone–criminality relationship. After measuring men's testosterone levels and interviewing them about their offending at various stages in their lives, the researchers found a moderate association between testosterone levels and offending rates (Booth and Osgood 1993). Higher

testosterone is thought to increase aggression, risk taking, and impulsiveness, and thus also low self-control, all important components of delinquency and crime.

However, several methodological problems indicate that the testosterone explanation might be weaker than these findings suggest. Consider, for example, the common assumption that testosterone produces aggression throughout the animal kingdom. Although this link is commonly found, it is also true that in many animal species, among them guinea pigs and lions, females are more aggressive than males even though they have lower testosterone. Moreover, neuroendocrinologists who study hormones and behavior caution against extrapolating from animal studies to human behavior. Although hormones strongly affect many behaviors of lower animals, including primates, the human central nervous system is so complex that simple endocrine influences cannot be assumed.

The evidence among humans of testosterone-induced offending is also open to question (Sapolsky 1998). Although many studies have found a link between testosterone and aggression or offending, other studies have found no such link. Moreover, a correlation among human males between high testosterone and high offending does not necessarily mean that testosterone affects offending. Methodologically, it is just as plausible that offending affects testosterone or that some third factor leads to both high testosterone and high offending. In the animal kingdom, for example, aggression and dominance lead to high testosterone in certain species. Although this has not been widely investigated among humans, delinquency and adult criminality may lead to feelings of dominance and thus to higher testosterone ((Miczek et al. 1994). The sex difference in testosterone and criminality is also obviously subject to other interpretations. As Chapter 3 discussed, gender-role socialization produces different behaviors in girls and boys and different opportunities for offending. To most sociologists, a testosterone-based explanation of the gender difference in crime seems much less plausible than one based on social and structural factors.

In view of these problems, a significant effect of testosterone on human aggression cannot be assumed. A review commissioned for the National Academy of Sciences concluded that the testosterone–aggression correlations often found among human males "are not high, they are sometimes difficult to replicate, and importantly, they do not demonstrate causation. In fact there is better evidence for the reverse relationship (behavior altering hormonal levels). . . . [W]inning—even in innocuous laboratory competitions—can increase testosterone" (Miczek et al. 1994: 6–7).

HORMONES: PMS AND CRIME BY WOMEN

Another hormonal explanation focuses on women's crime. In some women, hormonal changes in the days before menstruation appear to be linked to increased stress, tension, lethargy, and other problems. These women are said to suffer from **premenstrual syndrome,** or PMS. Thinking that this emotional condition might lead to aggression and other offending, some researchers study whether crime by women tends to occur in their premenstrual phase. If PMS were not related to women's crime, their offending would occur randomly throughout their menstrual cycles. If PMS did lead women to offend, their deviance would tend to occur during their premenstrual phases (see Figure 6.2).

To study this possibility, researchers ask women in prison to think back to when they committed the offense for which they were arrested and to remember the dates of their menstruation. From this information researchers can determine whether offenses occurred randomly throughout the women's cycles or instead were concentrated in their premenstrual phases. One researcher in this field, Katharina Dalton (1961), found such a concentration, with about half of prisoners she studied reporting committing their offenses in the eight-day period immediately preceding and during menstruation. Dalton attributed their criminality to their emotional condition and increased lethargy and clumsiness during this time: Their emotional condition prompted them to commit the crimes, and their lethargy and clumsiness made it more difficult for them to avoid detection and arrest. To

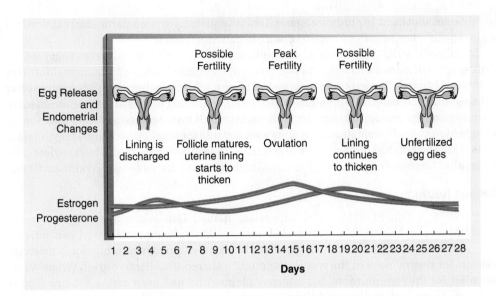

Possible Fertility   Peak Fertility   Possible Fertility

Egg Release and Endometrial Changes

Lining is discharged   Follicle matures, uterine lining starts to thicken   Ovulation   Lining continues to thicken   Unfertilized egg dies

Estrogen Progesterone

1 2 3 4 5 6 7 8 9 10 11 12 13 14 15 16 17 18 19 20 21 22 23 24 25 26 27 28
Days

FIGURE 6.2 ▸ The Menstrual Cycle

support her view of women's physical ineptitude, Dalton noted that half of women drivers involved in serious auto accidents are also in the eight-day premenstrual–menstrual phase. Such findings have led some attorneys representing women defendants to claim PMS as a defense. In England in 1980, for example, one woman murdered her boyfriend by driving her car into him, and another killed a coworker in a London pub. Both claimed that PMS led to their violence, and both received probation instead of imprisonment.

As you might expect, the PMS explanation for women's crime is very controversial. Many scholars feel that it takes us back to the days of "raging hormones," when women were considered unfit to be airplane pilots, to be president of the United States, and to hold other positions because they could not be trusted to act rationally during "that time of the month." Beyond these ideological concerns, the PMS research is also methodologically flawed (Katz and Chambliss 1995). It assumes that women can accurately remember when menstruation occurred; even a few days' error can place their crime outside the premenstrual phase. Some women are very regular and can remember the dates of their menstruation, but others cannot. More important, stress and other problems can disrupt women's cycles. If the stress of committing a crime or the stress leading up to the crime hastens menstruation, it may appear artificially that the crime occurred during a woman's premenstrual phase only because menstruation occurred sooner than normal. In recalling Dalton's finding that half of all women drivers in serious accidents were in the eight-day premenstrual–menstrual phase of their cycles, consider that half of all women passengers involved in accidents are also in the same phase. As Janet Katz and William J. Chambliss (1995: 290) aptly put it, "Unless we wish to argue that the passenger's lethargy somehow caused the accident, it would appear that the trauma of the accident triggered menstruation, not vice versa."

NEUROTRANSMITTERS

The human nervous system consists of billions of cells called *neurons* and bundles of neurons called *nerves*. Nerves carry messages from the brain throughout the body and messages from the body back to the brain and spinal cord. Certain neurons called *receptors* are found in the sense organs of the body, such as the eye. Receptors send messages, or impulses, through nerves back to the brain. After obtaining these messages, the brain sends instructions for particular actions back to various parts of the body. Neurons transmit impulses to each other across synapses with the aid of chemical substances called **neurotransmitters.** In studying aggression, scientists have been particularly interested in one specific neurotransmitter, *serotonin*, mentioned earlier

In animal studies, low levels of serotonin are linked with higher levels of aggression. Many studies of humans have found low levels of serotonin in violent offenders (Moffitt et al. 1998). Although the serotonin–aggression research is intriguing, it suffers from several of the methodological problems already discussed, including inconsistent measurement of offending and the possibility that serotonin levels result from aggression rather than the reverse, which make it premature to assume a strong role for serotonin in human aggression. Some studies even find *higher* levels of serotonin in aggressive individuals. A review concluded that "serotonin is not a very discriminating marker for violence" (Wallman 1999).

Diet and Nutrition

In late 1978, a San Francisco city supervisor named Dan White allegedly murdered George Moscone, the city's mayor, and Harvey Milk, a city supervisor and gay activist. The murders shocked the Bay Area. People even stopped shopping for Christmas presents for several days as the whole community shared in collective grief. When White was tried for the two murders, his attorney claimed he had been eating too much junk food. The sugar and various additives in the food supposedly deepened his depression and reduced his ability to tell right from wrong. White's "Twinkie defense" worked: He was convicted only of manslaughter, not first-degree murder. His conviction on the lower charge outraged Bay Area residents (Weiss 1984).

As this example indicates, diet and nutrition might play a role in aggression and crime. Researchers investigate this role with two kinds of studies. In the first kind, they control the levels of various nutrients given to animal or occasionally human subjects and then compare the behavior of these subjects to control groups. In the second kind, they compare the diet and nutrition of offenders, usually juveniles, to those of nonoffenders. From this body of evidence, several diet and nutritional factors have been identified as producing aggression and other forms of offending: high amounts of sugar and refined carbohydrates, excessive levels of chemical additives, and deficiencies in vitamin B and other vitamins. Yet this research, too, suffers from several methodological problems that cast doubt on its findings, including small samples, possibly spurious findings, and ambiguity in defining offending (Curran and Renzetti 2001). Moreover, several studies of diet and nutrition do not find them linked to antisocial behavior. A review concluded that diet and nutrition have at most a "relatively minor" effect on criminality (Kanarek 1994).

Although many people probably think that high levels of sugar and refined carbohydrates contribute to aggressive behavior, research on this issue is inconclusive.

Pregnancy and Birth Complications

Some of the most interesting biological research concerns the effects of pregnancy and birth complications. These complications are often referred to as *perinatal* problems. Poor nutrition and the use of alcohol, tobacco, and other drugs during pregnancy are thought to harm fetal development, with potentially long-lasting effects on central nervous system (CNS) functioning that in turn can lead to antisocial behavior. Many studies find that children born to women who smoke or use other drugs, including alcohol, during pregnancy are more likely to commit violence and other crimes by the time they reach adulthood (McGloin, Pratt, and Piquero 2006). CNS functioning can also be impaired by complications during difficult births. Such complications may also increase the potential for later criminal behavior (Brennan, Mednick, and Volavka 1995).

Although this body of research suggests a biological role in offending, other interpretations are possible. In particular, pregnancy and birth complications may often be the fault of mothers who fail to observe standard advice for promoting fetal health and development. If so, they may very well practice inadequate parenting after birth, making spurious the presumed relationship between offending and pregnancy and birth complications. To rule out this possibility, research must take parenting practices into account. Some studies of cigarette smoking during pregnancy have done this with limited measures of such practices, and they still find that the mother's offspring are more likely to commit crime later on (Gibson, Piquero, and Tibbetts 2000). This result increases confidence that smoking during pregnancy was the cause of their criminality, but studies using a wider range of parenting behaviors are still necessary.

Early Puberty

A growing body of research finds that adolescents who experience early puberty are more likely to commit delinquenct acts and other antisocial behavior (Felson and Haynie 2002; Haynie 2003). This effect is thought to occur for at least three reasons. First, early puberty prompts adolescents to associate with older adolescents who have already experienced puberty and, for this reason, to have more opportunity to get into trouble. Second, some early maturers resent the fact that they now look like adults but are not given the freedom by their parents to act like adults. Illegal behavior thus provides them a way to act out their resentment by rebelling against their parents. Third, some early maturers experience depression and other psychological problems that may prompt them to act in antisocial ways. To the extent that early puberty is a risk factor for both offending and victimization (see Chapter 4), parents, educators, and public health officials need to keep it in mind in addressing the needs of adolescents in their familial and professional capacities.

EVALUATION OF BIOLOGICAL EXPLANATIONS

Many scholars are enthusiastic about biological explanations. Modern biological theory, they say, has been unfairly stigmatized by the crude early work of Lombroso, Hooton, and others (Wright et al. 2008). This stigma has resulted in "misguided prejudice" among many criminologists toward biological explanations (DeLisi et al. 2010:82). Most sociologists who study crime are somewhat less enthusiastic but still recognize that "biological explanations have come to occupy a new place of respectability in criminology . . . [and] are taken more seriously today than at any other time since the early part of the 20th century" (Akers and Sellers 2009:53).

Despite this recognition, sociologists cite some problems with biological explanations. One problem is that crime is simply too diverse. Even if biological factors account for some violent aggression, they cannot explain most criminal behavior. Among other problems, they cannot easily account for the *relativity* of deviance; that is, they cannot explain why someone with a biological predisposition to violence turns to street crime instead of, say, football or any other activity involving physical violence. As Charles H. McCaghy and colleagues (McCaghy et al. 2008) point out, violence in a bar fight makes you a criminal, whereas violence in wartime makes you a hero. A biological explanation of violence is thus not the same thing as a biological explanation of *criminal* violence.

A second problem concerns *group-rate differences*. As we have seen in earlier chapters, sociologists try to understand the reasons for different crime rates among different groups or locations and for changes in crime rates. For example, they are more interested in why big cities have higher crime rates than rural areas than in why a particular individual in a big city commits a crime. Biological explanations cannot easily account for group-rate differences. Take the fact that the United States has a much higher homicide rate than Canada and Western European nations. How would you explain this biologically? Is it really conceivable that Americans are different biologically from Canadians, the English, Germans, or Danes in a way that leads to more homicide in the United States? Can the high crime rates of big cities as compared to rural areas really be attributed to biological problems in big-city residents? Can biological explanations account for why street crime rose

Crime and Controversy

Does Abortion Lower the Crime Rate?

A controversy erupted a decade ago when two economists proposed that almost half of the 1990s crime decline was the result of the large increase in abortions two decades earlier in the wake of the U.S. Supreme Court's famous 1973 *Roe v. Wade* decision. The drop in crime began, they said, when the children who were not born because of the abortion increase, much of it found among poor, unmarried teenagers, would have reached their late teenage years, when offending reaches its peak. The states that first legalized abortion before *Roe v. Wade* were the first to see their crime rates drop. States with the highest abortion rates after *Roe v. Wade* also had larger crime decreases than states with lower abortion rates.

The economists' claims met with immediate skepticism from criminologists and provoked concern from both sides of the abortion debate. Criminologists said the 1990s crime-rate decline stemmed from factors far more important than the rise in abortions two decades earlier. These included the thriving economy during the 1990s, a stabilization in gang wars over the sale and distribution of crack that began in the mid-1980s,

and perhaps more effective policing and community-based crime-control strategies.

Criminologists have since noted some weaknesses of the economists' study that ignited the controversy. For example, adolescent property-crime rates began to decline only in 1994, about a decade after what would have been expected if the legalization of abortion in 1973 had been responsible, and adolescent violent-crime rates were increasing during the 1980s at the very time they would have been expected to decline because of abortion's legalization. Moreover, African-American youths experienced the greatest increase in violence, even though African-American women were more likely than women of other races to receive abortions after *Roe v. Wade*.

Empirical efforts to replicate the original abortion–crime findings have also been inconsistent. Several studies have found that legalized abortion did not lower the crime rate; some have found it did lower the crime rate; and some have even found that it raised the crime rate. These mixed results indicate that a link between legalized abortion and higher crime rates cannot be assumed, and they promise that the abortion–crime controversy is not about to fade away.

Sources: Berk et al. 2003; Chamlin, Myer, and Sanders 2008; Donohue and Levitt 2001; Hay and Evans 2006; Kahane, Paton, and Simmons 2008.

in the United States during the 1960s and fell in the 1990s? Even if they might explain why some individuals commit crime, biological explanations cannot easily account for different crime rates among groups or locations or for changes in crime rates.

A final concern about biological explanations addresses their social policy implications. One implication is that to reduce crime we must correct the biological deficiency that causes it. However, short of some science fiction world that, thankfully, does not yet exist, we cannot easily change biology. And if we cannot change biology, we cannot reduce crime. Say, for example, that biochemical problems explain why people commit crime. If so, what can we do to reduce crime? Perform some genetic engineering? Give them drugs to correct the problems? Given the rapid rise in scientific advances, some of these measures are quickly becoming possible (DeLisi et al. 2010), but they remain rather frightening to some observers. Perinatal research is a notable exception. If it turns out to be true that perinatal problems predict later offending, then it may be possible to reduce crime with social policies aimed at better prenatal health care and nutrition, especially among the poor, where pregnancy and birth complications are more common.

Responding to the concern that biological explanations imply little chance for reducing crime, some scholars stress a *biosocial perspective*, which assumes that biological traits interact with environmental influences to produce crime: biological factors may predispose individuals to crime, but the extent and timing of their influence depend on environmental factors (Beaver 2009; DeLisi et al. 2010). For example, biological factors may be more likely to lead to crime if an individual comes from a family environment characterized by poor parenting; conversely, individuals with a biological predisposition to crime may be less likely to actually commit it if they come from a warm, loving home. If so, and reflecting a *dual hazard* hypothesis, individuals are most likely to commit crime if they have a biological predisposition for it and if they come from negative family environments (Cullen and Agnew 2011).

Although this perspective is more compatible with a sociological framework (Ledger 2009), it still suggests the need to do something about the biological traits. Thus some scholars recommend, for example, that children be screened for biological traits that may lead to later criminality. Proposals like this raise several ethical and other concerns, including the possibility that children targeted in this fashion may be labeled as potential criminals and treated that way (Arehart-Treichel 2006).

A related problem with biological explanations centers on their potential justification for appalling acts committed against people regarded as biologically different. It can be a short step from considering people biologically different to viewing them as biologically inferior. History is replete with acts of genocide, lynchings, hate crime, and other actions taken against people deemed biologically inferior to some ruling group, with their supposed inferiority justifying the inhumane treatment. In the early decades of the twentieth century, the eugenics movement in the United States led to the involuntary sterilization of some 70,000 people, almost all of them poor and many of them African American. Not too long thereafter, Nazi Germany slaughtered millions of Jews and others who were

It probably sounds silly to suggest that a biological problem leads corporate executives to break the law. Given our society's prejudices, however, it might not sound silly to suggest that a biological problem leads poor people, and especially persons of color, to commit violent crime.

thought to be inferior to the Aryan race. The "evidence" gathered by American eugenicists of biological inferiority reinforced Nazi ideology (Kuhl 1994).

If, then, we find that a biological trait makes certain people more likely to be criminals, history tells us it is very easy for these groups to be considered biologically inferior and in need of special, even inhumane, treatment, even if no biologists today advocate such treatment. These groups are usually the poor and people of color, because biological research on crime has centered on street crimes committed by the poor while ignoring the white-collar crimes committed by wealthier people. It might sound silly even to suggest that a defective gene or hormonal imbalance leads corporate executives to engage in price-fixing or to market unsafe products. Yet, given our society's prejudices, it might not sound as silly to suggest that a biological problem leads poor people to commit violent crime. Given continuing racial and ethnic prejudice, we must be very careful in interpreting the findings of contemporary research on biology and crime.

Proponents of biosocial criminology vigorously defend it against all these criticisms and argue for the importance of their perspective. As a recent review advocated, "Neuroscience is shining light on the mechanisms of nature and nurture that underscore human existence and human behavior. This scientific advance has already infiltrated criminology. If not now then very soon, biosocial theory, an area once completely marginalized and ridiculed within criminology, will become the definite statement of crime" (DeLisi et al. 2010:83). The value of biosocial explanations will undoubtedly remain a major source of vigorous controversy in criminology for some years to come.

Review and Discuss

What concerns do many sociologists and criminologists have about biological explanations of criminal behavior? How valid do you think these concerns are?

Psychological Explanations

Psychology offers a valuable explanation of individual behavior, but says little about the larger social and structural forces also at work. In the area of crime, sociology and psychology together provide a more comprehensive explanation than either discipline can provide separately. Sociology tries to explain why certain groups and locations have more crime than others, and psychology tries to explain why a few people with or without these backgrounds commit serious crime, whereas most do not (Andrews and Bonta 2010; Bartol and Bartol 2011).) This section examines the major psychological explanations (see Table 6.2) while leaving learning approaches, which are more compatible with a sociological framework, for Chapter 8.

PSYCHOANALYTIC EXPLANATIONS

Modern **psychoanalytic** explanations say delinquency and crime arise from internal disturbances developing in early childhood because of interaction problems between parents and children. These explanations derive from the work of Sigmund Freud (1856–1939), the founder of psychoanalysis (Freud 1935 [1920]; Freud 1961 [1930]). Although Freud focused more on mental disorders than on criminal behavior, his work provided a logical foundation for extensions into delinquency and crime by later theorists.

Freud and his followers see mental disorders as arising from a conflict between society and the instinctive needs of the individual. The individual personality consists of three parts: the id, the ego, and the superego. The **id,** present at birth, consists of instinctual desires that demand immediate gratification: infants get hungry and do not take no

TABLE 6.2 ▸ **Psychological Explanations in Brief**

THEORY	KEY FIGURE(S)	SYNOPSIS
Psychoanalytic Explanations	Sigmund Freud	The individual personality consists of the id, ego, and superego. Delinquency and crime result if the superego is too weak to control the id, or if the superego is so strong that individuals feel overly guilty and ashamed.
Moral Development	Lawrence Kohlberg	Children experience several stages of moral development. Incomplete moral development is a major reason for criminal and other antisocial behavior.
Intelligence (IQ)	—	Low intelligence (IQ) produces criminality, in part because low intelligence impairs moral reasoning and the ability to appreciate the consequences of one's actions.
Personality Explanations	Terrie A. Moffitt	Personality problems during childhood contribute to delinquency during adolescence and criminality during adulthood.

for an answer if not fed soon enough. Eventually the **ego** develops and represents the more rational part of personality. Children learn that they cannot always expect immediate gratification of their needs. The **superego** comes later and represents the internalization of society's moral code. This is the individual's conscience and leads the individual to feel guilty or ashamed for violating social norms. The development of these three parts of the personality is generally complete by about age 5.

Freud thought that people are inherently pleasure seeking because of the id, but that too much pleasure seeking can translate into antisocial behavior. The ego and superego thus need to restrain the id. This happens in mentally healthy individuals because the three parts of the personality coexist harmoniously. A lack of balance can result when a child's needs are not met because of parental deprivation, neglect, or overly harsh discipline. If the superego then becomes too weak to control the id's instinctive impulses, delinquency and crime result. They can also result if the superego is too strong, when individuals feel overly guilty and ashamed. The rational part of the personality, the ego, realizes that if individuals commit a crime they will be punished and thus reduce their guilt. Given this realization, the ego leads the person to break the law.

Psychoanalytic explanations have been valuable in emphasizing the importance of early childhood experiences for later behavior, but their value for understanding crime is limited for several reasons (Bernard, Snipes, and Gerould 2009). First, they suggest that antisocial behavior is mentally disordered behavior, which is not true for most individuals. Second, they neglect social factors and overemphasize childhood experiences; although these are undoubtedly important, later life-cycle influences are also important (see Chapter 8). Finally, psychoanalytic research relies on case histories of individuals under treatment or on samples of offenders in juvenile institutions, adult prisons, or mental institutions. This methodology ignores the possibilities that the subjects might not represent the vast majority of

Although psychoanalytic explanations have been valuable in emphasizing the influence of early childhood experiences on later behavior, their value for understanding crime is limited for several reasons.

offenders not under treatment or institutionalized and that any mental or emotional problems in the institutionalized subjects may be the result, and not the cause, of their institutionalization.

Before we leave psychoanalytic explanations, a comment on their view of women's criminality is in order. Although Freud is widely regarded as one of the greatest thinkers of the last two centuries, his views on women reflected the sexism of his day (Klein 1995). Freud viewed child rearing as women's natural role in life and thought that females who could not adjust to this role suffered from "penis envy" and hence mental disorder. To compensate for the lack of a penis, some women, he thought, tried to act like men in desiring careers. Extending Freud's views to delinquency and crime, Freudian scholars later attributed most girls' delinquency to their sexual needs. In a traditional Freudian framework, then, women and girls with mental disorders or histories of crime and delinquency need to be helped to adjust to their natural child-rearing roles. Thanks to critiques by feminist scholars, this view of female criminality lost popularity in the 1970s, but has not entirely disappeared.

MORAL DEVELOPMENT AND CRIME

Since the time of Jean Piaget (1896–1980), psychologists have been interested in children's mental and moral development. Piaget thought that children experience four stages of mental development. The *sensorimotor* period lasts until the age of 2 and involves learning about their immediate environment and developing their reflexes. The *preoperational* period lasts from ages 2 to 7 and consists of learning language, drawing, and other skills. A stage of *concrete operations* lasts from ages 7 to 11 and involves learning logical thinking and problem solving. The final *formal operations* stage occurs during ages 11 to 15 and concerns dealing with abstract ideas (Singer and Revenson 1997).

Following in Piaget's footsteps, psychologist Lawrence Kohlberg (1969) developed his theory of **moral development,** the ability to distinguish right from wrong and to determine the ethically correct course of action in complex circumstances. Kohlberg theorized that individuals pass through several stages in which they develop their ability to reason morally. In the early stages, children's moral reasoning is related solely to punishment: correct behavior is behavior that keeps them from getting punished. In later stages, as adolescents, they begin to realize that society and their parents have rules that deserve to be obeyed in and of themselves, not just to avoid punishment. They also realize that exhibiting the behaviors expected of them will lead others to view them positively. In the final stages of moral development, during late adolescence and early adulthood, people recognize that universal moral principles supersede the laws of any one society. Individuals reaching this stage may decide to disobey the law in the name of a higher law.

Kohlberg further theorized that not everyone makes it through all the stages of moral development. In particular, some people's moral development stops after only the early stages. Because their view of right and wrong is limited to what avoids punishment, they have not developed what many of us would call a conscience and may well engage in harmful behavior as long as they think they will not get punished for it. Kohlberg thus thought that incomplete moral development was a major reason for criminal and other antisocial behavior.

One problem with tests of Kohlberg's theory is the familiar chicken-and-egg question of causal order. Even if offenders do have a lower level of moral reasoning than nonoffenders, their offending may have affected their moral reasoning rather than the reverse. They might have begun to violate the law for other reasons, such as peer pressure or hostility toward their parents, and then adjusted their moral reasoning to accommodate their illegal behavior to minimize any guilt or shame.

INTELLIGENCE AND CRIME

Researchers have long blamed crime on low intelligence **(IQ).** Studies in the early twentieth century found low IQs among prisoners and juveniles in reform schools. Scholars later criticized this research on methodological grounds, and it lost popularity by the 1930s. In the late 1970s, however, a study by Travis Hirschi and Michael Hindelang (1977) renewed interest in the IQ–crime relationship. After determining from many studies that delinquents' IQ scores were about eight points lower than nondelinquents' scores on the average, the authors concluded that low IQ is an important cause of delinquency. More recent studies sometimes also link delinquency to low IQ, and some scholars go as far as to say that IQ is a stronger predictor of delinquency than either race or social class (Herrnstein and Murray 1994).

Several reasons might explain a possible causal link between IQ and delinquency. First, youths with low intelligence do poorly in school. Poor school performance in turn leads to less attachment to school and thus to higher rates of delinquency. Second, such youths also experience lower self-esteem and turn for support to youths with similar problems; because some of their new friends are involved in delinquency, they become delinquent themselves. Third, low intelligence leads to a lower ability to engage in moral reasoning and to delay gratification, increasing the likelihood of offending. Fourth, adolescents with low intelligence are less able to appreciate the consequences of their actions and to be more susceptible to the influence of delinquent friends (Hirschi and Hindelang 1977; Lynam, Moffitt, and Stouthamer-Loeber 1993).

Although a presumed low IQ–delinquency link sounds sensible, it has proven very controversial for several reasons (Nisbett 2009). The first is methodological. Without question, the early IQ research was rife with methodological problems, and serious questions remain regarding whether IQ tests measure native (inborn) intelligence or instead reflect the effects of schooling and familiarity with white, middle-class experiences. Recent IQ studies are more carefully designed, but some still use samples of offenders in adult prisons or juvenile institutions. Because incarcerated offenders represent only a very small proportion of all offenders, we cannot safely generalize these studies' findings to the entire offender population. In another issue, many researchers say the presumed IQ–delinquency link is not as strong as its proponents think and may not even exist at all. One study found that the effect of IQ on delinquency was weak initially and became spurious when other predictors of delinquency were taken into account (Cullen et al. 1997).

Race, IQ, and Crime

Contemporary research on IQ and crime also has troubling racial overtones that echo the first uses of the IQ test in the early twentieth century. Several studies have found African-American–white differences in IQ scores, with the average scores of African Americans about ten to fifteen points below those for whites. Some researchers think this difference reflects the lower natural intelligence of African Americans and further think it explains why they commit more street crimes than whites do (Herrnstein and Murray 1994).

Suppose we accept the assumptions guiding this research linking IQ, race, and crime: (1) IQ tests are valid measures of natural

Some research finds a link between low IQ and high levels of delinquency. However, methodological problems cast doubt on the validity of this finding, and many researchers think that the link may not really exist.

intelligence, (2) African Americans are intellectually inferior to whites, (3) low natural intelligence produces higher rates of delinquency and crime, and (4) low natural intelligence is perhaps the major reason for high rates of street crime by African Americans. What do these beliefs imply about efforts to reduce such crime? Because they discount social factors, they suggest, first of all, that efforts to reduce social inequality and other structural problems would do relatively little to reduce African-American crime rates. They also imply that to reduce African-American crime rates, we have to improve African Americans' innate intelligence. But to say that intelligence is innate suggests that efforts to raise it will probably be useless; if so, we can do little to reduce African-American crime. If we cannot reduce it, perhaps all we can do is to deter African Americans from committing crime by putting even more of them in prison.

This is certainly a pessimistic appraisal and perhaps a bit simplistic, but is it warranted? Not if the assumptions turn out to be questionable or even false, which is precisely what many critics charge (Menard and Morse 1984). If the IQ test is culturally biased, as many critics say, then African Americans' lower IQ scores reflect their poorer schooling and the fact that they are not white and often not middle class. In sum, race–IQ–crime assumptions are highly questionable at best and patently false at worst, with dangerous racial and class overtones. Although ruling out the presumed intelligence–criminality link in the race–IQ–crime chain may be premature, history tells us we must tread very cautiously in this area.

Review and Discuss

What does the research on intelligence and crime tell us? What are the methodological and other critiques of this line of research?

PERSONALITY AND CRIME

Some of the most important work today in psychology and crime focuses on **personality.** Early studies administered Rorschach (ink blot) tests or personality inventories to samples of incarcerated juvenile and adult offenders and to control groups of nonoffenders. Although this research found personality differences between offenders and nonoffenders, several problems limited the value of this finding (Akers and Sellers 2009). First, because most of this research examined institutionalized offenders, the offenders' personality problems may have been the result of their institutionalization and not the cause. Second, the personality–offending link that was found might have resulted from an effect of offending on personality traits rather than the reverse. Third, because many studies did not control for socioeconomic status, education, and other characteristics, their correlation between personality and criminality may have been spurious. These problems led many criminologists to discount the importance of personality traits for criminality (Andrews and Wormith 1989).

Much contemporary research avoids these problems by using random samples of the population and longitudinal data to clarify cause and effect. Important longitudinal research efforts in New Zealand and elsewhere follow individuals from infancy or adolescence into adulthood (see the International Focus box). Many of these studies focus on childhood **temperament,** which produces behavioral problems during childhood and also delinquency during adolescence and crime during adulthood. The long list of temperament problems includes such things as attention deficits, impulsiveness, hyperactivity, irritability, coldness, and suspiciousness. Although most children with temperament problems do not end up committing serious delinquency, the ones with the

International Focus

Psychological Research in New Zealand

New Zealand has been the site not only of the making of the award-winning *Lord of the Rings* movies, but also of some of the best-designed research on the biological, psychological, and developmental (family-based) causes of delinquency and crime. The researchers involved are psychologists Avshalom Caspi and Terrie A. Moffitt and their colleagues in New Zealand and elsewhere. The basis for much of their research is the Dunedin Multidisciplinary Health and Development Study, a longitudinal investigation begun in the 1970s. The researchers began studying more than 1,000 children born in 1972 and 1973 in New Zealand's province of Dunedin when they were 3 years old and studied them again periodically into early adulthood, gathering several kinds of medical, psychological, and sociological information each time. At the outset of the study, they also obtained perinatal data for when the subjects were born.

Caspi, Moffitt, and colleagues found correlations in one study between various personality characteristics and delinquency among their subjects and also a sample of Pittsburgh youths. The New Zealand data for this study were gathered when the youths were 18 years old. For both sexes, delinquency (as measured by self-reports) was higher in youths with the following traits: aggression (is willing to hurt or frighten others), alienation (feels victimized and betrayed), stress reaction (feels nervous and vulnerable or worries a lot), and social potency (is forceful and decisive). It was also lower in youths with these traits: traditionalism (favors high moral standards), harm avoidance (dislikes excitement and danger), and control (is reflective and cautious).

In other research, the New Zealand researchers have taken advantage of their study's longitudinal design and have found that behavioral, personality, and other problems during childhood predict several types of problems by adolescence and then young adulthood, including conflict in interacting with others, delinquency, employment problems, and domestic violence. They have also found that boys at age 13 with neuropsychological problems, such as poor language processing, poor memory, and difficulty in linking visual information to motor coordination, developed higher rates of delinquency, even after controlling for socioeconomic status. The researchers concluded that these neuropsychological problems impair communication between children and their parents, teachers, and peers and hamper school performance. These problems in turn promote delinquency.

According to Caspi, Moffitt, and their colleagues, their findings have important implications for preventing crime because childhood neuropsychological, personality, and behavioral problems often stem from issues in the social or family environment that can be prevented. These issues include poor nutrition during pregnancy, alcohol or drug use during pregnancy, birth complications, childhood head injuries, exposure to lead and other toxic substances, and inadequate parenting. Thus, efforts that successfully address all these problems will also help address the crime problem.

Sources: Caspi 2000; Moffitt 2003; Moffitt 2006.

worst problems are more likely to become delinquent and to continue to commit crime during adulthood. Further, most serious delinquents are thought to have had childhood temperament problems (Loeber et al. 2008). Strong links between certain personality traits and delinquency and crime have been found in several nations, for both genders, and among several racial and ethnic groups (Caspi et al. 1994; Thornberry 2009).

The new wave of personality research has led many criminologists to recognize the importance of personality and to begin to incorporate personality traits more explicitly into sociological theories of crime (Agnew et al. 2002; Miller and Lynam 2001), although other scholars find that neighborhood and other structural factors are more important than personality traits for the development of criminality (Sampson, Morenoff, Raudenbush 2005). Still, the new personality research has important implications reducing crime because it points to childhood temperament problems as an import contributor to criminality. If these problems do matter, then efforts such as preschool early family intervention programs that address them may also reduce delinquency crime (Welsh and Farrington 2007). Moreover, to the extent that temperament proble are more common among children raised in poverty and in disadvantaged neight hoods, the new personality research also highlights the need to address these aspect the social environment to reduce crime.

Two related problems still characterize the new personality research. First, person ity explanations of crime, like their biological counterparts, cannot adequately acco for the relativity of deviance: They cannot explain why individuals psychologica predisposed to thrill seeking or violence undertake criminal actions instead of legal o (McCaghy et al. 2008). Some people with the impulsiveness trait mentioned previous for example, may pursue car racing or parachute jumping as careers or hobbies; oth may choose crime. Personality explanations do not help us understand why a pers chooses one behavior instead of another. Second, because so many people with pers ality problems do not break the law, conclusions from the personality–crime resea should be interpreted cautiously.

Despite these problems, the new longitudinal personality research has succeeded highlighting the importance of childhood temperament problems for later criminality. doing so, it has also pointed to the need for social policies to reduce these problems o they emerge and, better yet, to prevent them from emerging at all.

EVALUATION OF PSYCHOLOGICAL EXPLANATIONS

In certain respects, psychological explanations complement sociological ones by fill in the smaller picture of crime that sociology's larger, structural approach leaves emp Some psychologists criticize the "antipsychological bias" they see in sociological cri nology (Andrews and Bonta 2010). Although valid to some extent, this charge is also severe. Although sociologists certainly look beyond the individual, many of their str tural explanations for crime rest on social psychological states such as frustration a alienation (see Chapter 7). Many of the social process theories favored by sociologists (Chapter 8) also rest on psychological concepts such as learning and role modeling. A personality traits are making their way, however belatedly, into sociological theor (Simons et al. 2007).

Despite the contributions of some psychological approaches to the understanding crime, several issues remain (Bernard, Snipes, and Gerould 2009). First, psychologi studies historically have often used small, unrepresentative samples of offenders prisons or mental institutions. Even if these offenders are psychologically different, difference may be the result of their institutionalization and not the cause. Secor psychological studies generally disregard structural factors such as poverty and can easily account for variations in crime by group and location or for changes in crime rat

Third, although these studies offer interesting statistical correlations, their cau order remains unclear. In this regard, the recent longitudinal studies of childho temperament and later delinquency have been very valuable because their research sign permits a conclusion that temperament problems precede initial delinquency, ev if delinquency might later in turn affect temperament. Finally, psychologists of crime jo their biological counterparts in rarely studying crimes by white-collar offenders, ev though these crimes result in much injury and death. The fact that researchers and public are attracted to suggestions of psychological problems in common criminals not in white-collar criminals may reflect stereotypical views of the poor and people color, who are much more likely to commit street crime than white-collar crime.

Abnormality or Normality?

Psychological approaches also suggest that criminals are psychologically abnormal and that crime thus results from psychological **abnormality.** Normal people do not commit crime; abnormal people do. As Chapter 1 noted, Émile Durkheim wrote that crime and deviance are indeed normal, meaning that they occur in every healthy society because people will always violate the norms of any society. Building on Durkheim's perspective, sociological criminology sees crime and deviance arising from normal social structures, institutions, and processes. Because psychological explanations assume that individuals have problems that lead them to commit crime, they imply that the way to reduce crime is to cure the few aberrant individuals who commit it. As we saw with eating disorders, a sociological perspective suggests that there will always be other deviants to take their place given the social and structural forces at work.

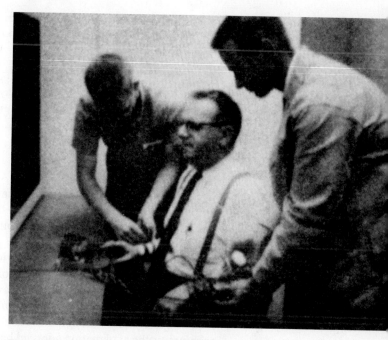

This photo shows part of Stanley Milgram's famous experiment involving electri shock and learning. His experiment indicated that psychologically normal peopl will follow orders and inflict serious injury.

It may also be mistaken to view most criminals as psychologically abnormal. A person can commit horrible violence and still be psychologically normal in other respects. Studies after World War II of prison guards in Nazi concentration camps found them to be good husbands and fathers who performed well on various psychological tests. Despite their apparent psychological normality, they were able to commit some of the worst crimes known to humanity.

Two famous psychological experiments are telling in this regard. The first took place in the early 1960s when Yale University psychologist Stanley Milgram recruited Yale students and residents of Bridgeport, Connecticut, to administer electric shock in a learning experiment (Milgram 1974). Subjects were told to apply electric shock to "learners" who performed poorly in word-pair tests. Unknown to the subjects, no electric shock was actually used, and the learners were all actors. Although they even screamed in pain and pleaded for the subjects to stop, the subjects proved all too ready to shock them. Because Milgram's experiment showed that psychologically normal people would follow orders and inflict serious injury on innocent people, it attracted wide attention and remains controversial to this day.

The other experiment was conducted at Stanford University. Psychologist Philip Zimbardo randomly assigned male student volunteers to be either guards or prisoners in a mock prison in the basement of a psychology building (Zimbardo 1972). Within a day, the guards began to treat the prisoners harshly, and within a few days some prisoners began suffering symptoms of a nervous breakdown. One prisoner even had to be convinced he was really a student. Because all the students had initially passed screening tests for mental disorder and drug and alcohol abuse and then were randomly assigned, the guards' abuse and prisoners' breakdowns could not have stemmed from any preexisting problems. Instead, their abnormal behaviors arose from the structural conditions and role expectations of the mock prison experience that led normal people to behave unacceptably.

Both of these experiments indicated that "normal" people are very capable of committing violent and abusive behavior under certain circumstances. Although people with mental disorders are at greater risk for committing violence (Silver and Teasdale 2005), most people who commit violence do not have mental disorders.

Review and Discuss

The question of abnormality versus normality lies at the heart of much psychological research on criminal behavior. Do you think many criminals are psychologically abnormal?

Conclusion

The explanations discussed in this chapter focus on the individual and attribute crime to individual biological or psychological traits. Ultimately, your view of the world influences the value you find in these explanations. If you think that people are responsible for their own behavior, then you will probably prefer the neoclassical views discussed in the previous chapter. If you think that behavioral problems arise primarily from individual failings, then you will probably prefer one or more of the explanations discussed in this chapter. If instead you think that behavioral problems derive primarily from problems in the larger society, then you will probably prefer sociological explanations discussed in the next few chapters. Although there is certainly room for more than one way to understand criminality, the explanation adopted has important implications for efforts to reduce crime.

Rational choice views attribute crime to the choices individuals make about their own behavior. Crime policies based on these views aim to affect these choices by making punishment more certain and more severe. However, it is unclear whether the decision making of potential criminals follows the rational choice model, as well as whether increasing the certainty and severity of punishment can reduce crime rates significantly. Moreover, the world of rational choice and deterrence theory is largely devoid of social inequality and social structure. To the extent that these social factors generate criminality, the rational choice model ignores important sources of crime.

Biological and psychological explanations both ultimately locate the origins of crime inside the individual. These explanations generally minimize the importance of social and structural factors. Even if the biological evidence were more conclusive, sociologists would continue to be troubled by its implications for social policy on crime. Several psychological approaches are more compatible with a sociological framework, but still minimize the importance of social factors.

Historically, biological research and, in its work on intelligence, psychological research have had damaging consequences for women, the poor, and people of color. Sensitivity to this history demands that biological and psychological evidence of criminality be interpreted cautiously.

These problems aside, biological and psychological research has made a valuable contribution in stressing the importance of early childhood for later delinquency and criminality. For example, certain approaches in both biology and psychology focus on childhood problems stemming from poor prenatal health and nutrition and inadequate parenting. These approaches suggest that programs focusing on families at risk for both sets of problems can achieve significant crime reduction. Because this risk is greatest for families living in poverty, this line of biological and psychological work complements sociological attention to the criminogenic effects of poverty and other structural conditions in the social environment explored in the next chapter. Chapter 8 examines social process theories in sociology that stress negative childhood social experiences, which again are more common for families living in poverty. Despite their differences, then, contemporary efforts in biology, psychology, and sociology all underscore the crime-reduction potential of well-designed and well-funded efforts that address the causes and consequences of poverty.

Summary

1. Biological explanations go back to phrenology in the early nineteenth century and Lombroso's theory of atavism several decades later. Explanations today focus on genetic transmission, neurochemical factors, diet and nutrition, and pregnancy and birth complications. To reduce crime, biological explanations imply the need to change the biological factors that produce it. They do not account well for group and location differences in crime rates and for the relativity of deviance. Because biological explanations historically were used to support racist ideologies, caution should be exercised in interpreting the findings of contemporary research on biology and crime.

2. Psychological explanations of crime include those emphasizing disturbances arising from negative early childhood experiences, inadequate moral development, low intelligence, and personality problems. Among other problems, these explanations generally minimize the importance of social factors, they cannot easily account for variations in crime by group or location for changes in crime rates, and they suggest that criminal behavior represents psychological abnormality. Research testing these explanations also often uses small, unrepresentative samples of offenders in prisons or mental institutions. Recent research using longitudinal data to investigate the impact of early childhood temperament problems is providing valuable evidence that such problems do predict later delinquency and crime.

Key Terms

abnormality 155	heredity 138	personality 152	superego 149
atavism 135	id 148	phrenology 135	temperament 152
concordance 139	IQ 151	premenstrual syndrome 142	testosterone 141
discordance 139	moral development 150	psychoanalytic 148	
ego 149	neurotransmitters 144	somatology 137	

What Would You Do?

1. You are working in a day care center that serves toddlers from working-class and middle-class backgrounds alike. On average, the working-class children seem more hyperactive than the middle-class children, but not very much so. One day, a university researcher approaches the manager of the day care center and requests permission to study the children to determine whether a relationship exists between their behavior and any personality problems they may have. The manager asks whether you think the researcher should be allowed to conduct this research. How do you respond?

2. The text notes that early childhood temperament problems can predict later delinquency and criminality. You are a teacher for grades 1 and 2 in a large city. The children are mostly African American or Latino and generally come from working-class families. Most are well behaved, but a few seem off the wall. Having worked in a school serving a wealthier neighborhood mostly populated by white families, you do not think your current children's behavior is very much out of the ordinary. One day school administrators propose giving all your school's children a battery of tests to determine which of them have temperament problems. The children targeted by the tests will receive special education and counseling for the next year. The principal organizes a meeting of all the teachers to hear their reactions to this proposal. What will your reaction be? Why?

CHAPTER

seven

Sociological Theories: Emphasis on Social Structure

Crime in the News

t was Mother's Day 2010, and hundreds of people in a high-crime area of Boston marched 3.6 miles in the fourteenth annual Mother's Day Walk for Peace. Just a day before, a local 14-year-old boy had been fatally shot on a basketball court. His second cousin cried as she held a poster displaying his photo and also a photo of her own son, who had been fatally shot three years earlier. Another marcher was mourning a stepson who had lost his life to gunfire a week before the march; six years earlier she had also lost a son the same way. A third marcher, 17, had lost her brother in 2007, and said she was marching because she "lost too many people to violence."

Source: Teehan 2010.

We begin this chapter with two mental exercises. (1) Pretend you could wave a magic wand and create a community that would have a lot of street crime. What kind of community would this be? How would it look? Write down four or five characteristics that immediately come to mind. (2) Now pretend that you could take an individual and clone her or him at birth. One grows up in a poor urban area and the other in a wealthy suburb. Who would be more likely to commit street crimes?

Your list for Exercise 1 probably looks something like many urban neighborhoods: poverty, overcrowding, unemployment, run-down housing and schools. Is this correct? If so, your answer to Exercise 2 was undoubtedly the individual in the urban area. Is this correct again? If these were your answers, you recognize that there is something about poor urban areas that leads to more street crime. This "something" is what sociologists call structural conditions or structural problems. Although we must avoid stereotyping urban areas as evil and suburbs as angelic, the sociological evidence on the structural problems of urban areas supports your hypotheses.

As we saw in Chapter 6, individual-level theories of crime cannot easily account for why some locations and groups have higher crime rates than others. Given their more macro-level orientation, sociologists highlight the role played by **social structure** or, as it is more popularly called, *social environment*, in these differences. As Chapter 1 indicated, social structure refers not only to the physical features of communities, but also to the way society is organized: the distribution of social and economic resources and the nature of social relationships. Specific aspects of the social structure are sometimes called *structural conditions* and include such things as the levels of poverty and unemployment and the amount of crowded housing. Structural conditions are social forces external to the individual that affect behavior and attitudes. These forces help explain why crime and other behaviors vary across locations and groups.

A structural approach helps us understand why poor urban areas have higher street-crime rates than wealthy suburbs. Although most urban residents still do not commit street crimes, structural conditions like the ones you listed in the mental exercise help explain why street crime is more likely in poor urban areas. All other things being equal, individuals growing up in poor urban environments are more likely to commit street crime than are ones raised in more affluent locations. The structural conditions of the community matter more than the particular individuals living in it.

The Legacy of Durkheim

Sociologists have recognized the impact of social structure on deviance and crime since Émile Durkheim's work more than a century ago. As Chapter 1 noted, Durkheim emphasized the influence of structural forces on individual behavior such as suicide. As a member of the conservative intellectual movement that arose after the French Revolution, Durkheim felt that human nature is basically selfish, with individuals having unlimited **aspirations** that, if left unchecked by a strong society, would result in chaos (Durkheim 1952 [1897]).

Durkheim emphasized two related mechanisms, **socialization** and **social ties,** by which society was able to hold individual impulses in check. Through socialization, we learn social norms and become good members of society. The ties we have to family, friends, and others further help socialize us, integrate us into society, and control our aspirations. Thus, a strong set of norms—or, to use Durkheim's term, a strong *collective conscience*—and solid social ties are both necessary for a stable society. A weakening in either of these elements destabilizes society and leads to many problems. This view lies at the heart of the "Durkheimian tradition" in sociology (Abrahamson 2010).

Durkheim's most notable application of this theory was to suicide (see Chapter 1). Although suicide is commonly considered the result of individual unhappiness,

Durkheim found that suicide rates were influenced by external forces. For example, they tended to be higher in times of rapid social change, when traditional norms become less applicable to new circumstances. Normlessness, or **anomie,** sets in. Aspirations that previously were controlled are now unlimited, leaving people feeling more adrift. They realize that not all their aspirations can be fulfilled, and the resulting frustration leads some to commit suicide.

Durkheim used a similar argument to explain why Protestants have higher suicide rates than Catholics. Protestants are not less happy than Catholics, which an individual-level explanation might propose. Instead, said Durkheim, Catholic doctrine is stricter than Protestant doctrine and thus better controls the aspirations of its adherents. Catholics also have clearer norms on which to rely for comfort in times of trouble, whereas Protestants are left more to fend for themselves. Finally, Catholic doctrine con-

The boys in the novel *Lord of the Flies*, about the ages of those pictured here, became savages after they were stranded on an island and were no longer living in their former society.

demns suicide in no uncertain terms; Protestant doctrine is less clear on the subject. Because of these factors, suicide rates are higher among Protestants than among Catholics.

Durkheim also explained that unmarried people have higher suicide rates than married people because of the former's lack of social ties. He reasoned that people with fewer ties have fewer sources of support in times of personal trouble and so have higher suicide rates.

These two structural conditions, anomie and low **social integration,** thus contribute to higher suicide rates. Obviously, not everyone in a society marked by anomie or low integration commits suicide. Individual-level explanations remain necessary to explain the specific suicides that do occur, but they cannot explain why suicide rates are higher for some groups and locations than others. Although Durkheim focused on suicide and only tangentially on crime, we will see in this and the next chapters that theorists have since applied his general views to various kinds of criminal behavior.

A modern literary application of Durkheim's (and the nineteenth-century conservative movement's) view of human nature and society appears in William Golding's (1954) famous novel *Lord of the Flies*, which you might have read in high school. To summarize a complex story far too simplistically, a group of young boys from England is stranded on an island after a plane crash. They have left their society behind and with it the norms, institutions, and social bonds that governed their behavior. Not sure how to proceed, they begin to devise new norms to deal with their extraordinary situation, but their backgrounds as well-behaved youngsters do them no good after the ripping away of their society. Slowly but surely they become savages, as the book calls them again and again, and the story ends in murder. Echoing the view of Durkheim and other conservative intellectuals, Golding's bleak vision of human nature remains compelling, if controversial, and is reflected in many contemporary treatments of crime.

Review and Discuss

How and why did Durkheim's work contribute to a structural understanding of deviance and crime? How does the book *Lord of the Flies* reflect this understanding?

TABLE 7.1 ▸ **Social Structure Theories in Brief**

THEORY	KEY FIGURE(S)	SYNOPSIS
Social Ecological Theories		
Social disorganization	Clifford R. Shaw Henry D. McKay	High neighborhood crime rates due to weakened norms, social bonds, and conventional social institutions; evidence of social disorganization includes dilapidation and high rates of poverty and divorce.
Deviant places	Rodney Stark	High neighborhood crime rates due to high rates of density, poverty, coexistence of residential and commercial property, transience, and dilapidation.
Anomie and Strain Theories		
Anomie	Robert K. Merton	Crime results from the failure to achieve the cultural goal of economic success through the institutional means of working.
General strain	Robert Agnew	Negative emotions and thus delinquency result from the failure to achieve desired goals, from the removal of positive stimuli, and from the introduction of negative stimuli.
Subcultural Theories		
Status frustration	Albert K. Cohen	Delinquency results from the failure of lower-class boys to do well in school because of its middle-class values.
Focal concerns	Walter B. Miller	Delinquency results from several lower-class subcultural focal concerns: trouble, toughness, smartness, excitement, fate, and autonomy.
Differential opportunity	Richard Cloward Lloyd Ohlin	Whether individuals respond to their lack of access to legitimate means with criminal behavior depends on their access to illegitimate means.
Subculture of violence	Marvin Wolfgang Franco Ferracuti	High rates of urban violence result from a subculture of violence that favors violent responses to insults and other interpersonal conflicts.
Code of the street	Elijah Anderson	A variation of a subculture-violence approach that emphasizes the use and threat of violence to maintain respect; the need for respect results from the despair and alienation in which the urban poor live.

We now turn to the major sociological theories of crime that emphasize aspects of the social structure. A summary of these theories appears in Table 7.1.

Social Disorganization and Social Ecology

Durkheim and other members of the conservative intellectual movement were concerned about industrialization and the rapid growth of large cities in the nineteenth century. To these thinkers, society was quickly changing from rural communities with close, personal relationships to larger, urban communities with impersonal relationships. These types of societies are less able to exert social control over individual behavior, leading to more deviance, crime, and other problems.

This view guided the work of U.S. sociologists and other social scientists who began to study crime and deviance in the late 1800s and early 1900s. Many of these scholars had grown up in small, rural communities with a strict Protestant upbringing condemning various acts of deviance as sins. In Chicago and other cities, they saw drinking, prostitution, and other deviance being committed by poor people, many of them Catholic immigrants. The social scientists' concern over urban crime was thus heightened by their bias against urban areas, Catholics, and immigrants and by their religious beliefs that drinking and other acts were sins. They viewed these "sins" as evidence of a sickness in society stemming from individuals' moral failings.

Although this **social pathology** school faded by the 1930s, a new approach emerged at the University of Chicago that emphasized structural causes of urban crime over moral failings. In particular, it attributed crime in certain neighborhoods to **social disorganization,** or a breakdown in social bonds and social control and on the accompanying confusion regarding how to behave (Shoemaker 2010). (In this sense the "society" in *Lord of the Flies* suffered from extreme social disorganization.) These were neighborhoods in transition, with poor immigrants and others moving in and long-standing residents moving out. High divorce rates, dilapidated housing, and other problems characterized these neighborhoods. In such conditions, these theorists thought, high crime rates were inevitable.

The concept of social disorganization first appeared in the work of W. I. Thomas and Florian Znaniecki (Thomas and Znaniecki 1927), who documented the troubles faced by Polish immigrants in Chicago, a huge, bustling city very different from the small, rural farms in their home country. These were stable areas where little change took place, whereas Chicago was undergoing rapid change in the early 1900s. In such a setting, the immigrants found their old ways not working as well; their children faced new, alien influences and weakened familial and other traditional sources of social control. Delinquency and crime thus became much more common in Polish neighborhoods in Chicago than they had been in the old country.

At about the same time, other social scientists at the University of Chicago, most notably Robert E. Park and Ernest W. Burgess, developed an ecological analysis of Chicago neighborhoods. Just as the relationship of plants and animals to their physical environment can be studied, said Park and Burgess, so can that of people to their environment. Their type of analysis has since been called a **social ecology** approach. Park and Burgess divided Chicago into five **concentric zones,** radiating from the central part of the city at the center of the circles to the outlying areas of Chicago on the outer circle. They found these zones differing widely in their physical and social characteristics. The outer areas had wealthier homes and more spacious streets, for example, whereas the inner zones had poorer, more crowded housing and other symptoms of social disorganization (Park, Burgess, and McKenzie 1925).

A social ecology approach recognizes that cities can be divided into different neighborhoods or zones that vary according to certain physical and social characteristics. These characteristics, in turn, are associated with different crime rates.

CLIFFORD R. SHAW AND HENRY D. MCKAY

This ecological model influenced the work of Clifford R. Shaw and Henry D. McKay, who studied delinquency rates in Chicago from 1900 to 1933. Shaw and McKay noted that the ethnic and racial backgrounds of inner-zone residents changed during this period. In the early 1900s, inner-zone residents came from English, German, and Irish backgrounds. By the 1920s, these residents had given way to Polish and other Eastern European immigrants, who in turn began to be replaced in the 1930s

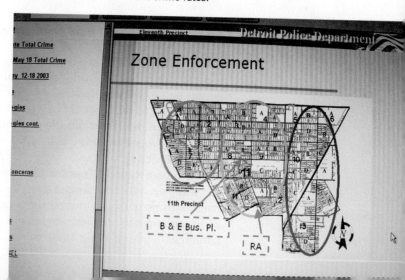

by African Americans migrating from the South. After painstakingly compiling data from some 56,000 juvenile court records on male delinquency in Chicago for this period, Shaw and McKay found that delinquency remained highest in the inner zones regardless of which ethnic groups lived there. They also found that the ethnic groups' delinquency fell after they moved to the outlying areas (Shaw and McKay 1942).

Shaw and McKay concluded that personal characteristics of the ethnic groups could not logically explain these two related phenomena. Instead, the social disorganization of the inner zones had to be at work. In such a climate, informal social control weakens, and deviant values emerge to flourish alongside conventional values. Adolescents grow up amid these conflicting values. Most adopt conventional values, but some adopt deviant beliefs, especially when influenced by delinquent peers. Shaw and McKay used their reasoning to reject the idea that crime was due to biological or psychological deficiencies of the people living in high-crime areas. Instead, their overall perspective was that "crime and deviance were simply the normal responses of normal people to abnormal social conditions." Although they acknowledged that individual-level factors help explain whether particular adolescents commit delinquency, Shaw and McKay argued that adolescents commit more delinquency if they are living in less advantaged neighborhoods because of these neighborhoods' social disorganization (Akers and Sellers 2009).

EVALUATION OF SOCIAL DISORGANIZATION THEORY

Shaw and McKay's social disorganization theory was popular for some time, but later gave way to several methodological critiques (Bursik 1988; Kornhauser 1978). The most devastating criticism concerned their reliance on official records for measuring delinquency rates, as middle-class delinquents may escape detection and not show up in official records, while bias against the poor and people of color may increase their appearance in official records. In a related criticism, scholars also noted that social disorganization theory cannot explain middle-class delinquency, because the middle classes do not, almost by definition, live in conditions of social disorganization.

Shaw and McKay were also faulted for imprecision in their concept of social disorganization. At times they engaged in circular reasoning by taking criminality as an indicator of disorganization. They also underestimated the amount of social organization in cities' inner zones. Rich ethnographic studies of inner-city neighborhoods find they can have high amounts of social order and social integration (Suttles 1968; Whyte 1943). In view of these and other problems, the causal power of the social disorganization model eventually came to be considered rather weak (Kornhauser 1978).

THE REVIVAL OF SOCIAL DISORGANIZATION THEORY

Since the mid-1980s, however, sociologists have rediscovered social disorganization theory and found it a powerful tool for explaining variation in crime and victimization across groups and locations (Kubrin and Weitzer 2003a; Pratt and Gau 2010). In response to the methodological critiques of Shaw and McKay's work, recent research uses self-report and victimization data (to avoid the problems of official crime measures) and more sophisticated, neighborhood-level measures of social disorganization than were available to Shaw and McKay.

Although the results of the new research depend on the type of crime examined and the way variables are measured, it generally finds crime and victimization highest in communities with (1) low participation in voluntary organizations; (2) few networks of friendship ties; (3) low levels of *collective efficacy*, or community supervision of adolescents and of other informal social control mechanisms; and (4) high degrees of residential mobility, population density, single-parent homes, dilapidated housing, and poverty (Lee and Thomas 2010; Mazerolle, Wickes, and McBroom 2010; Peterson and Krivo 2009; Pratt and Cullen 2005; Sampson 2006). These findings provide new and very strong empirical support for Shaw and McKay's decades-old theory, even if the findings may partly reflect the influence of crime on social disorganization rather than the reverse (Hipp 2010).

Consistent with Shaw and McKay's view, the new research assumes that social disorganization increases crime and delinquency because it weakens a neighborhood's social relationships and thus its informal social control, and also because it increases adolescents' associations with delinquent peers (Warner 2007). One reason for the latter effect is that social disorganization weakens the quality of parenting in a community. Poorer parenting in turn puts children at greater risk for delinquency because it weakens the parent–child bond and makes it more likely that children will spend time with delinquent peers (Hay et al. 2006).

OTHER ECOLOGICAL WORK

The revival of social disorganization theory reflects a growing and more general interest in the impact of ecological factors on community crime rates (Sampson 2006). This growing interest departs from the individual-level focus of biological and psychological explanations: "Instead of looking for what is wrong with people, these researchers are looking for what is wrong with society" (Turk 1993). Interestingly, some evidence suggests that high-risk neighborhoods (with high levels of social disorganization and economic deprivation) can lead even "well-adjusted children to become adolescent delinquents," to borrow from the title of a study of delinquency in Pittsburgh (Wikström and Loeber 2000). This study found that male delinquency was more common in more disadvantaged neighborhoods, but, perhaps more tellingly, it also found that neighborhood disadvantage affected whether individual risk factors translate into delinquency. Although high-risk boys were more delinquent no matter what type of neighborhood they lived in, average-risk and even low-risk boys were more delinquent when they lived in more disadvantaged neighborhoods. High-risk neighborhoods also have negative consequences for former prisoners, as recent research finds that released prisoners who settle in disadvantaged neighborhoods are more likely than those who settle in more advantaged neighborhoods to commit new crimes (Kirk 2009; Kubrin and Stewart 2006; Mears et al. 2008). The disadvantaged neighborhoods lack resources, including treatment clinics, job placement centers, and stable personal networks, that would help ex-offenders, and they also include other offenders with whom ex-offenders could get into trouble.

Extreme Poverty and Crime

As should be clear, a key emphasis of contemporary ecological work is the effect of extreme poverty (also termed **economic deprivation**) on community crime rates. At least two reasons explain why poverty might increase neighborhood criminality (Mears and Bhati 2006). Shaw and McKay thought that poverty fosters crime at the community level only because it first generates social disorganization and hence undermines traditional social control mechanisms. In this sense they considered the ecological effect of poverty on crime to be *indirect*. Although not rejecting this assumption, some scholars say that poverty also has a *direct* effect. In this view, some people, called the **underclass**, live in a continuing cycle of *concentrated disadvantage* characterized by extreme poverty, housing segregation, and racial and ethnic discrimination. As a result of these conditions, some members of the underclass commit violence and other crime out of frustration, anger, or economic need (Sampson and Wilson 1995).

Crime and Controversy

Closing the Window on Crime?

This chapter emphasizes that crime is more common in urban neighborhoods characterized by extreme poverty and other indicators of concentrated disadvantage. These neighborhoods are often rife with signs of physical disorder: graffiti, litter, abandoned cars, dilapidated stores and housing, public drinking, homeless people begging for a living, and so forth. Does such disorder contribute to their high crime rates? If so, then one way to reduce crime is to literally clean up the neighborhoods and remove the physical disorder that is an important component of urban blight.

This is precisely the view, popularly called *broken windows theory*, of scholars James Q. Wilson and George L. Kelling. In 1982 they penned an influential article in *The Atlantic Monthly* that argued that signs of disorder—such as a broken window—send a signal to potential criminals that neighborhood residents do not care about what happens in their surroundings, making crime more likely. The New York City police force embraced the theory during the 1990s when it formulated a zero-tolerance policing strategy aimed at getting petty criminals, vagrants, and other such nuisance people off the streets. The strategy was widely credited for lowering New York's crime rate, although many scholars think this credit is undeserved (see Chapter 16).

Since then, broken windows theory itself has come under careful scrutiny. A basic issue is whether it can be proved that physical disorder does, in fact, raise the crime rate. Because physical disorder is worse in the neighborhoods with the worst concentrated disadvantage, it is difficult to isolate the effects of the disorder from those of the other neighborhood problems. Crime may even produce disorder rather than the reverse, or both problems may stem from the same source, such as the poverty of the neighborhoods.

Most research investigating these possibilities has found only weak or even no evidence for the validity of the broken windows theory. One study found that correlations between neighborhood disorder and crime disappeared when factors such as poverty were taken into account. A study of Baltimore neighborhoods found that disorder was linked to only certain kinds of crimes. Another study of 2,400 city blocks in Chicago found only a weak correlation between physical disorder and violent crime that disappeared, except for robbery, when poverty and other factors were taken into account. This study concluded that crime and disorder both stem from the neighborhood structural characteristics, especially concentrated poverty. On the other hand, a study using Colorado Springs, Colorado, data did conclude that physical disorder induces crime, as broken windows theory predicts.

Critics say that broken windows theory and its implied anticrime strategy—to reduce physical disorder—take attention away from more important causes of crime such as extreme poverty, persistent unemployment, and racial discrimination. Given the importance of determining the most effective crime-control strategies, debate over broken windows theory will undoubtedly continue to engage scholars and criminal justice policy makers.

Sources: Gau and Pratt 2008; Harcourt and Ludwig 2007; Miller 2001; Sampson and Raudenbush 2001; Wilson and Kelling 1982; Xu, Fiedler, and Flaming 2005; Yang 2010.

Most ecological studies find the expected poverty–crime relationship. In some, an initial relationship disappears when social disorganization factors are held constant, supporting Shaw and McKay's view of how poverty generates crime. In other studies, concentrated disadvantage continues to predict crime even when social disorganization is taken into account, supporting the "direct" view of the causal process. Although these new ecological studies do not agree on how extreme poverty generates crime, they nonetheless underscore its importance for community differences in criminality (Akins 2009; Peterson and Krivo 2005; Pratt and Cullen 2005; Strom and MacDonald 2007).

One reason the poor become angry and frustrated might be their realization that other people in society have more money. This realization leads them to experience **relative deprivation:** It is one thing to be poor if everyone else is; it is another to be poor if many others are not (Hipp 2007; Webber 2007). Supporting this view, a study found that Houston adolescents who thought they were economically deprived compared to their friends, relatives, and the national population had lower feelings of self-worth and, as a result, higher rates of violent and property crime and drug use (Stiles, Liu, and Kaplan 2000). At the macro level, relative deprivation should be higher in poor neighborhoods located near affluent ones than in poor neighborhoods farther away, because people in the former neighborhoods see the wealth and possessions of richer residents more often than do their counterparts in the latter neighborhoods. If this is true, they should also be more angry and frustrated and, as a result, more likely to commit crime. Crime rates should thus be higher in poor neighborhoods bordering affluent areas than in poor neighborhoods farther away. Some studies find that this is indeed the case (Peterson and Krivo 2009).

The evidence on economic deprivation and community crime rates helps explain the relatively high crime rates of people of color. As Chapter 3 noted, it is possible to acknowledge and explain these groups' higher rates without resorting to biological and other racially biased explanations. The new ecological work on economic deprivation and crime provides one such explanation, suggesting that a primary reason is these groups' poverty, the seriously disadvantaged communities in which many live, and their resulting frustration and hostility. All these factors in turn generate violent crime and other offenses (Bellair and McNulty 2005; Kaufman 2005; Peterson and Krivo 2005). A complementary explanation has to do with the kinds of places in which many people of color live. We now discuss this view in some detail.

Kinds of Places Versus Kinds of People

The revival of an ecological focus reflects the belief of many scholars that **kinds of places** matter more than **kinds of people** (Kubrin and Weitzer 2003a). Recalling Shaw and McKay's central finding that neighborhoods can continue to have high crime rates despite changes in the kinds of people who live there, Rodney Stark (1987) observed that *"there must be something about places as such"* that sustains crime" (emphasis his). Drawing on ecological and other approaches, Stark then advanced thirty propositions, many of them focusing on neighborhood physical features, that offer a compelling ecological explanation for the high crime and delinquency of particular urban neighborhoods and more generally of the cities containing them. His view has since been referred to as the *theory of deviant places.*

Rodney Stark's theory of deviant places argues that crowded neighborhoods contribute to higher rates of street crime.

In one proposition, Stark assumed that the denser a neighborhood, the greater the likelihood that "good kids" will come into contact with "bad kids," increasing the pressures on the former to break the law. This helps explain why cities have more serious delinquency than other areas: adolescents who step out the door can easily find other teenagers. In suburbs and especially rural areas where housing is much more spread out, it is more difficult to get together with friends, especially if a car ride is necessary. In other propositions, Stark noted that poor urban neighborhoods contain many overcrowded homes, which generate family conflict and lead their inhabitants, especially adolescents, to spend extra time outside the home to have some elbow room. Once outside, they are freer to associate with delinquent peers, with more delinquency again resulting. The presence of convenience stores and other places to hang out in urban neighborhoods aggravates this problem, because these places can become targets for crime or at least foster communication about committing crime elsewhere. All these factors in turn increase these neighborhoods' criminality.

Taken together, Stark's propositions and other research on kinds of places provide a powerful ecological basis for the high crime rates of urban neighborhoods (Stucky and Ottensmann 2009). They suggest that normal people get caught in a vicious cycle of structural conditions that generate delinquency and crime, just as the normal people in Zimbardo's and Milgram's experiments (Chapter 6) committed abnormal behavior. Stark's theory and other ecological perspectives thus explain why neighborhoods can continue to have high crime rates even when some people move from the neighborhoods and others move in. They also provide yet another racially unbiased explanation of the high crime rates of African Americans and other people of color. As Stark noted (1987: 905–906), the particularly high crime rates of non-Southern African Americans can be seen as "the result of where they live," for example, the inner zones of cities. These areas, said Stark, are "precisely the kinds of places explored in this essay—areas where the probabilities of *anyone* committing a crime are high" (emphasis his). In the South, African Americans tend to live in rural areas and thus have lower crime rates than their northern counterparts. Kinds of places matter more than kinds of people.

Notice that we are *not* saying that kinds of people make *no* difference. Ecological theories do not mean we should "stop seeking and formulating 'kinds of people' explanations" (Stark 1987: 906) to explain why some individuals in damaging ecological conditions commit crime, whereas most do not. Chapter 8 discusses such explanations.

Whether you prefer kinds of places or kinds of people explanations depends on which level of analysis makes the most sense to you. Ecological theories remind us that, no matter what kinds of people we have in mind, their criminality would be lower if they grew up and lived in communities lacking the many structural conditions generating crime. We do not have to be stranded like the boys in *Lord of the Flies* to realize that where we live strongly affects our values and behavior, including crime. To return to a mental exercise that began this chapter, a clone growing up amid overcrowding, extreme poverty, and other disadvantaged structural conditions will often turn out very different from its match growing up in a more advantaged area.

Review and Discuss

What does the new ecological work on crime and victimization generally tell us about the factors that make crime more common?

Anomie and Strain Theory

Durkheim felt that anomie, or **strain,** results when people's aspirations become uncontrolled and unfulfilled. Although Durkheim discussed how anomie can lead to suicide, it remained to Columbia University sociologist Robert K. Merton to connect anomie to other forms of deviance. In his 1938 paper "Social Structure and Anomie," perhaps the most famous in the criminology literature, Merton discounted the assumption, popular then and still today, that criminality is rooted in biological impulses. He argued instead that "certain phases of social structure generate the circumstances in which infringement of social codes constitutes a 'normal' response" (Merton 1938). Assuming that most crime is committed by poor people, he intended his anomie theory to explain the high rates of crimes by the poor.

Merton reasoned as follows: Every society includes cultural goals and institutional means (norms) about how to reach these goals. These two dimensions are usually in harmony, meaning that, more often than not, members of society can reach the cultural goals, or at least have some hope of reaching them, by following certain socially approved means. A lack of harmony, or anomie, between the goals and the means results when either too much emphasis is given to goals or the means are inadequate to reach the goals.

In the United States, Merton reasoned, there is too much emphasis on the goal of economic success. As a result, U.S. residents often find they cannot fulfill "the American dream" unless they commit illegal activity. This problem is greatest for the poor in the United States, said Merton, because they also lack the ability, because of their poverty, to achieve economic success through the approved means of working. The strain they feel is heightened because they live in a society where it is widely believed that all people can pull themselves up by their bootstraps. Given this ideology, they are especially likely to feel frustrated. In response to their strain, the poor may either accept or reject the cultural goals of economic success and the legitimate means (working) of becoming economically successful. These possibilities result in the logical adaptations to anomie depicted in Table 7.2.

The first adaptation is *conformity*. Even given anomie, most poor people continue to accept the goal of economic success and the means of working; in short, they continue to be law-abiding members of society. Merton said it is not surprising that so many people continue to conform, because otherwise there could be no social order. Conformity is, of course, not deviant behavior, but a logical and by far the most common adaptation to anomie.

The second adaptation is *innovation*. Here people continue to accept the goal of economic success, but reject the means of working and undertake new means, or innovate, to achieve success. Unlike conformity, innovation thus involves illegal behavior, of which theft, fraud, and other economic crimes are prime examples. If we were to think about good grades as another kind of success, then cheating would be an example of innovation.

The third adaptation is *ritualism*. Here people reject the goal of economic success, but continue to accept the means of working. Examples include "bureaucrats" who come to work day after day as a ritual, not to achieve economic success. Though a logical adaptation to anomie, ritualism is not deviant per se and certainly not illegal, and Merton spent little time discussing it.

Retreatism is the fourth adaptation. Here people reject both the goal of economic success and the means of working. In effect, they give up. Merton included in this category alcoholics, drug addicts, and hobos.

TABLE 7.2 ▸ **Merton's Adaptations to Anomie**

ADAPTATION	CULTURAL GOALS	INSTITUTIONAL MEANS
1. Conformity	Accept	Accept
2. Innovation	Accept	Reject
3. Ritualism	Reject	Accept
4. Retreatism	Reject	Reject
5. Rebellion	Reject/substitute	Reject/substitute

The fifth and final adaptation is *rebellion*. People who rebel not only reject both the goal of economic success and the means of working, but also try to bring about a new society with different, more egalitarian goals. These are the radicals and revolutionaries of society who often break the law in an attempt to transform it.

Like social disorganization theory, Merton's anomie theory provides a structural explanation of criminality that assumes that problems in the way society is set up produce deviance among normal but poor people. In social disorganization theory, these problems involve structural conditions at the neighborhood level that generate deviance by weakening traditional social control mechanisms. In anomie theory, these issues involve a disjunction at the societal level between the goal of economic success and the means of working that generates deviance by creating strain. Although the theories disagree on how and why economic deprivation leads to deviance, they nonetheless locate the roots of deviance in the social structure, not in the properties or failings of individuals.

EVALUATION OF ANOMIE THEORY

Anomie theory (or strain theory, as it is often called) provides an important structural explanation for some crimes by the poor in the United States, but it falls short in other respects (Bernard, Snipes, and Gerould 2009). Many scholars question Merton's assumption that the poor commit more crime than the nonpoor, and they fault its failure to address either middle-class delinquency or the many serious white-collar offenses committed by the "respectable" elements of society. They also fault the theory for not explaining the violent crimes of homicide, assault, and rape, which do not readily fit into any of Merton's logical adaptations. Innovation applies to crimes such as theft that are committed for financial gain, but the motivation for these violent crimes is usually not financial. Instead, it is anger, jealousy, or the thrill of "doing evil" (Katz 1988). For rape, it is also hatred of women and perhaps sexual gratification (Brownmiller 1975; Felson and Krohn 1990). Even much theft is often done more for thrills than for money. Because the power of a theory of crime depends to a large degree on the number of different crimes it can explain, anomie theory's inability to explain most violent crimes and other noneconomic offenses is a serious failure.

Robert K. Merton's anomie theory assumes that drug users are retreatists, or double failures. This explanation overlooks the use of marijuana and other drugs by people who want to be financially successful and who accept the need to work hard to achieve such success.

Merton's retreatism adaptation is also problematic. He assumed that most alcoholism, drug addiction, and vagrancy occur when poor people reject both economic success and working. They are double failures who give up on society and withdraw from it. However, research since Merton's time finds that much alcohol and drug use occurs as a result of noneconomic factors such as peer influences (Jang 2002). Merton's explanation also overlooks the alcohol and drug abuse found among the nonpoor, including very successful occupational groups such as physicians. Friends of yours who have used marijuana and other illegal drugs might disagree with Merton's assumption that they have given up on making money by getting a good education and working!

Anomie theory also fails to explain why people choose one adaptation over another, and, more generally, cannot explain why, given anomie, some people commit crime and others do not. Finally, several tests of anomie theory have not supported it. In these studies, researchers measured adolescents' aspirations and expectations. Anomie theory predicts that strain and thus delinquency should be highest among juveniles with high aspirations and low expectations and among juveniles with the largest gap between their aspirations and expectations. However, empirical tests do not support these hypotheses (Elliott, Huizinga, and Ageton 1985).

DEFENSE AND EXTENSION OF ANOMIE THEORY

In response to these criticisms, anomie theory supporters have revised and extended it to explain some of the crimes that Merton's original formulation did not cover. They have also defended the theory against its critics (Adler and Laufer 1995; Agnew 2000). A first argument focuses on the issue of social class and offending. Even if Merton may have exaggerated class differences in delinquency by relying on official records, his assumption of these differences appears to be supported at least for serious offenses (see Chapter 3). The anomie concept can also be extended to cover middle-class delinquency and white-collar crime; given the intense importance in the United States of economic success, middle-class adolescents and corporate executives may still feel they do not have enough wealth and possessions and thus break the law (Passas 1990).

This view forms the basis for an influential extension of Merton's theory by Steven F. Messner and Richard Rosenfeld (2007), whose *institutional anomie theory* argues that crime in the United States results from several key cultural values, including achievement, individualism, universalism, and the fetishism of money. To achieve the American dream, people eagerly pursue economic success in a society whose universal ideology is that anyone, rich or poor, has a chance for success. Because economic success is so important, Americans often judge one another's merit by how much wealth and possessions they have. Because this creates intense pressures for the most economic success possible, many people, rich or poor, feel they lack enough money and turn to crime. At the same time, the exaggerated emphasis on monetary success makes the economic institution more prominent than other social institutions, such as the family and schools. This effect weakens these traditional social control institutions, making crime even more likely. For all these reasons, U.S. society itself is criminogenic, or, as Messner and Rosenfeld (p. 1) put it, a "society organized for crime." This in turn means, they say, that the "American Dream thus has a dark side that must be considered in any serious effort to uncover the social sources of crime" (p. 10). The same values that make the American dream attainable also make crime not only possible but likely.

A second argument of anomie theory supporters addresses the empirical tests of the theory. In these tests, strain is typically measured by examining the difference between expectations and educational or occupational aspirations. These aspirations, the theory's supporters say, are not the same as the *economic* aspirations that Merton addressed. Eventual

Institutional anomie theory argues that crime results from several key cultural values, including an exaggerated emphasis on economic success.

economic success might be more important to adolescents than their eventual education or occupational status. Supporting this view, a study of Seattle adolescents found delinquency more related to the imbalance between their economic goals and educational expectations than to the imbalance between their educational goals and expectations (Farnworth and Leiber 1989).

GENERAL STRAIN THEORY

A very influential extension of Merton's views is Robert Agnew's (1992; 2007) *general strain theory* (GST) of delinquency, which broadens strain theory's focus beyond economic goals and success. Agnew argued that adolescent strain results not only from failure to achieve economic goals, but also from failure to achieve noneconomic goals, the removal of positive stimuli (e.g., the death of a loved one, the ending of a romantic relationship), and the introduction of negative stimuli (e.g., arguments with parents, insults by teachers or friends). Events occurring closely in time cause more stress than events occurring far apart. Repeated stress leads to several negative emotions, including anger, frustration, and unhappiness. Of these, anger is particularly likely to occur when adolescents blame others for their misfortune. Because anger increases the desire for revenge and inhibits self-control, it, along with other negative emotions, can increase delinquency and drug use.

In short, as Agnew pointed out, GST "is very simple. It argues that if we treat people badly, they may get mad and engage in crime" (Agnew 2000). Whether someone does engage in crime depends on a variety of factors, including the individual's social support networks, relationships with delinquent friends, and personal characteristics such as self-esteem and self-efficacy (the sense that you are in control of your life). Agnew argues that most tests of strain theory examine the effects of only one or two of the types of strain adolescents experience and neglect the cumulative impact of stressful events. This weakness helps account for the tests' failure to support the theory. Agnew thus feels that Merton's version of strain theory should be supplemented by recognizing the noneconomic strains facing adolescents. He also thinks that certain types of strain should be especially likely to prompt delinquency. One such type is perceptions of unjust treatment, which can produce a great deal of anger.

The many tests of GST generally support it (Botchkovar, Tittle, and Antonaccio 2009; Moon et al. 2009). Various kinds of strain predict delinquency, including the death or serious injury of a family member or friend; a change in school or residence; victimization by physical and sexual abuse and other crimes; and unemployment.

Importantly, Agnew (1999) has also used GST to explain variation in crime and delinquency across communities. If strain produces anger at the individual level, he reasoned, negative social conditions should also produce strain, and in turn anger and frustration, at the macro level. Thus, the neighborhoods with the worst social conditions should have the most angry and frustrated residents and thus the most crime. This perspective nicely supplements the ecological emphasis on concentrated disadvantage discussed earlier.

Despite the empirical support for GST, more research is needed on several issues. A first issue concerns the reasons that strain leads to delinquency. For example, although the theory highlights the role played by anger, not all types of strain produce anger, and not all studies find that anger produces delinquency (Broidy 2001; Tittle, Broidy, and Gertz 2008). In a related issue, although some studies do support the presumed strain–anger–delinquency relationship, it is not always clear "whether strain creates anger, which then leads to crime, or whether people who are angry are more likely to create strain in their lives, which then leads to crime" (Lilly, Cullen, and Ball 2011).

Strain, Immigration, and Rioting in France

Strain theory in its various formulations emphasizes that crime results from the frustration and anger stemming from poverty, discrimination, and other strains. Rioting in France during the past decade illustrates this dynamic.

In May 2007, France elected a new president, Nicolas Sarkozy, a conservative who beat a socialist candidate. After his election, young people rioted in Paris and other cities across the nation, trashing and burning hundreds of cars and breaking a countless number of store windows. Observers said the rioters were protesting Sarkozy's perceived hostility toward labor unions, the poor, and immigrants. Similar rioting on a smaller scale had preceded the election.

The spurt of riots before and after the election recalled an even larger wave of rioting that overtook France about eighteen months earlier, in late fall 2005, in the immigrant-dominated suburbs of Paris and other large cities. The earlier rioting began after two youths were accidentally electrocuted while they hid from police. In the wake of their tragic deaths, thousands of young people from the immigrant suburbs set fire to cars and buildings and generally wreaked havoc in the Paris suburbs and elsewhere around the country. Sarkozy, then the state minister in charge of the police, called the rioting immigrants, most of them from North African or Arab backgrounds, "scum," and won acclaim in many circles for the actions he took in helping to quell the riots. This acclaim helped propel his candidacy and eventually his victory as France's next president. Some observers said his election would ironically help ensure that the conditions that led to the 2005 and more recent rioting would continue and perhaps lead to more rioting in the future.

What were these conditions? Large numbers of immigrants came to France during the 1950s and 1960s from its former colonies in Africa and found working-class industrial jobs in the suburbs of French cities, as France was then experiencing a labor shortage and needed their employment. Over time, though, many of the industrial jobs disappeared, and France's immigrant suburbs became beset with poverty; high rates of unemployment, reaching 30 percent in some locations; and related problems. A news report discussing the 2005 riots said that France's suburbs "have become the French equivalent of America's inner cities." According to many reports, racism against the residents of the suburbs, many of them now second- and third-generation citizens, was virulent and widespread, and residents of immigrant neighborhoods complained of routine police harassment. One resident said at the time of the 2005 riots, "It's the police who are provoking us. They don't like foreigners." Another resident complained, "On paper we're all the same, but if your name is Mohamed, even with a good education, you can only find a job as a porter at the airport." Another youth, one of the many who were unemployed, said, "I feel French 90 percent of the time. But when I go to look for a job, that's when I feel like a foreigner."

In hindsight, the rioting in France was not that surprising. The structural conditions of the immigrant suburbs were precisely those highlighted in strain theories of crime. The electrocution of two youths may have set off the 2005 rioting, but the rioting would likely not have occurred if these conditions had not existed. As a reporter who interviewed several unemployed youths observed, "These young men seethed with resentment that they were being denied the fruits of the system." One man he interviewed did not apologize for the rioting. "Violence is the language of the poor," he said.

Sources: Murray 2005; Smith 2005; Smith 2007.

Research also has to explore whether gender differences exist in the response to strain. For example, some studies have found that females are less likely than males to react to strain with anger and more likely to react with guilt or depression (Kaufman 2009). This raises the further point that it is still unclear "why some individuals are more likely than others to react to strain with delinquency" (Agnew et al. 2002).

GST and the other recent defenses, revisions, and extensions of anomie or strain theory have revived it as an important explanation of crime and delinquency. Additional research is needed to assess the importance of strain at the community and individual levels for crime and delinquency.

Review and Discuss

Why should anomie theory be considered a structural theory? How does general strain theory build on anomie theory?

Subcultural Theories

Recall that Merton's theory does not explain why some people unable to achieve economic success turn to crime, whereas others do not. Shaw and McKay gave an early clue to one of the processes involved when they noted that juveniles in socially disorganized neighborhoods grow up amid conflicting values, some of them law-abiding and some of them lawbreaking. Delinquency results when juveniles adopt the latter values. Beginning in the 1950s, scholars began to discuss various kinds of subcultures through which adolescents and others learn that it is acceptable to break the law. Explicitly or implicitly, most of these theorists traced these subcultures' origins to poverty and other kinds of strain.

ALBERT K. COHEN: SCHOOL FAILURE AND DELINQUENT SUBCULTURES

Extending Merton's anomie theory into noneconomic behavior, Albert K. Cohen (1955) developed the notion of a delinquent subculture in his influential book, *Delinquent Boys*. Like Merton, Cohen assumed that lower-class boys have high delinquency rates. He observed that much, and perhaps most, delinquency, such as fighting and vandalism, is noneconomic or nonutilitarian and that even delinquency involving theft—shoplifting, burglary, and the like—is often done more for thrills than for economic reasons. As a result, this delinquency cannot result from anomie as Merton conceived it.

Cohen adapted Merton's concept of strain but reasoned that a major adolescent goal involves making a favorable impression on others and thus feeling good about oneself. However, the school experience of lower-class boys makes it difficult to achieve this goal because schools are dominated by middle-class values such as courtesy and

Albert K. Cohen thought that poor school performance leads to status frustration that, in turn, leads to involvement in a delinquent gang subculture to regain status and respect.

hard work. Having not been raised with these values, lower-class boys do poorly in school and experience **status frustration,** or strain. To reduce their frustration, they turn to a delinquent gang subculture to regain status and respect. This subculture includes values, including hedonism and maliciousness, that help promote delinquency. *Hedonism*, or pleasure seeking, involves the immediate, impulsive gratification of the need for fun and excitement, whereas *maliciousness* involves a desire to hurt, and even delight in hurting, others. For obvious reasons, both values can lead gang members to pursue illegal activities. Their primary motive is not to acquire money or possessions, but rather to gain status in the eyes of their peers and to improve their self-esteem by defying authority.

Notice that Cohen's book is entitled *Delinquent Boys*. What about girls? For the most part, Cohen ignored them because he considered delinquency primarily a lower-class male phenomenon. He thought girls were not delinquent because they care less than boys about how well they do in school. Instead, they attach more importance to romantic relationships because they consider marriage their major goal in life. Girls' delinquency, Cohen thought, stems more from a poor romantic life than from poor school performance.

Evaluation of Cohen's Status Frustration Theory

When Cohen wrote his book in 1955, relatively little research on gang delinquency had been done since Shaw and McKay's work. Cohen's book helped change that, and delinquency research burgeoned in the ensuing years. Ironically, much of this research challenged Cohen's assumptions and conclusions (Bernard, Snipes, and Gerould 2009).

A first criticism should by now be familiar: Cohen overlooked middle-class delinquency, which his theory cannot explain. A second criticism concerns his assumption that most delinquency is nonutilitarian. Some researchers argue that delinquency is more utilitarian, or economically motivated, than Cohen assumed. The involvement of many urban gangs these days in drug trafficking is aimed more at making money than at finding cheap thrills. Critics also take issue with Cohen's explanation of why school failure leads to delinquency. Although the association between school failure and delinquency is a common finding in the literature, processes other than status frustration might be at work (see Chapter 8).

Another criticism is that Cohen failed to explain why many boys doing poorly in school do *not* become delinquent. Critics also charged that by placing more emphasis on delinquent subcultures than on the structural conditions in which poor adolescents live, Cohen implicitly blamed lower-class adolescents for their problems. A final criticism is that Cohen's view of girls and their delinquency was based on outmoded, sexist views.

WALTER B. MILLER: FOCAL CONCERNS

Three years after the publication of Cohen's book, Walter B. Miller (1958) published an influential article on lower-class subcultures and delinquency. Like Cohen, Miller emphasized that juveniles learn values conducive to delinquency from their subculture, but his views differed as to the nature of the subculture. Whereas Cohen attributed delinquency to involvement in a delinquent gang subculture after failure in school, Miller attributed it to the lower-class subculture itself. He thought that lower-class boys are exposed to this subculture, and are hence likely to commit delinquent acts, whether or not they do well in school.

Miller termed the values of the lower-class subculture **focal concerns** and thought that they contribute to delinquency. In order of importance, Miller presented the focal concerns as follows (see Figure 7.1):

1. *Trouble.* Miller wrote that an interest in "trouble" characterizes lower-class culture. Adults usually want their children to stay out of trouble, but lower-class adolescents sometimes gain prestige with their friends by getting into trouble.

2. *Toughness.* This concern evokes the John Wayne image of the strong, silent, brave cowboy adept at fighting and involves, Miller said, preoccupation with masculinity and extreme homophobia (hatred of homosexuals). Miller believed it arises from the fact that many lower-class boys are raised in female-headed households and thus lack adequate male role models.

3. *Smartness.* To be "smart" in the lower-class subculture is to outwit others and to avoid being outwitted yourself. It involves the ability to achieve a goal by the use of wits rather than physical force. Boys grow up outwitting each other in various activities, including the mutual trading of insults.

4. *Excitement.* Miller wrote that many aspects of lower-class life revolve around excitement and thrills. On weekends people typically drink, gamble, go out on the town, and have sex. Many men are involved in physical fights. Miller believed that the pursuit of excitement on weekends arises in part from boring lives led the rest of the week.

5. *Fate.* Lower-class people have a particularly fatalistic outlook on life, said Miller. Whether they succeed or fail is due less to their own efforts than to good luck or bad luck. This helps account for their high interest in gambling, he said.

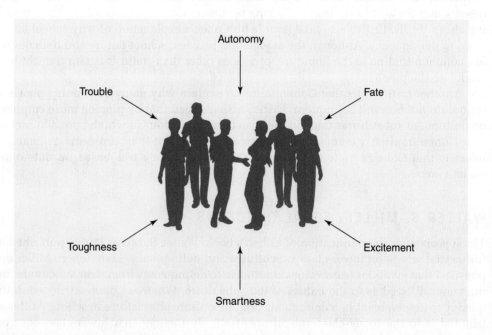

FIGURE 7.1 ▸ **Focal Concerns** Walter Miller felt that lower-class boys grow up amid several focal concerns that they learn from their subculture. These focal concerns, he thought, help explain their high rates of delinquency. Source: Based on Miller 1958.

6. *Autonomy.* This focal concern involves a rejection of authority and distaste for anyone trying to control one's behavior. Autonomy helps justify the violation of laws and other rules.

If adolescents grow up in a subculture valuing trouble, toughness, smartness, excitement, fate, and autonomy, said Miller, it is no surprise that they often end up being delinquent: By conforming to their culture, they violate the larger society's legal norms. Delinquents are thus normal adolescents who have learned from their subculture several attitudes that justify breaking the law.

Evaluation of Miller's View

Miller's analysis has been subject to some withering criticism (Bernard, Snipes, and Gerould 2009). The most pointed is that his discussion of lower-class culture "blames the victim" by ignoring the dire effects of economic deprivation. Much research since Miller's article also finds that poor and middle-class adolescents have similar values and attitudes: Middle-class boys appear to value excitement, toughness, autonomy, and other focal concerns as much as their poorer counterparts do (Cernkovich 1978). Moreover, to the extent that middle-class delinquency exists, Miller's theory cannot readily account for it because it attributes the focal concerns conducive to delinquency to the lower class. Miller also engaged in circular reasoning. He identified delinquent boys' focal concerns by observing their behavior and then used these concerns to explain their behavior. Finally, Miller's thesis, like Cohen's work, ignored female delinquency and thus was necessarily incomplete.

RICHARD CLOWARD AND LLOYD OHLIN: DIFFERENTIAL OPPORTUNITY THEORY

Recall that Merton's anomie theory fails to explain why people facing anomie choose a specific adaptation. In 1960, Richard Cloward and Lloyd Ohlin extended Merton's formulation to address this problem with their **differential opportunity** theory (Cloward and Ohlin 1960). Merton stressed that society provides *differential access to legitimate means*—working—to achieve monetary success. The nonpoor have such access; the poor often do not. Cloward and Ohlin argued there is also *differential access to illegitimate means*, or illegitimate opportunity structures. Given anomie, the type of adaptation one pursues depends on which illegitimate opportunities are available in a particular neighborhood. Where organized crime is a powerful presence, adolescents will gravitate toward it. In especially deprived areas where drug use and addiction are already rampant, adolescents will start using drugs.

The neighborhoods' deviant activities in turn reflect their social organization and resulting subculture. Some neighborhoods have a *criminal subculture*. These tend to be well-organized, highly integrated neighborhoods with adults who have become well-to-do through illegitimate means (e.g., organized crime). Adolescents look up to these adults as role models and turn to various forms of property crime themselves, just as middle-class youths who spend time with businesspeople may desire a business career. Delinquent gangs in these communities thus specialize in highly organized, well-planned criminal activities. Other adolescents live in disorganized neighborhoods in which a *conflict subculture* exists. Organized crime does not flourish, and there are few successful adult criminals to befriend impressionable adolescents. Because youths in these communities lack both legitimate and illegitimate opportunities, they join gangs and engage in high amounts of random, and often spontaneous, violence. Regardless of their type of neighborhood, some youths find it difficult to join gangs or fail to do well after they join and then drop out of the gang. These youths are *double failures*, and among them a *retreatist subculture* develops that involves heavy drug and alcohol use.

Evaluation of Differential Opportunity Theory

Cloward and Ohlin's theory was immediately popular and helped prompt many of the antipoverty programs of the 1960s. Its emphasis on differential access to illegitimate opportunities remains important in helping to explain various types of deviance and crime. However, it too has been criticized for neglecting middle-class delinquency and white-collar crime. Although some research supports Cloward and Ohlin's idea that gangs specialize in various illegitimate activities determined by neighborhood social organization, the type of specialization does not always correspond with their criminal, conflict, and retreatist typology. Many gangs also combine several different kinds of illegitimate activities (e.g., drug use and theft) and thus are unspecialized. In another criticism, urban adolescent drug users often do not appear to be the double failures depicted by Cloward and Ohlin. Instead, as noted earlier regarding Merton's view, they use drugs for other reasons.

Showing the contemporary relevance of differential opportunity theory, a recent study of Chicago neighborhoods found violence to be particularly high, relative to other crimes, in neighborhoods that had the highest levels of social disorganization. Reasoning that these were precisely the neighborhoods with conflict subcultures as discussed by Cloward and Ohlin, the authors of the study concluded that this finding supported Cloward and Ohlin's theory (Schreck, McGloin, and Kirk 2009).

MARVIN WOLFGANG AND FRANCO FERRACUTI: THE SUBCULTURE OF VIOLENCE

About the time that Miller published his influential article, Marvin Wolfgang said that a **subculture of violence** explains the high level of violence among poor, urban males. This subculture "does not define personal assaults as wrong or antisocial." Instead, it is a subculture in which "quick resort to physical aggression is a socially approved and expected concomitant of certain stimuli" (Wolfgang 1958:329). Wolfgang later expanded on this view in a book with Franco Ferracuti (Wolfgang and Ferracuti 1967). The two authors reasoned that when insults and other interpersonal conflicts occur, lower-class males often respond with physical force, whereas middle-class males tend to walk away. Echoing Miller's emphasis on lower-class males' obsession with masculinity, they thought this aggressive response stems from the need of lower-class males to defend their honor and masculinity.

Some scholars say that a subculture of violence, involving a physical response to insults and other interpersonal problems, characterizes urban neighborhoods.

Evaluation of the Subculture of Violence Theory

As the discussion of race and crime in Chapter 3 indicated, the subculture of violence theory is very controversial. Early research found that the urban poor disapprove of violence as much as other demographic subgroups do (Ball-Rokeach 1972; Erlanger 1974), and more recent research finds that blacks are no more likely than whites to approve of violence (Cao, Adams, and Jensen 1997; Sampson and Bartusch 1999). Although the disproportionate involvement of young urban males in street violence seems beyond dispute (see Chapter 3), this does not automatically mean that their behavior stems from a subculture of violence, as Wolfgang and Ferracuti argued. Their reasoning, like Miller's, is a bit circular: they infer a subculture of violence from the high level of violence among young urban men and then attribute the violence to the subculture they have inferred.

These criticisms notwithstanding, a growing body of work supports Wolfgang and Ferracuti's basic theme, but places it squarely in the context of the structural problems discussed earlier in this chapter. According to this view, urban violence stems from the combined stresses of economic deprivation, urban living, and racial discrimination, all of which lead to a subculture characterized by a desire for self-respect and angry aggression (Baron, Kennedy. and Forde 2001; Bernard 1990; Sampson and Wilson 1995). These factors in turn increase the willingness to use violence in interpersonal confrontations, especially as younger adolescents come under the influence of older adolescents and young adults who reject conventional values (Harding 2010).

ELIJAH ANDERSON: THE CODE OF THE STREET

The most influential contemporary view on the subcultural basis for violence comes from sociologist Elijah Anderson (1999), one of the most sensitive observers of urban life. Based on his years of ethnographic research in Philadelphia, Anderson documented a *code of the street* among young urban African Americans that arises from their despair and alienation and that helps explain their interpersonal violence. Its most central feature is the need and striving for respect. "People are being told day in and day out that they are not respectable," Anderson said. "This is the message young black people get every day from the system. If you perceive that you're getting those kinds of messages, it may be that you will crave respect—you've got to get it from a turnip if you can. So every encounter becomes an opportunity for salvaging respect" (Coughlin 1994:A8).

To help command respect, Anderson said, young urban men often adopt a certain "look" involving the way they dress, move, and talk; this persona helps deter verbal and physical assaults by other men and is an essential aspect of the conception of manhood in inner cities. Displaying nerve by initiating physical and verbal attacks is another way for a young male to prove his manhood and gain respect. Striving for respect in these ways thus leads masculinity in urban areas to take on an especially violent tone.

Distrust of the police and courts also helps explain urban violence, Anderson added. Like the frontier settlers of an earlier era, young urban males feel they cannot count on the legal system for help and deem it necessary to use violence to defend themselves, their families, and friends. Gang wars over drugs and the availability of ever more powerful firearms all make an explosive situation even more volatile.

Anderson's view presents a subcultural basis for urban violence that derives from the structural problems and conditions of urban areas. This clear structural underpinning and the richness of his discussion have revived subcultural explanations in the field of criminology. As a result, research has begun to stress the combined impact of structural problems and cultural influences on crime rates (Harding 2010; Kubrin and Weitzer 2003b; Warner 2003). It also supports his view that distrust of the police and the criminal justice system more generally leads some urban residents to turn to violence to resolve confrontations rather than call the police (Wilkinson, Beaty, and Lurry 2009).

Review and Discuss

Evaluate the value of the various subcultural theories of crime. To what extent do you agree with Anderson's "code of the street" thesis? Explain your answer.

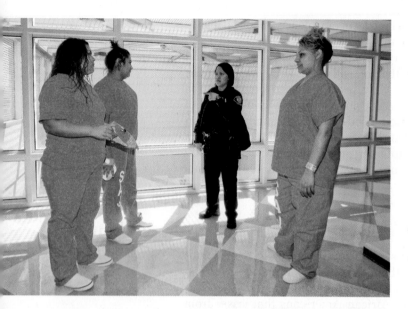

Structural theories help explain why some women are more likely than other women to commit crime. However, they do not help explain why female crime rates are lower than male crime rates.

Structural Theories and Gender

What if the stranded children in William Golding's *Lord of the Flies* had been girls instead of boys? Would they have become as savage as the boys? Would they have committed murder? If not, is Golding's view of human behavior really only a view of male behavior? Could he have written the same book with girls as the protagonists?

As these questions indicate, Golding's neglect of gender limits the value of his book, however powerful it is in other respects. The same neglect characterizes the structural theories of crime discussed in this chapter. Although social class and race lie at the heart of these theories, gender remains invisible. The work of the many scholars of anomie or strain, social disorganization, and subcultural theories was limited not only to lower-class delinquency and crime but also to male delinquency and crime. Hence, these theories may explain only male offending.

To address this neglect, scholars have begun to test the theories with samples of female offenders. They generally find that the theories do help explain variation in female offending, although they differ on whether the factors emphasized in the various theories have stronger effects on female offending or on male offending, if either (Agnew 2009; Piquero and Sealock 2004; Zahn and Browne 2009). Supporting an *economic marginality hypothesis*, studies find that the poverty resulting from women's low-paying jobs and increasing divorce rates plays a very important role in female offending, most of which involves petty property crime (Hunnicutt and Broidy 2004).

Although structural theories do seem to apply to female offending, they are less helpful in understanding why there is much less female offending than male offending. For example, because women's incomes are much lower than men's on the average, they should experience more anomie than men and thus, if Merton is correct, be more likely than men to commit crime (Leonard 1995). However, we know they commit less crime. Also, although contemporary ecological work stresses, as we have seen, the criminogenic effects of urban living conditions, concentrated disadvantage, and racial discrimination, males commit most of the crime in disadvantaged urban neighborhoods even though females experience the same strain-producing conditions. In this regard, Lisa Broidy's (2001) finding that girls are less apt than boys to have their strain-induced anger translate into delinquency may explain why similar structural conditions do not yield similar levels for both genders of crime and delinquency.

Review and Discuss

In what ways do structural theories ignore gender differences in criminal offending? Do you think these theories help us understand why these gender differences exist?

Conclusion

The structural theories presented in this chapter are distinctively sociological. They invoke Durkheim's classic view that external forces affect individual behavior and attitudes and remind us that normal people may be compelled to commit criminal behavior. This does not mean that we should excuse such behavior, but it does mean that we should be sensitive to the structural conditions underlying crime as we try to reduce it.

Social disorganization theory has recently been revived, and with good reason. Its focus on the criminogenic conditions of urban neighborhoods is perhaps more timely than ever, and its emphasis on kinds of places over kinds of people is an important corrective to continuing beliefs that crime is due to moral or other failings of individual offenders. Its recent revival in contemporary ecological work represents a major theoretical development with significant policy implications. Perhaps most important, it provides a nonracist explanation for the high crime rates of poor urban areas.

Merton's anomie theory has also been revived and calls attention to the strain and subsequent deviance produced by failure to reach economic and other goals. Such strain is heightened in a society whose ideology stresses equal opportunity for all. Anomie theory thus allows us to see that certain values of U.S. society are ironically criminogenic. The very ideology that drives many people to seek their fortunes legally drives others, poor or rich, to seek theirs illegally.

Subcultural theories were developed to help explain how and why structural conditions lead to crime and delinquency. Although they remind us that crime is a learned behavior, some come close to stereotyping the poor and blaming them totally for their behavior. Recent work that provides a strong structural underpinning for the subculture of urban areas provides an important corrective to these problems and is growing in popularity as an explanation for these areas' high crime rates.

All these theories try to explain crime and delinquency by the poor. This focus is both their blessing and their curse. Although it is important to explain why poor people disproportionately commit serious street crime, it is also important to recognize that wealthier people commit serious crimes themselves and to explain why they do so. Strain theory begins to provide part of the explanation for white-collar crime, but the other theories do not. Finally, all three theories suffer from their neglect of gender. Although females and males both experience social disorganization and anomie and both live in deviant subcultures, if they exist, males remain far more likely than females to commit serious crime and delinquency. None of the structural theories discussed in this chapter adequately accounts for this fact.

A final problem is that most people experiencing the structural problems presented in this chapter still do *not* commit serious crime and delinquency, whereas some not experiencing these problems do commit them. Structural theories cannot easily explain such individual variation. Several sociological theories have been developed to help us understand the more micro-level social processes that lead some individuals to commit crime and deviance. Chapter 8 discusses these theories.

Summary

1. Structural theories emphasize that crime is the result not of individual failings or abnormalities, but of certain physical and social aspects of communities, the distribution of social and economic power, and the nature of relationships among individuals and groups. They stress that normal people are led to commit crime because of these factors and that any individuals will be more likely to commit crime if they are subject to these factors. Structural explanations are particularly useful for explaining variation in crime rates across social groups and locations.

2. Structural theories are the legacy of Émile Durkheim, who focused on social integration and socialization as sources of individual behavior and attitudes. Durkheim argued that individual suicides are the result of normlessness and lack of social integration.

3. Shaw and McKay's social disorganization theory recognized that some urban areas continue to have high crime rates even after their residents are displaced by other types of residents. They said that the multiple social and economic problems of some neighborhoods create social disorganization that leads to conflicting values and weakens conventional social institutions. Crime and delinquency rates are thus higher in areas with greater social disorganization. Although social disorganization theory eventually fell out of favor, its recent revitalization has enriched criminological theory.

4. Merton's anomie theory stressed that U.S. culture is characterized by an exaggerated emphasis on economic success. Individuals living in poverty who cannot achieve economic success experience normlessness. Their possible adaptations in reaction to this strain include conformity, innovation, ritualism, retreatism, and rebellion. Although anomie theory, too, eventually fell out of favor, it has also been revitalized, especially with the advent of general strain theory.

5. Several subcultural theories attempt to explain why certain structural conditions lead to crime and deviance. Albert Cohen theorized that lower-class boys turn to delinquency because they lose self-esteem after doing poorly in school, where middle-class values conflict with their own. Walter Miller identified several focal concerns that guide the behavior of boys living in poverty and push them into delinquency. Richard Cloward and Lloyd Ohlin emphasized differential access to illegitimate opportunities afforded by different subcultures of poor urban areas, whereas Marvin Wolfgang emphasized the role played by a subculture of violence in the genesis of crime in nonwhite urban areas. In general, all these views come close to stereotyping the poor and blaming them for their deviance, but recent work provides a strong structural basis for subcultural problems and is attracting popularity as a reasonable explanation for the high crime rates of urban areas.

6. Structural theories generally ignore female crime and delinquency and cannot adequately explain gender difference in the rates of crime and delinquency. Some research does indicate that structural explanations help explain variation in female offending.

Key Terms

anomie 161

aspirations 160

concentric zones 163

differential opportunity 177

economic deprivation 165

focal concerns 176

kinds of people 167

kinds of places 167

relative deprivation 167

social disorganization 163

social ecology 163

social integration 161

socialization 160

social pathology 163

social structure 160

social ties 160

status frustration 175

strain 168

subculture of violence 178

underclass 165

What Would You Do?

1. Suppose you are driving a young child through a blighted urban neighborhood. After the child asks, "What happened here?" what do you tell her? How, if at all, would your answer reflect the structural understanding emphasized in this chapter?

2. Recall that part of Stark's theory of deviant places says that youths who step out of their homes are more likely to break the law because they have greater opportunity to do so. Because they are more likely to encounter peers in urban neighborhoods when they do step out, urban neighborhoods have more delinquency than rural areas. If you were the parent of an adolescent in a middle-class urban neighborhood, would you let your teen go out with friends on weekend nights whenever she or he wanted to? Would you have a curfew? Explain your answers.

CHAPTER

eight

Sociological Theories: Emphasis on Social Process

Crime in the News

igh school students were graduating in spring 2010, and headlines such as "Students Overcome Great Odds" showed that young people in the nation's poor and working-class neighborhoods can indeed beat the odds and not end up in a life of crime and other problems. In Savannah, Georgia, a young man named Richard was working 37 hours weekly to support his family and still maintained a 3.86 GPA while taking honors and Advanced Placement courses. He said, "I receive respect from my classmates, my teachers and my family. But even if nothing came of all my hard work, it's worth it knowing I'm building character and doing my best." Another Savannah student, Sharaina, maintained a 3.6 GPA while caring for her autistic brother when her single mother was at work.

Across the country in Rio Rancho, New Mexico, a city of 80,000 just north of Albuquerque, a student named April was especially being honored for her scholastic achievement and for overcoming adversity. After her father died when she was 10 and her mother died when she was 15, April and her seven siblings were raised by their grandmother. She planned to attend the University of New Mexico and major in education. A news report said that "she hopes to make an impact in children's lives just as her grandmother did in hers."

Sources: Few 2010; Rodrigo 2010.

I n Chapter 7, we said the behavior of the boys in *Lord of the Flies* arose from their extreme anomie and social disorganization. There are other ways to explain their behavior. We could talk instead about how they influenced each other to be violent. Or we could say their island lacked the law-abiding influence of parents, schools, and religion. The explanation in Chapter 7 emphasized social structure. The explanations just listed emphasize social processes such as peer influences, socialization, and social interaction. These processes help explain why many people turn to crime, but they also provide clues about why people like Richard, Sharaina, and April in the Crime in the News feature can manage to "beat the odds."

Such social process explanations see crime arising more from the interaction of individuals than from the way society is organized. Although structural and social process explanations both make sense, some scholars favor the macro view of structural approaches, whereas others favor the micro view of social process perspectives. The popularity of the latter view stems from scholarly recognition that most people living in criminogenic structural conditions do not commit serious crime. If this is true, then it is important to understand the social processes leading some people in these conditions to commit crime and others, like Richard, Sharaina, and April, not to do so.

While conceding the importance of criminogenic social processes, structural theorists still stress the underlying influence of structural problems in society or in specific neighborhoods. They argue that poor individuals would commit less street crime if they were living in more advantaged locations. A healthy tension exists today between the two approaches' proponents, with some scholars favoring integrated theories combining factors from both views. For a comprehensive explanation of crime, structural and social process factors are both necessary. We would have less crime if not for the structural conditions producing it, and we would have less crime if not for certain social processes increasing individuals' likelihood of committing crime. Those making efforts to reduce crime need to keep these basic facts in mind.

This chapter reviews the major social process theories of criminal behavior. Although some scholars consider them psychological theories (Widom and Toch 1993), their focus on social interaction normally places them under a sociological rubric. Whatever we call them, they incorporate ideas compatible with both sociological and psychological explanations, helping to explain their popularity today. A summary of the social process theories discussed in this chapter appears in Table 8.1.

Social processes such as peer influences, socialization, and social interaction affect our chances of becoming or not becoming criminal offenders. The more law-abiding friends we have, the more likely we are to be law-abiding ourselves.

Learning Theories

Sociologists consider **socialization** critical for social order. As Chapter 7 noted, Émile Durkheim emphasized the need for people to internalize the norms and values of society and learn how to get along with each other. In this way, society forms a "moral cocoon" around us and we become social beings who care about the welfare of others and the well-being of society as a whole (Collins 1994:190). Socialization makes this possible. Accordingly, almost every introduction to sociology text has an early chapter extolling the virtues of socialization and emphasizing its importance during childhood and adolescence and beyond.

TABLE 8.1 ▸ Social Process Theories in Brief

THEORY	KEY FIGURE(S)	SYNOPSIS
Learning Theories		
Differential association	Edwin H. Sutherland	Techniques of and attitudes regarding criminal behavior are learned within intimate personal groups; a person becomes delinquent from an excess of definitions favorable to the violation of law over definitions unfavorable to the violation of law.
Differential identification	Daniel Glaser	People pursue criminal behavior to the extent they identify with members of reference groups who engage in criminal behavior.
Social learning	Albert Bandura	Aggressive tendencies are learned through a process of rewards for such tendencies and imitation of aggressive behavior.
Differential reinforcement	Robert L. Burgess Ronald L. Akers	Criminal behavior and attitudes are more likely to be learned if they are rewarded by friends and/or family; when the rewards for criminal behavior outweigh the rewards for conforming behavior, differential reinforcement occurs and the criminal behavior is learned.
Control Theories		
Containment	Walter Reckless	Inner containments (e.g., a positive self-concept and tolerance for frustration) and outer containments (e.g., family influences) help prevent juvenile offending.
Neutralization and drift	Gresham M. Sykes David Matza	Before committing delinquent acts, adolescents develop techniques of neutralization, or rationalizations, to minimize any guilt they might feel from breaking the law; specific techniques include denial of responsibility, denial of injury, denial of the victim, condemnation of the condemners, and appeal to higher loyalties.
Social bonding	Travis Hirschi	Delinquency and crime are more common among individuals with weakened social bonds to conventional social institutions such as the family and school.
Self-control	Michael Gottfredson Travis Hirschi	Criminal behavior results from low self-control, which in turn results from ineffective parenting.
Control balance	Charles R. Tittle	People are more likely to engage in deviance when they are either very controlling or very controlled than when they have a balance of control.
Coercive control and social support	Mark Colvin Francis T. Cullen	Coercion at either the micro or macro level promotes criminal behavior, while social support at either level reduces it.
Life-Course Theories		
Integrated Strain Control	Delbert S. Elliott	Weak social bonds, strain, and delinquent peers contribute to delinquency; adolescents with weak bonds and strain are particularly vulnerable to the delinquent peers' influence. Strain may weaken even strong bonds and thus increase delinquent peer associations and delinquency.
Interactional	Terence P. Thornberry	Weak social bonds and delinquent peers contribute to delinquency; delinquency and delinquent peer associations may also weaken social bonds and increase delinquency further.
Life-course-persistent	Terrie E. Moffitt	Some individuals' antisocial behavior is serious; persists adolescence-limited through the life course, and begins during childhood because of neuropsychological and other problems. A much greater number of individuals' antisocial behavior occurs only during adolescence, is relatively minor, and is a way of expressing their growing maturity and independence from parents.
Age graded	Robert J. Sampson John H. Laub	Weak social bonds, inadequate parenting, and delinquent peers contribute to criminality, but turning points in the life course, such as marriage and employment, often lead to desistance from crime.

Just as most people learn to obey society's norms, however, others learn that it is okay to violate these norms. They learn these deviant norms and values from their **delinquent peers** and immediate environments, and perhaps also from the mass media. **Learning theories** of crime see criminality as the result of the socialization process we all experience. Because of their individual circumstances, some people learn and practice behaviors that the larger society condemns. Not surprisingly, children growing up in neighborhoods rife with crime often end up committing crime themselves. Middle-class kids often engage in shoplifting, vandalism, and other delinquency because of the influence of delinquent friends. White-collar executives learn to consider price-fixing and other financial crimes a normal and necessary part of doing business.

Learning theories start where structural theories leave off. Structural theories tell us why various attitudes and feelings arise that promote criminality. Learning theories tell us how people come to adopt these views and how and why these views result in crime. Several learning theories exist, and certain nuances distinguish them from one another. But they agree much more than they disagree, and all view crime and delinquency as a consequence of "wrong" socialization. In showing how individuals are socialized to commit crime, learning theories join with structural approaches in presenting a positivist view of crime that stresses the influences of external forces on the individual.

EDWIN H. SUTHERLAND: DIFFERENTIAL ASSOCIATION THEORY

Seven decades ago, sociologist Edwin Sutherland (1883–1950) presented the most famous learning theory of crime, which he termed **differential association** theory, in his text, *Principles of Criminology* (Sutherland 1939). As we noted in Chapter 1, Sutherland is a towering figure in the sociological study of crime. As a sociologist, he thought biological and psychological approaches presented a false picture of crime and criminals as abnormal. The work of Shaw and McKay and other Chicago sociologists had sensitized Sutherland to the consequences of growing up in neighborhoods abounding in crime and delinquency. Whereas Shaw and McKay aimed to explain why certain urban areas have high crime rates, Sutherland tried to explain why and how some people in such areas turn to crime while others do not. Sutherland later applied his theory to professional thieves and argued that differential association with different types of thieves (e.g., shoplifters, professional burglars, or pickpockets) influences what kind of thief someone becomes. He also applied it to white-collar criminals, who learn that it is okay to violate the law in a business climate that justifies lawbreaking to maximize profit (Sutherland 1940).

Sutherland presented his final version of differential association in a 1947 revision of his text (Sutherland 1947). His theory contained nine propositions that have appeared in most criminology textbooks since then:

1. *Criminal behavior is learned.* Sutherland declared that criminal behavior is not inherited biologically or otherwise the result of any biological traits.

2. *Criminal behavior is learned in interaction with other persons in a process of communication.* Here Sutherland said that the learning of criminal behavior occurs through interpersonal interaction.

3. *The principal part of the learning of criminal behavior occurs within intimate personal groups.* Following Tarde, Sutherland asserted that people learn crime from people who are close to them emotionally. He implied that criminal behavior is not learned from the mass media.

4. *When criminal behavior is learned, the learning includes (a) the techniques of committing the crime, which are sometimes very complicated, sometimes very simple; and (b) the specific direction of motives, drives, rationalizations, and attitudes.* This proposition says that the learning of criminal behavior involves mastering how to commit the crime and also deviant attitudes that justify committing it.

5. *The specific direction of motives and drives is learned from definitions of the legal codes as favorable or unfavorable.* Gaining knowledge of criminal behavior also involves learning whether to define laws as worthy of obedience or deserving of violation.

6. *A person becomes delinquent because of an excess of definitions favorable to the violation of law over definitions unfavorable to the violation of law.* This is the heart of Sutherland's differential association theory. People will break the law if they develop more lawbreaking attitudes than law-abiding attitudes.

7. *Differential association may vary in frequency, duration, priority, and intensity.* Associations do not affect one's views equally. Police come into frequent contact with criminals, but do not usually adopt these criminals' attitudes (Shoemaker 2010). In this proposition, Sutherland noted that the effects of associations vary according to four dimensions. *Frequency* simply means how often one spends time with friends. *Duration* means how much time on the average one spends with them during each association. *Priority* refers to how early in life the associations occur, and *intensity* means how much importance one places on one's associations. Although these dimensions often overlap, associations will likely have the greatest impact on one's views if they are of high frequency and duration, occur early in life, and involve people whose views and friendship one values highly.

8. *The process of learning criminal behavior by association with criminal and anticriminal patterns involves all the mechanisms that are involved in any other learning.* Here Sutherland emphasized that socialization into crime includes the same processes involved in socialization into law-abiding behavior.

9. *Although criminal behavior is an expression of general needs and values, it is not explained by these general needs and values, because noncriminal behavior is an expression of the same needs and values.* Sutherland believed that motives are not sufficient to explain crime. For example, the desire for money motivates some people to break the law, but motivates most people to get a good education and work hard. Similarly, jealousy may lead some people to commit murder, but most people who are jealous do not commit murder. Thus, other forces must also be at work.

Sutherland's theory of differential association assumes that criminal tendencies are learned from close friends and not from depictions of crime (such as this scene from *The Sopranos* television show) in the mass media.

Evaluation of Differential Association Theory

Along with Merton's anomie theory, Sutherland's theory of differential association is the most notable historically in the sociological study of crime (Bernard, Snipes, and Gerould 2009). By explicitly linking crime to learning and socialization, Sutherland emphasized its social nature and thus countered explanations emphasizing biological abnormalities.

By stressing the importance of differential associations, he helped to explain variation in offending among people experiencing similar structural conditions. And by extending his theory to white-collar crime, Sutherland helped understand how and why the wealthy commit their share of criminal behavior. For all these reasons, differential association theory has been called a "watershed in criminology" (Matsueda 1988:277).

Perhaps the major reason for its historical importance is that so much research supports its emphasis on the importance of learning and peer influences for lawbreaking. As a review observed, "No characteristic of individuals known to criminologists is a better predictor of criminal behavior than the number of delinquent friends an individual has. The strong correlation between delinquent behavior and delinquent friends has been documented in scores of studies from the 1950s up to the present day" (Warr 2002: 40). Peer networks also help explain gender and racial/ethnic differences in offending, as males, African Americans, and Latinos have greater numbers of delinquent peers than females and whites, respectively (Haynie and Payne 2006; McCarthy, Felmlee, and Hagan 2004). There is even evidence that antisocial individuals tend to have romantic relationships with other deviant individuals and that these relationships then foster more involvement in deviant activities (McCarthy and Casey 2008; Seffrin et al. 2009). Supporting one of Sutherland's assumptions, recent research also shows that many criminal offenders were drawn into and taught crime by a mentor in much the same way that someone working in a lawful occupation may benefit from the help of a mentor (Morselli, Tremblay, and McCarthy 2006).

Despite its important contributions, differential association theory has been criticized (Miller, Shutt, and Barnes 2010). A first criticism, and perhaps the most important, concerns causal order. Staying for a moment with delinquency, which comes first, associating with delinquent peers or one's own delinquency? It is possible that someone's delinquency produces friendships with delinquent peers rather than the reverse. People become delinquent for reasons other than differential association, but once they do, they find themselves spending more time with other delinquents, the reverse of what Sutherland and other learning theorists assume. To investigate this problem, some studies use longitudinal data and find a reciprocal relationship: Having delinquent peers influences delinquency, as differential association and other learning theories assume, and then delinquency increases involvement with delinquent peers. However, some research finds that the effect of delinquency on delinquent-peer associations is greater than that of the associations on delinquency (Matsueda 1988). Although the general importance of delinquent-peer associations seems beyond dispute, this research suggests that the exact nature of this relationship remains to be determined.

In a second criticism, Sutherland may have erred in talking about the influence of friends' definitions, or attitudes, favorable to violating the law while neglecting other influences of the friends' behavior. We might do what our friends do, not because we have adopted their attitudes, but simply because we want them to like us or because we find their behavior rewarding. We can adopt their behavior without necessarily adopting any deviant attitudes they might have. This view of the learning of crime supports other learning theories (discussed later) more than it does Sutherland's (Warr 2002).

A third criticism concerns Sutherland's implication that crime is committed in groups or, if done alone, is still influenced by "intimate personal groups." Differential association theory applies well to many crimes and especially to juvenile offenses such as shoplifting, vandalism, and drug use, in which peer influences loom large. But many criminal behaviors do not fit this pattern: They are committed by lone individuals and also do not stem from attitudes and techniques learned from friends. For example, most murders are committed by people acting alone, who cannot be said to have learned from their friends that it is acceptable to commit murder. Most rapes are similarly committed by lone offenders who cannot be said to have learned attitudes approving rape from their friends. Rape might derive from attitudes in the larger culture condoning rape (see Chapter 11), but this sort of explanation differs from Sutherland's emphasis on intimate personal groups.

Some critics also point to difficulties in testing differential association theory. As implied earlier, empirical tests of the theory usually examine the effects of the number of delinquent friends. To measure this variable, scholars might ask, "In the last year, how many of your friends have engaged in" shoplifting, marijuana use, and the like. But this focus differs from Sutherland's emphasis on the number of definitions favorable and unfavorable to violating the law. This concept is much more difficult to measure than the number of delinquent friends (Bernard, Snipes, and Gerould 2009). In another problem, some research finds that "recent rather than early friends have the greatest effect on delinquency" (Warr 1993:35). This finding suggests that Sutherland had his *priority* dimension backward, because he thought that earlier friendships have the greatest effect.

Finally, because Sutherland's focus was on male delinquency, he did not consider whether differential association works the same for females. Some studies suggest that it may not (Agnew 2009; Giordano 2009). Although girls often have more intimate relationships than boys do, their friends tend to be less delinquent than boys' friends are. Their relationships are thus less likely than boys' to promote delinquency. To put it another way, peer relationships may be a stronger determinant of male delinquency than of female delinquency, even if they do account for female delinquency. To the extent that this is true, Sutherland's theory applies more to males than to females. Despite this problem, differential association theory nonetheless helps explain the gender difference in criminality because females have fewer delinquent peers than males do.

Differential association theory is very applicable to juvenile crimes such as shoplifting, in which peer influences play an important role, but it is much less applicable to crimes such as homicide that are committed by lone individuals who are not reacting to peer influences.

These criticisms notwithstanding, differential association theory remains important for calling attention to the influence of peers and learning on delinquency. Notice that Sutherland did not say much about the processes by which individuals adopt deviant attitudes through differential associations. Other subsequent learning theories discuss some of these processes. We turn briefly to these theories.

Review and Discuss

What are the key assumptions of Sutherland's differential association theory? What are some criticisms of this theory?

OTHER LEARNING THEORIES

Daniel Glaser: Differential Identification Theory

Sociologist Daniel Glaser's (1956) *theory of differential identification* rests on the notion of *reference groups*, or groups whose values, attitudes, and behavior you admire and wish to copy. These can be groups to which you already belong, such as your circle of friends, or groups to which you do not belong, such as the clique of high school students who are the well-dressed school leaders, or even a popular music group. If your reference groups happen to be ones engaging in criminal or deviant behavior, you are more apt to engage in such behavior yourself.

As Glaser (1956:440) summarized his central thesis, "A person pursues criminal behavior to the extent that he identifies himself with real or imaginary persons from whose perspective his criminal behavior seems acceptable" (italics deleted). In contrast to differential association theory and the other learning theories discussed later, differential identification theory stressed that learning of criminal behavior can occur without actually interacting with the influencing group.

Albert Bandura: Social Learning Theory

Psychologist Albert Bandura (1973) developed his **social learning** theory of aggression more than forty years ago. He argued that aggressive tendencies are learned rather than inborn. We may see our friends or parents act aggressively, and we may see violence on TV and in other aspects of our popular culture. All these influences help us learn that aggression is acceptable behavior. In developing his theory, Bandura drew on a rich body of psychological research on classical and operant conditioning, which stresses that learning occurs from the association of a stimulus with a response (classical conditioning) or because of the rewarding of a particular behavior (operant conditioning). Although Bandura recognized the importance of rewards for learning behavior, he also stressed that learning can occur just through modeling, or imitating behavior, without any rewards being involved.

Robert L. Burgess and Ronald L. Akers: Differential Reinforcement Theory

In an influential 1966 article, Robert L. Burgess and Ronald L. Akers (1966) presented their *differential reinforcement theory of crime.* Akers developed this theory further in later work and, borrowing Bandura's term, named it a *social learning theory* (Akers 1977). Burgess and Akers argued that criminal behavior and attitudes are more likely to be learned if they are reinforced, or rewarded, usually by friends, family, or both. When the rewards for criminal behaviors outweigh the rewards for alternative behaviors, differential reinforcement occurs and the criminal behavior is learned. Although Burgess and Akers granted that much learning of criminal behavior occurs within the intimate personal groups emphasized by Sutherland, they said such learning can also stem from the influence of school authorities, police, the mass media, and other nonprimary group sources. These sources all provide rewards and punishments that influence the learning of behavior. As revised and extended by Akers, social learning theory is the dominant learning theory today and, in his words, "is more strongly and consistently supported by empirical data than any other social psychological explanation of crime and deviance" (Akers and Jensen 2006:37).

Control Theories

Theories of behavior, including theories of crime and deviance, are often based on assumptions about human nature. As Chapter 7 noted, Durkheim and other conservative thinkers of the 1800s thought that society needed to restrain individual impulses because human nature was selfish. Other thinkers have presented a less pessimistic view. The most notable statement is probably that of English philosopher John Locke in his 1690 work, *An Essay Concerning Human Understanding* (see Chapter 5). Locke believed that humans are naturally neither good nor bad and instead are born with a blank slate into which ideas are placed by experience.

Learning theories of crime share this view. Recall their basic assumption that individuals learn to be criminals. This view implies that individuals will not commit crime unless they first learn criminal attitudes and behaviors. This in turn implies that the individual is a blank slate who would generally not become a criminal without first learning about crime from society. With this assumption of human nature, learning theories thus ask: Why do people become criminals?

Control theories of crime take a different view of human nature and ask a different question about crime. Like the nineteenth-century conservative thinkers, they assume that people are naturally selfish and capable of committing crime and other antisocial behavior. Given this view, the key question control theories try to answer is not why people become criminals, but rather why people do *not* become criminals.

In answering this question, control theorists discuss two kinds of controls: personal and social (Reiss 1951). **Personal controls** concern such things as individual conscience, commitment to law, and a positive self-concept. **Social controls** concern attachments to and involvement in **conventional social institutions** such as the family, schools, and religion. Weak personal controls often result from weakened social controls. The basic argument is that a positive self-concept and other personal controls combine with strong attachments to conventional social institutions to keep individuals from becoming criminals. When either or both types of control weaken, individuals are freer to become criminals. In this regard, *Lord of the Flies* is a vivid example of the effects of weakened social attachments.

WALTER RECKLESS: CONTAINMENT THEORY

In the 1950s and 1960s, sociologist Walter C. Reckless (Reckless 1961; Reckless, Dinitz, and Murray 1956) developed his **containment** theory of delinquency, which stressed that inner and outer containments help prevent juvenile offending. *Inner containments* include a positive self-concept, tolerance for frustration, and an ability to set realistic goals; *outer containments* include institutions such as the family. Both types of containments are necessary, said Reckless, to keep juveniles from succumbing to internal pushes and external pressures and pulls that might otherwise prompt them to break the law. *Internal pushes* are social–psychological states, such as the need for immediate gratification, restlessness, and a hostile attitude. *External pressures* are structural problems and include poverty, unemployment, and other social conditions. *External pulls* are forces such as delinquent peers that draw or pull individuals into crime and delinquency.

Evaluation of Containment Theory

Critics of containment theory raise several issues. One is the familiar chicken-and-egg question. Although youths with delinquent records may have lower self-concepts, these may stem from their official label of delinquency (see Chapter 9) and not be the cause of the delinquency. It is also questionable whether a positive self-concept is the most important factor preventing delinquency, as containment theory asserts: Other factors, such as peer relationships and family influences, may be more important (Shoemaker 2010). Finally, empirical research does not always find the presumed link between self-concept and delinquency.

GRESHAM M. SYKES AND DAVID MATZA: NEUTRALIZATION AND DRIFT THEORY

Assume you believe there should be speed limits for cars. Now consider all the times you and your friends drive a car past the speed limit. You might be worried about getting a ticket, but do you ever feel a tiny twinge of guilt now and then? If so, why do you exceed the speed limit? Do you justify to yourself that it is acceptable to do so? If you don't feel any guilt, why not? Whether or not you feel guilty, do you reason that the speed limit is too low and that no one will get hurt if you exceed it?

As these questions suggest, law-abiding people may accept the validity of laws but violate them anyway. Part of this process involves justifying to themselves why it is okay to break the law, especially when they might feel guilty or ashamed for doing so. The theories discussed so far generally ignore this issue. Differential association theory suggests that the individual passively succumbs to peer influences to commit crime. Other learning theories say that the individual more actively calculates whether potential rewards for crime outweigh the risks. Yet even these theories generally disregard any guilt accompanying such calculations. Most control theories also allow little or no role for guilt or shame because they assume that people are naturally selfish.

Guilt and shame lie at the center of *neutralization* theory, developed by Gresham M. Sykes and David Matza in a classic 1957 article (Sykes and Matza 1957) They wrote that adolescents need to neutralize any guilt or shame they feel before committing delinquent acts by developing at least one of five rationalizations, or *techniques of neutralization*, about why it is okay to break the law. These rationalizations precede delinquency and comprise an important part of the definitions favorable to law violation stressed by differential association theory. The five techniques of neutralization follow:

1. *Denial of Responsibility.* Here adolescents say they are not responsible for the delinquent acts they intend to commit. Their behavior is due to forces beyond their control, such as abusive parents or deviant friends. Teenagers who drink or use illegal drugs with their friends may say that peer pressure made them do it.

2. *Denial of Injury.* Here adolescents reason that no one will be hurt by their intended illegal behavior. Borrowing a car for a joy ride is just fun-loving mischief, not a crime; because the owner will get the car back or at least has insurance, no one gets hurt. A large department store will not miss any items that are shoplifted.

3. *Denial of the Victim.* Even if offenders concede that they are about to harm someone or something, they may reason that their target deserves the harm. Robin Hood and his Merry Men felt it acceptable to rob from the rich and give to the poor. Shoplifters reason that the store has "ripped them off," so now it is their turn to rip off the store. People about to commit hate crimes say their targets are less than human and deserve to be beaten. Men who beat their wives/girlfriends say they should have kept the children more quiet, should not have looked at another man, or should have had dinner ready on time.

4. *Condemnation of the Condemners.* Here offenders question the motives and integrity of police, parents, teachers, and other parties who condemn the offenders' behavior: The police are corrupt, so it's okay for me to break the law. My parents used marijuana when they were my age, so why can't I?

5. *Appeal to Higher Loyalties.* Here offenders reason that their illegal behavior is necessary to help people dear to them. Members of gangs may conclude that loyalty to the gang justifies their taking part in illegal activities committed by the gangs. Poor people may steal food to help their starving families.

Matza (1964) later expanded the idea of neutralization with his **drift** theory of delinquency. (Sykes and Matza's views today are commonly referred to as *neutralization and drift theory*.) Matza argued that delinquents are not constantly delinquent and instead drift into and out of delinquency. Techniques of neutralization make their delinquency possible, but so do *subterranean* values from the larger culture such as daring and excitement, a belief that aggression is sometimes necessary, and the desire for wealth and possessions.

Although these values often underlie conforming behavior, they can also lead to deviant behavior, especially when peer influences help channel these values into illegal activity.

Evaluation of Neutralization and Drift Theory

Sykes and Matza's ideas have been popular, but they have also been criticized. Some scholars say that adolescents who are serious offenders do not feel guilty and have nothing to neutralize (Topalli 2005). Moreover, although several studies find that offenders do rationalize their behavior, it is difficult to prove that this happened *before* they broke the law, as Sykes and Matza assumed. Techniques of neutralization may thus be "after-the-fact rationalizations rather than before-the-fact neutralizations" (Hirschi 1969:207). In another criticism, Sykes and Matza believed that delinquents do not hold different values and are not chronic offenders because they drift into and out of delinquency. However, some offenders are chronic (see Chapter 3) and do appear to hold values different from those of nondelinquents.

Despite these criticisms, many scholars defend neutralization and drift theory, with some studies finding that most adolescents do disapprove of violence and other offending and thus indeed must neutralize guilt or shame before engaging in delinquent acts (Agnew 1994). This research "does much to provide support for the arguments of Sykes and Matza" (Agnew 1994:573).

Review and Discuss

What are the five techniques of neutralization discussed by Sykes and Matza? How have some scholars criticized their view of deviance and crime?

TRAVIS HIRSCHI: SOCIAL BONDING THEORY

Have you ever refused to join your friends in illegal behavior because you were worried about what your parents might think or about how it might affect your school record? Do you know people whose religious beliefs have led them to avoid drinking, using illegal drugs, or having sex? As these examples suggest, our bonds to conventional social institutions such as family, schools, and religion may keep us from committing deviant behavior. This is the central view of Travis Hirschi's *social bonding theory* (also called *social control theory*), which may be the most popular criminological theory today and certainly the most popular control theory. First presented in a 1969 book (Hirschi 1969), Hirschi's theory has since stimulated many investigations.

Strong parent–child attachment and other indicators of quality parenting are associated with lower delinquency.

Hirschi began his book by stating that human nature is selfish. Given this view, he said, the key question is why people do *not* commit crime. Drawing on Durkheim, his answer was that their bond to society's institutions keeps them from breaking the law. When that bond is weakened, they feel freer to deviate and crime results. Social bonding theory presents a social process or micro complement to the structural or macro view of social disorganization theory. If the latter theory says that crime flourishes in neighborhoods with weakened social institutions, social bonding theory argues that crime is more common among individuals with weakened bonds to the same institutions. Four elements of **social bonds** exist.

1. *Attachment.* **Attachment** is the most important social bond element and refers to the degree to which we care about the opinions of others, including parents and teachers. The more sensitive we are to their views, the less likely we are to violate norms, both because we have internalized their norms and because we do not want to

disappoint or hurt them. The opposite is also true: The less sensitive we are to their views, the more likely we are to break the law.

2. *Commitment.* This refers to an individual's investment of energy and emotion in conventional pursuits, such as getting a good education. The more committed people are in this sense, the more they have to lose if they break the law. People with low commitment to conventional pursuits thus are more likely to deviate.

3. *Involvement.* This is the amount of time an individual spends on a conventional pursuit. The argument here is that the more time spent, the less the opportunity to deviate.

4. *Belief.* This refers to acceptance of the norms of conventional society. People who believe in these norms are less likely to deviate than are those who reject them. Hirschi noted that all four elements are related, so that someone with a strong tie in one element tends to have strong ties in the others. For example, people who are strongly attached to parents and schools also tend to believe in conventional norms.

Hirschi tested his hypotheses with a sample of about 4,000 male junior and senior high school students from the San Francisco Bay area. He asked them many questions about their delinquency and the four social bond elements just outlined, including their feelings about their parents and teachers, the amount of time they spent on various school activities, and what they thought about conventional pursuits such as getting a good education. His analysis yielded considerable support for his theory. For example, youths who felt very close to their parents were less likely to be delinquent than youths who felt more distant.

Social bonding theory has won wide acclaim, with support for it found in dozens of studies of delinquency (Lilly, Cullen, and Ball 2011). These studies generally find that delinquency is lower among teens who feel close to their parents, who like their teachers, who value their schooling and take part in school activities, and who believe in the conventional rules of society.

Social Bonding Theory and the Context of Delinquency

Most of the research inspired by social bonding theory focuses on the family, school, and religious contexts of delinquency. We examine these briefly to indicate the theory's impact and application.

THE FAMILY

To study the role played by the family in delinquency, researchers distinguish between family structure and family functioning. **Family structure** refers to the way the family is set up or organized, whereas **family interaction** or *family functioning* refers to the nature of the interaction and relationships within the family.

Regarding family structure, the most studied component is *family disruption* in the form of a household headed by a single parent, usually the mother, because of divorce, birth out of wedlock, or, less commonly, the death of a parent (Fomby and Cherlin 2007). Because there is only one parent to supervise the children and father role models are lacking for sons, such households are popularly thought to contribute to delinquency. Supporting this view, many studies find that children from single-parent households are indeed more at risk for serious juvenile offending (Demuth and Brown 2004). Yet some studies do not find this presumed relationship once these households' low income is taken into account or find it limited to *status offenses*, such as truancy and running away from home, or to drinking and drug use (Rankin and Kern 1994). These studies conclude that if children from single-parent households are more likely to be delinquent, it is because their families are poor, not because their families have only one parent.

International Focus

Social Bonding in the Land of the Rising Sun

Japan has long had the lowest crime rate in the industrialized world, or nearly so. The 2004–2005 International Crime Victims Survey (ICVS) found that 9.9 percent of Japanese had been victimized by crime in the previous year; this figure ranked Japan as next to last among the thirty industrialized nations included in the ICVS. By contrast, 17.5 percent of U.S. residents had been victimized. Japan ranked lowest in assaults and threats, with only 0.6 percent reporting being assaulted or threatened during the past year; the U.S. rate was seven times higher at 4.3 percent. Japan is thus a very safe nation, even though its popular culture—films, TV shows, and so on—depicts a great deal of violence and its history is filled with war, murders of peasants, political assassinations, and other violence.

Given this background, why is Japan's crime rate so low? According to Hirschi's social bonding theory, the stronger an individual's bonds to conventional social institutions such as the family and schools are, the less likely the individual will be to break the law. Does Hirschi's view help understand Japan's low crime rate?

In explaining its low rate, several scholars emphasize the Japanese culture, in particular the value it places on *group-belonging*. From birth the Japanese are taught that the group is more important than the individual. The family, the school, and the workplace are the subjects of great respect and authority in Japanese culture. In school, individual achievement is not as important as a whole classroom's achievement. At home, Japanese families are known for their high levels of love and harmony. Children sleep with their parents from birth until they are about 5 years old. When they misbehave, parents punish them by locking them out of the house, whereas U.S. children are often punished by being "grounded," or kept within the house. As scholar David H. Bayley says, "The effect is that American children are taught that it is punishment to be locked up with one's family; Japanese children are taught that punishment is being excluded from one's family."

The emphasis on group-belonging in Japan promotes two other emphases, harmonious relationships and respect for authority. All three emphases contribute to especially strong social bonding in Japan and hence to its lower crime rates. Japanese children grow up strongly attached to their parents and teachers and very committed to obeying social norms. In contrast, U.S. children grow up much more independently, because U.S. culture emphasizes individualism rather than group-belonging. The ties U.S. children feel to parents, schools, and other conventional social institutions are weaker than those felt by Japanese children. With weaker bonds, U.S. adolescents are thus freer, as social bonding theory predicts, to violate social norms, which means they are freer to commit crime and delinquent acts.

Although some observers credit Japan's low crime rate to its criminal justice system, Japan's experience does seem to underscore the value of the social bond for reducing crime. It suggests that significant crime reduction could be achieved in the United States if children were more respectful of their parents and teachers and if family relationships were more harmonious. Are these qualities beyond the scope of social policy? For better or worse, the U.S. culture is not likely to become more similar to the Japanese culture. Japan's example suggests that it is possible to have an industrial society with low crime rates, but it also implies the difficulty of implementing the Japanese model in the United States. In this regard, family intervention programs for U.S. families at greatest risk for conflict may be an effective strategy for reducing crime.

Sources: Bayley 1996; Komiya 1999; Schneider and Silverman 2010; van Dijk, Kesteren, and Smit 2008.

Reflecting the impact of social bonding theory, most scholars believe that family interaction is more important than family structure for delinquency. Many studies link strong parent–child attachment and other indicators of quality parenting to lower delinquency. To turn that around, delinquency is more often found among children with cold and distant relationships with their parents and among children whose parents do not supervise them adequately. Children with such relationships are more apt to reject their parents' values and rules, as Hirschi thought, but are also more vulnerable to their friends' delinquent influences (Warr 2005).

In related research, harsh or erratic discipline and especially physical and sexual abuse are also thought to contribute to delinquency (Welsh and Farrington 2007). In contrast, *firm but fair* discipline, which involves clear but fair rules and positive feedback, seems to prevent delinquency, in part because it leads to greater internalization of parental values (Rankin and Wells 1990). Conversely, harsh discipline may lower children's affection for their parents and, as Hirschi noted, increase their delinquency potential. In addition, because corporal punishment teaches children that violence is an acceptable solution to interpersonal conflict, it may ironically lead to violent aggression in adolescence and adulthood, especially when the punishment becomes abusive (Teague et al. 2008).

These negative family influences are especially found among children born to teenage mothers. Their families tend to be unstable (male partners moving in and out), to have low incomes, and to live in disadvantaged neighborhoods, and the mothers are more likely to practice ineffective parenting. All these reasons are thought to explain why their children are more at risk for abuse and neglect, low school achievement, aggressive behavior during childhood, and delinquency during adolescence (Welsh and Farrington 2007).

Review and Discuss

If parents want to reduce their children's chances of growing up to be delinquents, what type of discipline should they practice? Why?

SCHOOLS

A large literature on schooling and delinquency also exists. Supporting social bonding theory views, adolescents with poor grades and negative attitudes about their teachers, their schools, and the importance of education are more likely to be delinquent than youths with good grades and positive attitudes (Kirk 2009; Payne 2009). Adolescents who are less involved in school extracurricular activities are also more likely to be delinquent. Once again, though, questions remain on causal order, as it is possible that delinquency and delinquent peers affect students' perceptions of their schools and involvement in school activities.

According to social bonding theory, students with poor grades and negative attitudes about their teachers and schools are more likely than those with good grades and positive attitudes to commit delinquent acts.

Social bonding theory's explanation of the relationship between various school factors and delinquency relationships is different from that of strain theory. As you m5ight recall from Chapter 7, Albert Cohen's status frustration theory argued that school failure leads to frustration and hence to delinquency to resolve that frustration. Control theory instead argues that failure in and negative attitudes about school prompt youths to reject the conformist values of school and the legitimacy of school authorities to tell them how to behave, with frustration playing no role.

An interesting controversy is whether dropping out of school promotes or reduces delinquency. The Crime and Controversy box discusses this issue further.

Crime and Controversy

Does Dropping Out of School Promote or Reduce Delinquency?

Most people would probably think that youths who drop out of school are at greater risk for committing delinquency. They have more time to spend with their friends and thus have more opportunity to get into trouble. Also, if strong bonds to school help reduce delinquency, as social bonding theory assumes, then teens who drop out of school should be at greater risk for delinquency because they eliminate all their school bonds.

However, Albert Cohen's status frustration theory (see Chapter 7) predicts that dropping out should reduce delinquency. Because Cohen thought delinquency arises from poor school performance that leads to status frustration, a logical prediction from his theory is that dropping out of school should reduce this frustration and thus reduce delinquency. The best studies that test this hypothesis take into account the age at which students drop out and also why they drop out (poor grades, problems at home, financial problems, etc.), and they

also control for important variables such as social class and prior delinquency. However, these studies report very inconsistent results: Some studies find that dropping out increases delinquency, some studies find that dropping out decreases delinquency, and some studies find that dropping out does not affect delinquency.

It is also possible that dropping out and delinquency are both the result of other problems, including having a mother who had her first child when she was a teenager and having a history of antisocial behavior since childhood, as recent research has found. To the extent this is true, the statistical correlations that are sometimes found between dropping out and delinquency may be spurious. As a recent study observed, "This finding suggests that concern about the event of dropout may be misplaced. Instead, attention must be focused on the process that leads to dropout and criminal involvement; this process seems to begin to take place at an early age."

Sources: Jarjoura 1993; Sweeten, Bushway, and Paternoster 2009.

RELIGION

Following Durkheim (1947 [1915]), sociologists have long considered religion an important force for social stability. Accordingly, many think that religious belief and practice (*religiosity*) should help to prevent delinquent and criminal behavior, as social bonding theory would predict.

A growing body of research finds that youths who are more religious are indeed less likely to be delinquent, although the effect may be stronger for drinking, drug use, and sexual behavior than for other kinds of delinquency (Petts 2009; Wallace et al. 2007). Extending the relationship to adults, studies of national and local data link religiosity to reduced criminality during adulthood (Evans et al. 1995; Petts 2009). Other national research even suggests that

Greater religiosity is associated in several studies with lower rates of juvenile delinquency and adult criminality.

religiosity reduces premarital sex among never-married adults (Barkan 2006). At the macro level, violent crime is lower in rural counties with more churches per capita than in those with fewer churches (Lee 2006).

One problem in interpreting the religiosity–delinquency relationship is that teens who crave excitement tend to be bored with religion, and are hence less religious and also more likely to commit delinquency. If so, the relationship may be at least partially spurious (Cochran, Wood, and Arneklev 1994). However, a test of this possibility with national longitudinal data found that religiosity had a nonspurious effect on delinquency, in part because it increased disapproval of delinquency and the proportion of law-abiding friends (Johnson et al. 2001).

Evaluation of Social Bonding Theory

The research just discussed on the social contexts of delinquency gives ready evidence of social bonding theory's importance. The theory has also been lauded for helping to understand gender and age differences in delinquency. Girls are less delinquent than boys in part because they are more attached to family and school, more likely to hold conventional beliefs, and more closely supervised by their parents (Agnew 2009). Turning to age, recall that criminality decreases as adolescents become adults (Chapter 3). One reason for this is that many young adults marry, join the workforce, and otherwise become more involved in conventional society. As social bonding theory predicts, these new conventional social bonds help reduce their criminality (Farrington 2003).

Still, critics note several problems with the theory. First, relationships between social bonding and delinquency in the research tend to be rather weak, suggesting that various social bonds may not matter as much as the theory assumes (Lilly, Cullen, and Ball 2011). Some research also finds that social bonds are more weakly related to serious delinquency than they are to minor delinquency, suggesting that the theory explains minor offending better than it explains serious offending.

Another problem concerns the familiar chicken-and-egg question of causal order. If, for example, youths with weak parental attachment are more delinquent than those with strong parental attachment, does this mean that parental attachment influences delinquency or that delinquency influences parental attachment? Fortunately, there are studies investigating this issue with longitudinal data (Liska and Reed 1985; Stewart et al. 2002). Significantly, they find a reciprocal relationship: Weak social bonds help produce delinquency, but delinquency also weakens social bonds (Liska and Reed 1985; Stewart et al. 2002). These findings do support social bonding theory, but they also indicate that the reason for some of the statistical support is the reverse of what the theory assumes.

Two final criticisms exist. First, the theory's concepts of commitment and involvement cannot easily be distinguished from each other: It is difficult to imagine someone spending a lot of time on a conventional pursuit who is not also committed to it (Krohn 2000). For example, is time spent on homework best seen as a measure of involvement in school or as a commitment to the importance of education? Second, the theory cannot easily explain certain geographical differences in crime (Bohm and Vogel 2011). If, say, Texas has a higher delinquency rate than Maine, it is doubtful that Texan children are less attached than Maine children to their parents.

In sum, Hirschi's social bonding theory has been very influential and for very good reasons. At the same time, questions remain about several issues, including the strength and direction of the social bond–criminality relationship that is so often found.

Review and Discuss

How does Hirschi's view of human nature relate to his social bonding theory of crime and deviance? In his theory, what are the four elements of the bonds that individuals have to their society?

MICHAEL GOTTFREDSON AND TRAVIS HIRSCHI: SELF-CONTROL THEORY

In 1990, Hirschi coauthored a book with Michael Gottfredson that revised social control theory to present a "general theory of crime," as the book was entitled (Gottfredson and Hirschi 1990). They argued that all crime stems from one problem: the lack of **self-control,** which results from ineffective child rearing and lasts throughout life. People with low self-control act impulsively and spontaneously, value risk and adventure, and care about themselves more than they do about others. They are thus more likely than people with high self-control to commit crime, because all types of crime, said the authors, are spontaneous and exciting and require little skill. This is as true for white-collar crime as for petty theft and assault. Self-control, or more precisely, low self-control, thus "explains all crime, at all times" (p. 117). Low self-control often continues into adulthood and thus explains adult criminality as well as juvenile delinquency. In stressing low self-control, Gottfredson and Hirschi explicitly minimized or ruled out the effects of other problems such as economic deprivation and peer influences. They thus declared that the only hope to reduce crime lies in improving child rearing. Policies focusing on structural causes of crime and on criminal opportunities will, they said, have little effect.

Self-control theory, as their theory has come to be called, has generated much research, most of which finds that individuals with low self-control are indeed more likely to commit various kinds of offenses and to have other kinds of problems as well (Miller, Jennings, and Alvarez-Rivera 2009; Vazsonyi and Klanjšek 2008; Meldrum, Young, and Weerman 2009; Piquero and Bouffard 2007). Studies also find that differences in self-control help to understand the gender difference in criminality: Males have less self-control than females and partly for this reason they commit more delinquent acts (Agnew 2009). As Chapter 4 noted, some research also finds that low self-control helps make people more vulnerable to being victimized by crime (Holtfreter, Reisig, and Pratt 2008). In another area, a recent study found that low self-control makes it more likely that suspects will be hostile toward police and thus be arrested (Beaver et al. 2009).

Evaluation of Self-Control Theory

Although self-control theory is very popular, it, too, has been criticized (Akers and Sellers 2009; Piquero and Piquero 2010). One problem is that it engages in circular (or *tautological*) reasoning: Because crime is considered evidence of low self-control, crime is being used to explain itself. To help avoid this problem, most tests of the theory use attitudinal measures of low self-control, such as losing one's temper and thinking only about short-term consequences, but critics say the theory remains somewhat tautological nonetheless.

Low self-control, including the tendency to act impulsively and to care about oneself more than others, develops during childhood and results from inadequate parenting.

A second problem is that the actual effects of low self-control are not very strong (Pratt and Cullen 2000) and that it overstates its case in claiming that low self-control is the only factor that matters for delinquency and crime. Contrary to this assumption, factors such as peer influences also matter and may even be more important than low self-control (Akers and Sellers 2009), and neuropsychological problems may also matter (Wright and Beaver 2005). In a third problem, critics say the theory, contrary to its assumptions, does not apply equally well across gender and racial categories of people (Morris, Wood, and Dunaway 2006).

Two additional problems concern other assumptions of the theory. Contrary to its assumption that low self-control and its effects on criminal behavior last throughout life, ample evidence exists that people with a history of offending can "straighten out" when they reach adulthood, thanks to marriage, employment, and other such influences (Doherty 2006; Laub, Sampson, and Sweeten 2006). The theory's assumption that ineffective child rearing is the sole source of low self-control has also been questioned. At the individual level, low self-control also results from neuropsychological deficits (Boutwell and Beaver 2010). At the structural level, low self-control results from living in socially disorganized neighborhoods—those with high levels of poverty and low levels of collective efficacy (see Chapter 7) (Gibson et al. 2010; Teasdale and Silver 2009).

A final criticism focuses on Gottfredson and Hirschi's assumption that all crime, including white-collar crime, is spontaneous and unskilled. To the contrary, many crimes do not fit this description, in particular corporate and other business crime, which involves much planning and skill (Geis 2000). Although low self-control may explain some types of crime, it does not appear to explain white-collar crime.

In sum, self-control theory helps explain some criminal and delinquent behavior, and the empirical support for it has been "fairly impressive" (Pratt and Cullen 2000:951). However, it does not seem to offer the all-powerful general theory of crime its authors intended and claimed.

Review and Discuss

What are any three problems associated with self-control theory? In your opinion, to what degree does self-control theory offer a better understanding of delinquency and crime than the other theories presented in this chapter?

CHARLES R. TITTLE: CONTROL BALANCE THEORY

Another control theory is Charles R. Tittle's (2004) *control balance theory*, which has been applauded as "one of the most important theoretical contributions to the sociology of deviance" (Braithwaite 1997:77). Tittle observed that some people, by virtue of their roles and personal qualities, can exercise considerable control over other people. At the same time, some people are more easily controlled by other people. When people are either very controlling or very controlled, Tittle said, they are more likely to engage in deviance than when their *control ratio*, the degree to which they exercise control versus the degree to which they experience control, is in balance. Thus, people with a *control surplus*, such as corporate executives, tend to commit crime, albeit of the white-collar variety, and those with a *control deficit*, such as the urban poor, also tend to commit crime.

Why does control ratio make a difference? Tittle assumed that people want to be as autonomous as possible. If they have a control deficit, they break the law to achieve more control over their lives, if only by victimizing someone else, and to lessen the feelings of humiliation and inferiority arising from their control deficit. If they have a control surplus, they break the law because they greedily want even more control and because they realize that the control they exert reduces their risk of sanctions for lawbreaking.

Tests of control balance theory generally support it (Baron and Forde 2007; Piquero and Piquero 2006). In one study, 146 college students were asked to read several scenarios in which individuals engaged in various deviant activities and then to indicate the likelihood that they would do the same. The students were also asked several questions to measure the amount of control they exercised and the amount of control they experienced. Supporting Tittle's theory, students with control surpluses and control deficits were both more likely than those with a control balance to indicate that they would engage in the deviant activities (Piquero and Hickman 1999).

MARK COLVIN AND FRANCIS T. CULLEN: COERCIVE CONTROL AND SOCIAL SUPPORT THEORY

A final control theory is Mark Colvin and Francis T. Cullen's *coercive control and social support theory* (Colvin, Cullen, and Ven 2002). Coercion is defined as "a force that compels or intimidates an individual to act because of the fear or anxiety it creates" (Colvin and Cullen 2002:19) and can be micro (e.g., someone threatens or humiliates you) or macro (e.g., poverty) in nature. Social support is defined as "assistance from communities, social networks, and confiding partners in meeting the instrumental and expressive needs of individuals" (p. 20) and can also be micro or macro in nature. The theory argues that coercion causes crime and that social support reduces or prevents it. Coercion promotes criminal behavior because it first leads to anger, frustration, alienation, weaker self-control and social bonds, and then to a belief that actions to avenge coercion are acceptable. Social support reduces crime because it helps people meet their emotional and practical needs.

The theory is still too new to have been adequately tested, but some research has supported it (Baron 2009; Unnever, Colvin, and Cullen 2004). One study used involved data on almost 2,500 students from six middle schools in Virginia. The students were asked to indicate the extent of their exposure to four types of coercion: (1) parental coercion (e.g., corporal punishment), (2) peer coercion (e.g., being bullied), (3) neighborhood coercion (e.g., whether they considered their neighborhood dangerous), and (4) school coercion (e.g., whether they considered their school dangerous). Supporting the theory, students with high scores on three types of coercion (all except peer coercion) were more likely to be delinquent and to be so partly because coercion weakened their parental and school bonding and made them more likely to favor revengeful actions after being coerced (Unnever, Colvin, and Cullen 2004).

Life-Course Theories

Learning and control theories typically focus on delinquency during adolescence. Aided by the growth of longitudinal data, however, criminologists have begun to pay attention to the onset and termination of antisocial behavior, delinquency, and crime at different stages over the **life course:** infancy, childhood, adolescence, young adulthood, and beyond. These criminologists have formulated and tested *life-course theories* (also called *developmental theories*), and their theories and research are together called *life-course criminology* (Farrington 2006; Loeber et al. 2008; Wright, Tibbetts, and Daigle 2008). Criminologists who favor this perspective come from biological, psychological, and sociological backgrounds, and their work draws on many of the explanations presented in this and the previous two chapters, while also drawing from important work in developmental psychology.

Their research addresses many questions, some of which we have already encountered, and include (1) Why are some children more at risk for engaging in antisocial behavior, including delinquency and crime? (2) To what degree do childhood behavioral problems predict similar problems during adolescence? (3) Why do

Life-course explanations emphasize the importance of parenting during childhood and adolescence on the likelihood of behavioral problems in young and older children alike.

some juvenile delinquents continue their criminal ways well into adulthood, whereas most desist after leaving their teenage years? (4) Why are delinquency and crime highest in middle to late adolescence, and why do they decline thereafter? (5) Which factors matter more for delinquency at different stages of adolescence? (6) Which factors help explain why some adolescents and adults who have been involved in crime later decide to desist from it? and (7) How does the importance of all these factors differ by gender or race and ethnicity?

In explaining the onset of offending, life-course research identifies many of the *risk factors* we have already reviewed: extreme poverty, inadequate parenting, poor family relationships and school performance, delinquent peers, and unemployment. Two insights from this research are especially valuable. First, many children with these risk factors do *not* end up committing delinquent acts because various events and processes during the life course—better parenting, positive school experiences, supportive friendships with law-abiding peers—may intervene. Second, criminal offenders may *desist* from crime because of certain *turning points*, such as marriage and employment, that increase social attachments, promote conventional beliefs, reduce the opportunity for offending (for example, by keeping someone busy at home or at work), and minimize the influence of criminal peers (Laub, Sampson, and Sweeten 2006; Thompson and Petrovic 2009).

SPECIFIC LIFE-COURSE THEORIES

Several life-course theories exist and share many features while having different emphases. Brief summaries of a few life-course theories follow.

Delbert S. Elliott: Integrated Strain-Control Theory

Delbert S. Elliott and colleagues (Elliott, Ageton, and Canter 1979; Elliott, Huizinga, and Ageton 1985) formulated one of the most popular integrated theories, which they termed an *integrated strain-control* theory. Although this theory was not originally conceived as a life-course theory, it nonetheless incorporates life-course components and thus may be regarded as a life-course perspective. Elliott and colleagues integrated strain, social learning, and social control theories into their approach, which they considered a better explanation of delinquency than any one of the three theories by itself.

In their view, childhood socialization affects whether bonds to society become weak or strong. Weak bonds are more likely for children living in very poor and otherwise socially disorganized areas. During adolescence, youths achieve success or failure in schooling and other conventional activities, with failure causing further strain. Peer influences become very important during this time. Adolescents with weak bonds to their parents and schools and experiencing strain from failure in conventional activities are particularly vulnerable to the criminogenic influence of delinquent peers. Failure and strain may also weaken the strong bonds that some adolescents initially have and prompt these adolescents to spend more time with delinquent friends and thus to engage in delinquent acts themselves. Thus, although delinquency most often results from weak bonds in childhood that then lead to associations with delinquent peers, even strong childhood bonds may weaken because of adolescent strains and open the door to delinquent peer associations and delinquency itself.

Terence P. Thornberry: Interactional Theory

Another life-course perspective is Terence P. Thornberry's *interactional theory* (Thornberry 1987; Thornberry 2009; Thornberry et al. 1994). This theory is similar to integrated strain-control theory, as it emphasizes that strong childhood bonds to parents reduce the risk for delinquency and weak bonds raise this risk, in particular by increasing associations with delinquent peers. But Thornberry adds that delinquency and association with delinquent peers can weaken parental and school bonds in a type of vicious cycle that increases delinquency even further. Thornberry also argues that the relative importance of parental and school bonds and peer associations for delinquency changes as youths become older. During early adolescence, parental bonds matter more, and during middle adolescence, school bonds and peer associations matter more. More generally, Thornberry emphasizes that parental and school bonds can change as other aspects of a youth's life change.

With colleague Marvin D. Krohn, Thornberry also used his theory to explain why antisocial behavior emerges at different stages of the life course (Thornberry and Krohn 2005). During childhood and early adolescence (up through age 11), youngsters who develop behavior problems tend to do so for several reasons: (1) they live in disadvantaged neighborhoods, (2) their parents' child rearing is inadequate, (3) they do poorly in school, and (4) and they associate with misbehaving friends. Such youths are at great risk for continuing their antisocial behavior well into adolescence, where it can take on very serious forms. During middle adolescence (ages 12 to 16), some teens who had previously been well behaved nonetheless begin to misbehave in relatively minor ways (e.g., drinking, experimental drug use, shoplifting), and they do so partly because of negative peer associations that they develop during this time. As these teens leave middle adolescence, they tend to end their minor misbehavior. During young adulthood, a relatively small number of individuals who had not really misbehaved earlier nonetheless begin to break the law. These tend to be individuals who had certain personal problems when they were younger that did not translate into delinquency because they were protected by strong parental and school bonds. When they reach young adulthood, however, they leave this protective environment, and negative peer influences may now have an impact. These individuals may also encounter employment and relationship problems, and these, too, may lead them to commit crime.

Terrie E. Moffitt: Life-Course-Persistent/Adolescence-Limited Theory

Terrie E. Moffitt's (1993; 2006) very influential *life-course-persistent/adolescence-limited theory*, related to her longitudinal research reviewed in Chapter 6, attempts to explain the onset and patterning of two distinct types of antisocial behavior. As the theory's name implies, it assumes that antisocial behavior either persists across the life course or instead is limited to adolescence. Individuals whose antisocial behavior is life-course persistent comprise less than 10 percent of the population. Their misbehavior begins during childhood and continues, often in very serious form, well into adulthood. To recall some terminology from Chapter 1, they are *chronic criminals*. According to the theory, these individuals suffer from neuropsychological problems that often begin during the prenatal period and then lead to psychological problems during childhood and in turn to serious misbehavior. Life-course-persistent offenders also tend to grow up in disadvantaged neighborhoods and to suffer from inadequate parenting.

In contrast, adolescence-limited offenders begin their offending during adolescence and largely end it once they leave adolescence. They drink, engage in experimental drug use, and commit minor forms of delinquency as a way of expressing their growing maturity and independence from their parents. In a sense, their offending is a normal pattern of behavior during this stage of life that is heavily influenced by peer associations. As they leave adolescence, they also end their pattern of minor offending as they take on new adult responsibilities, such as employment and marriage. In general, adolescence-limited offenders come from more advantaged social backgrounds and had parents who practiced effective parenting.

Some critics question Moffitt's assumption that offenders fall only into the two categories she has identified (Lilly, Cullen, and Ball 2011). For example, life-course-persistent offenders may not be as homogeneous as Moffitt assumes, as some commit serious offenses and others commit only minor offenses. Similarly, some adolescence-limited offenders commit serious offenses, even if most commit only minor offenses. These criticisms notwithstanding, Moffitt's taxonomy has been very influential in directing criminological attention to chronic offenders and to the reasons for their persistent offending over much of the life course.

Robert J. Sampson and John H. Laub: Age-Graded Theory

Another very influential theory is John H. Laub and Robert J. Sampson's *age-graded theory* (Laub and Sampson 2003; Sampson and Laub 1993; Sampson and Laub 2005). Laub and Sampson recognize the importance of the many factors outlined in other life-course perspectives, in particular bonds to parents and school during childhood and adolescence, the quality and effectiveness of parenting, and the influence of one's friends. However, they especially emphasize that key events over the life course act as turning points in helping individuals to desist from crime. These turning points during adulthood include marriage, stable employment, and military service. Individuals with a history of offending who enter adulthood and then get married and land a stable job, for example, may well stop their criminal behavior.

In emphasizing that such turning points can lead to desistance from crime, Laub and Sampson take issue with the idea that serious antisocial behavior that begins in childhood necessarily persists throughout the life course. In this regard, they challenge key assumptions of Moffitt's theory and of Gottfredson and Hirschi's self-control theory discussed earlier. Supporting Laub and Sampson's view, research finds that marriage and parenthood tend to inhibit criminality (Bersani, Laub, and Nieuwbeerta 2009; King, Massoglia, and MacMillan 2007; Kreager, Matsueda, and Erosheva 2010).

A recent study challenged one of Laub and Sampson's conclusions from their analysis of the data collected during the World War II era, that military service reduces criminality. This conclusion left unclear whether military service per se reduces offending or whether only military service during World War II reduced offending. Using data on youths from the Vietnam War era, Wright, Carter, and Cullen (2005) found that youths who served in Vietnam were more likely after leaving the military to use drugs and commit crime than their counterparts who did not serve in the military. Thus, although service in World War II may have been a positive turning point that led to desistance from crime, service in Vietnam was a negative turning point that led to increased drug use and criminal behavior.

THE PROMISE AND PROBLEM OF THEORETICAL INTEGRATION

Because life-course theories often combine factors highlighted in other theories, they are often considered *integrated theories*. Many scholars favor **theoretical integration** because they feel that neither a social process nor a structural approach can adequately explain crime by itself: Social process theories cannot easily account for structural variation in criminality, and structural theories cannot easily account for individual variation in crime among people living in similar structural conditions. A more comprehensive understanding of crime thus might be achieved by integrating social process and structural factors.

Several integrated theories of crime have been developed (Akers and Sellers 2009), and an example of an integrated model appears in Figure 8.1. In recent examples of models that combined structural and social process factors, Ronald L. Simons and colleagues (Simons et al. 2005) found that high-quality authoritative parenting is more common in neighborhoods with high levels of collective efficacy and that both authoritative parenting and collective efficacy reduce delinquency. They also found a stronger deterrent effect of authoritative parenting on delinquency in neighborhoods with high levels of collective efficacy than in those with low levels. Similarly, Dana L. Haynie and colleagues (Haynie, Silver, and Teasdale 2006) found that disadvantaged neighborhoods have higher rates of violence in part because they provide greater opportunities for youths to associate with violent peers.

More limited integrated models that combine only social process factors also exist. Combining social bonding and self-control theories, a recent study of teen offenders found

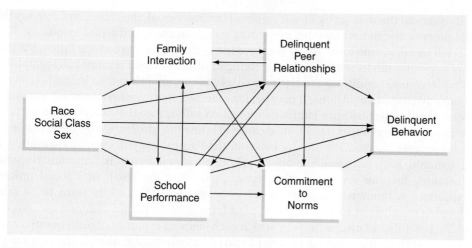

FIGURE 8.1 ▸ A Sample of an Integrated Model of Delinquency

that those with low self-control had weakened social bonds to family and school and, for that reason, were more likely to have a greater history of delinquency (Longshore, Chang, and Messina 2005). Similarly, combining social learning and self-control theories, another study found that teens with low self-control were more likely to develop ties to delinquent peers and, partly for this reason, to be more delinquent (Chapple 2005).

As surprising as it might seem, some scholars dispute the value of integrated theories. Self-control theory proponent Travis Hirschi (1989), for example, believes that theoretical integration does more harm than good. In his view, some theories are so different that to integrate them yields a "theoretical mush" (Akers 1989:24) that weakens their ability to explain crime. Even scholars who favor theoretical integration concede that it may nonetheless reduce the "clarity and strength" of the theories that are integrated (Thornberry 1989:56). In contrast, other scholars think theoretical integration can be useful if the theories to be integrated complement each other. This is particularly true, said learning theorist Ronald L. Akers (1989:28), for structural theories and social learning theory because "social learning is the basic process by which the structural variables specified in the macro-level theories have an effect on deviant behavior." Akers also notes the compatibility of social learning and social control theories.

As should be clear, theoretical integration in criminology holds much promise but is not without some risk. Future work will determine if it leads to useless "mush" or instead to a more comprehensive explanation of crime and delinquency. In this regard, life-course criminology offers a very promising approach to understand a myriad of issues regarding the onset and termination of crime and other antisocial behavior at different stages of our lives.

Review and Discuss

What are the advantages and disadvantages of integrated theories of criminality? What are the major questions that life-course and developmental theories try to answer?

Conclusion

Social process theories of crime emphasize learning, socialization, human interaction, and other social processes. They help us understand why some individuals are more likely than others to commit crime even if they live in similar circumstances. As such, they are an important complement to structural theories, which say much about the social and economic roots of crime, but little about the mechanisms through which structural conditions generate crime.

If structural theories err by forgetting about the individual, then it is also fair to say that social process theories err by often neglecting social structure and social inequality. They might tell us why some individuals are more likely than others to commit crime, but they do not explicitly tell us why individuals living in disadvantaged economic, geographical, or other structural conditions are also more likely to commit crime than individuals living in more advantaged conditions. It may be, for example, that street crime is more common in poor communities because family relationships suffer from the stresses of poverty, but such an explanation traces the ultimate cause of crime to a structural condition instead of a social process mechanism. Debate between the two camps will certainly continue, as well it should: Both have much to offer, but both are also deficient in important respects.

Learning theories remind us that deviance is often the result of a social process, socialization, without which social order is impossible. Most of us learn to be fairly conforming members of society, but some of us learn to be criminals. Different learning theories discuss different mechanisms by which such learning occurs. Although questions still remain about the causal sequence involved and other important problems, the emphasis of learning theories on socialization and on peer influences is one of the most important themes in criminology today.

Control theories assume a pessimistic view of human nature. People are basically selfish and hedonistic and will deviate unless controlled by society. Although different control theories focus on different kinds of constraints, all assume that there would be social chaos without these constraints. Hirschi's social bonding theory has been the most influential formulation, with his emphasis on the parent–child bond receiving the most attention. Although the theory has been criticized, it has greatly expanded our knowledge of the micro origins of criminal behavior and helps to explain the gendered patterning of criminal behavior.

Increasingly popular, life-course and developmental theories combine insights from biology, psychology, and sociology to examine the many factors affecting the onset, persistence, and termination of antisocial behavior over the many stages of our lives. Though not without some faults, integrated theories promise to offer a more comprehensive explanation of criminal behavior than any one theory can offer by itself.

We now turn to our final chapter on theory, in which we look at *critical* perspectives that challenge fundamental ideas in criminology and that also spend much more time than any of the theories already discussed on the social reaction to crime. Social inequality lies at the heart of these perspectives, so they are of special interest for the themes of this book. At the same time, some of these perspectives have been criticized by traditional criminologists at least as much as traditional criminology has been, and we will explore the controversy they generate.

8

Summary

1. Social process theories take up where social structural theories leave off. The latter cannot explain why some individuals living in criminogenic structural circumstances are led to commit crime, whereas most individuals in these same circumstances remain law-abiding citizens.

2. Learning theories say that criminal behavior is the result of socialization by peers and others with deviant values and lifestyles. Edwin Sutherland's differential association theory is the most influential learning theory. His basic emphasis on learning and peer pressure has received much empirical support

over the decades, although his theory has been criticized for several reasons, including the possibility that involvement in delinquency may influence associations with delinquent peers.

3. Control theories derive from Durkheim. They assume a selfish human nature and argue that individuals must be constrained by internal and external controls from following their natural impulses and committing antisocial behavior, including crime. Sykes and Matza's neutralization and drift theory assumes that adolescents rationalize that it is acceptable to break the law before actually committing delinquency in order to lessen any guilt or shame they might otherwise feel.

4. Hirschi's 1969 social bonding theory is the most influential control theory. It argues that strong social bonds to family and schools help prevent delinquency. Research inspired by social bonding theory finds that social bonds to parents, schooling, and religion all help reduce delinquency. This theory, too, is subject to causal order questions. Hirschi and Gottfredson's more recent self-control theory has also generated much interest but also much controversy, thanks in part to the authors' declaration that low self-control is by far the most important reason for all criminal behavior.

5. Tittle's control balance theory states that deviance results when people are very controlling or very controlled. The reason for this is that people want to be as autonomous as possible. Those with control deficits break the law to achieve more control over their lives, and those with a control surplus break the law because they desire even more control.

6. Life-course criminology focuses on the onset and termination of crime and delinquency stages over the life course. This perspective emphasizes developmental problems in infancy and childhood that create antisocial behavior that may continue into adolescence and even beyond. It also emphasizes that criminality lessens as people move into adulthood because of increasing stakes in conformity through strengthened bonds to family, work, and other conventional social institutions.

7. Some criminologists favor theoretical integration in which concepts or whole theories are blended to yield what is intended to be a more comprehensive and therefore better explanation of criminality. Others feel that theoretical integration reduces the clarity of the theories and their ability to explain crime.

Key Terms

attachment 195

containment 193

conventional social institutions 193

delinquent peers 188

differential association 188

drift 194

family interaction 196

family structure 196

learning theories 188

life course 203

personal controls 193

self-control 201

social bonds 195

social controls 193

socialization 186

social learning 192

theoretical integration 206

What Would You Do?

1. You have a son in first grade. It is about halfway through the school year. Your son has always been rambunctious, but lately his attention span and behavior seem even worse. You think this has happened because two of his new classmates are wild boys themselves. What do you do?

2. Your daughter, the oldest of your three children, just started ninth grade. She has always been a nice, well-behaved young woman, but one day you notice an empty can of beer when you are cleaning out her backpack. You confront her with the can and she says in an angry voice, "It's no big deal!" You want her to know that you trust her, but you also don't want her to be drinking. You are worried that if you come down too hard on her, your relationship with her will deteriorate. You are also worried that if you don't come down hard enough, she won't get the message. What do you do?

CHAPTER

nine

Sociological Theories: Critical Perspectives

Crime in the News

n May 2010, Reggie Deshawn Cole of Los Angeles was released from prison after a fourteen-year term for a murder and attempted robbery that someone else committed. DNA and fingerprint evidence at the scene of the crime did not point to Cole as the culprit, but he was arrested and convicted largely on the testimony of someone who said he had seen Cole shoot the victim. A three-year investigation by about two dozen lawyers and law students strongly suggested that this "eyewitness" gave false testimony and may have even been the person who committed the murder. A law professor who helped direct the investigation remarked, "Reggie's case is another example of a shoddy investigation leading to a wrongful conviction, I'm grateful that he is released, but there are many more people still in prison who have suffered the same injustice."

Source: KTLA-TV 2010.

Despite their many differences, the sociological theories examined in the preceding two chapters are similar in several ways. They are all *positivist* theories: They try to explain why crime occurs and they locate its causes in the immediate social environment or in the whole society. These theories do not ask how particular behaviors and people come to be defined as crimes and criminals, and they disregard how social networks and social institutions respond to crime. They also do not wonder how and why some people such as Reggie Cole are mistaken as criminals. Although many of the theories suggest the need for social reforms to reduce crime, none urges the drastic overhaul of society's social and economic foundations. In these various ways, these sociological theories might all be called *traditional theories*.

Critical perspectives on crime take a different view. Because they highlight the ways in which people and institutions respond to crime and criminals, they are often called *social reaction* theories. Although critical perspectives differ in many respects, they all consider the definition of crime *problematic*, meaning that the definition of a behavior as a crime and the defining of individuals as criminals are both something to explain. In explaining how these definitions originate, critical perspectives emphasize the concept of power and the inequality based on differences in power. Depending on the theory, power differences are based on social class, race or ethnicity, or gender. Whatever the source of the difference, the theories hold that behaviors by people or groups with power are less likely to be considered crimes than behaviors by those without power. The unfortunate story of Reggie Cole illustrates the importance of understanding how people come to be defined as criminals.

The various critical perspectives became popular in the 1960s and 1970s, a turbulent era highlighted by the civil rights movement, the Vietnam antiwar movement, and the beginning of the contemporary women's movement. Many sociology graduate students and younger sociology faculty took part in these movements, all of which questioned the status quo and emphasized the discriminatory and other damaging practices of social institutions. The civil rights movement and black power movements called attention to the racism pervading all aspects of society. The antiwar movement charged the U.S. government with committing genocide abroad and lying to its own citizens at home. The women's movement began to challenge the many inequities based on gender. "Question authority" and "don't trust anyone over 30" became rallying cries for a whole generation. Against this backdrop, it was perhaps inevitable that younger sociologists began to question traditional views of society, including those of crime. They wondered whether the chances of arrest and imprisonment had less to do with the crime itself and more to do with the suspect's race, social class, and gender.

This chapter discusses the major critical perspectives on crime. **Labeling** theory was the first critical perspective of the 1960s and was soon followed by various **conflict** theories. **Feminist** views on crime developed in the mid-1970s, in part because labeling and conflict theories neglected gender. Although all these theories stress the social reaction to crime, they also aim to explain the origins of crime. However, their explanations differ in important ways from those advanced by traditional theories. A summary of the critical perspectives discussed in this chapter appears in Table 9.1. We begin our discussion with labeling theory.

Labeling Theory

Labeling theory, which has been called "one of the most significant perspectives in the study of crime and deviance" (Matsueda 2001), addresses three major issues: (1) the definition of deviance and crime, (2) possible discrimination in the application of official labeling and sanctions, and (3) the effect of labeling on continued criminality.

TABLE 9.1 ▸ **Critical Perspectives in Brief**

THEORY	KEY FIGURE(S)	SYNOPSIS
Labeling Theory	Edwin Lemert Howard S. Becker	Deviance is not a quality of the act a person commits; some people and behaviors are more likely than others to be labeled deviant; the deviant label may lead to continued deviance.
Conflict and Radical Theories		
Conflict	Thorsten Sellin George Vold Austin T. Turk	Law and crime result from conflict among the various groups in society, not just economic classes.
Radical	Willem Bonger Jerome Hall William Chambliss Richard Quinney	The wealthy use the legal system to protect their dominance and to suppress the poor; the criminal law and justice system reflects the interests of the powerful.
Feminist Theories	Kathleen Daly Meda Chesney-Lind Sally S. Simpson	Crime cannot be fully understood and explained without appreciating the important role that gender plays; feminist theories can and should be used to reduce gender inequality in the areas of crime and criminal justice, as well as in the larger society.

THE RELATIVIST DEFINITION OF CRIME AND DEVIANCE

We start with labeling theory's definition of deviance. Traditional theories of deviance and crime adopt an *absolutist* definition of deviance as something real that is inherent in behavior. In contrast, labeling theory adopts a **relativist definition,** which we first encountered in Chapter 1, by assuming that nothing about a given behavior automatically makes it deviant. In this view, deviance is not a property of a behavior, but rather the result of how others regard the behavior. Howard S. Becker (1963:9), one of the originators of labeling theory, presented the theory's definition of deviance in perhaps the most widely quoted passage in the deviance and criminality literature in the last fifty years:

> Social groups create deviance by making the rules whose infraction constitutes deviance, and by applying those rules to particular people and labeling them as outsiders. From this point of view, deviance is not a quality of the act the person commits, but rather a consequence of the application by others of rules or sanctions to an "offender." The deviant is one to whom that label has been successfully applied; deviant behavior is behavior that people so label.

To illustrate this view, recall Chapter 1's discussion of murder, widely regarded as the most serious crime because it involves the taking of a human life. Labeling theory would say there is nothing inherent in murder that makes it deviant. Rather, murder is considered deviant because of the circumstances under which it occurs. Much killing occurs in wartime, but people who do the most killing in wars receive medals, not arrest records. We deem it acceptable and even necessary to kill in wartime, so we do not call it murder, as long as the rules of war are followed. A police officer who kills an armed criminal in self-defense does

Labeling theory assumes that wealthy, white people are less likely than other categories of people to be arrested or to suffer other legal sanctions.

not murder. Capital punishment also involves killing, but again, most of society does not consider an execution a murder.

THE IMPOSITION OF THE DEVIANT LABEL

In addition to defining deviance in an unusual way, labeling theory also discusses how official labeling (i.e., the identification of certain people as deviants) occurs. Traditional theories accept the accuracy of official labeling such as arrest and imprisonment. Labeling theory challenges this view and says that some people and behaviors are more likely than others to be labeled deviant. Simply put, people in power impose definitions of deviance on behaviors committed by people without power. Most tests of labeling theory focus on the effects of race and ethnicity, social class, and, more recently, gender on the chances of being labeled, with the argument being that official labeling discriminates against people of color, the poor, and women.

William Chambliss's (1973) famous discussion of the Saints and the Roughnecks provides a classic example of labeling theory's view. The Saints were eight extremely delinquent male high school students in a particular town. They drank routinely, committed truancy, drove recklessly, and engaged in petty theft and vandalism. One of their favorite activities was going to street construction sites at night and removing warning signals; they would then hide and watch cars bottom out in potholes and other cavities. As their name implies, the Saints, despite their behavior, were considered "good kids." They came from middle-class families and were never arrested because their offenses were dismissed as harmless pranks. When they grew into adulthood, they went to graduate and professional schools and became doctors, lawyers, and the like. The six Roughnecks fared much differently. They were also very delinquent and got into many fights, but caused less monetary damage than the Saints did. They came from poor families and were often in trouble with the police because everyone viewed them as troublemakers. When they grew into adulthood, they ended up in low-paying jobs and even prison.

Chambliss's analysis suggests that our impressions of people affect how likely they are to be officially labeled. Since the 1960s, many studies have examined whether *extralegal* factors such as race or ethnicity, social class, gender, and appearance affect the chances of arrest, imprisonment, and other official labeling. Overall, the evidence is inconsistent. Early studies found these variables to have the effects predicted by labeling theory, but later research found that official labeling was affected primarily by *legal* factors such as the weight of the evidence and the seriousness of the offense. Debate on the importance of extralegal factors continues to be among the most heated in the criminology literature (see Chapters 16 and 17). A reasonable view, shared by many but not all scholars, is that extralegal factors matter much less than legal factors. Race/ethnicity, social class, and gender do make a difference, but in more variable and subtle ways than depicted by labeling theory (Walker, Spohn, and DeLone 2007).

The evidence of only a fairly weak effect of extralegal factors leads many critics to dismiss labeling theory; they say that most people who are officially labeled have, in fact, committed the behavior for which they are labeled. Labeling proponents just as quickly point to the evidence supporting the theory. Regardless of where the weight of the evidence lies, it is fair to say that labeling theory generated a new focus forty years ago on the social reaction to crime and the operation of the legal system that continues to influence the study of crime and delinquency.

Review and Discuss

How does Chambliss's Saints and Roughnecks study provide support for labeling theory?

THE NEGATIVE CONSEQUENCES OF LABELING

One of the most important sociological principles is that our interaction with others shapes our conception of ourselves and affects our behavior. Labeling theorists build on this view, part of the *symbolic interactionist* approach in sociology (Abrahamson 2010), to present a similar dynamic. They stress that labeling someone deviant can produce a deviant self-image that prompts the person to commit more deviance. Frank Tannenbaum (1938), a historian of crime, called this process the **dramatization of evil** and said it "plays a greater role in making the criminal than perhaps any other experience." A person labeled deviant, said Tannenbaum, "becomes the thing he is described as being." Howard S. Becker (1963) highlighted a similar view twenty-five years later, noting that the "experience of being caught and publicly labeled as a deviant" is "one of the most crucial steps" leading to a deviant career, with "important consequences for one's further participation and self-image."

If labeling promotes continued deviance, says the theory, then *official* labeling by the legal system is counterproductive. In this view, arrest and imprisonment have the ironic effect of increasing deviance by generating a deviant self-image. The person labeled not only comes to accept the label, but also finds others treating her or him like a criminal. As a result, conventional opportunities and friendships are blocked: Jobs are hard to get with a criminal record, and friendships with law-abiding people are difficult to achieve. In a self-fulfilling prophecy, the social–psychological and practical consequences of official labeling thus lead to **deviance amplification,** or the commission of continued deviance and the adoption of a deviant lifestyle.

Labeling theory's focus is not on the initial act or two leading someone to be officially labeled, and labeling theory does not try to explain why these initial acts occur. In Edwin Lemert's (1951) term, these acts are examples of **primary deviance** and occur among wide segments of the population. We all transgress now and then: Some youths shoplift, others commit vandalism, and still others use illegal drugs. But suppose a youth, say a 15-year-old male, is caught vandalizing or using an illegal drug. His arrest, fingerprinting, and other legal measures make him think of himself as a young criminal. Parents, friends, teachers, and even the whole neighborhood hear about his crime. He is now

Labeling theory assumes that an arrest, conviction, or other criminal label produces a deviant self-image that may lead a person to commit additional deviance.

labeled a troublemaker, and people look at him differently. Perhaps some of his friends are even told not to spend time with him, and he might have trouble finding an after-school job for extra money. If some other offense occurs in the neighborhood, the youth might be suspected. He becomes angry and resentful and figures if they are all going to treat him this way, why not act this way? **Secondary deviance,** or continued deviance, follows.

Although this is admittedly a melodramatic scenario, it lies at the heart of labeling theory. Experimental evidence shows how deviance can reduce opportunities to succeed in the law-abiding world. In a study of fictitious job applications, Devah Pager (2009) had pairs of male college students apply for jobs in Milwaukee. The students were articulate and well dressed, but one in each pair claimed he had spent time in prison for cocaine possession. The applicants with the (supposed) criminal record were called back by the employers only half as often as those with a clean record. Reflecting racial discrimination, African-American applicants without a criminal record were slightly less likely than white applicants with a criminal record to be called back. Other kinds of studies also show that official labeling can reduce educational and employment opportunities. A record of juvenile delinquency reduces the likelihood of graduating from high school and hurts employment chances into young adulthood (Sweeten 2006), while incarceration during adulthood severely reduces employment opportunities after release from prison (Western 2006). These problems in turn are widely thought to increase the likelihood of continued criminality (Clear 2010).

In arguing that official labeling increases future criminality, labeling theory directly challenges deterrence theory's view (see Chapter 5) that official labeling has the opposite effect (specific deterrence). The two theories also disagree on the effects of official labeling on the offender's perceptions. Labeling theory argues that labeling causes or increases a deviant self-image, whereas deterrence theory argues that it increases the offender's perceived risk of arrest and aversion to arrest and punishment. Many tests of labeling theory have addressed these contradictory expectations. Some studies investigate whether official labeling is more likely to increase or decrease future criminality; others investigate whether official labeling increases deviant self-images or increases perceptions of risk.

The evidence on either effect of official labeling is mixed. As Chapter 5 indicated, research finds that legal punishment often increases future offending, as labeling theory predicts, in part because punishment reduces employment chances and educational attainment and increases involvement with peers who are also criminal offenders (Chiricos et al. 2007; Nagin, Cullen, and Jonson 2009; Nieuwbeerta, Nagin, and Blokland 2009; Wiesner, Kim, and Capaldi 2010). However, some research does find that punishment decreases future offending, as deterrence theory predicts. For example, a study of convicted offenders in Virginia found that their criminality declined after they were put on probation, probably because they feared going to prison if they committed any new offenses (MacKenzie and Li 2002). Still other studies find no effect in either direction.

Regarding self-image, research on juveniles generally finds that official labeling does not increase deviant self-images. Many youths already have deviant self-images before arrest, and the remainder seem able to keep their positive self-images intact despite arrest. A more negative self-image is likely to occur among youths involved in only minor delinquency (Thomas and Bishop 1984). The lack of consistent empirical support for labeling theory's predictions leads many observers to dismiss the theory. Commenting on these inconsistent findings, a recent review noted, "The soundest conclusion is that official sanctions by themselves have neither a strong deterrent nor a substantial labeling effect" (Akers and Sellers 2009).

Review and Discuss

To what extent does labeling have negative consequences for the people who are labeled?

EVALUATION OF LABELING THEORY

Labeling theory has certainly generated much controversy over the years, and scholars have criticized it since its inception (Akers 1968; Gove 1980). Several criticisms are worth noting (Bernburg 2010). First, labeling theory paints an overly passive view of the individual as quietly succumbing to the effects of the deviant label. Second, and as we have seen, empirical research fails to consistently support its arguments as to the influence of extralegal factors on labeling and the effect of labeling on self-image and continued deviance. Third, the theory implies that a life of crime, or secondary deviance, does not develop unless official labeling first occurs, even though many individuals end up with a life of crime without ever being labeled. Fourth, the theory fails to explain primary deviance and thus ignores the effects of family and peer relationships and more macro factors on deviance and crime.

Critics also take issue with labeling theory's prescription for reducing crime and delinquency. Because the theory stresses that official labeling promotes continued deviance, many labeling theorists urge caution in using the law to fight crime except for the most serious offenders. Critics, especially deterrence theory proponents, charge that following such a policy would increase crime and delinquency rather than reduce it. However, this criticism seems unjustified in view of the evidence cited earlier that imprisonment often leads to more offending, as labeling theory predicts.

Radical criminologists also criticize labeling theory. While liking its general perspective, they nonetheless charge it with focusing on "nuts, sluts, and perverts," or deviance by the powerless, and ignoring crimes by the powerful. They also criticize the theory for ignoring the sources of the power inequalities that affect the making of laws and the likelihood of official labeling for criminal behavior (Liazos 1972; Taylor, Walton, and Young 1973).

REVISING AND RENEWING LABELING THEORY

The withering attack from all sides has reduced the popularity of labeling theory (Akers and Sellers 2009). In response, the theory's proponents have attempted to revise it. Given the inconsistent evidence on the effects of official labeling, research has begun to return labeling theory to its symbolic interactionist roots by addressing the negative effects of *informal* labeling by social networks of friends, relatives, and loved ones (Bernburg 2010). Such labeling can be very influential for adults, but its influence is even greater during childhood and adolescence, when self-concepts are forming. Some studies find that informal labeling can result in many negative consequences, including resentment, a deviant self-image, and continued deviance (Bartusch and Matsueda 1996). Thus, even though labeling theory may overstate the effects of official labeling, refocusing the theory on unofficial labeling may illuminate the informal social processes leading to deviance and crime.

Other scholars note that official labeling promotes deviance for some people and deters it for others. If this is true, they say, then research must clarify the circumstances under which labeling has one effect or the other. In this regard, some scholars believe that continued deviance is more likely when offenders perceive that the police and courts

Crime and Controversy

How Should We Deal with Juvenile Offenders?

Labeling theory spawned new concern over the negative consequences of labeling, especially for adolescents who get into trouble with the law. Sociologists warned that treating juveniles like common criminals would only make them more likely to continue breaking the law. During the 1960s and 1970s, states across the nation heeded this warning and began to *divert* from the juvenile justice system adolescents who had committed minor delinquency or status offenses (running away from home, truancy, etc.). Instead of going into juvenile court and youth centers, these offenders stayed out of the system and experienced other sanctions, such as undergoing counseling, making restitution to their victims, or having their behavior monitored by juvenile probation officers or sometimes by their parents.

A rough consensus of studies since the 1970s is that diversion produces modest *decreases* in recidivism (repeat offending). Because it costs much less money to divert juvenile offenders than to place them in youth centers, diversion remains a popular legal sanction for adolescents, especially those charged with minor offenses.

However, as the public became more concerned about juvenile crime in the late 1970s, sentiment about juvenile delinquency began to change. Thinking that juvenile court sentencing is generally too lenient, many observers urged that the cases of serious juvenile offenders be transferred to adult criminal court, and states began to do so. Critics replied that even serious juvenile offenders are still too young to be able to fully comprehend their actions and, if tried as adults, would turn out worse than if they were processed through the juvenile justice system. This transfer movement eventually extended in many states to juveniles accused of property crime rather than just serious violent crime. Today twenty-seven states even permit children under the age of 13 to be tried as adults.

A major goal of treating juvenile offenders as adults is to reduce juvenile crime. However, there is little evidence that the transfer movement has had this general deterrent effect. There is even evidence, as labeling theory would predict, that juvenile offenders whose cases are handled by the (adult) criminal court have higher recidivism rates than those whose cases are retained by juvenile court, even when factors like the seriousness of the offense are taken into account. These results indicate that transferring juvenile cases to adult court ironically has the opposite effect of what is intended. As one of these studies concluded, "(G)et-tough policies that transfer juvenile cases to criminal court may backfire and have a criminogenic rather than deterrent effect."

Sources: Bishop 2006; Deitch et al. 2009; Lanza-Kaduce, Lane, and Bishop 2005.

are treating them unfairly or disrespectfully. In this situation, continued deviance is especially likely when offenders have few social ties to family, employment, and other social institutions (McCarthy and Hagan 2003; Sherman 1993).

John Braithwaite (2001) makes a similar point in his work on **shaming,** or social disapproval. Braithwaite distinguishes between *disintegrative shaming* and *reintegrative shaming.* Disintegrative shaming, or stigmatization, occurs when offenders are treated like outcasts and no effort is made to forgive them and to involve them in community affairs. It promotes continued deviance because it humiliates and angers offenders, denies them legitimate opportunities, and forces them to associate with criminal peers. Reintegrative shaming occurs when efforts are made to bring offenders back into the community. Such shaming reduces continued deviance, partly because it encourages offenders to feel ashamed, and is most common in *communitarian* societies marked by a high degree of concern for the welfare of others.

In the industrialized world, says Braithwaite, the key communitarian society stressing reintegrative shaming is Japan, where shame is keenly felt by all, including offenders. The Japanese are much more likely than Americans to think offenders can change for the better. As a result, Japanese social networks readily support offenders and try to reintegrate them into the community. These efforts help generate a lower rate of recidivism, or repeat offending, in Japan than in the United States. Although Braithwaite recognizes that industrialized nations are very different from Japan, he still believes that more reintegrative shaming could occur in these nations if they adopted more informal social

The Japanese are much more likely than Americans to think criminals can change for the better.

control processes. For example, some programs in Australia and New Zealand have juvenile offenders and their families meet with the offenders' victims and their families.

Despite many pessimistic assessments of labeling theory's value, research findings that legal sanctions do contribute to additional delinquency (see Crime and Controversy box) "attest to the viability of the labeling approach for explaining secondary deviance" (Bernburg and Krohn 2003). The new emphasis on informal labeling and on the conditions under which labeling increases or decreases deviance has further reinvigorated the theory and increased its importance for contemporary criminology.

Restorative Justice

Labeling theory's views in general, and Braithwaite's views in particular, are reflected in a new *restorative justice* movement that has been gaining popularity in recent years (Dorne 2008). Reflecting a philosophy that goes back to ancient times, restorative justice focuses on restoring the social bond between the offender and the community. In contrast to the *retributive model* guiding U.S. crime policy, which emphasizes punishment of the offender, restorative justice emphasizes the needs of the victim and of the community and, perhaps above all, the need to reintegrate the offender into the community. Often involving meetings between offenders, their victims, and community members, restorative justice is a more personal process that encourages offenders to take responsibility for their actions. A major goal of these efforts is to accomplish the reintegrative shaming that Braithwaite advocates.

Restorative justice has been tried in some areas of the United States and also in nations such as Australia, Canada, Japan, and New Zealand (Braithwaite 2007). It is also popular among native peoples in the United States and Canada and in some socialist nations. Although restorative justice practices differ, they include such things as *victim impact panels*, in which victims talk with offenders about their feelings as victims; *family group conferences* involving family members of both offenders and victims; *sentencing circles* involving offenders' and victims' relatives, friends, and other associates; and *citizen reparative boards* that determine the conditions of probation for convicted offenders (McGarrell and Hipple 2007).

The key question, of course, is whether restorative justice works. Does it reduce repeat offending, does it reduce community fear of crime, and does it enhance victims' satisfaction with the criminal justice system? Unfortunately, restorative justice is still too new for definitive answers to these questions. However, it does seem to increase victim satisfaction with the justice process and reduce their fear of revictimization by the same offender. Some studies also indicate that offenders who participate in restorative justice procedures are less likely to reoffend than control groups of offenders who experience more typical criminal justice outcomes (Morris 2002). In the United States, restorative justice has probably been used most often for juvenile offenders who commit relatively minor offenses. Whether it would work for more serious juvenile offenders and for their adult counterparts remains an important question.

Review and Discuss

On balance, does the empirical evidence support labeling theory's various assumptions, or does it fail to support them?

Conflict and Radical Theories

Conflict and radical theories take up where labeling theory leaves off. They argue that law is a key part of the struggle between powerful interests and the powerless. To preserve their dominance, the powerful use the law to control the powerless. This argument applies to both the formation of law and the operation of the legal system. In contrast, traditional theories stress the positive functions of law. They see law needed by every modern society to maintain social order, given that there will always be people deviating. Law and the criminal justice system are thus designed to benefit all of us, not just the powerful.

CONSENSUS AND CONFLICT PERSPECTIVES IN SOCIOLOGY

These competing theories reflect a more general division in sociology between functional or **consensus** perspectives and conflict perspectives. Reflecting the Durkheimian sociological tradition, consensus perspectives stress that social institutions help create social stability. In contrast, conflict theory says that social institutions serve the interests of the powerful in society and are dysfunctional for many other members of society.

Conflict theory lies at the heart of the *conflict tradition* in sociology, which goes back to the work of the German social philosopher and political activist Karl Marx (1818–1883), his collaborator Friedrich Engels (1820–1895), and the German sociologist Max Weber (1864–1920) (Abrahamson 2010). As is well known, Marx and Engels distinguished classes based on the ownership of the means of production—land, technology, factories, tools, and the like. In capitalist society, the two major classes are the **bourgeoisie** (sometimes called the **ruling class**), who own the factories and other modern means of production, and the **proletariat,** who work for the bourgeoisie. The bourgeoisie's primary interest is to maintain its dominance by exploiting and oppressing the proletariat; the proletariat's primary interest is to eliminate its oppression by overthrowing the bourgeoisie. Weber recognized economic classes, but, unlike Marx and Engels, he also recognized *status groups* with different amounts of power. Some status groups derive from their placement in the economic system, but others are based on religion, ethnicity, urban versus rural residence, and other noneconomic factors. Weber's concept of power and conflict is thus more multidimensional than that of Marx and Engels.

CONFLICT PERSPECTIVES IN CRIMINOLOGY

Because law is an important social institution, the debate between consensus and conflict views naturally entered the field of criminology. In the 1960s and 1970s, the civil rights, Vietnam antiwar, and other social movements affected a new generation of scholars interested in crime. They saw law used again and again to repress African Americans in the South and to harass antiwar protesters, and began to consider whether the criminal law and justice system similarly oppress or otherwise harm the powerless. These scholars looked back to Marx, Engels, and Weber for inspiration. Eventually, two strands of thought developed. The first, hereafter called *conflict* theory, is more Weberian in orientation. It considers law and crime the result of conflict among various kinds of groups in society, not just economic classes. Austin T. Turk's (1969) book *Criminality and Legal Order* is perhaps the most important statement of this perspective. He argued that the powerful impose the label of crime on the powerless to help reinforce their political power. From this vantage point, Turk developed a theory of **criminalization** that spelled out how criminal labels are applied. For example, criminalization is more likely when the subordinate groups are less sophisticated.

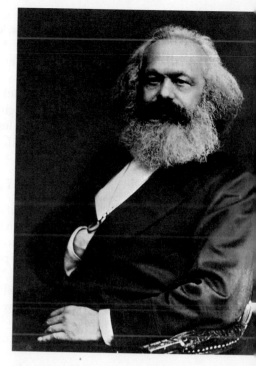

The conflict tradition in sociology derives from the work of Karl Marx, pictured here, and his collaborator Friedrich Engels.

Turk's Weberian orientation followed in the footsteps of earlier scholars Thorsten Sellin and George Vold. Sellin (1938) discussed immigration and crime in a short report, *Culture Conflict and Crime*. Because some behaviors considered acceptable in immigrant cultures are illegal in the eyes of the larger U.S. society, he said, many crimes they commit should be seen as the result of **culture conflict.** In a famous example, Sellin wrote about a Sicilian father in New Jersey who killed a teenage boy for having sex with his daughter. Because Sicilian culture approved this way of defending family honor, the man was surprised to be arrested.

Vold (1958) presented a *group conflict* theory of crime in his important book, *Theoretical Criminology*. He said that groups with legislative power have the power to decide which behaviors will be illegal and that crime stems from the conflict among various interest groups. Vold also argued that juvenile gangs arise from conflict between young people's values and those of the adult culture. Finally, he believed his theory was especially relevant for crimes involving political protest, labor disputes, and racial and ethnic hostility (see Chapter 14).

Evaluation of Conflict Theory

Conflict theory helps to explain the origins of some criminal laws and types of crime. In both areas, it seems especially relevant for crimes committed as part of social movement unrest, including labor strife, and for behaviors such as abortion, drug and alcohol use, and other consensual crimes on which people have many different views (see Chapter 15). However, as Vold himself conceded, it seems less relevant for conventional street crimes such as murder, assault, robbery, and burglary. Laws prohibiting these behaviors are meant to protect all segments of society, not just the powerful, who suffer less than the poor from these crimes. In another area, conflict theory shares labeling theory's view on disparities in the labeling process. However, evidence of these disparities is inconsistent, and scholars continue to disagree on their extent.

Some of the best evidence for conflict theory comes from historical studies. One such study was Joseph R. Gusfield's (1963) book *Symbolic Crusade*, which discussed the origins and dynamics of the temperance (prohibition) movement of the late 1800s and early 1900s. As his book's title implies, Gusfield saw the temperance movement as a symbolic attack of one group on another group. The movement was composed mostly of devout middle-class, small-town, or rural Protestants who considered alcohol use a sin. They disliked the drinking by poor Catholic immigrants in urban areas. To the minds of temperance advocates, these people had several strikes against them: They were poor, they were Catholic, they were immigrants, and they were urban residents. The temperance attack on their drinking is thus best seen as a symbolic attack against their poverty, religion, immigrant status, and urban residence. Rural Protestants, who dominated state legislatures and the Congress, were able to amend the U.S. Constitution to prohibit alcohol.

RADICAL THEORIES IN CRIMINOLOGY

Conflict theory was the first strand of thought that the new generation of scholars began developing in the 1960s. The second line of thinking is more Marxian than Weberian and views law and crime as the result of conflict between capitalists and workers, or the ruling class and the poor. This perspective has been variously called "critical," "new," "radical," "dialectical," "socialist," and "Marxist" criminology. Although these labels indicate certain differences, all of these approaches essentially adopt a Marxian approach to the study of crime and law (Lynch and Michalowski 2006). For the sake of simplicity, the term *radical theory* will refer to all these theories. Their basic views all stem from the work of Marx and Engels, to whom we now return.

Marx and Engels on Crime and Law

In contrast to other topics, Marx and Engels actually wrote relatively little about law and even less about crime, and what they did write is scattered throughout their various essays and books (Cain and Hunt 1979). They thought that law helps the ruling class in at least two ways: (1) it emphasizes and preserves private property, almost all of which belongs to the ruling class, and (2) it gives everyone various legal rights and thus appears to provide "equal justice for all." In promoting an appearance of legal equality, the law pacifies the powerless by making them feel good about the status quo and obscuring the true nature and extent of their oppression.

Marx and Engels presented several contrasting views of crime. In some of their writing, they depicted crime as stemming from the misery accompanying capitalism and as a necessary, logical response by the poor to the conditions in which they live. At other times, however, they depicted crime as political rebellion by the poor against their exploitation and an expression of their hostility toward the ruling class. And sometimes they harshly depicted criminals as a *lumpenproletariat*, or "the social scum, the positively rotting mass" composed of vagabonds, pimps, prostitutes, pickpockets, and the like (Marx and Engels 1962 [1848]). As might be evident from their language, Marx and Engels felt that the *lumpenproletariat* hindered the chances of a proletarian revolution.

Willem Bonger: Capitalism, Egoism, and Crime

Despite Marx and Engels's occasional concern with crime and law, for a long time Marxists neglected these subjects. Dutch criminologist Willem Bonger (1876–1940) was a major exception. Bonger (1916) argued, in his book *Criminality and Economic Conditions,* that a cultural emphasis on altruism characterized precapitalist, agricultural societies. In such societies, everyone was poor and looked out for each other's welfare. The development of capitalism led to a very different situation, because as an economic system it emphasizes competition for profit above all. Competition in turn means that someone wins and someone loses: Your success comes at the expense of someone else's failure.

This leads to a cultural emphasis on egoism and greed that makes people willing to break the law for economic gain and other advantages even if others get hurt. Bonger thought this was true for all social classes, not just the poor, but also noted that the poor are driven to crime by economic necessity. Although the wealthy commit crimes, he said, they escape legal punishment, because the law in capitalist societies is intended to help dominate the poor. Attributing crime to capitalism, Bonger thought it would largely disappear under socialism, which places much more importance on altruism. Supporting one of Bonger's views, a recent study of 100 nations found that their degree of capitalism was positively related to their homicide rates (Antonaccio and Tittle 2007).

 International Focus

Crime and the Economy in China, Vietnam, and Russia

Many radical criminologists blame capitalism for much of the crime the United States suffers: Crime results from the economic deprivation caused by capitalism and also from the selfish individualism that accompanies capitalism. If they are right, then as communist nations move toward a capitalist economy, crime of many types should increase. The experience of China, Vietnam, and Russia supports this prediction.

In 1984 the Communist Party in China initiated economic reforms to reduce government control over business activity as a move toward a market (capitalist) economy began. During the next few years, China's official crime rate rose sharply, although it still remains much lower than the U.S. rate. China's reported crime rate (keep in mind that official crime statistics in China may be even less reliable than those in the United States) quadrupled between 1985 and the early 1990s, and its serious crime rate (homicide, rape, aggravated assault, robbery, theft, and fraud) quintupled during that time. Political corruption in China is also thought to have soared during this period of economic change. The former director of international law enforcement research for China's Ministry of Public Security attributed the rising crime rate to the social changes and growing unemployment accompanying China's move to a market economy.

A crime increase also followed Vietnam's move toward a market economy. In the wake of this effort, theft, drug use and trafficking, delinquency, smuggling, and business-related crime grew into major problems. Experts blame the growth in crime on problems related to the move toward capitalism. As a Vietnamese social scientist explained, "Inequality and unemployment have increased, education and health care are no longer free, so Vietnamese people are losing the social protection they once had."

Russia's crime rate has also increased since it, too, began moving toward a market economy after the Soviet Union dissolved in the late 1980s. Its homicide rate doubled by 2000, and its rates of other crimes also soared. Homicide rates rose more rapidly in Russian regions that fared worse economically than in regions that did better economically. A study of Russia's crime rate increase concluded, "Unfortunately, it appears that increases in and high levels of violence are a price Russians must pay for a path chosen by their leaders and others."

The growth in crime problems in all three nations was doubtless the result of several factors. Their shift to market economies may have prompted greater inequality and selfish individualism, but it also involved other kinds of social changes. Following Durkheim, the resulting anomie, or normlessness, accompanying these changes may well be another factor accounting for rising crime in all three nations. Nevertheless, the experience of China, Vietnam, and Russia does support the radical criminology view that capitalism may be criminogenic.

Sources: Mel and Wang 2007; Mitton 2007; Pomfret 1999; Pridemore 2007; Ward 1995

Jerome Hall: The Law of Theft

Almost four decades after Bonger's book was published, historian Jerome Hall (1952) presented a Marxian analysis of the law of theft in his influential book *Theft, Law, and Society*, which discussed how the modern concept of theft developed in England some 500 years ago. At that time, England was emerging from a feudal, agricultural society into a mercantile economy. When a merchant sold goods to another merchant or landowner, poor people, or *carriers*, working for the merchant transported these goods on a horse-drawn cart. Because carriers were thought to technically own the goods while transporting them, they had the legal right to keep the goods for themselves, with no crime committed.

Fearing being fired or even physically attacked, most carriers simply transported their goods, but some did decide to keep them. Merchants naturally detested this practice, but the poor, by far the vast majority of English people, unsurprisingly supported it. Eventually, the issue reached the courts, and in the landmark 1473 *Carrier's Case* English judges established a new crime by ruling that carriers could no longer keep the goods. This decision, said Hall, protected the mercantile class's interests. Although today we all agree that carriers should not keep goods they are delivering (if you buy a flat-screen TV, you would certainly not want the truck driver to keep it!), the origins of this particular concept of theft do fit a Marxian perspective.

William Chambliss: The Law of Vagrancy

In 1964, William Chambliss authored a similar analysis of the development of vagrancy laws long ago. Before the 1340s, no law in England prohibited begging or loitering. Then the bubonic plague struck England in 1348 and killed about half of the population. With fewer people left to work on their land, landowners would have to pay higher wages. The passage of the first vagrancy law in 1349 aimed to prevent this by making it a crime for people to beg and to move from place to place to find employment. Both provisions in effect increased the size of the labor force, keeping wages lower than they would have been otherwise.

Vagrancy is illegal throughout the United States. Today's vagrancy laws originated during the 1348 bubonic plague that killed half of England's population. The first vagrancy law was enacted the next year to force people to work. By increasing the size of the labor force in this manner, the law kept wages lower than they would otherwise have been.

Chambliss (1964) said this law was "designed for one express purpose: to force laborers . . . to accept employment at a low wage in order to insure the landowner an adequate supply of labor at a price he could afford to pay." In the following centuries, Chambliss said, vagrancy laws were revived from time to time to benefit the mercantile class. Although Chambliss's analysis has been criticized for overemphasizing the economic motivation for vagrancy law development (Adler 1989), it remains a classic application of radical theory.

Contemporary Radical Views on Crime and Law

As radical perspectives on crime and law developed during the 1960s and 1970s, scholars drew on the work of Marx and Engels, Bonger, Hall, Chambliss, and others. Much of the new work was historical, but a good deal of it also looked at the law and crime in the contemporary United States and other nations, with the major emphasis on the formation of law and the punishment of criminals. Reflecting more general Marxist theory, radical work on law and crime is often categorized according to whether it embraces instrumental or structural Marxist views. The first radical scholars in the 1970s took an instrumental view, whereas more recent radical scholars espouse structural views.

Instrumental Marxism considers the ruling class a small, unified group that uses the law to dominate the poor and to advance its own interests. According to Richard Quinney (1974), a noted proponent of this view, law is simply "an instrument of the state that serves the interests of the developing capitalist ruling class." *Structural Marxism* considers this view too simplistic. If law were just a means of oppression, they ask, how can such advantages as civil liberties and unemployment insurance exist? Their answer is that the ruling class is less unified than instrumental Marxists think, as ruling class members disagree over important issues and compete among themselves for political and economic power. The state and its legal order must thus be "relatively autonomous" to ensure the long-term interests of capitalism by providing legal rights and other benefits that keep the public happy (Chambliss and Seidman 1982). Thus these benefits are sham, not real, because they serve in the long run to preserve capitalist interests.

A COMMON AGENDA

Despite their different views, radical criminologists generally agree on a common set of beliefs (Paternoster and Bachman 2001). First, a few people in capitalist societies have most of the wealth and power and the mass of people have little. Second, the wealthy use their power and the legal system to protect their dominance and to keep the poor and people of color in their place. Third, the criminal law reflects the interests of the powerful and not those of the general public. Fourth, criminals are normal people who commit crime because they are poor. Fifth, a harsh criminal justice system will not reduce crime because it does not address the causes of crime; instead, it will only worsen the lives of the poor. Finally, the criminal justice system must become fairer, and social and economic reform must occur.

Evaluation of Radical Criminology

Traditional criminologists have vigorously attacked radical criminology. One observer called the "new criminology" the "old baloney" and accused it of sentimentality in glorifying predatory crime by the poor (Toby 1980). Critics challenge radical criminology on other grounds (Arrigo and Williams 2010). Most generally, they say that radical criminologists unfairly malign the United States and other democracies and overlook the oppressive nature of authoritarian nations. Because crime also exists in these societies, say the critics, it is unfair to blame capitalism for crime, and it is utopian to think crime would disappear if socialism replaced capitalism. Critics also say that radical criminology exaggerates the importance of class relations in the genesis of crime and ignores the many other factors at work (Akers and Sellers 2009).

Radical criminologists believe that the wealthy use the legal system to keep the poor and people of color in their place.

In response, radical criminologists fault this criticism for focusing on instrumental Marxist approaches, which characterized the early work of radical criminologists in the 1970s. These views have been replaced by more structural views since that time. In fact, many radical criminologists have also criticized instrumental views. They thus claim that criticism by traditional criminologists focuses on a particular type of radical criminology that is no longer popular even in radical circles (Lynch and Michalowski 2006).

In sum, radical criminology has been harshly attacked and just as staunchly defended. Although some early radical views of crime presented an instrumental Marxist view that even other Marxists find too simplistic, more recent formulations present a richer understanding of crime and law formulation under capitalism. Marxist historical work on the development of the police, prisons, and other mechanisms of legal control has been especially useful (Harring 1993). Although not usually grounded in **Marxism,** the studies of inequality and crime discussed in Chapter 7 nonetheless support the basic thrust of radical criminology. Growing evidence of disparity in the legal treatment of street and white-collar crime also supports radical views (Reiman and Leighton 2010). However, radical theory has been less successful in presenting a "radical" explanation of street crime that differs substantially from the structural explanations discussed in Chapter 7 (Akers and Sellers 2009). Like conflict theory, radical theory's view on the origins of laws and operation of the criminal justice system seems less relevant for street crime than for consensual offenses and political criminality.

The debate between radical and traditional criminologists has cooled since the 1970s, but sharp differences of opinion remain. Although one critic concluded in 1979 that radical criminology's "capacity for contribution is exhausted" because of its "theoretical and empirical poverty" (Klockars 1979), a radical criminologist observed in 1993 that "Marxist criminology is healthier than it has ever been" (Greenberg 1993). Almost two decades later, radical and traditional criminologists continue to dispute the validity of radical criminology, even if the debate has become less heated.

Left Realism and Peacemaking Criminology

Before leaving radical criminology, we should address two recent developments. Recall that traditional criminologists criticized instrumental Marxist approaches for dismissing the seriousness of street crime. In the 1970s and 1980s, feminist criminologists also took instrumental Marxism to task for neglecting rape and family violence. These developments led some British criminologists in the 1980s to develop a radical approach to crime termed "left realist criminology," or **left realism** (Lea and Young 1984; Young 1986). This approach was a response to the "left idealism" of instrumental Marxists who viewed street crime as political rebellion and the result of the alienation caused by capitalism. The left realists instead insisted that crime causes real distress, not only for the poor and people of color, but also for women victimized by rape and family violence. Given this reality, left realists say, crime prevention and control are essential. They champion measures similar to those advanced by liberal observers, including improving the socioeconomic conditions underlying crime, community policing, victim compensation, and using imprisonment only for criminals posing a real threat to society. However, some left realists also call for increased police surveillance and more punitive treatment of criminals (Matthews and Young 1992). In turn, some radical criminologists criticize left realism for being too willing "to inflict punishment as a tool of social justice" and for deflecting blame for crime away from the capitalist system (Menzies 1992).

Another recent development in radical criminology is **peacemaking criminology,** which combines Gandhism, Marxism, Buddhism, and other humanistic strains of thought (Pepinsky 2006). Peacemaking criminology views crime as just one of the many forms of suffering that characterize human existence. To reduce such suffering, people must find inner peace and develop nonviolent ways of resolving conflict, including both crime and war. These efforts must involve a fundamental transformation of our social institutions so that they no longer cause suffering and oppression. Peacemaking criminologists also say that the criminal justice system is too authoritarian and violent to reduce crime and advocate using alternative types of punishment such as restitution and community service.

Review and Discuss

What are the elements of the common agenda of radical criminology? What kinds of evidence support the views of radical criminology and what kinds of evidence fail to support these views?

Feminist Theories

Previous chapters have noted that theories of crime developed before the 1970s were essentially theories of male crime, because scholars either ignored girls and women altogether or else discussed them in stereotypical ways. This combination of neglect and ignorance impoverished criminological theory. Thus, one of the most exciting developments in criminology is the growth of feminist theory and research that focuses on women and girls (Renzetti 2011).

AN OVERVIEW OF FEMINIST PERSPECTIVES IN CRIMINOLOGY

Just as there are many radical theories in criminology, so are there many feminist perspectives. Jody Miller and Christopher W. Mullins (2009) summarize several assumptions and beliefs that distinguish feminist theories and the work of feminist scholars from traditional theories and work in criminology. Two of these are particularly important for the discussion here. First, crime cannot be fully understood and explained without appreciating the important role that gender plays. Second, feminist theories can and should be used to reduce gender inequality in the areas of crime and criminal justice, as well as in the larger society.

Within this broad framework, feminist theories all highlight women's subordinate status, but feminist scholars differ in their explanations for this status and in their recommendations to improve it. *Liberal feminists* attribute gender differences in crime rates to gender differences in socialization and also call attention to gender discrimination in the criminal justice system. They advocate changes in socialization to reduce male criminality and reforms in the criminal justice system to reduce the gender discrimination found there. *Marxist feminists* say that women's subordination results from the development of capitalism, which forced women to depend on men for economic support. Women's subordination under capitalism is also thought to increase the amount of rape and other violence they suffer (Schwendinger and Schwendinger 1983).

Radical feminists argue that patriarchy precedes capitalism and that gender relations are more important than class relations. Instead of viewing violence against women as a by-product of capitalism, radical feminists see such violence as a primary means by which men in all societies maintain and extend their dominance over women (Dworkin 1989). *Socialist feminists* consider capitalism and patriarchy equally important (Messerschmidt 1986). In their view, the interaction of class and gender relations affects the opportunities available to people and thus both their likelihood of committing crime and being victimized by crime. Finally, scholars who favor *multicultural feminism* consider race and ethnicity, class, and gender simultaneously (Burgess-Proctor 2006). In their view, crime by and victimization of women of color can thus be understood only if we consider the intersection of gender, race and ethnicity, and class. Work on the gender–race–class intersection is one of the most important developments in contemporary criminology.

THE SCOPE OF FEMINIST THEORY AND RESEARCH

Whatever particular perspective it adopts, feminist work in criminology generally addresses four areas: (1) the victimization of women, (2) gender differences in crime, (3) explanations of women's criminality, and (4) women's experiences and gender discrimination in the criminal justice system (Griffin 2010; Renzetti 2011).

The Victimization of Women

The first feminist work in the 1970s focused mostly on the victimization of women by rape and domestic violence, which previously had received little attention. As Chapter 4 noted, a major accomplishment of this work was simply to bring these crimes to public attention. To do so, feminist criminologists began to document the extent of these crimes and their psychological and behavioral consequences. They also stressed the involvement of male intimates and other nonstrangers in these crimes, and they emphasized that women were not to blame for being victimized by them. (Chapter 11 discusses rape and domestic violence further.)

A growing focus of feminist work on victimization, and one that provides a bridge to its work on women's criminality, is the role played by sexual abuse in girls' delinquency (Makarios 2007). Although both girls and boys suffer physical abuse, girls are much more likely than boys to be sexually abused, and their history of sexual abuse "is at the heart of much of girls' and women's lawbreaking" (Chesney-Lind 2004).

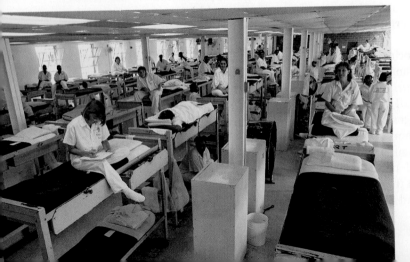

Feminist perspectives focus on many aspects of women's criminality, including the problems that women inmates face in jail and prison.

Gender Differences in Crime

A second area inspired by feminist work is often called the *gender-ratio* issue and seeks to understand why female rates of serious offending are so much lower than men's rates (or, conversely, why men's rates are so much higher). Chapter 7 noted that structural theories do not easily explain why women living in criminogenic conditions are less likely than their male counterparts to turn to crime. An exception to this conclusion is general strain theory, which, as used in some recent work, does seem to shed some light on this issue (Broidy 2001; Piquero and Sealock 2004). Chapter 7 discussed how various social process theories begin to fill in the gap left by structural explanations in helping to explain gender differences in crime rates. Traditional theories of (male) crime thus do seem to help explain why women and girls commit less serious crime than men and boys do (Agnew 2009).

MASCULINITY AND CRIME

An important focus of work on the gender-ratio issue goes beyond traditional theories to focus on the nature of masculinity. As Chapter 3 noted, we are already doing a good job of raising girls not to become criminals. The crime problem that so concerns us is really the *male* crime problem: If our national crime rates were no higher than women's crime rates, crime would concern us much less. Recognizing this fact, some scholars consider "maleness" and masculinity to be criminogenic conditions. To reduce crime, they argue, male socialization and notions of masculinity must be changed and male dominance reduced (Collier 2004; Messerschmidt 1997). This argument applies not only to rape, domestic violence, and other crimes that especially target women, but also to other street crimes and even to white-collar crime. Masculinity brings with it attitudes, values, and behavior that underlie a wide range of criminal activities.

Girls are socialized in ways that develop nurturing values and other traits that make it less likely they will commit crime.

Admittedly, some might regard women's low criminality merely as an unintended silver lining of their subordinate status, lack of freedom and opportunity, and socialization into feminine values. If so, their low criminality might not be something to praise. But neither is it something to overlook, because it might offer some insight into how we can lower men's criminality. In this regard, Ngaire Naffine (1995) argues that the nurturing values produced by female socialization should be welcomed as important, positive traits, not as evidence of weakness, passivity, and dependency. Reflecting this view, Kathleen Daly and Meda Chesney-Lind (1988:527) wrote that they see "some cause for hope" in the gender difference in crime:

> Of whatever age, race, or class and of whatever nation, men are more likely to be involved in crime, and in its most serious forms. . . . A large price is paid for structures of male domination and for the very qualities that drive men to be successful, to control others, and to wield uncompromising power. . . . Gender differences in crime suggest that crime may not be so normal after all. Such differences challenge us to see that in the lives of women, men have a great deal more to learn.

The mass media, public officials, and criminal justice professionals have ignored the essential link between masculinity and crime. They say little about the need to change masculinity and lessen male dominance if we want to be serious about reducing crime. The new work on masculinity and crime suggests an important but neglected avenue for public policy on the crime problem.

Review and Discuss

Why do men and boys commit more serious crime than women and girls? What are some of the social process and socialization factors that account for this difference?

Explanations of Women's Criminality

Because traditional criminological theories focused mostly on males and were tested primarily with data about males, feminist criminologists have asked whether these theories also apply to females. This third area is often called the *generalizability* issue. In this regard, Chapters 7 and 8 noted that certain structural and social process theories help explain variation in female offending, even if specific factors identified by these theories may be more important for one gender than the other. Traditional theories of (male) crime thus once again seem to apply generally to female criminality (Agnew 2009).

Other work goes beyond the generalizability issue in seeking to understand such things as the gendered nature of criminal behavior, the impact of gender stratification in offender networks on how crime happens, and the impact of families' gender processes on delinquency. We look at examples of research in all of these areas.

DOING GENDER

A first line of inquiry, on the gendered nature of crime and the impact of gender stratification in offender networks, reflects the idea that female and male offenders "do gender" (1987), as do women and men in other walks of life, in their daily activities in order to accomplish femininity and masculinity. In this regard, Jody Miller (2000) studied active (i.e., not imprisoned) robbers in St. Louis. Although both genders committed robbery for the same motives—money, possessions, and thrills—the ways they committed robbery differed, Miller found. Men generally robbed men instead of women and routinely threatened their victims with a gun and often hit them.

In contrast, women robbers more often targeted women instead of men and rarely used a gun to rob them. Sometimes they would show a knife, but only rarely would they stab them. Instead they typically hit, shoved, or beat up their female victims. When women robbed men, they usually used a gun in view of the men's greater size and strength. They also would pretend to be sexually interested in the men, either as prostitutes or just as women out to have a good time, and then rob the men when their guard, and sometimes their pants, were down. Miller concluded that all these differences reflected "a gender-stratified environment in which, on the whole, males are perceived as strong and women are perceived as weak" (p. 42).

Miller and Scott H. Decker (2001) also studied female gang members and found that gendered notions of behavior and gender stratification within the gangs shaped the girls' involvement in gang activities. Specifically, the girls were less likely than boys to take part in gang fighting and other dangerous gang activities. When the girls met up with rival gang members, they usually avoided fighting, but when a fight did occur, they typically used fists or sometimes knives, but not guns. Their reluctance to fight and to use guns when fighting stemmed from their understanding of gender roles. As one girl put it, "We ain't no supercommando girls" (p. 127)! Two other girls concurred: "Girls don't be up there shooting unless they really have to" and "We ladies, we not dudes for real . . . we don't got to be rowdy, all we do is fight" (p. 127).

This body of work provides striking evidence that the behavior of active robbers and gang members is influenced by their understanding of gender roles and by gender stratification in their criminal networks. Both types of female and male offenders "do gender" in the ways described and thus accomplish femininity and masculinity, respectively.

POWER-CONTROL THEORY

A second line of inquiry examines the gendered processes of family life that increase or decrease delinquency. The major perspective here is John Hagan and associates' (Hagan,

Simpson, and Gillis 1987) *power-control theory*, which remains one of the few explanations of delinquency that highlights the roles played by both gender and class. Hagan and associates distinguished between *patriarchal* and *egalitarian* households. In patriarchal households, the father works outside the home and the mother stays at home to take care of the children. The parents subscribe to traditional gender roles and teach those to their children. Boys learn the criminogenic masculine values discussed earlier, and girls learn anticrime feminine values. Reflecting her own situation, the mother controls her daughters' behavior much more than her sons' behavior. All these factors produce relatively high gender differences in delinquency.

In egalitarian households, both father and mother work outside the home in positions of authority. As a result, both sons and daughters receive less maternal supervision and, given their mothers' workplace autonomy, are encouraged to be more independent. Mothers treat their daughters more like their sons, increasing their daughters' potential for delinquency. The gender difference in delinquency in these households will thus be smaller than in patriarchal households where daughters are much more controlled.

Tests of power-control theory offer mixed results (Blackwell 2000). Supporting the theory, they generally find that working-class patriarchal families control their children more than do middle-class egalitarian families. However, contrary to the theory, they often do not find patriarchal families exhibiting greater gender differences in delinquency. Critics also fault the theory for ignoring criminogenic factors such as harsh punishment and negative school experiences and for assuming that the mother's employment leads to greater delinquency (Akers and Sellers 2009). They say this assumption smacks of the backlash to feminism underlying earlier arguments blaming increased female criminality on the women's movement (see Chapter 3). There is also little evidence linking maternal employment to increased delinquency (Loeber and Stouthamer-Loeber 1986). In a later article, Hagan and colleagues (McCarthy, Hagan, and Woodward 1999) conceded some of this criticism and revised their theory to argue that maternal employment decreases male delinquency by reducing sons' exposure to patriarchal attitudes.

Women in the Criminal Justice System

The fourth general area of feminist work addresses women's experiences and possible gender discrimination in the criminal justice system. This area discusses the experiences of offenders as well as criminal justice professionals. Many studies document the abuse and other problems that women prison and jail inmates face and the kinds of discrimination that women lawyers, police officers, and prisons guards face (Belknap 2007); Chapter 16 discusses women police further. Other studies focus on possible gender differences in the probability of arrest, sentencing, and other criminal justice outcomes. Three hypotheses on these differences have been developed. The *chivalry* hypothesis predicts that girls and women will be treated more leniently than boys and men. The *evil woman* hypothesis predicts the opposite: Because female criminality is so rare, a woman committing crime looks that much more terrible by comparison. Conflict and labeling theories would also expect more punitive treatment of women given their subordinate status to men. A third hypothesis, *equal treatment*, predicts that gender will not affect legal processing.

Empirical tests of these hypotheses are examined in Chapters 16 and 17. For now, it seems fair to say that the empirical evidence is very inconsistent. Although all three hypotheses receive support in one study or another, the most recent and best-designed studies find women treated somewhat more punitively for minor crimes and somewhat less punitively for serious crimes (with women up to 30 percent less likely than men to be imprisoned for similar crimes). At the same time, they conclude that the effect of gender is weak compared to the effects of legally relevant variables such as prior criminal record and offense severity (Steffensmeier, Ulmer, and Kramer 1998). Some evidence exists that any chivalry shown toward women is actually directed toward white women, not African-American women or other women of color (Spohn, Gruhl, and Welch 1987).

Review and Discuss

What are the four major areas that comprise the scope of feminist theory and research? According to recent research on girls' lives and delinquency, what factors inhibit the chances of girls becoming delinquent, and what factors raise the chances of girls becoming delinquent?

A FINAL WORD ON FEMINISM

Feminist work in criminology represents one of the most important advances in the field. At the same time, it is only about thirty to thirty-five years old, whereas the field of criminology has been around for more than a century if we go back to its early biological explanations. Historically, then, feminist criminology is still relatively new. Meda Chesney-Lind and Karlene Faith (2001:298–299) say that feminist perspectives "offer much to criminological theorizing" and that their insights promise "to improve the situation for all—girls and women as well as boys and men."

Conclusion

We are now leaving the world of theory, but will visit it again during the next several chapters on types of criminal behavior. Recall that we must understand the reasons for crime in order to reduce it. The theories reviewed in the past five chapters suggest several avenues for reducing crime.

Neoclassical theories suggest the need to increase the probability of arrest, to have harsher legal punishments, and to undertake situational crime prevention. Although situational crime prevention shows promise, the vast majority of studies show that efforts to reduce crime by relying on deterrence do not work and are very expensive. Although criminals often act and think in the ways that rational choice and deterrence theories assume, they also often fail to act in these ways. Hence, efforts to reduce crime must rely on other explanations of criminality if they are to succeed.

Biological theories suggest the need to change the biological factors involved in criminality. This, of course, is difficult and fraught with ethical and political problems. The "softer" biosocial view is that social factors such as poverty and stress trigger genetic and other biological predispositions toward crime. It might be possible to change these social factors, many of which are featured in sociological theories of crime. Biological explanations highlighting pregnancy and birth complications are also compatible with a sociological perspective, because many of these complications could be minimized or prevented with improved social and health programs and policies.

Psychological explanations focusing on personality also hold some promise for reducing crime, although ethical and practical questions remain about identifying children with temperament problems. Still, if our society can do something about the social factors underlying temperament problems—poverty, inadequate child rearing, and the like—then we should be able to reduce crime.

Structural theories in sociology point to several conditions underlying many types of crime: economic deprivation and inequality, overcrowding and dilapidated housing, and other aspects of what is sometimes called social disorganization. The physical and economic problems of urban living combine to produce especially high street criminality. Although we might not be able to reduce the emphasis on the American dream that leads people from many walks of life to commit crime, we might be able to address the other structural conditions producing street crime.

Social process theories highlight the importance of proper parenting, harmonious family relationships, associations with conventional peers, and positive school experiences for reducing the potential for delinquency and later criminality. Public-policy efforts designed to address family and school problems thus hold great potential for crime reduction.

In this chapter we discussed critical perspectives on crime and criminal justice. Although these theories' focus on the social reaction to crime represents their most distinctive contribution to criminology, they also have something to say about why crime occurs. Labeling theory contends that extralegal factors affect legal processing and that legal processing creates increased deviance by inducing deviant self-images and reducing conventional opportunities. The inconsistent empirical evidence for the theory leads many scholars to urge its abandonment. However, to the extent that legal processing may sometimes have unintended effects, as research indicates, we must be careful that attempts to control juvenile and adult offenders through the law do not increase the likelihood of future offending.

Conflict and radical theories attribute several types of crime and criminal laws to the self-interest of powerful groups in society. As with labeling theory, the empirical evidence for conflict and radical theories is inconsistent. While some scholars dismiss the theories, others consider them valuable. Conflict and radical theories echo certain structural theories in calling attention to the criminogenic effects of social inequality. Radical theories, of course, suggest the need to eliminate capitalism if we want to reduce crime significantly. Although that is not about to happen, this view underscores the reductions in crime that would occur if social inequality were diminished, even if capitalism itself remained.

Feminist perspectives alert us to the inadequacy of a criminology that ignores women or discusses them stereotypically. Feminist work stresses that certain features of a patriarchal society help account for both women's criminality and women's victimization, and it highlights the criminogenic effects of masculinity and the price women, men, and society pay for male dominance. In this regard, one of the most effective things we could do to reduce street crime and women's victimization would be to reduce male dominance and to change male socialization and notions of masculinity. Such change, of course, will not come soon and might even be impossible to achieve to any significant degree. However, as feminists emphasize, masculinity and male dominance can no longer be ignored as major causes of street crime and victimization.

We now turn to several types of criminal behavior, beginning with interpersonal violence. Here we will see the influence of masculinity and male domination, inequality, and several of the other factors discussed by the theories of crime and delinquency we have reviewed.

9

Summary

1. The traditional theories reviewed in previous chapters do not discuss the social reaction to crime, which critical theories do discuss. In explaining this reaction, these theories highlight the concept of power and the inequality based on differences in power.

2. Labeling theory addresses three major issues: (1) the definition of deviance and crime, (2) possible discrimination in the application of official labeling and sanctions, and (3) the effect of labeling on continued criminality. It adopts a relativist definition of deviance, saying that deviance is not a property of a behavior, but rather the result of how others regard that behavior, and it claims that extralegal factors such as gender and appearance affect the chances of being officially labeled. It also states that labeling acts to increase deviant behavior in the future. Empirical support for labeling theory's views is inconsistent, but recent efforts to revive and revise the theory, such as Braithwaite's work on reintegrative shaming, hold some promise.

3. Conflict and radical theories argue that law is a key part of the struggle between powerful interests and the powerless. To preserve their dominance, the powerful use the law to control the powerless. This argument applies to both the formation of law and the operation of the legal system.

4. Conflict theory focuses on group and culture conflict and helps to explain the origins of some criminal laws and types of crime. It seems especially relevant for crimes committed as part of social movement unrest, but less relevant for conventional street crimes. As with labeling theory, the empirical evidence for conflict theory's assumptions of disparities in legal processing is inconsistent.

5. Radical theories are generally Marxian in orientation and take several forms. However, they all share a common set of beliefs that are critical of the economic structure of U.S. society to which they attribute much street crime. They also emphasize the more lenient treatment of white-collar crime, which they say is the best evidence of social class disparities in the criminal justice system. Critics say that radical criminologists unfairly malign the United States, overlook the oppressive nature of socialism and communism, and exaggerate the importance of economic factors in the genesis of crime. Radical criminologists say that this criticism attacks oversimplified versions of radical theory. Like conflict theory, radical theory's views seem less relevant for street crime than for consensual offenses and political criminality.

6. Several feminist perspectives on crime and society exist, but they all generally address three areas: (1) the victimization of women, (2) gender differences in crime and explanations of women's criminality, and (3) gender discrimination in the criminal justice system. Feminist work on rape and domestic violence began in the 1970s and has brought these crimes to public attention. Feminist-inspired work also finds that traditional theories of crime help explain gender differences in crime and variation among women in criminality. A line of inquiry here highlights the criminogenic functions of masculinity and the anticrime implications of femininity. Gender seems to affect legal processing in complex ways, but it does appear that women's criminal sentences are somewhat more lenient owing to their child-rearing responsibilities.

Key Terms

bourgeoisie 220

conflict 212

consensus 220

criminalization 221

critical perspectives 212

culture conflict 221

deviance amplification 215

dramatization of evil 215

feminist 212

labeling 212

left realism 226

Marxism 226

peacemaking criminology 227

primary deviance 215

proletariat 220

relativist definition 213

ruling class 220

secondary deviance 216

shaming 218

What Would You Do?

1. Pretend you are again a high school student and have heard through the grapevine that a student who recently moved into your high school district and is in two of your classes was once arrested for armed robbery. The student's behavior seems okay, but he does have a rough edge to him and tends to keep to himself. You find yourself feeling kind of sorry for him, but you also wonder whether the rumor is true. At lunch in the cafeteria, he usually sits by himself as people whisper to each other when they walk by him. One day the cafeteria is crowded, but you notice an empty seat next to the new student. Do you sit next to him? Why or why not?

2. Suppose you have two friends, Susan and Joshua, who have been married for three years. They had their first child, William, about four months ago. Now you're out shopping with the whole family at the local mall as the holiday season approaches. Knowing that Susan has been concerned about gender roles as long as you have known her, you tell the proud parents that you'd like to buy William a baby doll. Susan says with delight, "Oh, how thoughtful!" But Joshua is less happy and even angry. "I won't have my son playing with a girl's toy!" he almost shouts. Susan looks at him in horror. What do you do?

CHAPTER

ten

Violent Crime: Homicid Assault, and Robbery

Crime in the News

n a single week in mid-May 2010, nineteen people died in homicides in Los Angeles County in Southern California. As high as this number might seem, it was about the weekly average for the county, as the nineteen deaths brought the homicide death toll for the year to 260. According to police, at least seven of the nineteen homicides were gang-related. A few victims had been walking down the street in separate incidents when they were approached by one or more persons who killed them as bystanders watched in shock. The bodies of a few other victims were discovered long after they were killed. Most of the victims had died from gunfire. Fifteen of the nineteen victims were under age 30; the youngest was 6 and the oldest was 65. Of the nineteen victims, fourteen were males.

Source: Ardanlani 2010.

eople fear senseless violence more than any other crime. It is the stuff of TV movies and the type of crime the news media favor, and it is the reason we lock our doors at night, buy firearms for protection, and build more prisons. Violent crime makes us afraid and drives public policy. The week of violence in Los Angeles County reminds us of the enormity of violence in the United States and of the need to understand why it occurs so that we can prevent it before it happens.

Much violence occurs between strangers, but much also occurs between acquaintances, friends, and even loved ones. Women and children are especially likely to be victims of nonstranger violence, such as rape and other forms of sexual and physical abuse. To emphasize this point and to underscore the seriousness of the crimes suffered, two chapters are devoted to violent crime. This chapter features homicide, assault, and robbery, and several special topics related to violence, while the next chapter discusses rape, sexual assault, and domestic violence. Continuing our earlier emphasis, the discussion in each chapter highlights the criminogenic effects of inequality and masculinity.

Both chapters focus on **interpersonal violence,** defined as the "threat, attempt, or actual use of physical force by one or more persons that results in physical or nonphysical harm to one or more other persons" (Weiner, Zahn, and Sagi 1990:xiii). *Nonphysical harm* here refers to fear, anxiety, and other emotional states. Thus, an armed robbery involving no physical injury would still be considered an act of interpersonal violence because it scares the victim. The adjective *interpersonal* rules out such things as pollution, unsafe products, and dangerous workplaces, which kill and harm many thousands of people each year. These practices are often called *corporate violence* because corporations commit them, but they do not involve interpersonal physical force. Another type of violence involving such acts as terrorism, sabotage, and genocide is often called *political violence.* Although most political violence is interpersonal, its special nature places it under the broader category of political crime. Later chapters discuss corporate and political violence.

Homicide and Assault

The subject of countless mystery novels, TV shows, and films, **homicide** captures the attention of the public, news media, and criminologists more than any other crime. Partly because of the presence of a corpse, homicides are also far more likely than other crimes to become known to the police. Hence we have more information about and a greater understanding of homicide than of any other crime.

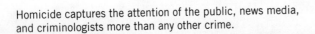
Homicide captures the attention of the public, news media, and criminologists more than any other crime.

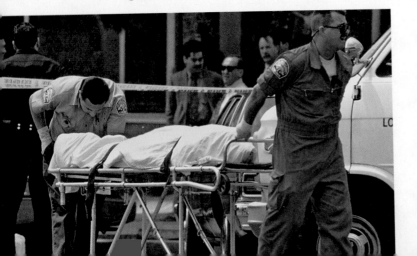

DEFINING HOMICIDE AND ASSAULT

The FBI's list of Part I crimes included in its Uniform Crime Reports (UCR) begins with murder and nonnegligent **manslaughter.** This category refers to the willful killing of one human being by another and excludes deaths caused by gross negligence, suicide, and justifiable homicide. *Justifiable homicide* refers to the killing of armed and dangerous felons by police or private citizens.

The criminal law divides murder and nonnegligent manslaughter into four subcategories: (1) first-degree murder, (2) second-degree murder, (3) voluntary manslaughter, and (4) involuntary manslaughter. The placing of a killing into one of these subcategories depends on the offender's intent and the amount and nature of the physical force that results in death. Traditionally, *first-degree murders* are committed with malice aforethought, meaning that the offender planned to kill someone and then did so. The popular term for this category, *premeditated murder*, has been extended in the past few decades to include *felony murders*, in which the commission of a felony such as rape, robbery, or arson causes someone's death. Thus, if an arsonist sets fire to a building and someone inside dies, even though that was not intended to happen, the arsonist may be charged with felony murder and hence first-degree murder. *Second-degree murders* refer to deaths in which an offender intended to do serious bodily harm short of killing the victim, but the victim died anyway. Deaths resulting from a "depraved heart" or extremely reckless conduct can also lead to second-degree murder charges. *Manslaughter* refers to killings considered less serious or less blameworthy but still not justifiable. *Voluntary manslaughter* alludes to killings committed out of intense emotion such as anger or fear. *Involuntary manslaughter* refers to killings committed because offenders have acted recklessly, as when a parent shakes a crying infant and accidentally kills the baby. Traffic fatalities constitute most involuntary manslaughter cases.

In practice, these four subcategories overlap, and it is often difficult to know which one best describes a particular killing. Prosecutors have great latitude in deciding which charge to bring against a murder defendant. Their decision depends heavily on whether the evidence will indicate beyond a reasonable doubt the intent, amount, and nature of physical force required for a particular charge. Sometimes other factors, such as the race of the offender and the victim, also influence, however unwittingly, the prosecutor's decision (see Chapter 17).

The UCR defines two types of **assault.** *Aggravated assault* is "an unlawful attack by one person upon another for the purpose of inflicting severe or aggravated bodily injury." Aggravated assault involves the use of a weapon or other "means likely to produce death or great bodily harm." *Simple assaults* are assaults "where no weapon is used and which do not result in serious or aggravated injury to the victim." Only aggravated assaults are included in the FBI's Part I crimes, but both types of assault are included in the National Crime Victimization Survey (NCVS). The major difference between homicide and aggravated assault is whether the victim dies. Because of the greater reliability of homicide data, most of our discussion focuses on homicide, but still pertains to aggravated assault. We will rely heavily on the UCR (from which all data are for 2008 unless otherwise indicated; Federal Bureau of Investigation 2009) for our understanding of homicide, because victimization surveys are obviously irrelevant.

PATTERNING AND SOCIAL DYNAMICS OF HOMICIDE

Race, Gender, and Age of Offenders and Victims

The race and gender makeup of homicide offenders and victims is very instructive. As depicted in Table 10.1, about half of offenders and victims are African American, even though African Americans comprise only about 13 percent of the U.S. population. Homicide is largely an **intraracial** crime: for single-offender, single-victim homicides, 92 percent of African-American murder victims are murdered by African-American offenders, and 86 percent of white murder victims are murdered by white offenders.

Turning to gender in Table 10.1, men are much more likely than women both to murder and be murdered. As these data suggest, homicide is a "distinctively masculine matter" (Polk 1994:5). When women murder men, the majority kill a current or former husband or boyfriend who has been battering them. That said, women are still much more likely than

TABLE 10.1 ▸ **Race and Sex of Murder Offenders and Victims, 2009 (percentage)**

VARIABLE	OFFENDERS[a]	VICTIMS[a]
Race		
White	46	49
African American	52	49
Other	2	3
Sex		
Male	90	77
Female	10	23

Source: Federal Bureau of Investigation 2010.
[a]Percentages are based on homicides for which information is known.

men to be murdered by a current or former spouse or partner. About 35 percent of all female murder victims are killed by male intimates, whereas less than 3 percent of male victims are killed by female intimates (Federal Bureau of Investigation 2009).

Young people are also disproportionately likely both to murder and be murdered. Although only 14 percent of the population is in the 15-to-24 age bracket, 48 percent of all homicide arrests in 2009 were of people in this age range. Their victims also tend to be in this range.

Geographic Patterns

As with much other crime, homicide is also patterned geographically. The homicide rate (number of homicides per 100,000 residents) is 10.2 in the nation's largest cities (population over 250,000) versus only 2.7 in towns with populations under 25,000 (see Figure 10.1).

Despite the impression given by this upscale neighborhood in Charleston, South Carolina, the South historically has had the nation's highest regional rate of homicide. Some scholars think that this fact arises from a southern subculture of violence in which disputes that might fade away in other regions become deadly in the South.

THE SOUTH

Looking at different regions of the United States, homicide rates are highest in the South (5.0) and lowest in the Northeast (3.8), with the Midwest and West in between (4.6 and 4.5, respectively). The South historically has had the nation's highest regional homicide rate. The most popular explanation for this is that the South has a regional subculture of violence in which disputes that might fade away in other regions become deadly. Southerners are thought to have a code of honor that demands responses, ones that are violent if necessary, to insults and other slights (Lee et al. 2007).

This subculture arose for several reasons. The first is the South's history of slavery, which, as a violent institution, made the South accustomed to the use of violence in everyday life. The South's history of lynching

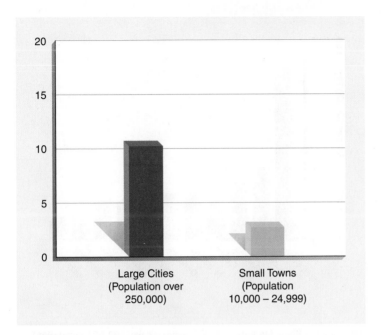

FIGURE 10.1 ▸ **City Size and Homicide Rates 2009** Source: Federal Bureau of Investigation 2010.

is presumed to have had a similar effect (Messner, Baller, and Zevenbergen 2005). A second reason is the South's warmer temperatures. As Chapter 3 indicated, higher temperatures seem associated with greater violence. Southerners may have originally been more violent because of their warmer temperatures, but over time this violence became part of their culture. A third reason is that the South's initial economy hundreds of years ago was primarily herding, not farming. Because animals that are herded make such tempting targets for potential rustlers, herders must be very willing to protect their herds with any means necessary, including violence. Thus, Southerners hundreds of years ago became oriented to violence for this reason.

Some scholars attribute the South's high homicide rate not to a subculture of violence, but instead to its level of economic deprivation, which is higher than in other regions (Parker 1989). Some scholars also attribute the South's high homicide rate to its gun-ownership rate, which is thought to be the highest regional rate in the United States. Countering this view, the South also has the highest rate of aggravated assault, suggesting that there is more serious violence in the South regardless of the presence of guns.

INTERNATIONAL COMPARISONS

Homicide is also patterned geographically across nations. In this regard, the United States has the highest homicide rate of the world's industrialized nations (see Figure 10.2). Here it is useful to compare the homicide rates of U.S. cities with those of other cities of similar size (see Figure 10.3). For example, Houston's homicide rate is five times greater than that for Toronto. It is instructive to note that the difference between the United States and other nations is much larger for homicide than it is for other types of serious violence (Zimring and Hawkins 1997). We revisit this issue later.

The Victim–Offender Relationship

According to the UCR, the relationship between the victim and offender was unknown for 44 percent of 2009 homicide victims. Of the remaining victims, about 78 percent were killed by someone they knew, and only 22 percent were murdered by a stranger.

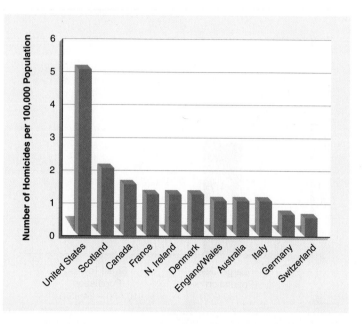

FIGURE 10.2 ▶ **International Homicide Rates, 2008 (homicides per 100,000 population)**
Sources: Federal Bureau of Investigation 2007; United Nations Office on Drugs and Crime 2006.

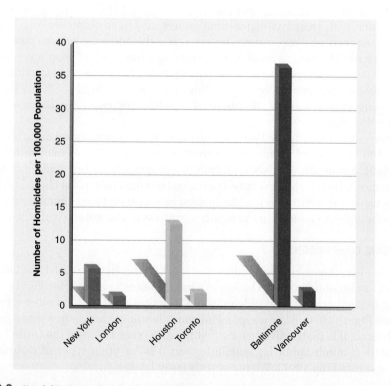

FIGURE 10.3 ▶ **Homicide Rates (homicides per 100,000 population) for Selected International Cities of Similar Sizes, 2008** Sources: www.csc-scc.gc.ca/text/faits/facts08-02_e.shtml; Coleman et al. 2007; Federal Bureau of Investigation 2007.

Note: Rate for London is for March 2005–March 2006.

Most of the "unknown relationship" cases arise from the fact that police often report homicides to the FBI before an arrest occurs. In such unsolved homicides, the **victim–offender relationship** is initially recorded as unknown. When arrests occur later, new information, including the victim–offender relationship, is added to the local police station's case files, but typically not sent to the FBI and not reported by the UCR. The unknown category in UCR homicide data is thus artificially high because this information is missing. When these new data are later anlayzed, the percentage of homicides committed by strangers is also under 25 percent (Messner, Deane, and Beaulieu 2002). Like violent crime in general (see Chapter 4), then, murder involves people who know each other much more than it involves strangers; murder victims are three times more likely to be killed by someone they know than by a stranger.

Type of Weapon

Another important fact about homicides is the type of weapon used (see Table 10.2). In 2009, firearms accounted for about two-thirds of all homicides, with handguns accounting for 47 percent. We revisit the issue of handguns and homicides later in this chapter.

Circumstances Leading to Homicides

We have seen that most homicides involve the use of handguns and other firearms among people who know each other. With this profile in mind, it is not surprising that the typical U.S. murder is a relatively spontaneous event arising from an argument that gets out of hand and escalates into lethal violence, usually involving a handgun. Early research by Marvin Wolfgang (1958) found that the victim precipitates about 25 percent of all homicides by starting the argument or being the first to use physical force. Depending on how precipitation is defined, some studies find that more than half of all homicides are victim precipitated (Felson and Steadman 1983). In a typical scenario, the victim insults and angers the eventual offender. The offender responds in kind and may even use physical force. The victim reacts with another verbal or physical attack and soon is killed. Often the offender, the victim, or both, have been drinking before their encounter, and alcohol use is thought to play a key role in the violence and death that eventually occur (Phillips, Matusko, and Tomasovic 2007).

TABLE 10.2 ▸ **Homicide and Type of Weapon Used, 2009**

WEAPON	PERCENTAGE
Firearms	67
Handguns	48
Shotguns	3
Rifles	3
Other or unknown type of firearm	14
Knives and cutting instruments	13
Personal (hands, fists, feet)	6
Blunt objects	4
Other	9

Source: Federal Bureau of Investigation 2010.

Review and Discuss

How does an understanding of the type of weapons involved in homicides help us understand why homicides occur?

TRENDS IN U.S. HOMICIDE RATES

The U.S. homicide rate rose sharply after the mid-1960s into the 1970s, before declining after 1980 and rising after 1985 into the early 1990s. It then dropped sharply before leveling off during the past few years. Figure 10.4 displays the trend since 1985. According to the UCR, 15,241 homicides occurred in the United States in 2009, for a rate of 5.0 homicides per 100,000 population. This rate was much lower than the beginning of the 1990s and in fact was as low as the rate during the mid-1960s.

The post-1985 homicide rise stemmed primarily from an increase in homicides by and against young males (under age 24) in urban areas (Blumstein 1995; Fox and Zawitz 1998).This increase stemmed from several factors: (1) the growing sense of despair resulting from declining economic opportunities in urban areas during the 1980s; (2) increased drug trafficking in inner cities because of the declining economic opportunities; and (3) the increased possession and use of powerful handguns in urban areas, partly because of drug-trafficking battles (Ousey and Lee 2007; Sampson and Wilson 1995). The drop in the homicide rate after the early 1990s reflected the general decline in crime since then. As Chapter 3 discussed, scholars attribute this crime decline to various social and economic factors, including a strong economy, declining numbers of people in the high-crime 15-to-25 age group, and fewer gang wars over drug trafficking. Most criminologists doubt the importance of the rising incarceration rate during this period (Blumstein and Wallman 2006). For example, sociologist Richard Rosenfeld (Rosenfeld 2006) found that rising imprisonment accounted for only about 25 percent of the homicide drop during the early 1990s, meaning that social and economic factors had much more of an impact.

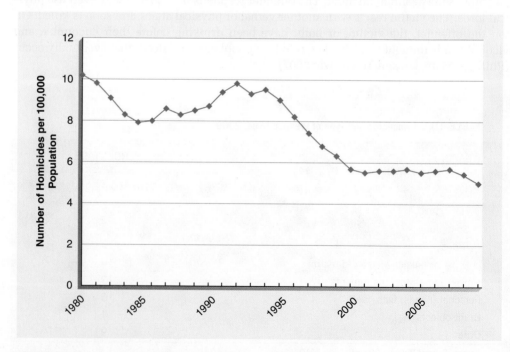

FIGURE 10.4 ▸ **U.S. Homicide Trend, 1980–2009** Sources: Federal Bureau of Investigation 2010; Pastore and Maguire 2010.

He estimated that each prevented homicide cost more than $13 million in annual prison costs and suggested that this sum would prevent more homicide and other crime if it were instead spent on drug treatment, preschool programs, and other prevention efforts.

One additional factor may have accounted for the decline in homicides since the early 1990s and possibly prevented many homicides even when the homicide rate was increasing before then. This factor is improved emergency medical technology and care. Whereas 5.6 percent of aggravated assaults in 1960 ended in death and thus became homicides, only 1.7 percent had the same result in 1999. As sociologist Anthony Harris observed, "People who would have ended up in morgues 20 years ago are now simply treated and released by a hospital, often in a matter of a few days" (Tynan 2002:A2). Harris and colleagues estimate that the number of homicides would be three to four times greater without the medical advances (Harris et al. 2002).

AGGRAVATED ASSAULT

Our discussion of homicide and aggravated assault has centered on homicide because its data are the most reliable and because the two crimes are generally so similar except for the fate of the victim. This discussion of aggravated assault is thus much briefer and presents the most important information for understanding this crime.

First, the trend data for homicide and social and geographical patterning of homicide apply generally to aggravated assault. The rate of aggravated assault declined after the early 1990s along with homicide, as we would expect, and the racial, ethnic, gender, age, and geographical patterning for homicide offending and victimization also apply to aggravated assault. Aggravated assaults are disproportionately committed by men, by people of color, by young people, and in the South and major urban centers.

Second, the dynamics of aggravated assault resemble those for homicide, an unsurprising conclusion given that the major difference between the two crimes is whether the victim dies. Aggravated assaults tend to be relatively spontaneous events in which the assailant acts out of anger, revenge, or other strong emotions.

Third, many aggravated assaults, about 53 percent, involve people who know each other, according to the NCVS, whereas 46 percent involve strangers. This latter percentage is greater than that for homicide, but, like robbery (discussed later), varies by gender. Strangers commit 52 percent of the aggravated assaults against men, but only 36 percent of the aggravated assaults against women; nonstrangers commit 47 percent of the aggravated assaults against men, but 65 percent of the aggravated assaults against women (Truman and Rand 2010).

Fourth, perhaps the major difference between aggravated assault and homicide involves the use of weapons. Whereas about two-thirds of homicides involve a firearm, only about one-fourth of aggravated assaults involve firearms. The much greater involvement of firearms in homicides obviously reflects the fact that firearms are much more lethal than other weapons. Because firearm victims are more likely to die, their assaults become classified as homicides.

Finally, the FBI reported that about 807,000 aggravated assaults occurred during 2009, for a rate of 262.8 per 100,000 residents. This rate was more than one-third lower than the early 1990s and as low as the rate in the late 1970s.

EXPLAINING HOMICIDE AND AGGRAVATED ASSAULT

An adequate explanation of homicide (and also aggravated assault) must answer the following questions arising from the central facts about this crime: (1) Why does the United States have a higher homicide rate than any other industrial nation? (2) Within the United States, why are homicide and aggravated assault rates highest in large, urban areas? (3) Why do men commit almost all homicides and aggravated assaults? and (4) Why do African Americans and other people of color have high rates of homicides and aggravated assaults, both as offenders and as victims? Sociological explanations are necessary to answer these questions.

Why Does the United States Have a Higher Homicide Rate than Other Industrial Nations?

Several studies find that homicide is higher in nations with greater economic inequality, measured as the difference between rich and poor, and greater levels of poverty (Chamlin and Cochran 2006; Pridemore 2008). The fact that the United States has more inequality than other industrial nations may be one reason for its higher homicide rate.

The difference between the United States and other industrial nations is much larger for homicide than for other types of serious violence, for which the U.S. ranking, according to the International Crime Victims Survey (ICVS), is only about average (see Chapter 4). According to Franklin E. Zimring and Gordon Hawkins (1997), a major reason for the especially high U.S. homicide rate is its high rate of handgun ownership compared to European nations. The much greater use of handguns by assailants in the United States than elsewhere increases the chance that their intended victims will die. What would have been an aggravated assault in another nation thus becomes a homicide in the United States (Hoskin 2001).

A third reason for the high U.S. homicide rate, and its historically high rate of serious violence, might be historical. Historian Richard Maxwell Brown (1990) argued that the expansive use of violence in the United States, beginning with the War for Independence against England and continuing with the Civil War, massacres of Native Americans, and lynchings of African Americans, among other experiences, helped integrate violence into the American character: "We have resorted so often to violence that we have long since become a trigger-happy people. Violence is clearly rejected by us as a part of the American value system, but so great has been our involvement with violence over the long sweep of our history that violence has truly become part of our unacknowledged (or underground) value structure" (Brown 1990:15).

Although this argument is appealing, other nations such as Japan and Scotland had very violent pasts but have much lower homicide rates today than the United States. In effect, they have succeeded in overcoming their violent pasts, even if the United States has not. Thus, although the violent U.S. past may be one factor, other forces must also be at work. The high level of inequality seems to be one such factor. Another might be the U.S. cultural emphasis on strong individualism and distrust of authority, values that may undermine nonviolent attempts to settle interpersonal disputes.

Review and Discuss

Why is the United States more violent than many other industrial nations?

Why Are U.S. Homicides and Aggravated Assaults More Common in Urban Areas than Elsewhere?

Social disorganization and anomie and strain theories (Chapter 7) help explain why urban areas have higher rates of homicide and aggravated assault than other areas: The population density, household overcrowding, dilapidated living conditions, weak social institutions, and concentrated disadvantage (e.g., extreme poverty and high unemployment) of many urban neighborhoods contribute to their high rates of violence. As Elliott Currie (1985:160) noted, "(H)arsh inequality is . . . enormously destructive of human personality and of social order. Brutal conditions breed brutal behavior." In addition to these problems, urban communities also have high numbers of bars, taverns, and other settings where

International Focus

Drug Cartels and Violence South of the Border

Mexico has been filled with bloodshed since the beginning of 2007, when its government began an all-out military offensive, involving police and some 50,000 soldiers, against drug cartels. Members of drug cartels have killed thousands of people—police, military personnel, civilians, politicians, and members of rival cartels—with bullets, hand grenades, and decapitations. Cartel members have also been killed by police and military.

In a single week in March 2010, some fifty people died in drug cartel violence throughout Mexico. The victims included employees of the U.S. consulate in a border town who were shot in broad daylight. After these murders, the U.S. State Department recommended that employees at consulates on the border evacuate their families to the United States.

Critics said the government's strategy was clearly not working and called on the Mexican government to address the economic conditions that lead young people to work for the drug cartels. Early on, Mexico's president defended the strategy: "This has to be done because the alternative is to leave people in the hands of criminals, to turn a blind eye, pretend nothing is happening, leave them open territory so they end up finishing off communities. That I will not allow." He also said that U.S. residents who used illegal drugs were partly responsible for the violence. "I have argued that this is a shared problem between the United States and Mexico. The principal cause . . . is the use of drugs. And [the United States] is the prime consumer in the world." The Mexican president added that many of the assault weapons the cartels were using were coming across the border from the United States and called on the U.S. government to clamp down on the gun flow.

As this war of words went on, residents of many of Mexico's towns were living in fear for their lives. Dozens of families fled the border town of El Porvenir into the United States after drug gangs burned down houses and killed many of the town's residents. One of these refugees said, "It's very hard over there. They are killing people over there who have nothing to do with drug trafficking. They kill you just for having seen what they are doing."

Sources: Associated Press 2007; Lacey and Thompson 2010; Lacey 2010; McKinley 2010.

---

violence is apt to occur, as routine activities theory would predict (Roncek and Maier 1991). Recent research suggests that the subcultures of urban neighborhoods also matter: The most disadvantaged neighborhoods respond with a code of honor featuring an exaggerated emphasis on respect and manhood that often translates into violence (Stewart and Simons 2006) (see Chapter 7).

Why Do Men Commit Almost All Homicides and Aggravated Assaults?

Chapter 9 emphasized the violent nature of **masculinity.** This gender difference takes on critical importance in adolescence as males become bigger and stronger and are more likely than females to commit various acts of violence (see Table 10.3). Gender differences in homicide thus stem from gender differences in nonlethal violence.

Poverty interacts with masculinity to explain why poor men have higher rates of homicide and aggravated assault than wealthier men. Masculinity means many things: academic and economic success, breadwinning for one's family; competitiveness, assertiveness, and aggressiveness; lack of emotionality; the willingness to "fight like a man" when necessary (Kimmel and Messner 2010). In U.S. society, a man's socioeconomic

TABLE 10.3 ▸ **Proportion of High School Seniors (Class of 2008) Reporting Involvement in Various Violent Acts in Past 12 Months (percentage saying at least once)**

ACTIVITY	MALES	FEMALES
Fought with group of friends against another group	21	12
Got into serious fight in school or at work	15	10
Hurt someone badly enough to need bandages or a doctor	18	7
Used a weapon to get something from a person	4	1
Hit instructor or supervisor	3	1

Source: Bachman, Johnston, and O'Malley 2009.

standing affects the way he expresses these ways of "being a man." As James W. Messerschmidt (1993:87–88) put it, "'Boys will be boys' differently, depending upon their position in social structures and, therefore, upon their access to power and resources."

Men at the middle and top of the socioeconomic ladder engage in a masculine behavior pattern involving economic competition and various forms of nonphysical dominating behavior (Connell 1995). In contrast, men at the bottom of the ladder are more apt to engage in *opposition masculinity* involving physical competition, violence, and drinking (Hobbs 1994). They are much more likely to regard insults and slights as major offenses meriting violent responses and thus to commit *confrontational homicides*. This violence permits these males to demonstrate their masculinity and to gain the respect their low economic standing denies them.

Review and Discuss

Why do men commit almost all serious violent crime? To what extent do you think the gender difference in crime is biologically caused?

Males at the bottom of the socioeconomic ladder are more likely than wealthier males to engage in opposition masculinity involving physical competition, violence, and drinking.

Why Do African Americans and Other People of Color Have High Rates of Homicide and Aggravated Assault?

As Darnell F. Hawkins (2003) notes, this question has long been emotional and contentious, in part because some researchers in the past responded in a racist manner by claiming that African Americans have an inborn disposition to be violent, are biologically inferior, or both. This problem has made criminologists hesitant "to engage in discussions of the extent and causes of racial differences in crime and violence" (Hawkins 2003: xxi).

As discussed in previous chapters, a nonracist explanation of African-American violent crime rates emphasizes certain criminogenic structural and ecological factors and their social–psychological effects: (1) the anger and frustration arising from racial discrimination and from economic deprivation; (2) the stress, social disorganization, and other criminogenic conditions that are especially severe in urban neighborhoods with the multiple problems social scientists call *concentrated disadvantage*; (3) negative family and school experiences; and (4) the influence of deviant peers and the "code of the street" that is especially common in these neighborhoods. These reasons all "come together" for African Americans, and particularly young African-American males, more than for any other group (Kaufman 2005; McNulty and Bellair 2003; Stewart, Schreck, and Simons 2006).

As Chapter 3 noted, the explanations for the high levels of African-American violence also appear to apply to the high levels found among Latinos and Native Americans (Phillips 2002). Compared to non-Latino whites, both these groups are more likely to live amid extreme poverty and the other structural and ecological conditions conducive to violent crime (Martinez 2002; McNulty and Bellair 2003). The conditions on many Native American reservations are thought to be especially desperate, accounting for their high rates of violent crime and victimization (Lanier and Huff-Corzine 2006).

Several structural, ecological, and cultural factors help account for African-American violent crime rates. These factors also help explain violent crime by Latinos and Native Americans.

VIOLENCE BY WOMEN

Most research on homicide and other violence explicitly or implicitly concerns men because men commit most violent crime. The studies we have of women's violence suggest that it has the same roots—extreme poverty, negative family and school experiences, and disadvantaged neighborhoods—as men's violence (Baskin and Sommers 1998; Kruttschnitt and Carbone-Lopez 2006; Steffensmeier and Haynie 2000). Much of the research on women's violence focuses on African-American women, whose violent crime rate is much higher than that for white women and sometimes exceeds that for white men, even though it remains much lower than that for African-American men.

Women's violence appears to have the same roots—extreme poverty, negative family and school experiences, and disadvantaged neighborhoods—as men's violence.

In his study of the "code of the street," Elijah Anderson (1999) noted that young African-American women seek respect as much as their male counterparts and in the same manner: through displays of bravado, verbal insults, and a willingness to use violence to settle disputes. Despite these similarities, young African-American women's violence lags behind that of their male counterparts because of gender socialization. When young urban women feel the need to retaliate violently, Anderson said, they typically enlist the aid of a brother, uncle, or cousin. When they do fight themselves, they rarely use guns because, as women, they do not feel a "macho" need to do so. Jody Miller and Scott H. Decker's (Miller and Decker 2001) research on female gang members, discussed in Chapter 9, found a similar phenomenon: Girls fought less often than boys because of their gender socialization, and they also used guns less often.

Recall that when women commit homicide their victims are usually men who have been battering them. This pattern holds true for women of color as well as for white women. Coramae Richey Mann (1990:198) wrote that African-American female homicide offenders are part of a *subculture of hopelessness*: "By the time these women reach age 30 or more, they feel the full impact of the hopelessness of their lives. When the last straw is broken, they finally strike back at the closest living representative of their plight."

An explanation of women's homicide by Robbin S. Ogle and colleagues (Ogle, Maier-Katkin, and Bernard 1995) supports Mann's view. They argued that women, like men, experience significant stress in their lives. Both sexes react to stress with anger, but men direct theirs at external targets through violence, whereas women tend to internalize theirs as guilt, hurt, and self-doubt. This leads to "overcontrolled personalities" that ordinarily commit no violence, but occasionally become overwhelmed and "erupt in extreme violence" such as homicide. The targets of this violence are often the men who abuse women and sometimes even a woman's own children.

Review and Discuss

Why do you think women commit violence? How are the reasons for their violence similar to the reasons for men's violence, and how do these reasons differ from those for men's violence?

Robbery

When people say they fear crime, they often have robbery (or mugging) in mind. What do we know about this crime?

DEFINING ROBBERY

Robbery is "the taking or attempting to take anything of value from the care, custody, or control of a person or persons by force or threat of force or violence and/or by putting the victim in fear" (Federal Bureau of Investigation 2010). As this definition implies, robbery involves both theft and interpersonal violence. The latter component distinguishes robbery from other property crimes and prompts both the UCR and NCVS to classify it as a violent crime. UCR robbery data include both personal and commercial (e.g., in convenience store) robberies, whereas the NCVS covers only personal robberies. This difference leads the two data sources to give us slightly different pictures of robbery, but together they give us a better understanding of robbery than either source provides alone.

EXTENT AND PATTERNING OF ROBBERY

The UCR reports a lower number of robberies than the NCVS (Federal Bureau of Investigation 2009; Rand 2009). The UCR reported 408,217 robberies of all types in 2009, a drop of more than one-third from the early 1990s. The NCVS estimates that 533,790 personal robberies occurred in 2009. Of all the UCR robberies, about 28 percent were cleared by arrest.

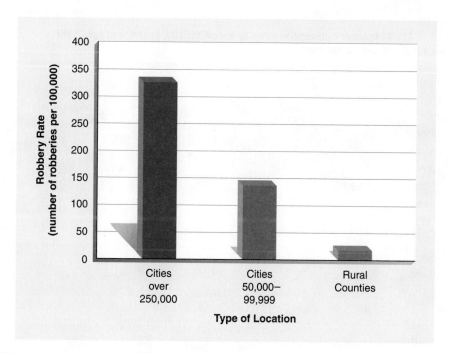

FIGURE 10.5 ▸ **UCR Robbery Rates and Population Size, 2009** Source: Federal Bureau of Investigation 2010.

Like homicide and assault, robbery is primarily a young person's crime: Persons under the age of 25 account for about two-thirds of all robbery arrests. Robbery is also much more common in large urban areas than elsewhere (see Figure 10.5). UCR robbery rates are highest in the South, where the rate is twice as high as other regions. Again like homicide and assault, robbery is disproportionately committed by men and by African Americans. Men comprised 88 percent of all robbery arrests in 2009, and African Americans comprised 55.5 percent. As Table 10.4 indicates, men and African Americans are also disproportionately likely to be victims of robberies, while Latinos are robbed more often than non-Latinos. Reflecting the victimization pattern for violent crime noted in Chapter 4, robbery victimization is also highest among young people and among people from low-income backgrounds.

In an important difference between robbery and other violent crime, robbery is more likely to be committed by a stranger than by someone the victim knows. According to the NCVS, 57 percent of personal robberies in 2009 involved a stranger, and 38 percent involved someone the victim knew. This latter figure masks a significant gender difference: about 46 percent of female victims are robbed by someone they know, compared to only 33 percent of male victims.

TYPES OF ROBBERS

Just as there are several types of murderers, there are also several types of robbers. John Conklin (1972) developed the standard classification. A first type is *professional robbers*. These people carefully plan their robberies, carry guns, and often work in groups. Their targets include "big scores" such as stores, banks, or other commercial targets. A second type is *opportunist robbers*, who commit robberies when the opportunity presents itself. They are usually young males who choose vulnerable targets, such as people walking alone at night, and they get relatively little money from each robbery. Conklin's third type, *addict robbers*, rob to acquire money to buy illegal drugs. They generally plan their robberies less

TABLE 10.4 ▸ **Robbery Victimization Rates by Race//Ethnicity, Gender, and Age, 2009 (per 1,000 persons 12 and older)**

VARIABLE	RATE
Race	
African American	5.6
White	1.6
Other	0.5
Two or more races	5.2
Ethnicity	
Latino	3.4
Non-Latino	1.9
Gender	
Male	2.7
Female	1.6
Age	
12–15	3.1
16–19	5.2
20–24	3.5
25–34	2.8
35–49	2.0
50–64	1.1
65 or older	0.4

Source: Truman and Rand 2010.

carefully than professional robbers, but more carefully than opportunistic robbers. *Alcoholic robbers* are Conklin's final type; they commit robberies when they are drunk and trying to get money to buy more alcohol. Their robberies are rarely planned and usually involve no firearms.

Because robbery is committed for economic gain, it is an example of innovation in Robert Merton's anomie theory.

EXPLAINING ROBBERY

Robbery is a violent crime committed for economic gain. As such, robbery is a prototypical example of *innovation* in Merton's anomie theory: In a society placing so much value on economic success, the poor often feel pressured to achieve this success through illegitimate means. Robbery is one of the crimes they commit.

This chapter's explanations for homicide and aggravated assault also apply to robbery. Like these other crimes, robbery stems from the criminogenic features of many urban neighborhoods, including extreme poverty, dilapidated living conditions, and other evidence of social disorganization (Cancino, Martinez, and Stowell 2009). Routine activities theory also helps explain robbery because robbery victimization is higher among people who put themselves at risk, for example, by going out at night at least once per week (Miethe, Stafford, and Long 1987). Further, certain locations promote robbery because they provide attractive targets without guardianship. For example, the advent of automated teller machines (ATMs) helped increase robbery rates because they provided a location where a lone target could be expected to have a fair amount of money. The growth of convenience stores has increased commercial robberies for similar reasons.

So far we have implied that the motivation for robbery is primarily economic. Other scholars take a different view. Jack Katz (1991) argued that the amount of money robbers obtain is too small for economic gain to be their primary motivation. If it were, he said, they would engage in more lucrative illegal activities such as drug trafficking or illegal gambling. Instead, robbers' primary goal is to sustain a "badass" identity involving "the portrayal of a personal character that is committed to violence beyond calculations of legal, material, or even physical costs to oneself" (p. 285). This motivation makes persistent robbers willing to risk arrest and renders them relatively immune to any deterrent effects that the threat of legal punishment might have. A related motivation is robbers' desire to look "cool" and "hip" through the spending of huge sums of money. To keep up this appearance, they often need money quickly and thus commit robberies with little concern for, or even attention to, the possible consequences (Jacobs and Wright 1999).

These motivations reflect the emphasis on respect so characteristic of the code of the streets in urban areas, discussed earlier. Katz (1991:298) observed that urban adolescents learn the need to use violence and exert a "fierceness of will" and "humiliating dominance" when faced with insults and assaults by peers. More than most crimes, robbery embodies these characteristics. Although most urban adolescents do not become robbers, those who do reflect their socialization into the code of the streets. As Elijah Anderson (1999) observed, masculinity is a fundamental part of this code. Although Katz (1991) did not stress the point, masculinity is thus fundamental to his own argument on the nature of robbery and helps explain why robbers are almost always men.

Review and Discuss

Should robbery be best understood as a crime that is done for economic gain or as one done for thrills and other reasons?

Special Topics in Violent Crime

This section examines some additional kinds of violence—mass murder and serial killing, workplace violence, hate crime, and child abuse—as well as two controversial issues—mass media and violence, and guns and gun control. The entire next chapter is devoted to the very important topic of violence against women, in view of its great importance and the amount of research on it.

MASS MURDER AND SERIAL KILLING

Mass murder and serial killing are examples of *multiple murder*, or *multicide*, in which several victims die either all at once or in a much longer time span. Despite the heavy attention it receives from the news media, this type of violence is actually very rare in the United States. As Chapter 2 noted, the number of serial killings is thought to range between 50 and 400 annually, or less than 3 percent of all homicides. This fact provides little comfort to the families and friends of serial-killing victims, but it does indicate that serial killing is rare and not typical of homicide.

Much has been written about mass murder and serial killing, and we have room here only for a brief summary of the research on these subjects (DeFronzo et al. 2007; Fox, Levin, and Quinet 2008). *Mass murder* involves the taking of several lives at once or within a very short time frame. There is no clear definition of how many lives must be taken or how short the time frame must be. Two lives would ordinarily not be enough for this term to be used; eight to ten lives would ordinarily suffice. Many scholars think that at least four people must be killed for an event to be labeled a mass murder (Alvarez and Bachman 2003). This issue aside, the very short time frame distinguishes mass murder from *serial killing*, which involves the methodical taking of a human life one at a time over a period of days, weeks, months, and even years. Once again, there is no clear definition of how many lives must be taken, but many scholars think at least three killings must happen for serial murder to have occurred (Alvarez and Bachman 2003).

Mass Murder

In April 2007, a student at Virginia Polytechnic Institute and State University (Virginia Tech) fatally shot thirty-two students and faculty before killing himself in one of the most shocking mass murders in U.S. history. When mass murder like this happens, we naturally want to know why it occurs. What do criminologist know about it?

Mass murder usually takes place at one of a low number of locations: a home, a workplace, a school, or, more rarely, a shopping mall or other public area. When mass murder occurs in a home, the offender is almost always a close male relative of the victims in the home. Scholars term this type of mass murderer a *family annihilator*. Typically, such men feel at the end of their ropes and kill out of despair and hopelessness, often committing suicide afterward. Although we have more to say about workplace violence later, it typically occurs because an employee or ex-employee is outraged over a firing or some perceived slight or other problem. Mass murder in schools, perhaps most infamously illustrated by the April 1999 killings at Columbine High School in Littleton, Colorado, also occurs because of perceived injustice. The students who commit mass murder typically feel harassed by other students for any number of things that often lead some students to be teased or ridiculed. The two students who committed the Columbine massacre were both seen as "nerds" and outcasts and hung out with other such students in a group called the Trench Coat Mafia. Their massacre was an act of revenge on the people and school that they felt had caused them so much suffering (Fox, Levin, and Quinet 2008).

Mass murderers are almost always males, as was certainly true of the Virginia Tech and Columbine killers. Although girls and women suffer the same indignities and problems as boys or men do and sometimes even worse, they do not respond with mass murder and, as we have seen in previous chapters, they also do not respond as often as males with other acts of violence. As always, gender differences in socialization must be kept in mind as we try to understand the problem of violence in America, whether we talk about mass murder or about more everyday acts of violence.

Most mass murderers, regardless of where they commit their horrible crimes, feel aggrieved by family members, workplace associates, or school peers and teachers and perhaps by life in general. However, this sense of grievance does not sufficiently explain mass murder, as many people obviously feel aggrieved and yet do not commit mass murder. Thus, a sense of grievance may be a necessary condition for mass murder but does not by itself explain why mass murder occurs.

Some dynamics of mass murder are also apparent from studies of various examples of this crime (Fox, Levin, and Quinet 2008). First, firearms are certainly the weapon of choice, and it is not an exaggeration to say that mass murder would not be possible without firearms. Second, most mass murderers plan their crime for days or weeks in advance. They compile their arsenal, plan the sequencing and locations of their attack, and determine other courses of action to help ensure that they will achieve their goal of mass murder. Mass murderers often also choose particular individuals or categories of individuals (e.g., women) that they perceive as responsible for their problems. Innocent bystanders may also be shot and killed, but most mass murderers have selected specific individuals or types of individuals as targets long before they start their rampage. In this regard, mass murderers seem to select women disproportionately for execution. Some experts think they do so because they are both misogynistic (hating women) and homophobic (hating gays), and that mass murder is, for them, a way of proving their manhood, especially if they have also experienced shame or humiliation in their personal lives (Herbert 2007).

Serial Killing

In contrast to mass murderers, serial killers tend to murder strangers, and these strangers are typically prostitutes, the homeless, and runaway youths and other individuals whom serial killers perceive as "easy targets." As Alex Alvarez and Ronet Bachman (2003:131) note, "Prostitutes, for example, are used to getting into vehicles with total strangers and driving to secluded areas. This behavior, of course, makes them very vulnerable to victimizations of many kinds, including serial killing."

Scholars distinguish several types of serial killers based on their motivation (Holmes and Holmes 1994). *Hedonistic lust killers* commit their murders for sexual pleasure, and may even have sex with a corpse. *Thrill killers* also kill for sexual pleasure, but obtain their pleasure by torturing or humiliating their victims before they die. *Comfort killers* commit their crimes for financial gain, while *power-control killers* commit their murders for the (nonsexual) satisfaction they obtain from dominating and then killing their victims. *Mission killers* are, as the name implies, "on a mission" to end the lives of types of people (e.g., prostitutes) whom they regard as immoral or inferior. Finally, *visionary killers* are psychotic and hear voices that tell them to kill.

Serial killer Danny Rolling, nicknamed the Gainesville Ripper, was convicted and executed in 2006 after murdering eight people, including five university students in Gainesville, FL in August 1990.

This last type of serial killer notwithstanding, many scholars think it a mistake to regard most serial killers as mentally ill, however horrible their crimes may be. As Alvarez and Bachman (2003:133) observe, "By definition, we want to believe that anyone who can kill, mutilate, and perhaps eat other human beings must be crazy. This is a natural reaction . . . [but] this conception of serial killers as crazy is not accurate. Most serial killers are not found to suffer from a psychosis and can typically distinguish right from wrong." Serial killers do tend to be *sociopaths,* in that they exhibit *antisocial personality disorder* traits such as lack of conscience and remorse and a desire for manipulation, but, as Fox and Levin (2005:112) note, this is a "disorder of character rather than that of the mind."

So why do they do it? Ultimately, there is no easy answer to this question. Many scholars attribute serial killing, and also mass murder, to childhood problems, including head injuries or brain trauma, parental neglect, and physical and/or sexual abuse (Begley 2007). Although some combination of these factors has been found in the backgrounds of many serial killers, these are common problems, and most everyone with them obviously does *not* become a serial killer. Thus, childhood problems by themselves do not explain why a few individuals commit serial murder years later. In a more sociological explanation, a recent study found that serial killers isproportionately grew up in the South, supporting the idea that they were influenced by the subculture of violence found in that region that was discussed earlier (DeFronzo et al. 2007). Despite many studies of serial killers, however, a good explanation for serial killing remains elusive.

Review and Discuss

Do you think mass murder and serial killing reflect psychological abnormality among the individuals who commit these crimes? Why or why not?

WORKPLACE VIOLENCE

"Going postal" entered the U.S. lexicon some time ago as disgruntled workers, some of them U.S. Post Office employees, went into their workplaces with handguns or other firearms and took a deadly toll on their bosses, coworkers, and former bosses and coworkers. Other workplace violence occurs when strangers enter to commit a robbery or when estranged lovers come to confront their partners, sometimes with deadly force. Sometimes workplace violence is random; in one example, a man who was angry over a broken door in his apartment building shot and killed the maintenance man and then shot and killed two more people at a nearby McDonald's and Burger King (Spangler 2000). Still other workplace violence is committed against people, such as police, who are performing their jobs but not technically in a workplace.

The Extent of Workplace Violence

Whatever its source, workplace violence is very common, and NCVS data paint a disturbing picture (Duhart 2001). From 1992 to 1999, about 1.7 million violent victimizations (equal to 18 percent of all violent victimizations) occurred in workplaces each year on the average, including 900 homicides, 325,000 aggravated assaults, 1.3 million simple assaults, 70,000 robberies, and 36,500 rapes and sexual assaults. According to victims, about 82 percent of the people committing workplace violence are men, 55 percent are white, and 43 percent are age 30 or older.

Somewhat more than half of all workplace violence is committed by a stranger to the victim, although this percentage varies by the type of workplace, as does the victimization rate in general. Table 10.5 provides the relevant information for several types of workplaces. Note that the workplaces included in the table actually involve several types of occupations, and that the victimization rate within each type of workplace can vary by type of occupation. Among teachers, for example, there are very large differences, ranging

TABLE 10.5 ▸ **Selected Information on Workplace Violent Victimization, 1993–1999**

TYPE OF WORKPLACE	AVERAGE ANNUAL VICTIMIZATION RATE PER 1,000 WORKERS	PERCENTAGE COMMITTED BY STRANGERS
Law enforcement	127	73
Medical	13	56
Mental health	55	25
Retail sales	20	52
Teaching	18	20
Transportation	16	51
Other	7	36

Source: Duhart 2001.

from highs of 68 (per 1,000) for special education teachers and 54 for junior high teachers to a low of 1.6 for college and university teachers. Your professor undoubtedly appreciates this!

HATE CRIME

Hate crimes are committed against individuals or groups or their property (destruction and theft) because of their race, ethnicity, religion, national origin, disability, or sexual orientation. The key factor distinguishing hate crime from "normal" violent crime is the motive of the offender(s). If the offender's motivation includes prejudice or hostility based on the victim's race, religion, and the like, then it is a hate crime (Perry 2008).

Defined this way, hate crimes have always been with us. In the United States, they go back at least to the 1600s, when Puritans in Massachusetts Bay Colony hanged Quakers (Brinton 1952). Although the term *hate crime* had not yet been coined in the days of slavery, the lynchings of African Americans, the killings of Native Americans, and the racial hostility underlying these acts classifies them as hate crimes carried out on a massive scale.

Although whites are sometimes the victims of racially motivated hate crime, most hate crime is committed by dominant or established groups against people perceived as different, many of them without power or at least statistically in the minority. In our history whites have committed hate crime against people of color, long-time citizens against immigrants, Protestants against Catholics, non-Jews against Jews, and heterosexuals against homosexuals. Sometimes hate crime takes the form of mob violence. Between 1830 and 1860, the major U.S. cities were racked by dozens of riots, many of them begun by native white Protestants who attacked African Americans, immigrants, Mormons, Catholics, and other non-WASP groups (Feldberg 1998).

Most hate crimes, however, are committed by organized groups or by individuals, not by mobs. Perhaps the most notorious U.S. example is the Ku Klux Klan (KKK), which committed many of the lynchings of African Americans and also terrorized Catholics, Jews, and other groups. Although the KKK is commonly associated with the South, it has had a strong presence elsewhere in the United States. During the 1920s, it numbered some 550,000 members in New England and held rallies across the region. Franco-Americans were a major target because their immigrant status and Catholic religion angered the Protestants who made up the KKK. During the rallies, Franco-Americans would darken their houses and hide under beds and in closets (Doty 1994). A newer hate group is neo-Nazis, including Skinheads (Hamm 1995). Skinhead gangs, typically composed of working-class young men and also some women, first formed in England in the 1970s, but spread to the United States, Germany, and other European nations by the 1980s. A specific type of hate crime, violence against lesbians and gay men, has attracted particular attention in recent years, especially after the brutal murder of Matthew Shepard in Wyoming in October 1998. Two men lured Shepard to a remote area, beat him with a gun, and tied him to a ranch fence in freezing temperatures. He was found after 18 hours and died a few days later (Swigonski, Mama, and Ward 2001).

Because the members of hate groups are, not surprisingly, difficult to study, we know relatively little about their social backgrounds or motivation beyond their racism or other prejudice. Sociologist Kathleen Blee (2002) interviewed thirty-four women in racist hate groups. Most of the women came from middle-class backgrounds and were not abused as children, and many worked in professional jobs. Although men tended to join the groups because of their racism and anti-Semitism, women joined for other reasons and then became more racist and anti-Semitic because of their participation.

Hate crime is vastly underreported, and the true number of hate crimes remains unknown. The FBI's count in the UCR is probably a serious underestimate, but the 2008 UCR listed 7,783 incidents of hate crime, involving 9,168 separate offenses, 6,927 offenders,

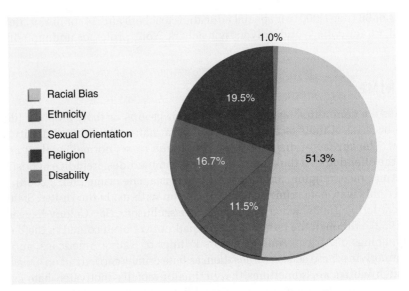

Racial Bias
Ethnicity
Sexual Orientation
Religion
Disability

1.0%
19.5%
16.7%
51.3%
11.5%

FIGURE 10.6 ▸ **Motivation for Hate Crime Offenses, 2008** Source: Federal Bureau of Investigation 2009.

and 9,691 victims (persons, businesses, locations). The FBI's total included 7 murders and 774 aggravated assaults. Racial prejudice motivated 51 percent of all incidents; religious bias motivated 17.5 percent; sexual-orientation bias motivated 17.7 percent; and ethnicity or national origin bias motivated another 12.5 percent (see Figure 10.6). About 60 percent of the offenses were crimes against persons, whereas 40 percent were crimes against property (Federal Bureau of Investigation 2009). The NCVS estimates a much higher figure of hate crimes, almost 200,000 annually, of which 56 percent were motivated by racial prejudice according to NCVS respondents (Harlow 2005).

VIOLENCE AGAINST CHILDREN: PHYSICAL AND SEXUAL ABUSE

One of the most tragic forms of violence in the United States and elsewhere is committed against children. This violence takes two forms: *physical abuse* and *sexual abuse*. Children can also suffer from neglect and other problems, and these are often included in discussions of **child abuse** and maltreatment. For the sake of simplicity and space, our discussion is limited to physical and sexual abuse and examines each problem in turn.

Extent of Physical and Sexual Abuse

We will never know how many children are abused each year. The major reason is that children are usually unlikely to report their abuse. The youngest ones, infants, obviously cannot even talk, and toddlers are little better. But even older children, say age 7, do not report their abuse for several reasons: They do not typically define their abuse as abuse, they may feel their parents have the right to hit them, they may feel they deserved to be hit and thus blame themselves, they may fear parental retaliation, or they may not know how or where to report the abuse. As a result, most child abuse remains hidden, and children can only hope that a teacher, nurse, physician, or other adult will notice their bruises and injuries.

We do have some idea of how many abused children there are, but this estimate represents only the tip of the iceberg. Each year the U.S. Department of Health and Human Services (HHS) gathers data from child protective service agencies across the nation. Using this information, HHS estimated that more than 122,000 cases of physical abuse and 69,000 cases of sexual abuse occurred in 2008. An estimated 1,740 children died in 2008 (Administration on Children Youth and Families 2010).

Some surveys ask parents whether they have committed various acts of violence against their children. The data from these surveys yield estimates of the number of physical abuse cases annually that are much higher than that reported by HHS. One survey estimate was 23 cases per 1,000 children, or about 1.7 million cases annually today, if the rate has not changed since the survey was done, while another survey estimate (by the Gallup company) was 44 cases per 1,000 children, or about 3.2 million cases today. These surveys estimates are thus up to twenty-six times greater than the annual HHS estimate, but even they are likely lower than the true amount because some parents do not disclose all the violence they have committed. The Gallup survey also estimated 19 cases of sexual abuse per 1,000 children, yielding an estimated 1.4 cases annually today; this figure is again much higher than the HHS estimate (English 1998).

Explaining Physical and Sexual Abuse

Whereas many theories of child physical abuse highlight psychological disorders in the adults who batter their children, sociological approaches instead emphasize the structural and cultural factor that make child violence inevitable. Following the theme of this book, we focus here on these factors.

One factor is inequality: Because of their size, intellectual immaturity, and lack of economic resources, children are a powerless group, perhaps the most powerless of all. Sociologically, it is no accident, and perhaps even inevitable, that children will suffer violence at the hands of adults (Gil 1979). This and earlier chapters have also emphasized that people are more likely to commit violence when they are very poor, and child physical abuse appears to be more common in poorer families than in wealthier families (English 1998). If so, this income patterning underlines yet another alarming consequence of poverty, even if most poor parents do not abuse their children. A key mechanism here is *stress* (Wauchope and Straus 1990). Many studies document that poverty can be a source of enormous stress as parents cope with paying bills, crowded housing conditions, and other problems. Given such stress, tempers often flare, with children a convenient target. Even in the best of circumstances, children often annoy parents; in worse circumstances, parents are annoyed more often and more intensely and can go over the edge.

Another important factor in child physical abuse is whether parents were physically abused themselves as children: Such parents are more likely to abuse their own children in a vicious cycle of violence (Widom and Maxfield 2001). Another explanation derives from the frequent use in the United States of spanking to discipline children. Reflecting the old saying, "spare the rod and spoil the child," most parents spank their children regularly, with some national surveys indicating that 90 percent of parents of toddlers spank them at least three times a week (Meltz 1995). Even if parents intend spanking for good purposes, it is still a violent act. Unfortunately, there is a very thin line between a "good, hard spanking" and physical abuse. Once parents are accustomed to using any force against a child, it is inevitable that undue force, or abuse, will occur. As Barbara A. Wauchope and Murray A. Straus (1990:147) pointed out, "Although most physical punishment does not turn into physical abuse, most physical abuse begins as ordinary physical punishment." Coupled with the vulnerability of children, cultural approval of violence against them in the form of spanking makes child physical abuse inevitable.

Turning to child sexual abuse, psychological explanations center on such factors as men's craving for love and affection, extreme jealousy and authoritarianism, and various personality disorders (Rowan 2006). A sociological explanation of child sexual abuse emphasizes power and gender inequality. Because the most typical episode of sexual abuse involves an adult man and a young girl, the power and gender inequality dimensions

Although many studies suggest that violence on TV and in the movies contributes to real-life violence, the actual effect of media violence remains unclear.

are apparent. These dimensions become especially important in incest, where fathers and stepfathers assume that their daughters are their sexual property (Russell 1984). Beyond this structural explanation, we cannot forget that girls and women in our society are still regarded as sex objects existing for men's pleasure. This belief contributes to our high levels of child sexual abuse and adult rape.

MASS MEDIA AND VIOLENCE

Violence portrayed in the **mass media,** particularly on TV shows and in Hollywood movies, is often blamed for the U.S. violent-crime problem, especially violence committed by juveniles. The key question is whether mass-media violence is a symptom of a violent culture or a cause of our violence. Both possibilities might be true: The United States might have mass-media violence because of its historical emphasis on violence, but mass-media violence in turn might promote additional violence in real life.

Much research establishes a strong statistical connection between mass-media violence and violent attitudes, behavior, or both, but causality is hard to prove (Glymour, Glymour, and Glymour 2008; Rhodes 2000; Surette 2011). Several lines of research exist. The most common study involves having children, teenagers, or college students watch violent videos; often a control group watches a nonviolent video. Typically, researchers measure the subjects' violent attitudes before and after they watch the videos by, for example, asking them how they would behave in various scenarios or whether they would approve of violence depicted in certain scenarios. When children are the subjects, researchers often watch them play before and after they view the videos. Regardless of the type of study, researchers typically find that viewing violent videos increases subjects' violent attitudes, behavior, or both.

At least two problems limit the value of such studies. First, because the studies are necessarily short term, they can find only short-term effects. Whether viewing violence has long-term effects, especially on criminal violence and not just on aggression, remains unclear. Second, because these are experimental studies, the effects occurring in the "laboratory" may not occur in the real world, where many other influences come into play (Lowry 2000).

Another line of research involves surveying children and teenagers and asking them how much TV, or how much violent TV, they watch. Their amount of time watching TV is then compared to their involvement in violent delinquency and other aggression. Researchers often find a statistical correlation between watching TV and committing aggression, and they conclude that watching TV increases aggression (Murray 2008). However, this correlation might be spurious. Youths might both watch TV and commit violence because they are interested in violence for other reasons. If so, both behaviors stem from this interest, and it cannot be said that watching TV causes their aggression.

Despite the evidence of mass-media effects on aggression and violent crime, the actual strength of these effects, especially compared with the importance of the other influences discussed earlier, remains unclear (Surette 2011). One critic even said that the notion that mass-media violence causes interpersonal violence amounts to nothing more than "hollow claims" (Rhodes 2000:19). A conservative conclusion is that mass-media violence does have an effect on real-life violence (Glymour, Glymour, and Glymour 2008), but that this effect is small and eclipsed by other influences. In view of the possible censorship involved in any legislative attempts to control the mass media, we should remain skeptical of mass-media effects until the empirical evidence becomes compelling. Even then, censorship remains an important issue that should be addressed.

Review and Discuss

What is the evidence for and against the proposition that mass-media violence plays a large role in real-life violence?

GUNS AND GUN CONTROL

Americans own more than 200 million firearms, one-third of which are handguns. The issue of guns and **handgun control** is one of the most controversial topics in criminal justice today. Scholars disagree on what the research evidence indicates about the relationship between firearms and crime and other violence (Wellford, Pepper, and Petrie 2004.) The major question addressed by this research is whether handguns deter crime or make firearm violence more likely. Another way of asking this is whether handgun ownership by law-abiding citizens raises or lowers their risk of becoming victims of gun crimes.

Gun-control opponents think reduction of handgun ownership by law-abiding citizens will make them more vulnerable to crime, not less. This is the "more guns, less crime" thesis (Lott 2000). A major problem with this argument lies in the nature of homicide. Recall that most homicides occur between people who know each other, often after an argument arising out of a minor dispute or as part of ongoing family violence. The presence of a handgun in law-abiding households greatly increases the chances that a gun will be used against a victim by someone he or she knows (Hoskin 2001). If no handgun were present, the offender would have to use a less lethal weapon, and a homicide would be less likely. Supporting this viewpoint, a widely cited study compared households with guns with ones without guns in the same neighborhoods and matched by age, sex, and race of household members (Kellerman et al. 1993). The researchers found that the households with guns were 2.7 times more likely to have someone in the house murdered, usually by a family member or close friend. This was true even when the researchers controlled for the use of alcohol or illegal drugs and a history of domestic violence. A more recent study analyzed the relationship between state rates of firearm ownership and homicide victimization. States with higher rates of firearm ownership had higher homicide victimization rates. Importantly, there was no relationship among the fifty states between firearm ownership and nonfirearm homicide victimization (Miller, Hemenway, and Azrael 2007).

If handgun ownership does deter crime, as gun-control opponents argue, then in communities that ban handguns, crime should go up, and in communities that require handgun ownership, crime should go down. Some interesting real-life tests of these possibilities occurred in the 1980s. In June 1981, Morton Grove, Illinois, banned handguns, and in September 1982 so did Evanston, Illinois. The bans received heavy publicity in the press. Despite the bans, burglaries in the two cities did not rise after the bans took effect. Meanwhile, in March 1982 the town of Kennesaw, Georgia, required every household to own a firearm. Research later found no evidence of a burglary reduction. A study of these cities said "there is currently no solid empirical support" for a deterrent effect of civilian firearm ownership on crime (McDowall, Lizotte, and Wiersema 1991: 556).

In a related issue, many states allow citizens to obtain police permits to carry concealed handguns. Advocates of concealed weapon laws believe they deter potential criminals from committing robberies and other crimes. If so, states that enact *right-to-carry* laws should see a drop in their crime rates. Several studies find such a deterrent effect (Lott 2000; Passmann and Whitley 2003), but other research challenges their findings (Black and Nagin 1998;

Packing Heat in the Land of Jefferson

What would you think if you were eating at a restaurant and you saw a table full of diners wearing handguns in plain view? This was a sight that confronted Virginians a few years ago, and it was a sight that prompted much debate over the wisdom and effects of "packing heat" out in the open.

The controversy began when the police in one Virginia town received a report in July 2004 that six men were sitting at a restaurant, all of them wearing guns. Four police hurried to the scene, only to be told by the men that they had a right to carry their guns in public. Much to many people's surprise and to some people's dismay, Virginia state law allows such a practice. At least three times that summer, members of the Virginia Citizens Defense League were seen carrying guns tied to their hips. Two of them were college students who had their guns taken by the police, who returned them the next day when they realized the students had broken no law. Police in various jurisdictions were then informed that carrying guns in public was perfectly legal under Virginia law. Ironically, Virginia, like many other states (and as discussed in the text), requires a permit to carry a concealed weapon, but not to carry one out in the open.

The situation arose from a quirk in the Virginia statute that bans the open carrying of firearms, but then defines firearms in a manner that excludes handguns, which, as a result, are not considered firearms under state law. A law that took effect on July 1, 2004, also contributed to the controversy: The law forbids any local gun-control regulation, and its enactment did away with local regulations that prohibited open carrying.

Virginia again made the news in early 2010 when it enacted a law that lets persons with concealed weapons permits take their guns into restaurants that serve alcohol, provided they do not also drink. The state senator who sponsored the bill said he wanted to enable women who carry guns in their purses to be safe when they eat at a Red Lobster restaurant, which he used as an example. A woman state senator who opposed the bill said, "I've really never been afraid for my life at the Red Lobster." Opponents said it would be difficult to enforce the no-drinking provision in the law, as gun-carrying diners could drink without anyone knowing they had guns because the guns would be concealed. A comment on a blog about the new law stated, "This is just what we need in Virginia. This law will ensure that the waiters and the cooks get the orders right."

Sources: Helderman 2010; Jackman 2004.

Handguns and handgun control remain one of the most controversial issues in criminal justice today.

Kovandzic and Marvell 2003). Additional research is needed to determine the effects of these laws.

Although gun ownership may not generally deter crime, once a crime has begun, a gun may help victims defend themselves or their property (*defensive gun use*, or DGU). Estimates of annual DGU in the United States come from the NCVS and other surveys and range widely from a low of 65,000 incidents annually to a high of 2.5 million (Wells 2002). The lower end of this range represents less than 1 percent of all violent crime, suggesting to some scholars that gun ownership provides little help (McDowall and Wiersema 1994). The higher end of the range suggests to other scholars that gun ownership provides significant help (Kleck and Gertz 1995). Regardless of whose interpretation is correct, DGU can prevent the intended victimization, but it may also increase the chance of victim injury or death (Schnebly 2002).

Review and Discuss

Do handguns make people safer or less safe? If effective gun control were possible, would it greatly reduce the number of gun-related crimes? Explain your answer.

Reducing Violent Crime

Although violent crime has declined since the early 1990s, it is still much more common than most Americans would want. What can be done to reduce it? Recall the explanations of violent crime stressed in this chapter: economic deprivation, criminogenic urban conditions, masculinity, racial discrimination, and inadequate and abusive parenting, among others. A sociological approach to reducing violent crime focuses on all these causes. Programs that might reduce poverty and joblessness, lessen urban blight, and improve the quality of parenting all hold potential for significant reductions in violent crime (see Chapter 18). Although they certainly have not been in fashion, such programs are essential if we want to make a dent in violent crime. To the extent that racial discrimination against African Americans and other people of color heightens their angry aggression and use of violence, successful efforts to reduce such discrimination would also help reduce violent crime.

A final focus for reducing violent crime must be masculinity. If men's violence rates were as low as women's rates, the U.S. violent-crime rate would be much, much lower. We must begin to raise our sons differently from the way we have been raising them. If we continue to accept the notions that "boys will be boys" and that they need to learn to "fight like a man," we are ensuring that interpersonal violence will continue.

WHAT HISTORY TELLS US

None of these roots of violent crime will be easy to eliminate, but if we do not begin to address them, our nation will continue to have much violent crime. Lest we despair too much over our situation, history tells us that reductions in violent crime *are* possible. Homicide rates in Europe were much higher in the Middle Ages than now, historians say (Eisner 2003). Amsterdam's rate in the mid-1400s was about 47 per 100,000, compared to about 1.5 per 100,000 in the early 1800s. Medieval England's rate was about ten times higher than it is now and almost twice as high as the current U.S. rate.

Most homicides in medieval England took place among farmers in their fields who fought over scarce resources (e.g., land) and over insults to honor they took very seriously. Because the courts were seen as slow and expensive, violence was a preferred way to resolve disputes. More generally, medieval people in England and other nations lived in a culture that "accepted, even glorified, many forms of brutality and aggressive behavior" (Gurr 1989:21). Knives and quarterstaffs, the heavy wooden stick used by Little John of Robin Hood fame, were their weapons of choice. The major reason for the drop in homicide rates in England and other European nations in the 1500s and 1600s was the development of a "civilizing process" marked by the rise of "courtly manners" and an increase in the use of courts to resolve private disputes (Elias 1978 [1939]).

A similar process later occurred in the United States, where the homicide rate peaked in the mid-1800s and then fell after the Civil War through the early 1900s, even though cities were growing rapidly (Monkkonen 1981). Scholars attribute this homicide decrease in the face of urban growth to the greater control that factories exerted over people's behavior, to the spread of public schools, and to the growth of the YMCA and other institutions that stressed moral behavior (Butterfield 1994). Looking at the historical decrease in homicides until the 1960s, historian Eric Monkkonen saw some hope: "What we are finding is that violence is not an immutable human problem. . . . The good news is violence can go down. The bad news is, we need to learn how to make it happen" (Butterfield 1994:16).

If history tells us that violence can go down, it also tells us that this will not happen if we do not provide economic opportunity for the poor and people of color. For example, despite the general decrease in U.S. homicide rates after the Civil War period, the African-American homicide rate did not decrease during this time, as African Americans continued to experience racial discrimination and declining economic opportunity (Lane 1986). Their rates finally did drop in the late 1940s and early 1950s, when increasing employment opportunities in factories and offices lowered African-American unemployment rates. Later in the 1950s, however, these unemployment rates rose as factories closed or moved from northern cities, and the urban decay that we see today accelerated. Not surprisingly, African-American homicide rates rose as a result (Lane 1989).

Conclusion

Violent crime remains one of the most serious problems in the United States. The fact that some groups—the poor, people of color, women—are more vulnerable to violent crime in general, or to specific types of violent crime, underscores the consequences of economic, racial, and gender inequality in U.S. society. Presenting a sociological understanding, this chapter emphasized that the roots of violent crime generally lie in the social environment. Even if we could somehow eliminate the violent individuals among us, others will soon take their place unless we also do something about the structural and cultural problems that make violence so common. A sociological understanding of violent crime thus underscores the need to reduce economic and racial inequality and to reshape masculinity if we want to reduce violent crime significantly (Currie 2010).

Another important theme of this chapter was that people we know, and in some cases know very well, account for much of the violence against us: Nonstrangers commit almost 80 percent of all homicides and more than half of all assaults. In Chapter 11 we examine several kinds of violence that women are especially likely to suffer from men they know, including spouses and partners.

10

Summary

1. Interpersonal violence involves the use or threat of physical force against one or more other people. This definition excludes two other types of violence, corporate and political violence, which also cause death, injury, and other harm, but are conceptually distinct from everyday interpersonal violence such as homicide, assault, and robbery.

2. Homicides include first- and second-degree murders and voluntary and involuntary manslaughter. In practice, these four categories often overlap, and

it is sometimes difficult to determine which category best describes a particular homicide.

3. Homicide and aggravated assault are patterned socially and geographically. Homicide rates are disproportionately high among African Americans, men, urban residents, and Southerners.

4. Certain characteristics of homicides are relevant. Regarding the victim–offender relationship, most homicide victims knew the person who killed them.

Homicides tend to be relatively spontaneous, emotionally charged events involving handguns.

5. Inequality and extreme poverty, cultural beliefs including masculinity, and other reasons rooted in the social environment help explain why the United States has the highest homicide rate among industrialized nations, why homicides are more common in urban areas than elsewhere within the United States, why men commit most homicides and aggravated assaults, and why African Americans and other people of color have disproportionately high homicide rates. Structural reasons also generally account for why some women commit violence while most do not.

6. Robbery is a crime that many Americans fear most of all. Like homicide and assault, it is patterned socially and geographically. Structural factors and a search for thrills help account for differences in robbery rates, and factors drawn from routine activities theory help account for differences in robbery victimization.

7. Mass murder and serial killing receive heavy media attention but are actually relatively rare events. Men commit most of these crimes, but accurate understanding of why specific individuals commit these crimes remains elusive. Almost one-fifth of violence occurs in the workplace, most often by strangers committing robberies. When coworkers "go postal" and go on shooting sprees in their workplaces, these incidents receive heavy media coverage.

8. TV shows, films, and other components of the mass media are filled with violence, much of it graphic, and many scholars and much of the public believe that mass-media violence is a prime contributor to violence by youths and other individuals. Although many studies find a correlation between exposure to mass-media violence and actual involvement in violent behavior, scholars disagree among themselves whether this correlation means that mass-media violence is, in fact, an important cause of real-life violence.

9. The issue of gun control is one of the most controversial in society at large and in the field of criminology, with scholars disagreeing among themselves on whether guns make people safer or less safe.

10. The homicide rate has decreased dramatically since several centuries ago. History tells us that increased economic opportunities for the poor and people of color are necessary to decrease their relatively high homicide rates.

Key Terms

assault 239

child abuse 258

handgun control 261

homicide 238

interpersonal violence 238

intraracial 239

manslaughter 238

masculinity 247

mass media 260

robbery 250

victim–offender relationship 243

What Would You Do?

1. Suppose you are driving a car on a city street and begin to stop for a traffic light. As you do so, you notice a burly, somewhat unkempt man come walking toward you rather quickly from the sidewalk. You naturally find yourself becoming tense as you see the man approaching. He may simply need some help, he may want to ask you for money, or he may want to steal your car. You have only a few more seconds until he reaches your window. What do you do?

2. This chapter included a discussion of guns and gun control. Pretend you are the mayor of a medium-sized city. A recent spate of robberies has captured a good deal of attention on local TV news shows and in the city's major newspaper. The public is clamoring for your office to do something about the robberies. A member of the city council introduces a resolution to allow private citizens to carry concealed handguns for their protection. What would your response be?

CHAPTER

eleven

Violence Against Women

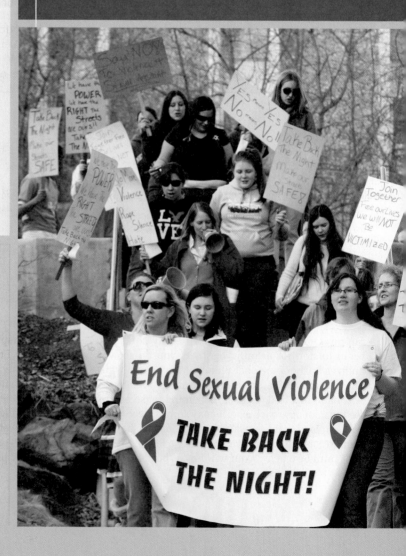

Crime in the News

In April 2010, 150 people marched downtown from the University of Wisconsin campus in Madison in a "Take Back the Night" march and rally to protest rape and domestic violence. Chanting "Two-four-six-eight, no more date rape" and carrying signs that read "Real men don't hurt women," they arrived downtown and held a candlelight vigil at which several women talked about their experience of being raped and others spoke about the problem of violence against women. "I don't just want the night back," one speaker told the crowd. "I want my hopes and my dreams and my peace of mind and my body back." One of the organizers of the event said, "It's the type of thing where all of us here have been touched by it, whether we know it or not."

Source: Brazy 2010.

Before the 1970s, rape and domestic violence were hardly ever discussed inside or outside the college classroom, even though they had been occurring for centuries. Then these crimes began to capture the attention of the modern women's movement, which was still in its early stages. Because of the feminist movement, there are now countless numbers of scholarly studies and popular accounts of rape and domestic violence (Miller 2006). Many college courses now deal with these crimes, and many campuses, as the Crime in the News story illustrates, have Rape Awareness Weeks, Take Back the Night marches, and other events. This chapter discusses the major findings from the burgeoning research on violence against women and continues the book's emphasis on the sociological roots of criminal behavior.

Overview: The Gendered Nature of Violent Crime

Women, like men, are victims of the crimes examined in Chapter 10: homicide, aggravated assault, and robbery. For all these crimes, their rates of victimization are much lower than men's rates. However, there are two broad categories of crimes for which women's rates of victimization are much higher: rape and sexual assault and domestic violence, also called *battering*. Moreover, when women are victims of homicide, assault, and robbery they are more likely than men to be attacked by people they know, including intimate partners (current and former husbands and boyfriends). Nonstrangers commit 68 percent of all nonlethal violence against women, but only 45 percent of all violence against men (Truman and Rand 2010). As Chapter 10 indicated, about 35 percent of all female murder victims are killed by male intimates, whereas less than 3 percent of male victims are killed by female intimates (Federal Bureau of Investigation 2009). These figures all demonstrate the gendered nature of violent crime, and especially of rape (and sexual assault) and domestic violence. Women are the primary targets of these latter crimes precisely because they are women.

Sociologically, this is not surprising. Socially, economically, and physically, women have less power than men. As the discussion (in Chapter 10) of hate violence against African Americans, immigrants, and other subordinate groups illustrates, powerless groups are often the victims of violence by those with power. Rape and domestic violence are no different. We cannot understand violence against women unless we recognize men's social, economic, political, and physical dominance and women's lack of such dominance. It is no accident that men are almost always the ones who rape and batter or that women are their targets. Given this context, rape and domestic violence may even be regarded as the equivalent of hate crimes against women.

AN INTERNATIONAL PROBLEM

As we look around the globe, violence against women is a worldwide phenomenon of "epidemic proportions" (Robinson and Maxwell 2008; Websdale and Chesney-Lind 2004:304). Amnesty International (2004:10) calls violence against women "the greatest human rights scandal of our times." Summarizing the results of hundreds of studies, a report from the Johns Hopkins University School of Public Health estimated that one-third of women across the world have been raped, beaten, or otherwise abused (Heise, Ellsberg, and Gottemoeller 1999). Female **genital mutilation,** a routine practice in many countries, affects more than 100 million women worldwide.

In Pakistan, women in police custody are often sexually and physically abused. In Kuwait, male employers routinely rape their foreign maids. About half of married men in Northern India say they have physically or sexually abused their wives (Martin et al. 1999). In Uganda, more than half of women have been victims of physical and/or sexual violence. while the government does little to prevent it or to punish the men who commit it. One young woman recalled her beatings after she got married: "At first all he did was beat me, and then he began to have sex with me by force as well. When I told him to wear a condom because I suspected he had been sleeping with other women, he would beat me some more. . . . I know that even if I go to the Local Council, they won't do anything; the same thing happens to my friends and nothing is done when they report it" (Amnesty International 2010b:12).

Violence against women is an international problem. About one-third of women across the world have been raped, beaten, or otherwise abused.

In India and Pakistan, **dowry deaths** claim the lives of thousands of women annually (Kethineni and Srinivasan 2009; Rastogi and Therly 2006). Brides in those two nations are supposed to pay the groom money or goods. If they do not, the groom often beats his wife, or he and his relatives murder her. To hide their crime, they often burn the woman with kerosene and claim she caught fire accidentally in the kitchen. Police then accept bribes from the husband and/or his relatives to pretend the murder was an accident. A Pakistani human rights attorney noted, "These cases are some of the most horrifying and gruesome human rights abuses in the world." Although they are common in Pakistan, she said they reflect a more general international problem: "It is really, at bottom, simply about violence and cruelty to women. That is not a story unique to Pakistan" (Sennott 1995:1).

The nations mentioned in these examples are neither wealthy nor industrialized, but international human rights groups emphasize that violence against women is very common in the industrialized world as well, as this chapter will illustrate for the United States. Amnesty International reported that emergency service agencies in the United Kingdom receive one phone call each minute about domestic violence. A woman there explained why she finally called the police after being beaten by her partner for eight years:

> I really don't know what it was that evening that made me decide to call the police, but I always say it was the sight of cleaning up my own blood. People have asked me why I didn't just leave, but my partner made lots of threats to me which he always carried out. I was very, very frightened of him. So you get to the point where you live with it, it becomes a normal pattern of life, you adapt, you cope, you hide it (Amnesty International 2004:1).

Some of the worst abuses of women occur in wartime. In one of the first books on rape, Susan Brownmiller (1975) wrote that wartime rape has been occurring for centuries. In nations that are dissimilar geographically and culturally, such as Mexico and Bosnia, women have been routinely raped and genitally mutilated over the past two decades during ethnic and political conflicts. After a war began in eastern Congo in

1998 between rebels and government forces, the latter routinely used rape as a weapon to quell the rebellion. It is estimated that over the next five years, soldiers raped almost one-third of eastern Congolese women, leaving thousands of them with vaginal fistula (a medical term for an abnormal duct or passage resulting from an injury or disease) and unable to work or to have sex or children. In protest, hundreds of women took off their clothes in the center of one town in March 2003 and shouted for the rapes to stop. One woman called out, "If you are going to rape us, rape us now because this must stop today." She later told a reporter, "So many women have it [fistula], and so many were raped. Some were even raped by men sticking branches and guns up their vaginas. We couldn't just cry. . . . We had to fight back" (Wax 2003:A88). Another epidemic of wartime rape occurred in Sudan during bloody ethnic conflict that racked the Darfur region of that Northern African nation in 2003 and 2004. A government-sponsored militia known as the *Janjaweed* (translated as "armed men on horses") attacked village after village and routinely raped the women they found there, often in front of their husbands and other villagers (Amnesty International 2004).

Rape and battering in the United States are thus part of a larger, international pattern of violence against women that also includes murder, torture, sexual slavery, incest, genital mutilation, and involuntary sterilization. Jane Caputi and Diana E. H. Russell (1992:15) termed these acts *sexist terrorism*. They are directed against women because they are women and the acts are motivated by "hatred, contempt, pleasure, or a sense of ownership of women." In its most severe form, such violence involves what Caputi and Russell called **femicide,** or the murder of women. They likened femicide and other anti-women violence to the lynchings of African Americans that were designed to reinforce white dominance over African Americans. In a similar fashion, they wrote, men's violence against women helps maintain their dominance over them. Femicide goes back at least to the witch hunting in medieval Europe that killed some 300,000 people, most of them poor women (Demos 2008). The gendered nature of these witch killings led one scholar, Marianne Hester (1992:36), to see them as "part of the ongoing attempt by men . . . to ensure the continuance of male supremacy." In the modern era, women in the United States and elsewhere are murdered by men who have been battering them. In other countries they are also killed during ethnic and political conflicts or because they violate rigid cultural codes of sexuality. Whatever the reason and the context, women are murdered or assaulted because they are women. Men are not killed or assaulted for the same reasons.

DEFINING RAPE AND BATTERING

Put most simply, **rape** may be defined as forced sexual intercourse. The National Crime Victimization Survey (NCVS) defines rape as "carnal knowledge through the use of force or threat of force, including attempts; attempted rape may consist of verbal threats of rape." The NCVS interviewer's manual is more specific: "Rape is forced sexual intercourse and includes both psychological coercion as well as physical force. Forced sexual intercourse means vaginal, anal, or oral penetration by the offender(s). The category also includes incidents where the penetration is from a foreign object such as a bottle." A related crime, **sexual assault,** involves unwanted sexual contact that does not involve sexual intercourse. The NCVS says that sexual assaults "include attacks or attempted attacks generally involving (unwanted) sexual contact between victim and offender. Sexual assaults may or may not involve force and include such things as grabbing or fondling. Sexual assault also includes verbal threats" (Bachman and Saltzman 1995:6–7).

Battering, or domestic violence, may be defined as physical attacks committed by intimates: spouses or ex-spouses, boyfriends or girlfriends, and ex-boyfriends or ex-girlfriends. This form of violence is also called *intimate-partner violence* or more simply, *intimate violence*. The attacks by intimates include both aggravated assaults, in which a weapon is used or a serious injury occurs, and simple assaults, in which no weapon is used and only a minor injury occurs. Although the definition of battering allows for men to be battered, almost all battering is done against women, as is discussed later. One problem with defining battering as physical attacks is that doing so excludes psychological abuse, which is often as harmful or even more harmful than physical abuse. Because there is much more research on physical abuse than on psychological abuse by intimates, most of our discussion addresses the physical dimension.

Most battering involves assaults against women by male intimates.

EXTENT OF RAPE AND BATTERING

Rape

When the U.S. women's movement turned its attention to rape in the early 1970s, it documented the role that rape played in women's daily lives. Thus Susan Griffin (1971) began her classic essay, "Rape: The All-American Crime," by saying, "I have never been free of the fear of rape. From a very early age I, like most women, have thought of rape as a part of my natural environment—something to be feared and prayed against like fire or lightning. I never asked why men raped; I simply thought it one of the many mysteries of human nature."

Research since the early 1970s confirms the magnitude of the rape problem. The NCVS estimates that almost 126,000 rapes and sexual assaults occurred in 2009 against people age 12 or older. Of this number, 84 percent were committed against females for a rate of 0.8 per 1,000 women; 79 percent of these were committed by someone the woman knew and only 21 percent by a stranger (see Table 11.1).

While the NCVS focuses on crimes in the past year, other studies estimate how many women have been raped at some point in their lifetime. The National Violence Against Women Survey (NVAW) found that 18 percent of women had been raped at least once in their lifetime, with 83 percent of the rapes committed by men they knew (Tjaden and Thoennes 2000). Other studies find that about 20 to 25 percent of women have experienced a rape or an attempted rape, with 70 to 80 percent of the rapes committed by men they know (Koss, Gidycz, and Wisniewski 1987; Russell 1984).

A study of a random sample of 420 women in Toronto found even more alarming figures. Melanie Randall and Lori Haskell (1995) supervised face-to-face interviews with the subjects that lasted about two hours each. Of the 420 women, 56 percent reported at

OFFENDER	PERCENTAGE
Nonstranger	79
Intimate	41
Other relative	<1
Friend or acquaintance	39
Stranger	21
Unknown	<1

TABLE 11.1 ▸ **Victim–Offender Relationship for Rape and Sexual Assault (percentage of all offenses committed against women), NCVS, 2009**

Source: Truman and Rand 2010.

 # International Focus

Rape in the Nordic Nations

The Nordic nations of Denmark, Finland, Norway, and Sweden are widely regarded as among the wealthiest and most progressive in the world, with a strong record of gender equality throughout their societies. Despite this reputation, rape remains a serious problem in these nations that is compounded by the failure of their governments to take it seriously. A recent Amnesty International report declared that "rape and other forms of sexual violence remain an alarming reality that affects the lives of many thousands of girls and women every year in all Nordic countries." The report went on to discuss many ways in which the Nordic governments compound the problem.

For example, Denmark's rape laws fall short of international human rights standards in at least two respects. First, they provide lower penalties for men who have sex with women who are in a helpless state, for example, because of mental illness or drug use, because physical force was not used or threatened; if a husband rapes his wife who is in a helpless state, there are no penalties. According to the Danish Minister of Justice, "It is not natural to call it a 'rape,' if the perpetrator has not used physical coercion or has not threatened the victim or placed that victim in a state where that person is unable to resist." Second, the laws allow for reduced penalties if a rape is committed by a husband against a wife even when she is not in a helpless state. The government was reconsidering this latter problem at the time of this writing.

Finland's rape laws take into account the seriousness of the violence used against a woman and include a category called "coercion into sexual intercourse." The average prison term for this type of rape is only seven months, even though the "coercion" often involves very serious violence. Two examples illustrate this problem. In one case, a man raped a woman in a restaurant bathroom after banging her head against the wall, twisting her arm behind her, and covering her mouth with his hand to prevent her from screaming. He was convicted of coercion into sexual intercourse and received a seven-month sentence that was suspended. In a second case, a case "where a woman was held captive for several days, raped repeatedly and denied her medication," according to Amnesty International, also resulted in a prosecution and conviction only for coercion into sexual intercourse.

In these and other ways, the Nordic nations fail to protect women who are raped or otherwise sexually abused. The Amnesty International report called on their governments to take several measures to help their women, including: (1) adopting legal definitions of rape that conform to international human rights standards; (2) undertaking education and other preventive efforts to reduce rape; and (3) improving the quality of the investigation and judicial handling of rape cases.

Source: Amnesty International 2010a.

least one experience of forced or attempted forced sexual intercourse, with 83 percent of these rapes committed by someone they knew. When Randall and Haskell included other forms of sexual assault, including unwanted sexual touching of the breasts or genitals, two-thirds of the subjects reported at least one completed or attempted sexual assault, including rape. The researchers concluded that "it is more common than not for a woman to have an experience of sexual assault during her lifetime" (p. 22).

Review and Discuss

How common are rape and sexual assault? How might the way the answer to this question is determined affect the estimates that are found?

INTIMATE RAPE

Table 11.1 shows from NCVS figures that intimates accounted for 41 percent of all rapes and sexual assaults in 2009. The National Women's Survey, a federally sponsored survey of a random sample of 4,000 women, similarly found that intimates had committed about one-fifth of the rapes reported by its respondents (Skorneck 1992). The NVAW survey found that intimates, including dates, committed 62 percent of the rapes its respondents reported. The Toronto study found that intimates committed 30 percent of all sexual assaults occurring after a woman reached the age of 16.

Taking all these studies together, a fair estimate is that intimates commit at least 20 percent of all rapes. Such rapes are especially likely to occur in marriages or relationships that also include battering: In the Toronto study, half of the women reporting a physical assault by an intimate had also been sexually assaulted by the same man. Intimate rapes, whether or not they occur without other physical violence, are often more traumatic for women than stranger rapes for at least two reasons. First, they cause a woman to feel betrayed and to question whether she can trust *any* man. Second, women raped by husbands or boyfriends they live with often have to continue living with them (Bergen 2006).

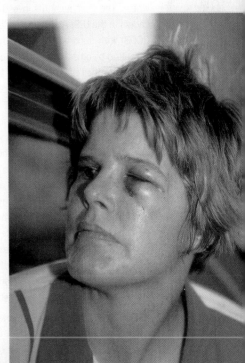

The National Crime Victimization Survey estimates that tens of thousands of assaults are committed by male intimates against women every year.

Review and Discuss

How does an understanding of the victim–offender relationship help us understand why rapes occur?

Battering

What about battering? The best evidence indicates that battering is even more common than rape. According to the NCVS, about 52,000 aggravated assaults and 401,000 simple assaults were committed by intimates against women in 2009, or about 453,000 overall for a rate of about 3.5 assaults per 1,000 women. The National Family Violence Survey (NFVS) yielded a much higher annual estimate of 6.25 million violent acts (ranging from using a weapon or beating to slapping, shoving, or pushing), for a rate of 110 per 1,000 women (Straus and Gelles 1986). The NVAW Survey, discussed earlier for rape, concluded that 22 percent of women are assaulted in their lifetime by a partner, including 1.3 percent (or 13 per 1,000) in the past year, for an estimate of 1.3 million assaults annually (Tjaden and Thoennes 2000). Drawing on various studies, the American Psychological Association reported that about one-third of all U.S. women will be assaulted by a male partner during their lifetime (Elias 1994). A nationwide survey of Canadian women

"All I See Is Blood": Rape and Battering in the Military

Women who serve our country in the military often find that the greatest threat to their safety comes from the men with whom they serve. As the title of a news report put it, "they fear ambush, snipers—and an enemy within." From 2002 to 2006, more than 500 military women in Afghanistan or Iraq reported being raped or sexually assaulted by U.S. military personnel; the actual number was probably much greater than this, since many women keep quiet about being attacked because they fear retaliation and because they do not think the military will take any action.

Reports of these assaults first surfaced in early 2004. Congress held hearings and told the military to issue an annual report on sexual assaults against members of the U.S. military around the world. The fiscal 2008 number was almost 3,000, but, again, this is probably a serious underestimate due to underreporting. According to some estimates, almost one-third of women in the military are raped or sexually assaulted.

The reports of the sexual assaults in Iraq and Afghanistan followed on the heels of a *Denver Post* report in November 2003 that documented thousands of rapes and acts of battering of U.S. military women on bases in the United States and elsewhere. The *Post* began its investigation after dozens of women cadets in the U.S. Air Force Academy came forward in February 2003 with reports that they had been raped or sexually assaulted by other cadets. The Academy, they said, did little or nothing to their offenders, while they, the victims, were intimidated and even punished for reporting the crimes. The *Post's* investigation found that sexual assault and battering were rampant throughout the armed forces and estimated that the number of women over the years who have been raped or sexually assaulted while serving in the military may be as high as 200,000. The number of cases of battering was more than 10,000 annually between 1997 and 2001.

According to the *Post*, many military women keep quiet about their victimization, but when they do report it, military officials usually treat the offenders with kid gloves, if they investigate the cases at all. For example, although more than 12,000 cases of battering within the armed forces were reported in 2000, only 26 resulted in courts-martial, and almost 5,000 army men accused of rape and sexual assault since 1992 were never criminally prosecuted; instead, if they were punished at all, they received administrative sanctions such as loss of rank. As these figures indicate, "the obstacles to pursuing justice are wrenching," as the *Post* put it. "Many (victims) fear retaliation, damage to their careers and being portrayed as disloyal. And those who do report are often punished, intimidated, ostracized or told they are crazy by their superiors."

Many women said the crimes committed against them and the callous responses of military officials amounted to a betrayal of trust. One woman, who was raped on a South Korea base by an army sergeant, said, "These people were supposed to be my family. All through basic training, that's what you're taught. Now I know that's not true."

Women veterans testify to the emotional trauma caused by their rape and battering. One woman, Rebekah, who was assaulted by her captain in Iraq, recalled, "The first two days after the incident, I just got physically ill. I just kept throwing up. After two days with the medics, I came back to the unit. But after that happened, I was so paranoid. It screwed me up for a while." Another woman, Sharon, was a combat medic during Operation Desert Storm in 1991 when she was gang-raped by fellow soldiers after being drugged. Although her rapists threatened to kill her if she reported what happened, she did so anyway, only to hear the military police officer respond, "What did you expect, being a female in Saudi Arabia?" In 1999 she suffered an emotional breakdown and was diagnosed with post-traumatic stress disorder.

A third woman, Marian, was 18 and just out of basic training when she was gang-raped by her drill sergeant and four other soldiers. In addition to the repeated rapes, they fractured several bones including her spine, urinated on her, and burned her with cigarettes. Her assailants were never brought to justice. Years later, she was continuing to have many serious health problems arising from her gang rape and beating when she was diagnosed with cervical cancer and given just a few years to live. Her will specifies that if her daughters join the military, they will not inherit any of her money. She will also not display the American flag: "When I looked at the American flag, I used to see red, white, and blue. Now, all I see is blood."

Sources: Gibbs 2010; Harris 2007; Herdy and Moffeit 2004; Schmitt 2004.

concluded that 25 percent had been assaulted by a husband or common-law (i.e., living together) partner (Randall and Haskell 1995).

Studies like these suggest that one-fifth to one-third of U.S. and Canadian women have been physically assaulted by a husband or other male intimate. This evidence leads domestic violence scholar Angela Browne to conclude that women "are more likely to be attacked and injured by a male partner than any other category of person. They are also more likely to be killed by a male partner than any other category of person" (Reynolds 1987:A18).

SOCIAL PATTERNING OF RAPE AND BATTERING

Age

The NCVS has reported detailed sociodemographic patterns for a combined measure of intimate-partner violence (IPV) that includes rape and sexual assault, aggravated and simple assault, and robbery (Catalano 2007). Because robberies are only 10 percent or less of the total measure, the patterns revealed by NCVS IPV data safely apply to rape and battering. With this in mind, rape and battering are, like many other crimes, more common among some demographic subgroups than others. One of the biggest risk factors is age: Young women are much more likely than older women to experience IPV (see Figure 11.1).

Social Class

Many discussions emphasize that rape and battering transcend social class boundaries. Although this is true, the NCVS does find that the poorest women have rates of IPV 6.6 times higher than those for women in the highest income bracket (see Figure 11.2). This social class difference underscores an important consequence of economic inequality in society.

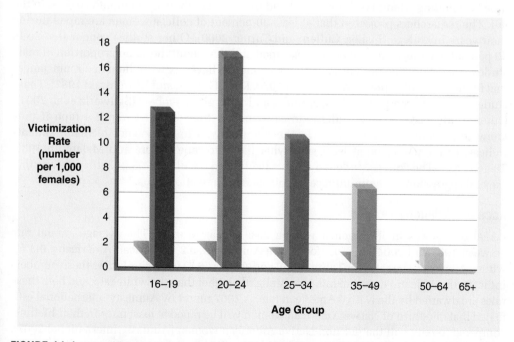

FIGURE 11.1 ▶ **Age and Average Annual Intimate-Partner Violence Committed Against Women 1993–2004**
Source: Catalano 2006a.

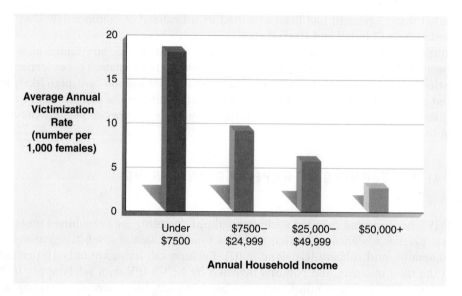

FIGURE 11.2 ▸ **Household Income and Average Annual Intimate-Partner Violence Committed Against Women, 1993–2004** Source: Catalano 2006.

That said, it remains true that rape and battering also occur among the middle and upper classes. As the notorious case of O. J. Simpson illustrates, men in all walks of life commit these crimes. In 1989 police responding to a "domestic dispute" saw Nicole Brown Simpson, "her lip bloodied, face swollen and eye blackened," running across the lawn and collapsing. At that point she screamed, "He's going to kill me, he's going to kill me!" When the police asked her who, she said, "O. J." (McGrory 1994:12).

Studies of college students reinforce this point (Gross et al. 2006). A survey of almost 4,500 college women nationwide in the spring of 1997 found that 2.8 percent had been raped (including attempts) since school had begun fewer than seven months earlier in the fall. The researchers projected that at least 20 percent of college women are raped during their years in college (Fisher, Cullen, and Turner 2000). Other studies concur that 20 to 30 percent of college women have been raped and that about the same proportion of male students have forced or attempted to force women to have sex with them in circumstances that fit the legal definition of rape (Kanin 1970; Koss, Gidycz, and Wisniewski 1987). These students include campus leaders, athletes, and fraternity members (Schwartz et al. 2001). Other studies asked male students to say whether they would commit a rape if they knew they would not be caught. In these studies, 25 to 40 percent of male students indicated they would be at least somewhat likely to rape (Briere and Malamuth 1983; Tieger 1981). The college student evidence leads Diana Scully (1995:207) to conclude that "sexual aggression is commonplace in college dating relationships."

Race and Ethnicity

Racial differences in IPV against women also appear to exist. The average annual rate between 1993 and 2004 was 18.2 for Native Americans, 8.2 for African Americans, 6.3 for whites. However, the rates for Latinas (6.0) and Anglos (6.5) were similar. As these numbers indicate, the African-American rate is only slightly higher than the white rate, and both these rates are dwarfed by the Native American rate. A 2007 report by Amnesty International estimated that one-third of Native American women will be raped at least once in their lifetime, compared to only half that for non-Native American women (Amnesty International 2007). In another contrast, although IPV against whites and African Americans is usually committed by men from their own race, most rapes of Native American women are committed by non-Native American men. Scholars attribute the higher rates for African Americans and Native Americans to several factors, including (1) their greater poverty, (2) their greater likelihood of living in high-crime areas, and (3) a lack of adequate legal help and social service provision for IPV survivors (Benson et al. 2004; Rasche 1988; Stark 2004).

In addition to their higher victimization, women of color also face greater problems in seeking help from rape crisis centers, battered women's shelters, social service agencies, the police, and other sources (Huisman 1996; Potter 2006). A major problem is that the antirape and battered women's movements were begun by white feminists and over the years have included few women of color. As a result, rape crisis centers and battered women's shelters continue to be relatively absent in inner cities and other areas, such as Native American reservations, where women of color live. For women

Native American women experience especially high rates of intimate partner violence.

in the United States who do not speak English, another problem is the language barrier (Klevens et al. 2007). Even when rape crisis centers and battered women's shelters do exist, they do not always have interpreters to whom these women can talk. The same problem applies when a non-English-speaking woman calls the police for help. Many times her husband or partner may speak English better than she and thus be able to convince the police there is no real problem. Sometimes the husband or partner even has to translate the woman's words to the police; as you might expect, they cannot be trusted to tell the police what the woman is saying. For immigrant women and undocumented workers, the problem is even worse (Rasche 1988). In addition to the language barrier, these women also face possible legal problems, including deportation or arrest, should they seek help from the police or social service agencies.

Certain racial or ethnic groups also have cultural traditions that make battered or raped women especially reluctant to seek help (Huisman 1996; Klevens et al. 2007; Rasche 1988). For example, a strong norm on Native American reservations is that one does not seek help outside one's own community. Reservations are usually in isolated rural areas, and a woman may not be able to get off the reservation even if she wants to get help. If she decides to seek help on the reservation, it is likely that law enforcement officers and social service agency workers know her and/or her abuser. In Asian-American communities, hostility toward the larger, white society may inhibit women from reporting their victimization. The particularly high respect in Asian-American families for men leads to the same inhibition.

Another problem affecting many women of color is fear of and hostility toward the police. A good deal of evidence suggests that people of color of either sex are more likely than whites to distrust the police (see Chapter 2). This feeling may lead women of color to be less likely than white women to call the police in cases of battering or rape. One additional problem facing battered African-American women is that the police may have more trouble noticing bruises on their bodies than they would on white women's bodies (Rasche 1988).

Review and Discuss

What special problems do women of color face in regard to intimate violence?

EXPLAINING RAPE AND BATTERING

A basic issue in explaining rape and battering is whether the crimes are more psychological or sociological in origin. A psychological perspective assumes that many and even most rapists and batterers have psychological problems that predispose them to commit their crimes. A noted proponent of this view is A. Nicholas Groth (1979:5), who wrote, "Rape is always a symptom of some psychological disfunction, either temporary and transient or chronic and repetitive." Although three decades have passed since Groth wrote this, this view remains popular within the field of psychology (Lalumière et al. 2005). In contrast, a sociological approach emphasizes the structural and cultural roots of rape and battering. Adopting this view, Diana Scully (1995:199) said it is wrong to assume that "individual psychopathology is the predisposing factor that best explains the majority of sexual violence against women." This assumption, she said, overlooks the social sources of this violence and implies that it is "unusual or strange" (p. 204), rather than a common phenomenon of everyday life.

In evaluating this debate, recall from Chapter 6 that psychologically normal people are very capable of committing antisocial and even violent behavior. Although it might be difficult to understand how psychologically normal men could rape and batter, there is ample evidence that such men commonly commit these crimes. Although no one will deny that some rapists, batterers, and other criminals have mental disorders, these individuals comprise only a small proportion of all criminals. The remainder are as psychologically normal as you or people you know.

Support for this view comes from the evidence on the prevalence of rape and battering. If these crimes are so common, it becomes very difficult to argue that they stem from psychological abnormality, unless we want to assume that 20 to 30 percent or more of all men are psychologically abnormal. That, of course, would be silly. Instead, these figures indicate that structural and cultural forces must be at work.

Gender and Economic Inequality

A key force here is gender inequality. Feminist scholars see rape and battering as inevitable consequences of **patriarchy,** or **male dominance.** These crimes reflect women's social and economic inequality and allow men to exert and maintain their power over women (Garcia and Clifford 2010). This does not mean that all men rape or batter women, but that a gender-based analysis of violence against women is necessary.

Anthropological evidence supports this view. Peggy Reeves Sanday (1981) studied 95 tribal societies on which a wide variety of information had been gathered. In forty-seven of these societies, rape was unknown or rare, and in eighteen rape was common. She then compared the two types of societies and found that women in the rape-prone tribes had less decision-making and other power than did women in the rape-absent tribes. A similar study by Rae Lesser Blumberg (1979) focused on women's economic power in sixty-one preindustrial societies. Beatings of women by male partners were more common in societies in which women had less economic power.

Anthropological evidence supports the view that gender inequality helps to explain violence against women.

Some U.S. evidence complements this anthropological evidence, but the evidence is complex overall (Vieraitis, Britto, and Kovandzic 2007). Studies using city and state data usually find that rape rates are higher where women have lower levels of income and education, but some also find that rape rates are higher where women have higher levels of employment and occupational prestige. Complicating matters further, studies often also find that rape rates are higher where women have greater equality relative to men (e.g., when relative measures, such as women's income divided by men's income, are used). This latter evidence is interpreted as supporting a *backlash hypothesis* that violence against women is higher when men feel threatened by women's growing equality compared to what men already have. The U.S. ecological evidence, then, does suggest that gender inequality matters for rape rates, but also that it matters in a complex manner that future research will have to clarify.

If gender inequality might contribute to rape, so does economic inequality. In her classic essay, Susan Griffin (1971) observed that women become convenient scapegoats for the anger some men feel over their low socioeconomic status: "For every man there is always someone lower on the social scale on whom he can take out his aggressions. And that is any woman alive." In this regard, recall the discussion in Chapter 10 of masculinity and violence. We saw that men with low socioeconomic status use violent, "opposition" masculine behavior against each other to gain the respect their low status deprives them of. A similar argument holds for their interaction with women; rape and battering allow them to take out on women their frustration over their economic inequality and to prove their masculinity (Petrik, Olson, and Subotnik 1994).

Supporting this view, several ecological studies find economic deprivation linked to higher rates of rape (Martin, Vieraitis, and Britto 2006). In a study of the fifty states, Larry Baron and Murray A. Straus (1987:843) found that states with higher economic inequality had higher rape rates. The authors concluded that "rape may be a way for some men to assert their masculinity in the absence of viable avenues of economic success." Making this same point, a study of rape and battering by African-American men cited their anger over their poverty and perceptions of racial mistreatment (Marsh 1993).

Cultural Myths Supporting Rape and Battering

If economic and gender inequality make rape and battering inevitable, so do cultural beliefs that either minimize the harm these crimes cause or somehow blame women for their victimization (Garcia and Clifford 2010). Because these beliefs distort reality, they are often called **cultural myths**. The myths about the two crimes are similar in many ways, but for clarity's sake receive separate discussions here.

RAPE MYTHS

Two of the most common rape myths are that women like to be raped and "ask" to be raped by their dress, behavior, or both (Melton 2010). Regarding the first myth, one of the most famous scenes in U.S. cinema occurs in *Gone with the Wind*, when Rhett Butler carries a struggling, resisting Scarlett O'Hara upstairs to have sex with her—in short, to rape her. The next scene we see takes place the following morning, when Scarlett awakens with a satisfied, loving smile on her face.

Unfortunately, traditional psychoanalytic views of women support the idea that they want to be raped. Psychoanalyst Karen Horney (1973:24) once wrote, "The specific satisfactions sought and found in female sex life and motherhood are of a masochistic nature. . . . What the woman secretly desires in intercourse is rape and violence, or in the mental sphere, humiliation." Another psychoanalyst, Ner Littner (1973), distinguished between "professional victims" of rape and "true victims." The former unconsciously want to be raped and thus act unknowingly in a way that invites rape, whereas the former do not unconsciously want to be raped. Although psychoanalysts have begun to abandon such notions, they remain common in both psychoanalytic and popular circles (Melton 2010).

Decades after *Gone with the Wind*, attitudes have changed, but many men still believe that women enjoy being forced to have sex and thus do not take her no for an answer. Despite the antirape movement's dictum that "no means no," this cultural myth is still very much with us. The traditional dating ritual demanding that men "make the first move" feeds into this myth. So does the traditional component of masculinity that says men are more masculine, or "studs," if they have a lot of sex. As we saw from the studies of approval by male college students for hypothetical rapes, many men, even those who do not rape, find the idea of forcing a woman to submit to them to be sexually stimulating. This notion combines with the cultural myth that women enjoy being forced to have sex to produce tragic consequences for women and their loved ones.

The other myth is that women "ask" or "deserve" to be raped by the way they dress and/or behave and thus precipitate their own victimization. In this view, if a woman dresses attractively, drinks, walks into a bar by herself, or hitchhikes, she wants to have sex. If a rape then occurs in these circumstances, it is thought that she really wanted it to happen anyway or at least was asking for it to happen. Either way, she bears some blame for the rape. As writer Tim Beneke (1995) put it, "A woman who assumes freedoms normally restricted to a man (like going out alone at night) and is raped is doing the same thing as a woman who goes out in the rain without an umbrella and catches a cold. Both are considered responsible for what happens to them." In turn, the man who rapes her is held only partly responsible, or perhaps not even responsible at all.

This reaction is especially common if the woman has been sexually active in the past. Unless a woman in any of these circumstances suffers physical injuries in addition to the rape, it is often assumed that she consented to have sex and thus was not raped. Many people believe a "real rape" has not occurred unless all the following are true: (1) An injury or other evidence indicates forced intercourse, (2) the woman has not been sexually active, and (3) the woman did not dress or act in any way that might suggest she wanted to have sex (Melton 2010). This way of thinking ignores the fact that women are often raped without visible injuries. Often they do not physically resist the rape out of fear of even worse consequences or out of paralysis induced by the sheer terror of the situation.

These rape myths start early in life. A study of Rhode Island students in sixth through ninth grades found more than half saying it is okay for a man to force a woman to have sex if they have been dating at least six months. About a fifth said it is acceptable for him to force her to have sex if he has spent money on her on a date. About half said a woman who dresses "seductively" and walks alone at night is asking to be raped. More than 80 percent said rape is okay when a couple is married, and almost a third said it "would not be wrong" for a man to rape a sexually active woman (Hood 1995; White and Humphrey 1995).

One myth about rape is that a woman who dresses attractively wants to have sex. If a rape then occurs in these circumstances, it is thought that she really wanted it to happen anyway or at least was "asking" for it to happen.

BATTERING MYTHS

Myths about battering also abound (Jackson 2010). One myth blames battered women for being hit and says that they must have done something to anger their male partners. This myth is akin to the victim-precipitation myth that women ask to be raped. Feeding into this myth, a batterer often says he hit his wife or partner only because she did something to provoke him (Smith 1990).

Another myth is that, because many women do not leave their batterers or call the police, the battering cannot be that bad. If it were bad, the reasoning goes, then they would leave or call for help. This myth distorts reality in at least two ways. First, most battered women *do* try to leave their batterers or at least call the police. Second, when women do not leave, they typically have many practical reasons for being hesitant to leave or to otherwise seek help. Perhaps you even know a woman who has been beaten but who has not tried to end the relationship or call the police. Did you ever wonder why she did not take either action? Let's examine her possible reasons (Kim and Gray 2008).

First, there is often nowhere to go, especially if a woman has children. Battered women's shelters are only a short-term solution and are often filled to capacity. Relatives or friends may be able to house a battered woman and her children for a while. However, this again is only a short-term solution, and many women cannot find a relative or friend to stay with. Second, the question of money applies particularly to wives and other women living with their batterers: Because many battered women have no income independent of their husband's or partner's, economically they simply cannot afford to leave.

Next, women may fear that if they do try to leave their batterer, he will track them down and hurt them even worse than before. They may fear the same consequence if they call the police. Unfortunately, this fear is often warranted (DeKeseredy et al. 2006). Studies indicate that at least 50 percent of women who do try to leave their batterers are harassed or further assaulted and that more battered women are killed while trying to leave their abusers than at any other time (Browne 2004). As family violence researcher Angela Browne observed, "If a woman attempts to end or ends the relationship, there's often an escalation in violence just at that point because the man believes he's losing the woman" (Elias 1994:10). Echoing these views, one batterer said about beating his wife, "Every time, Karen would have ugly bruises on her face and neck. She would cry and beg me for a divorce, and I would tell her, 'If I can't have you for my wife, you will die. No one else will have you if you ever try to leave me'" (Browne 1995:232). In this context, the O. J. Simpson case again serves as a reminder. As sociologist Saundra Gardner (1994:A9) wrote at the time, "Nicole Simpson left. Not only did she leave, she took legal action and divorced her husband. And, she is dead."

Another reason battered women stay is that many continue to love their batterers. Most relationships and marriages begin in love, and battered women often continue to love their batterers and to hope things will improve. Feeding this hope, many batterers are very apologetic after hitting their wives or girlfriends and say it won't happen again. It is also true that women often blame themselves for being battered, just as rape survivors often blame themselves for being raped, feeling they should not have "dressed that way," led the guy on, and so forth. In short, battered women often accept the myth that the battering is their fault. Helping this to happen, a man might tell a woman he's battering her for any number of reasons: The kids are noisy, the dinner was cold, she allegedly looked at another man. He thus tries to get her to think it was her fault she had to be hit, and she often believes him. If she does blame herself for being battered, she is less apt to try to leave or call the police.

Finally, experts on women's violence talk about a sense of *learned helplessness* that some women develop from repeated battering

Battered women's shelters like the one depicted here are of great help to women who experience domestic violence, but are also only a short-term solution and are often filled to capacity

(Walker 1984). This self-defense mechanism helps a battered woman cope by giving up any hope of improvement and by becoming passive. Social scientists have identified a similar personality syndrome in victims of natural disasters and wars (Walker and Browne 1985).

With these reasons in mind, the surprising thing might be that so many battered women *do* try to leave or call the police. Certainly, if a woman takes neither action, it should not be assumed that the battering "can't be that bad."

Review and Discuss

What are any three cultural myths that help explain the amount of rape and battering in the United States today?

Other Factors and Perspectives

Gender and economic inequality and cultural myths help explain why rape and battering occur, but other factors also matter. Specific factors highlighted in recent research include the overuse of alcohol, unemployment and other stressful life events, and male peer support (Armstrong, Hamilton, and Sweeney 2006; DeKeseredy et al. 2006; Fisher, Daigle, and Cullen 2010). Thus, rape and battering stem both from the inequality and myths highlighted in a feminist perspective on violence against women and also from other sources.

Disputing a feminist perspective, Richard B. Felson (2006; Felson and Lane 2010) contends that violence against women is not qualitatively different from violence against men. By this he means that the same factors that explain violence against men explain violence against women and that patriarchy, misogyny, and other concepts basic to a feminist perspective play no role in violence against women. As an analogy, he says that although the Nazis killed millions of women, it would be a mistake to say they did so out of sexism because they also killed millions of men. Thus Felson (2006:21) asks, "Perhaps this same kind of selective focus affects our understanding of violence against women today. Are the offenders sexist or just violent men? Are women victimized because of their gender, or because they make up half the population?" His answer is that "sexism plays at most a trivial role in rape and in physical assault on wives. Typically, men who commit these crimes commit other crimes as well, and their backgrounds and attitudes toward women are similar to those of other criminals." In this *violence perspective*, then, violence against women is no different from violence against men in its origins and dynamics, and the feminist perspective has no basis.

Feminist scholars dispute Felson's violence perspective (Brush, Hattery, and Smith 2007). Among other objections, they say it ignores the gendered nature of violence against women, including the fact that so much of it is committed by male intimates, and the roots of violence against women in male dominance. Although Felson's argument has forced feminist scholars to sharpen their own arguments, it seems beyond question, as this chapter observed at the outset, that women are raped and battered precisely because they are women and that violence against women is in many ways qualitatively different from violence against men. The issue of battered men, to which we now turn, again reflects the tension between the violence and feminist perspectives on the violence women experience.

BATTERED MEN: FACT OR FICTION?

The violence perspective also assumes that men are assaulted by their wives and girlfriends as often as women are assaulted by their husbands and boyfriends. If this is true, there is nothing special about the battering of women because both sexes commit violence against the other sex, and women victims should not be singled out for extra attention. This in turn implies that the physical harm men do to women is less reprehensible because women inflict the same kind of harm on men. As you might expect, this issue is the source of a heated debate among criminologists and other observers.

Murray A. Straus (1993), a noted family violence researcher, says that the prevalence of violence by wives against husbands (and, by extension, female intimate partners against other men) is at least as great as that by husbands against wives. About 12 percent of each sex committed at least one act of violence (contained in a Conflict Tactics Scales [CTS] list ranging from slapping to using a knife or gun) against a spouse in a given year (Straus 1993). Studies using the CTS to examine dating relationships also report such gender equivalence in battering (Marshall and Rose 1990).

In his early work, Straus argued that this gender similarity obscures important differences that make battering a far more serious problem for women (Straus 1980). One difference is that a woman's violence is usually in self-defense or the result of being battered, whereas a man's violence is meant simply to injure and dominate his wife or partner. Another difference is that women tend to commit more minor acts of violence (e.g., slapping or pushing), whereas men tend to commit more serious acts (e.g., beating or using a weapon). Men are also much more likely to repeat their violence. In another difference, even when women and men both slap or punch, the man's greater strength allows him to inflict a far more severe injury. A final difference is that male batterers tend to be especially likely to hit a pregnant partner.

In his later work, Straus abandoned this argument. Instead, he concluded that women often initiate violence against their husbands and are not acting in self-defense or in response to a history of battering, and he has called for more research on this topic (Straus 2006). The title of one his articles called their violence a "major social problem" (Straus 1993). This assertion of *gender symmetry in intimate-partner violence*, as it is often called, has received considerable attention in the popular media and has often been cited as evidence that the attention given to the battering of women is at least partly misdirected because it ignores the battering of men (Kay 2008; Young 2006).

Critics heavily criticize the gender symmetry claim as yet another myth that obscures the true nature of intimate-partner violence (DeKeseredy 2006; Dobash 2003; Johnson 2006). Ironically, the reasons for their criticism echo those that Straus noted in his early work, that is, most women's "violence" against men is best considered self-defense or the result of repeated battering and men injure women far more than women injure men. Among other things, critics also say that CTS measures ignore the context of violence and do not include rapes and other acts that men inflict. Another problem is that some CTS measures are overly broad. For example, one measure is "bit, kicked, or hit with fist." A woman who bites gets the same score as a man who uses his fist (Dobash et al. 1992).

Perhaps the most important evidence against the gender symmetry claim comes from victimization surveys such as the government's NCVS, which, contrary to CTS studies, find that about 85 percent of all intimate violence is committed against women (Catalano 2007; Lauritsen and Heimer 2008). Similarly, the NVAW survey discussed earlier found that women were seven to fourteen times more likely than men to report serious violence by an intimate partner (Tjaden and Thoennes 2000). Drawing on such evidence, reviews conclude that evidence overall fails to support the gender symmetry claim (Kimmel 2002; Saunders 2002).

Michael P. Johnson (2006) says the different findings about gender symmetry in IPV stem from different sampling strategies and different measurement of IPV. He adds that different types of IPV exist, including *intimate terrorism*, in which one individual (almost always a man) is extremely violent and controlling, and *situational couple* violence, in which both partners commit relatively minor and limited violence and neither partner is controlling. The studies that find gender symmetry, he says, typically rely on representative surveys of the

In 2009, Erin Andrews, a sideline reporter for ESPN, was stalked by a man who spied on her in hotel rooms and posted videos on the Internet of her unclothed body.

population, but these surveys have high refusal rates (many people refuse to answer the questions), and the people who refuse are likely those who are either committing or experiencing the most serious IPV. For this reason, these surveys underestimate the serious, one-sided violence men commit and overestimate gender symmetry. Johnson urges future research on the issue to explicitly recognize that IPV is not a "unitary phenomenon" (p. 1015).

Scholars and other observers will no doubt continue to debate the belief that the battering of men is as bad as the battering of women. For now, it seems fair to say that male battering is certainly not fiction, but that it is also not the huge problem that some observers assert. Claims of gender symmetry in IPV are not justified and do an injustice to the tens of thousands of women each year who fear for their lives from men they once loved and from men they sometimes continue to love despite the violence they experience.

STALKING

In 2009, Erin Andrews, a sideline reporter for ESPN, was stalked by a man who spied on her in hotel rooms. He filmed her through peepholes he made and posted videos of her unclothed body on the Internet. He was later arrested and sentenced to thirty months in prison (Dillon 2010).

Although rape, sexual assault, and battering are the most serious forms of violence that target women because of their gender, **stalking,** or the persistent following, observing, and/or harassment of an individual, "has come to be seen as a new and increasingly prevalent form of criminal behavior" (Mullen and Pathé 2002:275). Although this behavior has undoubtedly existed for many years, only since the early 1990s have the public and media come to recognize it as a serious problem and criminal laws have been passed against it. Although celebrities of either sex can be stalked by persons of either sex, stalking has become generally seen as a violent crime that a man does against a woman. A common goal is to intimidate the woman into staying in a romantic relationship (Melton 2007; Nobles et al. 2009).

How common is stalking against women? Perhaps the best evidence comes from the NVAW survey discussed earlier. Respondents were asked whether they had been followed or harassed (including by phone calls and letters) at least twice by the same individual in such a way that they felt very afraid. Eight percent of women (and 2 percent of men) reported that they had been stalked at least once in their lives, and 1 percent of women and 0.4 percent of men said they had been stalked at least once in the previous year. These annual figures translate to about 1 million female victims of stalking and 370,000 male victims. Using an alternative definition of stalking that required the victim to be only somewhat or a little afraid of a stalker, 12 percent of women and 4 percent of men said they had been stalked at least once in their lives. The authors of the survey concluded that "stalking should be considered a serious criminal justice and public health concern" (Tjaden and Thoennes 1998:1).

The survey of 4,500 college women discussed earlier also found that stalking was fairly common (Fisher, Cullen, and Turner 2002). Slightly more than 13 percent of the women, who were surveyed during the spring semester, reported being stalked at least once since the beginning of the academic year about seven months earlier. Four of every five stalking victims knew their offender. In some 43 percent of all stalking incidents, the victim tried to avoid the stalker, and in 16 percent she confronted the stalker. Less than one-fifth of all stalking incidents were reported to campus security or local police.

Stalking can last for many months and can produce severe stress and psychological trauma (Logan et al. 2006). Besides the fear they feel, victims also perceive that they have little or no control over what happens and that the criminal justice system offers little help. An important question about stalking is how often it actually results in a physical attack on the victim. Although more research is needed, it is estimated that 30 to 40 percent of stalking victims are eventually attacked, with this risk being the highest for stalking by an intimate or ex-intimate (Mullen and Pathé 2002). In 15 percent of all stalking incidents reported in the college women survey, the offender threatened the victim, attempted to harm her, or actually harmed her (Fisher, Cullen, and Turner 2002).

REDUCING VIOLENCE AGAINST WOMEN

Along with crime rates generally, IPV against women has decreased dramatically since the early 1990s. The IPV rate was 9.8 per 1,000 in 1993 and less than one-third of that, 3.1, in 2005, a drop of 68 percent in just a dozen years (Catalano 2007; Catalano 2006). Experts attribute the decline to greater awareness of such violence, to improved services for battered and raped women, and to improved policing, despite the problems that still exist in these areas. Although the decline in IPV is welcome, several policies and measures would help reduce it even further.

If violence against women is a consequence of gender inequality, then to reduce it we must first reduce male dominance. As Melanie Randall and Lori Haskell (1995:27) put it, "Understanding the causes and context of sexual [and physical] violence in women's lives, and examining how and why it continues to happen on a massive scale, means calling into question the organization of sexual inequality in our society." Similarly, if economic inequality precipitates violence against women, then efforts to reduce poverty should also reduce violence against women. Reducing male dominance and economic inequality are, of course, easier said than done. But unless these underlying causes are addressed, rape and battering will surely continue.

A related solution focuses on the nature of masculinity. As Chapter 10 stressed, the violent nature of masculinity underlies much violent crime. If men in the United States and elsewhere learn to be violent, then it is no surprise that they commit violence against women as well as against men. To reduce violence against women, we must begin to change the way we raise our boys.

In another area, one of the major accomplishments of the women's movement has been the establishment of rape crisis centers and battered women's shelters. These have been an invaluable aid to women who have been raped and/or battered. There is a need for even more crisis centers and shelters in urban and rural areas alike. To this end, more money should be spent to expand the network of existing rape crisis centers and battered women's shelters.

One final possible solution to violence against women lies in the criminal justice system. Compared to thirty years ago, police, prosecutors, and judges are more likely to view rape and battering as real crimes, not just as private matters in which the woman is to blame. That said, many of these legal professionals still subscribe to the myths discussed earlier. A study of police reactions to male-on-female spousal violence illustrates this problem (Fyfe, Klinger, and Flavin 1997). It found that police were only half as likely to make an arrest in such assaults as they were in other types of serious assaults. As this study indicates, efforts to educate criminal justice officials on the true nature of intimate violence continue to be needed, as are efforts involving collaboration between criminal justice officials and community groups (Visher et al. 2008).

Other problems include the fact that women who are raped and battered often face a difficult time if they choose to bring charges. If they testify on the witness stand, defense attorneys often question their character and try to vigorously suggest that they share the blame for their victimization. More women might bring charges if this line of questioning were limited or prohibited.

Recognizing this, just about all states now have *rape-shield* laws that restrict the use of a woman's sexual history in rape cases. However, the degree of this restriction varies from state to state. Some states prohibit any such evidence unless it concerns a prior sexual relationship between the defendant and his accuser, whereas other states allow this evidence if the judge decides it is relevant. Many states allow evidence of a woman's sexual history if it might show that sexual activity with a third person accounted for any semen that was found. All states permit evidence of a sexual history with the defendant.

Rape-shield laws have been controversial, with some observers thinking they are not restrictive enough to protect a woman who brings rape charges, and other observers thinking they are too restrictive to afford defendants a fair trial. This controversy was reignited after rape charges were brought in 2003 against professional basketball player Kobe Bryant in Colorado. Some observers warned that his accuser would face harsh questions about her sexual past despite that state's rape-shield law (Estrich 2003). In contrast, other observers thought that the law was so restrictive that Bryant would not get a fair trial (Burton 2004). The controversy intensified when the judge in his case ruled that evidence of his accuser's sex life during the days surrounding their encounter could be admitted into trial (Johnson 2004). The charges were later dismissed after Bryant's accuser said she did not want to testify.

Arresting Batterers: Deterrence or Escalation?

Does arresting batterers make it more or less likely that they will batter again? Because batterers traditionally have often not been arrested, the answer to this question is important for both theoretical and practical reasons. Theoretically, it addresses the more general issue of the degree to which arrest, prosecution, and punishment deter criminal behavior. Practically, it holds important implications for how we can best protect battered women. If arresting batterers does indeed help keep them from battering again, as deterrence theory would predict, then batterers should be routinely arrested. However, if arrest increases the chances for future battering, as labeling theory would predict, then arresting batterers may put battered women even more at risk. What does the research say?

In a widely cited investigation of this issue in Minneapolis in the early 1980s, the government sponsored a study in which police randomly did one of the following when called to the scene of a battering: (1) arrested the batterer, (2) separated him from his wife or partner for 8 hours, or (3) advised the batterer as the officer saw fit, but did not arrest or separate him. Researchers then compared the battering recidivism (repeat offending) rate in the three groups. They found that arrest produced the lowest recidivism rate in the six months after the police were called (Sherman and Berk 1984). The finding that arrest worked prompted many jurisdictions across the country to begin arresting battering suspects routinely, even when their victims did not want an arrest to occur (Sherman and Cohn 1989).

However, the Minneapolis experiment suffered from methodological problems that cast doubt on its conclusions (Sherman 1992). For example, its measurement of recidivism neglected the seriousness of repeat offending in terms of injury and hospitalization. In another problem, it examined recidivism only for the six-month follow-up period. It is possible that arrest may reduce recidivism during this period, but increase it beyond this period. Further, because Minneapolis differs from other cities in its racial composition and other factors, its results were not necessarily generalizable to other locations.

These concerns led the government to sponsor several replication experiments in other cities: Charlotte, North Carolina, Colorado Springs, Colorado, Miami, Milwaukee, and Omaha, Nebraska (Sherman 1992). In two of the cities, arrest generally reduced future battering, but in the other three cities, arrest often increased battering after first decreasing it. The effects of arrest depended to a large extent on certain offender characteristics. In three of the cities, arrest reduced recidivism by employed offenders, but increased it by unemployed offenders. In one city, arrest increased recidivism by unmarried offenders, but did not increase it among married offenders.

Lawrence W. Sherman (1992), the primary architect of the Min-

Scholars disagree over whether police should be required to arrest any man accused or suspected of committing intimate partner violence, even if the woman does not favor an arrest.

neapolis study, noted that the equivocal results of the replication studies leave police and other officials with some major policy dilemmas. Because arrest apparently increases battering in some cities but reduces it in others, we cannot tell whether a city will experience an increase or a decrease. As Sherman observed, "Cities that do not adopt an arrest policy may pass up an opportunity to help the victims of domestic violence. But cities that do adopt arrest policies—or have them imposed by state law—may catalyze more domestic violence than would otherwise occur" (p. 19).

Further, because arrest may increase battering by unemployed men but reduce it among employed men, mandatory arrest policies may protect women whose husbands or partners work, but harm those whose husbands or partners do not work. As Sherman noted, "Even in cities where arrest reduces domestic violence overall, as an unintended side effect it may increase violence against the poorest victims" (p. 19). Another dilemma arises from the finding in some cities that arrest reduces battering in the short term, but increases it in the long term. With such evidence in mind, it becomes difficult to know whether arrest would do more harm than good.

Mandatory arrest policies raise other issues as well (Chesney-Lind 2002; Humphries 2002). First, because they obviously increase the number of arrests for domestic violence, they can be very costly in terms of prosecutorial and court resources. This effect can undermine the intent of mandatory arrest. For example, after domestic violence prosecutions increased in Milwaukee during the mid-1990s, such cases took much longer to process and convictions for domestic violence decreased, as did victims' satisfaction with the handling and outcome of their cases. The researchers who uncovered these unintended effects concluded, "Good intentions do not always result in good public policy. Arresting more batterers does not necessarily result in more prosecutions" (Davis, Smith, and Taylor 2003:280).

Second, mandatory arrest policies lead to more women being arrested for domestic violence even though their violence is much less serious than men's violence. Women's arrests may trigger child-custody actions and other difficulties. Third, mandatory arrest, as we have seen, may put some women in more danger. Fourth, mandatory arrest deprives victims of any role in the decision to arrest even though they may have good reasons for not desiring an arrest: It might put them more at risk for future battering, for example, or affect their family's financial stability. For his part, Sherman (1992) concluded from all the evidence that mandatory arrest laws should be repealed where they now exist, especially in locations with high unemployment rates.

Kathleen J. Ferraro (1995) believes that arrest helps define battering as a real crime, but she also fears that police will enforce mandatory arrest policies more against poor people and people of color than against wealthy whites. Although arrest may be needed, she said, to help women in great danger, battering and other violence against women will be reduced only to the extent that the patriarchy underlying these crimes is also reduced. The criminal justice system may deal with individual batterers, but more will take their place as long as patriarchy continues to exist.

A recent study analyzed the arrest issue with NCVS data. It found that arrest did not reduce repeated domestic violence, but it also found that victims' reporting of domestic violence to the police did reduce repeated violence. The researchers concluded that "the best policies for deterrence will be those that encourage victims and third parties to report violence by intimate partners to the police" (Felson, Ackerman, and Gallagher 2005: 563). As should be clear, the appropriate legal handling of batterers will remain an important issue for some time to come (Guzik 2008).

Review and Discuss

Do you think men who abuse their female partners should always be arrested? Why or why not?

Conclusion

This chapter continued the Chapter 10 emphases on the huge amount of violence by nonstrangers, on the inequality lying at the heart of much of this violence, and on the psychological normality of the offenders who commit violence. As long as the structural and cultural forces responsible for violence, including violence against women, continue to exist, the crimes resulting from them will continue as well.

Violence against women is an international problem that manifests itself in the United States through rape, battering, and other behaviors. Although it is true that most men do not rape and batter, it is also true that rape and battering are two of the most dire consequences of patriarchy and gender inequality. It might not be too much of an exaggeration to say that men who do rape and batter are fulfilling, in an extreme and terrible way, certain notions of masculinity. We certainly must hold individual men responsible for their violence against women, but at the same time we must also seek to reduce gender inequality and change the norms of masculinity if we want to reduce this violence. Because women have much more to fear from men they know than from men who are strangers, it is not enough to focus on making the streets safer for women. The problem goes far beyond popular conceptions of strangers lurking in alleyways.

It is time now to leave interpersonal violence to turn to property crime. We will return to the issue of violence in later chapters on white-collar crime, where we discuss corporate violence, and on political crime, where we examine political violence. These chapters will show that violence takes many forms and is even more common than this and the previous chapter indicated.

Summary

1. Violence against women is an international problem in poor and wealthy nations alike. Human rights organizations estimate that one-third of women worldwide have been sexually or physically abused. Other forms of violence against women include murder, torture, genital mutilation, and involuntary sterilization.

2. Rape and battering are two common crimes within the United States. Various studies estimate that 20 to 30 percent of U.S. women will be raped or sexually assaulted at least once in their lifetime and that the same proportion of women will be physically assaulted by a husband or intimate partner.

3. Rape and battering seem more common among people who are young adults and who are poor or near-poor. The evidence on racial or ethnic differences in rape and battering is inconsistent, but substantial differences do not seem to exist. If they do exist, they are likely due to the greater poverty and other criminogenic circumstances in which people of color are more likely than non-Latino whites to live.

4. A sociological understanding of rape and battering emphasizes gender and economic inequality. Cultural myths also matter and include such ideas as a woman "asking" to be raped or a woman not leaving her batterer because his behavior is not that bad.

5. One of the most heated controversies in the study of domestic violence is the issue of battered males. The best evidence indicates that women are far more likely than men to be battered.

6. A study in the early 1980s in Minneapolis suggested that the mandatory arrest of batterers would reduce battering. Replications of this study suggested that the issue is much more complex, and it is not clear whether mandatory arrest overall helps battered women to be safer or less safe.

Key Terms

battering 271

cultural myths 279

dowry deaths 269

femicide 270

genital mutilation 268

male dominance 278

patriarchy 278

rape 270

sexual assault 270

stalking 284

What Would You Do?

1. Your friend Susan went to a movie with a guy she had met in one of her classes. Afterward they went out to get a bite to eat and then he took her back to her dorm room. She invited him in and they began to kiss, when suddenly he forced himself on her, threatened her with bodily harm if she screamed, and raped her. Paralyzed with fear, she kept quiet and did not fight back. The next morning she tells you what happened. She wonders what she might have done to provoke him, and she also fears that no one will believe her story. What do you advise her to do or not to do? Why?

2. Suppose one of your neighbors, a good friend, confesses that her husband recently hit her because she was late putting dinner on the table. She says this was "only the second time" that he had hit her and urges you not to say or do anything about it. Although you want to respect your friend's wishes, you also worry about her safety. What do you do?

CHAPTER

twelve

Property Crime
and Fraud

Crime in the News

ven a police officer's house may not be safe. The headline in May 2010 said it all: "Homes of Two Officers Burglarized." The officers lived and worked in Chicago and lived in the city's Southwest Side neighborhood. In the first of the burglaries, the thief or thieves stole the officer's gun, bullets, badge, and bulletproof vest, and they also took several TV sets for good measure. In the second burglary, one or more persons broke into the garage at the officer's home and stole a uniform shirt and a pair of handcuffs. They also helped themselves to a car stereo.

Source: Sadovi 2010.

As this Crime in the News story reminds us, property crime can happen anywhere and to anyone. Legendary folk singer Woody Guthrie used to sing that some people rob you with a gun, while others rob you with a fountain pen. As his words imply, crimes for economic gain occur in different ways. The next two chapters discuss these crimes. We look at property crime and several types of fraud in this chapter and at white-collar crime and organized crime in the next chapter. Although these types of crime differ greatly, they all aim to improve the offender's financial status. Most property criminals are not as desperate as the proverbial parent who steals bread to feed a starving family, but they are still fairly poor. In contrast, white-collar criminals are often wealthy, with their crimes smacking more of greed. To the extent that this is true, the motivation of white-collar criminals is perhaps more shameful than that of property criminals. As we will see, white-collar criminals also cause more financial loss, injury, and death than do property criminals.

Nevertheless, as Chapter 2 pointed out, the public fears property crime far more than white-collar crime. There is no doubt that property crime is very costly. The FBI estimates that more than $15 billion in property is stolen annually, including cash, jewelry, clothing and furs, motor vehicles, office equipment, televisions and stereos, firearms, household goods, and livestock (Federal Bureau of Investigation 2010). The National Crime Victimization Survey (NCVS) estimates that property crime costs the nation more than $18 billion annually in total economic loss (property loss, medical expenses, time lost from work) (Maston and Klaus 2010). By any measure, property crime is a serious problem. We thus need to understand the causes and dynamics of the many types of property crime that exist.

Defining Property Crime

There are many types of property crime. The FBI classifies four types—burglary, larceny–theft, motor vehicle theft, and arson—as Part I offenses and several others as Part II offenses. Most of this chapter's discussion focuses on the Index offenses. The following definitions come from the Uniform Crime Reports (UCR).

Burglary is attempted or completed "unlawful entry of a structure to commit a felony or a theft." Most burglarized structures are homes and businesses.

Larceny–theft (hereafter *larceny*) is attempted or completed "unlawful taking, carrying, leading, or riding away of property from the possession or constructive possession of another." Larceny's key feature is that it involves stealth, but does not involve force, the threat of force, or deception. It is a miscellaneous category that includes such behaviors as shoplifting, pickpocketing, purse snatching, the theft of contents from autos, and bicycle theft, but it excludes property crimes involving deception, such as embezzlement, fraud, and forgery.

Burglary, larceny, and *robbery* (see Chapter 10) all involve theft. How something is stolen determines what kind of crime is committed. For example, if someone stops you at gunpoint on a street and demands your purse, wallet, or any jewelry you might be wearing, this is a robbery because it involves the use or threat of physical force. The involvement of physical force in robbery classifies it as a violent crime even though it is committed for economic gain. If someone runs down the street and grabs your purse or snatches a gold chain from your neck before you realize what is happening and then runs away, this is larceny. If he pickpockets your wallet, it is also larceny.

If someone steals an object from a store while the store is open for business, this is larceny (shoplifting) because the person had the right to be in the store. If the offender breaks into the store at night and steals the same object, it is a burglary. If someone breaks into your house and steals an object, this is also a burglary. If you invite someone into your house and he or she steals the same object, it is larceny. If you answer the doorbell and someone holds you up at gunpoint, it is a robbery. In one other area of confusion, if someone steals your car's hubcaps, CD player, or cell phone, this is larceny. But if the offender takes the whole car, it is motor vehicle theft.

To return to our definitions, *motor vehicle theft* is, as the name implies, the attempted or completed theft of a motor vehicle. Such vehicles include cars, trucks, buses, snowmobiles, and motorcycles, but exclude boats, farming equipment, airplanes, and construction equipment. About 80 percent of all motor vehicle thefts involve cars, including minivans and SUVs.

Arson, the final Part I property crime, is "any willful or malicious burning or attempt to burn, with or without intent to defraud, a dwelling house, public building, motor vehicle or aircraft, personal property of another, etc." To be counted by the UCR, arson must definitely be proved. Fires of unknown or suspicious origins are not counted. The FBI did not classify arson as a Part I crime until 1979. The reporting system is still not fully in place, as many law enforcement agencies

About 80 percent of all motor vehicle thefts involve cars, including minivans and SUVs.

do not submit arson reports for all twelve months or are spotty when they do report it. For these reasons, the FBI does not include arson in its estimate of the annual crime rate.

The UCR's Part II offenses include several other property crimes, all of which involve deception of some kind. *Forgery* and *counterfeiting* involve "making, altering, uttering, or possessing, with intent to defraud, anything false in the semblance of that which is true." *Fraud* involves "obtaining money or property by false pretenses." *Buying, receiving, and possessing stolen property* is another Part II property offense and is just what its name implies. We will take a further look at forgery, fraud, and stolen property offenses later. A final Part II property offense is *embezzlement*, defined as the "misappropriation or misapplication of money or property entrusted to one's care, custody, or control." This crime is examined in Chapter 13.

Extent of Property Crime

Although the UCR and NCVS provide different estimates of the amount of property crime, they both indicate how common it is. Table 12.1 reports UCR and NCVS estimates for burglary, larceny, and motor vehicle theft. With so much property crime, it is not surprising

TABLE 12.1 ▸ Number of Property Crimes, UCR and NCVS Data, 2009

TYPE OF CRIME	UCR	NCVS
Burglary	2,199,125	3,134,920
Larceny–theft	6,327,230	11,843,040
Motor vehicle theft	794,616	735,770
Total crimes	9,320,971	15,713,730
Source: Pastore and Maguire 2010.		

that the risk of becoming a property-crime victim adds up over time. The NCVS estimates that 72 percent of U.S. households will suffer at least one burglary over a twenty-year period (Koppel 1987).

The UCR and NCVS also report different pictures of trends in property crime. The UCR show that property crime rose sharply from 1960 until the mid-1970s and then rose again from the late 1970s before peaking by 1980. It then dropped before rising in the late 1980s and then declining after the early 1990s. In contrast, the NCVS shows that property-crime victimization has declined fairly steadily since 1973, the first year of the NCVS. These different pictures stem from the different definitions and coverage of property crime in the data sets. The exclusion of commercial crime from the NCVS makes comparisons especially difficult. But because both data sets tell us that property crime has declined since the early 1990s, we can be fairly sure that this is in fact what happened.

Property crime has declined not only in the United States, but also in most other Western nations (Bernasco 2009). What accounts for this decline? No one is sure, but experts offer several possible reasons: *target hardening* (discussed later), involving the greater use of alarm systems and other measures; less cash being carried because of the greater use of credit and debit cards; and the fact that people probably stay at home more to watch cable TV and videos (Felson and Boba 2010). Some of the reasons for the more general crime decline since the early 1990s, such as demographic changes in the population, may also apply to U.S. property crime (see Chapter 3).

Patterning of Property Crime

Like violent crime, property crime in the United States is patterned both geographically and demographically. Let's look first at geographical differences and then at demographic (gender, race, class, age) differences.

Figure 12.1 displays regional differences in UCR property crime for the United States in 2009; property crime is highest in the South and lowest in the Northeast. Figure 12.2 displays UCR urban–rural differences in property crime. Like violent crime, property crime is lowest in rural areas.

Turning to demographic differences, property crime tends to be a young person's offense; people under 25 years of age account for 56 percent of all property-crime arrests. Self-report

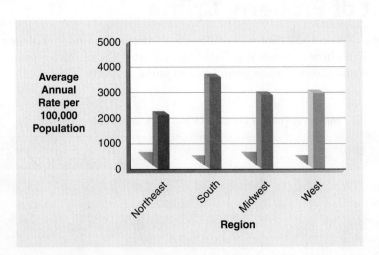

FIGURE 12.1 ▸ Regional Differences in Property Crime, 2009 Source: Federal Bureau of Investigation 2010.

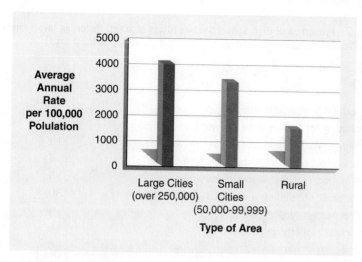

FIGURE 12.2 ▸ **Urban–Rural Differences in Property Crime, 2009**
Source: Federal Bureau of Investigation 2010.

data from high school seniors indicate that various kinds of theft and property damage are very common during adolescence (see Table 12.2).

Property crime also exhibits a significant gender pattern, with males accounting for about 85 percent of all burglary arrests, 82 percent of all motor vehicle theft arrests, 83 percent of all arson arrests, and 56 percent of all larceny arrests (2009 figures). The male proportion of larceny arrests is lower than for the other crimes because females are more involved in one type of larceny, shoplifting, than they are in other crimes. As the high school survey reported in Table 12.2 indicates, however, more males than females shoplift. Male shoplifters steal more items, and also more expensive items, than do female shoplifters and are also more likely to be professional shoplifters instead of amateurs (discussed later).

According to arrest data, the typical property offender is white, although African Americans are disproportionately represented (see Table 12.3). Although the UCR and NCVS do not report the social class backgrounds of property offenders, it is safe to say that the typical property offender is poor or near-poor.

Social Organization of Property Crime

A rich literature describes the social organization of property crime. **Social organization** refers to the roles that different property criminals play and the social networks that support their criminal ways. This literature makes a useful distinction between **amateur theft** and **professional theft** (Hepburn 1984) similar to that for robbery (see Chapter 10). *Amateur* criminals (also called *opportunistic* or *occasional* criminals) comprise the vast majority of property offenders. Most are in their teens or early twenties; they are unskilled and commit crimes when the opportunity arises, rather

Although males are more likely than females to shoplift, store personnel monitor female customers' behavior more closely because they believe women are more likely than men to shoplift.

TABLE 12.2 ▶ **Proportion of High School Seniors (Class of 2008) Reporting Involvement in Various Property Crimes in Last 12 Months (percentage saying at least once)**

ACTIVITY	MALE	FEMALE
Taken something from a store without paying for it	31	26
Taken something not belonging to you worth under $50	35	23
Taken something not belonging to you worth over $50	12	6
Taken a car without owner's (nonrelative) permission	6	4
Taken part of a car without owner's permission	5	2
Gone into a house or building when not supposed to be there	30	21
Set fire to someone's property on purpose	4	1
Damaged school property on purpose	16	7
Damaged property at work on purpose	8	3

Source: Bachman, Johnston, and O'Malley 2009.

TABLE 12.3 ▶ **Race and Property Crime Arrests, 2009 (percentage of all arrests)**

CRIME	WHITE	AFRICAN AMERICAN
Burglary	67	32
Larceny-theft	68	29
Motor vehicle theft	61	36
Arson	75	23

Source: Federal Bureau of Investigation 2010.

than planning them far in advance. In another defining feature, their illegal profit from any one property crime is relatively small.

In contrast, professional property criminals, first studied by Edwin Sutherland (1937), are older and much more skilled at what they do. They plan their offenses carefully, and the illegal profit from each crime can be high. Often they learn their craft from other professional criminals who serve as tutors by introducing them into the world of professional crime. Professional property criminals excite our imagination. Cat burglars and other professional thieves have been the subject of many movies and books over the years. We treat them somewhat like Robin Hood: Although intellectually we condemn their crimes, we secretly admire their brave daring, perhaps because of our own longing for economic success.

The amateur–professional distinction helps us understand the different types of offenders committing the different property crimes. In a classic study of shoplifting, Mary Owen Cameron (1964) categorized shoplifters as **snitches** and **boosters.** Most shoplifters are snitches, or amateurs, who steal merchandise of little value that they keep for themselves. Boosters, some 10 percent of all shoplifters, are skilled professionals who sell their stolen goods to fences or pawnshops.

Motor vehicle theft exhibits a similar distinction between amateur and professional offenders. Most analysts divide motor vehicle theft into two kinds, joyriding or professional theft (Clarke and Harris 1992). **Joyriding** is committed primarily by teenage boys working in groups as amateur motor vehicle thieves. As their name implies, these joy riders steal cars for a lark, take them for a short ride, and then dump them, often before the owner even knows the car is gone. They target unlocked cars with the key in the ignition or else crudely break into locked cars and hot-wire them. Because they abandon their stolen vehicles so soon, it is difficult to arrest them. Professional car thieves are older and more skilled. They can get into very secure vehicles, drive them away, and quickly dismantle them for parts in *chop shops* or otherwise deposit them into a very sophisticated auto resale market where they will be sold for a tidy profit. These professionals are so skilled that they are rarely discovered and arrested.

Review and Discuss

How does the distinction between amateur and professional criminals help us understand the nature and dynamics of property crime?

BURGLARY

The literature on the social organization of burglary is especially extensive. Although the image of a solitary professional cat burglar crawling up buildings and breaking into heavily guarded structures has been the stuff of many movies and books, most burglars are not nearly so skillful or specialized. They enter buildings through unlocked doors or windows or break into them in crude, unskilled ways. Most burglars do not specialize in burglary and instead commit other crimes over the long haul, but some do specialize in burglary for short periods (Wright and Decker 1994). Unlike the legendary cat burglar, many burglars work in groups of two or more, evidently feeling there is safety in numbers.

Beyond these generalizations, burglars differ in other ways. Mike Maguire (1982) identified three categories of burglars: low level, middle range, and high level. *Low-level* burglars are adolescents and young adults who get together to commit spontaneous, unskilled burglaries as a lark. They typically spend only a few minutes in the residence they enter and steal only small amounts of money and videos and other items popular in their age group. They do not think of themselves as criminals and lack access to fences and other members of what might be called the *burglary support system.*

Middle-range burglars tend to be older than low-level ones and more apt to spend time searching for attractive targets. They tend to act alone and often choose suburban areas featuring wealthy, isolated homes. They are more skilled than low-level burglars and more able to defeat home security systems. Middle-range burglars spend a fair amount of time in the residences they enter in order to find the most valuable items.

High-level burglars are the most skilled of all and tend to act in groups of two or more. They spend a lot of time planning their burglaries and are ready and willing to travel long distances to their targets. They also plan how to dispose of the items they steal through fences and other parts of the burglary support network. Neal Shover (1991) likened their burglary method to "military commando operations."

To determine how the experiences of female and male burglars differ, Scott Decker and associates (Decker et al. 1993) interviewed 105 urban residential burglars, 18 women and 87 men, and found some interesting similarities and differences. Female and male burglars were similar in their extent of drug and alcohol use and in their degree of specialization in burglary. Compared with the male burglars, however, female burglars began their crimes at a later age, were more likely to commit burglaries with other burglars, and were less likely to have been convicted of burglary. Additional studies of women burglars are needed to determine how they compare to male burglars and to yield a more complete understanding of the genesis and dynamics of burglary overall.

Tipsters and Fences

The burglary literature also describes the **support system** for burglars involving tipsters and fences (Shover 1973). *Tipsters* let burglars know of safe, attractive targets. They come not only from the criminal world, but also from legitimate occupations: Unscrupulous attorneys, repair people, police, bartenders, and the like, all tip off burglars about residences and businesses ripe for the taking. No one really knows how many tipsters exist or how much of a role they play in burglary, but it is safe to say that they often help middle-range and high-level burglars.

If you were to enter a home and steal an expensive stereo system and valuable jewels and silver, what would you do with these items? You might keep the stereo, but want to get rid of the jewels and silver in return for money. How would you dispose of the latter items? You cannot just walk into a jewelry store and say you found the items. It might also sound suspicious if you say they were in your family and you need money to pay your bills. As these problems suggest, burglars often need *fences* to dispose of their stolen goods and give them money in return (Cromwell and McElrath 1994). Fences sell the stolen goods to customers, many of whom are in legitimate occupations and recognize the shady nature of their transaction, but still want to buy the stolen goods for much less than they would otherwise cost. The world of professional burglars thus cannot exist without the help of otherwise law-abiding citizens.

Darrell J. Steffensmeier (1986) sees fences as working "in the shadow of two worlds," to quote the subtitle of his book on fencing. One world is that of any legitimate businessperson, whose activities a fence's functions resemble. Financial success in both fencing and legitimate business depends on marketing and management skills and on the ability to be reliable and punctual. As noted, fences also deal with law-abiding customers, further placing them in the world of legitimate business. The other world is the criminal world. The fence not only engages in illegal activity, but also interacts with many types of criminals.

DECISION MAKING IN BURGLARY

Another topic in the burglary literature is burglars' **decision-making processes.** Studies try to get into the minds of burglars to see how and why they decide whether to commit a crime and how they proceed once they decide to commit it. Most studies draw on in-depth interviews of small samples of burglars (Cromwell 1994; Tunnell 2006; Wright, Logie, and Decker 1995).

As Chapter 5 noted, these studies disagree on whether burglars pay much attention to their risk of arrest and imprisonment. On other points there is some consensus. In choosing a geographic area in which to commit a crime, burglars (and also other property criminals) rely on their knowledge of the area from their noncriminal activities (Bursik 2000). Once they choose an area, they tend to select homes less visible to neighbors and homes they believe to be unoccupied. As the police and news media remind us, burglars look for signs, including accumulating mail and newspapers, that people are away on vacation. Some burglars even scan newspaper obituaries to determine when homes will be empty while families attend funeral services. Other homes at risk are those whose residents are away at work or school for long periods.

Burglars tend to target homes that are less visible to possible scrutiny by neighbors and people passing by.

Property-Crime Victimization: Costs and Circumstances

To understand property crime further, we now examine its costs and the circumstances under which it occurs. The costs of property crime are both economic and psychological and are especially high for burglary. Homeowners and businesses spend tens of millions of dollars annually on elaborate security systems, firearms, and other items to prevent burglaries and protect themselves from intruders. Although burglary rates have been declining, this spending continues apace, and burglary remains very costly. The UCR estimates that burglary victims lost $4.4 billion in 2009, with an average loss per residential burglary of $2,100. About 70 percent of all reported burglaries are residential; the remainder are commercial.

Although burglary typically does not threaten its victims with injury, it still violates their privacy and sense of "personal space." Accordingly, about one-third of burglary victims become depressed, lose sleep, or suffer other similar problems. Female burglary victims are more likely than male victims to report being afraid and upset, whereas male victims are more apt to report being angry or annoyed. Women burglary victims who live alone are the most likely to feel afraid, evidently reflecting their concern over their physical vulnerability and the possibility of rape (Burt and Katz 1984; Shover 1991).

The NCVS has compiled some interesting figures on residential burglaries (Maston and Klaus 2010). Burglaries are slightly more likely to occur during the day than at night. Burglary victimization rates are much higher for poorer households; those with annual incomes under $7,500 are three times more likely to be burglarized than those with incomes of at least $75,000. In about one-fourth of all burglaries, a household member was at home, either asleep or doing various activities; another one-fourth were at work or on the way to or from work. Half of all burglaries are reported to the police, although this figure depends on the value of cash and/or property that was stolen: 84 percent of burglaries involving an economic loss of at least $1,000 are reported to the police, compared to less than 25 percent of burglaries with loss less than $100. When burglaries are reported, the police fail to visit the burglarized home 11 percent of the time; when they do visit the home, they arrive within ten minutes about one-third of the time, and within an hour three-fourths of the time.

Other property crimes are also costly. Turning to larceny, the UCR estimates that each 2009 larceny cost its victim an average $864, for a total loss from reported larcenies of about $5.5 billion. Because so many larcenies are not reported, the true property loss is undoubtedly much higher. As Table 12.4 indicates, the amount per larceny varies widely by the type of larceny.

TABLE 12.4 ▸ **Average Property Loss by Type of Larceny, UCR, 2009**

TYPE OF LARCENY	AMOUNT LOST
Thefts from buildings	$1,234
Motor vehicle contents	742
Pocket picking	504
Purse snatching	445
Coin machines	364
Bicycles	318
Shoplifting	81

Source: Federal Bureau of Investigation 2010.

Motor vehicle theft also adds up to billions of dollars annually. The FBI reported that about 795,000 million motor vehicles were stolen in 2009. Most of these vehicles 72.1 percent, were cars, with the remainder being trucks, buses, or other vehicles. The estimated value of all motor vehicles stolen was more than $5 billion, or $6,505 per vehicle. According to the NCVS, most motor vehicle theft occurs at night and either near the victim's home or in a parking lot or garage. In recent years, motor vehicle theft has become a worldwide phenomenon that the International Focus box discusses in more detail.

The average arson in 2009 cost $17,411 in property loss, for a total loss of about $1 billion. About 45 percent of all arson involved buildings; 28 percent involved motor vehicles and other mobile property; and 27 percent involved other types of property, such as crops and fences.

Explaining Property Crime

Explanations of property crime echo theories discussed in previous chapters. We first review several explanations of property crime generally and then turn to explanations of specific crimes.

CULTURAL EMPHASIS ON ECONOMIC SUCCESS

An important reason for property crime lies in the U.S. culture, which emphasizes economic success above other goals. As the discussion of anomie and the American dream in Chapter 7 indicated, the high emphasis on economic success underlies economic crime. The poor want more because they have not fulfilled the American dream; the rich want more because one can never have enough in a society that stresses economic success.

To explore this argument further, consider auto theft. Both as a status symbol and as a vehicle for transportation, cars are a vital part of our culture and economy. Auto manufacturers spend billions of dollars annually on advertising, with many of their ads targeting young men and stressing the excitement and even the sex appeal of owning a car. Against this backdrop, if you are a young man who cannot afford a car, you might well be tempted to steal one. With so many cars around, it is very easy to find one to steal. Given their advertisement-induced fascination with cars, many young men "borrow" them for a quick thrill. Other auto thieves are more economically motivated. Because cars are so expensive and have to be repaired so often, these thieves realize they can make a lot of money by stealing cars and either reselling them or dismantling them to sell their parts for repairs. For several reasons, then, auto theft is an inevitable property crime in our society.

Although this cultural emphasis seems to matter, it is also true that social class affects the way people break the law for economic gain. An important principle of criminology is that people have differential access to illegitimate means or, to put it another way, different opportunities for illegal gain (Cloward and Ohlin 1960). Poor people commit property crimes because they are not in a position to engage in complex financial schemes or to sell unsafe products. Wealthy people would not

Many motor vehicle thefts involve young men who take cars for quick, thrilling joyrides. Because of the speed involved, sometimes these joyrides end in tragedy.

International Focus

The Globalization of Motor Vehicle Theft

Like so many things in the world today, motor vehicle theft is becoming globalized. Motor vehicles are increasingly being stolen from the United States and other countries and then driven or shipped to other nations. Two international developments account for this increasing problem.

The first development is the rise of drug trafficking from Mexico and other nations south of the border into the United States. Of the ten urban areas with the highest amount of motor vehicle theft, seven are on or near the border with Mexico. Drug trafficking groups use the stolen vehicles to carry illicit drugs, weapons, and cash from drug sales into and out of the United States, and they also sell the stolen vehicles to help finance their drug trafficking.

The second development is the fall of the Soviet Union in 1991. This historic event freed the former Soviet nations to move toward capitalist economies. As they did so, they increased their demand for luxury cars and other vehicles. Because the supply of these vehicles in their nations was too small to meet demand, a market was created for vehicles stolen from other nations. Demand for imported stolen vehicles has also increased in other parts of the world, including the Middle East, parts of Africa, and China. The vehicles these nations receive come from the United States, western Europe, and Japan.

The number of stolen vehicles that are exported to other nations is estimated to be 500,000 annually. About 200,000 come from the United States, 20,000 from Canada, and as many as 300,000 from western Europe. Most are cars, but some are motorcycles and commercial trucks and vans. Different nations desire different types of imported stolen vehicles. German cars such as BMWs and Mercedes are a hot item in eastern Europe, but SUVs are the desired vehicle in African and South American nations.

China favors the Lexus and other luxury cars made in Japan.

Several groups ironically benefit from the massive exporting of stolen vehicles. Automobile insurance companies raise their rates to cover the loss of the vehicles and may increase their profits as a result. The companies that ship the stolen vehicles across oceans and other bodies of water also make a profit. Auto manufacturers also profit by selling new cars to the people whose vehicles were stolen. Finally, the economy of the nation from which a stolen vehicle is exported profits when the people responsible for the theft spend the illegal income they receive for their crime.

Certain "practical" conditions contribute to the exportation of stolen vehicles. First, many vehicles are driven across national borders each day, making it relatively easy to drive a stolen one across a border. Second, customs officials rarely examine the huge containers routinely carried on cargo ships. Third, many used cars are legally shipped from one nation to another, and stolen car rings are able to set up their activities as legitimate enterprises of this type. Fourth, the content and appearance of motor vehicle documents differ greatly from one nation to the next and are obviously written in different languages. These problems make it difficult for customs officials to know whether the documents are forged or changed. Fifth, officials in the countries receiving stolen vehicles are often corrupt and take bribes to look the other way. Sixth, motor vehicle theft is simply not a high priority for law-enforcement officials in the poor countries that receive stolen vehicles, because these nations face much more serious crime. For all these reasons, international trafficking in stolen vehicles is flourishing and shows no signs of abating.

Sources: Binagman 2010; Clarke and Brown 2003.

dream of breaking into a house or robbing someone on a street, but think nothing of defrauding the government, private citizens, and other parties in any number of ways.

TECHNIQUES OF NEUTRALIZATION

Chapter 8 noted that offenders engage in techniques of neutralization, or **rationalizations,** to justify their illegal behavior. Another underpinning of property crime is the rationalizations property offenders use. A store or other business is ripping us off or charging us too much, so we will rip it off. Everyone else does it, so why not me? The business is so big and rich, it won't miss what I take. Although most of us have not stolen a car or burglarized a home, many of us have done other things like shoplifting or taking items from hotels and motels, with many rationalizations for why our crimes are not really crimes.

Fencing

Rationalizations play an important role in **fencing,** as illustrated in Darrel J. Steffensmeier's (1986; Steffensmeier and Ulmer 2005) account of the experiences of a fence he called Sam Goodman (an alias). Goodman was close to 60 years old when Steffensmeier met him in January 1980 while Sam was serving a three-year prison term for receiving stolen property. Sam denied he was a thief: "A thief is out there stealing, breaking into people's places. . . . A fence would not do that. A fence is just buying what the thief brings, he is not the one crawling in windows" (1986:238–239). Sam also thought his fencing did burglary victims little harm because most of them would have insurance pay for their losses, and he likened fencing to legitimate businesses. As Steffensmeier (1986:243) put it, "Sam is in his store every day of the week. He buys and sells things, waits on customers, transports merchandise, and advertises in the yellow pages."

Sam also emphasized that his work benefited many people. The Red Cross sent him victims of fires to pick out home furnishings, and he then billed the Red Cross for what they chose. At Christmas he gave church groups household goods for poor families and toys for children. He added that many legitimate businesses deceive their customers, citing funeral directors who persuade the bereaved to buy expensive caskets and building contractors who exaggerate the effectiveness of security systems. As Sam put it, "Your fence really isn't much more crooked than your average businessman, who are many times very shady" (p. 243).

Review and Discuss

How does an understanding of techniques of neutralization help us understand the behavior and motivation of fences and other people involved in property crime?

ECONOMIC DEPRIVATION AND UNEMPLOYMENT

The explanation of property crime so far has highlighted cultural factors. Structural factors (see Chapter 7) also matter, as research links economic deprivation and urban living conditions to such crime (Walsh and Taylor 2007). A related body of research examines the effects of unemployment on property crime by comparing areas or individuals with different unemployment rates (Arvanites and Defina 2006). Despite many reasons to expect a strong unemployment–property crime link (Hagan 1993), research findings are inconsistent. Some find the expected link, others do not, and some studies have even found higher unemployment related to less property crime (Bursik 2000). Methodological differences appear to account for these inconsistent findings. In particular, individual-level studies find a link more often than community studies do.

In a related puzzle, property crime does not always rise when the economy sours, which might ordinarily be expected, as the evidence on this relationship is mixed (Wilson 2009). For example, the property-crime rate rose during the 1960s, when the economy thrived; it declined during the 1990s, when the economy also thrived; and it declined during 2009, when the economy was in a serious recession. An explanation for the mixed evidence comes from the routine activities and lifestyles literature (Felson and Boba 2010). Although unemployment may increase the motivation to commit property crime, it may also reduce the opportunities for property crime. For example, in areas and times of high unemployment, fewer people will be working or, because of their reduced incomes, vacationing, eating out, or engaging in other leisure activities. For these reasons, they will be more likely to be at home, ironically making their homes safer from burglars and themselves safer from robbers.

Complicating the issue, a recent study suggested that consumer sentiment about the economy might matter more for property crime than objective indicators such as the unemployment rate. Richard Rosenfeld and Robert Fornango (2007) found that property-crime rates between 1970 and 2003 rose when consumer sentiment as measured by the government was more pessimistic, and declined when sentiment was more optimistic. Drawing on this study and other recent research, Rosenfeld (2009:302) concluded, "Property crime rises during economic downturns and falls during recoveries."

ROUTINE ACTIVITIES AND SOCIAL PROCESS FACTORS

As the discussion of unemployment implied, the routine activities/lifestyles literature provides yet another explanation for property crime (Coupe and Blake 2006). Simply put, certain activities and lifestyles put people more at risk for burglary, larceny, and motor vehicle theft. For example, people whose homes are vacant for long periods of time because of work or vacationing are more apt to suffer burglaries, and those who often walk on crowded streets are more likely to become the victims of pickpockets or purse snatchers.

Social process factors such as learning and negative family and school influences also contribute to property crime. As Chapter 8 indicated, a large body of literature documents the effects of criminal peer influences, dysfunctional family environments, and negative school experiences on criminality, including property crime.

PROPERTY CRIME FOR THRILLS

In a novel formulation, Jack Katz (1988) argued that much violent and property crime is done for excitement and thrills. He described property offenses as **sneaky thrill crimes** that offenders commit because they are excited by the idea of stealing and by the prospect of obtaining objects they desire. Katz's view is both commended for calling attention to the importance of thrills and emotion for criminal behavior and criticized for overstating this importance (Hagan 1990; Turk 1991). Nevertheless, his theory helps explain why young males have especially high rates of property crime: they are more "seduced" than adults and women by objects that they want to steal, for example, motor vehicles (McCarthy 1995).

Importantly, Katz also found that, although socioeconomic status did not affect whether someone was attracted to an object he or she did not own, it did affect the likelihood of considering stealing the object. Whether people act illegally on their material seductions, then, may well depend on their social class. As Bill McCarthy (1995:533) put it, "People desire goods regardless of their structural conditions, whereas only those lacking (economic) opportunities are more willing to consider future theft if seduced."

Shoplifters rationalize their criminal behavior: The store charges them too much, makes them wait in line too long, treats them impersonally, or is so big it will not miss the shoplifted items.

A LOOK AT SHOPLIFTING

The several kinds of explanations just discussed—cultural emphasis on economic success, techniques of neutralization, routine activities, and sneaky thrills—all help explain why property crime occurs. A discussion of shoplifting and arson will emphasize this point.

Shoplifting is very common. The high school survey reported in Table 12.2 indicated that more than one-fourth of seniors had shoplifted in the last year. It is estimated that 8 to 10 percent of all shoppers shoplift, that about $13 billion in merchandise is stolen annually, and that the number of shoplifting incidents each year falls between 225 million and 300 million (Grannis 2009; Hayes International 2009). Most shoplifters, even professional ones, would condemn anyone robbing a store cashier at gunpoint of $10 or $20, yet they rationalize their own behavior. If you have friends who have shoplifted, you might have heard some of these justifications: The store charges them too much, makes them wait in line too long, treats them impersonally, or is so big it won't miss the shoplifted items. Like Sam the fence, shoplifters see crime and deviance as something other people do, even though the estimated annual loss from shoplifting runs into the billions of dollars.

Why else is shoplifting so common? For one reason, it is exciting, especially for the many adolescent shoplifters who act in groups of two or more to see what they can get away with. But cultural, gender, and social class forces also explain adolescent shoplifting. The teen subculture is so consumer oriented that youths feel pressured to steal items they cannot afford. This consumer subculture is a natural outcome of the cultural emphasis in the larger society on possessions and appearance. This emphasis leads girls to be especially interested in shoplifting cosmetics and clothes. For teens of both sexes, shoplifting stems from "the bombarding of young people with images of looks and goods attainable only with money many of them do not have" (Chesney-Lind and Sheldon 1992:44).

Routine activities theory also helps explain why shoplifting is so common (Dabney, Hollinger, and Dugan 2004). One reason shoplifting rose in the 1960s was the rapid development of large department and discount stores and especially of shopping malls, which did not exist before the late 1950s and early 1960s. For obvious reasons, it is easier to shoplift in large stores and malls than in smaller establishments. Large stores and malls thus presented the combination of motivated offenders, attractive targets, and lack of guardianship that, as routine activities theory stresses, results in crime and victimization. The rise in shoplifting was both predictable and inevitable.

Reducing Property Crime

Property crime has declined since the early 1970s, according to the NCVS. Popular efforts today to reduce property crime even further focus on the criminal justice system, on making it more difficult for property criminals to gain access to their targets, and on neighborhood watch groups.

THE CRIMINAL JUSTICE SYSTEM

Regarding the criminal justice system, federal and state governments have provided more money for additional police and mandated longer prison terms for persons convicted of serious property crime. As noted earlier, however, many and perhaps most property criminals do not weigh their chances of arrest and imprisonment as they decide whether to commit a crime. We also saw in Chapter 3 that only 18.6 percent of reported property crime is cleared by arrest. Because so much property crime is not reported to the police in the first place, the actual percentage of property crime that is cleared by arrest is much less than 18.6 percent. Because property criminals tend not to think and act in a way that makes their crimes deterrable, and because so few are arrested anyway, efforts to reduce property crime by increasing prison terms hold little or no potential for success (Shover and Copes 2010). Certain proactive policing strategies might help, and Chapter 16 discusses those further.

SITUATIONAL PREVENTION

Another popular response to property crime has been *situational prevention* strategies such as camera surveillance at street intersections, improved lighting, and exact change on buses. Situational prevention occurs at both the individual and community levels. Michael Tonry (2009:8) says "there is no doubt that situational prevention methods . . . can reduce crime rates, especially for kinds of crime that are often committed impulsively."

Target Hardening

At the individual level, situational prevention especially focuses on burglary and motor vehicle theft and takes the form of **target hardening:** efforts to make residences and businesses more difficult to burglarize, and motor vehicles less vulnerable to theft of the vehicle and/or of its contents. These efforts include stronger locks, burglar alarms, and other home security measures, all of which can reduce burglaries; and alarm systems, keyless locks, and other devices to make it more difficult to break into vehicles and to drive them away.

Target hardening seems to work, although it is difficult to determine exactly how effective it is. As one review put it, "the evidence has not always been compelling" (Bernasco 2009:185). For example, British data show that having window locks and deadbolt locks on doors appears to greatly lower the risk of burglary: Only 2.5 percent of households with these simple security measures are burglarized annually, compared to 22.5 percent of those without any locks (Felson and Clarke 2010). However, these households may differ in other respects that affect their burglary risk, making it difficult to draw any firm conclusions (Bernasco 2009). Still, the British experience suggests that target hardening and other measures do help. Britain began a comprehensive antiburglary strategy about two decades ago that involved target hardening, neighborhood watch groups, and publicity that warns homeowners about the risk of burglary and that indicates to potential burglars that homes will be difficult to break into. Evaluation of this strategy finds that it has helped lower the burglary rate (Bernasco 2009).

Experts also believe that target hardening has reduced motor vehicle theft. As a recent review noted, "Vehicles are now more difficult to steal than ever before as people have begun to take proactive measures to protect their vehicles by purchasing alarms, clubs, and other security devices" (Cherbonneau and Wright 2009:214). Vehicles are also

One of the most effective deterrents to burglary is a dog. Large dogs pose physical threats to burglars, and small dogs may yap and attract attention.

now being manufactured with sophisticated security systems and keyless entry systems. An additional target-hardening device is the electronic immobilizer, which is required on vehicles in Australia, Canada, and Europe and is becoming more common in the United States. This device involves a computer chip on the key that prevents thieves from jump-starting the vehicle. Evidence indicates that these vehicles indeed have a lower rate of theft than vehicles without the device. However, there is some evidence that thieves have simply switched to vehicles without the device and are finding ways to defeat it and steal the vehicle anyway. Ironically, increased security devices for vehicles may make vehicle theft more of a professional crime than it used to be, because the new measures often frustrate the efforts of joy riders to steal cars.

Two effective burglary deterrents are simply the presence of someone at home and a dog, both of which provide guardianship, to use a key term from routine activities theory. As Paul Cromwell (1994:43) observed, "Large dogs represent a physical threat to the burglar, and small ones are often noisy, attracting attention to his or her activities." Active burglars interviewed by Cromwell named dogs as the second most effective burglary deterrent, or "no go" factor, topped only by the presence of someone at home. One burglar said, "I don't mess with no dogs. If they got dogs, I go someplace else" (p. 44). Supporting this point, a study of college students at nine campuses found that theft victimization was lower for those who owned dogs than for those without a dog (Mustaine and Tewksbury 1998). The Crime and Controversy box discusses the issue of attacks by dogs on property criminals and innocent citizens.

Community Prevention

In addition to target hardening, situational prevention at the community level has also been used. This form of prevention focuses on streets and whole neighborhoods. Examples of community-level situational strategies include better street lighting, camera surveillance, and the reconfiguring of physical space to establish clearer sight lines. Tonry (2009: 9) concludes that "the evidence on the effectiveness of community prevention approaches is mixed, though some programs appear to be successful."

One form of community prevention does not appear to be successful, and that is the establishment of neighborhood watch organizations. Although these groups sound appealing, several problems limit their impact. The neighborhoods with the worst burglary and other crime problems are the least likely to start neighborhood watch groups, and when such groups are started, the households most likely to be burglarized are the least likely to join the groups. When groups do begin, people are enthusiastic at the outset but, as with many voluntary enterprises, quickly lose their interest (Shover 1991). Although research on neighborhood watch organizations suffers from methodological problems, the best-designed studies find that their efforts have only limited success or even no success. An additional problem is that, even if their efforts do succeed, the crime they prevent is often displaced to other locations (Sherman et al. 1998). The weak evidence overall leads Tonry (2009:9) to conclude, "There is no credible evidence that such

Crime and Controversy

Vicious Dogs and Property Crime

A dog can be a very good deterrent to burglary. One reason many people own a dog is to provide them some protection against burglars and other criminals and, in this way, to give themselves a feeling of security. For better or worse, many of the dogs that people own for protection are those with aggressive tendencies, such as a Doberman, rottweiler, pit bull, or German shepherd. These dogs may provide excellent protection against burglars, but on occasion they have attacked innocent people without provocation and seriously injured or even killed them.

One question that arises from such tragic incidents is the dog owner's legal liability. Owners can be sued for harboring a dangerous dog, and homeowner insurance companies are increasingly charging larger premiums for homes in which dogs from certain breeds reside, or refusing to cover such homes altogether. But some dog owners have also been criminally prosecuted after their dog has attacked someone without provocation. In a case that won national media attention, a San Francisco resident, Diane Whipple, was mauled to death in 2001 by her neighbors' two large dogs, both Presa Canario, a breed known for its ferocity. The attack, which lasted several minutes, occurred as Whipple was returning home, and the dogs bolted from their apartment. Their owner tried to stop them but to no avail. She and her husband, both lawyers, were arrested and indicted with various homicide charges. The trial judge called their dogs "a canine time bomb that would at some inevitable point explode with disastrous consequences." Both defendants were found guilty of involuntary manslaughter and sentenced to the maximum four years in state prison allowed under state law.

In a more recent incident from May 2010, a dog attacked a 6-year-old child in Southern California while the child, three siblings, and their mother were walking near their home. The dog kept biting the child until her 14-year-old brother hit the dog and it let go. The child was treated by paramedics for bites to her face, leg, arm, and shoulder.

What if a dog attacks a burglar? Although most jurisdictions have statutes that stipulate legal punishment for vicious, unprovoked attacks by dogs and that allow for these dogs to be put to death, these statutes typically exclude attacks on intruders or other people posing a threat to the dog's owner. For example, New York State law stipulates that a dog owner may be found guilty of a Class A misdemeanor if the dog "shall without justification kill or cause the death of any person who is peaceably conducting himself or herself in any place where he or she may lawfully be." However, the law exempts owners whose dog "was coming to the aid or defense of a person during the commission or attempted commission of a murder, robbery, burglary, arson, (or) rape in the first degree."

Sources: Animal Legal & Historical Center 2010; Associated Press 2004; Linthicum 2010.

organizations, usually organized in low-crime neighborhoods, have any significant effects on crime."

In sum, certain forms of situational prevention appear to help reduce property crime. Beyond these efforts, what else can we do? A sociological prescription for crime reduction would involve the cultural emphasis on economic success, economic deprivation, and social process factors. Perhaps it is too much to hope that the United States will soon decrease its emphasis on economic success and conspicuous consumption, but it is possible that public policy can do something about the economic deprivation, urban conditions, family dysfunction, and other by now familiar factors that set the stage for much property and other crime. Chapter 18 returns to this issue.

Review and Discuss

Evaluate the desirability and effectiveness of target hardening as a means of reducing property crime.

Fraud

Another type of economic crime in addition to property crime is fraud. **Fraud** involves deceit or trickery used for financial gain or for some other material advantage. Many types of crime fall under the broad category of fraud. We have saved these types of crime for last because they serve as a bridge between the property crime already discussed and the white-collar crime examined in Chapter 13. Many fraud cases could easily be considered white-collar crime, as they are committed by businesses and wealthy professionals as part of their occupations. We will keep most of our discussion of these types of fraud until Chapter 13 and will instead focus here on selected types of fraud committed by individuals and not as part of their occupations. These characteristics indicate that these types of fraud should not be classified as white-collar crime, although the proper classification is often difficult to determine (Copes and Vieraitis 2009b).

IDENTITY THEFT

Identity theft involves acquiring someone else's credit card number, Social Security number, bank account information, or other information that is then used for illegal economic gain, including the draining of an individual's bank account. The arrival of the Internet, as many people know all too well, increased identity theft by enabling hackers to access credit card numbers from individuals' purchases or from company databases. The NCVS estimates that 6.4 million households suffer identity theft annually, or 5.5 percent of all households, for a financial loss of $3.2 billion (Baum 2007). The Federal Trade Commission estimates that identity theft affects 8 million people annually for a financial loss of almost $16 billion (Copes and Vieraitis 2009a). Whatever the actual figures, identity theft is obviously widespread and costly and is estimated to cost more than $50 billion annually: approximately $5 billion for individuals and $48 billion for businesses (Abagnale 2005; Gilpin 2003).

Two specific types of identity theft involve check fraud and credit card fraud. Check fraud is a common crime, especially with the advent of high-speed printers, scanners, and other equipment to produce counterfeit checks. It is estimated that check fraud costs about $20 billion annually and involves more than 1 million fraudulent checks used or deposited each day (Abagnale 2005). In the days before modern technology, check fraud was less common and relied on the stealing of checks, a practice still in use today. Edwin Lemert's (1953) classic study of check forgers at that time distinguished two types of check forgers: *naive* and *systematic*. The former were the equivalent of amateur

Credit card fraud amounts to at least $1 billion annually and involves lost or stolen cards, the theft of card numbers from the Internet, or their acquisition through deceptive phone calls or from someone's mail or trash.

property criminals in that they worked alone and committed their crimes with relatively little skill, whereas the latter were more like professional property criminals in that they worked in groups and had fairly elaborate schemes for stealing and using checks.

A crime similar to check fraud is credit card fraud, which amounts to at least $1 billion a year and usually involves lost or stolen cards, the theft of card numbers from the Internet (described later), or their acquisition through deceptive phone calls or from someone's mail or trash (Berner and Carter 2005). As with motor vehicles, the abundance of credit cards provides tempting targets for motivated criminals. Some robbers or burglars acquire credit cards along with money and then use the cards until the victim informs the credit card company of the theft.

TAX FRAUD

Tax fraud, or *tax evasion,* involves the intentional failure to pay all taxes owed. The Internal Revenue Service refers to this problem as the *tax gap,* the difference between taxes that are legally owed and revenue that is actually collected, with almost all of it due to fraud. The IRS estimates that the tax gap in 2001 (the last year for which it has an estimate) was $345 billion, or about 16 percent of all taxes due by April 15. Of this amount, $55 billion was eventually collected through enforcement and voluntary compliance, yielding a net tax gap of $290 billion (U.S. Department of the Treasury 2009). Of this amount, $260 billion comes from individuals and small businesses and $30 billion from corporations. As high as this gap is, auditors for the U.S. Treasury Department think it may be even higher than the IRS's estimate because of deficiencies in the way the IRS compiled its estimate (Darymple 2006). Whatever the actual figure, the amount of tax fraud is far greater than the total value of all property losses from the other property crimes described in this chapter. Because of who is involved, tax fraud could easily also be considered white-collar crime. It is discussed here to reinforce the fact that economic crime is found in all walks of life.

It is difficult for the average person whose taxes are withheld from paychecks to cheat the IRS. Much tax fraud thus arises from the failure to report self-employment income and also from the claiming of false deductions (Braithwaite 2009). A common example of the former practice is the failure of restaurant employees to report their tips. But much more self-employment income is hidden from the IRS by small businesses and self-employed individuals, both blue collar (such as a plumber) and white collar (such as a physician). Much, and perhaps most, of such income belongs to middle- and upper-class professionals. However, the IRS has little way of knowing their income and thus must rely on them to report their incomes honestly. Many do not. Because of their occupations, investments, and other aspects of their status, many are also in a position to claim phony deductions that might sound plausible for them, but implausible for less wealthy people. Some also hide their assets in offshore bank accounts and undertake other sophisticated schemes.

Corporations also commit much tax fraud. In 1991 the U.S. General Accounting Office estimated that two-thirds of all U.S. corporations fail to report some of their income (*New York Times* 1991). The IRS's 2001 estimate of the tax gap listed $30 billion in unpaid corporate income tax, but this is probably an underestimate, as the IRS conceded (Darymple 2006).

Despite the enormity of tax fraud, our society does not condemn it. In fact, almost one-fifth of Americans say there is nothing wrong with cheating on their taxes (Bishop 2004). Nobody likes the IRS, so "ripping it off" is considered acceptable. As a technique of neutralization, we reason that because our taxes are so high it is okay to lower the tax bite through fraudulent means. The IRS gets so much money each year that it will not miss the relatively small sum of money we individually keep from it. We criticize, as we should, crimes such as burglary and larceny, but readily minimize the harm of tax fraud that costs many times more than these crimes combined.

INSURANCE FRAUD

Another type of fraud is *insurance fraud,* which accounts for about 10 percent of all U.S. insurance claims (South Carolina Attorney General's Office 2005). Insurance fraud is estimated to cost between $85 billion and $120 billion per year. Even the lower figure is almost five times greater than the FBI's estimate of the loss due to the street property crimes that worry us much more. The billions of dollars lost to insurance fraud do not come from us at gunpoint, but are costly nonetheless, as they raise the average household's insurance premiums by more than $1,000 per year. As with tax evasion, many otherwise law-abiding citizens think insurance fraud is acceptable, with almost one-third approving of exaggerating an insurance claim to compensate for paying a deductible (see Figure 12.3).

Several types of insurance fraud exist. One type involves arson to collect fire insurance. Health insurance fraud is also very costly and is covered in Chapter 13 as a type of white-collar crime because it so often involves medical professionals. Another common type of insurance fraud involves cars and other motor vehicles. Auto insurance fraud, as it is usually called, amounts to $14 billion annually and increases the average auto insurance policy by $200, or about $5 billion to $6 billion nationwide. About one-third of all claims for bodily injury in motor vehicle accidents are at least somewhat fraudulent (South Carolina Attorney General's Office 2005).

Auto insurance fraud occurs in several ways: (1) "paper" accidents in which no accident occurred but false reports are filed to collect insurance money, (2) minor accidents (e.g., the side-swiping of an innocent driver's car) deliberately committed to

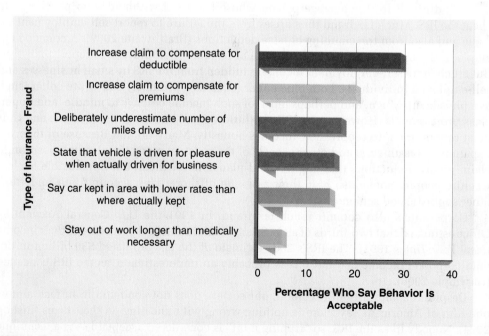

FIGURE 12.3 ▸ **Public Approval of Types of Insurance Fraud, 2002** Data from Insurance Research Council 2003.

collect insurance, and (3) staged accidents in which cars already damaged are driven to the same location so the drivers could pretend an accident occurred; (4) exaggeration of whiplash and other injuries after real accidents occurred; (5) abandoning or hiding a car and pretending it was stolen; (6) arriving at the scene of an accident and pretending one has been injured (Associated Press 1995).

After Hurricane Katrina hit Louisiana and Mississippi in August 2005, much insurance and related fraud occurred to claim some of the $5 billion made available for hurricane relief and rebuilding. Thousands of people committed at least $1 billion of fraud to get some of these funds. Some falsely claimed to be hurricane victims, and some falsely claimed to be helping real victims (Cohen 2007). Although much of the fraud was committed by ordinary citizens, some was also traced to public officials, small business owners, and employees of the Federal Emergency Management Agency and the Army Corps of Engineers.

Review and Discuss

Does tax and insurance fraud occur for the same reasons as burglary and larceny? Why or why not?

COMPUTER FRAUD AND COMPUTER CRIME

ATTENTION—FBI E-MAIL HOAX ALERT!! The FBI has become aware of e-mails being generated with the subject line "FBI Investigation" and implying the e-mail originated from the FBI. The e-mail requests the recipient's assistance by purchasing merchandise via the Internet. This e-mail is fictitious, and its origin is being investigated. The FBI would never direct someone to expend personal funds in furtherance of an investigation. If you've received the e-mail, please contact the FBI at www.ifccfbi.gov.

This warning appeared on the FBI's home page in July 2004 and is just one example of the many types of *computer crime* (also called *cybercrime*) that plague the Internet and affect so many people in the United States and abroad (Brenner 2010; McQuade 2009). Not long ago, this type of crime hardly existed, because personal computers were still rare before the 1990s. But just as the invention of automobiles more than a century ago enabled a new type of crime, motor vehicle theft, so the rapid growth of personal computer ownership has enabled many types of crimes that could not have been imagined a generation ago. Now that computers and the Internet are ubiquitous, so are opportunities for many types of offenses involving them.

With so many offenses, computer crime does not fit neatly into any crime category. For example, a man who makes a woman's acquaintance in a chat room and then rapes or robs her when he finally meets her is not just a computer criminal. Instead, his computer-related act is a violent crime. There are also reports that some juvenile gangs are planning their meetings, fights, and other activities over

Computer crime is a growing problem and involves such offenses as hacking and phishing.

the Internet, but most of us would not call them computer criminals. As we have seen, much fraud involves computers, e-mail, and the Internet, so computer crime could easily fall into the earlier identity theft section. But because of its growing importance, we examine computer crime here in a separate category.

Much computer crime involves *hacking*, in which, as you know, someone breaks into a Website or acquires information from someone's computer. Often the goal is identity theft: to steal someone's credit card number, social security number, or other information that can then be used to acquire money, other valuables, or important information fraudulently. Sometimes hacking is just done for thrills. A behavior related to hacking is *phishing*, which involves the use of e-mail or instant messaging to gain sensitive information. A popular type of phishing involves e-mails that purportedly come from a bank or other financial institution and ask the target to provide information so that a supposed account problem can be corrected. These e-mails look real and have fooled many people; it is estimated that phishing victimizes 1 million households annually with a loss of $650 million (Consumer Reports 2010). There are far too many examples of hacking or phishing to list here, but one notorious example involved the January 2007 hacking of the TJ Maxx and Marshall's clothing stores. Information was obtained on 46 million credit and debit cards that had been used beginning more than two years earlier (Kerber 2007). Eleven people from more than three different nations were accused of hacking into the accounts of these and other stores. The ringleader was eventually sentenced to a twenty-year prison term.

Other computer crime involves infringement of copyright laws and plagiarism. Term-paper mills, which a generation ago consisted of stacks of old papers in an offender's room that he or she made known were for sale, now exist at any number of sites on the Internet. A click of a mouse button can access these sites, and a quick (and expensive) credit card purchase allows a user to download some very well-written, and other not so well-written, term papers. As you know, students can also use the Internet to access electronic journal indexes; a quick click and drag of a mouse or touchpad can copy parts of these articles into a student's term paper. Some instructors are becoming more reluctant to assign the traditional term paper because such plagiarism is now so easy to do.

Cybercrime is difficult to control for many reasons, including the fact that it is often difficult to determine the identity of the person committing the crime. Someone can obviously be wreaking havoc over the Internet from halfway around the world. Hackers and other sophisticated computer criminals are very skilled and can keep one step ahead of investigators. They may eventually be discovered and apprehended, but in the meantime they will have done much damage.

THE COST OF FRAUD

It is instructive to compare the cost of "street" property crime—burglary, larceny, motor vehicle theft, and arson—with that of the many types of fraud just discussed. Recall that property crime costs the nation between $17 billion and $18 billion annually. Now recall the annual estimates of the various types of fraud: (1) check fraud, $20 billion; (2) identity theft, $53 billion; (3) tax fraud, $290 billion; and (5) insurance fraud, $85 billion to $120 billion. Taking the lower end of this last estimate, fraud amounts to at least $448 billion annually. This amount dwarfs the $17–18 billion lost to the property crime that worries us so much more (see Figure 12.4).

FIGURE 12.4 ▸ **Estimated Annual Economic Cost of Property Crime and Fraud**

Conclusion

Several theories and factors introduced in previous chapters help explain property crime, especially by the poor. Anomie, economic deprivation, and social process and routine activities factors all contribute to the higher involvement of the poor in robbery, burglary, and related crimes. We also cannot underestimate the role of gender, given that males account for the majority of larceny and more than 80 percent of other serious property crime. We previously explained this basic gender difference in terms of what masculinity means in modern U.S. society. Involvement in most of the property crimes in this chapter also demands the various traits that we associate with masculinity. The role that race plays is a bit more complex. Most property criminals are white, but African-American involvement in property crime exceeds the African-American proportion of the population. This latter fact once again underscores the criminogenic conditions in which many African Americans live.

The criminals in many property crimes can be divided into two basic types. Amateurs are the vast majority of all property criminals, but professionals steal more on the average because of their higher skills, greater willingness to take risks, and more frequent criminal involvement. People and organizations committing tax and insurance fraud could also be divided along these lines, with many white-collar criminals sounding and behaving very much like fences and other professional property criminals. Chapter 13 discusses this point further.

If nothing else, this chapter showed that economic crime in the United States is rampant. Many people have doubtless stolen or damaged property at some time in their lives. This is especially true if we include employee theft and other crimes to be discussed in Chapter 13. The poor commit the economic crimes we fear the most, but the middle class and the wealthy also commit many economic crimes. As emphasized at the outset, the kind of economic crime we commit depends on our opportunities. To recall Woody Guthrie's famous line, quoted at the beginning of this chapter, "some people rob you with a gun, while others rob you with a fountain pen." The next chapter examines the many forms of white-collar crime committed by the wealthy and respectable elements, individuals and businesses alike, of our society.

Summary

1. The legendary folk singer Woody Guthrie's observation that some people rob you with a gun while others rob you with a fountain pen reminds us that many types of economic crime exist. Property crime tends to be committed by the poor or near-poor, whereas white-collar crime tends to be committed by the wealthy.

2. The major forms of property crime are burglary, larceny, motor vehicle theft, arson, and fraud. The first four types cost their victims more than $15 billion annually. Property crime is least common in the Northeast and in rural areas. Most of it is committed by males. Although whites commit the majority of property crime, African Americans have disproportionately high rates.

3. Most property criminals are amateurs who tend to commit their crimes with little skill and planning and for little economic gain. Professional property criminals are much more skilled, commit their crimes with more planning, and reap much greater economic gain.

4. The external support system for burglars includes tipsters and fences. Tipsters include other criminals, but also people in legitimate occupations, who inform burglars of attractive targets. Fences sell the stolen merchandise, sometimes to otherwise law-abiding citizens.

5. Many types of fraud exist. Check forgery involves the writing of bad checks and is committed by both amateur and professional forgers. Its modern equivalent is credit card fraud. Before welfare reform in the mid-1990s, welfare fraud involved no more than 4 percent of people on welfare and amounted to $1 billion. In contrast, tax fraud amounts to almost $300 billion annually and involves many wealthy people and large organizations.

6. Insurance fraud is also common and costs tens of billions of dollars annually. A major type is auto insurance fraud, which adds an estimated $200 to the insurance premium for the average car.

7. Explanations of property crime include a cultural emphasis on economic success and conspicuous consumption, the use of techniques of neutralization, economic deprivation, routine activities and social process factors, and the desire for excitement and thrills.

8. Harsher criminal justice measures, target hardening, and neighborhood watch groups have been touted to reduce property crime, but the evidence does not indicate that they are very effective. The factors emphasized in sociological explanations of property crime should be addressed to reduce property crime beyond its current levels.

9. Computer crime plagues the Internet and affects people worldwide. Many forms of computer crime exist, helping to make such crime difficult to control.

Key Terms

amateur theft 295

booster 296

decision-making processes 298

fencing 302

fraud 308

identity theft 308

joyriding 296

professional theft 295

rationalization 302

sneaky thrill crimes 303

snitch 296

social organization 295

support system 298

target hardening 305

tax fraud 309

What Would You Do?

1. The text points out that a surprisingly high proportion of residential burglaries in which a household member saw the intruder is committed by someone the household member knew. Suppose you are the parent of a 16-year-old boy. One day you are returning from a trip to the supermarket and notice that your front door is ajar. You figure you must not have closed it properly and go inside. Suddenly you see a friend of your son looking in a kitchen drawer. He stammers that he was looking for paper and a pencil to leave a note for your son, but you notice some jewelry on the counter next to him. You demand that he leave the house immediately, and he goes without protest. Which of the following, if any, will you now do? (1) Call the police. (2) Call the boy's parents. (3) Tell your son. Explain your answers.

2. Suppose Joe from work says you can buy some expensive stereo equipment cheap. The equipment is almost brand new, he says. When you ask why he's selling the equipment at such a low price, he replies that someone gave it to him. When you ask why, he just shrugs his shoulders and says you don't want to know. Do you buy the stereo equipment? Why or why not?

CHAPTER
thirteen

White-Collar

and Organized

Crime

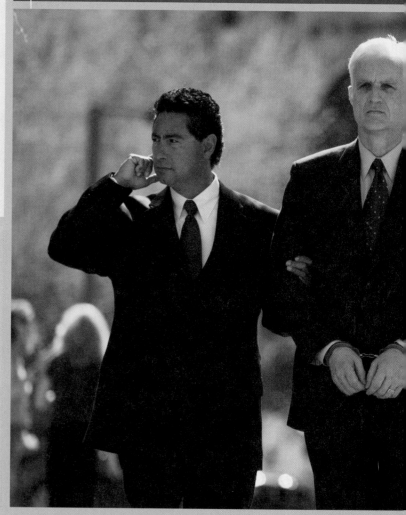

Crime in the News

oal mining is a dangerous activity, but events in 2010 indicated that some of the danger stems from neglect by coal-mining companies. In April 2010, an explosion in a coal mine in West Virginia killed twenty-nine workers. Experts attributed the explosion to a buildup of deadly methane gas and coal dust. The explosion was the worst mine disaster in the United States in several decades. In the aftermath of the disaster, news reports indicated that the mine had been cited by federal officials for potentially fatal safety violations, including inadequate ventilation of methane and unsafe levels of coal dust. Miners had reportedly been evacuated from the mine three times in the preceding two months because of methane buildup. A news report called the safety record of the mine's corporate owner "dismal" and said that federal officials and miners were suggesting that the explosion "might have been preventable." Just three weeks after this explosion, two miners died when a Kentucky mine roof collapsed. A news report noted that the mine had been cited dozens of times for safety violations during the past sixteen months; some of these citations were for roof bolts that were too far apart.

Sources: Urbina and Cooper 2010:67; Wilson 2010.

Almost forty years before these tragic coal mine deaths, 125 people died in the mining company of Buffalo Creek, West Virginia, when a 20-foot-high flood surged into a peaceful valley of several thousand homes, destroying everything in its path. The water had built up behind an artificial dam composed of the mine waste, or slag, which remains after coal has been mined and washed. After days of torrential rain, the 132 million gallons of "black water" used to wash the coal finally broke through the dam and destroyed Buffalo Creek in seconds.

The sad thing is that this tragedy could have been prevented. Despite the rain and flood, this was entirely a human disaster, not an act of God. The danger the dam posed to the people of Buffalo Creek was certainly no secret; they themselves had worried about its safety. Although the dam violated safety regulations, no one from the mining company was indicted or prosecuted for homicide. Nor were the 125 deaths it caused added to the list of homicides known to the police in 1972, the year the flood occurred. The company did pay $13.5 million to the flood survivors to settle a lawsuit, but this was an amount the company could easily afford because it was owned by a large corporation.

Some forty years later, the Buffalo Creek disaster remains a poignant example of corporate wrongdoing that may have been repeated in the mine disasters described in the Crime in the News feature. Many aspects of the disaster are common to other corporate misconduct: reckless behavior by corporate officials in the name of profit; their denial of any wrongdoing; death, injury or illness, and property loss; and little or no legal punishment (Rosoff, Pontell, and Tillman 2010). Despite growing awareness of these problems, the public, elected officials, and the news media remain much more concerned about street crime.

This chapter discusses white-collar crime and organized crime. Their grouping within the same chapter reflects the fact that much white-collar crime is committed by organizations (corporations and small businesses) whose motivations and strategies are similar in many ways to those characterizing organized crime. In addition, white-collar crime and organized crime both have dire economic consequences and endanger the health and safety of people across the country.

Andrew Carnegie was one of the pioneers of the Industrial Revolution in the United States after the Civil War and a very generous philanthropist. Most of the leading financial and industrial figures of this era repeatedly broke the law or at least engaged in questionable business practices. Their crimes included bribery, kickbacks, and other complex financial schemes, and their industries established factories and other work settings with inhumane working conditions.

White-Collar Crime

As cities grew rapidly in nineteenth-century Europe and the United States because of industrialization, public concern over the "dangerous classes" of the poor in these cities also grew (Shelden 2008). Industrialization fueled this concern, but it also ironically spawned a new form of crime that was much less visible and mostly ignored. This was the crime of a new type of business organization, the industrial corporation, that changed the face and economy of the United States after the Civil War. In this period, the oil, steel, railroad, and other industries brought the United States squarely into the Industrial Revolution. Men such as Andrew Carnegie (steel), J. P. Morgan (banking), John D. Rockefeller (oil), and Jay Gould, Leland Stanford, and Cornelius Vanderbilt (railroads) acquired massive fortunes. They are still honored today as the pioneers of the Industrial Revolution and as philanthropists who donated hundreds of millions of dollars to worthy causes.

Yet most of them repeatedly broke the law or at a minimum engaged in questionable business practices. Although some call these men "captains of industry," others call them "robber barons" (Josephson 1962). Their crimes included bribery, kickbacks, and other complex financial schemes, and their industries established factories and other work settings with inhumane working conditions. In the early 1900s, the **muckrakers** bitterly criticized business and political corruption and condemned the cruel treatment of workers. Ida M. Tarbell (1904) wrote a scathing history of Rockefeller's Standard Oil Company; Upton Sinclair (1990 [1906]) wrote a famous novel, *The Jungle* (1990 [1906]), that discussed the horrible sanitary and work conditions in the U.S. meatpacking industry; and Lincoln Steffens (1904) wrote his classic book on political corruption, *The Shame of the Cities*.

At about the same time, sociologist Edward A. Ross (1965 [1907]) authored a book about the corrupt and dangerous practices of corporate leaders, whom he called "criminaloids." Like the muckrakers, he noted that the actions of industrial leaders and their corporations often caused great financial and physical harm, even if they did not violate any criminal laws. Ross blamed corporate wrongdoing on the intense pursuit of profit that he saw as the hallmark of industrialization and capitalism.

EDWIN SUTHERLAND AND WHITE-COLLAR CRIME

Despite the work of the muckrakers and sociologist Ross, criminologists continued to focus on street crime. In the 1940s, however, Edwin Sutherland wrote some important works about white-collar crime, a term he coined. Sutherland (1949) studied the seventy largest U.S. corporations and found that they had violated antitrust, false advertising, bribery, and other laws 980 times, or 14 each on the average. Their crimes were deliberate, repeated, extensive, and harmful. He wrote that any common criminal committing this number of offenses would be considered a habitual offender and harshly punished by the law. Many of the corporations had been charged with engaging in crimes during World Wars I and II, including illegal profiteering, the manufacture of defective military parts, the sale of rancid food to the army, and the sale of munitions and other war materials to Germany. This history led Sutherland to observe that "profits are more important to large corporations than patriotism, even in the midst of an international struggle which endangered Western civilization" (p. 174). The widespread corporate lawbreaking also led him to question the assumption of "conventional theories that crime is due to poverty or to the personal and social pathologies connected with poverty" (p. 25).

DEFINING WHITE-COLLAR CRIME

In one of criminology's most famous definitions, Sutherland (1949:9) said **white-collar crime** is "a crime committed by a person of respectability and high social status in the course of his occupation." Sutherland's definition has two major components. First, the crime must be committed by someone of "respectability and high social status"; Sutherland's definition thus excluded crime by blue-collar workers. Second, the crime must be committed "in the course of" one's occupation. Thus, a wealthy corporate executive who murders a lover would not have committed white-collar crime. Like Ross and the muckrakers, Sutherland stressed that behavior of respectable persons can be very harmful even if it does not violate any criminal laws.

Over the years, Sutherland's definition of white-collar crime has been criticized and revised (Piquero and Schoepfer 2010). Some early critics argued that behavior that does not violate criminal law should not be considered a crime, no matter how harmful it may be. Others said his definition excluded crimes by blue-collar workers and businesses that, notwithstanding the color of the collar, share many features of crimes committed by persons of high social status. One other problem arose from Sutherland's own application of his definition. Although his definition focused on crime committed by an individual, his 1949 book *White-Collar Crime* focused almost entirely on crime by corporations, or *corporate crime.* This inconsistency led to some confusion over whether white-collar crime is something individuals do or something corporations and other businesses do (Geis 1992).

Contemporary Views

Given the complexity of white-collar crime, many substitute terms have been proposed over the years and many categories of white-collar crime developed. Given the popularity of Sutherland's coinage, most scholars continue to favor *white-collar crime,* but many favor other terms and definitions. Marshall Clinard and Richard Quinney (1973) divided white-collar crime into two types, occupational and corporate. **Occupational crime** is committed by individuals in the course of their occupation for *personal* gain, whereas **corporate crime** is committed by corporations. Corporate executives obviously plan and commit the crime, but they do so for their corporations' financial gain. Although they may then benefit along with their corporations, their primary intention is to benefit the corporation. While liking Clinard and Quinney's typology, some scholars prefer the name **organizational crime** over the term *corporate crime* (Shover and Scroggins 2009). This term emphasizes that crime can be done by and on behalf of organizations, many of them corporations, but some of them small businesses, including blue-collar businesses such as auto-repair shops.

We will use the typology of occupational and organizational crime. With this typology in mind, sociologist James W. Coleman (2006:6) defines white-collar crime (borrowing from the National White Collar Crime Center) as "illegal or unethical acts . . . committed by an individual or organization, usually during the course of legitimate occupational activity, by persons of high or respectable social status for personal or organizational gain." One advantage of this definition is that it includes harmful but legal behavior. Thus, the term *corporate crime* is typically used to cover harmful corporate behavior whether or not it violates any criminal law (Rosoff, Pontell, and Tillman 2010).

Review and Discuss

What are some of the conceptual problems in defining white-collar crime? What do you think is the best definition of such crime?

OCCUPATIONAL CRIME: LAWBREAKING FOR PERSONAL GAIN

Employee Theft: Pilferage and Embezzlement

If you are or ever have been employed, write down everything you have taken without permission from your workplace without paying for it: pens and pencils, dishes or glassware, food, and so forth. Next to each item, note its approximate value. Now write down how much cash you might have taken. Finally, if you ever were paid for more hours than you worked because you misreported your time, write down the amount you were overpaid. Now add up the value of all the items on your list to yield the total value of *employee theft* you have committed. Even if the average employee theft per student were only, say, $20, that would still mean that students at a 10,000-student campus would in effect have stolen $200,000 from their workplaces.

As this exercise might indicate, employee theft is very common and, indeed, has been called a "widespread, pervasive, and costly form of crime" (Langton, Piquero, and Hollinger 2006:539). About three-fourths of all workers are thought to steal from their employers at least once, with half of these stealing more than once. The annual amount of employee theft is estimated at $19.5 billion (National Retail Federation 2007). Consumers pay in the long run for employee theft because businesses raise their prices to help compensate for it. The U.S. Chamber of Commerce estimates that employee theft causes almost one-third of all business failures (Challenger 2004).

PILFERAGE

Employee theft may be divided into *pilferage* and *embezzlement.* **Pilferage** involves the theft of merchandise, tools, stationery, and other items. The most common reason for pilferage is employee dissatisfaction with pay, working conditions, and treatment by supervisors and the company itself. Another reason is what might be called the *workplace culture.* In many workplaces, employees develop informal norms of what is acceptable and not acceptable to steal. These norms generally dictate that expensive, important company property should not be stolen, but that inexpensive, less important property is up for grabs. The workplace culture also includes techniques of neutralization (see Chapter 8) that help employees rationalize their theft: They do not pay us enough, they treat us too harshly, the business won't miss the property we take.

Many types of items are stolen through pilferage. Pens, pencils, paper clips, cell phones, food, cleaning supplies, toilet paper—just about anything an employee can get away with is fair game. Even body parts: In March 2004, two UCLA employees were placed on leave and criminally investigated for allegedly selling body parts from dozens of cadavers donated to the university's medical school over a five-year period (Ornstein 2004).

EMBEZZLEMENT

The second type of employee theft is **embezzlement,** which involves the theft of cash and the misappropriation or misuse of funds. In a classic study, Donald R. Cressey (1971 [1953]) observed that embezzlers have financial problems they want to keep secret because of their embarrassment or shame. To use Cressey's term, their financial problems are *nonshareable.* They typically rationalize that they are only borrowing the money or that their company will not miss the funds. An individual act of embezzlement ranges from the tens of dollars to the millions. In a multimillion-dollar example, the head cashier at the University of California at San Francisco was sentenced to seven years in prison for embezzling more than $4 million over a three-year period (Chiang 2004).

Although embezzlement is usually a solo activity, a new type, **collective embezzlement,** emerged in the 1980s in the savings and loan and other financial industries (Rosoff, Pontell, and Tillman 2010). This scandal involved the stealing of company funds by top executives who often worked in groups of two or more and conspired with "outsiders" such as real estate developers and stock brokerage executives. A common activity was the practice of "land flips" by selling each other land back and forth, with each transaction involving a higher price in a process that artificially inflated the land's value. The executives also spent millions of dollars of company money on artwork and worldwide travel and took salaries and fees that exceeded federal limits. Their collective embezzlement led to the failure of more than 450 savings and loans institutions and the criminal conviction of some 2,300 defendants. It is estimated that this embezzlement will cost the federal government at least $500 billion by 2030 (Calavita, Tillman, and Pontell 1997).

Professional Fraud: Focus on Health Care

Physicians, lawyers, and other professionals are in a tempting position to defraud their patients, clients, and the government. Their work is private and complex, and it is difficult for investigators to know when fraud occurs. They are also more autonomous than most other workers and able to work without someone looking over their shoulder. Their patients and clients thus cannot know whether their bills are truthful and accurate. As one example, lawyers sometimes bill their clients for more time than they actually put in

Physicians and other health care professionals commit an estimated $100 billion of health care fraud annually.

or even charge them for work never done. The clients, of course, have no way of knowing this.

Most professions practice *self-regulation* by establishing rules for their members' behavior. Unfortunately, this is often like the proverbial fox guarding the chicken coop. Regulations often allow professionals great latitude in their behavior, and enforcement and punishment are often lax. Professionals also rationalize wrongdoing just as other kinds of criminals do. This allows them to view their crimes as justifiable and even necessary, however illegal they may be. The particular rationalizations depend on the profession and the type of crime involved, but all of them help ease any guilt professionals might feel from breaking the law.

Health care fraud, which is estimated at about $100 billion annually, has received perhaps the most attention of any **professional fraud** (Rosoff, Pontell, and Tillman 2010). This fraud is committed by physicians, pharmacists, medical equipment companies, nursing homes, medical testing laboratories, home health care providers, medical billing services, and ambulance services. Several types of health care fraud exist, but they often involve overbilling Medicare and other insurance. These types include (1) exaggerating charges, (2) billing for services not rendered for a real patient, (3) billing for services for fictitious or dead patients, (4) "pingponging" (sending patients to other doctors for unnecessary visits), (5) family "ganging" (examining all members of a family when only one is sick), (6) "churning" (asking patients to come in for unnecessary office visits), (7) "unbundling" (billing a medical procedure or piece of equipment as many separate procedures or equipment parts), (8) providing inferior products to patients, (9) paying kickbacks and bribes for referrals of patients, (10) falsifying medical records to make an individual eligible for benefits, (11) billing for inferior products or for items never provided, (12) falsifying prescriptions, and (13) inflating charges for ambulance services (Cohen 1994).

Review and Discuss

What are three types of health care fraud? Why does such fraud occur? To what degree do techniques of neutralization help us understand the origins of such fraud?

UNNECESSARY SURGERY

Another common medical practice is unnecessary surgery. What is considered unnecessary, of course, is often a matter of interpretation. Physicians and patients naturally want to err on the side of caution and often decide on surgery as the safest course of action to treat a disease or injury. However, studies have determined that a surprising amount of surgery exceeds any reasonable exercise of caution and is clearly unnecessary. The major reason unnecessary surgery occurs is that physicians profit from it. As evidence, more operations are performed on patients with private insurance (thus giving physicians a high fee for each operation) than on those belonging to prepaid health plans in which doctors receive a set salary regardless of the operations they perform (Coleman 2006). It is estimated that several million unnecessary surgeries occur each year and that

12,000 to 16,000 people die from medical complications resulting from these surgeries (Reiman and Leighton 2010).

Financial Fraud

The collective embezzlement discussed earlier is just one example of financial crime in financial institutions and corporations. Some of this crime is committed for the benefit of the companies and is thus discussed later in the organizational crime section, but other financial crime is committed for personal gain. In addition to collective embezzlement, another financial crime is *insider trading.* Here a company executive, stockbroker, or investment banker with special knowledge of a company's economic fortunes (such as a proposed merger) buys or sells stock in that company before this information is shared with the public. Lifestyle celebrity Martha Stewart's prison term in 2004 for lying to investigators arose from an insider trading scandal involving a friend who was convicted of insider trading (White 2003).

Police and Political Corruption: Violations of Public Trust

Another form of occupational crime is corruption by police and politicians, who violate the public trust by accepting bribes and kickbacks and by occasionally engaging in extortion and blackmail. Such public corruption was the subject of Lincoln Steffens's *The Shame of the Cities,* mentioned earlier. In the twentieth century it reached into the upper echelons of mayors' and governors' offices, police administration, Congress, and the White House. We will explore political corruption further in Chapter 14 and police corruption in Chapter 16.

ORGANIZATIONAL CRIMINALITY AND CORPORATE CRIME

Much white-collar crime is committed for the sake of corporations and other businesses. The primary intent of the persons committing the crime is to benefit the organization for which they work. They know, of course, that if they help their business, the business will "help" them. But their primary goal of helping the business classifies their crime as organizational, not occupational, although this classification becomes somewhat tricky when the owner of a business is involved.

Many blue-collar or small businesses cheat their customers and otherwise commit fraud. Auto-repair shops are notorious in this regard. Auto-repair fraud (overcharging and unnecessary or faulty repairs) costs more than an estimated $20 billion annually and accounts for 30 to 40 percent of all auto-repair expenses (Best Wire 2003; Fleck 2002). Auto-repair fraud is conducted by legitimate businesses that defraud the public as part of their business practice. Other organizational criminality involves illegitimate businesses that are fraudulent from the outset and have the sole purpose of defrauding the public. Examples include phony home improvement businesses, contests, and charities. Some of the health care and savings and loan fraud discussed earlier was committed by illegitimate enterprises formed specifically to defraud the public and/or the government.

Auto repair fraud consists of overcharging for repairs and unnecessary or faulty repairs. This type of business fraud costs more than an estimated $20 billion annually and accounts for 30 to 40 percent of all auto-repair expenses.

We now come to crime by corporations, which, because of their size and scope, commit great harm (Reiman and Leighton 2010). Corporate crime has continued long after Sutherland first wrote about it. During the mid-1970s, the federal government accused almost two-thirds of Fortune 500 corporations of violating the law and almost one-fourth of these were convicted of (or did not contest) at least one criminal or civil offense (*U.S. News & World Report* 1982). During the 1990s, more than 100 top corporations were criminally fined after pleading guilty or no contest to criminal charges involving behavior such as price-fixing, environmental law violations, and the marketing of drugs to doctors without Food and Drug Administration approval (Mokhiber and Weissman 1999). During the 2000s, major financial scandals broke involving Enron and many other corporations that exaggerated their assets (discussed later). In the following two years, major pharmaceutical companies paid hundreds of millions of dollars to settle accusations that they overcharged Medicaid by illegally failing to offer it their lowest prices or marketed drugs for uses that the FDA had not approved (Abelson 2004; Farrell 2004). In 2009, two pharmaceutical companies were fined almost $4 billion for illegal marketing of drugs. A news report observed, "Marketing fraud cases against pharmaceutical companies have become almost routine, with almost every major drug maker having been accused of giving kickbacks to doctors or shortchanging the Medicaid program on prices" (Harris 2009:B4).

Corporate crime takes two general forms: *financial* and *violent*. The major distinction between the two is whether people are injured or killed by corporate misconduct. We will first examine financial crime by corporations and then discuss the violence they commit.

Corporate Financial Crime

The economic cost of corporate crime is enormous. A 1982 investigation estimated that financial crime by corporations, including price-fixing, false advertising, bribery, and tax evasion, costs the public $200 billion per year (*U.S. News & World Report* 1982). In 2010 dollars, this amount would be about $445 billion. Several types of corporate financial crime exist.

CORPORATE FRAUD, CHEATING, AND CORRUPTION

A first type of corporate financial crime involves fraud, cheating, bribery, and other corruption not falling into the antitrust or false advertising categories that we examine later. Much of this fraud and corruption parallels what individuals do for personal gain as occupational crime. The difference here is that the fraud and corruption are performed primarily for the corporation's benefit, not for the benefit of the corporate executives engaging in these crimes.

Fraud and corruption, including conspiracy, securities fraud, and wire fraud, were widely suspected in the financial crisis involving the collapse of several huge financial and securities firms in 2008 and 2009 (Cohan 2010). These companies insured or invested heavily in subprime (high-risk) mortgages and collapsed when the housing market bottomed out and mortgage owners could no longer pay off their loans. In the wake of their collapse, reports indicated that executives at some of the companies had deceived creditors and investors about the companies' poor financial health and/or violated certain regulatory laws in taking such unnecessary risks in their investments. As the headline of one news column put it, these executives were "looters in loafers" (Krugman 2010).

While this financial crisis was occurring, the case of the notorious financial investor, Bernard Madoff, emerged. Madoff was discovered to have

Financier Bernard Madoff used a *Ponzi scheme* for some fifteen years to enrich himself and other people who worked with him. This scheme defrauded thousands of investors of an estimated $50 billion. Madoff pleaded guilty in February 2009 to eleven felonies and was sentenced to a 150-year prison term.

been using a *Ponzi scheme* (in which new investments are used to pay the interest on old investments) for some fifteen years to enrich himself and other people who worked with him. His scheme defrauded thousands of investors of an estimated $50 billion. Madoff eventually pleaded guilty in February 2009 to eleven felonies and was sentenced to a 150-year prison term (Henriques and Healy 2009).

There have been many other examples of high-finance fraud over the decades, but those that came to light in the early 2000s stand out for their enormity and audacity. Many of them involved accounting fraud, as numerous companies exaggerated their assets during the economic boom and stock market bubble of the late 1990s to artificially inflate the value of their stock. In doing so, they violated securities laws by defrauding their investors. When their scandalous behavior came to light and their stock value plummeted, many of their workers lost their jobs, and countless investors lost billions of dollars, including funds in their pension plans.

The most notorious accounting scandal involved Enron, a global energy company that had been the darling of Wall Street. In December 2000 its stock sold for $84 a share and the company employed some 20,000 people worldwide. Fewer than twelve months later, it was worth less than a dollar a share after the company revealed that it had over-stated earnings and hidden losses, with the total sum surpassing $1 billion. A month later it filed for bankruptcy and laid off more than 4,000 workers. The plummeting of its stock cost investors tens of billions of dollars (Behr and Whitt 2002). More than thirty people involved in the Enron scandal were eventually indicted, including its top executives, both of whom were convicted. Other corporations implicated in financial scandals at the same time were Adelphia, Halliburton, Rite Aid, and WorldCom. Top executives at Rite Aid, the national drugstore chain, were convicted of various charges relating to the hiding of operating losses, including bribing some employees and intimidating others to remain quiet (Johnson 2004).

PRICE-FIXING AND RESTRAINT OF TRADE

A second type of corporate financial crime involves antitrust violations. If corporations conspire to set high prices for goods and services rather than allowing the free market to work, consumers pay more than they should. Such **price-fixing** thus constitutes a form of theft from the public, which costs about $60 billion annually (Simon 2008). Also, if one company buys out all the others, does not have to worry about competition and can raise its prices without fear of losing sales to another company. This action, too, constitutes a theft from the public as **restraint of trade** violates antitrust law. Restraint of trade goes back to the post-Civil War period, when Standard Oil and other corporations bought up competitors or used questionable practices to prevent others from springing up or to drive them out of business. Congress passed the 1890 Sherman Antitrust Act to counter such behavior. One additional type of restraint of trade prohibited by antitrust laws involves *anticompetitive agreements,* in which a manufacturer sells its products only to retailers who agree not to sell rival manufacturers' products. Although some of the fines and legal settlements for price-fixing and other antitrust crimes range in the millions of dollars, the corporations involved are usually so wealthy that these financial penalties scarcely worry them.

Perhaps the most celebrated price-fixing scandal was uncovered in 1959–1960 and involved General Electric, Westinghouse, and twenty-seven other heavy electrical equipment manufacturers that controlled 95 percent of the electrical industry (Geis 1987). These companies' executives conspired over several years to fix prices on $7 billion of electrical equipment, costing the public about $1.7 billion in illegal profit. After pleading guilty in 1961, seven of the electrical executives received thirty-day jail terms for their conspiracy, and twenty-one others got suspended sentences. These were obviously light sentences compared to what a typical property criminal might get for stealing only a few dollars. In somewhat stiffer punishment, the corporations were fined a total of $1.8 million. This sum amounted to only $1 of every $1,000 the corporations stole from the public and still left them holding almost $1.7 billion in illegal profit. Of the total fines, GE's share came to $437,000. This might be a lot of money for you to pay, but for GE it was the equivalent of someone with an annual income of $175,000 paying a $3 fine. To bring this down to more meaningful figures, if you had an income of $17,000 and knew that your punishment for robbing a bank would be only 30 cents, would you rob the bank?

FALSE ADVERTISING

Another common corporate financial crime is false advertising. Advertisers obviously do their best to sell their products and engage legally in exaggerated claims, or *puffery*. A particular product, for example, may claim to be the best of its kind or, as in the case of cigarettes and beer, imply that using it will make you popular. But much advertising goes beyond puffery and makes patently false and illegal claims. Such deceptive advertising is very common, with the cosmetic, food, pharmaceutical, and many other industries accused of it (Jackson and Jamieson 2007). There have also been many examples of *bait-and-switch* advertising, in which a store advertises a low-priced item that is not actually available or available only in small quantities. The item is gone when customers come in to buy it, and the sales clerk switches them to a more expensive product in the same line.

Corporate Violence: Threats to Health and Safety

If you heard that corporations kill many more people each year than all murders combined, would you believe it? Even if corporations are corrupt, you may be thinking, they do not murder. Yet their actions do, in fact, kill more people each year than all murders combined. It is difficult for any of us to believe that corporations maim and kill. We equate violence with interpersonal violence, which dominates public discussion, fills us with fear, and even controls our lives. **Corporate violence,** in contrast, is less visible and has been called "quiet violence" (Frank and Lynch 1992). The term *corporate violence* refers to actions by corporations that cause injury, illness, and even death. These lives are lost in the name of profit, as corporations pursue profits with reckless disregard for the health, safety, and lives of their workers, consumers, and the general public (Reiman and Leighton 2010).

WORKERS AND UNSAFE WORKPLACES

Each year many workers die or become injured or ill because of hazardous occupational conditions; others suffer long-lasting psychological effects (Rosoff, Pontell, and Tillman 2010). Some hazardous workplace conditions violate federal and state laws, whereas others are technically not illegal but still pose dangers to workers. Most hazardous conditions involve worker exposure to various toxic substances that cause cancer and serious respiratory illnesses. Working with dangerous equipment and in dangerous circumstances also causes injury and death.

It does not have to be this way, as the mine disasters discussed at the beginning of this chapter indicate. Although some jobs and workplaces are inevitably hazardous, the primary reason for the nation's high rate of occupational injury, illness, and death is that corporations disregard their workers' health and safety in the name of profit. Moreover, the government has lax rules on workplace conditions and does relatively little to enforce the ones that do exist.

Estimates of the Problem

Exact data on workplace illness, injury, and death are difficult to determine for several reasons (Reiman and Leighton 2010). First, it is often difficult to establish that illness and death are work-related. Second, the U.S. Bureau of Labor Statistics, a major source of workplace data, gathers data only from workplaces with at least eleven employees. Its annual count of the number of workplace injuries is thought to miss from 33 to 69 percent of the actual number of injuries (Leigh, Marcin, and Miller 2004). Third, corporations and smaller businesses often hide workplace injuries and illnesses.

Not surprisingly, estimates of preventable workplace illness and disease, injury, and death vary widely, but reasonable estimates include the following: (1) 50,000 deaths from illness/disease; (2) between 100 and 2,500 deaths from injury; (2) 150,000 serious illnesses; and (3) as many as 2 million or more injuries (AFL-CIO 2007; Reiman and Leighton 2010; Simon 2008). Because of underreporting and other measurement problems, the true toll of work-related death, illness, and injury may well be much higher.

Examples of the Problem

Sometimes the harm done to workers is immediate and visible, as the coal-mine disasters at the beginning of this chapter again illustrate. In another example, an explosion occurred in 2001 at a refinery in Delaware when a crew was working near a tank filled with sulfuric acid; the refinery had a history of safety violations. The crew was told to work there even though employees had warned that the tank was corroded. The explosion occurred when a welding torch ignited vapors leaking from the tank and hurled one of the workers into the acid. The only remains that were found were some steel parts of his boots (Barstow 2003).

Usually, however, the harm done to workers takes much more time to kill them. The coal-mining industry is a prime example. Long-term breathing of coal dust leads to several respiratory problems, including black lung disease, which has killed some 100,000 coal miners over the last century and still kills about 1,500 annually. According to one investigation, many coal-mining companies "cheat on air-quality tests to conceal lethal dust levels. And while the federal government has known of the widespread cheating for more than 20 years, it has done little to stop it because of other priorities and a reluctance to confront coal operators" (Harris 1998:A1).

The asbestos industry has also killed many workers. Beginning in the late 1960s, medical researchers began to discover that asbestos, long used as a fire retardant in schools, homes, and other buildings and as an insulator in high-temperature equipment, can cause asbestosis, a virulent lung disease. Because this disease takes a long time to develop, it is estimated that more than 200,000 people, mostly asbestos workers, but also consumers, will eventually die from asbestos-related cancer and lung disease within the next few decades (Brodeur 1985).

"Where's the crime?" you might be asking. What if no one happened to know that asbestos was dangerous? If this were the case, then asbestos deaths would be a tragic problem, but not one for which the industry should be blamed. Unfortunately, there is plenty of blame, and even murderous criminal neglect, to go around. It turns out that the asbestos industry began to suspect at least as early as the 1930s that asbestos was dangerous, as it saw its workers coming down with serious lung disease. Instead of reporting their suspicions to the appropriate federal and state authorities, asbestos companies kept quiet and settled workers' claims out of court to avoid publicity (Lilienfeld 1991). For more than thirty years, they continued to manufacture a product they

The asbestos industry hid the dangers of asbestos for several decades.

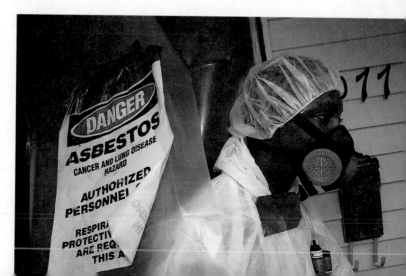

Crime and Controversy

Harvest of Shame: Pesticide Poisoning of Farm Workers

Each year in California, hundreds of farm workers, almost all of them Mexican American, become ill every year from inhaling pesticides used in the fruit and vegetable fields in which they work. About 75,000 tons of pesticides are used in California's fields annually to control the many types of insects that could decimate crops. Many of these pesticides cause cancer and/or damage the nervous and reproductive systems. Often the pesticides are sprayed by helicopter. Sometimes the wind blows the pesticide spray hundreds of yards until it reaches an area where farm workers are picking crops.

State pesticide officials say that such *pesticide drifts,* which officially number about forty per year, are rare, given the hundreds of thousands of pesticide applications occurring each year. A member of Californians for Pesticide Reform disputes this contention: "Everywhere I go to all the little rural communities, everybody has a story to tell about being drifted on by pesticides — that they were outside barbecuing or they were having a birthday party," de Anda says. "It just happens so commonplace, people don't report it."

According to official reports, 1,316 farm workers were sickened by pesticide drifts in 2002. During one drift from a potato field, workers began fainting or vomiting. The pesticide that sickened them was related to nerve gas, and exposure to it can result in seizures and even death. When farm workers are sickened by pesticides, they have the right to apply for workers' compensation. Because many speak little English, however, they might not know about workers' comp, and some who are aware of it still fear having anything to do with the government. They also realize they would lose time from work

if they get involved with the workers' compensation process and even fear losing their jobs. For all these reasons, they often get no help at all in paying their medical expenses. Because they so often do not report pesticide exposure, the actual number of workers sickened by pesticide drifts is probably much higher than the number indicated in official reports.

As with other types of workplace illnesses and injuries, investigation of pesticide violations in California's fields is lax, as is the enforcement of safety regulations. In 2002 a pesticide drift sickened 250 people. The company involved eventually paid only $60,000 to settle charges against it, but the farm workers who were sickened did not receive any of this money.

Farm workers are not the only people harmed by pesticide drifts. Children, who are especially vulnerable to pesticide-caused medical problems, are often exposed to pesticide drift at school or on their way to or from school. Many California counties have "protection zones" that restrict how close to a school pesticide spraying can occur, but eleven counties have no such zones, while six counties have rules that apply only if classes are in session. An Associated Press investigation found "that over the past decade, hundreds, possibly thousands, of schoolchildren in California and other agricultural states have been exposed to farm chemicals linked to sickness, brain damage, and birth defects."

In spring 2009, two children were waiting for their school bus when a pesticide cloud from a vineyard across the street drifted over and drenched them. One of the children later recalled, "And then I told the bus driver that I wasn't feeling good, like I was feeling sick. My head hurt, I wanted to throw up and everything."

Sources: Barbassa 2004; Burke 2007; Californians for Pesticide Reform 2010; Khokha 2010; Reeves, Katten, and Guzmán 2003.

knew was dangerous. During that time, workers continued to handle asbestos, and asbestos was put into many schools and other new buildings. It is no exaggeration to say that the companies' concern for profit was and will be responsible for more than 200,000 deaths and that the asbestos industry was guilty of "corporate malfeasance and inhumanity . . . that is unparalleled in the annals of the private-enterprise system" (Brodeur 1985:7).

CONSUMERS AND UNSAFE PRODUCTS

Even if you work in a safe workplace, you are not necessarily safe from corporate violence. Every year companies market dangerous products that injure us, make us sick, and even kill us. The Consumer Product Safety Commission (2009) estimates that unsafe products are associated with about 4,500 deaths and more than 14 million injuries annually. It is not known how many of these deaths and injuries are from products that were unsafe as manufactured versus those that were unsafe because they had aged past safe use (e.g., an old toaster with a frayed electric cord). However not all deaths and injuries from unsafe products come to the commission's attention. Meanwhile, the U.S. Centers for Disease Control and Prevention (CDC) estimates that each year about 5,000 people die and 325,000 are hospitalized from eating contaminated food (Young 2010), almost all of it because of processing violations. Again, not all such deaths come to the CDC's attention. Combining the two agencies' death estimates, about 9,500 people die from unsafe products each year, including food.

Children seem to be at special risk from unsafe products. About three dozen infants have died in recent years in accidents involving cribs whose sides drop down (Callahan 2010). A report in 2000 indicated that seventeen companies "kept quiet about products that were seriously injuring children until the government stepped in" (O'Donnell 2000:1A). These products included cribs and infant carriers, and the injuries included amputated fingers, broken bones, and skull fractures. Some of the companies had received thousands of complaints from parents and had investigated their products' safety, but they hid the evidence of their products' dangers from the government.

Three industries posing a great danger to consumers are the automobile, pharmaceutical, and food industries.

The automobile industry. Beginning in late 2009, news reports indicated that certain Toyota models were subject to sudden acceleration that may have caused eighty-nine deaths since 2000. Toyota eventually recalled millions of vehicles and paid a fine of $16.4 million (but without admitting any wrongdoing) for delay in reporting the problem to the federal government for four months. The Department of Transportation said Toyota had "knowingly hid a dangerous defect for months from U.S. officials and did not take action to protect millions of drivers and their families" (Bensinger and Vartabedian 2010:A1; Maynard 2010; Thomas 2010).

The complexity of motor vehicles means that some defects are inevitable. But as the Toyota example suggests, there have been many tragic cases in which automobile manufacturers knew of safety defects that killed and injured many people, but decided not to do anything in order to save money.

The most infamous case is probably that of the Ford Pinto, which was put on the market in 1971 even though Ford knew the Pinto's gas tank could easily explode in minor rear-end collisions. Ford did a cost–benefit analysis to determine whether it would cost more money to fix each Pinto, at $11 per car, or to pay settlements in lawsuits after people died or burned in accidents. Ford determined that it would cost $49.5 million to settle lawsuits from the 180 burn deaths, 180 serious burn injuries, and 2,100 burned cars it anticipated would occur, versus $137 million to fix the 12.5 million Pintos and other Fords with the problem. Because not fixing the problem would save Ford about $87 million, Ford executives decided to do nothing, even though they knew people would die and be seriously burned. About 500 people eventually did die (although one estimate puts the number at "only" some two dozen) when Pintos were hit from behind, often by cars traveling at relatively low speeds, before the Pinto was finally recalled (Cullen, Maakestad, and Cavender 2006).

Ford was responsible for more deaths and injuries beginning a few years earlier because of faulty automatic transmission that slipped from park into reverse. Drivers would put their cars in park and leave the engine running while they got out to get groceries from the trunk and to do other tasks. The transmission would shift unexpectedly into reverse, causing the car to roll backward and hit or run over the driver. By 1971 Ford was receiving six letters per month on this problem, but did nothing. In fact, for years it denied that its vehicles had any reversal problem at all. Instead of ordering a recall, the Department of Transportation allowed Ford in 1980 to send warning stickers to owners of all Ford vehicles manufactured between 1966 and 1979. Because many original owners had sold their cars, about 2.7 million owners of used Fords never received the stickers. At least eighty people died in Ford reversal accidents from 1980, when the stickers were mailed, to 1985. By this time, an estimated 207 deaths and 4,597 injuries had occurred from Ford vehicles rolling backward onto people (*Consumer Reports* 1985; Kahn 1986).

Ford claimed that its vehicles were no worse than any other manufacturer's and blamed the problem on drivers' failure to actually put their cars in park initially. Unfortunately for Ford, although the National Highway Traffic Safety Administration (NHTSA) recorded the eighty deaths from Ford cars between 1980 and 1985, it recorded only thirty-one similar fatalities for General Motors, Chrysler, and American Motors combined. Unless we are to assume that Ford drivers were somehow more inept than others at putting their vehicles into park, the Ford transmission had to be at fault. Ford eventually corrected the problem.

Beginning in the 1980s, thousands of Ford drivers reported that their cars were stalling on highways and when making left turns. Although Ford told the government that this problem was not due to any defect, its officials and engineers knew that the cars did, in fact, have a significant defect: an ignition system that would become too hot and then shut off the engine. Determining that it would cost almost half a billion dollars to fix the problem in millions of cars, Ford kept quiet about the defect for nine years, even as it led to serious car accidents, some of them fatal. Ford finally fixed the problem (Labaton and Bergman 2000).

The pharmaceutical industry. The pharmaceutical industry has also put profits above people by knowingly marketing dangerous drugs. As one scholar wrote, "Time after time, respected pharmaceutical firms have shown a cavalier disregard for the lives and safety of the people who use their products" (Coleman 2006:83).

One example of pharmaceutical misconduct involved Eli Lilly and Company, which in the 1980s put a new arthritis drug, Oraflex, on the market overseas. Shortly after taking the drug, at least twenty-six people died. These patients' doctors reported the deaths to Lilly. Because the patients were usually elderly, any individual physician could not assume that Oraflex was the cause of death. After getting several reports of such deaths, however, a responsible company would have told the government, conducted more tests, and perhaps taken the drug off the market. Lilly instead kept the deaths a secret, and the Food and Drug Administration allowed Lilly to market the drug in the United States in April 1982. More deaths took place, and Lilly pleaded guilty in August 1985 to deceiving the government. By this time, Oraflex had killed at least 62 people and made almost 1,000 more seriously ill. Lilly's total legal punishment was a $25,000 fine for the company and a $15,000 fine for one of its executives (Coleman 2006).

In a more recent case of a dangerous pharmaceutical product, the Wyeth company withdrew two diet drugs from the market after many reports of heart valve damage associated with using the drugs and allegations that the company had hid evidence of the problem. Wyeth eventually paid more than $1 billion to settle class-action lawsuits (Feeley and McCarty 2004).

One of the most publicized examples of pharmaceutical corporate violence involved the A. H. Robins Company and its Dalkon Shield IUD, or intrauterine device (Hicks 1994). Robins distributed more than 4 million Dalkon Shield IUDs between 1971 and 1975 in 80 nations, including 2.2 million in the United States, after falsifying safety tests. The IUD turned out to be a time bomb ticking inside women because its "tail string" carried bacteria from the vagina into the uterus, where it caused pelvic inflammatory disease for thousands of women, leading to sterility, miscarriage, or, for at least eighteen U.S. women, death. More than 100,000 U.S. women became pregnant despite using the IUD. Sixty percent of these women miscarried, and hundreds of those who did not miscarry gave birth to babies with severe defects, including blindness, cerebral palsy, and mental retardation; other women had stillborn babies. After finally recalling the IUD in 1974, Robins continued to sell it overseas for up to nine months. The company eventually paid more than $400 million to settle numerous lawsuits. Like other corporations, wrote Morton Mintz (Mintz 1985:247), a former investigative reporter for the *Washington Post*, A. H. Robins "put corporate greed before welfare, suppressed scientific studies that would ascertain safety and effectiveness, (and) concealed hazards from consumers." He added that "almost every other major drug company" has done similar things, often repeatedly.

The food industry. A third industry that has put profit over people is the food industry. Recall that about 5,000 people die each year and another 325,000 are hospitalized from eating contaminated food. Historically, one of the worst food offenders is the meatpacking industry, which has supplied spoiled meat to U.S. soldiers in more than one war. Upton Sinclair, in his muckraking novel *The Jungle,* wrote that rats routinely would get into meat in meatpacking plants. Workers used poisoned bread to try to kill the rats. The meat sold to the public thus included dead rats, rat feces, and poisoned bread. Sinclair's novel led to the Federal Meat Inspection Act in 1906 (Frank and Lynch 1992).

Despite this act and other regulations, some meatpacking companies still endanger our health, thanks in large part to lax federal monitoring of the meat industry. A 2010 report concluded that "beef containing harmful pesticides, veterinary antibiotics and heavy metals is being sold to the public because federal agencies have failed to set limits for the contaminants or adequately test for them" (Eisler 2010:A1) . In just two examples of tainted meat, four Los Angeles companies were charged in 2004 with violating federal food safety laws for, among other actions, selling meat containing rat feces (Rosenzweig 2004); and a 2003 news report revealed that a Georgia meat company that supplies schools, supermarkets, and restaurants across the nation had been cited for safety violations hundreds of times during the previous three years (Petersen and Drew 2003).

THE PUBLIC AND ENVIRONMENTAL POLLUTION

No doubt some pollution of our air, land, and water is inevitable in an industrial society. If people become ill or die from it, that is unfortunate, but unavoidable. But much of our pollution *is* preventable. Federal environmental laws are weak or nonexistent, corporations often violate the laws that do exist, federal monitoring and enforcement of these laws are lax, and the penalties for environmental violations are minimal (Rosoff, Pontell, and Tillman 2010). As a result, an estimated 20 percent of U.S. landfills and incinerators, 25 percent of drinking water systems, and 50 percent of wastewater treatment facilities violate health regulations (Armstrong 1999).

The consequences of these problems are illness, disease, and death. For many reasons, it is difficult to determine how many people die or become ill each year from pollution, but it is clear that pollution causes many deaths and illnesses every year. A study by the American Cancer Society that followed 500,000 people for sixteen years found that air pollution contributes to both heart disease and lung cancer and is as dangerous as secondhand smoke or being overweight or a former smoker (Pope et al. 2004). Scientists estimate that air pollution kills between 50,000 and 100,000 Americans and more than 300,000 Europeans each year from the heart disease, cancer, and respiratory diseases it causes (BBC News 2005; Reiman and Leighton 2010). The key question, and one that is almost impossible to answer, is: How many of these deaths could be prevented if corporations acted responsibly and put people above profit? A conservative estimate of annual pollution deaths in the United States due to corporate crime and neglect would be 35,000.

In this regard, an investigative report deplored several major corporations, including General Motors, Standard Oil, and Du Pont, for engaging in a "sad and sordid commercial venture" by conspiring from the beginning of the automobile age to manufacture and market gasoline containing lead, a deadly poison, even though the companies knew there were safe alternatives. Along the way they suppressed evidence of the health dangers of lead. More than sixty years after it was first used, lead was finally banned as a gasoline additive in 1986 (Kitman 2000).

Another environmental problem is the dumping of toxic waste. The United States produces close to 300 million tons of toxic waste each year, and as much as 90 percent of this is disposed of improperly into some 600,000 contaminated sites across the nation (Simon 2008). Perhaps the most infamous toxic-waste dumping crime occurred in an area known as Love Canal, near Niagara Falls, New York. For years a chemical company had dumped toxic wastes at Love Canal—and then it donated the land to the Niagara Falls School Board in 1953. The school board sold the land to a developer, and houses were eventually built on top of the toxic waste. Eventually, the waste leaked into the surrounding land and water, causing birth defects, miscarriages, and other health problems. By the 1980s, more than 500 families had to leave their homes, which were later destroyed. The company had also dumped toxic wastes in several other communities (Levine 1982).

The underlying motive for much of the pollution and environmental problems discussed in this section is profit. Companies make more money when they do not take measures to reduce the pollution they emit or to safely dispose of their toxic waste. A terrible example of this dynamic occurred in April 2010, when an oil rig owned by BP, the British global energy company, exploded in the Gulf of Mexico. The resulting oil spill lasted several months and became the largest oil spill in U.S. history. Reports several weeks after the explosion indicated that BP officials may have chosen to save money by using an inferior type of casing for the oil well. The casing was known to be more likely to release certain gases, and gas leaks were widely thought to have caused the explosion (Urbina 2010).

Review and Discuss

What are the ways in which corporations cause illness, injury, and/or death?

In April 2010, an oil rig owned by BP, the British global energy company, exploded in the Gulf of Mexico. The resulting oil spill lasted many months and became the largest oil spill in U.S. history. Reports after the explosion indicated that BP officials may have chosen to save money by using an inferior type of casing for the oil well that may have led to the explosion.

ECONOMIC AND HUMAN COSTS OF WHITE-COLLAR CRIME

Many criminologists believe that white-collar crime costs us more in lives and money than street crime (Reiman and Leighton 2010; Rosoff, Pontell, and Tillman 2010). We can collect the various figures that have been presented on the costs of both types of crime to see why they feel this way.

We will start with the value of property and money stolen annually from the public, government, and/or private sector by street crime and white-collar crime. Our figure for street crime is $18 billion, the FBI's upper estimate of the economic loss from all property crime and robbery. For white-collar crime, we will add several estimates presented earlier in this and the previous chapter: (1) $445 billion (the *U.S. News & World Report* estimate in today's dollars) for the cost of all corporate crime, including price-fixing, false advertising, tax evasion, and various types of fraud; (2) $100 billion in health care fraud; (3) and $19.5 billion in employee theft. These amounts add up to $564.5 billion annually. As you can see in Figure 13.1, this amount towers over the annual loss from street crime. Many forms of tax fraud (see Chapter 12) could also be considered white-collar crime, and if they were included in the estimation of white-collar crime costs, the total estimate would be many billions of dollars larger.

Now we will do a similar calculation for the number of people killed each year by street crime (murder and non-negligent manslaughter) and white-collar crime and misconduct. The UCR's estimate for 2008 homicides was 16,272. For white-collar crime (and misconduct), we again use the estimates presented earlier in this chapter and previous chapters: (1) 50,000 workplace-related deaths from disease and another 1,300 from injury (to take the midpoint of the estimate that was given), or 51,300 altogether; (2) 9,500 deaths from unsafe products; (3) 35,000 deaths from environmental pollution; and (4) and 14,000 deaths from unnecessary surgery (to again take the midpoint of the estimate). Adding these figures together, about 109,800 people a year, admittedly a very rough number, die from corporate and professional crime and misconduct. As Figure 13.2 illustrates, this number far exceeds the number of people murdered each year.

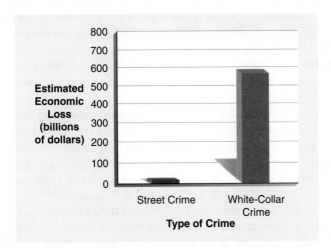

FIGURE 13.1 ▸ **Estimated Annual Economic Loss from Street Crime and White-Collar Crime**

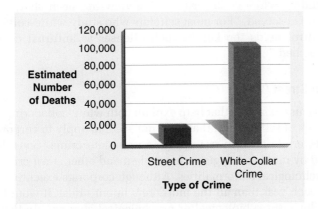

FIGURE 13.2 ▸ **Estimated Annual Number of Deaths from Homicide and White-Collar Crime**

EXPLAINING WHITE-COLLAR CRIME

In many ways, white-collar criminals are not that different from street criminals. Both groups steal and commit violence, even if their methods differ in ways already discussed. In addition, certain explanations of street crime also apply to white-collar crime. At the same time, there are obvious differences between the two types of crime and their respective offenders. To help understand why white-collar crime occurs, it is useful to examine its similarities with and differences from street crime. Because so many types of white-collar crime exist, our discussion will focus on the most serious type, corporate crime.

Similarities with Street Crime

A basic similarity between white-collar crime and street crime is that both types of crime involve stealing and violence. To again recall Woody Guthrie's line at the beginning of Chapter 12, some people rob you with a gun, while others rob you with a fountain pen (or, in the modern era, a computer). Beyond this basic similarity, both types of crime also share some other features and dynamics.

Like street criminals, white-collar criminals do not usually break the law unless they have both the opportunity and the motivation to do so (Shover and Hochstetler 2000). But the opportunity for corruption and other white-collar crime differs across occupations and industries. This helps us understand why some occupations and industries have more crime than others. For example, financial corruption is, to the best of our knowledge, much less common among professors than among businesspeople, physicians, and politicians. Are professors that much more virtuous than these other professionals? Professors would certainly like to think so! But, to be objective, we have to concede that the reason might simply be that professors have much less opportunity than the other professionals to make a buck through illegal means.

Also like street criminals, white-collar criminals use many techniques of neutralization to justify their crimes and other misconduct. At the corporate level, executives and middle managers see their behavior as necessary to compete in very competitive markets. Despite massive evidence to the contrary, corporate executives deny again and again that their workplaces harm their workers, that their products harm consumers, and that their pollutants harm the public. We will never know if they actually believe what they are saying or if they are lying to protect themselves and their companies. Probably, some do believe what they say, whereas others know full well the harm they have caused.

Another similarity has been hotly debated, and this is whether white-collar criminals join with street criminals in lacking self-control. Recall that Michael Gottfredson and Travis Hirschi (1990) put lack of self-control at the root of all criminality (see Chapter 8), including white-collar crime. This view has been sharply challenged. As Gilbert Geis (1995) observed, "For most scholars who study white-collar crime, the idea that low self-control holds the key to such offenses as antitrust conspiracies seems exceedingly farfetched."

Differences from Street Crime

So far we have discussed factors that help explain both white-collar crime and street crime and one factor, lack of self-control, that does not seem to apply to corporate crime. Other reasons for street crime also do not apply to corporate crime. Consider, for example, the view, rejected by most sociologists, that violent and other street criminals suffer from biological or psychological abnormalities. Although corporate executives are responsible for more deaths each year than all the murderers in our midst, it would probably sound silly to say they have some biological or psychological abnormality that causes them to allow people to die.

Turning to sociological explanations of conventional crime, it would also sound silly to say that corporate executives fleece the public because as children they grew up amid social disorganization, suffered negative family and school experiences, and consorted with delinquent friends. Corporate executives are, after all, successful. They have achieved the American dream, and one reason for this is that many were raised in the best of surroundings and went to the best schools. Nor can we blame their present economic circumstances. As Sutherland (1949) noted more than sixty years ago, we cannot attribute the crime of corporate executives to economic deprivation because they are, by definition, wealthy to begin with.

Cultural and Social Bases for White-Collar Crime

To explain the behavior of white-collar criminals, then, we must look beyond explanations stressing individual failings and instead consider a combination of structural and cultural forces. Here we again go back to Sutherland (1949), who said that white-collar crime stems from a process of differential association in which business offenders learn shared views on the desirability of their criminal conduct. Most contemporary scholars of white-collar crime agree with his view, especially where corporate crime is concerned, because many corporations develop "subcultures of resistance" that encourage corporate lawbreaking to enhance corporate profits (Braithwaite 1989). Here the views of top management matter greatly. According to one business professor, "Of all the factors that lead to corporate crime, none comes close in importance to the role top management plays in tolerating, even shaping, a culture that allows for it" (Leaf 2002).

Many scholars also blame white-collar crime on an insatiable thirst for money and the power accompanying it. This greed in turn arises from the stress placed in our society on economic success (Passas 1990). Even if we are already wealthy, we can never have enough. As discussed in Chapter 7, the pursuit of profit in a capitalist society can be ruthless at times, and individuals and organizations will often do whatever is necessary to acquire even more money, wealth, and power.

Lenient Treatment

Another reason corporate crime occurs is the lenient treatment afforded corporate criminals. As an article in *Fortune* magazine, a business publication, put it, "The double standard in criminal justice in this country is starker and more embedded than many realize. Bob Dylan was right: Steal a little, and they put you in jail. Steal a lot, and you're likely to walk away with a lecture and a court-ordered promised not to do it again" (Leaf 2002: 62). The problem of lenient treatment involves several components (Benson and Simpson 2009).

Despite some recent publicized prosecutions of prominent individuals accused of corporate crime, the legal treatment of corporate criminals continues to be fairly lenient.

WEAK OR ABSENT REGULATIONS

First, regulations forbidding corporate misconduct are either weak or nonexistent. Part of the reason for this is that corporations, whether you like them or not, are very powerful and influential and are often able to prevent or water down regulatory legislation. Also, because federal and state regulatory agencies are woefully underfunded and understaffed, much corporate misconduct goes undetected.

DIFFICULTY OF PROVING CORPORATE CRIME

Second, corporate crime is difficult to prove and punish even when it is suspected. A major reason for this is again corporate power. Simply put, corporations have more resources, including sheer wealth and highly paid, skilled attorneys, than do enforcement agencies and district attorney offices. A regulatory agency or district attorney bringing charges against a major corporation is like David fighting Goliath. In the Bible, David won, but in the contemporary world of corporate crime, Goliath usually wins. Regulatory agencies and district attorneys often have to settle for promises by corporations that they will stop their misconduct, which they often do not even admit they were doing (Rosoff, Pontell, and Tillman 2010).

The complexity of corporate crime is also a factor in the difficulty of proving it. As prosecutors realize, juries often find it difficult to understand complicated financial transactions and shenanigans. It is also often difficult to determine when and how a law or regulation was violated, who made the decision to violate it, and whether the alleged offender acted with criminal intent. For all these reasons, in many cases criminal indictments and prosecutions never occur.

WEAK PUNISHMENT

The third component of lenient treatment of white-collar criminals is weak punishment (Pontell 2010). As a business writer for the *New York Times* noted, "It's an all-too-familiar pattern: a corporation—usually a big name, with broad business and political influence—gets enmeshed in scandal. Shocking revelations portray a pattern of wrongdoing. The damages run into the billions . . . and then, not very much happens. Not many people go to jail, and if they do, it's not for very long" (Eichenwald 2002:A1). The writer then recounted several corporate scandals; although the companies involved in the scandals paid millions of dollars in fines, not a single senior executive was imprisoned.

As this writer noted, most corporate violations that are punished involve fines, not imprisonment. Although the fines may run into hundreds of thousands or even tens of millions of dollars, they are the proverbial drop in the bucket for the people or corporations who must pay them. We saw this earlier with the electrical price-fixing scandal of 1961, for which the fines might sound stiff for an ordinary person, but were very affordable for the corporations that broke the law. Many contemporary examples could also be cited. To take just one, Bank of America was fined $10 million several years ago for delaying the delivery of documentation on possible securities trading violations. The Securities and Exchange Commission (SEC), which levied the fine, noted it was the largest it had ever imposed for failing to produce evidence requested in an investigation. The $10 million fine was a lot of money in absolute terms. However, Bank of America took in $48 billion in revenue in 2003 and cleared a profit of $10.8 billion, and its total assets are almost $1 trillion. Thus, the fine amounted to 0.02 percent of its revenue, less than 1 percent of its profit, and 0.001 percent of its assets. To translate the first and last figures to ones that are more understandable, the $10 million fine was equivalent to $8 for someone with an annual income of $40,000 and to $2 for someone with a net worth (say from savings, stocks, and equity in a home) of $200,000. Thus, fines for corporations have little impact and are often seen as just the cost of doing business.

Imprisonment also has little impact on corporate criminals and other high-status offenders because it only rarely occurs and involves a light sentence (either no jail time or just a short sentence) when it does occur (Rosoff, Pontell, and Tillman 2010). This remains true despite some relatively long prison sentences handed out in the aftermath of the Enron scandal and the stiffening of prison terms under federal sentencing guidelines. Part of the reason for this problem are the high-powered attorneys and other resources that wealthy defendants can afford and the unwillingness of judges to regard them as real criminals deserving actual punishment. Another part of the reason is that the law often does not provide in a stiff prison term. Turning to financial crime, the executives convicted of crimes in the savings and loan scandal discussed earlier each stole at least $100,000, but received an average of only thirty-six months in prison. In contrast, burglars (who generally steal only a few hundred dollars' worth of goods) receive a sentence of almost fifty-six months (Calavita, Tillman, and Pontell 1997). Among convicted offenders in California, only 38 percent of physicians and other persons who defrauded Medicaid were incarcerated, compared to 79 percent of grand-theft defendants, even though thes economic loss from Medicaid fraud was ten times greater than the loss from grand theft (Tillman and Pontell 1992).

Lack of News Media Coverage

A final factor contributing to corporate crime is that the news media gloss over the damage it causes. This is unfortunate, because the threat of publicity can deter such crime (Scott 1989). Morton Mintz (1992), the former *Washington Post* investigative reporter cited earlier, attributed the media's neglect to cowardice, friendships, libel risks, and its "pro-business orientation." Although Mintz conceded that the press was covering corporate crime more than in the past (and, more than a decade after his statement, probably more now in the aftermath of the Enron scandal and others), he said it was still guilty of a "pro-corporate tilt" that led to a lack of adequate coverage of corporate crime and other misconduct.

Review and Discuss

Why, generally, does white-collar crime occur?

REDUCING WHITE-COLLAR CRIME

To reduce corporate and other white-collar crime, several measures are necessary (Piquero and Schoepfer 2010). To list but a few, federal and state regulatory agencies must be provided much larger budgets so they will become at least somewhat stronger Davids against corporate Goliaths. The media would have to focus as much or more attention on corporate and other white-collar crime as they now do on street crime. More severe punishment might also work. Because the major corporations can easily afford to pay even millions of dollars in fines, these would have to be increased substantially to have a noticeable deterrent effect. Because so few corporate executives and other high-status offenders are threatened with imprisonment, many scholars think the increased use of even short prison terms may induce these offenders to obey the law (Pontell 2010). Agreeing with this view, a writer for *Fortune* magazine observed that "the problem will not go away until white-collar thieves face a consequence they're actually scared of: time in jail" (Leaf 2002:62).

Other observers say that stiffer fines and greater use of imprisonment will not work and will lead only to further problems, including overburdening a legal system already stretched beyond its means. These observers think that self-regulation and compliance strategies emphasizing informal sanctions, such as negative publicity campaigns, would ultimately reduce corporate crime more effectively (Braithwaite 1995). However, Henry Pontell and Kitty Calavita (Pontell and Calavita 1993) think this approach would not have prevented the 1980s savings and loan fraud, partly because savings and loan executives looted their own institutions and would thus not have cared about their institutions' reputations.

Organized Crime

When the public demands **goods** or **services,** organized crime is all too ready to provide them. Sometimes this is true even if the products and services are legal. For example, organized crime is thought to be involved in several legitimate businesses, including trash-hauling operations and the vending and amusement machine industries (Lyman and Potter 2011). It is also believed to be involved in the toxic-waste dumping industry, often working hand in hand with the legitimate businesses that produce toxic waste and want to dispose of it quickly and quietly (Block and Scarpitti 1985).

Despite its involvement in these kinds of businesses, however, organized crime's primary source of income remains illegal activities and products: drugs, prostitution, pornography, gambling, loan sharking (loaning money at extraordinarily high interest rates), and extortion (obtaining money through threats). Throughout its history, organized crime has flourished because it has catered to the public's desires and has had the active or passive cooperation of political, legal, and business officials. The rest of this section explores these themes.

HISTORY OF ORGANIZED CRIME

If by organized crime we mean coordinated efforts to acquire illegal profits, then organized crime has existed for centuries. The earliest example of organized crime is **piracy,** in which pirates roamed the high seas and plundered ships. Piracy was common among ancient Phoenicians on the Mediterranean Sea and, many centuries later, among Vikings in what is now western Europe. In the 1600s, buccaneers—Dutch, English, and French pirates—began plundering ships carrying goods to and from the Spanish colonies in the New World and then branched out to colonies farther north. By the end of the 1600s, pirates openly traded their plunder with merchants in Boston, New York, Philadelphia, and other port cities in what is called the "golden age of piracy." The merchants bought the pirated booty at low cost and sold the pirates food and other provisions. Royal governors and other public officials took bribes to look the other way, with corruption especially rampant in the New York colony.

Eventually, merchants realized that they could get greater profits by trading with England rather than with pirates, and by the late 1720s piracy had faded. "At that point," wrote criminologists Dennis J. Kenney and James O. Finckenauer (1995:70), "the markets for pirate goods dried up, and the public demand for their services and support for their existence disappeared." The merchants who once traded with pirates now called them a public menace. One lesson of the golden age of piracy is that "colonial piracy flourished only because the colonists wanted it to" (Kenney and Finckenauer 1995:70). Piracy's success depended on the willingness of merchants to trade with pirates, the public's willingness to buy the pirates' plunder from the merchants, and the readiness of political officials to take bribes. The situation today with organized crime is not much different.

Organized crime began anew in New York City in the early 1800s, where almost 1 million people—most of them poor, half of them immigrants, and many of them unemployed—lived crammed into two square miles. Amid such conditions, stealing and other crime were inevitable. Young women were forced to turn to prostitution, and young men formed gangs, enabling them to commit crime more effectively and protecting them from the police. These gangs were the forerunners of today's organized crime groups and, like the pirates before them, had a cozy relationship with public officials. Crooked city politicians used them at polling places to stuff ballot boxes and intimidate voters (Kenney and Finckenauer 1995).

By the end of the century, the gangs in New York and elsewhere had developed into extensive operations, many of them involving vice crime such as prostitution and gambling. The ethnic makeup of these organized crime groups reflected the great waves of immigration into the United States during the nineteenth century. Most immigrants settled in the nation's major cities and faced abject poverty and horrible living conditions. As cities grew and the vice trade developed, it was inevitable that many immigrants would turn to organized crime to make ends meet. Irish Americans were the first to take up organized crime and eventually became very dominant in many cities. Later in the century, Italians and Jews immigrated into the country in enormous numbers and soon got their share of the vice trade, working closely, as the Irish had before them, with politicians, police, and various legitimate businesses. In the twentieth century, African Americans, Asian-Americans, and Latinos became more involved in organized crime. Although many scholars question whether the United States has been, as popularly thought, one big "melting pot" of various ethnic and racial groups, organized crime ironically is one area in which diverse groups have pursued economic opportunity and the American dream (O'Kane 1992).

If New York and other city gangs were the forerunners of organized crime, the nineteenth-century robber barons were the role models (Abadinsky 2007). To extend our earlier discussion, railroad baron Leland Stanford bribed members of Congress and other officials to gain land grants and federal loans for his Central Pacific Railroad. John D. Rockefeller's Standard Oil Company forced competitors out of business with price wars and occasionally dynamite. The Du Pont family, which made its fortune on gunpowder, cornered its market after the Civil War with bribery and explosions of competing firms. These and other examples are evidence of the corruption and violence characterizing much of U.S. business history. Organized crime since the nineteenth century is merely its latest manifestation.

The robber baron analogy indicates that organized crime and corporate crime might be more similar than we think. Taking up this theme, many scholars see little difference between the two (Abadinsky 2007). Both kinds of crime involve careful planning and coordinated effort to acquire illegal profits. Both rely on active or passive collusion of public officials and on public willingness to buy the goods and services they provide. Although organized crime is more willing to use interpersonal violence to acquire its profits, corporate crime, as we saw earlier, can also be very violent.

Organized crime's power and wealth increased enormously during Prohibition (Okrent 2010). Before this time, organized crime was primarily a local phenomenon with little coordination across cities. Bootlegging demanded much more coordination, because it involved the manufacture, distribution, and sale of alcohol. Organized crime groups in different cities now had to coordinate their activities, and organized crime became more organized to maximize the enormous profits from bootlegging. At the same time, rival gangs fought each other to control bootlegging turf. Politicians and federal and local law enforcement officials were all too willing to take bribes. For these reasons, Prohibition fueled the rise and power of organized crime. Bribery of politicians and police was common in cities such as Chicago, where organized crime acquired enormous influence.

According to the alien conspiracy model, U.S. organized crime is controlled by a small group of Italian families. This model was depicted in the popular TV series, The Sopranos, shown here.

After Prohibition ended, organized crime's primary source of income for several decades was gambling. Starting in the 1960s, it moved more into the illegal drug trade, which now provides an important source of organized crime's annual income, estimated between $50 billion and $150 billion in the United States, with gambling a fairly distant second. Due in large part to drug trafficking, organized crime in recent years has taken on an international focus, with cocaine smuggled into the United States from Colombia and elsewhere (McGee 1995).

ALIEN CONSPIRACY MODEL AND MYTH

One of the most controversial scholarly issues in U.S. organized crime today is whether it is controlled by a highly organized, hierarchical group of some twenty-four Italian *families*. This view, often called the **alien conspiracy model** or the *Mafia mystique,* was popularized in important congressional hearings beginning in the 1950s (Albanese 1982). It was later featured in the various *Godfather* films and many other movies and books, and lived again in the TV series *The Sopranos.* In addition to specifying a hierarchical, Italian-dominated structure of organized crime, the model argues that organized crime was largely unknown before Italians immigrated to the United States in the late 1800s. It also assumes that organized crime exists because immigrants, first Italians and later Asians and others, corrupt righteous U.S. citizens and prey on their weaknesses.

As with many other criminological topics, the alien conspiracy model is best regarded as a myth (Kappeler and Potter 2005). In emphasizing Italian domination, this particular myth ignores the long history of organized crime before Italian immigration and overlooks the involvement of many other ethnic and racial groups. It also diverts attention from organized crime's roots in poverty, in the readiness of citizens to pay for the goods and services it provides, and in the willingness of politicians, law enforcement agents, and legitimate businesses to take bribes and otherwise cooperate with organized crime.

As the history of organized crime indicates, the public, politicians, and other officials are not very righteous after all. This is still true today. As Gary W. Potter (1994:147) observed, "It is a fallacy that organized crime produces the desire for vice. Organized crime doesn't force people to gamble, snort cocaine, or read pornography. It merely fills an already existing social gap. The law has made organized crime inevitable because it denies people legal sources for those desired goods and services."

Nor does organized crime seduce honest politicians, police, and other officials and owners of legitimate businesses. Instead, these keepers of the public trust are often very willing to take bribes and otherwise cooperate with organized crime. In a Seattle, Washington, study, William Chambliss (1988) found organized crime, business leaders, politicians, and police working hand in hand. In a study of organized crime in "Morrisburg," a pseudonym for an East Coast city of 98,000, Potter (1994:101–102) concluded, "It is quite clear to anyone walking the streets of 'Morrisburg' that the political fix is in and extends from the cop on the beat to the most senior political officials."

International Focus

Organized Crime in Japan

The experience of Japan reminds us that organized crime is a global phenomenon. In April 2007, an assassin who belonged to Japan's largest organized crime gang fatally shot the mayor of Nagasaki, Japan. The shooting took place amid dozens of commuters at a train station and alarmed Japan, a country known, as we have seen in previous chapters, for its low crime rate. One Japanese resident said, "We can no longer let organized crime run rampant in Japan. I'm outraged." A news report indicated that in some cities organized crime gangs, known as *yakuza,* toted business cards and, like any legitimate business, had signs outside their offices to advertise their location. Officials estimated that about 85,000 Japanese belong to organized crime gangs.

Japan has a long history of organized crime, which for many years enjoyed a positive image in the nation because it reportedly helped control street crime. A news reporter noted, "Historians say these groups often kept cozy relations with politicians and the police, and were a widely accepted part of the social fabric." That image began to change a few years ago as organized crime experienced an economic downturn and began to prey on ordinary citizens to increase its income.

Although the confessed killer of the Nagasaki mayor was a member of organized crime, some police thought he shot the mayor because the city had refused to reimburse him the Japanese equivalent of $23,000 for a car accident he suffered from a construction site pothole. But other observers thought the killing was indeed related to the killer's organized crime involvement. As evidence, they noted that organized crime groups in Japan get much of their income from public works projects and that the confessed killer had been angry because the city had denied a contract to a construction company in which he had a financial interest. In recent years, Nagasaki had begun awarding construction contracts to companies with no ties to organized crime, and the nation as a whole had also decreased spending on public works projects more generally because of budgetary problems. In response, organized crime was using violence to scare public officials into spending more money on public works and to award contracts to companies with ties to organized crime, and the murder of Nagasaki's mayor may have been yet another example of such violence.

Sources: Adelstein 2009; Fackler 2007.

Such corruption, he noted, "is critical to the survival of organized crime. In fact, organized crime could not operate at all without the direct complicity and connivance of the political machinery in its area of operation" (p. 149).

Like Chambliss and other organized crime researchers, Potter also found legitimate businesses cooperating with organized crime in Morrisburg and noted, "The close interrelationships between legitimate and illicit businesses have been documented time and again in every local study of organized crime groups" (p. 135).

Chambliss, Potter, and other scholars also argue that the alien conspiracy model exaggerates the hierarchical nature of organized crime and the degree to which it is Italian-dominated. Instead, they say, organized crime today is best seen as a loose confederation of local groups consisting of people from many different ethnic backgrounds. Organized crime's decentralized, fluid structure permits it to adapt quickly to the ebb and flow of the vice trade and government's efforts to control it.

CONTROLLING ORGANIZED CRIME

Organized crime has been around for so long because it provides goods and services that the public desires. For this reason, it will not go away soon. Here the debate over the alien conspiracy model has important implications for how we should try to control organized crime and even for whether any effort will succeed. If the alien conspiracy model is correct, arrests and prosecutions of selected organized crime "bosses" should eliminate its leadership and thus weaken its ability to entice the public to use its goods and services and various officials to take bribes. The government has used this strategy at least since the days of Al Capone.

If, however, organized crime has a more fluid, decentralized structure whose success depends on public and official readiness to cooperate with its illegal activities, this strategy will not work. As long as public demand for illicit goods and services remains, the financial incentives for organized crime will also remain. And as long as politicians, police, and the business community are eager to cooperate, organized crime will be able to operate with impunity. Organized crime, in short, is too much a part of our economic, political, and social systems for the law enforcement strategy to work well (Albanese 2000).

To reduce organized crime's influence, then, we first must reduce public demand for its illicit goods and services. For better or worse, this is probably a futile goal. If so, a more effective way to fight organized crime might be to admit defeat and to legalize drugs, gambling, and prostitution, because the laws against these crimes have ironically generated opportunities for organized crime to realize huge financial gains (Kappeler and Potter 2005). Legalizing these crimes would be a very controversial step (see Chapter 15), but would at least lessen organized crime's influence. Legalization might weaken organized crime in an additional way, because current enforcement of the laws in fact strengthens organized crime. The reason is that organized crime figures who get arrested tend to be the smallest, weakest, and most inefficient operators. Their removal from the world of organized crime allows the stronger and more efficient organized crime figures to gain even more control over illicit goods and services. They can also charge more for the goods and services they provide, increasing their profits even further (Kappeler and Potter 2005).

Of course, legalization of drugs and other illicit products and activities is not about to happen soon. Given that fact, another way to fight organized crime would be to concentrate on the cooperation given it by politicians, police, and legitimate businesses. Unfortunately, this would entail a law enforcement focus that has not really been tried before. It is unlikely that the government would want to take this approach, given that in some ways it would be investigating itself.

One final way to weaken organized crime would be to provide alternative economic opportunities for the young people who become involved in it each year. Thus, if we could effectively reduce poverty and provide decent-paying, meaningful jobs, we could reduce the attractiveness of organized crime to the new recruits it needs to perpetuate itself. Unfortunately, there are no signs that our nation is eager to launch a new "war on poverty" with the same fervor that has guided our war against drugs and other illicit goods and services that now make so much money for organized crime.

Review and Discuss

The text says that organized crime has often had the cooperation of political, legal, and business officials. What evidence does the text provide for this allegation?

Conclusion

There once was an editorial cartoon depicting two men. One was middle-aged, dressed in a slick business suit, and listed as a corporate executive; the other was young and shabbily dressed with unkempt hair and a day-old beard. Under the cartoon was the question: Who's the criminal? This chapter has attempted to answer this question. By any objective standard, white-collar crime causes more financial loss, injury and illness, and death than street crime. However, street crimes remain the ones we worry about. We lock our doors, arm ourselves with guns, and take many other precautions to protect ourselves from muggers, rapists, burglars, and other criminals. These are all dangerous people, and we should be concerned about them. Because white-collar crime is more indirect and invisible than street crime, it worries us far less, no matter how much harm it causes. White-collar crime is less visible partly because of its nature and partly because of press inattention. One consequence of its invisibility is that white-collar crime victims often do not realize that they are being victimized.

As a result, most white-collar crime remains hidden from regulatory agencies and law enforcement personnel. If someone poisoned a bottle of aspirin or other consumer product, the press would publicize this crime heavily. We would all be alarmed and refuse to buy the product, and its manufacturer would probably take it off retail shelves. Meanwhile, we use dangerous products that kill many people each year because we are unaware of their danger. Even when we are aware of two other kinds of corporate violence, unsafe workplaces and environmental pollution, there is often little we can do. Workers have to go to work each day to pay their bills. Locked doors will not keep out air, water, or land pollution. The same is true for economic white-collar crime that steals from the public: locked doors, guns, and mace will not protect the average family of four from losing $1,000 to price-fixing each year.

White-collar crime remains an elusive concept. As used here, it encompasses petty workplace theft by blue-collar workers as well as complex financial schemes by wealthy professionals and major corporations. The inclusion of crime by blue-collar workers and businesses takes us far from Sutherland's original focus on corporate and other crime by high-status offenders. But it does remind us that crime takes on a variety of forms and involves many otherwise law-abiding people who would denounce robbers and burglars, but see nothing wrong with occasionally helping themselves to a few items from their workplaces or cheating a customer now and then.

However, given the power and influence of corporations, wealthy professionals, and other high-status offenders, it is important to keep their behavior at the forefront of the study of white-collar crime. As Sutherland reminded us, crime is not just something that poor nonwhite people do. And as he also reminded us, the harm caused by corporate and other high-status crime greatly exceeds the harm caused by the street crime of the poor. Sutherland and other like-minded scholars are not saying we should minimize the problem of street crime. This would not be fair to its many victims, most of them poor and many of them people of color. But they are saying that it is time to give white-collar crime the concern and attention it so richly deserves.

Organized crime has certainly received much attention over the decades and for good reason. It is a powerful influence in U.S. life and, as least as depicted in film and on TV, has colorful characters ready to commit violence. Although we know much about organized crime, this does not mean it is very possible to weaken it. As long as people continue to desire the goods and services organized crime provides, this type of crime will remain with us.

If white-collar crime has still received relatively little scholarly and other attention, political crime has received even less. This crime again challenges traditional views of criminality and forces us to question the nature and legitimacy of law when lawbreaking is committed by the government itself or by members of the public, acting not for personal gain, but for a higher end. We will examine this fascinating topic in Chapter 14.

13

Summary

1. In 1949, Edwin Sutherland examined lawbreaking by major U.S. corporations. Despite his pathbreaking work, the study of white-collar crime lagged until the 1970s. Sutherland defined white-collar crime as "a crime committed by a person of respectability and high social status in the course of his occupation." There has been much discussion of the value of this definition. A useful typology of white-collar crime distinguishes between occupational crime and organizational crime.

2. A major type of occupational crime is employee theft, composed of pilferage and embezzling. Much of this crime occurs because of the dissatisfaction of employees with their pay and various aspects of their working conditions. The savings and loan scandal of the 1980s involved a new form of crime called collective embezzlement, in which top executives stole from their own institutions.

3. Professional fraud occurs for many reasons, among them the fact that professional work is autonomous and self-regulated. Professionals who commit fraud invoke many techniques of neutralization. A very common type of professional fraud is health care fraud, which costs the nation about $100 billion annually. Unnecessary surgery costs about 12,000 lives per year.

4. Blue-collar businesses and corporations also commit financial crimes. The auto-repair industry is notoriously rife with fraud that costs consumers billions of dollars annually. Financial fraud by corporations received much attention in the beginning of this decade thanks to accounting scandals at Enron and other major corporations. These scandals resulted in the loss of thousands of jobs and of tens of billions of dollars held by investors. Corporate financial fraud takes several forms, including accounting improprieties, price-fixing and other antitrust violations, and false advertising. Financial fraud of all types by corporations may amount to almost $400 billion annually, and the total economic cost of all economic crime reaches more than $800 billion.

5. Corporate violence refers to actions by corporations that cause injury, illness, or death. Examples of corporate violence include unsafe workplaces, unsafe products, and environmental pollution. The number of annual estimated deaths in the United States from white-collar crime of all types is more than 118,000.

6. Many of the factors implicated in street crime (e.g., extreme poverty, negative childhood experiences, and low self-control) do not seem to explain white-collar crime by corporate executives and other high-status professionals. Instead, white-collar crime arises from an insatiable thirst for money and power, a workplace culture that condones lawbreaking, and a system of lax law enforcement.

7. Although many scholars and other observers think that longer and more certain prison terms would significantly deter white-collar crime in general and corporate crime in particular, other observers think this strategy would prove ineffective and overburden a legal system that is already stretched beyond its means.

8. Organized crime goes back to the days of pirates and exists because it provides citizens goods and services they desire. The popular image of organized crime dominated by a few Italian families and corrupting innocent individuals is a myth. Instead, organized crime is relatively decentralized and composed of many groups of different ethnicities and other backgrounds.

Key Terms

alien conspiracy model 340	embezzlement 321	organizational crime 320	professional fraud 322
collective embezzlement 321	goods 338	pilferage 321	restraint of trade 325
corporate crime 320	muckrakers 319	piracy 338	services 338
corporate violence 326	occupational crime 320	price-fixing 325	white-collar crime 319

What Would You Do?

1. One day you are hired for a summer job as a cashier in the clothing section of a large department store in a tourist area. At any one time, there are four cashiers working in your section. Because the hours of all the cashiers are staggered, over the next two weeks you meet a dozen other cashiers who were all hired just for the summer. By the end of this period, you have also become aware that most of them have stolen clothing from the store by taking the security tags off articles of clothing and putting the articles in their backpacks. Just about everyone but you has taken a couple of shirts and one or two pairs of pants. Because your store is so large and so busy, it is likely that the store will not realize what is happening until long after the summer is over, if then. Would you join the other cashiers in taking clothing, tell the store manager, or do nothing? Explain your answer.

2. You are working full-time in a summer job in a hamburger joint so that you can afford to pay your tuition for the fall semester at the state university. One day you notice that someone forgot to put a shipment of raw meat into the freezer immediately after arrival, as store regulations require, and instead let it lie around for several hours. Concerned that the meat may not be safe to eat, you notify the store manager. The manager says the meat is probably safe to eat and that, if he throws it out, the cost would come out of his salary. He then instructs you and one of your coworkers to put the meat in the freezer. What do you do? Why?

CHAPTER

fourteen

Political Crime

Crime in the News

n spring 2010, a professor and six students from California State University-Northridge (CSUN) were arrested for protesting campus budget cuts. They were part of a group of twenty-five people who marched to a traffic intersection and promptly sat down to block traffic. The police ordered them to disperse and arrested the protesters who refused to do so. The protest was part of a national "Day of Action" to protest budget cuts at campuses across the United States.

Source: Morales 2010.

The behavior for which the CSUN protesters were arrested was very different from the crimes covered in earlier chapters. Those crimes were either committed for economic gain (property crime or white-collar crime) or out of hatred, anger, jealousy, and other emotions (violent crime). The CSUN activists had none of these reasons in mind. Instead, their motivation was *ideological:* They aimed to call attention to the impact that budget cuts were having on students and to put pressure on their university administration to limit or rescind the cuts. The behavior for which they were arrested was a *political crime.* Political crime has existed for centuries and takes many forms. People like the CSUN protesters commit political crime, but so do governments. And although the CSUN traffic sit-in was a relatively benign, if disruptive, act of civil disobedience, the unforgettable attacks on 9/11 were obviously very deadly acts of terrorism. This chapter discusses these and the many other types of political crime. As we will see, political crime often plays a key role in the struggle between government and dissenters.

Defining Political Crime

Like *white-collar crime,* **political crime** is an ambiguous term. For example, we could say that all crimes are political crimes because all crimes by definition violate criminal laws passed by legislative bodies. However, this conceptualization would render the term *political crime* meaningless. As another example, political officials, as we will see, often take legal actions that violate standards of human decency and democracy. Should we consider their actions political crimes? Should social problems such as hunger, poverty, corporate violence, and institutionalized sexism and racism be considered political crimes, as some scholars argue? Should African Americans and other poor people of color languishing in our prisons for street crime be considered political prisoners, as some radicals argued a generation ago (Lefcourt 1971)? Were the urban riots of the 1960s political revolts or just common violence? What about politicians who take bribes and are otherwise corrupt for personal gain? Are their crimes political crimes?

None of these questions is easy to answer. A major part of the struggle between any government and its dissenters is to influence public views of the legitimacy and necessity of actions taken by both sides. The state does its best to frame its own actions, however harmful, as necessary to protect the social order from violent and even irrational individuals. Meanwhile, dissenters call attention to the evils of state policies and frame their own activities, even if illegal, as necessary for a more just society. Public officials call an urban uprising a riot, whereas dissenters call it a revolt. Against this backdrop, any attempt to define and categorize political crime is itself a political act. Omitting harmful, unethical, and even illegal actions by the state risks obscuring behaviors that are often far worse than what any common criminal does. In contrast, calling any state policy or social condition that oppresses some deprived group (the poor, women, people of color) a political crime might dilute the concept's analytic power.

As with white-collar crime, it seems best to take an eclectic view of political crime that encompasses what many people mean by the concept without being overly broad. A reasonable definition of political crime might then be *any illegal or socially harmful act aimed at preserving or changing the existing political and social order.* This is not a perfect definition because it leaves open, for example, the question of who defines whether a given act is "socially harmful," but it does get at what most scholars mean by political crime (Ross 2003). Although the actual behavior involved in political crime (e.g., murder) may be very similar to that involved in conventional crimes, the key difference is that political crime is performed for ideological reasons. Thus tax evasion intended for personal gain is fraud, whereas nonpayment of taxes to protest U.S. military or taxation policy is a political crime. A killing during a robbery is a homicide, whereas a killing by an act of terrorism is a homicide but also a political crime.

MAJOR CATEGORIES OF POLITICAL CRIME

Let us further divide political crime into two major categories: crime by government and crime against government. *Crime by government,* also called *state crime* or *state criminality* (Chambliss, Kramer, and Michalowski 2010; Rothe and Kauzlarich 2010), aims to preserve the existing order and includes (1) political repression and human rights violations (genocide, torture, assassination, and other violence; surveillance and infiltration; and arrest, prosecution, and imprisonment), (2) unethical or illegal experimentation, and (3) the aiding and abetting of corporate crime. Many governments, including the United States and other democracies, commit some or all of these crimes, which occur inside or outside their national borders. A fourth type of crime by government is *political corruption.* As Chapter 13 noted, many scholars place this corruption in the occupational crime category. But because political corruption violates the public trust by enhancing the wealth and influence of political officials, other scholars consider it a form of political crime, especially when it involves conspiracies of people at the highest levels of government, such as in the Watergate and Iran–Contra scandals (discussed later).

   Crime against government aims to change the existing order and includes (1) terrorism, assassination, and other political violence, (2) nonviolent civil disobedience, and (3) espionage and treason. It might be more accurate to call this category "crime against government and other established interests." For example, although much illegal protest is directed against government, as it was during the Vietnam War, much is also aimed against corporations and other targets. Illegal protest by organized labor, nuclear arms opponents, and animal rights activists are just a few that fall into this category.

   With these broad categories of political crime in mind, we now explore its nature and extent by turning to specific examples.

Crime by Government

POLITICAL REPRESSION AND HUMAN RIGHTS VIOLATIONS

In the ideal world of political theory, all societies would be democratic and egalitarian, treating their citizens and those of other nations with dignity and respect. This ideal world has never existed. History is replete with governments that have used both violent and legal means to repress dissent and to preserve inequality. The worst offenders are typically totalitarian regimes, but even democratic governments, including the United States, have engaged in various types of **repression,** including mass murder. To do justice to all victims of repression would take too much space, but several examples should give you an idea of its use in both totalitarian and democratic societies.

Genocide

The ultimate act of repression is genocide (Hagan and Rymond-Richmond 2008). **Genocide,** a term coined during World War II, refers to the deliberate extermination of a group because of its race, religion, ethnicity, or nationality. By definition, genocide is the worst crime by government of all and is often called a *crime against humanity.* The most infamous example of genocide, of course, is the Nazi slaughter of 6 million Jews during World War II, more than two-thirds of all the Jews in Europe, and up to 6 million other people,

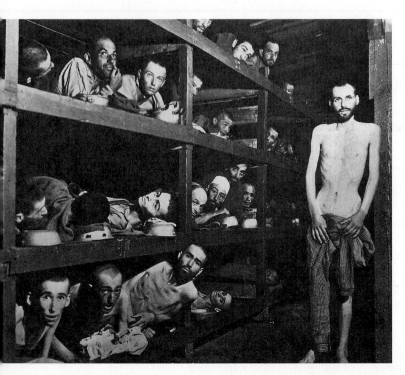

During World War II, the Nazis imprisoned Jews and other groups in concentration camps such as this one and eventually slaughtered some 6 million Jews and 5 million to 6 million other people.

including Poles, Slavs, Catholics, homosexuals, and gypsies (Safrian 2010). In the late 1800s, Russia also committed Jewish genocide by murdering hundreds of Jews in massacres called *pogroms.* More than 2 million Russian Jews fled their homeland for the safety of the United States, Palestine, and other areas (Klier and Lambroza 1992). In yet another act of genocide, about 1 million Armenians died from thirst, starvation, or attacks by roving tribes after Turkey forced them into the surrounding desert in 1915 (Balakian 2003).

Genocide did not end with the Nazis. In the last decade, the mass murder of Africans in Sudan by a militia group called the Janjaweed amounted to genocide. Political unrest in the western region of Darfur led the Sudanese government to pay the Janjaweed to quell the rebellion. The Janjaweed did so through mass terror, including murder, rape, torture, and the burning of whole villages (Hagan, Raymond-Richmond, and Parker 2005). By July 2004, more than 1 million Africans had been displaced and hundreds of thousands died from murder and starvation (Hagan and Rymond-Richmond 2008). A decade earlier, political violence in two other regions of the world, Bosnia in eastern Europe and Rwanda in Africa, also led to tens of thousands of deaths and repeated charges of genocide (Lynch 1995; Post 1994). And during the late 1970s, the Khmer Rouge regime of dictator Pol Pot slaughtered hundreds of thousands of Cambodians (Martin 1994).

Genocide is typically linked to totalitarian governments, but democracies can also commit it. Here the U.S. treatment of Native Americans is widely cited. When Europeans first came to this continent, about 1 million Native Americans lived here. Over the decades, tens of thousands were killed by white settlers and then U.S. troops, while many others died from disease introduced by the Europeans. Deaths from these two sources reduced the Indian population to less than 240,000 by 1900. Many historians and other scholars say the killings constituted genocide against American Indians (Johansen 2005).

The term *genocide* was used again during the Vietnam War years. The Vietnam War killed some 58,000 U.S. soldiers and other personnel and almost 2 million Vietnamese. The United States dropped four times as many tons of bombs, many targeting civilian populations, as the Allies had dropped over Germany in World War II. Some were strictly antipersonnel in nature, sending out small nails able to shred muscles and body organs but not able to dent military equipment, or steel pellets able to penetrate flesh but not trucks (Branfman 1972). Many bombs contained napalm, a jellied gasoline that would ignite when dropped from the plane, splatter across a wide area, and burn anything it touched. Often the "anything" was children and other civilians. In 1968, U.S. troops massacred up to 200 civilians at My Lai village. Although this massacre received wide attention after it was publicized, Vietnam veterans later revealed many other civilian massacres that never came to light (Meyrowitz and Campbell 1992).

Review and Discuss

The text mentions that some critics claimed that the United States was committing genocide during the Vietnam War. How valid is this charge?

Torture, Assassination, and Related Violence

Governments often resort to political violence that stops short of genocide. This violence includes torture and beatings; assassination, execution, and mass murder; and related actions, including forced expulsion. This is government rule by terror and is called **state terrorism** (Bushnell 1991). One of the most notorious examples of state terrorism of the last century occurred under Soviet Union dictator Joseph Stalin in the 1930s and 1940s. In that period, a purge of Communist Party leaders who might have threatened Stalin's reign resulted in the execution of thousands as Stalin's secret police terrorized the Soviet citizenry (Tzouliadis 2008).

State terrorism did not end with Stalin. International human rights groups have documented thousands of government-sponsored murders, beatings, and related violence across the world. In Latin America, the Middle East, Africa, and elsewhere, dissenters are kidnapped, tortured, and murdered, and government troops have raped women routinely. These human rights violations are once again much more common under totalitarian regimes than in democratic societies, but, as we will see shortly, the United States has seen its share of government violence over the years.

Governments also assassinate selected dissenters whom they perceive as special threats. As just one example, in the late 1970s peasants and other poor citizens in El Salvador began demanding that the government provide land, jobs, and other help to the poor. Many Roman Catholic priests and nuns supported the protesters. One of the most vocal clergy was Archbishop Oscar Arnulfo Romero, who was assassinated by government troops in March 1980. His death became a rallying cry for dissident forces for several years (Goldston 1990).

GOVERNMENT VIOLENCE IN THE UNITED STATES

The United States has also seen its share of political violence committed against dissenters, especially those in the labor movement. One of the several labor massacres remembered by history occurred in Ludlow, Colorado, in April 1914, at a tent city of striking miners and their families evicted from their company-owned homes. On Easter night, April 20, company guards and National Guard troops poured oil on the tents, set them afire, and machine-gunned the families as they fled from the tents. Thirteen children, one woman, and five men died from bullet wounds or smoke inhalation (McGovern and Guttridge 1972).

During the 1960s, violence against Southern civil rights activists by police, state troopers, and white civilians was common. Several dozen civil rights workers were murdered and hundreds more beaten. The murdered included Southern blacks as well as Northerners who had come to help the movement. Other violence greeted civil rights demonstrators engaging in protest campaigns, especially those in Selma, Alabama, in April and May 1963 and in Birmingham, Alabama, in March 1965. In Birmingham, police clubbed nonviolent demonstrators, attacked them with police dogs, and swept them away with powerful fire hoses. In Selma, state troopers again clubbed the demonstrators with nightsticks, attacked them with police horses, and used tear gas. Both episodes shocked the nation and helped win passage of federal civil rights legislation (Branch 1998).

The kind of official violence used against Southern civil rights activists was much less common during the Vietnam antiwar movement, but some still occurred. On May 4, 1970, National Guard troops fired into an antiwar rally at Kent State University in Ohio,

Political violence by governments includes torture, beatings, and other forms of physical abuse. In this famous photo from 2004, a prisoner of U.S. forces in Iraq is hooded, apparently wired to an electrical device, and forced to stand on a small box.

killing four students and wounding nine others. Several of the students were just watching the rally or walking to classes (Davies 1973). Ten days later, campus protest not related to the war brought police and state troopers onto the campus of Jackson State College, a historically black college in Mississippi. At one point they fired rifles, shotguns, and submachine guns into a dormitory, killing two students and wounding twelve others (Spofford 1988).

At the federal level, the U.S. government has conspired in or otherwise supported the torture and murder of dissidents and the assassination of political leaders in other nations in the last half century. During the Vietnam War, for example, the Central Intelligence Agency (CIA) established the notorious Operation Phoenix program that arrested, tortured, and murdered some 40,000 Vietnamese civilians (Chomsky and Herman 1979). Following orders of the White House and State Department, the CIA has supported coups that deposed and often killed national leaders in countries such as Chile, the Dominican Republic, Guatemala, Iran, and South Vietnam. These assassinations and coups often plunged these nations further into civil war or led to despotic governments that terrorized their citizenry (Moyers 1988).

Since 2001, U.S. military and civilian personnel have also participated in the torture and abuse of an unknown number of persons of Middle Eastern backgrounds, both during the war in Iraq and in the effort to stop international terrorism (Cole 2009; Miles 2009). Later investigation also uncovered a policy called *extraordinary rendition*. Under this policy, the CIA arrested or kidnapped suspected terrorists in several nations and transported them, blindfolded and shackled, to secret CIA prisons in the Middle East and eastern Europe, where they were reportedly tortured (Moore 2007). All these policies aroused outrage around the world when they came to light.

During the Vietnam War, the FBI and other intelligence groups spied on thousands of antiwar dissidents involved in lawful protest and sometimes infiltrated groups opposed to the war.

SURVEILLANCE, INFILTRATION, AND DISRUPTION

In George Orwell's (1949) classic novel *1984*, Big Brother was always watching, and citizens had no freedom of movement. Orwell's novel remains a frightening indictment of societies that today still have police and other agents spy on the citizenry, infiltrate dissident groups, and harass and disrupt their activities.

One cornerstone of democracy is freedom of movement and lawful dissent. Yet from the 1940s to the 1970s in the United States, the FBI, CIA, and other federal, state, and local law enforcement agencies systematically and illegally spied on hundreds of thousands of U.S. citizens who were lawfully involved in civil rights, antiwar, and other protests (Finan 2007). These agencies also infiltrated many dissident groups and did their best to disrupt their activities. The FBI's efforts were part of its counterintelligence program called **COINTELPRO,** begun in 1941 to target the Communist and Socialist Workers parties. During the 1960s, the FBI turned its attention to the civil rights, antiwar, and other social movements that began during that decade. Using wiretaps and informants, it monitored the activities of tens of thousands of citizens, some of them leaders of these movements, but most of them unknown except to their families and friends. Perhaps the most famous target of FBI harassment was the great civil rights leader, Martin Luther King, Jr. The FBI bugged motel rooms in which King stayed to gather evidence of alleged extramarital affairs and at one point wrote him anonymously, urging him to commit suicide before this evidence became public (Garrow 1981).

After the terrorist acts of 9/11, the U.S. government increased its surveillance of people suspected of terrorism. Critics said the government surveillance eroded civil liberties and included people who were engaging in activities protected by the First Amendment. The Crime and Controversy box reviews this debate.

Review and Discuss

In a democracy like the United States, is it legitimate for police and other law enforcement agents to conduct surveillance against and to infiltrate dissenting groups? To what degree does your response depend on whether the dissenting groups have indicated that they intend to break the law and/or to commit violence?

Legal Repression

A favorite repression strategy in totalitarian nations is to arrest and imprison dissidents. The aim here is to use the guise of law to legitimate political repression, even though the arrests and prosecutions are based on trumped-up charges. Stalin's reign of terror involved many *show trials* that depicted his opponents as dangerous threats to law and order. Yet repressive uses of the law also occur in democratic societies, where officials hope that arrests and prosecutions will prompt the public to view dissidents as common criminals. They also hope to intimidate dissidents and their movements and force them to spend large amounts of time, money, and energy on their legal defense.

U.S. history has been filled with legal repression (Finan 2007). To cite one example, federal law prohibited virtually all criticism of World War I. Arrests and prosecutions of some 2,000 labor radicals and socialists during the war muffled dissent and destroyed the Industrial Workers of the World, a radical labor union. After the war ended, federal agents raided homes, restaurants, and other places in thirty-three cities across the country and arrested some 10,000 radicals in what became known as the *Palmer raids,* named after the U.S. attorney general at the time. Legal repression was also used during the Southern civil rights movement of the 1960s, when thousands of activists were arrested and jailed on trumped-up charges, forced to spend large sums of money on their defense, and subjected to beatings and the very real possibility of death in Southern jails. Convictions by white judges and juries were a foregone conclusion. Several Southern cities used mass arrests and prosecutions to thwart civil rights protest campaigns. By avoiding police violence, these cities' efforts seemed reasonable and even won plaudits from the press and federal officials (Barkan 1985).

UNETHICAL OR ILLEGAL EXPERIMENTATION

In the concentration camps of World War II, Nazi scientists performed some hideous experiments in the name of science (Gilbert 1987). In a typical experiment, they would strip camp prisoners naked and leave them outside in subfreezing temperatures to see

Crime and Controversy

Civil Liberties in an Age of Terrorism

A fundamental dilemma of any democratic society is how best to strike the right balance between keeping the society safe and keeping the society free. This dilemma became a national controversy after the 9/11 terrorist attacks. In their wake, the federal government arrested thousands of people of Middle Eastern backgrounds living in the United States. They were detained in secret locations for months, and many were not permitted to contact family or friends or even an attorney. Many also had no charges filed against them, and the government refused to reveal their names or locations of detainment. When some were allowed to meet with an attorney, the government monitored their communication in violation of attorney–client privilege.

Forty-five days after 9/11, Congress passed—with hardly any debate—the so-called Patriot Act that greatly expanded the powers of the federal government to combat terrorism. President Bush quickly signed the bill. The act was 342 pages long and most members of Congress did not read it all (or at all). Among other provisions, it gave the FBI the power to gain access to anyone's medical, library, or student records without having to show probable cause or acquire a search warrant. It also expanded the power of law enforcement agents to conduct wiretapping and other surveillance.

In the months that followed, the government increased its surveillance of individuals and groups suspected not only of terrorist activity but also of dissent in general. In one case, a 60-year-old retired telephone company worker said at a gym that "Bush has nothing to be proud of. He is a servant of the big oil companies and his only interest in the Middle East is oil." Shortly afterward, FBI agents visited the man to question him about his statement. FBI agents also questioned many other people about statements and activities such as displaying artwork critical of the government, which is protected by the First Amendment.

The government's detainment of Middle Eastern individuals, the Patriot Act, and the other actions taken in the wake of 9/11 aroused enormous controversy. Civil liberties advocates denounced the erosion of civil liberties, and many cities across the country passed resolutions calling for reforms to the act or its outright elimination. Defenders of the government's actions said they were necessary to keep America safe from terrorism.

The war of words escalated when U.S. Attorney General John Ashcroft questioned the patriotism of his critics in testimony before the Senate Judiciary Committee: "To those who pit Americans against immigrants, citizens against noncitizens, those who scare peace-loving people with phantoms of lost liberty, my message is this: Your tactics only aid terrorists for they erode our national unity and diminish our resolve. They give ammunition to America's enemies and pause to America's friends." The American Civil Liberties Union sharply criticized this statement, saying "that our wealth and power derive from the democratic values expressed in our Declaration of Independence and Constitution. If we are intimidated to the point of restricting our freedoms and undermining our democracy, the terrorists will have won a resounding victory indeed."

Further fuel was provided for civil liberties advocates' fears in March 2007, when it was disclosed that the FBI "may have violated the law or government policies as many as 3,000 times since 2003 as agents secretly collected the telephone, bank and credit card records of U.S. citizens and foreign nationals residing here," according to a news report. Six hundred of the violations were called "serious misconduct" because they involved the use of national security letters, equivalent to subpoenas but not approved by a judge, issued by the FBI.

The civil liberties debate in the aftermath of 9/11 goes to the heart of fundamental questions regarding crime and society. As terrorism will be with us for many years to come, so will the questions about the extent to which a government in a free society should curtail the civil rights and liberties of its residents and citizens.

Sources: Cohen and Wells 2004; Cole and Lobel 2007; Smith 2007.

how long it would take them to freeze to death. These experiments outraged the world community when they came to light.

This outrage did not prevent similar government-sponsored experiments from occurring in the United States during the next few decades. This is a strong charge, to be sure, but the evidence supports the accusation. Perhaps the most notorious experiment began before the Holocaust and lasted forty years. In 1932 the U.S. Public Health Service identified some 400 poor, illiterate African-American men in Tuskegee, Alabama, who had syphilis, a deadly venereal disease that was incurable at the time. To gather information on the progression of this disease, the government decided to monitor these men for many years. When a cure for syphilis, penicillin, was discovered in the 1940s, the government decided to withhold it from the men to avoid ruining the study. They remained untreated for three more decades, when the press finally revealed the Tuskegee experiment in 1972. During that time, their wives who caught syphilis from them also remained untreated, as did any of their children born with syphilis (Washington 2006). After the experiment was disclosed in 1972, commentators compared it to the worst Nazi experiments and charged that it would not have occurred if the subjects had been white and wealthy.

The Tuskegee experiment was not the only one in which the U.S. government treated U.S. citizens as human guinea pigs. Congressional and other investigations since the 1970s have revealed many secret experiments conducted by the military and the CIA over the years. Many of these involved radiation. From 1946 to 1963, for example, the military subjected up to 300,000 soldiers and civilians to radiation during atomic bomb tests in Nevada and elsewhere. Many times soldiers were made to stand near the sites of the bomb tests; in others, nuclear fallout was spread in the air over civilian populations in the Southwest (Kershaw 2004; Schneider 1993). The exposed groups ended up with abnormally high levels of leukemia and cancer, and medical records of their exposure either disappeared or were destroyed.

During that period, federal agencies also injected people with plutonium, uranium, and radium or gave them high doses of X-rays. These "government guinea pigs" included prisoners, mentally retarded individuals, and others who were not fully informed of the nature of the experiments (Lee 1995). In Idaho, radioactive iodine was added to land and drinking water. The CIA conducted its own medical experiments, one of them involving spiking army scientists' drinks with LSD. Two days later one of the scientists jumped from a hotel window and died. The CIA hid the true circumstances of his death from his family for more than two decades (Thomas 1989).

STATE–CORPORATE CRIME

Chapter 13 indicated that much corporate crime occurs because of the government's inability or unwillingness to have stronger regulations and more effective law enforcement. Along this line, some scholars have discussed episodes in which government agencies and corporations *cooperate* to commit illegal or socially harmful activities. Such **state–corporate crime** represents the intersection of corporate crime and crime by government (Rothe and Kauzlarich 2010).

A notorious example of state–corporate criminality was the January 1986 explosion of the *Challenger* space shuttle that killed six astronauts and schoolteacher Christa McAuliffe. When people around the nation watched in horror as the *Challenger* exploded, little did they know that the explosion was, as Ronald C. Kramer noted (1992:214), the "collective product of the interaction between" the National Aeronautics and Space Administration (NASA) and Morton Thiokol, Inc., the corporation that built the flawed O-ring seals that caused the explosion. After the United States finally reached the moon in the late 1960s, support for NASA began to dry up. The space shuttle program

International Focus

Cracking Down on Dissent and Dress in Iran

So many nations around the world suppress dissent that it would take a whole book or more to recount the nature and extent of their efforts. Activities of the government in Iran a few years ago illustrate what happens far too often in far too many locations—the harassment and arrest of dissenters and the control of the press—while also illustrating how the national context can affect what kinds of dissent are targeted for suppression.

During the spring and summer of 2007, Iran was in the middle of an economic downturn and, not coincidentally, was also experiencing what a news report described as "one of its most ferocious crackdowns on dissent in years." The crackdown targeted students, labor unions, and women's rights activists and was seen as an effort to deflect attention from the faltering economy. The crackdown began when police went into the streets and stopped and questioned an estimated 150,000 people for wearing clothing that was deemed to violate Islamic norms. Police followed the dress crackdown with arrests of student activists and labor union leaders. Iran's intelligence minister declared, "Those who damage the system under any guise will be punished," and he contended that individuals and groups who were trying to lessen Iran's harsh rules were really trying to overturn the government itself.

As part of its attempt to suppress dissent, the government banned the press from reporting on the crackdown to reduce the publicity it received outside Iran. Instead, the government-controlled press focused on the growing tension between Iran and the United States and the controversy created after a former Iranian president supposedly committed an immoral act by shaking hands with a woman he did not know at the conclusion of a speech he gave in Rome. Western journalists in Iran worried about what might happen if they reported on the crackdown, with one journalist saying, "There are many things that I would like to write about, but can't. They would shut down our office and kick us out."

In some cases, police used violence against young people accused of wearing Western dress. Cell phone videos of the violence soon appeared on the Internet and, in an act of protest, young people played music on their car radios at an unusually loud level. One woman said defiantly, "I dress how I dress and wear my hair like this because I like it. They [the police] bother me on the streets. They've thrown me up against the wall. They've told me to change how I look. The next day, I go out like this again."

Sources: Daragahi 2007; MacFarquhar 2007.

became its salvation. However, NASA was under orders to implement the program at relatively low cost. As a result, said Kramer, "NASA began to promise the impossible in order to build the shuttle and save the agency" (p. 220).

This pressure mounted in the 1980s as the Reagan administration became eager to use the shuttle system for commercial and military purposes. In July 1982, President Reagan declared the shuttle system "fully operational," meaning that all bugs had been eliminated and it was ready to deploy. As it turned out, however, the president's declaration was premature because NASA had not finished developing the shuttle. Despite this problem, the president's declaration led to "relentless pressure on NASA to launch shuttle missions on an accelerated schedule" (Kramer 1992:221). This pressure in turn led NASA officials to overlook evidence of problems in the O-ring design.

Morton Thiokol was also to blame for the *Challenger* disaster. Thiokol tests in the 1970s indicated problems with the O-ring seal design. The company reported these problems to NASA, but said they were no cause for concern. Engineers at NASA's Marshall Space Flight Center reported similar problems in the late 1970s, more than six years before the disaster. One 1978 memo warned that the O-ring seal design could produce "hot gas leaks and resulting catastrophic failure" (Kramer 1992:225). Although Marshall managers initially did not tell higher NASA officials about these concerns, in 1982 they finally did classify the O-ring seals as a hazard, but called them an "acceptable risk." In 1985, Marshall and Thiokol engineers repeatedly warned that the O-ring design could cause a catastrophe. High-level officials at both NASA and Thiokol ignored these warnings and certified the O-ring seals as safe. To do otherwise would have scuttled the shuttle and reduced Thiokol's profits.

The explosion of the *Challenger* space shuttle resulted from the failure of NASA and Morton Thiokol officials to heed warnings about problems with the O-ring seals.

The launch of the *Challenger* was set for January 28, 1986. With very cold weather predicted, Thiokol engineers became concerned that the O-rings would become brittle and even more risky. On January 27 they alerted Marshall officials, who pressured Thiokol officials into overriding their engineers' concerns and into recommending that the launch proceed. The *Challenger* went up the next day and seconds later exploded in a ball of flame, killing everyone on board.

POLITICAL CORRUPTION

Political corruption is committed either for personal economic gain or for political influence. We look at each of these types in turn.

Personal Economic Gain

Officials at the local, state, and national levels of government may misuse their offices for personal economic gain, most often by accepting bribes and kick backs for favors they give businesses and individuals. These favors include approving the purchase of goods and services from certain companies and awarding construction contracts to other companies. This form of graft goes back at least to the nineteenth century, when public officials in the major U.S. cities were notorious for corruption, documented by muckraker Lincoln Steffens in his famous 1904 book *The Shame of the Cities,* in which he detailed corruption in many cities, including Chicago, Minneapolis, New York, Philadelphia, Pittsburgh, and St. Louis. Perhaps the worst offender was William March "Boss" Tweed, the head of New York City's Democratic Party organization after the Civil War. Tweed and his associates robbed New York of up to $200 million (about $3.4 billion in today's dollars) in a ten-year span, as more than two-thirds of every municipal contract went into their pockets (Hershkowitz 1977).

One of the most infamous national scandals, Teapot Dome, occurred during President Warren G. Harding's administration in the early 1920s. Secretary of the Interior Albert B. Fall took bribes in 1922 of more than $400,000 (more than $4.5 million in today's dollars) for leasing government-owned oil fields to private oil companies. Fall then resigned in 1923 to join one of the companies. He was convicted in 1929 of accepting a

The governor of Illinois, Rod Blagojevich, was impeached and removed from office in 2009 after being arrested on federal charges of bribery and other corruption.

bribe, fined $100,000, and sentenced to one year in prison. Harding's attorney general was tried but not convicted in 1926 for other corruption. In yet another scandal, the director and legal adviser of Harding's Veterans Bureau were accused of embezzling bureau funds. The director was convicted and imprisoned, and the legal adviser committed suicide (Noggle 1965).

Three decades ago, Vice President Spiro Agnew was forced to resign his office because of his own political corruption. During the 1960s, Agnew was a Baltimore County executive and then Maryland's governor. During this period, he and other officials took kickbacks from contractors and engineering and architectural firms to approve various construction projects. Agnew continued to receive these kickbacks while he was governor and later vice president. He eventually resigned in 1971 and pleaded no contest to one charge of income tax evasion. His punishment was a $10,000 fine and three years' probation (Cohen and Witcover 1974).

Any number of more recent political corruption scandals could be cited, but one example involved the governor of Illinois, Rod Blagojevich, who was impeached and removed from office in 2009 after being arrested on federal charges of bribery and other corruption (Long and Pearson 2009).

Political Power and Influence

Officials may also misuse their office for political power and influence. There are too many examples of such corruption, including campaign fraud, to recount here, but the most celebrated examples of the last quarter century, the Watergate and Iran–Contra scandals, do deserve some mention.

The well-known **Watergate scandal** began with a mysterious burglary in June 1972 at Democratic Party headquarters in the Watergate office complex and hotel in Washington, DC, and two years later toppled President Nixon and many of his chief aides and cabinet members, including the U.S. attorney general. It involved illegal campaign contributions running to the millions of dollars from corporations and wealthy individuals, dirty tricks against potential Democratic nominees for president, lie after lie to Congress and the public, obstruction of justice, and the secret wiretapping of people critical of Nixon presidency (Bernstein and Woodward 1974).

A decade later, the **Iran–Contra scandal** had the potential to topple the Reagan presidency. It involved key figures in the upper levels of the U.S. government, including the CIA director and National Security Council advisers, who allegedly helped supply weapons to Iran in exchange for the release of hostages held in Lebanon. The money gained from the Iranian arms sales was then used illegally to help arm the Contras in Nicaragua, a group of right-wing rebels trying to overthrow the left-wing, democratically elected Nicaraguan government. The arming of the Contras in this manner violated congressional prohibitions on Contra funding. Some of the illegal funds for the Contras also came from drug smuggling in Latin America that was aided and abetted by military and CIA officials. There is strong evidence that President Reagan knew of and approved the arms sale to Iran despite his denials, and several officials later lied to Congress (Arnson 1989).

Crimes Against Government

The torture, experimentation, and other crimes just discussed account for only one side of the political crime picture. The other side consists of crimes by individuals and organizations opposed to government and other established interests. The motivation for their criminality is largely ideological: They want to change the existing order (Ross 2003). The strong political convictions underlying their illegal behavior lead some scholars to call them "convictional criminals" (Schafer 1974). These political criminals can be on the left or the right side of the political spectrum, and they can be violent or nonviolent. They usually act as members of organized protest groups, but they can also act alone.

Whatever form it takes, crime against government is an important part of the dissent occurring in most societies. Some of the most important people in world history—Socrates, Jesus, Joan of Arc, Sir Thomas More, Mahatma Gandhi, and Martin Luther King, Jr., to name just a few—were political criminals who were arrested, tried, imprisoned, and, in some cases, executed for opposing the state. Though condemned at the time, their illegality contributed to the freedom of thought many societies enjoy today, as Durkheim (1962 [1895]) recognized long ago. History now honors them for opposing oppression and arbitrary power.

Of course, not all crime against government is so admirable. History is also filled with terrorism and other political violence in which innocent victims die, as America learned firsthand on 9/11. Other illegal dissent has evoked very different reactions at the time it occurred. During the civil rights movement, for example, many white Southerners condemned civil rights protest as anarchy and communism, whereas most Northerners saw Southern governments and police as the real criminals. Vietnam antiwar protest aroused similar passions pro and con. What people think about a particular crime against government obviously depends on their own ideological views. Some of us may liken political criminals to common lawbreakers, whereas others may consider them heroes. Americans and people across the world condemned the 9/11 terrorists, but some Middle Eastern residents deemed them martyrs for a just cause.

MASS POLITICAL VIOLENCE: REBELLION, RIOTS, TERRORISM

Individuals and groups often commit terrorism and other **political violence** to change the status quo. Although it is tempting to think of this violence as irrational acts of demented minds, its motivation and purpose are very rational: to force established interests to grant social and political reforms or even to give up power altogether. In this sense, mass political violence is no less rational, and its users no more deranged, than the government violence discussed earlier. Just as the people ordering and committing government violence know exactly what they are doing, so do those committing violence against government (Tilly 1989).

Not surprisingly, mass political violence has deep historical roots. Peasant revolts were common in preindustrial Europe, with labor riots replacing them after industrialization. Agrarian revolts also marked early U.S. history. Two you might remember from your history classes are Shays' Rebellion in Massachusetts in 1786–1787 and the Whiskey Rebellion in Pennsylvania in 1794. There were also farmer revolts after the Civil War and in the early 1900s. Historian Richard Maxwell Brown (1989:45) wrote that these agrarian revolts "formed one of the longest and most enduring chronicles in the history of American reform—one that was often violent."

Violent labor strife was common in the many strikes in the United States after the Civil War. Workers often turned to violence to protect themselves when police and company guards used violence to suppress strikes, but they also rioted and used other violence to force concessions. One of the most violent labor groups was the Molly Maguires, a secret organization of Irish miners in 1870s Pennsylvania who murdered company officials and committed terrorism. They took their name from an Irish folk hero said to have led a peasant revolt in the 1600s (Broehl 1964).

Over the years African Americans have also used violence to improve their lot. The first slave uprising occurred in New York City in 1712, with several more occurring before slavery ended with the Civil War. The most famous took place in Virginia in 1831 and was led by Nat Turner, whose rebellion involved more than sixty slaves who killed some sixty whites, including the family of Turner's owner. Twenty of the slaves, including Turner, were later hanged, and some 100 other slaves who had not participated in the revolt were also murdered by vengeful whites (Oates 1983).

African Americans also rioted in major U.S. cities in the twentieth century. This was a change from the past, when many cities in the 1800s and early 1900s were the scenes of race riots begun by whites, who typically encountered no resistance as they beat and slaughtered African Americans (Feldberg 1980). Beginning in the early 1900s, African Americans began to fight back when attacked by white mobs in cities such as Chicago and Washington, DC, in 1919 and Detroit in 1943. In the 1960s, urban violence assumed a new character as African Americans struck out against white-owned businesses, white police, and the National Guard in many cities. These riots were met with lethal force and a massive legal response, but led to increased federal funding to urban areas and other gains for African Americans (Button 1989). Many scholars view these riots as small-scale political revolts stemming from blacks' anger over their poverty and other aspects of racial oppression by a white society (Baldassare 1994).

Political scientist Richard E. Rubenstein (1970) wrote that the United States has long been characterized by a "myth of peaceful progress," which assumes that deprived groups have historically made social and economic gains by working within the electoral system. Looking at the expanse of U.S. history, Rubenstein said the myth of peaceful progress is just that—a myth: "For more than two hundred years, from the Indian wars and farmer uprisings of the eighteenth century to the labor–management and racial disturbances of the twentieth, the United States has experienced regular episodes of serious mass violence related to the social, political and economic objectives of insurgent groups" (p. 7). Against this historical backdrop, he said, the 1960s' urban riots and other episodes of insurgent violence over the years are hardly atypical; instead they are understandable as normal, if extreme, responses to racial and economic deprivation.

This photo of the World Trade Center after the September 11 attack reminds us of the horror of terrorism. However irrational terrorism might seem, it is best seen as a strategy for achieving political goals.

TERRORISM

If revolts and riots are often hard for us to understand, **terrorism** is even more baffling because it usually involves the killing and maiming of innocent bystanders. Wartime violence is understandable, if tragic, because the soldiers being killed and wounded are appropriate targets. But the innocent lives lost through terrorism are senseless killings that fill us with rage. This was the common reaction in the United States after the 9/11 attacks and after the April 1995 bombing of the Oklahoma City Federal Building by U.S. citizens linked to right-wing militia (Serrano 1998).

It is tempting to view 9/11 and other terrorism as irrational, demented acts, but such a view would obscure the rational, political purposes of terrorism, which is best seen as a strategy, however horrible and desperate, for achieving political goals (Dugan 2009; LaFree and Dugan 2009). This understanding of terrorism is reflected in its definition: "The use of unexpected violence to intimidate or coerce people in the pursuit of political or social objectives" (Gurr 1989:201). The motivation here is to frighten or demoralize one's political targets or the public at large.

Several types of terrorism exist (Gurr 1989). A first type is *state terrorism*, which involves the use of police and other government agents to repress their citizenry through violent means. As we saw, state terrorism is common in totalitarian nations, but has also occurred in the United States. A second type is *vigilante terrorism*, initiated by private groups against other private groups to preserve the status quo. Much vigilante terrorism takes the form of the hate crime discussed in Chapter 9. Bombings of abortion and family planning clinics and the murders of physicians performing abortions in the 1990s were other examples of vigilante terrorism (Dugan 2009). Many feminists also consider rape and battering to be a form of vigilante terrorism against women.

A third type of political terrorism, and the one falling under the crime against government rubric now being discussed, is *insurgent terrorism*, which is designed to bring about political change. The violence involved includes bombings, shootings, kidnappings, and hijackings, and its targets include public figures and the general public, public buildings, and buses and other means of transportation. The Oklahoma City federal building bombing was a particularly deadly example of insurgent terrorism.

This example notwithstanding, the terrorism that now most concerns Americans originates in the Middle East. The 9/11 terrorism is an example of the fourth type of terrorism, *transnational terrorism* (also called *global terrorism*), that is committed by residents of one or more nations against human and property targets in another nation. In addition to 9/11, other examples of transnational terrorism in the world in recent decades include bombings of buses, public buildings, and other targets by Palestinian nationalists in Israel.

Review and Discuss

What are the four major types of terrorism? Why should terrorism be considered *political* violence?

POLITICAL ASSASSINATION

A related form of political violence is political assassination, or the murder of public figures for political reasons. Political assassinations are often part of a larger campaign of political terrorism, but they also are sometimes committed by lone individuals bearing a political grudge. Murders of public figures are considered political assassinations only if they are politically motivated. If someone kills a public figure out of jealousy or because of mental illness, it is not a political assassination and thus not a political crime. Like terrorism, political assassination has a long history. One of its most famous victims was Roman dictator Julius Caesar, who was killed by a group that included his friend Brutus and memorialized in Shakespeare's famous play. Moving much further forward in European history, the assassination of Archduke Ferdinand of Austria in 1914 helped start World War I. In the United States, the assassination of Abraham Lincoln was an early tragic example.

The list of public figures assassinated since the 1960s is dismaying. It includes Medgar Evers, Southern civil rights leader; Indira Gandhi, prime minister of India; John F. Kennedy; Robert Kennedy; Martin Luther King, Jr.; Malcolm X; Yitzhak Rabin, prime minister of Israel; and Anwar Sadat, president

President John F. Kennedy (left) and his brother Robert (right) were both gunned down by assassins during the 1960s.

of Egypt. Two lesser known figures, San Francisco Mayor George Moscone and Supervisor Harvey Milk, were assassinated in late November 1978 by a former supervisor with personal and political grudges. Other notable figures were also the targets of assassination attempts: former Georgia governor George Wallace, President Gerald Ford (twice), and President Ronald Reagan.

CIVIL DISOBEDIENCE

Civil disobedience is the violation of law for reasons of conscience and is usually nonviolent and public (Lovell 2009). In the classic act of civil disobedience, protesters violate a law they consider morally unjust and wait to be arrested. Political and legal philosophers have long debated the definition and justification of civil disobedience in a democratic society, but this debate lies beyond our scope. Instead, we sketch the history of civil disobedience in the United States to give some idea of its use to bring about social change.

History of Civil Disobedience

The idea of civil disobedience goes back at least to ancient Greece. After the death of King Oedipus, according to Greek mythology, his two sons killed each other in a battle for the throne. The new king, Creon, considered one of the sons a traitor and ordered that he not be given a proper burial. His sister, Antigone, thought this order violated divine law and defiantly buried the son. In response, Creon sentenced her to death. She soon disappeared, and Greek mythology differs on whether she was executed, committed suicide, or fled (Bushnell 1988). The ancient Greek philosopher Socrates was also sentenced to death for defying the state by teaching unorthodox religious views. After his sentence, he declined several opportunities to escape from prison and eventually committed suicide by drinking a cup of hemlock (Stone 1989). Antigone and Socrates remain symbols of courageous, conscientious resistance to unjust state authority.

Civil disobedience also appears in the Bible. In the New Testament, Jesus' disciples disobeyed government orders to stop their teachings because they felt their loyalty was to God rather than to the state. Jesus himself can also be regarded as a civil disobedient who died for refusing state orders to stop his religious teaching. The conflict between religious belief and state decrees recurred during the medieval period, when Sir Thomas More was executed for adhering to his religious faith. More was lord chancellor, the highest judicial authority in England, from 1529 to 1532. During that time King Henry VIII wanted a divorce so that he could marry Anne Boleyn. The pope refused to grant permission. More resigned his post to protest the king's actions. Two years later he was imprisoned for refusing to take an oath that the king ranked higher than other rulers, including the pope, and he was beheaded in July 1535 (Kaufman 2007).

Disobedience to the law for religious reasons continued during colonial America, as pacifist Quakers refused to pay taxes to support the colonial effort in the war against England (Brock 1968). Depending on how civil disobedience is defined, many of the colonists' acts of resistance to British rule can also be considered civil disobedience.

A major event in the history of civil disobedience occurred in 1849 with the publication of Henry David Thoreau's (1969) famous essay on the subject. Thoreau had spent a night in jail in 1846 for refusing to pay taxes to protest slavery and the Mexican War, and the essay arose from a public lecture he gave in 1848 to justify his tax resistance. It is one of the most famous essays in U.S. history and profoundly influenced such important literary and political figures as Leo Tolstoy, Mahatma Gandhi, and Martin Luther King, Jr. The abolitionist period during which Thoreau wrote was marked by civil disobedience against the 1850 Fugitive Slave Law. Abolitionists were arrested for helping slaves escape in the South and for obstructing their capture or freeing them once imprisoned in the North (Friedman 1971). Two decades later, suffragist Susan B. Anthony voted in November 1872 in violation of a federal law prohibiting people (including all women) from voting when they had no right to vote. At her June 1873 trial in Canandaigua, New York, the judge refused to let her say anything in her defense and ordered the jury to find her guilty. Anthony was allowed to give a statement before sentencing that attracted wide attention and ended with the stirring words, "I shall earnestly and persistently continue to urge all women to the practical recognition of the old revolutionary maxim, 'Resistance to tyranny is obedience to God'" (Barry 1988).

In 1955, Rosa Parks was arrested in Montgomery, AL for refusing to move to the back of a city bus. Her act of civil disobedience helped spark the Southern civil rights movement.

Moving forward almost a century, nonviolent civil disobedience was the key strategy of the Southern civil rights movement. Rosa Parks's heroic refusal to move to the back of the bus was only the beginning of civil disobedience aimed at protesting and ending segregation. Southern blacks were arrested for sitting-in at segregated lunch counters, libraries, and movie theaters and for "kneeling-in" at segregated churches. They were also arrested countless times for peacefully marching after being unfairly denied parade permits. One such arrest landed Martin Luther King, Jr., in jail in Birmingham, Alabama, where he wrote an essay, "Letter from Birmingham City Jail" (King 1969), which rivals Thoreau's essay in its fame and impact.

The civil rights movement's use of nonviolent civil disobedience inspired similar protest by other social movements of the 1960s and the decades since. There are too many instances to detail here, but some of the most dramatic occurred during the Vietnam War when devout Catholics burned draft files. Wearing clerical clothing or otherwise dressed neatly, they went into about thirty draft board offices across the country, seized their files, took them outside and then poured blood on them or burned them, and they prayed while they waited to be arrested. These events involved more than 150 Catholic priests, nuns, and lay Catholics and destroyed more than 400,000 draft files (Bannan and Bannan 1974).

Other examples of civil disobedience abound. A decade ago, many people broke the law and were arrested for protesting the U.S. government's intention to invade Iraq in March 2003, and close to 2,000 protesters were arrested at the Republican National Convention in New York in August 2004. As the Crime in the News story that began this chapter illustrated, college students have also committed civil disobedience in regard to campus issues.

Review and Discuss

What were Henry David Thoreau's and Martin Luther King, Jr.'s arguments justifying civil disobedience?

ESPIONAGE AND TREASON

A final category of crime against government is espionage and treason. **Espionage,** or spying, has been called the world's "second oldest profession" and has probably been with us for thousands of years (Knightley 1987). In the Old Testament, Moses sent spies into Canaan. During the Revolutionary War, George Washington used many spies, including the celebrated Nathan Hale, to obtain information on British forces. Espionage remains the stuff of James Bond movies and countless spy thrillers. Today, many governments employ spies, and spying by the United States and the Soviet Union was a virtual industry during the Cold War (Kessler 1988).

Treason involves the aiding and abetting of a country's enemy by, for example, providing the enemy military secrets or other important information that puts the country at risk.

Historically, the terms *treason* and *traitor* have been used rather loosely to condemn legitimate dissent falling far short of treacherous conduct. During much of the Vietnam War, for example, much of the country considered antiwar protest unpatriotic at best and traitorous at worst (DeBenedetti and Chatfield 1990). Similar charges were made against early critics of the war in Iraq and as late as 2007 against Democrats in Congress who opposed continued funding for the war (Conte 2007).

The most famous traitor in U.S. history is certainly Benedict Arnold, the decorated Revolutionary War general who conspired in 1780 to surrender the West Point military base he commanded to the British. Today his name in the United States is synonymous with treason.

When citizens spy on their own country, espionage and treason become the same. Some do so for ideological reasons, and some for money and other personal reasons (Hagan 1989). One of the most controversial cases of espionage for ideological reasons involved the 1953 execution of Ethel and Julius Rosenberg for allegedly conspiring as members of the Communist Party to supply the Soviet Union with U.S. atomic bomb secrets. In a case of espionage for money, CIA operative Aldrich Ames spied for the Soviet Union as a "mole" from 1985 to 1994 and was paid or promised more than $4 million for his efforts. He gave the KGB, the Soviet CIA counterpart, the names of dozens of Soviet citizens whom the CIA had recruited. The Soviets executed ten of these people and imprisoned others. Aldrich also supplied the KGB with information about hundreds of CIA operations. He was later sentenced to life in prison (Adams 1995).

Explaining and Reducing Political Crime

Political crime is perhaps best seen as a consequence of power. Crime by government and other established interests is crime by those with power. Crime against government and other established interests is crime by those without power. The history of nations around the world indicates that governments are ready to use violence, the law, and other means to intimidate dissenters and the masses at the bottom of society. Powerful individuals within government are similarly ready to use their offices for personal economic gain and political influence.

By the same token, the history of nations also indicates that the lack of power motivates crime and other dissent against government. Explanations of why people dissent fall into the sociological subfield of social movements. Some of these explanations emphasize social–psychological factors, whereas others emphasize structural ones (Snow and Soule 2009). Social–psychological explanations emphasize emotions and other psychological states that motivate people to engage in protest. Thus, people are considered more apt to protest when conditions worsen and they become more upset or when they compare themselves to more successful groups and feel relatively deprived. Structural explanations focus on *micro-structural* factors such as preexisting friendship and organizational ties: People having friends or belonging to organizations already involved in social movements are considered more likely to join themselves. Another type of structural explanation, *political opportunity* theory, stresses that movements are more likely to arise when changes in the national government promise it will prove receptive or vulnerable to movement challenges.

In explaining terrorism, we might be tempted to believe that anyone who is able to commit such random, senseless violence must be psychologically abnormal or at least have certain psychological problems. However, this does not appear to be the case. "Most terrorists are no more or less fanatical than the young men who charged into Union cannonfire at Gettysburg or those who parachuted behind German lines into France. They are no more or less cruel and cold-blooded than the Resistance fighters who executed Nazi officials and collaborators in Europe, or the American GI's ordered to 'pacify' Vietnamese villages" (Rubenstein 1987:5). As Chapter 6 discussed, people can commit extreme violence without necessarily being psychologically abnormal.

THE SOCIAL PATTERNING OF POLITICAL CRIME

So far we have said little about the race, class, and gender of the people who commit either crime by government or crime against government. Understanding political crime as a function of power helps us in turn to understand the sociodemographic makeup of the people who commit this crime. Simply put, their race, class, and gender often mirror those of the powerful and powerless in any particular society.

Thus, in the United States and other Western nations, crime by government is almost always committed by white men of middle- or upper-class status, if only because privileged white men occupy almost all positions of political power in these societies. It is true that working-class soldiers, police, and other individuals, often nonwhite and occasionally female, carry out repression and other government crimes, but they do so in Western nations under orders from privileged white men. In non-Western nations, men are in positions of power, and race is sometimes less of a factor depending on the nation involved. However, in such nations ethnicity and/or religion often become more important, and the privileged men with political power usually belong to the dominant ethnicity or religion in the nation. Such men are thus responsible for the government crime that occurs.

The targets of government crime are typically those without power; in non-Western and Western nations alike, this often means the poor and people belonging to subordinate races, ethnicities, and religions. Which sociodemographic factor becomes most important in determining government crime targets depends on the particular society. For the Nazis, religion, nationality, and ethnicity were what mattered. They considered people not belonging to the Aryan "race" to be less than human and thus suitable targets for genocide. Jews had the same skin color as Nazis, but not the "correct" religion. In the United States, however, skin color has often mattered, as a similar dehumanization process made it possible for white Europeans to target Native Americans for slaughter and Africans for slavery. Race has also played an important role in determining the targets of vigilante terrorism and other hate crimes.

Whether race, class, or gender affects the targets of government repression in the United States has depended on the specific social movement that the government wishes to repress. The targets of repression during the labor movement were obviously working-class people, men and women, usually white but sometimes black or of other races. In the South, the victims of government crime during the civil rights movement were obviously black, although whites who supported the movement were also arrested, attacked, and sometimes murdered. During the Vietnam antiwar movement, however, the targets of surveillance and other government crime were often middle- and upper middle-class whites, because many of them were involved in the movement (DeBenedetti and Chatfield 1990). People from these social-class backgrounds were also the targets of government surveillance of Central American protest groups in the 1980s and gay rights groups in the early 1990s.

The targets of U.S. government experimentation often come from the ranks of the poor and nonwhite, but not always. It is difficult to imagine the government deciding to conduct the equivalent of the Tuskegee syphilis experiment on the children of corporate executives. Likewise, because most soldiers are from the working class, the soldiers upon whom the government conducted its radiation and other tests did not come from the ranks of the wealthy. Yet when the government spread nuclear fallout into the air and groundwater, everyone was vulnerable, white or black, male or female, rich or poor.

We have seen that most crime against government is committed by members of various social movements. Not surprisingly, the kinds of people who are the targets of government crime are usually those who commit crimes against government. What we have said about the racial, class, and gender makeup of the targets of government crime thus applies to the makeup of the perpetrators of crime against government. In non-Western nations, they are usually the poor or members of subjugated ethnicities and religions. In Western nations, including the United States, their specific makeup depends on the particular social movement. Thus, the abolitionists and women's suffragists who broke the law were white and middle class, while labor movement activists who broke the law were working class and mostly white, but sometimes of color. In nonlabor social movements, U.S. activists tend to be fairly well educated and at least middle class.

REDUCING POLITICAL CRIME

Compared to the literature on reducing the kinds of crimes discussed in earlier chapters, generally less attention is paid to reducing crime by or against government. Part of the reason for this inattention is that the political crime literature is relatively scant to begin with. Another reason is that political crime is so universal, both historically and cross-nationally, that it almost seems natural and inevitable. If, as we have argued, political crime is best understood as a function of power, then to reduce political crime we must reduce the disparities of power that characterize many societies. At a minimum, this means moving from authoritarian to democratic rule.

As we have seen, however, even democracies have their share of political crime, and the U.S. historical record yields little hope that crime by government and by political officials will soon end. The historical record also indicates that dissenters will turn to civil disobedience and other illegal activities as long as they perceive flawed governmental policies. One way to reduce their political crime, then, would be to reduce poverty, racial discrimination, military adventurism, and other conditions and policies that promote dissent. It would be more difficult, and even antidemocratic, to change governmental policies in such a way as to placate right-wing militia and other groups and individuals committed to terrorism and hate crime. At a minimum, responsible political officials from all sides of the political spectrum must state in no uncertain terms their opposition to these activities.

COUNTERING TERRORISM

The 9/11 attacks and other examples of transnational terrorism before and since have stimulated much thinking on how best to combat this form of political violence. For better or worse, however, the *counterterrorism* literature is filled with disagreement. Many counterterrorism experts support a combined law enforcement and military approach that emphasizes military strikes, arrests, and harsh prison terms (Simonsen and Spindlove 2007); this is the approach the United States used, along with abuse and torture, after 9/11. Terrorist groups in the Middle East and elsewhere have remained strong despite the measures. Some terrorism experts think a law enforcement and military approach may ironically strengthen terrorist groups by giving them more resolve and by winning them at least some public sympathy. As Laura Dugan (2009:447) writes, "Most terrorist organizations are unlikely to be deterred by traditional sanctions, especially because they are often wholly willing to exchange their lives or their freedom to strike a blow against their enemies."

Another way to combat terrorism is to address the problems underlying the grievances that terrorists have. The key question, of course, is whether doing so would only encourage terrorists to commit more random violence. And it is obviously not possible to appease the many Middle Eastern terrorists who detest the American way of life without doing away with America itself or at least drastically changing our culture. That said, some experts cite American imperialism as a major reason that much of the world, including terrorists, dislikes the United States (Rubenstein 1987). Eliminating U.S. intervention overseas, they feel, could thus help to reduce terrorism.

Conclusion

Political crime is part of the perpetual struggle between established interests, especially the state, and forces for social change. Because of the ideological issues and goals so often at stake, political crime differs in many ways from the other kinds of crime to which criminology devotes far more attention.

Crime by government takes many forms, including political repression involving torture and other violence. Political repression is almost a given in totalitarian societies, but occurs surprisingly often in and by democratic nations such as the United States. It is tempting to dismiss U.S. repression as historically abnormal, but there has been so much of it over the years that it would be wrong to succumb to such a temptation. To say that the United States is not as repressive as totalitarian nations is of small comfort. Our own Declaration of Independence, after all, speaks eloquently of God's gift to humanity of "certain unalienable rights" including "life, liberty, and the pursuit of happiness." The Pledge of Allegiance we have recited throughout our lives speaks of "one nation, under God, indivisible, with liberty and justice for all." U.S. government repression takes us far from these democratic ideals, as our country has too often denied its own citizens, and those living elsewhere, their liberty, their happiness, and even their lives. Surely we should aspire to a higher standard than this.

If much crime by government deprives its opponents of liberty and justice, the goal of a good amount of crime against government is to secure these elusive states. The United States and other nations have a long history of mass political violence and nonviolent civil disobedience aimed at producing fundamental social change. Whether or not we agree with the means and/or the goals of such lawbreaking, history would be very different if people had refrained from it. The "myth of peaceful progress" notwithstanding, change often does not come unless and until aggrieved populations resist their government. Often their protest is legal, but sometimes it is illegal and even deadly. Although it is easy to dismiss terrorism, assassination, and other political violence as the desperate acts of fanatical minds, it would be neither correct nor wise to obscure the political motivation and goals of politically violent actors. This is true even of terrorism on the scale of 9/11, however much we detest the destruction of that day and the people who caused it.

Political crime raises some fascinating questions about the nature of law, order, and social change in democratic and nondemocratic societies. Unless some utopian state is finally reached, governments and their opponents will continue to struggle for political power. If history is any guide to the future, this struggle will inevitably include repression by the government and law-breaking by its opponents. Whatever form it takes, political crime reminds us that what is *legally* right or wrong sometimes differs from what is *morally* right or wrong. For these and other reasons, political crime deserves more attention than it has received from criminologists and other social scientists.

Summary

1. Political crime is any illegal or socially harmful act aimed at preserving or changing the existing political and social order. It takes on many forms and falls into two major categories, crime by government and crime against government.

2. A major form of crime by government involves political repression and human rights violations. The ultimate act of repression is genocide, which has resulted in the deaths of millions of people over the last century. Governments also commit torture and murder against dissenters that stops short of genocide but is deadly nonetheless. Other acts of government oppression include surveillance and the use of the law to quell dissent.

3. Governments have also used illegal or unethical experimentation. The Nazis performed hideous experiments in concentration camps, but the U.S. government has also sponsored experiments involving syphilis and radiation that resulted in much death and illness.

4. State–corporate crime involves cooperation between government agencies and corporations that results in illegal or harmful activities. A major example involved the *Challenger* space shuttle that exploded because of defective O-rings.

5. Many political officials have engaged in political corruption for personal economic gain by taking bribes or kickbacks, with some notable scandals involving people at the highest reaches of government. Vice President Spiro Agnew was forced to resign his office when it was discovered that he had received kickbacks as the governor of Maryland and also as vice president. Corruption scandals regarding political influence include the Watergate and Iran–Contra scandals.

6. A major form of crime against government involves mass political violence that takes the form of rebellion, rioting, or terrorism. The United States and many other nations have experienced such violence throughout much of their history. Of the several types of terrorism, the one that most concerns Americans is transnational (or global) terrorism.

7. Civil disobedience is the violation of law for reasons of conscience. In the classic act of civil disobedience, protesters violate a law that is felt to be unjust and then wait to be arrested. The idea of civil disobedience goes back to ancient Greece and is a recurring theme in U.S. history. Two essays on civil disobedience by Henry David Thoreau and Martin Luther King, Jr., are among the most famous writings in U.S. history.

8. Two final forms of political crime are espionage and treason, which have also been common in the history of many nations. In U.S. history, the most famous spy is Nathan Hale, and the most famous traitor is Benedict Arnold.

9. The counterterrorism literature is divided over the potential effectiveness of a military and law enforcement approach to combat terrorism. This approach may work to some extent, but leaves untouched the roots of terrorism and may endanger civil liberties. It may also give terrorists more resolve and win them some public support. Although some experts thus believe that strategies focusing on the social problems that lead to terrorism could reduce this form of violence, others say that such efforts are too weak and would encourage terrorists to commit further violence.

Key Terms

civil disobedience 362	Iran–Contra scandal 358	state–corporate crime 355	treason 363
COINTELPRO 353	political crime 348	state terrorism 351	Watergate scandal 358
espionage 363	political violence 359	terrorism 360	
genocide 349	repression 349		

What Would You Do?

1. You are a member of the jury in a trial involving four people who poured their own blood on a nuclear submarine to protest the proliferation and possible use of nuclear weapons. After committing their act of protest, they waited to be arrested. They are accused of trespassing and defacing government property. They admit to this in court, but say their actions were necessary to call attention to the threat of nuclear war. As a juror, do you vote to find them guilty or not guilty? Explain your answer.

2. Suppose that someday you are elected to the U.S. House of Representatives. During your second term in office, the president seeks an expansion of the powers of the FBI to combat terrorism by giving it the right to subject suspected terrorists to what the president calls "mild" psychological and physical punishment, including sleep and food deprivation and minor electric shocking. A physician would supervise any such treatment. Do you vote for the bill that would allow the FBI to undertake these actions? Why or why not?

CHAPTER

fifteen

Consensual Crime

Crime in the News

n May 2010, the federal government issued its National Drug Control Strategy report that called for increasing spending on antidrug efforts to $15.6 billion. Of this amount, $10 billion would be spent on law enforcement efforts, including a beefed-up effort by the Coast Guard to stop drug shipments. The remainder would be spent on education and treatment programs and other efforts to reduce demand for drugs.

Drug reform organizations immediately criticized the strategy for allocating twice as much money to enforcement as to demand reduction. According to a news report, the organizations argued that "targeting shipments of drugs will not stop production so long as high demand encourages cartels." The organizations also said that crackdowns on drug trafficking in Colombia and Mexico just encourage drug trafficking in other locations. As one reform advocate put it, "It's like a balloon; if you press down in one area it will push out in another because there is still demand." A second advocate added, "Coming only a couple of weeks after the drug czar testified under oath that eradication in Colombia and Afghanistan and elsewhere had no impact on the availability of drugs in the US, to then put out a strategy embracing what he said was least effective is quite disturbing."

Mexcio's ambassador to the United States acknowledged that anticartel efforts in his nation had increased cartel activity in several Central American nations. He also acknowledged that Plan Colombia, the U.S. $6 billion military-aid effort to reduce cocaine trafficking in Colombia, had not been "a big success."

Sources: Risen 2010; Smith et al. 2010.

What should be done about illegal drugs? What should be done about other illegal behaviors, such as prostitution and much gambling, in which people engage voluntarily? Drugs, prostitution, and gambling raise the important issue of whether and to what degree the law should be used to enforce notions of how morally proper people should behave. Reasonable people hold very different views on these behaviors. Many oppose them for moral or pragmatic reasons and think the law should be used to punish their participants. Other people think individuals should have the right in a free society to engage in some or all of these consensual behaviors.

This chapter examines the debate over the major consensual crimes: drug use, prostitution and pornography, and gambling. We will discuss why people engage in them, and we will explore possible alternatives to the current criminalization of these behaviors. Two general themes will guide the discussion. First, consensual crime laws are often arbitrary and even illogical. For example, some gambling is legal, whereas other gambling is illegal, and some of the most harmful drugs are the legal ones. Second (and using drugs as the prime example), the laws against consensual crimes may do more harm than good.

Overview of the Consensual Crime Debate

Unlike most of the crimes we have studied so far that involve unwilling victims, *consensual crimes* (also called *vice crimes, public order crimes,* or *victimless crimes*) involve people who participate in these behaviors willingly. Some scholars say people should be free in a democratic society to engage in these behaviors, however unwise these behaviors may be, as the state should not enforce morality. Other scholars say people engaging in these behaviors do not just hurt themselves. Illegal drug use and gambling, for example, may also hurt the offenders' families and even lead to other crimes involving unwilling victims. If so, consensual crimes are less a matter of morality than of protecting society.

Critics of laws against these behaviors reply that families are often hurt by many things a family member may do, including starting a business that fails, clogging one's arteries with "fat food," and other normal, legal practices. Just as the law cannot begin to prohibit these practices, so it should not prohibit other practices that sound less socially acceptable. They also emphasize that laws against these behaviors might do **more harm than good** (Meier and Geis 2007). Among other things, these laws may (1) increase police and other official corruption, (2) lead consensual offenders to commit other types of crime that they would not commit if their behaviors were legal, (3) generate public disrespect for the law, (4) divert much time, money, and energy from fighting more serious crime to futile efforts to stop what so many people want to do, (5) prompt law enforcement agencies to engage in wiretapping and other possible violations of civil liberties, and (6) provide much of the revenue for organized crime, which is all too willing to supply the goods and services prohibited by consensual crime laws but remaining in demand by large segments of the population (see Chapter 13).

We now explore these issues further by looking more closely at the major consensual crimes, starting with drug use.

Illegal Drug Use

Illegal drug use and trafficking continue to be the most publicized consensual crimes in the United States. We hear from public officials and news media accounts of a drug crisis, and many statistics about the drug problem exist (http://www.whitehousedrugpolicy.gov/).

The federal, state, and local governments spend almost $49 billion yearly on law enforcement expenses related to illegal drugs (McVay 2010). Almost one-fifth of state prisoners say they committed their offense to get money for drugs, and one-third say they committed their offense while under the influence of drugs. Meanwhile, about two-thirds of adult arrestees test positive for an illegal drug. In many of our cities, drug dealers operate openly at street corners and drug gangs control entire neighborhoods.

Amid public concern over illegal drugs, it is easy to get caught up in a frenzy of mythology and misinformation and lose sight of carefully gathered, scientific evidence. Perhaps nowhere is this truer than for the drug problem. As Samuel Walker (2011:304) observes, "Public hysteria over drugs and drug-related crime inhibits sensible discussion of policy."

The federal and state governments spend about $49 billion annually on law enforcement expenses related to illegal drugs.

DRUG USE IN HISTORY

Drug use in contemporary life is hardly a new phenomenon. In fact, a society with little or no drug use is rare in human history. Primitive people during the Stone Age drank alcohol; South American Indians have chewed coca leaves containing cocaine since before the time of the Incas; people in ancient China, Greece, and India smoked marijuana; Mexican Indians have chewed hallucinogenic mushrooms since before the time of the Aztecs (Goode 2008).

Drug use was very common in the United States in the late nineteenth century (Musto 2002). Dozens of over-the-counter products containing opium and its derivatives (such as morphine) were used across the country by people with headaches, toothaches, menstrual cramps, sleeplessness, depression, and other problems. About 500,000 Americans, many of them middle-aged, middle-class women, were addicted to opium at the turn of the twentieth century. These addicts were not considered criminals because their drugs were legal and readily available. Instead, they were considered unfortunate individuals in need of help. Only slightly less popular was cocaine, which was used in many over-the-counter products and as an anesthetic for some surgeries. It was also a major ingredient in Coca-Cola, which was first marketed in 1894 and, not surprisingly, became very popular. Marijuana, another common drug, was used as a painkiller by people with menstrual cramps, migraine headaches, and other aches and pains.

CONTEMPORARY U.S. DRUG USE

Drug use is certainly common in the United States today. To illustrate this, let us first define a psychoactive drug as any substance that physiologically affects our behavior by changing our mood, emotion, perception, or other mental states. Defined this way, each of the following substances is a psychoactive drug or contains a drug: beer, wine, and other alcohol; Coca-Cola, Pepsi, and other colas; coffee and tea; chocolate; cigarettes and other tobacco products; cocaine and crack; heroin; No-Doz and other over-the-counter products that help us stay awake; Valium and other antianxiety drugs; and Prozac and other antidepressant drugs.

The United States is a nation of drug users, even if many of the drugs we use, such as nicotine in tobacco, are legal.

As this list makes clear, most of us use drugs at one time or another, and many of us use at least some of these drugs daily. Some drugs, such as caffeine (found, of course, in coffee, colas, chocolate, and many other products) are "good drugs": Their use is socially acceptable, celebrated in advertising, and very much a part of our culture. Alcohol, too, would fall into this category, despite recognition of its contribution to drunk driving, domestic violence, rape, and other crimes. Cigarettes (tobacco) were another "good drug" not too long ago and are still the subject of much advertising, but have become much less socially acceptable since the 1970s. Other drugs are "bad drugs": Their use is not only socially unacceptable but also illegal, and we view users of these drugs much more negatively than someone who drinks coffee or has a beer every day. Both good and bad drugs can cause physiological and/or psychological dependence, as anyone smoking a pack of cigarettes or drinking several cups of coffee daily can attest.

Prevalence of Legal Drug Use

It is no exaggeration to say that the United States is a nation of drug users, even if we disregard such common products as aspirin, Tylenol, and cold and allergy medications. A few figures help illustrate this point (Goode 2008; Johnston et al. 2008; U.S. Census Bureau 2010). Starting with legal drugs, more than 80 percent of Americans use coffee and other caffeine products regularly, with the average person consuming about 16 pounds of caffeine yearly from all sources. Physicians write about 250 million prescriptions annually for psychoactive drugs such as Valium. One-fifth of adults, or 45 million people, smoke cigarettes. Smokers include 20 percent of high school seniors and 18 percent of college students.

Turning to alcohol, two-thirds of adults drink alcohol occasionally or regularly. About one-third of students in grades 6 through 8 have drunk alcohol during the past year; this figure rises to about 70 percent for high school seniors. More than half of high school seniors have drunk alcohol, and more than one-third have engaged in binge drinking during the past month. More than three-fourths of college students have drunk alcohol during the past year; almost 70 percent have drunk alcohol during the past month; and 45 percent have been drunk during the past month.

Prevalence of Illegal Drug Use

We have just seen that legal drug use (including by minors) is commonplace. Illegal drug use is less common but far from rare: *About 47 percent of people 12 or older, or some 117 million individuals, have used an illegal drug at least once in their lifetime* (Substance Abuse and Mental Health Services Administration 2009). Americans spend more than $60 billion on these drugs annually (Office of National Drug Control Policy 2001). This amount includes $35 billion on cocaine and crack, $10 billion on heroin, and $10.5 billion on marijuana. The proportion of the U.S. population using selected illegal drugs in 2008 appears in Table 15.1, with the data taken from the annual National Survey on Drug Use and Health that is administered to people age 12 or older. To look at just a few numbers in

TABLE 15.1 ▸ Prevalence (percentage) of Illegal Drug Use, 2008 (National Survey on Drug Use and Health)

	AGE 12 AND OLDER			18–25		
	EVER USED	PAST YEAR	PAST MONTH	EVER[a] USED	PAST[a] YEAR	PAST MONTH
Any illicit drug	47	14	8	57	33	20
Marijuana	41	10	6	51	28	17
Psychotherapeutic	21	6	3	30	15	6
Cocaine or crack	15	2	1	15	6	2
Hallucinogens	14	2	<1	19	6	2
Heroin	2	<1	<1	1	<1	<1

Source: Substance Abuse and Mental Health Services Administration 2009.
[a]Data are for 2007.

the table, 41 percent of this population, or about 113 million people, have used marijuana, with 10 percent, or about 28 million people, using it in the last year. Fifteen percent of the population, or about 41 million people, have used cocaine, with 2 percent, or about 6 million people, using it in the last year. These figures represent a good deal of illegal drug use, but a more valid indicator of *serious* (i.e., current) drug use, as opposed to experimental or occasional use, involves people who used a drug in the past month. Only 8 percent of the population 12 or older had used an illicit drug in the past month, with marijuana the drug of choice. Past-month use is only 3 percent for psychotherapeutic drugs (painkillers, tranquilizers, etc.) and 1 percent or less for other illegal drugs.

Most of these percentages are higher for people 18 to 25 years old than for the general population of 12 and older, which obviously includes young teenagers and much older people who are unlikely to use illegal drugs. Yet even in this population, current illegal drug use other than marijuana is uncommon. In contrast, 61 percent of the 18-to-25 group drank alcohol in the past month, and 42 percent "used" tobacco. Alcohol and tobacco use is thus more common—and, statistically speaking, much more of a problem—than illegal drug use for this and the other age groups.

National self-report surveys of drug use exclude people whose illegal drug use may be especially high, such as the homeless, prisoners, and runaway teenagers.

A Drug Crisis?

Scholars dispute whether these data on illegal drug use show a nation in a drug crisis (Goode 2008). Stressing that illegal drug use other than marijuana is low, some say the data do *not* show a crisis, and they add that illegal drug use has declined since the early 1980s. In terms of sheer numbers, they say, if there is a nationwide drug crisis, it is a crisis of alcohol and tobacco, not of illegal drugs.

Other observers say that this portrait of low illegal drug use is misleading for two reasons (MacCoun and Martin 2009; Walker 2011). First, the low percentages for drugs other than marijuana still translate into millions of people. For example, the 1 percent of the 12 and older population using cocaine in the past month (Table 15.1) translates into about 2.7 million monthly users. Thus, although illegal drug use is low in percentage terms, it is high in absolute numbers. Whether you think illegal drug use is "low" or "high" thus depends on whether you think percentages or actual numbers are better measures of such use.

Second, the national self-report surveys that provide this portrait exclude people whose illegal drug use is especially high: youths in juvenile

detention centers, the homeless, runaway teenagers, and high school dropouts, all of whom are concentrated in our largest cities. The national surveys also obviously include many people living in smaller towns and rural areas, where illegal drug use is less common. For these reasons, the national portrait of low illegal drug use overlooks high use of cocaine/crack, heroin, and some other drugs in many poor, urban neighborhoods. Thus, although there might not be a drug crisis for the national population, there *is* one for "America's have-nots," as sociologist Elliott Currie (1994:3) called them. As Currie observed, "Serious drug abuse is not evenly distributed: it runs 'along the fault lines of our society.' It is concentrated among some groups and not others, and has been for at least half a century" (pp. 4–5).

Review and Discuss

It is often said that the United States has a "drug culture." What evidence does the text give that such a culture exists?

EXPLAINING ILLEGAL DRUG USE

Structural and social process factors help explain illegal drug use. As Currie's comment indicates, much of the illegal drug problem is an urban phenomenon reflecting the many urban problems that also prompt high rates of other crimes. Accordingly, scholars attribute today's urban drug use to economic decline in U.S. cities after World War II and especially during the 1970s and 1980s. Unemployment soared during these decades for urban youths, federal aid to the poor decreased, and poverty rates increased. Amid such growing economic despair, it is not surprising that drug abuse also worsened in inner cities during this period. As Currie (1994:123–124) observed, the "drug crisis of the 1980s flourished in the context of an unparalleled social and economic disaster that swept low-income communities in America in ways that virtually ensured that the drug problem would worsen." When crack was introduced during the mid-1980s, the most blighted urban neighborhoods saw the highest levels of crack sales and use. Amid the despair and frustration created by economic deprivation (see Chapter 7), illegal drug use induces psychoactive effects that provide temporary relief. Drug dealing is another response to this frustration because of the high income it promises.

Peers and families also matter for illegal drug use. Not surprisingly, many studies confirm peers' use of drugs as an important influence on one's own use, and also note the importance of inadequate parenting and other family problems (Crosnoe, Muller, and Frank 2004; Ford 2009). As Chapter 8 discussed, peer influences are greater in neighborhoods with chronic joblessness and poverty because families there are weaker. Delinquency and crime are higher in these neighborhoods, and so is illegal drug use.

It is also true that illegal drug use creates more illegal drug use in a vicious cycle: In poor, urban neighborhoods, drug use and drug trafficking make neighborhoods even more blighted, and this consequence in turn leads to more drug use (Currie 1994). In a related problem, addicted parents are especially unable to keep their own kids from using drugs. Because their families are likely to be poor and jobless, their children may well turn to drug dealing as a source of income. All these factors create a drug spiral from which there is little escape as long as economic deprivation continues.

If this sociological explanation makes sense, then it is shortsighted to view drug abuse by the urban poor mainly as an individual problem with biochemical and psychological roots. Such a view ignores the systematic social inequality lying at the heart of the problem. Urban drug abuse occurs, wrote Currie (1994:122), because it helps in many ways "to meet human needs that are systematically thwarted by the social and economic structures of the world the users live in." Urban drug abuse, then, is best regarded not as a decadent, aberrant act, but rather as "a predictable response to social conditions that destroy self-esteem, hope, solidarity, stability, and a sense of purpose" (Currie 1994:123).

Gender and Illegal Drug Use

Gender also helps explain illegal drug use. Increased scholarly attention to women's illegal drug use has provided a more complete picture of drug use than previously existed. What has the research found?

The best evidence is that women tend to use illegal drugs somewhat less than men do. According to the National Survey on Drug Use and Health, 41.8 percent of women have used an illegal drug sometime in their lives, compared to 50.6 percent of men. About 5.8 percent of women report illegal drug use in the past month, compared to 10.4 percent of men (Substance Abuse and Mental Health Services Administration 2009). Women's illegal drug use appears to arise from the same structural and social process factors underlying men's use, as female users resemble male users in their economic and family backgrounds (Fagan 1994; Inciardi, Lockwood, and Pottieger 1993).

However, certain gender differences also exist. Females are more likely than males to use illegal drugs to cope with depression and other psychological distress, often stemming from sexual abuse, whereas men are more likely to use illegal drugs for excitement (Chesney-Lind and Pasko 2004). One other gender difference in motivation for illegal drug use is financial. Because they have fewer job opportunities than men and more often have children to support, young women face economic crisis more often than young men do. In a study of female crack users in New York City, Lisa Maher and Richard Curtis (1995) argued that the 1980s' economic decay in U.S. cities affected women more than men and contributed especially heavily to their increased use of crack and other illegal drugs in that decade.

A final gender difference concerns the reaction to women who use illegal drugs during pregnancy. In the 1980s and early 1990s, the news media and public officials sounded an alarm about illegal drug use during pregnancy. Prosecutors charged dozens of drug-using pregnant women with child abuse or drug trafficking, and the term *crack babies* became a household word. In response, several scholars noted that (1) the much more common use of alcohol, tobacco, and even caffeine during pregnancy was at least as dangerous to the fetus as illegal drug use; (2) prosecuting pregnant women for using illegal drugs would discourage them from seeking prenatal medical care or drug treatment; and (3) prosecutions of "crack mothers" obscured the many other problems these women faced (Humphries et al. 1995).

THE DRUGS–CRIME CONNECTION

One question that comes up repeatedly is whether drugs cause crime. Although many people believe that drugs are a major cause of crime, we have seen in previous chapters that popular beliefs do not always square with scientific evidence. Keeping this in mind, what does the evidence say about the drugs–crime connection?

Before we can answer this question, we must first be clear on what we mean when we say that drugs "cause" crime (Zilney 2011). We could mean that drugs cause crime because of their physiological and psychological effects on drug users. Or, we could mean that people using illegal drugs commit other crimes, such as robbery, burglary, and prostitution, to get money to help pay for their drug habits. Or, finally, we could mean that drug traffickers go to war against each other to control "turf" for drug sales (Ousey and Lee 2007). One thing is clear: A very strong correlation exists between illegal drug use and other types of crime. People who regularly use illegal drugs tend to commit more crime than people using illegal drugs less often or not at all.

Does this mean that illegal drug use causes crime? Not necessarily. At least two reasons cast doubt on a simple drug–crime causal relationship. First, most illegal drug use is experimental or recreational, and very few of the millions of illegal drug users each year go on to commit other kinds of crime. Second, the drugs–crime correlation might mean that drug use leads to other crime, but it might also mean that committing other crime leads to drug use, say because you get involved with other offenders who already use drugs. The correlation may even be spurious: Perhaps the same factors, such as economic deprivation and inadequate parenting, lead to both drug use and other criminality.

Scholars have examined these possibilities with juvenile offenders and young adults. Although the evidence is complex, a rough consensus is that much of the illegal drugs–crime connection is indeed spurious, with both kinds of illegal behavior the result of the various structural and social process factors examined in this and previous chapters (Faupel, Horowitz, and Weaver. 2010). It also seems that delinquency more often precedes drug use rather than the reverse: Adolescents begin to commit delinquent acts and then start using drugs, perhaps because of the influence of delinquent friends or because their delinquency worsens their relationship with their parents (Menard, Mihalic, and Huizinga 2001). Once that process has started, illegal drug use does seem to increase the likelihood of future offending. The drugs–crime connection is thus best explained partly as a spurious correlation and partly as one indicating that crime causes drug use. The "illegal drug use causes crime" belief thus turns out to be largely, if not totally, a myth (Kappeler and Potter 2005).

What about drugs leading to crime because of their physiological and psychological effects? Although anecdotal evidence suggests that people using certain illegal drugs can become violent, there does not appear to be a systematic, cause-and-effect relationship (Roth 1994). Any such violence tends to occur only rarely and is committed primarily by individuals with histories of emotional problems or antisocial behavior. Some drugs, notably marijuana and opiates, reduce violent behavior. Ironically, the one psychoactive drug consistently linked to interpersonal violence is a legal drug, alcohol: "Alcohol is the only psychoactive drug that in many individuals tends to increase aggressive behavior temporarily while it is taking effect" (Felson, Teasdale, and Burchfield 2008; Roth 1994:4).

Illegal drug users do commit crimes to get money to pay for their drug habit. Yet here the drug–crime connection is not due to the illegal drug use itself, but rather to the fact that the drugs being used are illegal. When drugs are illegal, simple supply-and-demand economics dictates that their prices will be higher than if they were legal. Their users, most of them very poor, cannot afford to pay for them unless they steal the necessary funds. Such theft thus results from the laws against the drugs, not from the drugs themselves (MacCoun and Martin 2009).

This logic also applies to drug users who commit crime because they start associating with other drug users and, in general, become more involved in the criminal community. Although this might sound a bit simplistic, if the drugs they were using were not illegal, they would not start associating with other criminals. To the extent that they then would not become involved in the criminal community, they would not commit other crimes. Even here, then, the drugs–crime connection is the result of the laws against drugs, rather than the drugs themselves.

When people talk about drugs causing crime, they often mean the violence between drug gangs that can harm innocent bystanders (Bellair and McNulty 2009). Once again, such violence, as horrible as it is, results from the fact that the drugs the gangs are selling are illegal, not from the drugs themselves. We do not see such violence from the "traffickers" of legal drug products such as coffee and cigarettes (large supermarkets, convenience stores, etc.), who, because their products are legal, can instead rely on advertising and friendly service.

To summarize, the answer to the question of whether drugs cause crime is yes, if we are talking about alcohol, and generally no, if we are talking about illegal drugs. To the extent that illegal drugs are connected to crime, the connection results primarily from laws against these drugs, rather than from their physiological or social effects. Ironically, the war against drugs aggravates one of the very problems it is intended to stop (Faupel, Horowitz, and Weaver 2010).

Review and Discuss

What is the evidence for and against the argument that drugs cause crime?

THE LEGALIZATION DEBATE

Earlier we outlined the debate over laws against consensual crimes. One dimension of the debate is *philosophical:* In a democratic society people should be free to engage in self-destructive behavior, and it is arbitrary and even hypocritical for a society to decide which such behaviors it will allow and prohibit. A second dimension is more *social-scientific:* Consensual crime laws do more harm than good, or so some scholars think. Perhaps nowhere is the debate over consensual crime laws more important—and also more controversial—than on the issue of illegal drugs.

The Philosophical Argument

We first explore the philosophical argument against drug laws, which is a libertarian position: In a free society, people should be allowed to engage in risky behavior, including drug use. For example, eating the all-too-typical U.S. diet of red meat, butter, ice cream, and other fat-laden food causes far more death and illness—with incalculable social harm from increased health care costs, lost economic productivity, and the tears of bereaved spouses and children—than does drug use. If our society allows such a diet, why should it not allow drug use?

Like most nations, the United States has obviously not adopted this position. Instead, it has decided to permit the use of many drugs and ban the use of many other drugs. For practical purposes, then, the philosophical question becomes: Which drugs should the state prohibit, and which drugs should the state allow?

Any answer to this question has to be arbitrary, because any drug is potentially harmful if taken in large enough doses. Someone downing a bottle of aspirin causes more personal, familial, and social harm (medical costs, lost economic productivity, etc.) than someone smoking a marijuana joint or even snorting a typical amount of cocaine, but the state is not about to prohibit aspirin use. Moreover, sometimes the harm a drug causes has little to do with whether it is permitted or prohibited. Surely, however, we can distinguish more harmful drugs from less harmful drugs and prohibit the former while allowing, however grudgingly, the latter. Yet even here our decisions have less to do with the harm of the drugs than with various political and social factors, including how many people use the drug, the extent to which it is ingrained in our culture, and the influence of the organizations manufacturing and selling the drug.

To explore this issue further, let us consider two groups of drugs. Our first group consists of alcohol and tobacco (nicotine), both legal drugs when used by those beyond a certain age. Our second group consists of cocaine, heroin, marijuana, and all other illegal drugs. How many people die in the United States each year from taking these two groups of drugs? Death is not the only harm drugs cause, of course, but it is their ultimate harm and can be counted by federal agencies (Mokdad et al. 2004). The deadliest drug of all is tobacco, which kills about 435,000 people each year from lung cancer, emphysema, heart disease, and other

Marijuana smoking, which has killed few, if any, people, causes less death and illness than the typical U.S. high-fat diet of red meat, ice cream, and other such foods.

illnesses. Next on the list is alcohol, with almost 102,000 people dying each year from alcohol-induced liver disease and other illness, alcohol-related motor vehicle accidents, and homicides committed under the influence of alcohol. Tobacco and alcohol together thus kill approximately 537,000 people every year.

In contrast, the physiological effects of all illegal drugs kill about 17,000 people annually (Mokdad et al. 2004). Many of these deaths occur not from the physiological effect of the drug itself, but from the fact that it has been laced with other toxic substances or from the fact that the user overdoses because the drug's potency is greater than expected. No deaths occur from marijuana use. Although constant use of high doses of marijuana might in the long run have health effects similar to those of tobacco, very few people use this much marijuana for that long. This does not mean that marijuana is a safe drug, only that it is not a lethal one (Goode 2008). Figure 15.1 depicts the disparity in the deaths caused by legal and illegal drugs, respectively.

It might be argued that illegal drugs would kill more people if they were legal because more people would then use them (Goode 2008). If so, the disparity in Figure 15.1 might indicate the success of the laws prohibiting illegal drugs. We discuss this argument later, but for now simply ask, If the legal drugs kill far more than the illegal ones, then where is the logic behind our drug laws? The answer is that there is little logic here. Tobacco is legal not because it is safe—far from it—but because so many people for so long have smoked cigarettes and because tobacco companies provide thousands of jobs to people in the South and millions of dollars in campaign contributions to members of Congress. Although tobacco does not distort perception and motor skills as many other psychoactive drugs do, it is nonetheless a slow, deadly poison. If it were just invented by a small, entrepreneurial company, the Food and Drug Administration would never approve its

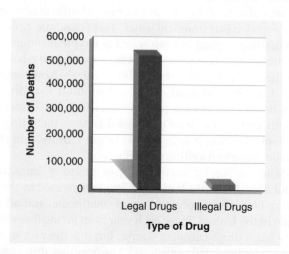

FIGURE 15.1 ▶ Estimated Annual U.S. Deaths from Legal and Illegal Drugs, 2000 Source: Mokdad et al. 2004.

sale and use. Alcohol is legal not because it is safe—again, far from it—but because so many people for so long have drunk alcohol that it is an integral part of our culture, and because the alcohol industry spends millions of dollars each year advertising its drug's supposed ability to help people be popular and to have a good time.

Review and Discuss

Summarize the philosophical debate regarding laws against consensual behaviors.

The Social Science Argument

The social science dimension of the drug law debate considers the very important question of whether drug laws do more harm than good. When then-U.S. Surgeon General Jocelyn Elders in December 1993 proposed considering drug **legalization,** a firestorm greeted her remarks (Labaton 1993). Yet several prominent people, including noted conservatives William F. Buckley, Milton Friedman, and George Schultz, as well as the then-mayors of Baltimore and San Francisco and the former police chiefs of Minneapolis, Minnesota, New York City, and San Jose, California, had already made the same proposal or have made it since (Kappeler and Potter 2005). In October 1999, the governor of New Mexico, Gary Johnson, also endorsed legalization:

> I hate to say it, but the majority of people who use drugs use them responsibly. They choose when to do it. They do them at home. It's not a financial burden. For the amount of money we're putting into the war on drugs, I suggest it's an absolute failure. Make drugs a controlled substance like alcohol. Legalize it, control it, regulate it, tax it. If you legalize it, we might actually have a healthier society (Jackson 1999:A19).

ARGUMENT FOR LEGALIZATION

Several drug scholars and drug reform advocates also advocate some form of legalization or at least harm reduction (discussed later). Their belief rests on the harms they now see in drug laws and the benefits they say would result if the laws were abolished or extensively modified (Nadelmann 2008; Zilney 2011). In making their case, legalization proponents often cite Prohibition. In 1920, a constitutional amendment banned alcohol manufacture and sale and began the Prohibition era. Although alcohol use probably declined during Prohibition (Jensen 2000), bootlegging was still widespread, with many otherwise law-abiding people obtaining alcohol in speakeasies and elsewhere. When Prohibition began, there were 15,000 saloons in New York City; this number more than doubled to 32,000 within a few years (Lerner 2007).

Worse yet, Prohibition had many unintended negative effects (Okrent 2010). The potential illegal profits from bootlegging were so enormous that organized crime decided to provide this service and in a few short years became much wealthier and more powerful, with Al Capone, the famous organized crime leader, making $200 million a year (equivalent to $2 billion in today's dollars) (Rorabaugh 1995). In attempts to control bootlegging turf, organized crime groups fought each other with machine guns and engaged in drive-by shootings. Police and other parts of the criminal justice system devoted much time, energy, and money to stopping the bootlegging. Many police were wounded or killed by organized crime members. Thus, even though Prohibition probably decreased alcohol use and some of the deaths associated with drinking, it caused even more deaths—of organized crime figures, innocent bystanders, and police—and made the nation more murderous overall. As sociologist Gary F. Jensen (2000:31) concluded, "Despite the fact that alcohol consumption is a positive correlate of homicide . . . . Prohibition and its enforcement increased the homicide rate." Prohibition also increased official corruption, as police, politicians, and other public servants took bribes to look the other way (Rorabaugh 1995). Finally, several thousand Americans reportedly died from drinking "bad liquor" during Prohibition, as they could never know exactly what was in their beverage (Lerner 2007). Prohibition, in short, was a disaster, and the nation repealed the Prohibition amendment in 1933.

In recalling Prohibition, legalization proponents make the following points. First, drug laws, as we have already seen, create the very crime and other problems they are intended to stop. Addicts commit robberies and other crimes to obtain money to support their habit, drug gangs terrorize neighborhoods with deadly violence to control turf, and people taking illegal drugs become involved in the criminal community and then commit other crimes themselves. Drawing on his study of Prohibition, Jensen (2000) thinks legalization would reduce all this violence. Drug laws are also responsible for most of the 17,000 annual deaths from using illegal drugs. Most of these deaths result from the adulteration of the drugs with various toxic substances and from their users' willingness to take the drugs in an unsafe manner (for example, smoking crack instead of snorting cocaine) to get the most intense "high" because of the drugs' expense. If the drugs were legalized with some government regulation, many of these deaths would be prevented. The drugs would not be adulterated, and their lower expense would allow users to take them in a safer manner.

Second, drug laws cost almost $49 billion annually to enforce even though millions of people still use illegal drugs (McVay 2010). This money could be better spent on prevention and treatment programs that ultimately would be more effective in lowering drug abuse. Third, in a related point, the drug war fills our prisons and jails with hundreds of thousands of people who would otherwise not be there. In 2009, for example, almost 1.7 million arrests occurred for drug abuse (including some 750,000 for marijuana possession) in the United States, a figure almost three times greater than the number of arrests for violent crime (homicide, rape, robbery, aggravated assault) (Federal Bureau of Investigation 2010). The large number of drug arrests has flooded the nation's prisons over the last two decades (see Figure 15.2) and forced the criminal justice system to release violent criminals who pose much more of a threat to society.

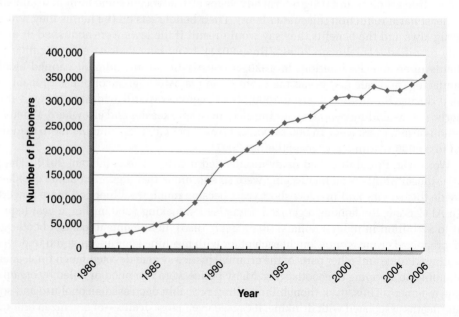

FIGURE 15.2 ▸ **State and Federal Prisoners Sentenced for Drug Offenses, 1980–2006** Sources: Maguire and Pastore 2007; www.ojp.usdoj.gov/bjs/dcf/correct.htm#state.

Fourth, drug laws are good for organized crime. As happened during Prohibition, drugs are a major source of organized crime's money and influence (see Chapter 13). Fifth, drug laws create opportunities for official corruption throughout the criminal justice system. **Bribery** of police and thefts by police of confiscated drugs are common. Over the years, police forces in major cities have been plagued with many scandals involving officers taking bribes from drug dealers, robbing dealers, or selling confiscated drugs themselves. Most of this corruption would disappear if drugs were legalized.

Sixth, if illegal drugs were legalized and sold like any other product, they could be taxed like any other product. The taxes on the drugs would add an estimated $34 billion annually to federal and state revenues (McVay 2010). Much or all of this money could, if we wished, be used for drug treatment and prevention programs.

Seventh and last, enforcement of drug laws often involves the use of informants, wiretapping, and other legally distasteful procedures. Drug testing in the workplace and in the schools has become commonplace. Like many other consensual crime laws, drug laws, say their critics, thus threaten the nation's civil liberties by turning us all into "a society of suspects" (Wisotsky 1995).

ARGUMENT AGAINST LEGALIZATION

Opponents of legalization concede some of these points but argue that drug laws have indeed reduced the use of illegal drugs, even if many people still use them. They predict that many more people would use illegal drugs if they were made legal, leading to more drug addicts and much more of the death and disease that we now see with tobacco and alcohol. Although they concede that these two drugs would be illegal in an ideal world, they say we should not compound the problem by legalizing other drugs. The increase in drug abuse after legalization would be especially great in the nation's inner cities. As Currie (1994:188) observed, "If consumption increased, it would almost certainly increase most among the strata already most vulnerable to hard-drug use—thus exacerbating the social stratification of the drug crisis."

REBUTTAL BY LEGALIZATION PROPONENTS

Legalization proponents counter that it is by no means certain that more people would use illegal drugs if they were made legal. Illegal drugs are so easy to get now that anyone who wants to use them already does. If people are not using them now, it is because they dislike drugs or fear their effects, not because the drugs are illegal.

Support for this argument comes from a federally funded national survey of high school seniors (Bachman, Johnston, and O'Malley 2009). The proportion of seniors using illegal drugs is far smaller than the proportion feeling they could obtain the drugs "fairly easily" or "easily." For example, although 87 percent of seniors in 2008 reported they could easily obtain marijuana, only 32 percent reported using it in the past year. Similarly, although 39 percent of the seniors said they could easily obtain cocaine, only 4 percent had used it in the past year (Bachman, Johnston, and O'Malley 2009). These data suggest to legalization proponents that people, including the urban poor, who do not use illegal drugs now also would not use them if they were legalized.

To support their views, legalization proponents point to marijuana use. When marijuana was decriminalized in many states in the 1970s, marijuana use did not go up in these states as compared to other states that did not decriminalize it; in fact, marijuana use declined nationally. Marijuana use in the Netherlands also declined after it was decriminalized there in the 1970s (Nadelmann 1992). A recent study that compared marijuana use in Amsterdam, the largest city in the Netherlands, and San Francisco, where marijuana use is subject to arrest and prosecution despite that city's reputation, concluded, "Our findings do not support claims that criminalization reduces cannabis use and that decriminalization increases cannabis use" (Reinarman, Cohen, and Hendrien 2004:841). Legalization opponents counter that what might be true for marijuana might not hold true for other illegal drugs, which are much more enticing and addictive (Currie 1994).

A Final Word

Both sides to the legalization debate make valid points. Unfortunately, we cannot test their views unless we first legalize drugs, which is not about to happen soon. Thus, as Walker (2011:330) noted, "The impact of legalizing drugs on serious crime is not known at this time." The key questions are whether more people would use illegal drugs if they were made legal, and, if so, how many and at what social cost. Assuming for the sake of argument that there would be some increased use, the question then becomes whether this risk is worth taking to obtain the benefits of legalization. New Mexico's governor Gary Johnson thought the risk was worth it: "There are going to be new problems under legalization. But I submit to you they are going to be about half of what they are today under the prohibition model" (Kelley 1999:A7). Because the war on drugs has been so ineffective and has cost billions of dollars and led to other problems, alternatives like legalization deserve the careful consideration for which the Surgeon General called two decades ago.

Before we leave the legalization debate, it is important to note one specific dimension of the controversy surrounding it, the issue of medical marijuana. The Crime and Controversy box examines this issue further.

Review and Discuss

What are the arguments for and against legalizing some of the drugs that are now illegal? Do you think any illegal drugs should be made legal? Why or why not?

HARM REDUCTION AND DRUG COURTS

Many drug experts who think legalization goes too far, and even those who favor some form of it, think our nation should adopt a **harm reduction** policy regarding illegal drug use and drug offenders (Stimson and O'Hare 2010). Under this policy, drug use is treated as a public health problem and not as a crime problem. Drug users would be treated not as criminals but as persons in need of medical, psychological, and other help, and much more money would be spent on drug prevention and treatment programs and much less on criminal justice approaches. Sterile needles would be made available to known drug users to reduce the spread of AIDS and other diseases. Several European nations have adopted harm reduction policies along these lines (see the International Focus box).

In the United States, harm reduction has been much slower to develop, but there are signs of some change. In the late 1990s, for example, Baltimore adopted some harm reduction measures in what was called "an unusual social experiment" (Gammage 1997:A1). One-ninth of Baltimore's adult population was addicted to heroin or other illegal drugs. Aided by a $25 million contribution from a philanthropist, Baltimore funded drug treatment and other efforts, including needle exchange, to deal with its drug problem. The city estimated that every nonviolent drug offender who was imprisoned was costing taxpayers about $20,000 a year, but would cost only about $3,000 to $4,000 in a treatment program. In early 2004, Baltimore's approach became state policy in Maryland after the passage of a bill that authorized the diversion of nonviolent drug offenders into

Crime and Controversy

Pot Shops and the Medical Marijuana Debate

As the text notes, 41 percent of Americans age 12 or older, equivalent to 113 million people, say they have used marijuana, and about 750,000 arrests for marijuana possession occurred in 2008. Although marijuana penalties are much less severe now than they were a generation ago, marijuana is obviously still an illegal drug no matter how many tens of millions of people have used it. One important dimension of the controversy over the legal war against drugs involves the issue of marijuana used for medical purposes, especially for the following illnesses or conditions: AIDS, cancer pain, the severe nausea resulting from chemotherapy, epilepsy, glaucoma, and multiple sclerosis.

Two key questions, of course, are whether marijuana is an effective drug for any or all of these medical problems and, if so, whether it is more effective than legal medications. Many medical experts say yes to both questions, but other experts say no. A few years ago the Institute of Medicine, one of the four National Academies that provide independent advice to the federal government on scientific and medical issues, issued a report that assessed the health benefits of marijuana. The report found that marijuana can indeed relieve the symptoms of several illnesses and diseases, but it also found that existing prescription medicines are generally more effective in providing relief. For patients who have AIDS or who suffer from chemotherapy-induced nausea and whose symptoms are unrelieved by existing medicines, the report said that marijuana would be a suitable treatment. It found that marijuana could be useful to reduce some of the eye pressure caused by glaucoma, but it also concluded that the health risks of long-term marijuana use outweighed this particular benefit.

The report found that smoking marijuana may pose a threat of lung cancer, and it cautioned that marijuana should be smoked only by patients who are terminally ill or who suffer debilitating symptoms unrelieved by existing medicines. For other patients, the report recommended that cannabinoids, the chemical components of marijuana, could be usefully combined with existing medicines to provide additional benefits beyond those achieved by these medicines alone. The report recommended rigorous assessment of the potential health benefits of cannabinoids through clinical trials that would involve the delivery of these components through means other than smoking. In one other finding, the report concluded that there is no evidence that the medical use of marijuana would increase its use by the general population.

The debate over medical marijuana has gone beyond the scientific domain and into the public arena. Since 1996, 14 states and the District of Columbia have passed legislation that permits the possession of medical marijuana under certain circumstances. In California and some locations, "pot shops" have emerged to sell marijuana to people who need it for medical reasons. Critics say the shops often sell marijuana to people without a medical need for it. A recent news article said that California "allowed the pot industry to grow so out of control that at one point Los Angeles had more medical marijuana shops than Starbucks." Some people were so angered by the pot shops that they committed vandalism against them, including one episode in Montana that involved Molotov cocktails thrown through two shops' windows.

Sources: Mack and Joy 2000; Volz 2010.

drug treatment programs instead of prison, at a savings of millions of dollars annually. Several other states, including Arizona, California, and Texas, adopted similar programs (Wagner 2004). Harm reduction efforts are no panacea for drug use, but they do seem to help reduce drug use while costing much less than arrest and incarceration (Ritter and Cameron 2006).

International Focus

Harm Reduction in the Netherlands

In beginning, however slowly, to apply a harm reduction approach to the drug problem involving drug courts and treatment programs, the United States is following in the footsteps of some other nations, most notably the Netherlands, an urban nation of 15.5 million people in western Europe. Although the experience of other nations is not always transferable to the United States, given all the differences among the nations of the world, the history of the Netherlands' drug policy does suggest that a harm reduction approach may work.

The Netherlands' current drug policy has its roots in the 1970s, when a serious heroin problem there led to the establishment of the Baan Commission to develop recommendations for a new approach to illegal drugs. The commission's recommendations were a precursor to today's harm reduction strategy. It recognized that drug use is a problem that will not go away, and it recommended that drug users be treated as people in need of help, not as criminals. The aim of national policy, it said, should be to try to reduce the use of drugs through means other than law enforcement and to help people with drug problems by providing them with suitable treatment.

Adopting the commission's recommendations in 1976, the Netherlands established an important distinction between drug traffickers and drug users. The former are subject to arrest and prosecution if they possess or are selling large amounts of hard drugs, but are not normally arrested for small amounts of hard drugs. Meanwhile, drug users are also not normally subject to arrest merely for possessing and using drugs. If drug users are arrested for some other reason, they are required to undergo drug treatment. The Netherlands also established an important distinction between hard and soft drugs. Cannabis (marijuana) is the primary soft drug, and possession of small amounts of marijuana for one's own use is legal. Moreover, coffee shops are permitted to sell quantities of cannabis products up to 5 grams to persons 18 or older. They are not permitted to advertise cannabis, and they are not allowed to sell hard drugs. The Dutch believe that this method of making marijuana available helps to isolate marijuana users from traffickers and users of hard drugs.

What consequences has the Netherlands' drug policy had for drug use there? As the text notes, marijuana use in the Netherlands decreased after it was decriminalized during the 1970s. The prevalence of marijuana use in the Netherlands does not appear to be higher than that in other western European nations, and the use of hard drugs appears to be lower than in these other nations. Moreover, the use of marijuana and hard drugs also appears to be lower in the Netherlands than in the United States. Survey data from 2001 show that the proportion of the Dutch (17 percent) who have ever used marijuana is less than half that of the United States (37 percent), and the proportion (4 percent) who have ever used cocaine is only one-third that of the United States (12 percent). Similarly, the proportion of the Dutch (0.4 percent) who have ever used heroin is less than one-third that of the United States (1.4 percent). The Dutch are also slightly less likely to have ever used ecstasy. Although obvious differences exist between the two nations, the Dutch experience does suggest that it is possible to decriminalize marijuana and avoid an all-encompassing law enforcement approach without significantly raising drug use. Other nations in western Europe, including Belgium, Germany, Spain, and Switzerland, have also decriminalized marijuana and undertaken other harm reduction strategies without apparent adverse consequences.

Sources: Drug Policy Alliance 2010; Netherlands Ministry of Foreign Affairs 2008; Reinarman, Cohen, and Hendrien 2004.

A complementary harm reduction approach involves the use of drug courts, which typically sentence drug users to drug treatment and counseling rather than to jail. This approach again saves money and is thought to hold much more potential for weaning users from drugs. Drug courts have become more popular in recent years. In the mid-1990s there were only twelve in the nation, but now they operate in virtually every state and number in the hundreds. Research evidence indicates that they provide a promising, cost-effective alternative to prison for helping nonviolent drug offenders (Stinchcomb 2010; Walker 2011). Critics feel they still treat drug users as criminals and rob offenders of their rights to due process and privacy because they often require a defendant to plead guilty to be allowed to enter a drug treatment,s program (Cole 1999). They also say that not everyone who uses drugs needs treatment, because the use of marijuana and other drugs ordinarily does not cause serious problems. In a final criticism, critics fear that drug courts may, because of their lower expense, ironically lead to more arrests for drug use, increasing the harm caused by the war against drugs.

Sexual Offenses: Prostitution and Pornography

PROSTITUTION

Prostitution is often called the world's oldest profession, and it might well be. It existed in ancient Mesopotamia, where priests had sex with women whose religious duty was to help procreate the species. In ancient Greece, legal **brothels** (houses of prostitution) were common. One class of prostitutes served the needs of Greek political officials, and another class served the common citizenry. Prostitution also flourished in ancient Rome. In the Old Testament, prostitution "was accepted as a more or less necessary fact of life and it was more or less expected that many men would turn to prostitutes" (Bullough and Bullough 1977:137–138). Licensed brothels providing much tax revenue were found throughout Europe during the Middle Ages. The church disapproved but still tolerated the practice as one that prevented more wanton lust. In the 1500s, however, brothels were shut down across Europe when the church and political officials became alarmed by the possibility that prostitutes were spreading syphilis. Brothels and certainly prostitution did not disappear, and in the 1700s and 1800s many European cities permitted licensed brothels and required regular medical exams of their employees (Bullough and Bullough 1987).

Prostitution was also common in the United States in the 1800s, as poor young women chose it as one of the few jobs available to them (Bullough and Bullough 1987). Individual prostitutes solicited business at street corners and respectable hotels and businesses throughout many cities, and camps of prostitutes would travel to railroad construction sites and other locations where men lacking wives or other female partners would be found. Railroad workers visiting prostitutes would hang their red signal lamps outside the women's tents so that they could be found in case they were needed suddenly for railroad work. The term *red-light district* comes from the red glow illuminating the prostitutes' encampments on busy nights. Earlier, during the Civil War, men in either side's army were potential customers for prostitutes. The modern term *hooker* comes from the prostitutes who had sex with soldiers under the command of Union General Joseph Hooker.

Through the early 1900s many U.S. cities had legal brothels, which were often segregated in certain parts of the cities. A **moral crusade** against brothels, carried out by the same white, middle-class Protestants behind the temperance movement, began in the United States about 1910 and sounded the alarm about prostitution's influence on middle-class girls lured into sexual depravation by the promise of lots of money for little time and effort. The crusade was especially strong in Chicago, and its brothels ceased

Prostitution is often called the world's oldest profession; it was legal in brothels in many U.S. cities through the early 1900s. Today it is legal only in certain parts of Nevada.

business by late 1912. Dozens of other cities shut down their brothels during the next six years (Hobson 1987).

Despite the bans on brothels, some have continued their business over the years. In Nevada, of course, brothels are legal outside the counties containing Las Vegas and Reno, and these *ranches,* as they are called, are a favorite tourist attraction for men. Some illegal brothels in other states have also received their share of publicity. During World War II, Sally Stanford ran a fancy brothel in San Francisco, where the customers included many of the city's leading politicians, law enforcement officers, and businessmen. Stanford required regular health exams of her employees to guard against venereal disease, and her rather luxurious enterprise ensured that the employees would not suffer the various problems that streetwalkers often experience. Stanford later became mayor of a town across the bay from San Francisco and published her autobiography with a major publishing house (Stanford 1966). Another elegant brothel was run in the 1980s by Sydney Biddle Barrows in a posh New York City neighborhood. Barrows, a descendant of the *Mayflower* settlers, quickly became known as the Mayflower Madam after her brothel was uncovered. She eventually also published her autobiography (Barrows and Novak 1986).

Explaining Prostitution

Most prostitutes are women, and the majority of the 71,000 arrests in 2009 for prostitution and commercialized vice were of women (Federal Bureau of Investigation 2010). The men arrested are usually male prostitutes serving a male clientele. Pimps are only occasionally arrested, and male customers of female prostitutes hardly at all, notwithstanding the widely publicized 1995 arrest of British actor Hugh Grant for "lewd conduct" in a car with a California prostitute. Although the exact number is difficult to determine, the United States has an estimated 70,000 full-time female prostitutes; they each have an average of 700 male sex partners annually, for a yearly total of about 50 million acts of prostitution (Brewer et al. 2000). A national survey on sexual attitudes and behavior estimated that 5 million U.S. women had engaged in acts fitting the definition of prostitution (Janus and Janus 1993); the survey also estimated that 20 percent of U.S. adult males had had sex with a prostitute.

Prostitution is widely disliked because it involves sex in exchange for money or other economic gain. Not surprisingly, our negative attitudes toward prostitution apply much more to (female) prostitutes than to their (male) customers, many of whom are middle-class businessmen and other so-called respectable individuals. Over the years, critics have condemned prostitutes as immoral women with uncontrolled sexual desire, but they have said little about their customers. Scholars have studied why women become prostitutes, yet few, if any, studies exist of why men become their customers. The message is that it is normal for men, often in a sort of rite of passage, to have sex with a prostitute, but abnormal for women to take money for sex with these men.

Many scholars say that prostitution symbolizes the many ways society victimizes women (Miller 2009). It is no accident, they say, that most prostitutes are poor. Poor women turn to prostitution because they lack the income alternatives available to men, even poor men. Also, prostitution is a particularly tempting option if money is needed to support an illegal drug habit. Women also commit prostitution because, in a society that continues to regard women as "sex objects" that exist for the pleasure of men, female prostitution is inevitable and perhaps even a logical extension of "normal" female–male relationships in which men continue to be dominant. Further, many young women turn to prostitution as a tragic, complex psychological response to long histories of incest and other childhood and adolescent sexual abuse and family disorder (Chesney-Lind and Pasko 2004). In prostitution, then, we see a striking manifestation of the many ways women suffer in a sexist society.

Some scholars also note that prostitution, however disagreeable to many people, still provides several important functions for prostitutes and their customers (McCaghy et al. 2008). For prostitutes, their behavior is a source of income. For their customers, prostitution is a sexual outlet for those who have no other sexual alternatives. Some of these are men who lack female partners because they are at locations, such as military bases, where few women live; others lack partners because of a physical disability or other problem; still others lack partners because they have unusual sexual desires. In 1937, sociologist Kingsley Davis (1937) proposed that prostitution even lowers the divorce rate by providing married men unhappy with their marital sex with a love-free sexual outlet. Otherwise, a married man might have to have an affair and could more easily fall in love with another woman.

The Legalization Debate

As with drugs, various observers debate whether prostitution should be legalized, with their arguments echoing some of those at the center of the drug debate. Proponents say that legalizing prostitution would reduce some of the problems now associated with it, whereas opponents fear that legalization would increase prostitution and victimize women even further (Meier and Geis 2007; Miller 2009).

Proponents offer both philosophical and social-scientific arguments. Philosophically, prostitution is an act involving two individuals consenting to the behavior. Although many people do not like the idea of exchanging sex for money, this is ultimately a moral view on which the state should not legislate. Other people, including athletes and models, "sell their bodies." Some women and men go out on dates in which, even today, the man still expects sex in return for showing the woman a good time and spending lavishly on their evening together. Any sex that then occurs is thus not too different from what the law bans.

Perhaps more important, say legalization proponents, the problems associated with prostitution stem from the laws against it and would be reduced greatly, and perhaps eliminated, if it were decriminalized. Sometimes prostitutes are beaten and robbed by their customers, and sometimes customers are robbed by prostitutes or their pimps. Prostitution also is a source of money for organized crime and helps spread AIDS and other venereal disease. All these problems would be reduced if prostitution were legalized and regulated like any other business. In short, we should adopt and improve on the licensed brothel model common in the United States for much of its history and now common in many parts of Nevada and in several western European nations. Under this model, regular health exams could be required to check for venereal disease, and the use of condoms could be required to reduce the spread of venereal disease. In addition, hundreds of millions of dollars of tax money would be added to federal, state, and local government revenues. Moreover, the time, energy, and money the criminal justice system now spends on the 70,000 to 80,000 prostitute arrests each year would be more wisely used against the truly violent criminals who are real threats to public safety.

Opponents of legalization take issue with many of these arguments. Some say prostitution is so immoral that society should not implicitly condone it by making it legal. Other opponents with a more feminist orientation say that, because prostitution inherently victimizes the women who engage in it, any effort to legalize it and thus possibly expand the number of prostitutes would only victimize more women (Hughes 1999). The brothel model might work to some degree, they add, but the problems associated with prostitution would still continue.

PORNOGRAPHY

Like prostitution, pornography has been around since ancient times. The term comes from the Greek word *pornographos* and literally means "writings about prostitutes." As the history of the term suggests, pornography, which for now is defined as sexually explicit materials, was common in ancient Greece and Rome and especially popular in ancient India and Japan. It persisted through the Middle Ages, but lost popularity in the West because of rigid Judeo-Christian views on sexuality. Like prostitution, the church tolerated pornography but did not approve it. Pornography remained uncommon in the United States until the late 1800s, when it became more popular amid the great social and economic upheaval after the Civil War (Kendrick 1987; Richlin 1992).

The years since have seen various federal, state, and local efforts to ban or control the distribution of pornography. These efforts were filled with controversy over the definition of pornography and over questions of censorship in a democratic society. Finally, in 1973 the U.S. Supreme Court said that pornography could be considered obscene and therefore banned (1) if an average person applying current community views would conclude that the work appealed to the "prurient" interest, (2) if the work depicts sexual conduct in a "patently offensive way," and (3) if the work taken as a whole lacks "serious literary, artistic, political, or scientific value" (*Miller v. California,* 413 U.S. 15). As critics pointed out, even this definition raised more questions than it answered. For example, who is an "average person"? Who should decide whether the way a work depicts sexual conduct is "patently offensive" or, alternatively, just unpleasant or even appealing? Who should decide whether a work lacks serious literary or other value? What if a few people think it has such value and most do not? How much value constitutes *serious* value?

In 1987 the Court modified its 1973 ruling when it noted that a work could be judged obscene and thus banned if a "reasonable person," applying a national standard, would conclude that the work lacked any social value (*Pope v. Illinois,* 107 S. Ct. 1918). This ruling still left unanswered several questions, including who is a "reasonable person" and how we know what the national standard would be (Albanese 1996).

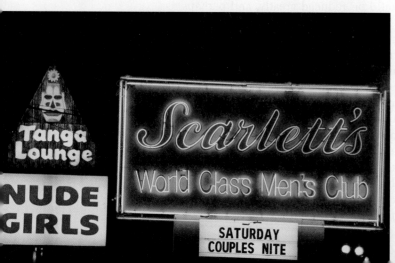

The popularity of pornography reflects a more general widespread interest among many Americans in nudity and sexual encounters.

Defining and Debating Pornography

As the questions about the Supreme Court rulings suggest, one of the most important issues regarding pornography is how to define it. Related to this issue is the question of censorship. Just as beauty is in the eye of the beholder, so may be pornography. Some of the greatest works in art history depict nudes in paintings or sculpture. Many of these were considered pornographic by various secular or religious authorities at the time of their creation. Some books now hailed as literary masterpieces, such as James Joyce's *Ulysses,* were considered obscene and even banned when they were first published. If pornography is defined as sexually explicit or sexually arousing material, then even the most benign works have the potential to be considered pornographic. In the 1950s, for example, adolescent boys would look at pictures of seminude women in *National Geographic* to become sexually aroused. Not surprisingly, some religious groups considered the pictures pornographic and urged the magazine to omit them. More recently, a classic episode in the 1990s TV comedy *Seinfeld* began with one of the characters, George, telling his friends that he had been caught by his mother in the act of masturbating while reading *Glamour* magazine. As these examples indicate, any effort to ban pornography, no matter how disgusting the vast majority of the public finds certain kinds of pornography, inevitably raises the question of censorship (Bauder 2007).

Those in favor of banning pornography say that censorship is not an issue. Even in a democratic society, they note, some speech is prohibited without it being considered censorship. People may not shout "fire" in a crowded theater, nor may they libel or slander other individuals. Given these exceptions to the First Amendment, they say that banning pornography is not a question of censorship, but rather one of protecting society (Kammeyer 2008).

The kind of protection urged depends on why one opposes pornography in the first place. Two otherwise very different groups, religious moralists and antipornography feminists, have been especially vocal in criticizing pornography and calling for its ban. Religious moralists condemn the sexual aspect of pornography. Representing traditional Judeo-Christian views, they feel that sexual pleasure is a means to an end—reproduction of the species—and not an end in itself. Depictions of nudity and sexual behavior thus violate their religious views, which prompt them to feel that pornography both offends and threatens society's moral order.

Many feminists also call for the banning of pornography, but for very different reasons. To them pornography, like rape, is not about sex but rather about male domination and violence against women (Cornell 2000). It is no accident, say these feminists, that virtually all pornography depicts women rather than men and that, when men are also depicted, they usually dominate women sexually and/or violently. Whether or not it involves violence, pornography expresses contempt for women and degrades them as sexual objects existing solely for men's pleasure. Perhaps the worst aspect of pornography, say many feminists, is that it contributes to rape by reinforcing men's beliefs that women like or need to be raped. As Robin Morgan (1977:169) asserted thirty-five years ago in a now-famous phrase, "Pornography is the theory, and rape the practice."

In criticizing pornography, some feminists distinguish between **violent pornography,** which depicts sexual violence against women, and **erotica,** which depicts respectful nudity and consensual, loving sexual interaction between adults. They also distinguish violent pornography from **nonviolent pornography,** which falls short of the respect and loving nature of erotica, but does not include violence against women. Other feminists make no such distinctions; they consider nudity such as that appearing in *Playboy* or *Penthouse* little better than violent pornography. They would thus ban virtually any pornography. Other feminists feel that this goes too far and believe only the most violent pornography should be banned. Still other feminists criticize pornography, but oppose its banning because they worry about the censorship issue. They and other free-speech advocates fear that any bans on pornography would inevitably extend to erotica and even to feminist depictions of the nature of rape, prostitution, and crimes involving women.

Pornography and Rape

Does pornography cause rape or other violence against women, as many feminists charge? Anecdotal evidence indicates that the homes of convicted rapists often contain a good deal of violent pornography. Some people interpret such evidence as proof of a pornography–rape causal connection, but it may simply mean that men with violent sexual attitudes are likely both to read and view violent pornography and to rape women. Several studies show that men (usually male college students) who view violent pornography in laboratory experiments often, but not always, exhibit short-term increases in aggressive attitudes toward women and in acceptance of rape myths (Donnerstein, Linz, and Penrod 1987). However, these laboratory studies do not necessarily mean that pornography actually causes men to go out and rape in real life.

A recent review of these and other studies concluded that pornography does not cause rape and argued that "it is time to discard the hypothesis that pornography contributes to increased sexual assault behavior" (Ferguson and Hartley 2009:323). As Chapter 11 indicated, there are many structural and cultural sources of rape, and pornography is probably more a symptom of these structural and cultural conditions than an independent cause of rape. However, even if pornography does not cause rape, much pornography, depending on how it is defined, degrades women by portraying them as men's sexual playthings. No matter what pornographers try to tell us, women are far more than collections of attractive body parts. Unfortunately, many men, subscribing to antiquated notions of masculinity and femininity, cannot see beyond these limits.

Certainly, opponents of pornography are not about to stop their efforts to ban offensive sexual material. However repugnant many people find much pornography, though, the civil liberties issues raised by calls for its prohibition demand that we proceed with the greatest caution in this area. Judging from the other consensual crimes already discussed, any outright ban on pornography may well prove futile. For better or worse, there is simply too much interest in pornography, however it is defined, for such a ban to work well and too many individuals and organizations willing to provide it, especially in the modern era of the Internet.

Review and Discuss

Do you think pornography helps cause rape? Why or why not?

Gambling

Like the other behaviors discussed in this chapter, gambling has a very long history punctuated by laws designed to regulate the conduct of society's poor (Meier and Geis 2007). In ancient Egypt, authorities prohibited gambling because they worried it would distract workers from mining and other labor. A similar concern prompted the kings of England and France in the late twelfth century to prohibit gambling for the poor, while allowing it for the nobility. Several centuries later, vagrancy laws expanded in England in 1743 to forbid certain types of gambling. Additional legislation in 1853 further outlawed most of the types of betting in which the English poor were involved, although they flouted the law and continued to bet anyway.

In the U.S. colonies, Massachusetts Bay Puritans considered gambling a sin and banned it in 1638, but gambling eventually became very popular in the colonies (Fenster 1994). Lotteries were the game of choice, as lottery revenue helped finance the construction of public buildings and early universities such as Harvard and Yale. Lotteries eventually fell prey to corruption and were abolished during the 1800s. In their place grew illegal betting, most commonly in the form of bookmaking and *numbers running,* in which people bet on the last few numbers of stock exchange and other numerical indicators. Over the years, illegal gambling has provided much of the revenue for organized crime and fueled corruption by police, politicians, and other public officials.

Of all the behaviors discussed in this chapter, gambling is the most common and by far the most accepted. Most U.S. residents gamble at one time or another, and many gamble repeatedly. About 85 percent of Americans say they have gambled at least once in their lives, and 60 percent say they have gambled in the past year (MayoClinic.com 2004). Estimates say that more than 20 million Americans either have gambling problems or are at risk for developing them and put the number of addicted gamblers between 2 million and 5 million. One study estimated that gambling addiction costs the

About 60 percent of Americans say they have gambled during the past year. More than $300 billion is spent each year at casinos and race tracks and on state lotteries.

nation $5 billion each year in lost wages, bankruptcy, and legal fees for divorce and other problems (Arnold 1999). It is not an exaggeration to say we are a "nation of gamblers" suffering from "gambling fever," as the titles of gambling studies put it (Fenster 1994; Welles 1989). We spend more hundreds of billions of dollars every year on legal gambling at **casinos,** horse- and dog-racing tracks, state lotteries, and church bingo, and probably tens of billions on illegal gambling, much of it sports related, and on gambling on the Internet.

THE GROWTH OF GAMBLING

For better or worse, gambling has become increasingly legal (Dombrink 2009). As Walker (2011:295) noted, "The legal status of gambling in the United States has undergone a massive change in recent years. The old moralistic objections to gambling have collapsed as many states have created lotteries and authorized casino gambling." After more than a century of no legal lotteries, most states now have them, and land- and water-based casinos can be found around the country. Americans spend more than $1 trillion every year on legal gambling (Lange 2007). Reflecting the growth in legal gambling and police decisions to de-emphasize control of illegal gambling, gambling arrests have dropped dramatically in the last few decades, from some 123,000 in 1960 to only 9,811 in 2008 (Federal Bureau of Investigation 2009).

At least three reasons explain the growth of legal gambling (Rosecrance 1988). First, the United States in general has become more tolerant in the last few decades of the various consensual or vice crimes. Given such a relaxation of attitudes, legalization of gambling was probably inevitable. Second, and perhaps more important, states and cities have turned to lotteries and casinos as sources of much-needed revenue. The lotteries are very profitable for the states, with the odds against winning many millions to one. A third reason for casino growth lies in decisions by various Native American tribes to start casinos on their reservations, again as a source of much-needed revenue; two very successful Connecticut casinos, Foxwoods and Mohegan Sun, are prime examples.

THE GAMBLING DEBATE

Despite the growing acceptance and legalization of gambling, religious groups warn against it. In addition to worrying about the money people lose from legal gambling and the harm done to their families, they view gambling as an immoral attempt to get something for nothing, which destroys personal character (Kennedy 2004). The position of the United Methodist Church is representative: "Gambling is a menace to society, deadly to the best interests of moral, social, economic, and spiritual life, and destructive of good government" (Keating 2004). Interestingly, despite the religious condemnation of gambling, various churches and synagogues (as well as other nonprofit organizations) have long held regular bingo or beano games to raise funds.

This inconsistency aside, their concern over legal gambling's economic harm is worth restating. There is little question that the growth of lotteries and casinos has increased the number of gamblers and the amount of money spent on gambling (Dombrink 2009). Noting that the poor and near-poor are the major players of state lotteries, many observers charge that lotteries and casinos exploit the poor and worsen their financial condition (Lange 2007). Still others point to compulsive gambling that ravages hundreds of thousands of families, even if compulsive gamblers comprise only a minuscule fraction of all gamblers, and they worry that the growth of casinos will only worsen this problem (Eckenrode 2007).

As these warnings attest, gambling, like the other behaviors in this chapter, cannot be truly victimless. But it is a choice that people make, and critics of laws against gambling and other risky consensual behaviors question whether we should stop people from making unwise choices. So much gambling occurs anyway, they add, that there is little hope of banning it effectively. Despite the problems it may cause, the growing legalization of gambling may be keeping some gambling revenue from organized crime, and the great decrease in gambling arrests has freed up scarce criminal justice resources for more important crime fighting. Like the other behaviors discussed in this chapter, gambling remains an activity that provides thrills and excitement for millions of people, even as it causes some of them to suffer. For better or worse, gambling is here to stay, and its legalization, however distasteful to some, may lead to more good than harm.

Review and Discuss

The text argues that there may be no logical distinction between the types of gambling that are legal and the types that are illegal. Do you agree? Why or why not?

Reducing Consensual Crime

We have seen that consensual crime laws generally do not work and may even do more harm than good. Because drug use, prostitution, pornography, and gambling have been around for centuries, they are not about to disappear, and the historical record provides little hope that we can do much about them. That said, economic deprivation does seem to underlie some illegal drug use and much prostitution. To the extent that this is true, efforts to reduce poverty hold much potential for reducing these two crimes. Unfortunately, because current approaches to these two crimes, including the legal war against drugs and education and treatment programs for drug users, ignore their structural roots in economic inequality, they ultimately offer little promise for reducing these crimes.

For better or worse, one way to reduce consensual criminal behaviors is to legalize the behaviors, as was done for alcohol use with the repeal of Prohibition in 1933. People would still engage in the behaviors, as they do now, but they would no longer be committing a crime when they do so. The problems of the consensual behaviors discussed in this chapter would continue, but the problems caused by the enforcement of the laws against these behaviors would diminish or disappear altogether. This is a basic rationale of the legalization argument for all consensual crimes. Legalization may be a risky solution and may even be entirely wrongheaded but, as Surgeon General Elders said in 1993 about the drug problem, it at least deserves careful consideration, which it has not yet received in the United States.

Conclusion

The behaviors we call consensual or vice crimes have existed since ancient times and will doubtless continue far into the future. Illegal drug use, prostitution, pornography, and gambling occur because many people desire them. This is a fact. The question is what, if anything, society should do about this fact.

One problem with consensual crime laws is that the distinction between legal and illegal behavior can be blurry and artificial. We prohibit some drugs, but allow the use of others such as alcohol and tobacco that kill hundreds of thousands annually and cost tens of billions of dollars in health care costs, lost economic productivity, and other expenses. We prohibit prostitutes from selling their bodies for sex, but pay athletes, models, and other people large sums of money to sell their bodies. We allow some forms of gambling but prohibit others, with no logical reason for why some are allowed but others are banned. We try to ban pornography even as reasonable people disagree on what is pornographic and what is merely erotic.

Vice behavior raises some fascinating philosophical and social-scientific questions regarding the role of the state and the nature of individual freedom. The major philosophical question is how far the state should go in prohibiting people from engaging in consensual behavior that may harm themselves or indirectly harm others. The major social-scientific question is whether laws against consensual behaviors do more harm than good. There are many things wrong and even counterproductive about our current approach to illegal drugs, prostitution, pornography, and gambling. Unfortunately, it is easier to note these problems than to come up with workable solutions. Should we pour even more time, money, and energy into fighting consensual crimes? Or should we instead consider a radically different approach such as legalization? Reasonable people will debate these questions for many years to come.

Summary

1. The debate over consensual crime centers on two issues. First, to what degree should the state prohibit consensual behaviors that may directly harm their participants and indirectly harm the participants' family and friends? Second, do the laws against consensual behaviors do more harm than good?

2. Drug use has been common throughout human history, and it is not an exaggeration to say that the United States is a nation of drug users. Many types of legal drugs exist, and almost everyone uses them. Illegal drug use is also very common, although most such use is of marijuana and is often experimental or occasional, rather than frequent or habitual. National surveys of illegal drug use obscure its high concentration in poor, urban areas.

3. Economic deprivation, peer influences, and dysfunctional families account for much illegal drug use. Although women use illegal drugs slightly less often than men do, they are more likely to use drugs because of depression and a history of sexual abuse.

4. Illegal drug use and criminal behavior are highly correlated, but this does not necessarily mean that drug use causes criminal behavior. Much of the relationship between using drugs and committing crimes is spurious, because both behaviors result from the same kinds of structural and social process factors. The drug–crime connection is clearest for alcohol, which in U.S. culture produces violent behavior.

5. All drugs can be dangerous, at least in large quantities, and the state must decide which drugs it will ban and which it will allow. Two legal drugs, tobacco and alcohol, cause many more deaths than all the illegal drugs combined. The laws against certain drugs are said by critics to do more harm than good. The harms they have in mind include the many criminal behaviors resulting from the fact that the drugs are illegal, many of the deaths associated with using illegal drugs, the billions of dollars spent on the legal war against drugs, the bolstering that the illegality of drugs gives to organized crime, the corruption of police and other public servants and individuals resulting from the illegality of certain drugs, and the use of legally unsavory investigative procedures such as wiretapping. If the laws against certain drugs were repealed, it is uncertain whether and how much use of those drugs would increase. Harm reduction involving drug treatment alternatives to imprisonment is gaining a foothold in the United States.

6. Prostitution is called the world's oldest profession, and legal brothels existed for much of U.S. history and still operate in many parts of Nevada. Economic deprivation and a history of sexual abuse underlie the decisions of many women to turn to prostitution. Prostitution is said to perform several important functions for prostitutes and their customers. It gives prostitutes a source of income and their customers a sexual outlet.

7. A key issue in the nation's response to pornography is that pornography is very difficult and perhaps impossible to define precisely. Attempts to outlaw pornography raise important issues of censorship in a free society. Although many people believe that pornography causes rape, empirical evidence of such a causal connection is not conclusive.

8. Like other consensual behaviors, gambling, both legal and illegal, is very common. Thanks to lotteries and casinos, legal gambling has grown rapidly in recent decades. Critics of gambling laws say it is not clear why some gambling is legal and some is illegal.

9. Because drug use, prostitution, pornography, and gambling are historically and currently very common, society can do little to eliminate these behaviors. The legal war against them has not proved effective. In 1933 the United Stated repealed Prohibition because it decided that Prohibition was causing more harm than good. Critics of consensual crime laws say that the nation should carefully consider whether to maintain these laws.

Key Terms

bribery 383

brothel 387

casino 393

erotica 391

harm reduction 384

legalization 381

moral crusade 387

more harm than good 372

nonviolent pornography 391

violent pornography 391

What Would You Do?

1. You have a 16-year-old daughter and a 14-year-old son. Most days they are involved in after-school activities, but sometimes they both come home right after school and are by themselves until you and your spouse come home from work. One day you leave work early and go home because you are not feeling well. When you get home and go upstairs, you think you smell marijuana, an odor with which you are familiar because you used to smoke it occasionally in college. You knock on your daughter's bedroom door and open it right away without waiting to hear her reply. Inside you see your daughter and son, who were obviously sharing a joint, which your son is now frantically trying to hide in a cup of soda. What do you do and say?

2. You are 51 years old and living in the suburbs. Your daughter and her best friend go to different colleges out of state, but they are now home for Christmas break. One day you overhear your daughter talking with her friend when you come home unexpectedly, and you are shocked to hear the friend telling your daughter that she is now a call girl a few times a month, meeting men at a four-star hotel near her college, to help pay her tuition. Your daughter sounds very upset to hear the news. What, if anything, do you do or say?

CHAPTER

sixteen

Policing: Dilemmas

of Crime Control

in a Democratic Society

Crime in the News

In May 2010, a task force appointed by the governor of New York concluded that unconscious racial bias was responsible for an alarming number of incidents in which police accidentally killed other police, some of them off-duty, whom they mistakenly assumed were criminals. Of fourteen police who had died for this reason since 1995, ten were officers of color. Out of ten officers who were off-duty when they were killed by police, nine were African American or Latino. Data like these led the report to conclude, "Inherent or unconscious racial bias plays a role in 'shoot/don't-shoot' decisions made by officers of all races and ethnicities." As the vice chair of the task force explained, "Research reveals that race may play a role in an officer's instantaneous assessment of whether a particular person presents a danger or not."

Source: Baker 2010a.

This Crime in the News story is a striking and tragic reminder that the police have great powers over us and may make arrests and use deadly force when necessary. Sometimes, they make mistakes, and sometimes, as the task force concluded, they act consciously or unconsciously out of racial and other biases. The role and power of police are central issues in the study of crime. How far should the police go in a democracy in their efforts to control crime? Should they be allowed to search our cars or homes without permission? Should they be allowed to threaten suspects to get them to confess? Many U.S. Supreme Court rulings limit police powers, and questions such as these lie at the heart of contemporary debate over police and crime.

In a well-known distinction, law professor Herbert L. Packer (1964) outlined two competing models of the criminal justice system. These **crime-control** and **due process** models, as Packer labeled them, reflect the tensions of crime-control in a **democratic society.** As its name implies, the crime-control model's key concerns are the apprehension and punishment of criminals, and it stresses the criminal justice system's need to capture and process criminals in the most efficient manner possible. In contrast, the due process model stresses the need of the criminal justice system to protect suspects from honest mistakes or deliberate deception and bias by police and other criminal justice actors.

These two models have long been in tension as the United States decides how best to deal with crime. The due process model had its heyday during the 1960s, in which the Supreme Court under the direction of Chief Justice Earl Warren expanded the rights of criminal suspects and defendants. In the late 1980s and especially the 1990s, a more conservative Court limited some of the rights conferred by the Warren Court. Efforts to deal with terrorism after 9/11 illustrate the tension between the two models, as the nation debated then and today how many legal rights suspected terrorists should enjoy (Cole and Lobel 2007).

Crime Control in a Democratic Society

This tension goes to the heart of fundamental questions in criminology. Simply put, the more crime control we want, the less due process we can have; the more due process we want, the less crime control we can expect. In a classic book about police first published in 1966 and reissued with added material, Jerome H. Skolnick (1994:1) referred to this problem as a "dilemma of democratic society." This dilemma is perhaps best illustrated by using an exaggerated example of the crime-control model. Consider a society with no due process. In such a society, the police can arrest suspects without probable cause, torture them to extract confessions, and throw them in jail and even execute them without a trial. Suppose further that this system of "justice" applies not just to political dissidents but also to the most common criminals, such as pickpockets, who could have their arms amputated. Crime in such a society would likely be very low because people would live in terror of doing anything wrong, however minor.

Of course, no reasonable crime-control advocate in the United States proposes such an exaggerated model. The question then becomes which balance to strike between the polar opposites of the crime-control and due process models. Do we err on the side of crime control and sacrifice individual freedom, or do we err on the side of due process and perhaps sacrifice public safety? Crime might well be lower in the exaggerated model. But is this the kind of society we want? Émile Durkheim (1962 [1895]) noted long ago that a society (such as the United States) valuing freedom of thought will also have high levels of deviance because both concepts presuppose a weak "collective conscience" that permits people both to think individually and to violate social norms. One does not occur without the other. As one criminologist observed, "Crime may be one of the prices we pay for the individualism that we have in this society" (Rosen 1995:109), The dilemma of crime control in a democratic society becomes one of deciding what kind of society we want to have.

In considering this dilemma, it is important to keep in mind that it is possible to have a democracy that is relatively crime free; several democratic nations have lower crime rates than the United States (see Chapter 3), even though they do not follow the U.S. tough crime-control model. These nations have less crime than the United States in part because they have lower inequality and do more to help children most at risk for committing delinquent acts and crime when they get older. In the long run, these nations point to directions the United States could pursue to lower its own crime rate.

In a democratic society, a key question is how much power to give to the police to preserve law and order.

THE IDEAL OF BLIND JUSTICE

So far, we have been discussing the problem of civil liberty as a democracy like the United States considers how to deal with crime. But if one of the cornerstones of democracy is freedom, another is equality. In the legal system, this means that justice should be *blind* to personal differences—that is, people should be treated the same regardless of their race, ethnicity, social class, gender, or other **extralegal** characteristics. Crime control in a democratic society thus also raises the problem of civil rights. As we try to control crime, we have to be careful that citizens are not singled out because of who they are instead of what they did and how they did it. If one dilemma of crime control in a democratic society involves striking the right balance between public safety and individual freedom, another dilemma concerns striking the right balance between public safety and equality of treatment. Civil rights advocates and *law and order* champions often have different views on where this balance should be struck.

A PREVIEW OF THE DISCUSSION

This and the next chapter explore some aspects of these two basic dilemmas of crime control in democratic society. We will discuss the major issues facing the police, courts, and prisons as they try to control crime and the issues facing our society as it uses the criminal justice system as its primary means of dealing with crime. We will also discuss the complex evidence on inequality in crime control and explore how aspects of the social structure affect how the criminal justice system operates. Anticipating the book's final chapter on reducing crime, we will, in addition, critically examine the effectiveness of our criminal justice system. Our view will stress what Packer (1968) called "the limits of the criminal sanction." Simply put, the amount of crime control tolerable in a democratic society can ultimately do little to prevent criminality. Given this reality, "get tough" approaches to crime will do little to reduce crime; efforts to address the roots of crime hold more promise.

This chapter begins our discussion with a look at police. We begin by reviewing the history of police and then discuss sociological research on police behavior and the impact of policing. For the most part, research on police did not exist before the 1960s, as criminological work before then focused on the causes of criminal and delinquent behavior.

The social and political upheaval of the 1960s awakened interest in the social reaction to crime. In particular, the possibility of police racial bias in arrest practices motivated the government-sponsored, observational studies of police behavior discussed later.

Development of the Modern Police Force

The concept of police goes back to ancient times. Ancient Egypt, Mesopotamia, and Rome all used police forces to maintain public order (Mosse 1975). Although this sounds like a benign function, the police forces in effect were private bodyguards whose primary purpose was to protect the societies' rulers from uprisings and other threatening conduct by the masses.

In eleventh-century England, a system of community policing called the *frankpledge* developed, in which groups of ten families, called *tithings,* were required to maintain order within each tithing. Ten tithings living on a particular noble's estate were called a *hundred.* The noble appointed an unpaid **constable** to monitor their behavior; one of his main duties was to control poaching on the noble's land. Several hundreds eventually constituted a *shire,* or county, which were put under the charge of a *shire reeve,* the root of the modern term *sheriff.* Eventually, English units of government called *parishes* developed and appointed unpaid constables to watch out for disorderly conduct and perform various services such as trash collection. The constables in turn appointed watchmen as assistants (Critchley 1972).

By the early 1800s, the constable system was no longer working. London was the scene of repeated riots and crime by the poor. There were too few constables who were too poorly trained to handle these problems. A call began for a larger, more organized police force to quell the social chaos, but some people worried that this step would endanger individual freedom. Finally, Prime Minister Sir Robert Peel persuaded Parliament in 1829 to establish the first paid, specialized police force in London, whose police soon became known as *bobbies* because of Peel's influence. London was divided into small districts called *beats,* and police were given jurisdiction over specific beats.

The development of police forces in the United States followed the English model. In the colonial era, the constable and watch system was typical. As in England, by the early 1800s this system had outlived its usefulness. Cities were growing rapidly and were the scenes of repeated mob violence in the decades preceding the Civil War, most of it instigated by bands of white youths who preyed on immigrants and African Americans. This violence prompted calls for organized police forces similar to London's. In 1838, Boston created a daytime police force to complement the night watchmen, and then in 1844, New York City established the first full-time force. Within a decade, most big U.S. cities had gone the same route. Although Northern cities developed police forces because they feared mob violence, Southern cities developed them because they feared slave revolts. In Southern cities police forces evolved from the "slave patrols" that tracked down runaway slaves (Walker 1998).

These early U.S. police forces were notoriously corrupt and brutal and were of little help against crime. Many police officers drank heavily while they patrolled and used their nightsticks freely on suspects, most of them poor immigrants, who were widely considered by "respectable society" to be "dangerous classes" in need of careful monitoring (Shelden 2008). Police forces grew in size beginning in the 1870s to deal with thousands of strikes by workers across the country against their pitiful wages and wretched living and working conditions (Shelden 2008). In the early 1900s, cities began to reform their police departments by developing a professional model of policing in which police were hired on their qualifications and properly trained to carry out their jobs efficiently and honestly. As we will see later, police brutality and corruption may be less common today than a century ago, but they are still a problem.

Review and Discuss

How and why did the modern police force develop? Do the operation and behavior of today's police forces resemble those of their historical counterparts? Why or why not?

Working Personality and Police Behavior

Police spend a surprisingly low amount of their time responding to 911 calls, questioning witnesses, arresting suspects, and performing other aspects of crime control. Only about 20 percent of police time is spent on these activities, with most police time spent on activities such as directing traffic, responding to traffic accidents, and other much more mundane matters. It is also true that policing is less dangerous in terms of fatality rates than occupations such as construction and mining (Kappeler and Potter 2005).

These facts notwithstanding, police remain afraid for their safety, especially in urban areas. They realize that anyone they confront, even in a routine traffic stop, poses a potential threat of injury and even death. As a result, they are constantly on the alert for any signs that their safety is in danger when they interact with citizens. The fact that these citizens are not exactly happy when being questioned by police (and often become downright hostile) only heightens an officer's concern. The importance of this basic feature of policing cannot be underestimated because it has important implications for all other aspects of police behavior.

In his classic book on policing, Jerome Skolnick (1994) developed the very influential concept of the police officer's **working personality.** Skolnick noted that the work people do affects the way they view the world and even their personalities. The working personality of the police, wrote Skolnick, stems from the danger of their job. This inevitably makes police suspicious of and even hostile toward the public and reinforces police solidarity, or mutual loyalty. The public's hostility toward the police reinforces police solidarity and creates among police an "us against them" mentality (Lyman 2010). These and other aspects of policing prompt police officers to develop a working personality that is authoritarian, cynical, and suspicious, which prompts them to be ready and willing to use violence when they feel it is necessary.

This structural basis for police behavior is dramatically illustrated in a classic article by George L. Kirkham (1984), a criminology professor who became a police officer. In the classroom, Kirkham often criticized police behavior. Many of his students were police, and they told him that he "could not possibly understand what a police officer has to endure in modern society until I had been one myself" (p. 78). At the age of 31, Kirkham took up their challenge and, after completing police academy training, joined the Jacksonville, Florida, police force and quickly began to learn his "street lessons."

As a professor, Kirkham had always thought that police exaggerated the disrespect

Many citizens are hostile to the presence of police. In turn, police are constantly on alert for any signs that their own lives are in danger.

they encountered from the public. On his first day on the beat in Jacksonville, Kirkham learned how wrong he had been. He wrote, "As a college professor, I had grown accustomed to being treated with uniform respect and deference by those I encountered. I somehow naively assumed that this same quality of respect would carry over into my new role as a policeman . . . [but] quickly found that my badge and uniform . . . only acted as a magnet which drew me toward many individuals who hated what I represented" (p. 81).

In one of his first encounters, Kirkham asked a drunk to leave a bar. Smiling "pleasantly" at the man, Kirkham asked him, "Excuse me, sir, but I wonder if I could ask you to step outside and talk with me for just a minute?" Kirkham described what happened next: "Without warning . . . he swung at me, luckily missing my face and striking me on the right shoulder. I couldn't believe it. What on earth had I done to provoke such a reaction?" (p. 81). Kirkham recalled how startled he was that his "gentle, rapport-building approach," which had worked so well in other settings, had failed him here.

In the weeks that followed, fear "became something which I regularly experienced," Kirkham wrote (p. 82). In one incident in which he and his partner tried to arrest a young male in a poor neighborhood, an ugly crowd threatened their safety. Kirkham felt a "sickening sensation of cold terror" as he put out a distress call on his police car radio and grabbed a shotgun to protect himself and his partner. He wrote, "How readily as a criminology professor I would have condemned the officer who was now myself, trembling with fear and anxiety and menacing an 'unarmed' assembly" with a shotgun (p. 83). Circumstances, he noted, "had dramatically changed my perspective, for now it was my life and safety that were in danger, my wife and child who might be mourning" (p. 84). Kirkham wrote later in the article that as a criminology professor he could always take his time to make decisions, but as a police officer he was "forced to make the most critical choices in a time frame of seconds, rather than days: to shoot or not to shoot, to arrest or not to arrest, to give chase or let go" (p. 85).

Review and Discuss

What explains the working personality of police? How does the working personality of police help us understand their behavior?

POLICE MISCONDUCT: BRUTALITY

The picture Kirkham and other observers present of policing helps explain why police brutality and corruption occur. We look first at **brutality,** more neutrally called the excessive, unjustified, or undue use of force.

A defining feature of the police is that they are authorized to use physical force when necessary to subdue suspects (Westley 1970). As we have seen, the police are often in tense situations in which their safety and lives might be on the line. They confront suspects who are often hostile and who often insult them. Tempers flare. Inevitably, police will use force when none was needed or will sometimes use more force than was needed to subdue a suspect. The result is police brutality.

Measuring Excessive Force

No one really knows how many cases of police use of excessive force occur each year (Fyfe 2002). Usually its only witnesses are the police and their victims. Their solidarity usually leads the police to keep quiet about these incidents. The victims are often reluctant to lodge a complaint because they feel they will not be believed or it will not do any good. After the notorious beating of Rodney King by Los Angeles police in 1991, which was captured on home video and seen around the nation, the number of police brutality complaints reportedly increased in many jurisdictions.

SURVEYS

The two primary methods of measuring excessive force are surveys and direct observation. A prominent survey for this purpose is the Police–Public Contact Survey (PPCS), a random sample of about 64,000 persons 16 or older interviewed nationwide in 2005 (Durose, Smith, and Langan 2007). About one-fifth of the sample had face-to-face contact with the police during the previous year. Just over half of these contacts were for traffic stops; many of the remainder occurred when people reported a crime or sought other help. The people with any police contact were asked whether the police used any force against them. About 1.6 percent, equivalent to about 700,000 people, responded yes. These persons were then asked whether they considered the force excessive. About 83 percent again said yes, with the force typically involving grabbing or shoving. Putting all these numbers together, about 1.3 percent of all po-

A defining feature of the police is that they are authorized to use physical force when necessary to subdue suspects.

lice contacts in 2005, involving some 590,000 people, were considered excessive by the civilians against whom the force was used. To turn this around, 98.7 percent of all police contacts involved no excessive force. An interesting gender difference emerged in the PPCS: Males comprised 53.6 percent of all police contacts, but 72.4 percent of all contacts involving police use of force (see Figure 16.1). This difference may indicate police gender bias, but it may also reflect the possibility that males behave more aggressively than females toward a police officer.

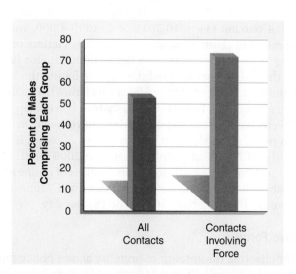

FIGURE 16.1 ▸ **Males, Police Contacts, and Perceived Police Use of Force, 2005 Police–Public Contact Survey** Source: Durose, Schmitt, and Langan 2007.

One problem with the PPCS estimate of 590,000 cases of excessive force is that the police use of force may not actually have been excessive even if the individual thought it was. The actual number of cases of excessive force may thus be at least somewhat lower than the survey implies. However, the reported 1.3 percent prevalence of police brutality may also be misleading in the other direction, because it is based on all police contacts and not just those involving criminal suspects (only 2.8 percent of all police contacts in the survey), against whom excessive force is most often used. Of those respondents whose police contact involved suspicion of a crime, 14 percent said excessive force was used. In this regard, the PPCS's sample excluded the nation's more than 2 million jail and prison inmates, who may be particularly likely to have experienced excessive force.

The PPCS assessed police use of force during just the past year. A decade earlier, a Gallup poll assessed lifetime prevalence of (perceptions of) police brutality by asking whether respondents had "ever been physically mistreated or abused by the police" (Blumberg 1994). Five percent of the respondents, equivalent to more than 8 million adults, answered yes. As with the PPCS, it is possible that at least some of the respondents were behaving in a way that justified the police behavior in question.

DIRECT OBSERVATION

Police behavior, including excessive force, has also been measured via direct observation by trained researchers. One of the earliest and still best such studies occurred in the summer of 1966, when thirty-six observers funded by the federal government accompanied police officers in Boston, Chicago, Illinois, and Washington, DC, on their patrols for seven weeks. The observers recorded several kinds of information on the 3,826 encounters that officers had with suspects and other citizens. Some of this information concerned brutality. In the seven-week study, the observers found 37 cases of brutality involving 44 citizens. Because the police knew they were being observed, it is possible that more brutality would have occurred had they been unobserved. Typically, the police committing brutality falsely claimed they were acting in self-defense, and some even carried guns and knives to plant on suspects to support these bogus claims (Reiss 1980b).

Albert J. Reiss (1980b), the study's director, later discussed whether these 37 cases represented a high or low level of brutality. Because there were 3,826 encounters in the study, "only" 1 percent (37 ÷ 3,826) involved brutality. Of the 10,564 citizens in these encounters, "only" 0.4 percent (44 ÷ 10,564), or 4 out of 1,000, were beaten. However, said Reiss, because many of these encounters were with victims or witnesses, who are not the "logical" targets of police violence, a better denominator is the number of suspects, 1,394, whom the police encountered. Using this figure, the brutality rate rises to 44 of 1,394, or 3.16 percent. Reiss concluded from this figure that police brutality in large cities is "far from rare" (p. 288). This is especially true if we keep in mind that Reiss's police knew they were being observed and might have been on their best behavior. Moreover, even 3.16 percent translates to large numbers of cases. If we venture to apply this rate to the roughly 13.7 million people arrested in 2009 for all offenses, then about 432,000 people (3.16 percent of 13.7 million) were victims of police brutality in that year. In California alone, about 1.47 million people were arrested. Our estimate of police brutality in California would thus be about 46,000, or 127 per day.

Explaining Excessive Force

One important factor affecting the amount of brutality across police forces is their culture and operating philosophy (Terrill III and Manning 2003). In cities in which police administrators make it very clear that brutality will not be tolerated, brutality rates appear lower than in cities in which administrators make no such proclamations. Police killings of civilians are also less common in police departments in which administrators set clear limits on police use of force (Fyfe 1993). The philosophies and policies of individual police departments thus seem to have an important effect on how much police violence occurs.

RACISM AND POLICE BRUTALITY

The issue of racism in police brutality remains highly controversial. Many consider the Rodney King beating typical: King was African American, and the police who beat him were white. African Americans have long listed brutality as one of their major grievances against the police, and beatings of African-American suspects were widely blamed for igniting many of the 1960s urban riots (Kerner Commission 1968). After King's beating, many observers deplored the racial pattern in the brutality he experienced as all too common. As an official of the National Association for the Advancement of Colored People (NAACP) testified to Congress, "The problem of police brutality is pervasive, deep-rooted and alarming. . . . For too long, African Americans and other racial minorities have been among the special targets of police abuse. . . . [T]oo often innocent black people—including many of our youngsters—find themselves the victims of the abuse of authority and law" (Henderson 1991:23, 28).

How true is this? To the extent that police brutality exists, how much of it is directed at African Americans or Latinos because of their race or ethnicity? The PPCS data discussed earlier exhibit an ambiguous picture. Whereas only 1.2 percent of whites with police contact experienced use of force, 2.3 percent of Latinos and 4.4 percent of African Americans with police contact experienced use of force. However, among those who did experience use of force, Latinos and African Americans were not more likely than whites to say the force was excessive. This latter finding does not support the view that African Americans or Latinos are more likely than whites to be victims of police brutality.

Although African Americans and Latinos are more likely to experience police use of force in general, this fact does not necessarily indicate police racial/ethnic bias. Some scholars believe that the many instances each year of police excessive force against people of color simply reflect their urban locations. African Americans and Latinos in large cities may suffer police violence not because of police racism, but because they are the suspects that police encounter, and suspects in general are at risk for brutality. They might be suspects because a racist society denies them full equality (see Chapters 7 and 10), but that does not necessarily mean that racism motivates the police brutality they suffer.

Evidence for this view comes from the 1966 Reiss study discussed earlier. Although Reiss's observers recorded brutality for 31.6 of every 1,000 suspects, this rate broke down to 41.9 for every 1,000 white suspects and 22.6 for every 1,000 black suspects (Reiss 1980b). The risk of white suspects for brutality was thus twice as great as that of black suspects. Reiss's observers also found no evidence that white police were more likely to beat black suspects than white suspects. (Keep in mind, however, that Reiss's police knew they were being watched and thus might not have beaten suspects they normally would have beaten.) Although Reiss readily acknowledged that white officers were racially prejudiced, in his study he concluded that racism did not motivate the use of excessive force by the white police against African Americans.

Reiss's view is certainly not the final word on the subject of police brutality and racism, but it does reinforce the complexity of the issue. At a minimum, however, there is ample evidence, as Reiss himself acknowledged, of racist attitudes among white police (Skolnick 1994), and also of unconscious racial bias, as this chapter's Crime in the News story indicated. The key question is whether these attitudes lead white police to treat African Americans and whites differently.

RACISM AND POLICE USE OF DEADLY FORCE

Scholars have also considered whether racism affects police use of deadly force. As with brutality, a disproportionate number of the civilians killed by police, more than 50 percent, are people of color, especially African American. Espousing a *community violence hypothesis,* many scholars think this fact simply reflects the disproportionate number of felons and other suspects who are people of color (Fyfe 1993). Espousing a *conflict hypothesis,* other scholars think it reflects police racism, with one scholar asserting that police have "one trigger finger for whites and another for African Americans" (Takagi 1974:30).

Which view is correct? Here again, the evidence is complex and ambiguous. Supporting the community violence view, several studies find that police killings of civilians are highest in areas with high violent-crime rates and that white officers tend to kill white suspects and black officers tend to kill black suspects. Such findings suggest that "the application of deadly force by officers is not racially motivated" (Sorensen, Marquart, and Brock 1993:429). Supporting the conflict view, however, other studies find that police killings of civilians are highest in areas with the greatest racial inequality and with higher proportions of African Americans (Jacobs and O'Brien 1998). These results suggest that the "police response in these areas is higher than is warranted by the levels of violent crime" (Sorensen et al. 1993:437).

Review and Discuss

To what extent does racial bias play a role in the use of violence by police?

POLICE VIOLENCE AGAINST WOMEN

The available evidence indicates that women are rarely the victims of police brutality as it is usually defined. Turning around the PPCS findings on males reported earlier, women comprise 47 percent of all police contacts but only 13 percent of all force contacts. Of the forty-four citizens beaten by police in Reiss's study, only two, both African Americans, were women. Several reasons probably account for women's low incidence of brutality victimization. Compared to men, few women are suspects (and thus less at risk than men for brutality) because their crime rates are far lower than men's. Because of socialization differences in aggressiveness, when women do become suspects they are probably less likely than male suspects to act belligerently and thus are less likely to arouse police ire. It is also possible that police may be reluctant to hit female suspects because of notions of chivalry or embarrassment.

Although women's gender may protect them from police beatings, it subjects them to **police sexual violence (PSV).** Such violence includes rape and other sexual assaults and unnecessary strip searches and body cavity searches by male officers. Peter B. Kraska and Victor E. Kappeler (Kraska and Kappeler 1995) examined newspaper accounts of PSV between 1991 and 1993 and federal lawsuits between 1978 and 1992 alleging PSV. Their research revealed 124 cases of PSV, with many more, they assumed, not reaching press or judicial attention. About 30 percent of the cases involved rape and other sexual assaults; 56 percent, strip and body cavity searches; and 15 percent, violations of privacy such as voyeurism.

The authors blamed PSV on at least three factors. The first is male officers' sexist ideology, which, as Chapter 11 noted, helps explain sexual violence against women in general. The remaining factors are more structural. The first of these concerns the "extreme power differential between policemen and female citizens" (Kraska and Kappeler 1995:106), which is even greater than the normal power differential underlying sexual violence in our society. The second structural factor concerns the "situational opportunity of the police to commit acts of PSV" (p. 107). Just as police are corrupt because they have many opportunities to be corrupt (see the following section), so do they commit PSV because they have opportunities to do so. As Kraska and Kappeler (p. 107) put it, "The police possess exceptional access to women, often in situations with little or no direct accountability."

POLICE MISCONDUCT: CORRUPTION

As they accompanied officers on their patrols, the observers in Reiss's 1966 government study also noticed police **corruption.** More than one-fifth of the officers engaged in at least one act of corruption, including taking bribes and stealing objects from stores they were checking (Reiss 1980a). As this figure suggests, the police corruption that existed during the 1800s remains common despite periodic investigations and exposés by the press and government commissions. The police in Reiss's study may even have been less corrupt than usual because they knew they were being observed.

Perhaps the most famous investigation was conducted in 1972 by the Knapp Commission (1973). The commission was established after New York City police officer Frank Serpico disclosed corruption by his fellow officers and then was set up by some of them and almost murdered. The commission found corruption throughout New York's police force that stemmed primarily from illegal drug trafficking and gambling. It divided corrupt officers into **meat-eaters** and **grass-eaters.** The former were a small percentage of all corrupt officers who pursued corruption aggressively and made the most money. Grass-eaters were more passive in their corruption and made less money, but lay at the heart of the problem by making corruption respectable, keeping quiet about the corruption, and threatening any officer who disobeyed this "code of silence" with physical injury or worse. One such officer was Serpico.

Police corruption arises from structural roots similar to those motivating brutality. The nature of police work fuels police perceptions that the public not only dislikes the police, but also fails to appreciate the hard job they do. Combine these perceptions with the many opportunities for police to obtain money through bribes and other forms of corruption and you inevitably end up with much corruption. This sort of explanation suggests that the problem of such "blue-coat crime" extends far beyond a "few rotten apples" and instead reflects a "rotten barrel" that will remain even if the "apples" are removed from the force. As a former Philadelphia police officer put it, "[P]olice corruption results from a system where honest police recruits are placed into a dishonest police subculture" (Birch 1984:120). As Chapter 15 discussed and as the Knapp Commission documented, illegal drug trafficking, gambling, and other consensual crimes are responsible for most of this corruption. This was true more than a century ago and remains true now. Legalizing these behaviors should reduce the corruption by drying up the opportunities police have for acquiring money illegally.

POLICE SCANDALS

Sometimes police brutality, corruption, and other misconduct become so rampant that, when discovered, they take on a new life as a full-fledged police *scandal* that reminds us of the dangers of having out-of-control police in a democratic society. One of the worst scandals occurred in Los Angeles and was revealed in early 2000. Months earlier, an LA police officer, Rafael Perez, had been arrested for stealing drugs. In return for a plea bargain, he told authorities that dozens of LA antigang police and supervisors in the city's Rampart Division and elsewhere had engaged in massive corruption, brutality, and other wrongdoing. Their acts included many beatings, several unjustified police shootings, the planting of weapons on their victims, the planting of illegal drugs on other citizens to justify false arrests, false testimony at trials, and the stealing of drugs and money. More than seventy officers eventually were investigated for either engaging in these acts or for covering them up.

In one case, Perez said he saw an officer plant a gun on a dying suspect and a supervisor delay an ambulance so that the officers involved in the unjustified shooting would have time to make up a story. In another act, police allegedly shot an unarmed man who was in handcuffs. In still another act, police allegedly used a suspect as a battering ram by banging his head on a wall when he would not lead police to a gun they were trying to find. Sometimes officers even reportedly had "shooting parties" in which they got awards for wounding or killing people. Because of the scandal, dozens of criminal convictions were overturned (Glover and Lait 2000a; Glover and Lait 2000b).

A similar scandal came to light a few years earlier in Philadelphia. There a group of police engaged in practices similar to those in Los Angeles, including false testimony, beatings, and planted evidence. About 300 convictions were overturned because of the scandal (Fazlollah 1997).

Review and Discuss

Why does police corruption occur? To what extent does the major blame lie with a few corrupt officers versus the nature of policing itself?

Police Discretion: To Arrest or Not to Arrest?

Officials make decisions at every stage of the criminal justice system. Police decide whether to arrest someone once they have identified a suspect. Once a person is arrested, a prosecutor decides whether to prosecute the case and which charges to bring against the defendant. The judge determines whether to require bail and how much bail should be required. A judge or jury decides whether to find the defendant guilty, and the judge determines how severe the sentence for a convicted offender will be. Such discretionary justice helps the criminal justice system remain flexible and individualized, but it also opens the system to the possibility of disparate treatment of suspects and defendants based on their race, social class, gender, and other extralegal variables.

The first stage of discretionary justice is the police officer's decision to arrest or cite someone for an alleged offense. As Shakespeare might have put it, to arrest or not to arrest, that is the **discretion.** The police arrest only a small percentage of all the suspects they encounter (Lyman 2010). What factors influence the chances of arrest? The two most important factors are the seriousness of the alleged offense and the strength of the evidence. Another factor is the relationship between the offender and victim. Arrest is more likely if the alleged offender and victim are strangers than if they know each other. Yet another factor is the *complainant's preference:* Arrest is more likely when complainants (i.e., victims) prefer arrest than when they do not. A final factor is the suspect's *demeanor:* suspects who are hostile toward the police are more likely to be arrested than respectful suspects (Engel, Sobol, and Worden 2000).

RACE, ETHNICITY, AND ARREST

Perhaps the most controversial issue in police discretion is whether arrest practices are racially discriminatory, an issue introduced in Chapter 3. In 2009, 28 percent of all persons arrested were African American, a figure that rose to 39 percent for violent crimes

International Focus

Police and Policing in Japan

In the United States, there are as many police forces as there are cities and towns, and they all have many different styles and sets of procedures. As a result, there is little standardization among U.S. police regarding training, equipment, or procedures. The situation is very different in Japan, because the Japanese police force is a branch of the national government called the National Police Agency (NPA). This allows the Japanese police to be more standardized than their U.S. counterparts. They all receive the same type of training and are expected to conform to the same sets of rules. At the same time, Japanese police are much more oriented toward community policing than most U.S. police are, because they operate at the level of the immediate neighborhood.

A key feature of the Japanese model of policing is a type of mini police station located in neighborhoods across the country. The mini station in urban neighborhoods is called the *koban,* and the mini station in rural areas is called the *chuzaisho.* Both sets of police stations are small operations. The *koban* usually has fewer than fifteen officers per shift and the *chuzaisho* is staffed by one officer.

The police at either kind of station integrate law enforcement with community service functions, and they typically solicit community input on crime and other problems. To do this, they often make house calls and use these calls to allow them and citizens to get to know one another better. They keep petty cash funds to help the homeless and other people in need of money, and their mini stations often include counseling rooms in which specially trained officers sit down to talk with families or individuals in need of help.

Another difference between U.S. and Japanese police lies in police decision making. In the United States, police management style follows a top-down model in which police supervisors command the officers under them and make almost all policy decisions. In Japan, police decision making is more consensual. Police officials still make decisions, but are expected to be aware of what the average officer thinks and to take rank-and-file views into account.

Compared to their U.S. counterparts, the Japanese police enjoy two significant advantages. One is the respect and gratitude of the public. In the United States, a cultural value of autonomy and distrust of authority underlies the hostility with which much of the public views police. In Japan, a cultural value of respect for authority and of harmonious relations prompts the Japanese citizenry to respect the police and to regard them as important public servants. The Japanese community-policing orientation reinforces the positive way the public views the police.

The other advantage enjoyed by the Japanese police is their nation's low crime rate. The high U.S. crime rate puts pressure on police to see themselves as law enforcement officers first and foremost and to view the public with suspicion. It also leads the U.S. public to see the police as inefficient and harassing. In contrast, the low Japanese crime rate allows the police to act more as public servants than as law enforcers and reinforces the public's positive view of police and policing in that nation.

Sources: Adelstein 2009; Parker 2001; Ueno 1994.

and 49 and 55.5 percent for homicides and robberies, respectively (Federal Bureau of Investigation 2009). Because African Americans comprise only 13 percent of the total population, there is ready evidence of disproportionate arrest of African Americans. The Uniform Crime Reports does not report arrest information for Latinos, who also comprise about 13 percent of the population, but they, too, are thought to be arrested disproportionately (Walker, Spohn, and DeLone 2007).

Perhaps the most controversial issue in policing is whether arrest practices are racially discriminatory.

The major debate is whether these groups' disproportionate arrests reflect police/ethnic racial prejudice, including unconscious bias, or, instead, simply their disproportionate involvement in street crime (see Chapter 3). The research evidence, as we will now see, is both complex and ambiguous.

A Review of the Evidence

Many white police, like many white civilians, are racially prejudiced, and there is ample evidence that police routinely harass African Americans and Latinos by stopping and questioning them for no apparent reason and by verbally abusing them (Brunson 2007; Stewart 2007). This practice became known a decade ago as *racial profiling,* or, more caustically when applied to traffic violations, *DWB (driving while black).* The Crime and Controversy box takes a further look at racial profiling.

If the police do engage in racial profiling involving harassment and traffic offenses, does that also mean they are more likely to *arrest* people of color for criminal offenses? Reiss's 1966 police observation study found police arresting a greater proportion of African-American suspects than white suspects, but it attributed this disparity to three reasons other than police racism: (1) African Americans tended to be suspected of more serious crimes than whites; (2) African-American suspects were more hostile than white suspects toward police; and (3) complainants (who were usually African American) in cases involving black suspects preferred arrest more often than did the (mostly white) complainants in cases involving white suspects (Black 1980). Other observation studies reach similar conclusions (Riksheim and Chermak 1993). Whether police might again be on their best behavior because they are being watched is an important question in interpreting these studies' results.

Further support for a conclusion of nonracism in arrest comes from the similarity of racial disparity in arrest data to that found in self-report and victimization studies. As Chapter 3 noted, self-report surveys and the National Crime Victimization Survey (NCVS) indicate disproportionate involvement in crime by people of color, including African Americans. To the extent that these crime measures are more valid measures of crime than the Uniform Crime Reports (UCR), they bolster the conclusion that racial disparities in arrest do not reflect police racism.

Other evidence disputes this conclusion. For one thing, the proportion of African Americans arrested exceeds the proportion of offenders identified by victims in the NCVS as being African American (see Figure 16.2). This difference suggests to some observers that African Americans are disproportionately likely to be arrested (Reiman and Leighton 2010). However, whether this is due to police racism or to some other factors (e.g., the nature of the crimes or even the possibility that victims are more likely to report crimes to the police when their offenders are black) remains unclear.

Better evidence for actual racial bias in arrest would come from observational studies. Although the observational studies cited earlier found no racial bias in arrest, others have found such evidence (Walker, Spohn, and DeLone 2007). Further, despite the finding in some studies that African-American suspects' hostile demeanor helps account for their

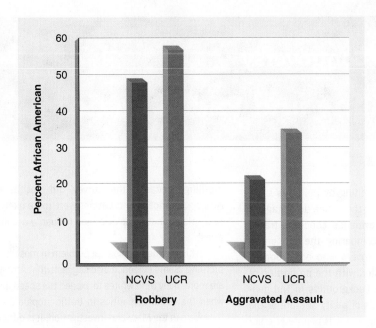

FIGURE 16.2 ▸ **Perceived Race of Offenders (NCVS) and Race of Persons Arrested (UCR), 2007**
Sources: Federal Bureau of Investigation 2008; Maston 2010.

greater likelihood of arrest, their demeanor may stem from hostile treatment by police and even from the arrest itself. Thus, "arrest may cause disrespect as much as disrespect causes arrest" (Sherman 1980:80).

In a more subtle form of police discrimination, race/ethnicity affects the strength of the evidence needed for arrest: Police tend not to arrest whites unless the evidence against them is fairly strong, whereas they often arrest African Americans and Latinos even when the evidence is fairly weak (Hagan and Zatz 1985; Petersilia 1983).

Where do all these findings leave us? A fair conclusion is that police arrest practices are racially biased to a degree, but that racial and ethnic disparities in arrest reflect disproportionate racial involvement in crime more than police bias (Tonry and Melewski 2008; Walker, Spohn, and DeLone 2007). As with police brutality, some arrests are undoubtedly racially motivated, but overall the higher arrest rates for African Americans and other people of color "are not substantially the result of bias" (Tonry 1994:71). This conclusion notwithstanding, the evidence that does exist of racial and ethnic bias in arrest and also the use of brutal and deadly force is troubling in a society whose Pledge of Allegiance professes "liberty and justice for all."

Race, Arrest, and the War on Drugs

So far we have explored racial and ethnic discrimination in arrest by focusing on the proportion of African Americans, Latinos, and whites who get arrested. This focus led to the conclusion of a lack of substantial bias in arrest. A much harsher conclusion is reached if we focus on arrests for one type of crime, illegal drug use (Golub, Johnson, and Dunlap 2007; Tonry and Melewski 2008). *Simply put, even though African Americans are no more likely than whites to use illegal drugs, they have been much more likely than whites to be arrested for the use of illegal drugs.* This disparity began in the mid-1980s, when the government intensified its legal war on drugs. This was mainly a war against crack cocaine, which African Americans tend to use and sell. In contrast, whites

Crime and Controversy

Racial Profiling and Racial Justice

The evidence on racial profiling by police is complex but does suggest that the police do engage in profiling. Much of the evidence concerns traffic stops, with the typical study comparing the proportion of African-American or Latino drivers who are stopped, ticketed, searched, and/or arrested with the proportion of people from these racial/ethnic backgrounds in the general population (i.e., the residents of a city or state or the drivers on a particular road or highway). If people of color are overrepresented among drivers who receive such treatment, this is evidence of a racial disparity that may reflect racial profiling.

Investigations in Maryland and New Jersey found strong evidence of profiling. In Maryland, for example, African Americans were 17 percent of the drivers on a major highway but 77 percent of all the drivers stopped by state troopers. The New Jersey investigation found that state troopers had targeted African-American and Latino drivers for alleged traffic violations and were three times more likely to search their cars than those of white drivers they stopped.

In the 2005 Police–Public Contact Survey discussed earlier in the text, equal proportions of African-American, Latino, and white drivers reported being stopped by police, but among all drivers stopped, African Americans (9.5 percent) and Latinos (8.8 percent) were more likely than whites (3.6 percent) to be searched by police. African Americans (4.5 percent) were also more likely than whites (2.1 percent) to be arrested during traffic stops. A government report that summarized the PPCS findings cautioned that they do not necessarily indicate racial and ethnic profiling, because the survey did not assess whether African Americans and Latinos were more likely than whites to display behavior or evidence to justify a police search or arrest.

This is a methodological problem in most studies of racial profiling. Some evidence also suggests that African Americans are more likely than whites to exceed the speed limit. However, when the racial disparities in traffic stops are very large, as they were in the Maryland investigation, it is difficult to believe that the driving behavior of people of color is so much worse than that of whites. In addition, African-American drivers in the PPCS were less likely than white and Latino drivers to say the police had a legitimate reason to stop them. Two criminologists said this finding suggests "more frequent police recourse to pretext when stopping drivers of color." In studies where racial disparities in traffic stops are smaller, racial profiling has been found to affect what happens to drivers after they are stopped.

Racial profiling may also affect which citizens get stopped and frisked while walking down the street or simply hanging out. A recent investigation in New York City found that African Americans and Latinos were much more likely than whites to be stopped by police and, once stopped, to be frisked. However, once stopped, they were not more likely to be arrested. In making these stops, police gave as the most common reasons "furtive movements" and "casing a victim or location." Because the three groups had the same arrest rates once stopped, the data strongly suggested that police were especially suspicious of the behavior of African Americans and Latinos simply because of their race/ethnicity.

Sources: Alpert, Dunham, and Smith 2007; Baker 2010b; Durose, Smith, and Langan 2007; Lundman and Kaufman 2003; Lundman and Kowalski 2009; Tomaskovic-Devey and Warren 2009.

prefer powder cocaine. Taking their cue from the congressional, media, and public concern over crack, police departments focused their efforts in poor African-American neighborhoods and ignored the use and sale of powder cocaine and other illegal drugs in wealthier white neighborhoods. The problem was aggravated by federal penalties that involved the same sentence for selling only 5 grams of crack as for selling 500 grams of powder cocaine.

Accordingly, drug arrests since the 1980s have had a huge racial impact, with African Americans, most of them young males, accounting for more than one-third of all drug arrests. This figure held true in 2009, when African Americans still comprised 34 percent of all drug arrests (Federal Bureau of Investigation 2010). As Figure 16.3 illustrates, the African-American arrest rate for drug offenses that year was 3.4 times higher than the white rate.

The racial discrimination suggested by these figures troubles many observers. As Alfred Blumstein (Blumstein 1993:4–5), a former president of the American Society of Criminology, observed, "What is particularly troublesome . . . is the degree to which the impact [of the drug war] has been so disproportionately imposed on nonwhites. There is no clear indication that the racial differences in arrest truly reflect different levels of [drug] activity or of harm imposed." Calling the war on drugs "a major assault on the

Evidence of racial discrimination in arrest is very complex. Some observation studies find such evidence, but other observation studies do not.

black community," Blumstein commented, "One can be reasonably confident that if a similar assault was affecting the white community, there would be a strong and effective effort to change either the laws or the enforcement policy" (p. 5). In addition to arrest, the drug war has also had a significant racial impact on incarceration, an issue examined further in Chapter 17.

Ecological Evidence for Racial Discrimination in Policing

The example of the war on drugs shows that racial discrimination in policing occurs if the police target a behavior popular among a subordinate racial group while ignoring similar behavior popular among wealthier whites. Similar discrimination occurs if police

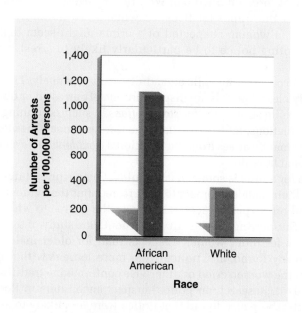

FIGURE 16.3 ▸ **Race and Arrest Rates for Drug Offenses, 2009** Sources: Federal Bureau of Investigation 2010; U.S. Bureau of the Census 2010.

resources are focused more on communities with high proportions of people of color than on those with lower proportions but similar crime rates. Drawing on Hubert Blalock's (1967) *racial-threat theory,* the idea here is that dominant groups (whites) feel more threatened as the size and power of minority groups grow, and they respond with legal measures and other actions to protect their dominant status.

Supporting this view, several studies find police-force size and police expenditures higher in cities with higher proportions of African Americans, even after controlling for crime rates (Kent and Jacobs 2005). Research also finds that increases in the 1960s and 1970s in spending on police resources were highest in cities with the greatest increases in black population, even with crime rates held constant (Jackson 1989).

Review and Discuss

To what degree does racial prejudice affect police decisions to arrest suspects? Explain your answer.

GENDER AND ARREST

The issue of gender discrimination in arrest is perhaps less controversial than its racial counterpart but no less interesting. In 2009, 74.7 percent of all people arrested were men, and more than 81 percent of people arrested for violent crimes (including more than 88 percent of those arrested for homicide and robbery) were men (Federal Bureau of Investigation 2010). Although almost all scholars say these high percentages reflect heavier male involvement in crime (Steffensmeier et al. 2006), they may also reflect more lenient treatment of women by police. This is the view of the *chivalry hypothesis,* which says that male police do not arrest female suspects because of notions of chivalry: They feel that women need to be protected, not punished; that arrest would harm them and their families; and that women do not pose a threat to society. Police may also be reluctant to arrest women because they do not want to have to use physical force on a woman who resists arrest. A contrasting *evil woman hypothesis* predicts the opposite: Because women are normally regarded as more virtuous than men, a woman suspected of a crime might seem that much worse by comparison, prompting police to be particularly likely to arrest her. What does the evidence say?

Here we have to consider juvenile and adult arrests separately. The evidence for juvenile arrests is fairly clear that girls are disproportionately arrested or otherwise brought to the attention of juvenile authorities for *status offenses,* such as running away from home, parental curfew violations, and premarital sexual intercourse (Chesney-Lind and Pasko 2004). This discrimination arises from the traditional *double-standard* view that girls need protection more than boys do.

The evidence for adults is somewhat complex. Female prostitutes, of course, are far more likely than their male customers to be arrested, but the evidence for other crimes appears to depend on suspects' race and age and the degree to which female suspects act "femininely." Supporting the chivalry argument, one study of the elderly found that arrest is less likely for older women suspects than for older male suspects (Shichor 1985). Another study found that police were more lenient with young women than young men only if the women cried or otherwise conformed to traditional female stereotypes (DeFleur 1975). Research on police–suspect encounters in Rochester, St. Louis, and Tampa–St. Petersburg also found that police were less likely to arrest older women and women who acted femininely. This study also found that police treated white women more leniently than they did black women, who were treated no more leniently than black men (Visher 1983).

Although receiving a traffic ticket for speeding is less serious than being arrested for a criminal offense, it is worth noting that the Police–Public Contact Survey discussed earlier found only a small gender difference in the chance of being ticketed after being stopped for speeding. Of the males stopped, 59.2 percent received a ticket; of the females stopped, 54.4 percent received a ticket, for a difference of less than 5 percent. The survey did not ask respondents how much they were exceeding the speed limit when stopped. If males tend to driver faster than females even if both sexes are speeding, it is possible that this may help account for the small gender difference in being ticketed. Although the PPCS ticketing data indicate that gender does not affect ticketing, or does so only to a small extent, a study of traffic-stop data from Florida found that males were more likely to be arrested after a stop. The authors of the study said their results may indicate "unconscious police bias" against males and in favor of females (Smith, Makarios, and Alpert 2006:289).

Impact of Policing on Crime

Do police make a difference in crime? On the face of it, this is an absurd question. Of course police make a difference in crime. If we had no police, we would probably have chaos. But when we ask whether police make a difference in crime, we are not posing an all-or-nothing alternative. Instead, we are asking whether more police (once some minimal threshold is reached) are more effective than fewer police in controlling crime, whether more arrests (again assuming a minimal threshold) are more effective than fewer arrests, and whether certain police practices are more effective than other practices. Answers to these questions obviously have important criminal justice policy implications. What does the evidence say?

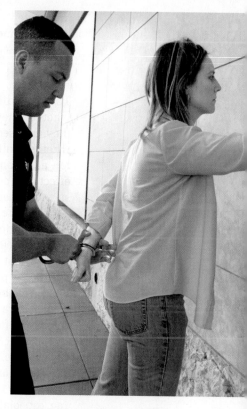

Whether women receive harsher or more lenient treatment in arrest compared to men appears to depend on the race and age of suspects and on the degree to which female suspects act in a feminine manner.

DO ADDITIONAL POLICE DETER CRIME?

Most studies find that additional police do not reduce the crime rate. For example, cities that have more police relative to their population size do not have lower crime rates than cities with fewer police (Worrall and Kovandzic 2007). However, one well-designed study did find that additional police reduce crime (Marvell and Moody 1996), suggesting to some scholars that additional police might indeed make a difference (Sherman et al. 1998). A widely cited study in Kansas City varied the number of patrol cars in different neighborhoods and found that the number of cars did not affect the crime rate (Kelling et al. 1974). Although this study suggested to many observers that additional police do not deter crime, it was criticized for several methodological problems (Larson 1975).

Several reasons explain why additional police may not matter or may not matter very much (Walker 2011). Even when additional police are hired by a city, the actual presence of police at a given place and at a given time hardly increases. Further, many violent crimes involve people who know each other and also occur indoors, where the police cannot see them and cannot prevent them. Even when more police are added, the risk of detection and arrest for public crimes such as robbery still remains low. Finally, as noted in Chapter 5, many criminals give little thought to their chances of arrest, and those who do so assume they can get away with it.

HOW POLICE ARE USED

The preceding discussion suggests that *how* police are used is at least as important as whether they are used in the first place. Evidence that the police can reduce crime if they are used properly arises from several kinds of research. One type of study explores whether police can deter crime in closed environments such as subway stations. Even a few additional officers in a subway station will be very visible, suggesting that a deterrent effect will occur, and research involving New York City subway and train stations finds such an effect (Chaiken, Lawless, and Stevenson 1975).

Other research examines the effects of *directed* police patrol, in which the police focus their attention on *hot spots* of crime, the relatively few locations at which most of the city's serious street crime occurs. A number of studies find that additional police patrol, by car and/on foot, of hot spots reduces crime in these locations compared to locations where additional patrol does not occur (Braga and Bond 2008; Mastrofski, Weisburd, and Braga 2010; Weisburd et al. 2006). Related research involves directed patrol in hot spots for *gun crime*. Here another experiment in Kansas City was telling. The experiment involved intensive efforts to take handguns from people who had them illegally. In a high-crime area of Kansas City, police officers trained in detecting concealed firearms stopped cars and pedestrians for legitimate reasons. They found many illegal handguns on the people they stopped. Gun seizures rose by 60 percent, and gun crimes dropped by 49 percent (Sherman and Rogan 1995). This and other studies suggest that efforts targeted at reducing gun carrying, especially that by urban youths, can reduce gun crimes (Walker 2011).

Crackdowns and Zero-Tolerance Policing

If directed patrol in hot spots can reduce crime at least in those locations, what about an even more intense police presence in the form of a police **crackdown?** Here police suddenly saturate a small area and arrest drug pushers, prostitutes, gang members, and others committing visible crime. For better or worse, research on crackdowns suggests that they offer little hope for reducing crime. Some studies find that crackdowns reduce drug trafficking and other crime in the target areas, but other research finds that crackdowns have no such effect (Sherman et al. 1998). Even when a deterrent effect is found, it tends to be short term only, as crime rates eventually return to their initial levels. Often the drug trafficking and other crimes are simply displaced to other neighborhoods. In another problem, crackdowns raise serious civil liberties questions for drug dealers and law-abiding citizens alike and flood the courts and jails with new defendants and inmates. Crackdowns thus appear to be at best a quick fix to the crime problem with no long-term effects, and have had little success in the war against drugs. As Elliott Currie (1994:206) put it, "On balance, it is not that crackdowns make no difference, but that, especially where drug dealing is heaviest and most widespread, any effects they have are likely to be short-lived."

Directed police patrolling, in which the police focus on hot-spot locations for crime, appears to be able to reduce the amount of crime at these locations.

ZERO-TOLERANCE POLICING

If crackdowns do have short-term effects, these results probably stem from the heightened visibility of police. Assuming this connection, several police departments, especially those in New York City, began in the 1990s to use an ongoing, aggressive style of **zero-tolerance policing** that falls short of a crackdown, but is more intense than directed policing. It involves frequent traffic stops and questioning of suspicious persons and frequent arrests for disorderly conduct, vagrancy, and other minor offenses. It is possible that such visible, aggressive policing may lower crime rates by increasing the chances that criminals get arrested and by deterring potential criminals from breaking the law. Zero-tolerance policing may also reduce *incivilities* such as disorderly youth and public drunkenness, which prompt potential offenders to think that residents do not care what happens in their neighborhoods—in short, that "anything goes." This may be another reason such aggressive policing can lower crime rates (Kelling and Coles 1998).

Zero-tolerance policing raises important civil liberties questions, and complaints of racial harassment by police increased after zero-tolerance policing was begun in New York City (Herbert 2000). Moreover, zero-tolerance policing may not live up to its advocates' claims. For example, although New York's crime rate declined after it introduced zero-tolerance policing, crime rates also declined in many other large cities where zero-tolerance policing was not used (Butterfield 2000). New York's crime rate had also begun declining before zero-tolerance policing began.

Actual research on New York's zero-tolerance policing yields only mixed results (Kubrin et al. 2010); some studies conclude it did not reduce New York's crime rate at all (Harcourt and Ludwig 2007), and some studies conclude it had a small effect on the city's crime but that "substantial crime reductions" would probably have occurred even without it (Messner et al. 2007:377; Rosenfeld, Fornango, and Rengifo 2007). However, a study of a similar policy, *proactive policing* (measured as the number of arrests for drunk driving and disorderly conduct divided by the number of police officers), in cities across the country found a link between such policing and lower robbery rates (Kubrin et al. 2010). The authors still cautioned that "whatever the deterrent effects of proactive or any other policing style might prove to be, policy decisions need to be informed not only by considerations of crime control but by the fundamental values of a democratic society" (Kubrin et al. 2010:85).

Review and Discuss

Would a change in policing strategy help to reduce the crime rate? Why or why not?

DOES ARREST MAKE A DIFFERENCE?

When we ask whether arrest makes a difference in crime rates, we are not talking about some arrests versus no arrests; instead we are considering more arrests versus fewer arrests. A common line of investigation determines an arrest or *certainty* ratio for states or cities by dividing a location's number of annual arrests by its official number of crimes for that location. The resulting ratio provides a rough measure of the chances that a crime will lead to an arrest.

A police **deterrence** hypothesis would predict that locations with higher certainty ratios should have lower crime rates than locations with lower ratios. This correlation is usually found, but it is difficult to interpret because of the familiar chicken-and-egg question: Which comes first, the certainty of arrest or the crime rate? Although a deterrence view would interpret this correlation as support for its perspective, it is also possible that crime rates affect certainty rates. In this view, police in areas with low crime rates will be able to devote more resources to solving the few crimes they do have and thus be able to solve more crimes through arrest, creating high certainty ratios. Conversely, police in areas with high crime rates will simply not have the time or resources to investigate many crimes, resulting in low certainty ratios. These possibilities support a *system capacity* argument (see Chapter 5) and are at least as compelling as deterrence views (Decker and Kohfeld 1985; Pontell 1984). If so, the evidence on certainty ratios and crime rates cannot be interpreted as supporting the deterrence hypothesis.

To investigate these possibilities, studies looking at certainty ratios and crime rates over time are necessary. Several such studies find little or no impact of arrest certainty (or, to be more precise, changes in arrest certainty) on crime rates. A review concluded that these studies "provide little, if any, evidence consistent with the general deterrence perspective" (Chamlin 1991:188). However, a later study indicated that arrest does make a difference. Stewart J. D'Alessio and Lisa Stolzenberg (1998) studied arrests and the number of crimes in greater Orlando, Florida over a 184-day period. The number of daily arrests ranged from 8 to 104, with an average of almost 54 per day. The authors concluded that "as the number of arrests made by police increases, criminal activity decreases substantially the following day" (p. 748), probably because word gets around after an arrest and deters potential offenders from committing a crime.

A fair conclusion from the arrest-deterrence literature is that arrests reduce crime only to the extent that potential offenders become more concerned about being arrested. This might happen because they hear about an arrest, as in the Orlando study, or because they see more police out and about, as the directed patrol research discussed in the last section suggests.

COMMUNITY POLICING

Community policing (also called *problem-oriented policing*) has become more popular. In this style of policing, police work closely with community groups and residents on various activities designed to reduce crime, including youth programs, cleanup projects, meetings with juvenile gangs, and replacing car patrol with foot patrol. These strategies allow police officers and citizens to get to know each other better and humanize the police to the citizenry. In return, citizens are more likely to trust the police, to report crimes to them, and to work with them on community projects. Foot patrol also allows officers to notice trash and other neighborhood incivilities that contribute to fear of crime and to bring these incivilities to the attention of local officials (Peak and W. Glensor 2008). Several very comprehensive community policing programs have been implemented in several cities, and research shows that these programs reduce crime (Braga et al. 2008; Weisburd et al. 2010). As Walker (2011:347) concludes from this body of research, "Focused, problem-oriented policing programs that involve partnerships and utilize a range of strategies can reduce serious crime."

LEGAL TECHNICALITIES AND POLICE EFFECTIVENESS

Many critics charge that the Warren Court's rulings in the 1960s forced the police to fight crime with one hand tied behind their backs. Suspects and defendants now have too many rights, the critics say, forcing the police not to arrest them or prosecutors to release them. In either case, public safety suffers as the law shackles police and prevents them from doing their job. Reduce the controls on police and they will be able to arrest more criminals and otherwise do a better job of keeping the public safe.

The two Court rulings most under attack are the ones that developed the **exclusionary rule** and the *Miranda* warning. In the first case, the Court ruled in *Mapp v. Ohio* (367 U.S. 643 [1961]) that evidence obtained by police in violation of the Fourth Amendment of the Constitution cannot be used in court. In the second case, the Court ruled in *Miranda v. Arizona* (384 U.S. 436 [1966]) that police must advise suspects that they may remain silent, that anything they say may be used against them, and that they have the right to have an attorney present during questioning.

How valid is the argument that these rules restrict arrests, let criminals go free, and raise our crime rates? Several considerations suggest that it is not valid at all. For example, because so few offenders are arrested at all (see Chapter 3), even if the police could arrest more people if legal **technicalities** were reduced, these extra arrests would probably have little effect on the crime rate.

Moreover, legal technicalities do not even seem to inhibit arrests. The clear conclusion from many studies is that very few suspects are freed because of the exclusionary rule. Of more than 500,000 felony arrests in California between 1976 and 1979, for example, prosecutors dismissed only 4,130 cases, or less than 1 percent, because of illegally obtained evidence (Fyfe 1983). The cases dismissed tend to be drug cases, in which police sometimes conduct improper searches to find the drugs, and not violent crimes. Walker (2011:113) concludes, "The exclusionary rule does not let 'thousands' of dangerous criminals loose on the streets, and it has almost no effect on violent crime."

The *Miranda* warning also has not impeded the police. Walker (2011) points out that most suspects confess anyway, because the evidence against them is often substantial and they want to plea bargain to reduce their sentence. Police also have various ways of getting around the *Miranda* warning. They are required to give suspects the warning only when they are about to ask them questions. If a suspect confesses or provides other information before questioning has begun, this evidence is admissible. Some officers also continue questioning suspects even after they give the *Miranda* warning and eventually wear them down, sometimes leading to confessions by innocent people (Hoffman 1998). Walker (2011:117) concludes that "repeal or modification of the *Miranda* warning will not result in more convictions."

IMPACT OF POLICING ON CRIME REVISITED

Overall, the literature on police, arrest, and crime rates suggests that intelligent policing strategies can reduce crime rates. These strategies include directed patrol and community policing, but they do not include crackdowns, or the simple addition of police officers without regard to how they are used. Zero-tolerance policing might also work, but the mixed results overall leave its actual impact unclear, and such policing may lead to abuse of police powers and worsen civilian–police relationships, if New York City's experience is any indication.

It is less clear how these policing strategies can reduce the many crimes of violence, including much homicide and assault, rape, domestic violence, and child abuse, that typically occur behind closed doors among people who know each other. Also, these policing strategies certainly leave white-collar crime untouched, which should not be forgotten in this discussion. Another problem is money. Even if additional police and directed patrol could reduce subway crime and some robberies and burglaries, the financial cost of each deterred crime is large and perhaps prohibitive. For example, the study of police in New York City subway and trains stations (cited earlier) determined that each reduced felony cost the city some $125,000 in today's dollars (Chaiken, Lawless, and Stevenson 1975). Finally, intensified police efforts at crime control also raise serious civil liberties questions for a democratic society.

Women and People of Color in Police Forces

In a democratic society in which everyone is held equal under the law, everyone should also be equal *in* the law. All citizens, regardless of gender, race, or ethnicity, should have the same opportunity to become police officers and should be treated equally if and when they do join the police. Because police are our first line of defense in creating order under law, anything less than equitable recruitment and treatment is unacceptable. Thus, another dilemma of crime control in a democratic society is ensuring that equality prevails in the recruitment of police and in their treatment once on the job.

With these ideals in mind, how equitable is our law enforcement institution? Not too long ago, few people of color and hardly any women were on our police forces. In the past few decades, more women and people of color have joined police forces, and conditions for them on the job have improved. As the old saying goes, however, the more things change, the more they stay the same. People of color and women still face obstacles in joining police forces and in their treatment by other officers and opportunities for advancement once they are on the job.

Let's look first at race and ethnicity issues in police work. On the eve of World War II more than a half century ago, only 1 percent of all U.S. police officers were people of color. This figure rose to 2 percent in 1950, almost 4 percent in 1960, and about 6 percent by 1970. One result of the urban riots of the 1960s was increased pressure for the recruitment of more people of color. Coupled with new affirmative-action hiring regulations, recruitment of people of color into police forces accelerated in the 1980s. Today about 20 percent, or one-fifth, of all sworn officers in the United States are people of color, although their proportion varies greatly from one city to another (Walker, Spohn, and DeLone 2007). This variation reflects differences not only in city racial composition, but also in the cities' police recruitment policies and efforts.

Once they are on the police force, people of color face obstacles that their white counterparts do not (Lyman 2010). They tend to be denied prestigious positions on special anticrime units and undercover patrols and are far less likely than their white peers to be promoted. Their chances for promotion are greatest in cities with the largest populations of people of color. Not surprisingly, the racial prejudice of many white officers often contaminates their relationships with officers who are not white. African-American officers in Los Angeles and elsewhere have reported bigoted comments and discriminatory treatment by white officers.

Women police officers also face **discrimination,** but of a different sort (Lord and Peak 2005). Women comprise about 10 percent of all police officers, but policing is still seen as "men's work" in many police departments. Women officers thus confront many of the same problems that women entering other male-dominated occupations have faced, including sexual harassment. But because police work sometimes involves dangerous confrontations with suspects, women officers face the additional burden of overcoming widespread doubts about their

Women and people of color have joined police forces in increasing numbers, but still face many obstacles.

ability to handle themselves during such incidents. Studies of this issue find women officers at least as capable as male officers in persuading or subduing suspects to submit to arrest (Harrington and Lonsway 2004).

Research on African-American and other women officers of color indicate that they face a **double burden** of both racism and sexism (Martin 2004). In an early example, an African-American officer, Cheryl Gomez-Preston, was transferred to the largest precinct in Detroit in 1982, only to receive from fellow officers written racial slurs such as "n——bitch," "die, bitch," and "go back to Africa." When she went to her commanding officer to tell him about these notes, he responded by showing her pictures of nude women in pornographic magazines. Once, when she and six other officers were chasing an armed robbery suspect, the other officers failed to back her up when she confronted the suspect as he tried to pull out his gun. Gomez-Preston eventually sued the Detroit Police Department for sexual harassment and won a jury award of $675,000 (Gomez-Preston and Trescott 1995).

Susan E. Martin (2004) wrote that, historically, white women have been "put on a pedestal" by being considered frail and in need of male protection. In contrast, African-American women have been considered very capable of performing physical labor. These stereotypes contribute to differences in the tasks assigned to African-American and white female officers. In particular, white women are more likely than African-American women to be given station house duties instead of more dangerous street patrol assignments. On patrol, white male officers typically back up white female officers, but often fail to back up African-American female officers, as Gomez-Preston's experience illustrates. In the station house, women of both races encounter hostility from male officers, but African-American women experience more problems than white women. Martin found that African-American women officers resent the preferential treatment that their white counterparts receive, and white women accept many of the racially stereotyped views that white male officers espouse. All these differences contribute to deep divisions between African-American and white women in police forces and prevent them from acting together to fight sexism in policing.

Conclusion

Policing in a democratic society is filled with dilemmas. First and foremost, the police must enforce the law while staying within it. The delicate balance between police powers and democratic rights remains a hotly debated topic. The evidence is clear, however, that judicial restrictions on police powers do not hamper police officers' ability to fight crime and protect public safety. Directed patrol does appear to reduce crime, but cost and civil liberties questions remain significant issues. Problem-oriented policy also appears to reduce crime, but cost again is a significant issue.

In a democratic society, police also need to exercise their discretion without regard to race, gender, or other extralegal variables. Experts continue to disagree on whether police practices in arrest and brutality differ by race/ethnicity and gender. Certainly, there is evidence to support very different conclusions. A fair conclusion, but one with which partisans on either side of the discretion debate will disagree, is that race/ethnicity and gender play a small but significant role in police behavior.

Regardless of this issue, it is clear that, for better or worse, the police pay more attention to crimes by the poor than by the wealthy. Historically, the police arrested and beat up workers who were protesting horrible wages and working conditions, but they did not arrest company officials for their mistreatment of their workers. In contemporary times, the police arrest poor street criminals, but largely ignore wealthy white-collar criminals. This social class difference in today's policing reflects larger social and institutional priorities, including the public's concern over street crime and lack of concern over its white-collar counterpart.

We now turn to the remaining stages of the criminal justice system and continue focusing on the two major themes introduced in this chapter: the extent to which race or ethnicity, gender, and class biases affect the exercise of legal discretion and the ability of the criminal justice system to control crime.

16

Summary

1. Herbert Packer's crime-control and due process models remind us that democratic societies face difficult questions of maintaining order while remaining a free society. Because the police have great powers over civilians, it is important, but very difficult, for society to strike the correct balance between crime control and due process. It is also important for a democratic society to ensure that the criminal justice system treats people the same regardless of their race, ethnicity, social class, gender, or other extralegal characteristics.

2. A major impetus for the development of the modern police force in England and later the United States was mob violence and the general unruliness of what were called the "dangerous classes." Early U.S. police forces were notoriously corrupt and brutal and of little help against crime.

3. The nature of police work contributes to a working personality of police officers that tends to be authoritarian, cynical, and suspicious. It also contributes to a strong feeling of loyalty among police officers and an "us against them" mentality in their relations with the public.

4. Although tens of thousands of acts of excessive force by police may occur annually, these acts comprise a very small proportion of all police–citizen encounters. Although the evidence is complex, it does not appear that racial prejudice plays a large role in the excessive force experienced by African Americans. To the extent that prejudice plays any such role, policing is not as blind as it should be in a democracy.

5. Police corruption in the form of bribery and other illegal behavior arises from the nature of police work and from the opportunities available to police to be corrupt. Scholars believe that police corruption extends beyond a few "rotten apples" to the entire culture of policing.

6. Legal factors such as the strength of the evidence play the largest role in decisions by police to arrest suspects. The evidence on racial bias in arrests is again very complex, but such bias does not appear to play a substantial role. The legal war against drugs has had a strong racially discriminatory effect, given that African Americans and Latinos are being arrested for drug offenses far out of proportion to their actual use of illegal drugs.

7. The evidence on gender bias and arrest is also complex. Whether women receive favorable treatment depends on whether they act femininely and perhaps also on their race. White women seem more likely than black women to avoid arrest for similar offenses.

8. Additional police do not appear to deter crime in and of themselves. What appears more important is how additional police are deployed, with directed policing in high-crime areas a promising strategy. Aggressive, zero-tolerance policing has won much

acclaim in the popular media, but research on its crime-reduction effects is very mixed.

9. Community policing is another popular crime-control strategy. It appears to produce more positive civilian perceptions of the police, but studies of its effectiveness in lowering the crime rate yield mixed results.

10. The *Miranda* ruling and the exclusionary rule are two examples of legal technicalities that are popularly thought to hamper the police. However, studies of this possible effect do not confirm this belief.

11. Women and people of color have joined the ranks of police forces in recent decades, but they continue to face many kinds of obstacles in their workplaces. Black women officers face a double burden of being both black and female that hampers their ability to achieve respect and promotions in their careers.

Key Terms

brutality 404

community policing 420

constable 402

corruption 409

crackdown 418

crime control 400

democratic society 400

deterrence 419

discretion 410

discrimination 422

double burden 423

due process 400

exclusionary rule 421

extralegal 401

grass-eaters 409

meat-eaters 409

police sexual violence (PSV) 408

technicalities 421

working personality 403

zero-tolerance policing 419

What Would You Do?

1. It's Saturday morning and you just began a 400-mile trip to visit some close friends in a nearby state for the weekend. Although the speed limit is 65 mph, you're cruising along at about 75. Even so, many cars have already passed you. Suddenly you see some flashing lights in your rearview mirror. You pull over, and the officer approaches your car and asks to see your license, registration, and proof of insurance. The officer then tells you you were going 75. When you begin to protest that you were probably the slowest car on the road, the officer gets angry, tells you to be quiet, and asks for permission to search your car. What is your reaction?

2. You're a server at a local restaurant and have been waiting on a table occupied by two police officers eating lunch. When they finish, you bring them the check. One of the officers says, "You don't expect us to pay that bill, do you?" and they both get up to leave. What do you do?

CHAPTER

seventeen

Prosecution
and Punishment

Crime in the News

onald Kitchen is lucky to be alive. In July 2009, he was released from prison in Illinois after spending thirteen years on death row, and twenty-one years behind bars altogether, for five murders he did not commit. In 1988, he and a codefendant, who was given a life sentence, were convicted in the deaths of two women and three children. Kitchen said he confessed to the murders after being beaten by police. According to a news report, the beating included "being hit in the head with a telephone, punched in the face, struck in the groin and kicked." Evidence at his trial also included testimony by a friend who was in prison at the time. The witness claimed that Kitchen had revealed his involvement in the murders in two telephone calls between them. Prosecutors failed to tell the defense that this informant was released from prison early in return for his testimony, and phone records later showed the two men did not talk on the dates the witness said they talked.

In commenting on Kitchen and his codefendant, a state official said, "In this case it became extraordinarily clear that justice required the release of these two men." Kitchen became the nation's 133rd death row inmate to be freed since the early 1970s after investigations determined their innocence or raised serious doubts about their guilt.

Sources: Walberg and Sadovi 2009; Walberg 2009.

Policing is only the first stage of the criminal justice process. After an arrest, the prosecutor determines whether to prosecute the case or to drop it, and the judge decides how much bail to require. If the decision is to prosecute, the prosecutor then determines what charges to bring against the defendant. The defendant must decide whether to plead guilty, which most do, or to plead not guilty and have a trial. At the end of the trial a jury or judge decides on the verdict. If the defendant pleads guilty or is found guilty after a trial, the judge next determines the punishment. Here the judge's major decision is whether to incarcerate the defendant by putting him or her behind bars. If the decision is to incarcerate, the judge must also determine the length of the sentence.

No doubt you are already familiar with these basic stages of the legal process. But notice that decisions are made at every stage, with each creating the possibility of mistakes and/or bias for or against defendants because of their race or ethnicity, gender, social class, or other extralegal factors. The Ronald Kitchen case described in the Crime in the News story is just one example of the injustice that can result. Much of this chapter examines the extent to which mistakes and bias exist. As with arrest, we will see that the evidence is very complex.

Another major issue in criminal justice today is whether a "get tough" approach involving mandatory sentences and longer prison terms can reduce crime. This chapter examines this issue. Most criminologists think this approach is short-sighted, even as most politicians and members of the public call for tougher treatment of criminals involving longer prison terms and the building of more prisons.

This chapter, then, continues the themes of the last chapter on policing: the extent to which social inequality affects the exercise of legal **discretion** and the extent to which reliance on the criminal justice system can reduce crime. These are arguably the two most important issues for a sociological understanding of criminal justice and they deserve our full attention.

Criminal Courts and the Adversary System

The United States has long been said to have an **adversary system** of criminal justice. The adversary model is one of combat. Like the knights of old, prosecutor and defense attorney fight each other with all the weapons at their disposal. Their weapons are not lances or swords, but rather their legal skills and powers of oratory, with which they vigorously contest the evidence as the judge referees their fight. The fate of the defendant lies in the balance, just as the fate of the proverbial "fair maiden" lay in the balance in the old, and probably sexist, knightly tales of mortal combat.

This exciting image of the courtroom process is the setting for many novels, films, and TV shows. Unfortunately, the adversary system is largely a myth. Although the most serious and/or publicized cases do follow the adversary model, most cases involve poor, unknown defendants. Few of these run-of-the-mill defendants can afford expensive attorneys and instead are forced to go with overworked and underpaid public defenders or court-appointed attorneys who

The adversary system, in which a prosecutor and defense attorney are said to vigorously contest the evidence at a trial refereed by a judge, is largely a myth.

usually provide them only perfunctory representation. Not surprisingly, most of these defendants plead guilty.

This was the central finding of work by sociologists and other scholars that began in the 1960s, as researchers studied how the criminal courts really worked, not how they claimed to work. A series of scholarly articles and books and journalistic accounts documenting the lack of equal justice and adversarial justice came out in rapid succession.

NORMAL CRIMES AND THE FATE OF POOR DEFENDANTS

In one of the most influential studies, David Sudnow (1965) developed the concept of the *normal crime* and applied it to cases involving poor defendants. He argued that prosecutors and public defenders develop the same idea of what constitutes a typical or "normal" crime based on the strength of the evidence, the seriousness of the charges, and the defendant's prior record. These assumptions allow them to classify particular crimes as either serious or minor cases and to quickly dispose of them through guilty pleas by agreeing on appropriate punishment for the defendant.

Sudnow concluded that the courts feature much more cooperation than combat between prosecutors and public defenders. Other work extended his view to private counsel assigned by judges to represent poor defendants and even to private defense attorneys paid by defendants. Abraham S. Blumberg (1967) said that the latter sell out their clients in a "confidence game" in which they do little for their clients, but pretend to do a lot. Their object is to collect their fees while minimizing the time spent on any one case. Blumberg further termed defense attorneys "double agents" for cooperating with prosecutors to obtain guilty pleas instead of vigorously defending their clients.

In short, this early body of work charged that poor but innocent defendants were being railroaded into pleading guilty by lawyers who cared more for courts' administrative needs and their own professional needs than for their clients' well-being. Urban courts were depicted as assembly lines in which the typical defendant, accused of a misdemeanor or minor felony, spends at most a few moments with a public defender or assigned counsel before pleading guilty. Public defenders and assigned counsel were depicted as undertrained and overworked and urban courtrooms as dismal, dirty, and crowded settings (Downie 1972; Mather 1973). These works were especially critical of rampant **plea bargaining,** which was said to deny defendants due process: "A lawyer who knows next to nothing about his client or the facts of the crime with which he is charged barters away a man's right to a trial, and, along with it, the presumption that a defendant is innocent until proved guilty" (Downie 1972:23).

PROSECUTORS, THE COURTROOM WORK GROUP, AND PLEA BARGAINING

Like other members of the courtroom work group, judges recognize that plea bargaining expedites the processing of large caseloads.

This early body of work was soon followed by a new wave of scholarship, much of it by political scientists, that refined our understanding of the flow of criminal cases after arrest. It stressed that heavy **caseloads** burden prosecutors, public defenders and other defense attorneys, and judges alike. Recognizing this, the **courtroom work group** consisting of all three parties realizes that the best thing for everyone is to resolve the case as quickly as possible through a guilty plea. Plea bargaining thus accounts for at least 90 percent of all guilty verdicts in many jurisdictions, and judge or jury trials are relatively rare (Eisenstein and Jacob 1977).

For prosecutors, who simply cannot afford to prosecute all the cases the police hand them, plea bargaining ensures convictions and helps process huge caseloads as quickly as possible. Prosecutors usually do not proceed with a case without being fairly confident that a jury would find the defendant guilty. They thus drop up to half of all felony arrests because of weak evidence or lack of cooperation from victims and other witnesses. To decide which cases to drop or plea bargain, prosecutors determine whether the case is a strong one from their perspective.

Several elements make up such a case: (1) a serious offense (e.g., murder compared to simple assault); (2) an injured victim; (3) strong evidence, including eyewitnesses or recovered weapons or stolen property; (4) the defendant's use of a weapon; (5) defendants with serious prior records; and (6) a "stand-up" victim whom "the jury would believe and consider undeserving of victimization" (Myers 2000:452). Ideally, these are victims who are articulate, who have no criminal background, who did not know their offender, and who did nothing to cause their victimization. If victims do not fit this profile or are unwilling to cooperate, prosecutors often drop the charges altogether or reduce them as part of a plea bargain.

The cases remaining after this initial screening are those in which the evidence is strongest and the charges the most serious. These are the best cases from the prosecutor's stand point because most of these defendants are probably guilty of the crime for which they were arrested. Given this likelihood, the new scholarship said, plea bargaining does not constitute the miscarriage of justice that earlier critics had cited. If anything, it helps defendants because they cannot be certain what sentence they would receive if they insisted on their right to a jury trial and were then found guilty. Recognizing this, most defendants in fact favor guilty pleas. Guilty pleas also resolve their cases much sooner, which shortens the time until defendants can resume their normal lives. Because defense attorneys realize all this, they are usually very willing to plea bargain instead of taking the case to trial (Eisenstein and Jacob 1977).

The new scholarship further challenged critics' charges that plea bargaining lets serious offenders off too lightly. When the courtroom work group determines the sentence for serious offenses and chronic offenders, little actual bargaining over the sentence occurs, because the courtroom work group already knows what the sentence will be. Suspects guilty of serious crimes thus receive stiff sentences even if they plead guilty (Feeley 1979). These sentences are at least as harsh as those for similar crimes in other Western nations and often harsher (Kappeler and Potter 2005).

Although the new scholarship took a more benign view of plea bargaining than did the earlier critiques, it still supported their view that courtroom work groups usually fail to vigorously contest the guilt of defendants. For better or worse, the adversary model is largely a myth for most criminal cases.

Review and Discuss

How does the concept of the courtroom work group help us understand why so much plea bargaining occurs? Do you think plea bargaining is good or bad? Why?

Punishment, Social Structure, and Inequality

Since the time of Émile Durkheim, punishment has been central to sociological theories of law and society. Durkheim (1933 [1893]) thought that punishment reinforced social stability by clarifying social norms and uniting conventional society against the deviants who are punished. He further argued that the social structure of a society helps determine the type of punishment it adopts. In small, traditional societies, the *collective conscience* (see Chapter 7) is extremely strong. When deviance occurs, these societies engage in **repressive law** marked by harsh physical punishment of deviants. In contrast, because the collective conscience is weaker in larger, modern societies, these societies deal with deviance through **restitutive law** marked by an interest in restoring relationships to their previous state. Restitution, such as payments to aggrieved parties, becomes a primary punishment. Such societies also develop prisons as a substitute for physical punishment (Durkheim 1983 [1901]).

Although some scholars question Durkheim's view of social evolution and punishment, his basic theme that a society's social structure influences its type of punishment remains compelling (Garland 1990). It is a basic theme, of course, of the work that falls under the broad rubric of conflict and radical theories (see Chapter 9). These theories see the inequality in society as a central influence on the type and severity of punishment and view legal punishment as a way for the ruling class to preserve its power by controlling the poor, people of color, and other subordinate groups.

ECONOMIC CONDITIONS AND PUNISHMENT

The classic statement on social structure and punishment is that of George Rusche and Otto Kirchheimer (1939), who contended that imprisonment increases when unemployment increases. Higher unemployment, they said, generates anger and rebellion. To counter this, the ruling class puts more of the poor behind bars when unemployment rises. This action helps intimidate the poor from rebelling and also reduces their labor supply, leaving fewer of them to compete for scarce jobs. The greater job prospects that result reduce the poor's anger and thus their potential for revolt.

Research on Unemployment and Imprisonment

Several studies have since tested Rusche and Kirchheimer's view. The evidence is inconsistent. Some studies have found that unemployed defendants are more likely than their employed counterparts to be imprisoned and that **incarceration** is higher in locations with higher unemployment (Chiricos and Delone 1992), but other studies have not found the presumed relationship or have found it in some locations but not in others (Nobiling, Spohn, and DeLone 1998).

These mixed results suggest that Rusche and Kirchheimer overestimated the importance of unemployment and underestimated the importance of other factors affecting incarceration rates (Sutton 2004). However, Raymond J. Michalowski and Susan M. Carlson (1999) found that the unemployment–imprisonment relationship is stronger for some periods of U.S. history than for others and speculated that the inconsistent findings reflect the fact that various studies have used data from various periods of U.S. history. Yet a recent study of business cycles and imprisonment in fifteen Western democracies did not find the presumed unemployment–imprisonment link once certain political and institutional factors were taken into account (Sutton 2004). As these contradictory findings suggest, the link between unemployment and incarceration remains unproven.

Research on the Postbellum South

Another line of research on economic conditions and punishment focuses on the African-American experience in the postbellum (post–Civil War) South. Much of this research is inspired by Blalock's (1967) *racial-threat theory* (see Chapter 16). Supporting the theory,

Crime and Controversy

Should Felons Lose the Right to Vote?

When they are sentenced to prison or jail, convicted criminals lose certain rights, most importantly their freedom. In recent years the loss of another right, voting, has become a controversial social, political, and policy issue. All but two states, Maine and Vermont, prohibit prison inmates from voting if they were convicted of a felony. The key difference among states regarding felony disenfranchisement occurs after felons are released from prison. Fifteen states, including Maine and Vermont, permit felons to vote once they are released from prison, even if they are on parole, but thirty-five states do not let them vote while they are on parole. Two states deny felons the right to vote permanently, and nine (Gotsch 2007) states deny the right to vote to certain kinds of ex-offenders or allow certain released convicts to vote only after several years have passed.

The estimated number of felons and ex-felons who are prohibited from voting permanently or currently is 5.3 million, equal to about 2.4 percent of all U.S. adults. This figure includes 1.4 million African-American men, equal to 13 percent of these men; in several states, this proportion is much higher. It is estimated that 30 percent of African-American men will be disenfranchised for a felony conviction at some point in their lives.

Felony disenfranchisement became an issue in the 2000 and 2004 presidential elections, but also raises larger questions of criminal justice policy. In 2000, 600,000 ex-felons were not allowed to vote in Florida. Because George Bush was deemed by the U.S. Supreme Court to have won Florida and its electoral votes (and thus the presidential election) by the narrowest of margins, 537 votes, the exclusion of

felons from the voting booths took on enormous importance. Most of the felons were African American, and most would probably have voted for Bush's opponent, Vice President Al Gore, had they been allowed to vote. Because Bush won Florida by so few votes, the felon vote would certainly have enabled Gore to win Florida and, with it, the presidency.

Florida's experience raises the issue of the political impact of prohibiting felons from voting. In a comprehensive study of this issue, Jeff Manza and Christopher Uggen found that felony disenfranchisement has affected the outcome of at least seven U.S. Senate elections and helped to ensure a Republican majority in the Senate in the early 1980s and mid-1990s. Other evidence suggests that felony disenfranchisement laws reduce voting even among people still allowed to vote, because going to the polls on election day is often a family event. If a member of the family is not allowed to vote, that person's spouse or partner may therefore not bother to vote.

The prohibition of felon voting also has important implications for criminal justice policy. Because hundreds of thousands of prisoners are released back into society each year, it is important that their reentry go as smoothly as possible to help keep them from committing new crimes. Many scholars feel that by refusing to let felons vote, society sends the wrong message and only embitters these ex-convicts. If they have served their sentences and paid their debt to society, these scholars say, then they should be allowed to vote. Presenting a different view, other observers say that felons should permanently forfeit their right to vote because they have indicated their disdain for society's rules and a lack of respect for society itself.

Sources: Manza and Uggen 2006; The Sentencing Project 2010.

imprisonment of African Americans for various offenses increased steadily during this period as Southern whites feared that the freed slaves would gain political and economic power (Myers 1990). Lynchings increased when African-American economic gains relative to whites were greatest and when the price of cotton was falling and threatening employment (Tolnay and Beck 1995). Imprisonment rates and sentence lengths of young African-American males accused of rape in Georgia also increased when cotton prices fell. Ironically, the increased imprisonment of African-American males for rape appears to have reduced their lynchings for the same accusation (Myers 1995).

Most contemporary work on punishment, social structure, and inequality focuses on class, racial or ethnic, and gender differences in prosecution and sentencing. Most studies analyze data on samples of individual defendants, but some analyze macro-level data from states, cities, and other areas. This body of work is both important and complex, and we explore it here in some detail, looking first at social class and then at race or ethnicity and gender.

SOCIAL CLASS AND LEGAL OUTCOMES

To test whether social class influences legal outcomes, researchers have examined the conviction and imprisonment rate and the average sentence length of criminal defendants. Although most of these defendants are

Lynchings were common in the South after the Civil War and well into the twentieth century. This picture of a New York lynching indicates that they also occurred outside the South.

poor, this research finds that the poorest defendants do not fare worse than less poor defendants after offense seriousness, prior record, and other factors are held constant (Myers 2000). Some observers view this lack of class differences in sentencing as contradicting conflict theory views (Chiricos and Waldo 1975).

Other scholars challenge this conclusion. Because most defendants are from lower- and working-class backgrounds, these scholars argue, there is too little income variation among them to allow class differences in outcomes to emerge, and there are too few middle- and upper-income defendants accused of street crimes with whom to compare them. Wealthy people, after all, rarely commit robbery, burglary, auto theft, or the like. Tests of class differences in sentencing and other outcomes are therefore meaningless (Shelden 1982). Further, wealthy defendants are certainly far more able than poor defendants to contest the evidence, because they can afford to hire highly skilled attorneys, private investigators, and other experts. In this manner, wealthy defendants are much more able to vigorously contest the evidence as envisioned by the adversary model. As Herbert Jacob (1978:185–186) observed,

> Those few defendants who are not poor can often escape the worst consequences of their involvement. . . . They can afford bail and thus avoid pretrial detention. They can obtain a private attorney who specializes in criminal work. They can usually obtain delays that help weaken the prosecution case. . . . They can enroll in diversion programs by seeking private psychiatric treatment or other medical assistance. They can keep their jobs and maintain their family relationships and, therefore, qualify as good probation risks. They can appeal their conviction (if, indeed, they are convicted) and delay serving their sentence.

Here the prosecution of O.J. Simpson (1994–1995) is instructive. Simpson was accused of two ghastly murders. Most poor defendants in his situation would have pleaded guilty or had a much shorter and more perfunctory trial handled by a lone public defender. Simpson's "dream team" defense cost $10 million, hundreds of thousands of

Criminal defendants who are wealthy are much more able than poor defendants to afford bail, to hire a skilled defense attorney, and to pay for investigators.

dollars of which helped pay for expert forensic and DNA witnesses who effectively challenged the credibility of the evidence against the wealthy, celebrated defendant, who was found not guilty (Barkan 1996).

The clearest class disparity in legal outcomes is seen by comparing poor defendants accused of street crime with much wealthier defendants accused of white-collar crime (Reiman and Leighton 2010). To recall a study mentioned in Chapter 13, Robert Tillman and Henry N. Pontell (1992) compared sentences received in California by Medicaid fraud defendants (physicians and other health care professionals) and grand theft defendants. Only 38 percent of the former were incarcerated, compared to 79 percent of the latter, even though the median economic loss from Medicaid fraud was ten times greater than the loss from grand theft.

Some may argue, of course, that street crimes should be treated more harshly than white-collar crimes because the public is so much more concerned about them. Notwithstanding this argument, the fact remains that criminal courts are "fundamentally courts against the poor" (Jacob 1978:185). The reason for this, wrote James Eisenstein and Herbert Jacob (1977:289), is that "the behaviors most severely punished by governmental power are those in which persons on the fringes of American society most readily engage. . . . Crimes (especially white-collar crimes) committed by other segments of the population attract less public attention, less scrutiny from the police, and less vigorous prosecution."

Community Context of Social Class and Sentencing

Most studies of social class and sentencing for street crime use individual-level data. Recent research has begun to explore a possible relationship at the community level. Prosecutors and judges may feel that defendants from poorer neighborhoods pose a greater threat than defendants who come from less poor neighborhoods. If so, the former defendants should receive harsher sentences than the latter defendants. Testing this hypothesis, John Wooldredge (2007) analyzed the sentences of almost 3,000 convicted felony defendants in Ohio. He found that defendants were indeed more likely to receive a prison term if they came from poorer neighborhoods, but that neighborhood disadvantage was unrelated to the sentence length among those who were incarcerated.

Review and Discuss

To what extent does social class affect legal outcomes?

IMPACT OF RACE AND ETHNICITY

Much research examines whether race and ethnicity influence the decisions of prosecutors, judges, and juries (Lynch, Patterson, and Childs 2008). We look first at research on prosecutorial decisions and then at studies of conviction and sentencing.

Prosecutorial Decisions

Several studies have explored whether race/ethnicity affects prosecutorial decisions to drop charges against defendants, or to bring more serious charges against defendants whose cases are not dropped. The evidence is mixed; some studies do find white defendants more likely than African-American and Latino defendants to have their charges dropped or reduced (Adams and Cutshall 1987; Hartley, Maddan, and Spohn 2007; Spohn, Gruhl, and Welch 1987), but other studies do not find this dynamic (Shermer and Johnson 2010).

In another type of racial discrimination, some studies have found that prosecutors bring more serious charges in homicide and rape cases when whites were victims than when African Americans were victims (Myers 2000). For example, people accused of killing whites are more likely to be indicted for first-degree murder, and thus are more likely to receive the death penalty if convicted, than people accused of killing African Americans. The charges in homicide and rape cases tend to be the most severe when African Americans are accused of victimizing whites. Such findings "raise the disturbing possibility that some prosecutors define the victimization of whites, especially when African Americans are perpetrators, as more serious criminal events than the comparable victimization of African Americans" (Myers 2000:451).

Conviction and Sentencing

African Americans and Latinos in the United States are far more likely than whites (non-Latino) to be in prison. In 2008, 38.4 percent of all prison inmates were African Americans and about 20.3 percent were Latinos, even though these groups comprise only 13 and 15 percent of the U.S. population respectively. Incarceration rates (the number of inmates per 100,000 residents of each race) present an even more vivid picture of racial disparity (see Figure 17.1). The rate for African Americans and Latinos of both sexes is much higher than that for whites. These rates reflect our chances of going to prison sometime in our lifetime, which again are much higher for African Americans and Latinos than for whites (see Figure 17.2).

Do these large racial and ethnic disparities reflect systematic racial/ethnic discrimination in the criminal justice system, especially at the sentencing stage, or do they simply reflect disproportionate involvement of African Americans and Latinos in street crime? Once again the evidence is very complex, and scholars dispute what it is saying. Several,

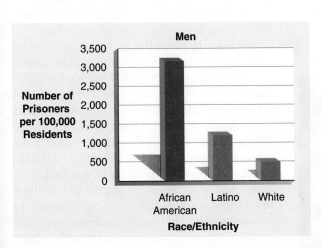
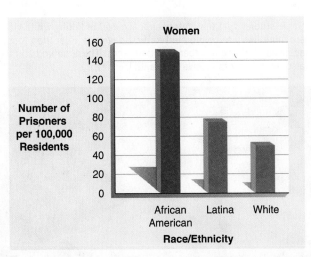

FIGURE 17.1 ▸ **Race, Ethnicity, Gender, and Imprisonment Rates, 2008 (federal and state prisoners)** Source: Sabol et al. 2010.
The African-American and white categories exclude Latinos.

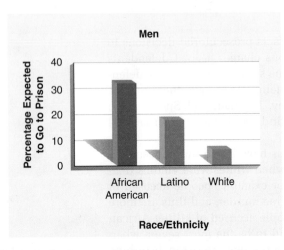

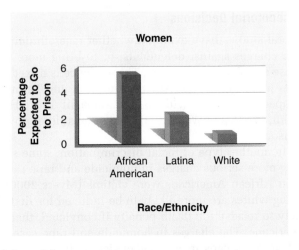

FIGURE 17.2 ▸ **Race, Ethnicity, Gender, and Lifetime Likelihood of Going to Prison** Source: Bonczar 2003.
The black and white categories exclude Hispanics.

but by no means all, recent studies find that African-American and Latino defendants are more likely than white defendants to be sentenced to prison after conviction, and some find that they also receive longer prison terms (Doerner and Demuth 2010). Other studies find that African Americans are treated more harshly than whites in these ways, but that Latinos are treated the same as whites (Brennan and Spohn 2009). Yet other studies find few or no racial/ethnic differences in sentencing outcomes (Harris et al. 2009).

Race-related factors other than the defendant's own race have also been studied. One of these factors is the victim's race, as several studies, especially of rape and capital (death sentence) offenses, uncover more punitive sentencing when whites are victims than when African Americans are victims (Sorensen and Wallace 1999). A second factor is the seriousness of the crime, as harsher sentencing for African Americans and Latinos seems to be more likely in less serious crimes than in more serious crimes (Chen 2008; Steen, Engen, and Gainey 2005). Reflecting a **liberation hypothesis,** the idea here is that in the most serious cases, there is little room for prosecutorial or judicial discretion to affect the sentence, because a severe sentence is clearly in order. In less serious cases, however, more discretion is possible, and thus greater opportunity exists for racial bias.

Less serious cases thus "liberate" judges to use their discretion and also, perhaps, to base sentencing decisions on racial prejudice.

A third factor is the structural and social makeup of states and local communities. Supporting Blalock's (1967) racial-threat hypothesis noted earlier, some (but again, not all) studies find harsher sentencing in states and counties with higher proportions of African Americans after controlling for crime rates and other relevant variables. African-American imprisonment rates are higher in states and counties with higher proportions of African Americans, and death-penalty sentences are also more common in such states (Bridges and Crutchfield 1988; Bridges, Crutchfield, and Simpson 1987; Jacobs, Carmichael, and Kent 2005).

Some studies find that defendants accused of killing white victims are more likely to be indicted for first-degree murder than those accused of killing members of other races. These defendants are also more likely to receive the death penalty.

Looking at all the evidence, how much of a difference do race and ethnicity make? Evidence on racial/ethnic discrimination in the juvenile justice system seems more consistent than the evidence for the adult criminal justice system, with much research finding that African-American and Latino youths receive harsher treatment than white youths at the various stages of the juvenile justice process even after relevant legal factors are taken into account (Hayes-Smith and Hayes-Smith 2009; Pope and Snyder 2003; Rodriguez 2007; Shook and Goodkind 2009).

The evidence on the adult criminal justice system is less clear (Walker, Spohn, and DeLone 2007). As already noted, some studies find racial/ethnic discrimination in sentencing, and some do not. Some find that African Americans and Latinos are both treated more harshly than whites, and some find that only one of these two groups receives harsher treatment. To the extent that racial/ethnic discrimination does occur in sentencing, it occurs primarily for young males and not among females (Brennan and Spohn 2009; Spohn and Holleran 2000; Steffensmeier and Demuth 2006). Complicating the picture further, racial/ethnic discrimination is more often found for the decision to incarcerate (the **in/out decision**) than for sentence lengths among those incarcerated. It is also more often found, as we have seen, for less serious offenses than for more serious offenses.

Discrimination also sometimes appears in the way judges determine sentences: Some studies find that judges place more emphasis on prior record and/or on offense seriousness when defendants are African American or Latino than when they are white.

So what should we conclude about race and ethnicity and sentencing from all the research? For better or worse, no clear picture quickly emerges. As Walker and colleagues (2007:279–280) concede, "a definitive answer to the question, 'Are racial minorities sentenced more harshly than whites?' remains elusive. Although a number of studies have uncovered evidence of racial discrimination in sentencing, others have found that there are no significant racial differences . . . .[D]iscrimination against racial minorities is not universal but is confined to certain types of cases, certain types of settings, and certain types of defendants."

To return to the issue of disproportionate imprisonment of African Americans and Latinos, many criminologists believe that this situation largely reflects the disproportionate involvement of these two groups in serious street crime (Harris et al. 2009; Tonry and Melewski 2008). As Alfred Blumstein (2009:183) concludes, any racial discrimination "cannot account for more than a fraction of" the racial disproportionality in the criminal justice system. To address this disproportionality, he says, "will require larger changes in the society outside the criminal justice system."

Other criminologists think that racial bias and other race-related factors do play a large role in producing the disproportionate incarceration, especially in certain states. As sentencing expert Marc Mauer (2009:3) says, "Thus, while greater involvement in some crimes is related to higher rates of incarceration for African Americans, the weight of the evidence to date suggests that a significant proportion of the disparities we currently observe is not a function of disproportionate criminal behavior."

The evidence on racial and ethnic discrimination in criminal sentencing is very complex. A fair conclusion is that race and ethnicity sometimes play a small but significant role in sentencing and other court outcomes.

The Drug War Revisited

Although the research on racial/ethnic discrimination in adult sentencing is rather inconsistent, it is very consistent for two specific types of sentencing. The first is the death penalty, for which the evidence consistently indicates pervasive racial discrimination. We discuss this evidence later in this chapter. The other type of sentencing derives from the war on drugs, which, as we saw in Chapter 16, has targeted African Americans, and especially young African-American males, far out of proportion to their actual illegal drug use. That chapter noted the disproportionate arrests of African Americans for illegal drug use and sale. Not surprisingly, they are also disproportionately imprisoned.

The drug war's focus on crack cocaine and its much higher penalties for crack than for similar amounts of powder cocaine account for much of these proportions. As Chapter 16 noted, the legal penalties for crack are much harsher than for powder cocaine, even though the two drugs are identical pharmacologically. Given racial differences in the use of crack and powder, it was inevitable that African Americans would be imprisoned in greater numbers and for longer periods than whites when the nation began cracking down on crack in the 1980s.

This is exactly what happened. In states across the nation, the African-American prison admission rate (number of African Americans imprisoned per 100,000 African Americans in the population) increased by a much greater amount than the white prison admission rate during the 1980s and 1990s. Today African Americans comprise about 44 percent of all state prisoners sentenced for drug offenses (Sabol, West, and Cooper 2009). Partly reflecting this disparity, some one-third of young African-American males (ages 20 to 29) nationally are under **correctional supervision,** meaning that they are either in prison, in jail, or on probation or parole. In some cities more than half of young African-American males are under correctional supervision (Mauer 2006). Of all men born between 1965 and 1969, 20 percent of African Americans had gone to prison by 1999, compared to only 3 percent of whites. The figure for African-American males rises to 30 percent of those without a college education and, astoundingly, almost 60 percent of those who had dropped out of high school (Western 2006). The war against drugs, whether intended or not, is clearly racially discriminatory.

Review and Discuss

To what extent do race and ethnicity affect conviction and sentencing?

GENDER AND SENTENCING

Gender disparity is readily evident in imprisonment, with men comprising 93 percent of all prison inmates in the United States (Sabol, West, and Cooper 2009). Earlier chapters noted that men are much more likely than women to commit serious offenses, and this fundamental gender difference in criminality undoubtedly accounts for most of the gender differences in imprisonment. However, gender may still affect sentencing. Perhaps women would be more likely to be imprisoned were it not for the chivalry of prosecutors and judges. Perhaps there are crimes for which women are more likely than men to be imprisoned. What does the evidence say?

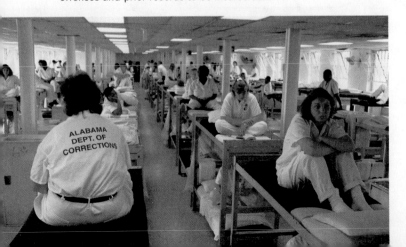

Women appear 10 to 25 percent less likely than men with similar offenses and prior records to be incarcerated.

The data on gender and sentencing parallel those for gender and arrest (see Chapter 16). In the juvenile justice system, girls are treated more harshly than boys for status offenses, but a bit less harshly for more serious offenses.

Nonwhite girls are less likely than their white counterparts to benefit from chivalrous treatment (Chesney-Lind and Pasko 2004).

In the adult criminal justice system, the best-designed studies generally find that women are 10 to 25 percent less likely than men with similar offenses and prior records to be incarcerated (Brennan and Spohn 2009; Griffin and Wooldredge 2006; Steffensmeier and Demuth 2006), but generally do not find that gender affects the length of their sentence for people who are incarcerated. This difference stems from prosecutors' and judges' beliefs that women are less of a threat than men to society, that their families and children would suffer if they were incarcerated, that they are less blameworthy than men for the crimes they committed, and that they have more community ties. Some scholars view these reasons as evidence of "warranted disparity in judicial decision making" involving women and men (Daly 1994:268).

Impact of Punishment on Crime

During the past few decades, a "get tough" attitude has guided the U.S. approach to crime (Tonry 2009). The federal government and states and cities across the country have established longer prison terms and mandatory minimum prison terms for many crimes. The war on drugs that began in the mid-1980s involved drastic crime-control efforts in our large cities and was targeted largely at African Americans. Beginning in 1994, two dozen states and the federal government enacted "three strikes and you're out" legislation requiring that defendants convicted of a third felony receive very long sentences, including life imprisonment. The death penalty has also been part of the "get tough" approach, with the number of death row inmates rising from 134 in 1973 to 3,207 at the end of 2008. This U.S. approach stands out in the Western world; as Michael Tory (2004:viii) observed, "[P]ractices that many Americans endorse—capital punishment, three-strikes laws, prison sentences measured in decades or lifetimes—are as unthinkable in other Western countries as are lynchings and public torture in America." (The International Focus box discusses a different approach to crime control undertaken by Denmark and the Netherlands.)

The result of these "get tough" efforts has been an enormous increase in the United States in the number of people incarcerated in our jails and prisons. These new prison admissions have swelled already overcrowded prisons far beyond capacity and forced states to spend billions of dollars on new prisons. As Figure 17.3 illustrates, the

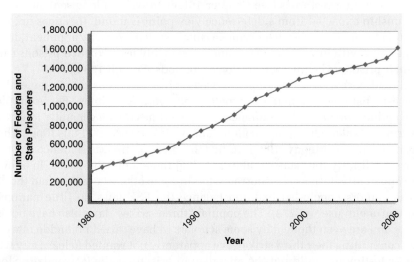

FIGURE 17.3 ▸ **Number of Adults in Federal and State Prison, 1980–2009** Source: http://bjs.ojp.usdoj.gov/content/glance/corr2.cfm.

number of federal and state prisoners quintupled from 1980 through 2009, rising from just over 300,000 in 1980 to about 1.6 million in 2009. The number of people in jail more than quadrupled during this period, from about 180,000 to more than 785,000. Meanwhile, the number on probation or parole quadrupled, rising from 1.3 million in 1980 to about 5.1 million. Adding up all these figures, the number of adults under correctional supervision (in prison or jail or on probation or parole) rose from 1.84 million to 7.3 million in just 29 years. By any standard, this is a very high number. In fact, the United States has the highest incarceration rate of any Western nation, with 748 of every 100,000 Americans behind bars in 2009. Despite this fact, the United States also has, as we know, higher crime rates than those of many other Western nations.

The "get tough" approach reflects the widespread belief among the public and politicians alike that harsher and more certain punishment deters crime and protects society by keeping dangerous criminals behind bars; these are called the **deterrence** and **incapacitation** arguments, respectively. As we have seen earlier in this book, however, what people believe about crime and criminal justice sometimes turns out to be a myth. What, then, does the evidence say about the effect of harsher punishment on crime rates? The conclusion here is clear: *Harsher punishment does not reduce crime.* This conclusion is probably shared by most criminologists and is supported by many kinds of evidence (Doob and Webster 2003; Kovandzic and Vieraitis 2006; Walker 2011). Let's examine this evidence, looking first at deterrence and then at incapacitation.

EVIDENCE AGAINST A DETERRENT EFFECT

First, decreases in crime rates have not always accompanied the huge increases in incarceration over the past two decades. For example, and as Chapter 3 noted, even though incarceration rose throughout the 1980s, the violent-crime rate also rose after the mid-1980s. Although the crime rate fell throughout the 1990s as incarceration continued to rise, factors other than incarceration seem to explain the drop in the crime rate then.

Second, at the state level only a weak and inconsistent relationship exists between severity of punishment (e.g., length of prison terms) and crime rates. Many states with longer prison terms have higher crime rates than states with shorter terms. As with similar research on arrest rates (see Chapter 16), even when a long sentence–low crime rate relationship expected from a deterrence viewpoint is found, this does not necessarily mean that harsh sentences deter crime. Using a *system capacity* argument, it is just as likely that states with lower crime rates and presumably less crowded prisons can afford to keep their prisoners behind bars for longer periods (Pontell 1984).

Third, and perhaps most tellingly, decreases in crime rates do not generally occur after the establishment of harsher penalties for various crimes. For example, laws mandating minimum or harsher sentences for gun crimes do not generally lower the rates of these crimes (Walker 2011). In a comprehensive investigation of this topic, Thomas B. Marvell and Carlisle E. Moody (1995) studied the effects of firearm sentence enhancement (FSE) laws in all forty-four states that established them since the 1960s. In a few states, FSE laws apparently decreased crime rates, but in some other states they had the opposite effect. The authors concluded that "on balance the FSE laws do little nationwide to reduce crime or gun use" (p. 274). The popular "three-strikes" laws also have not lowered crime rates and are even thought by some scholars to have raised homicide rates because offenders committing their third strike have apparently not wanted to leave any witnesses alive whose testimony could put the offenders in prison for life (Kovandzic, Sloan, and Vieraitis 2004).

International Focus

Punishing Criminals in Denmark and the Netherlands

The U.S. response to crime has focused on harsher imprisonment of criminals. Although this policy is politically popular, it arguably has done very little, if anything, to reduce crime. In Europe, various nations have confronted rising crime with very different measures and have rates of imprisonment (number of inmates per 100,000 population) up to ten times lower than the U.S. rate. Let's take a look at the European experience and focus on Denmark and the Netherlands.

Europe in general is far more pessimistic than the United States about the effectiveness of imprisonment. Almost all European criminal justice officials surveyed by the Helsinki Institute think prison often makes offenders worse and that alternative sanctions should be used whenever possible. They also acknowledge that prisons are very expensive and that prison overcrowding increases the chances that prisoners will come out of prison worse than when they went in.

These views lead Europe to favor probation and community service as alternatives to prison. Although these are not a cure-all for crime, say two criminologists, they "are at least as successful as sentences of imprisonment on several important counts, and . . . lack many of the drawbacks of imprisonment." The experience of Denmark and the Netherlands illustrates the European approach.

Denmark began to face a growing crime problem in the 1960s, which continued into the next decade. According to H. H. Brydensholt of Denmark's Prison and Probation Administration, the increase in crime stemmed from several reasons, including growing industrialization, rising youth drug use, and increasing unemployment. In response, Denmark devised a multifaceted response in 1973 that in many ways was the opposite of U.S. crime policy. It replaced longer indeterminate sentences (e.g., 3 to 7 years) with shorter fixed ones, reduced the length of prison terms and the number of offenses (especially nonviolent property offenses) leading to imprisonment, and reallocated funds from prisons to community-based corrections. These measures reduced the number of Danish prisoners during the next several years.

Denmark had several reasons for wanting to reduce imprisonment. First, it considered imprisonment a harsh measure because it stigmatized inmates and hurt their families. Second, it feared that imprisonment would lessen inmates' self-respect and increase their aggressiveness and other problems. Third, it considered imprisonment too harsh a penalty for many nonviolent property offenses. Finally, Denmark realized that it would be prohibitively expensive to put more people in prison.

The Netherlands' view of and experience with imprisonment is similar to Denmark's. Like Denmark, it considers imprisonment a costly, ineffective alternative to be avoided whenever possible, and it favors relatively short prison terms for offenders who need to be imprisoned. Although the number of Dutch prisoners has risen since the 1960s because of growing crime rates, the Dutch policy of short prison terms has kept this number from rising as high as it would have otherwise.

The United States is admittedly very different from Denmark, the Netherlands, and other European nations. Even so, their experience reminds us that it is possible to address crime without resorting to the "get tough" approach the United States has been following. This approach has cost the United States tens of billions of dollars that could be spent on crime prevention and alternatives to incarceration that would be at least as effective and less expensive.

Sources: Bijleveld and Smit 2005; Brydensholt 1992; Downes 2007; Joutsen and Bishop 1994.

Fourth, the dramatic increase in prisoners during the past two decades has forced the early release of convicted offenders already there. If harsher punishment makes a difference, these offenders should have higher rates of repeat offending (recidivism) than offenders convicted of similar crimes who are not released early. However, studies of this issue find that released offenders do not generally have higher recidivism rates than their counterparts who stay in prison, and they sometimes even have lower recidivism rates. As labeling theory predicts, longer stays in prison may embitter offenders and increase their exposure to the prison's criminal subculture. These and other problems make some offenders more crime prone when they leave prison than when they went in (Nagin, Cullen, and Jonson 2009).

In many respects, it is not so surprising that harsher punishment does not deter crime. When people commit violent offenses, they usually do so fairly spontaneously (see Chapter 5). At the time they lash out, they are not carefully weighing the possible penalties for their actions. Property offenses are more planned, allowing time for potential offenders to consider the prison term they may receive. Yet many property offenders either pay little attention to their chances of arrest or punishment or, at a minimum, simply assume that they will not get caught. Given this basic understanding of violent and property crimes, it would be surprising if harsher or more certain punishment did deter criminal behavior.

EVIDENCE AGAINST AN INCAPACITATION EFFECT

If harsher punishment does not work, perhaps we could at least keep society safer by imprisoning larger numbers of criminals, especially chronic, hard-core offenders and keeping them off the streets for longer amounts of time. Unfortunately, this incapacitation argument is faulty for several reasons (Walker 2011). It assumes that we do not have enough people already in prison. As this chapter has shown, however, our prisons are already stretched to the limit with little impact on the crime rate. This argument also assumes that we can easily identify the dangerous offenders who need to be incapacitated. However, it is not clear whether we can accurately identify such offenders and predict their future behavior (Auerhahn 2006). The incapacitation argument also ignores the fact that any extra people we put in prison represent only a small percentage of all offenders and that they will quickly be replaced on the streets by other offenders. The billions of dollars we would have to spend to house them will thus be largely wasted. Finally, the incapacitation argument overlooks the fact that the dangerous offenders it addresses must be caught in the first place, which may not happen given the low arrest rates for crimes of all types.

Putting all these factors together, incarcerating a much larger number of offenders (*gross incapacitation*) might reduce the crime rate, but only by a very small amount. This is what happened during the 1990s, when the number of prison and jail inmates increased by 67 percent. Although this increase cost tens of billions of dollars, its incapacitation effect accounted for no more than one-fourth of the crime drop during the 1990s (Spelman 2006). Empirical research confirms that the actual crime reduction stemming from gross incapacitation is very small and not cost-efficient. For example, Bruce Western (2006) found that a 10 percent rise in the incarceration rate produces a decrease of 1 percent in the crime rate. This means that the United States would have to imprison an additional 160,000 inmates (10 percent of the current 1.6 million in prison) to reduce the crime rate by only 1 percent. Because each inmate costs about $29,000 annually to house (Warren 2009), these new inmates would cost about $4.6 billion annually. And because prisons are filled beyond capacity, many new prisons would have to be built to house them, at a cost of many more billions of dollars.

Figures like these lead many criminologists to sharply question the wisdom of the "get tough" policy that relies on incapacitation. As Samuel Walker (2011:160) observes, "The evidence indicates no clear link between incarceration and crime rates. Moreover, gross incapacitation locks up many low-rate offenders at a great dollar cost to society." Elliott Currie (1985:88) is equally pessimistic: "No one seriously doubts that a modicum of crime can be prevented by incapacitating offenders. . . . [But] the potential reduction in serious crime is disturbingly small, especially when balanced against the social and economic costs of pursuing this strategy strenuously enough to make much difference to public safety."

Ironically, the massive increase in incarceration of the past few decades may eventually make the crime problem worse for at least two reasons. First, the hundreds of thousands of extra offenders now behind bars or with prison and jail records include many minor offenders. As many studies have found, their experiences in the criminal justice system may embitter them and reduce their employment chances, and thus make them more likely to commit additional and more serious crime (Nagin, Cullen, and Jonson 2009). Second, the increase in incarceration is also damaging our urban communities, as the imprisonment of so many of their young men weakens the communities' families and other social institutions. When these men return to their communities after being released from prison, their criminal orientation may be a bad influence on some community residents. By intensifying the communities' social disorganization in these ways, massive incarceration may ironically raise their crime rates and worsen the very problem it has been trying to stop (Clear 2008; Hipp and Yates 2009; Western and Wildeman 2009).

Ultimately, then, "get tough" measures involving harsher punishment do little, if anything, to reduce our crime rate, no matter how much common sense and popular opinion tell us otherwise, and any crime reduction they achieve is very small, costs billions of dollars, and causes many kinds of "collateral consequences" for the nation's cities (Foster and Hagan 2009). To reduce crime, another approach is required. Chapter 18 sketches what such an approach might look like.

Review and Discuss

To what extent does legal punishment prevent potential criminal behavior?

The Death-Penalty Debate

The themes of this chapter—discrimination in sentencing and the deterrent effect of punishment—come together in the debate over the death penalty, which produces passions pro and con as perhaps no other issue in criminal justice. The number of death row inmates has risen dramatically since the early 1970s despite a recent decrease (see Figure 17.4). Let's look at the death-penalty debate in detail.

Death-penalty proponents make at least three arguments: (1) people convicted of heinous murders deserve to be executed, (2) the death penalty saves the money that would be spent on years of confinement were the offender to serve a life sentence, and (3) the death penalty sends a message to potential murderers and thus has a general deterrent effect on homicide.

Death-penalty opponents, probably including most criminologists, attack all these arguments. The first argument, that vicious murderers deserve to be executed, raises philosophical and religious issues that are beyond the scope of this book. Whether it is moral for the state to take a life, even that of a vicious murderer, is a philosophical or religious question, not a sociological one. But criminologists do point out that the United States is the only remaining Western nation to use the death penalty, the rest having

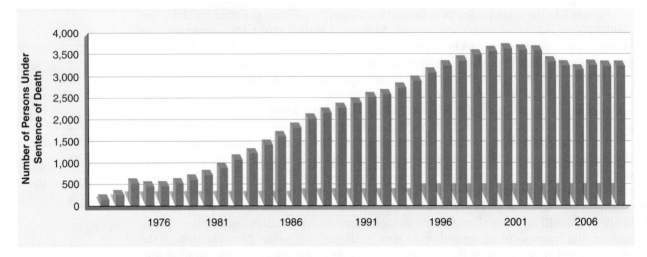

FIGURE 17.4 ▶ **Persons Under Sentence of Death, 1973–2008** Source: Pastore and Maguire 2010.

decided long ago that civilized nations should not commit what opponents call *legal murders* against those who have murdered. As a slogan of death-penalty opponents asks: Why do we kill people to show that killing people is wrong?

COST OF THE DEATH PENALTY

The second argument, that the death penalty saves money, is an appropriate one for social scientists to address. Here the evidence is clear: The death penalty actually costs more than life imprisonment in constant dollars. Keeping someone in prison for life, say forty years, would cost about $29,000 per year in constant dollars, or $1 million overall. Because someone's life is at stake, death-penalty cases are especially complicated from pretrial motions through sentencing and appeals, with the state usually having to pay for all costs at least through appeals to state courts. Although the cost of death-penalty cases varies by state, each capital case on the average costs $1 million *beyond* the cost of a noncapital case ending with a life sentence (Dieter 2009). With about 3,200 people on death row, the death-penalty cost to the states that sentenced them to death is an extra $2.2 billion.

The death penalty remains one of the most controversial issues in criminal justice today.

GENERAL DETERRENCE AND THE DEATH PENALTY

The third argument, that the death penalty has a general deterrent effect, is one that social scientists have tested for several decades. With few exceptions (Land, Teske, and Zheng 2009), studies find that the death penalty does not have this effect (Bohm 2007; Kovandzic, Vieraitis, and Boots 2009). This conclusion comes from several kinds of studies. Some of the earliest research compared the homicide rates of states with and without the death penalty. Contrary to the general-deterrence argument, states with the death penalty do not have lower homicide rates than those without it. States that eliminated the death penalty a few decades ago did not see their homicide rates rise compared with states that retained the death penalty. Conversely, states that established the death penalty did not see their homicide rates decrease compared with states that did not have the death penalty.

Scholars have also examined the consequences of well-publicized executions. If the death penalty does deter homicide, homicide should go down in the month or so after stories about these executions appear in the press. Although a few studies find this effect (Stack 1987), most find no effect (Peterson and Bailey 1991). Some studies even show that homicide actually increases after executions occur. This is called the **brutalization effect.** The argument here is that executions desensitize the public to the immorality of killing and thus increase the likelihood that some people will decide to kill. Executions may also increase homicide as a sort of imitation (Bowers and Pierce 1980).

In a demonstration of this effect, John K. Cochran and colleagues (Cochran, Chamlin, and Seth 1994) studied the aftermath of a September 1990 execution in Oklahoma, the first execution in the state in twenty-five years. In the three years following the execution, the general Oklahoma homicide rate did not change. There was, however, "an abrupt and lasting increase in the level of stranger homicides" (p. 129), which on the average rose by one per month. A replication of their study found that newspaper coverage of executions outside Oklahoma also increased other kinds of homicides in Oklahoma (Bailey 1998). Such evidence indicates that capital punishment may increase the number of homicides rather than reduce them. A study of California executions found that both effects may occur: The California executions apparently decreased felony murders (i.e., murders committed in the course of committing another felony), but increased stranger murders stemming from an argument (Cochran and Chamlin 2000).

It would be surprising if the death penalty did deter homicide. Most people who commit violence do not weigh the punishment they might receive before they strike. Most homicides are fairly spontaneous events, and offenders certainly do not pause to mull over their chances of being executed before they kill their victims. Felony murders are somewhat less spontaneous because offenders (usually armed robbers) have "at least a tacit understanding that lethal force may be necessary during the commission of the crime" (Cochran and Chamlin 2000:690). If so, this may account for the finding in the California study just cited. This finding notwithstanding, the vast majority of studies do not find a general-deterrent effect of executions on homicide.

ARBITRARINESS AND RACIAL DISCRIMINATION IN APPLICATION OF THE DEATH PENALTY

In addition to challenging the arguments of death-penalty proponents, opponents of the death penalty cite other problems with capital punishment. Many of these have to do with the way the death penalty is applied. In 1972, the U.S. Supreme Court ruled 5 to 4 in *Furman* v. *Georgia* (408 U.S. 238) that capital punishment as it was then practiced violated the Eighth Amendment's prohibition of cruel and unusual punishment. The Court found that jurors in capital cases had few standards to guide their decision to impose the death penalty, leading them to impose death sentences in some murder cases but not in others that were equally appalling. Far from logical and rational, the capital punishment process was, the Court declared, both capricious and arbitrary and held the potential for racial discrimination.

In the wake of *Furman,* states revised their death-penalty laws and procedures to reduce **arbitrariness** in the application of the penalty. Some mandated death sentences for any convictions of first-degree murder, and others devised a system of *bifurcated* juries that would first decide on the guilt of the defendant and then decide whether to impose the death penalty. In this second phase, juries would have to consider both *aggravating* (e.g., the murder was committed while the defendant was committing another felony) and *mitigating* (e.g., the defendant had no prior history of criminality) factors as they determined whether a death sentence was appropriate.

In a series of decisions in 1976, the Supreme Court struck down the mandatory death-penalty statutes, but upheld in *Gregg v. Georgia* (428 U.S. 153) the statutes establishing bifurcated juries and aggravating and mitigating factors. Social scientists since that time have studied whether the new, post-*Furman* system of capital punishment has continued to exhibit the same arbitrariness, capriciousness, and racial discrimination that motivated the *Furman* decision (Smith 2000).

Continuing Arbitrariness

On the issue of arbitrariness the evidence is clear: Throughout the country, defendants accused of similar murders are treated differently for no logical reasons (Bohm 2007). Some are charged with capital murders, whereas others are not. Some receive the death penalty after conviction, whereas others do not. Even within the same state, murder defendants are more likely to receive the death penalty in some jurisdictions than in others. Although such disparities inevitably exist in the criminal justice system for all kinds of crimes, they have even more ominous implications when a defendant's life is at stake. Researchers conclude that the capital punishment process is akin to a lottery system and that "being sentenced to death is the result of a process that may be no more rational than being struck by lightning" (Paternoster 1991:183).

Here again the 1994–1995 O. J. Simpson case is illustrative. Simpson was accused of the extremely vicious murders of two people. Many aspects of the alleged murders fit circumstances that often lead California prosecutors to ask for the death penalty when they charge defendants. Simpson's prosecutors chose not to ask for the death penalty in his case. Legal observers attributed this to Simpson's celebrity and assumed that the prosecutors thought a jury would never convict such a famous, well-liked defendant if they knew he could be executed. Thus Simpson did not face the death penalty, even though many poor, unknown defendants accused of far less vicious murders have faced it and continue to face it.

Racial Discrimination

Another line of research has focused on racial discrimination. Several studies have found one type of racial discrimination in the application of the death penalty: The lives of white victims are seemingly valued more than the lives of African-American victims (Paternoster and Brame 2008; Sorensen and Wallace 1999). Prosecutors in homicide cases are more likely to impose a first-degree murder charge (the only charge for which the death penalty is allowed) and also to seek the death penalty after conviction when the victim is white than when the victim is African American. Further, among defendants indicted for first-degree murder, death sentences from juries are also more likely when the victim is white than when the victim is African American. Some evidence indicates that death sentences are particularly likely when the victim is both white and female (Williams, Demuth, and Holcomb 2007). Although not all studies find that the victim's race makes a difference (Berk, Li, and Hickman 2005), the bulk of the evidence does indicate that death sentences are more likely when the victim is white. A recent study also yielded the same findings that death sentences are more likely when victims are relatively wealthy and otherwise "respectable" members of society (Phillips 2009).

The evidence for harsher treatment of African-American defendants once the race of the victim is held constant is less consistent. Some studies find African-American defendants more likely to be indicted for first-degree murder and also to receive the death penalty eventually, but some studies do not find this difference. When this difference is found, African-American offenders who murder white victims are much more likely than other combinations to be charged with first-degree murder, to have the death penalty sought by prosecutors, and to receive death sentences after conviction. Several scholars conclude that racial discrimination on the basis of the defendant's race has declined or even disappeared after *Furman,* but that discrimination on the basis of the victim's race has continued (Smith 2000).

Figures from perhaps the best study of racial discrimination in the death penalty underscore the difference that the victim's race makes. David C. Baldus and colleagues (Baldus, Woodworth, and Pulaski 1990) studied 594 murder cases from Georgia. Before they controlled for legally relevant variables such as the number of aggravating factors (evidence of clear premeditation, committing the murder during the course of committing other felonies), the authors found that prosecutors sought the death penalty in 45 percent of the cases with white victims, but in only 15 percent of the cases with African-American victims. Combining the races of the victim and the defendant, they found that prosecutors sought the death penalty in 58 percent of the African-American-defendant–white-victim cases; 38 percent of white-defendant–white-victim cases; and only 15 percent of African-American-defendant–African-American-victim cases. Juries imposed the death penalty in 57 percent of cases with white victims but only 42 percent of cases with African-American victims. After controlling for legally relevant factors, the racial disparities stemming from the victim's race increased: In cases with white victims, prosecutors were 5.5 times more likely to seek the death penalty and juries were 7 times more likely to impose it. The authors concluded that the race of the victim had a "potent influence" on the likelihood of the death penalty (p. 185).

Interestingly, they also found this influence greater in cases in which the number of aggravating factors was neither very high nor very low. In this middle range of cases, in which the murders were neither the most terrible nor the least terrible, prosecutors and juries are most likely to take the victim's race into account as they decide to seek or impose the death penalty. Although the authors did not note it, their finding supported the liberation hypothesis outlined earlier. An earlier study of capital murders in South Carolina also found support for the liberation hypothesis (Paternoster 1984). Although this study found that prosecutors were more likely to seek the death penalty in cases involving white victims, this effect was especially noted in cases involving fewer aggravating felonies. Moreover, in cases with white victims, prosecutors tended to seek the death penalty when there was only one aggravating felony; in cases with African-American victims, prosecutors were likely to seek the death penalty only when there was more than one aggravating felony. Thus, murders of African Americans had to be more appalling for the death penalty to be sought.

QUALITY OF LEGAL REPRESENTATION OF CAPITAL DEFENDANTS

Another criticism of the death penalty addresses the quality of legal representation of capital defendants (Perez-Pena 2000). Recall that almost all criminal defendants are poor and receive inadequate legal representation. This is no less true for defendants facing the death penalty. Capital cases are extraordinarily complex and can cost at least $250,000 to defend. Most public defenders and assigned counsel simply are not equipped to handle them and have little time to do so. They thus do not raise evidentiary and other issues at trial that may be grounds for later appeals, and they certainly do not have the funds and other resources to mount an effective defense in the first place. In many states their pay is also inadequate. For example, Mississippi pays attorneys assigned to capital cases only $1,000 in fees, whereas private attorneys would charge much more than $100 an hour.

Similar problems affect the appeals process after defendants are sentenced to death. Because almost all of them cannot afford to hire private counsel to launch an appeal, they must rely on assigned counsel. Once again, public attorneys are usually less able to handle death-penalty appeals than are more experienced, and much more expensive, private attorneys. Once appeals are denied by state courts, the defendant's only recourse lies in the federal courts. At this level, public funding for defense counsel is not available. The defendant thus must usually rely on volunteer attorneys, but very few attorneys are willing to serve in this capacity. Those who do volunteer their time usually do not have the resources to put forward the best appeal possible.

Sometimes defense attorneys in death-penalty cases are downright incompetent or corrupt. Some fail to present witnesses or evidence or do so ineptly, and some have even fallen asleep during the trials of their clients. Others have questionable legal credentials: In one death-penalty case, the attorney was a former leader of the Ku Klux Klan, and in another case the attorney was facing disbarment at the same time the trial of his client was occurring. According to various studies, 25 percent of Kentucky death row inmates were represented by attorneys who were later disbarred or who resigned to avoid this fate, 13 percent of Louisiana defendants who had been executed were represented by attorneys who had been disciplined for various kinds of misconduct, and 33 defendants sentenced to death in Illinois had lawyers who were later disbarred or suspended (Berlow 1999; Johnson 2000b; Perez-Pena 2000).

In short, defendants facing the death penalty receive inadequate representation at all levels of the legal process even though their lives are at stake. This is especially true in the South, where most death-penalty cases occur; few capable attorneys there are willing to take on capital cases. When they do so, their regular legal practice might suffer because of hostility from the public and other legal professionals.

WRONGFUL EXECUTIONS

A final criticism of the death penalty centers on the possibility of **wrongful executions.** Mistakes do occur in criminal justice, either out of honest errors or downright prejudice. It is estimated that slightly under 1 percent of all felony convictions are mistaken (Huff 2002; Zalman, Smith, and Kiger 2008). If a person is mistakenly found guilty, he or she can be released from prison once the mistake is discovered. But if that person is executed, he or she obviously cannot be brought back to life. Evidence of mistaken convictions abounds. At least 350 defendants during the twentieth century were convicted of potentially capital crimes even though they were probably or certainly innocent. Of these defendants, 139 received the death penalty and 23 were executed (Radelet, Bedau, and Putnam 1992). At least 381 homicide defendants had their convictions overturned between 1963 and the late 1990s because prosecutors presented false evidence or hid evidence they knew would favor the defendant (Berlow 1999). And, as the Crime in the News story that began this chapter reminds us, 138 death row inmates (as of June 2010) have been released from prison since the early1970s after new evidence, sometimes gathered by college and graduate students, established their innocence or raised serious doubts about their guilt.

Although these inmates won their freedom and their lives, it is estimated that at least a dozen people who have been executed during the past four decades were probably innocent of the capital crime for which they were sentenced to death (Bohm 2007). One of these was Cameron Todd Willingham, who was executed in Texas in 2004 for setting a fire to his home that killed his three daughters. According to later investigations, his court-appointed attorneys often seemed incompetent, and a major witness was a jail inmate and drug addict who claimed that Willingham had confessed to him. Most damning, forensic evidence strongly indicated that his house fire was an accident, not arson (Grann 2009). Another wrongful execution was probably that of Gary Graham, executed in 2000 in Texas for murdering a drug dealer. No physical evidence linked Graham to the murder. A witness's testimony was the only evidence against him, and two witnesses who could have cleared Graham were never called by his attorney to testify (Miller 2000). Another was Wilburn Henderson, convicted of the 1980 murder of a furniture store dealer in a robbery. The evidence against Henderson was so thin that an appellate court over-turned his conviction and ordered a new trial; the court's decision listed several other sus-pects, including the victim's husband, who had abused the victim and wondered aloud the day before she died where she would want to be buried. Henderson was again found guilty at his second trial and executed in 1998 (Mills, Possley, and Armstrong 2000).

Why are innocent people sometimes convicted of murder and sentenced to death? Ac-cording to legal writer Alan Berlow (1999:68), the reasons "range from simple police and prosecutorial error to the most outrageous misconduct, such as the framing of innocent people, and everything in between: perjured testimony, erroneous eyewitness testimony, false confessions (including the confessions of innocent defendants), racial bias, incom-petent defense counsel, and overzealous police officers and prosecutors." Ronald Kitchen's case, discussed at the beginning of this chapter, typifies some of these reasons. So does the case of Rolando Cruz, convicted in 1985 of the murder, rape, and kidnapping of a 10-year-old girl who was abducted from her home in a Chicago suburb by a man who kicked in her front door. Cruz was sentenced to die even though no physical evidence link-ing him to the rape and murder was introduced at his trial. DNA evidence later implicated another man who confessed to the crimes, and four police officers and three former pros-ecutors were eventually indicted for perjury and obstruction of justice in Cruz's case. He was released from prison after serving more than ten years on death row (Berlow 1999).

The possibility of wrongful convictions and executions and other problems in the appli-cation of the death penalty have led the American Bar Association and other organizations to call for a moratorium on executions. In early 2000, revelations that thirteen innocent men had been put on death row in Illinois led the state's governor, George Ryan, a Republican, to im-pose a moratorium on executions until it could be established that Illinois death-penalty cases were free from error or bias. His action led to calls for moratoriums in other states (Johnson 2000a). Ryan eventually commuted the sentences of all 167 death row inmates in Illinois be-cause of his concern over the possibility of wrongful executions. When he did so, he declared, "Our capital system is haunted by the demon of error: error in determining guilt and error in determining who among the guilty deserves to die" (Wilgoren 2003:A1).

Review and Discuss

What are the arguments for and against the death penalty? Are you in favor of the death penalty? Why or why not?

Conclusion

This chapter's focus on the prosecution and punishment of criminals completes our brief overview of the criminal justice system. Many issues were omitted for lack of space, but we did deal with the most important ones for a sociological understanding of crime and criminal justice: the inequality of legal outcomes and the crime-reduction effects of legal punishment.

We saw that structural context often shapes post-arrest legal decision making. In particular, we reviewed the extensive literature on class, racial and ethnic, and gender discrimination in sentencing. We saw that disparities do exist in many jurisdictions and at different stages of the legal process, even if legal factors exert the major influence on sentencing. There is thus evidence here to support both consensus and conflict views of law and criminal justice. Whether the system is fair or not overall is up to you to decide. What we have tried to provide is a sociological lens through which to view the evidence so that you can draw your own conclusions.

The chapter also reviewed the evidence on the crime-reduction effect of harsher sentences and reached a pessimistic conclusion: "Get tough" approaches offer little hope of reducing crime. This, of course, has been the dominant approach to the crime problem in the past few decades, as politicians continue to compete to show who is toughest on criminals. Amid all the calls for cracking down on criminals, it is easy to forget that the social policy may not always have its desired effects. The best evidence indicates that recent social policy on crime and drugs has failed in its most important professed goal, that of reducing the crime problem.

The United States holds the dubious honor of having a high crime rate even though it also has the highest imprisonment rate of all Western nations and longer prison terms than most of these nations. A quadrupling of imprisonment since 1980 has not lowered the crime rate, and a very punitive war on drugs has neither reduced the drug trade appreciably nor lowered drug use. Instead, they have swelled the number and occupation of our jails and prisons, cost us billions of dollars that could have been put to better use, and otherwise done much more harm than good. There must be a better way.

We have now come full circle. Near the beginning of the book, Chapter 2 tried to show that public opinion on crime and politicians' calls for cracking down on crime have little to do with actual crime-rate trends. Later chapters discussed explanations of crime and examined its nature and dynamics. More recently, we have considered the extent of discrimination in the criminal justice system and questioned whether a "get tough" approach is the most promising way to tackle the crime problem. This approach cannot and does not work for several reasons, not the least of which have to do with the sociological causes and nature of criminality that earlier chapters presented. Now that we have reached the end of the book, we will spend a few pages in the final chapter spelling out a sociological prescription for crime reduction.

17

Summary

1. The United States is popularly thought to have an adversary system of criminal justice. However, courtrooms feature much more cooperation than combat between prosecutors and defense attorneys. Sociological and journalistic accounts beginning in the 1960s painted a picture of criminal courts as assembly lines in which poor defendants did not receive justice.

2. Research beginning in the 1970s said that plea bargaining was an inevitable and not unwelcome dynamic for all sides to criminal court proceedings. For the prosecutor, it helps ensure convictions, whereas for the defendant it helps to some extent to minimize sentence severity, even though defendants accused of the most serious crimes still receive severe sentences.

3. Since the time of Durkheim, the study of punishment has been of particular interest to criminologists and law and society scholars. Much research has explored whether unemployment at the micro and macro levels increases the likelihood of incarceration, but evidence for this linkage is inconsistent. Historical research on the incarceration and lynchings of African Americans in the post–Civil War South supports the

presumed link between punishment and economic problems and unemployment. Although research on social class and criminal case outcomes does not find that social class makes a difference, there is too little income variation among criminal defendants to adequately test this hypothesis.

4. The evidence on racial and ethnic biases in sentencing is very complex, and scholars interpret this evidence in many different ways. To the extent that racial and ethnic discrimination in sentencing exists, it is most often seen in regard to the race of the defendant and for less serious crimes and for the in/out (incarceration) decision rather than for sentence lengths once the decision is made to incarcerate. Evidence for racial and ethnic discrimination in punishment is much stronger and clearer for drug offenses and capital cases.

5. The evidence on gender and sentencing indicates that women are somewhat less likely than men convicted of like crimes to be incarcerated. However, once the decision is made to incarcerate, gender does not appear to affect the length of prison terms.

6. The number of prison and jail inmates now is tens of thousands greater than two decades ago, but the huge increase in imprisonment does not seem to have had a large effect, if any, on the crime rate. The evidence indicates that imprisonment has neither a strong deterrent effect nor a strong incapacitation effect.

7. Research on the death penalty does not support the arguments of its proponents. In particular, the death penalty costs more than life imprisonment and does not deter homicide. It also is applied arbitrarily and in a discriminatory manner in regard to the race of the victim. In other problems, the legal representation of capital defendants is often of poor quality, and many wrongful convictions and even executions of such defendants in capital cases have occurred.

Key Terms

adversary system 428	correctional supervision 438	incapacitation 440	plea bargaining 429
arbitrariness 445	courtroom work group 429	incarceration 431	repressive law 431
brutalization effect 445	deterrence 440	in/out decision 437	restitutive law 431
caseloads 429	discretion 428	liberation hypothesis 436	wrongful execution 448

What Would You Do?

1. Suppose you are a juror in a homicide case for which the defendant could receive the death penalty if found guilty. As is true of the other jurors, you generally support the death penalty, but you also think it should be used only when there is clear and convincing evidence of the defendant's guilt and when the defendant committed a particularly vicious crime. In the case before you, the defendant is accused of fatally shooting a cashier during a robbery of a store after the cashier tried to grab the robber's gun. Although the robber ran from the store, an eyewitness who was in the store identified the defendant in a police lineup, but the murder weapon was never found. The prosecution's case rests almost entirely on the one eyewitness's testimony. Two other people shopping in the store at the time said they did not get a good look at the robber. Based on this description of the case, would you vote to convict the defendant and, if so, would you vote to execute him? Explain your answer.

2. You are a judge in a case in which a 22-year-old woman is on trial for possessing a small amount of heroin. She is employed part-time in a fast-food restaurant and has a 2-year-old daughter; the defendant's only previous arrest and conviction is for shoplifting when she was 18. The jury has found her guilty, and it is now your turn to impose the sentence. What sentence do you impose? Why?

CHAPTER

eighteen

Conclusion: How Can We Reduce Crime?

We have reached the end of our journey into the world of sociological criminology. In this world, crime and victimization are rooted in the social and physical characteristics of communities and in the structured social inequalities of race and ethnicity, social class, and gender. While not excusing any criminal's action, our sociological imagination allows us to understand that any individual's criminality is just one example of a public issue affecting masses of people. Our sociological imagination also forces us to realize that to reduce crime we must address its structural and cultural roots. Even if we could somehow "cure" all the criminals, new ones will replace them unless the structural and cultural conditions underlying crime are changed.

The need to address these conditions becomes even more paramount when we consider the criminal justice system's inability to reduce the crime problem. As we saw in the last two chapters, increasing the certainty and severity of arrest and punishment offers only false hope. The "get tough" approach to crime during the past few decades has had at most a small impact on the crime rate and has cost hundreds of billions of dollars. In addition to costing so much and achieving so little, the mass incarceration at the heart of the "get tough" approach has created many problems (as Chapter 17 noted) that have been called *collateral consequences* (Clear 2008; Foster and Hagan 2009). These consequences include (1) the release of some 735,000 ex-prisoners every year back into their home communities; (2) joblessness, drug addiction, and other problems among these ex-inmates; (3) the resulting prospect of many additional crimes committed by these former prisoners; (4) a generation of children raised with one parent in prison or jail; and (5) community-level problems including homelessness and AIDS and other infectious diseases. All these problems suggest the need to look to a different type of strategy to reduce crime.

The field of public health offers one such strategy. If we tried to prevent a disease by only curing those having it and not attacking the underlying causes, that disease would certainly continue. Recognizing this, the **public health model** stresses the need to identify the social and other causes of disease so that efforts can be launched to target these causes (Hemenway 2004; Moore 1995). Unfortunately, the U.S. approach to crime has not followed this sensible strategy. Instead, it has focused on "curing" those "afflicted" with crime by arresting as many as possible and putting them behind bars, all to little avail, and creating many other problems in the process.

More than a decade ago, public health experts began to treat violent crime as a public health problem (Friedman 1994; Hemenway 2004; Kellerman 1996). Their aim was to uncover the social causes of violence so that these causes could be addressed by public policy. In the spirit of this approach, this chapter offers a sociological prescription for reducing crime.

The Criminal Justice System Funnel

Before considering a sociological prescription for crime reduction, we will examine one more bit of evidence that underscores the cost-*ineffectiveness* of the "get tough" approach. This evidence concerns what is often called the **criminal justice funnel.** The funnel image comes from the fact that as we move from the number of crimes committed, the top of the funnel, to the number of offenders going to prison or jail, the bottom of the funnel, a sharp drop in numbers occurs at every stage of the criminal justice process. As the previous two chapters discussed, the reason for this is that decision makers at every stage of the process determine whether a crime, or someone suspected of the crime, filters down to the next level. Inevitably, these decisions "kick out" many crimes and suspects from the criminal justice system or at least from consideration for incarceration, so only a few remain by the time we get to prison and jail at the bottom of the funnel. Let's see how this happens.

As we saw in Chapter 3, many victimizations are not reported to the police. Of the crimes known to the police, only about one-fifth overall are cleared by arrest. What happens to the people arrested? Relatively few are convicted of felonies, and even fewer of these are sentenced to prison or jail. As we saw in Chapter 17, many cases are either dropped for lack of sufficient evidence or are plea bargained to a misdemeanor, for which incarceration is unlikely. Of those convicted of a felony, some receive probation and/or fines instead of imprisonment.

Now we will illustrate the criminal justice system funnel with some real data in Table 18.1 for 2006 (the latest year for which complete information was available at the time of writing). The data come from the National Crime Victimization Survey (NCVS), the Uniform Crime Reports (UCR), and government reports on the judicial processing of defendants. The table includes only the UCR Part I crimes of homicide, rape, aggravated assault, robbery, burglary, larceny, and auto theft. Thus, it excludes simple assaults, even

TABLE 18.1 ▸ **The Criminal Justice System Funnel for UCR Part I Crime, 2006[a]**

VARIABLE	TOTAL
NCVS victimizations	21,147,190
UCR offenses known to police	11,401,611
Number of arrests	2,151,820
Felony convictions in state and federal courts	435,629
Sentenced to prison or jail	320,908

Sources: Calculated from Durose, Farole, and Rosenmerkel 2009; Pastore and Maguire 2010.
[a]All figures include homicides and exclude arson.

TABLE 18.2 ▸ **The Criminal Justice System Funnel for UCR Violent Crime, 2006[a]**

VARIABLE	TOTAL
NCVS victimizations	2,355,400
UCR offenses known to police	1,418,043
Number of arrests	611,523
Felony convictions in state courts	208,260
Sentenced to prison or jail	160,628

Sources: Calculated from Durose, Farole, and Rosenmerkel 2009; Pastore and Maguire 2010.
[a]All figures include homicides and exclude arson.

though the NCVS reports them. Keep in mind that the NCVS itself excludes homicides, commercial burglaries, shoplifting, and other crimes included in the other figures in the table. The UCR's number of homicides has been added into the NCVS figure for total victimizations.

As you can see, we start with more than 21 million personal victimizations at the top of the funnel and end up with just 320,908 persons going to prison or jail at the bottom of the funnel. This number of incarcerated offenders represents only about 1.5 percent of the total number of victimizations estimated by the NCVS.

Perhaps the funnel effect for violent crimes is less severe. We consider this in Table 18.2, which presents the relevant data for the UCR violent crimes of homicide, aggravated assault, rape, and robbery. Once again, the NCVS figure in the table excludes simple assaults but includes homicides.

Here we start with more than 2.3 million personal violent victimizations at the top of the funnel and end up with 160,628 going to prison or jail. This number of incarcerated offenders represents about 6.8 percent of the total number of victimizations estimated by the NCVS. Although the drop throughout the violent crime funnel is a little less severe than the drop for the funnel combining violent and property offenses, it is still noticeable.

Besides making you want to live in a low-crime state or even move out of the country, what are the implications of the funnel effect for public policy on crime? One implication is that efforts concentrating on offenders and offenses at the bottom of the funnel will have only a limited impact, if that, on overall crime. Even if all people convicted of a violent felony each year were sentenced to prison for life, for example, they would still represent only a very small proportion of all people committing such felonies, leaving the crime rate essentially intact. This is true even if each person put into prison had committed more than one crime in a given year and therefore accounted for more than one of the crimes at the top of the funnel.

Suppose you decided you wanted to double the number of people going to prison for felonies. How much would that cost, and would the money be worth it? To answer these questions, let us go back to the data in

Building even more prisons will cost the nation billions of dollars but will not reduce crime significantly.

Table 18.1. Suppose we wanted to double the number of people going to prison or jail. This would mean that, instead of about 1.5 percent of all victimizations leading to someone being incarcerated, we would now have about 3 percent. How much safer would you feel? Even if the people incarcerated had accounted for, say, five crimes each in a given year, you would be increasing the proportion of all crimes accounted for by imprisonment from 7.5 to 15 percent. This would still leave 85 percent of all crimes unaccounted for. Would you feel much safer? Even if we just tried to "fix" the violent crime funnel depicted in Table 18.2, doubling the number at the bottom would still leave the vast majority of violent crimes unaccounted for.

How much would it cost to double the small number of people at the bottom of the funnel depicted in Table 18.1 who are incarcerated? To keep things simple, say we would eventually have to double the number of prison cells because our prisons are already stretched beyond capacity. Because we now have about 1.6 million people in our prisons, we would have to build at least 1,600 more prisons, each containing 1,000 beds. With the cost of each such prison averaging about $100 million or more, the cost of prison construction alone would come to about $160 billion, with another $160 billion or so in interest on construction loans. Because it also costs about $29,000 per year to keep each person in prison, it would eventually cost an extra $46 billion annually, in constant dollars, to house the new prisoners. In recent years, California, Texas, and other states have spent huge sums of money on new prisons to incarcerate more and more offenders. These expenditures have reduced funds for higher education and other uses and have severely strained the states' finances (Wood 2008).

Let's say further that to double the number of people going to prison each year, it would help to double the number of police. With about 650,000 local police in the United States, each earning an average annual income of about $50,000, the extra salaries alone would come to about $32 billion annually. The additional operating expenses, $55,000 (benefits, equipment, etc.), for each police officer would amount to another $36 billion. We would also have to build new courthouses, hire new prosecutors and other court personnel, and elect or appoint more judges, all at an expense that would easily run into the billions of dollars. We are now up to well over $270 billion in immediate and annual costs (excluding prison construction loan interest), just to double the proportion of victimizations leading to imprisonment from 1.5 to 3 percent. If you were a businessperson, how cost-effective would you consider this expenditure? If you ran your business this way, how long would you stay in business?

As this brief discussion suggests, it might make more sense to concentrate on the top of the funnel instead of on the bottom. To the extent this is true, we must focus more on crime prevention than on crime control and do so by addressing crime's structural and cultural roots. This is the view of many criminologists. Stressing perhaps the most important structural factor, Elliott Currie (1998:131) observed, "There is little question that growing up in extreme poverty exerts powerful pressures toward crime." It does so, he said, by impairing children's cognitive development, increasing their abuse and neglect, and hampering the quality of parenting in other respects. To reduce crime, he said, requires only that poverty be reduced, not eliminated. The next section outlines a reasonable crime-reduction strategy informed by sound social research on poverty and the other structural and cultural roots of criminal behavior.

Review and Discuss

About what percentage of all serious crime victimizations end up with someone going to prison or jail? How does this criminal justice funnel help us understand what might work or not work to reduce the crime rate?

A Sociological Prescription for Crime Reduction

Earlier we outlined a public health approach to violence and other crime. A public health strategy emphasizes the need for prevention. Here the public health community stresses three kinds of prevention: primary, secondary, and tertiary.

Primary prevention "seeks to prevent the occurrence of disease or injury entirely" by focusing on aspects of the social or physical environment that contribute to the disease or injury (Moore 1995:247). Thus, public health advocates underscore poverty as a cause of poor health and toxic dump sites and other environmental hazards as a cause of cancer. A primary prevention approach to crime, then, addresses features of our society, culture, and local communities that contribute to our high crime rates. We discussed many of these features in Chapter 6.

Secondary prevention aims to identify practices and situations that put certain individuals at risk for illness or injury. Thus, public health advocates emphasize that poor children are especially at risk for serious childhood diseases because they often do not get needed vaccinations. To address this problem, public health workers champion high-profile government vaccination and public education efforts. A secondary prevention approach to crime, then, addresses the developmental processes, especially those in early childhood, that make crime even more likely among individuals living in criminogenic social environments. We discussed many of these processes in Chapter 7.

Finally, **tertiary prevention** occurs after an illness has begun or an injury has occurred and "seeks to minimize the long-term consequences" of the health problem (Moore 1995:247). When you visit a physician for an illness or injury, the physician is engaging in tertiary prevention. A tertiary prevention approach to crime, then, focuses on preventing recidivism, or repeat offending, by offenders and on protecting society from these offenders. This, of course, is how the United States has traditionally responded to crime. Although the last two chapters discussed the limitations of this approach, there are some criminal justice–related policies that should be considered.

The following proposals represent a reasonable approach to crime reduction. They rest on the vast body of criminological theory and research presented in previous chapters and are advocated by highly regarded criminologists (Barlow and Decker 2010; Currie 2010; Frost, Freilich, and Clear 2010; Lab 2010; Tonry 2004; Welsh and Farrington 2007). The proposals are grouped according to three categories: (1) social, cultural, and community; (2) developmental (social processes); and (3) criminal justice. These categories roughly correspond to primary, secondary, and tertiary prevention, respectively.

Physicians' prescriptions sometimes do not cure illnesses immediately or at all, and not every aspect of this sociological prescription for crime reduction may have its intended effects. Some of the proposals will undoubtedly sound like pipe dreams and will be difficult or almost impossible to achieve, either because we do not have the national will to accomplish them or because the issues they address are intractable. But even some success in achieving these proposals' objectives offers real hope to reduce crime. Most of the proposals speak generally to street crime; some speak to violence against women; a few speak to white-collar crime.

SOCIAL, CULTURAL, AND COMMUNITY CRIME PREVENTION (PRIMARY PREVENTION)

A primary prevention approach to U.S. crime recognizes the geographical and sociodemographic patterning of street crime outlined in earlier chapters. The most important elements of this patterning are these: (1) serious violent crime in the United States is among the highest of all Western nations and (2) serious street crime, both violent and property, in the United States is committed disproportionately by young people, the poor, males, urban residents, and African Americans. Combining these characteristics, crime rates are highest among young, poor, urban, African-American men.

If we could wave a magic wand, we could probably reduce crime significantly, including white-collar crime, by giving our country a new value system. This value system would place less emphasis on economic success, individualism, and competition, and more emphasis on cooperation and multiple kinds of success. If Bonger (1916) and other critics of capitalism are correct (see Chapter 9), our capitalist economic system is responsible for many of the criminogenic values that need to be replaced. However, the United States is certainly not about to abandon capitalism and not about to adopt a new value system, although other industrial and nonindustrial nations, Western and non-Western alike, with lower crime rates all feature value systems that stress community and cooperation (Adler 1983; Clinard 1978; Westermann and Burfeind 1991).

If we had a magic wand, we could also reduce crime significantly by wiping out economic deprivation and racial discrimination. The high degree of economic deprivation in the United States is at least partly responsible for its high crime rate, and economic deprivation and racial discrimination help account for much of the relatively high criminality of urban African Americans and Latinos.

Finally, if we could wave a magic wand, we could reduce crime significantly by eliminating the many aspects of masculinity that prompt males to be so much more crime prone than females. If the male crime rate were as low as the female rate, crime in the United States would probably not be considered a serious problem.

Unfortunately, of course, magic wands do not exist except at Hogwarts Castle and in the Land of Oz, and we are not about to overhaul U.S. values, abolish poverty and racial discrimination, and eliminate the worst aspects of masculinity in any of our lifetimes. More practical strategies that address the structural and cultural roots of crime are therefore necessary. The following proposals outline several such strategies.

1. *Undertake social policies to create decent-paying jobs for the poor, especially those in urban communities.* The U.S. poverty rate has grown since 2000. Even when the nation's economy was thriving during the middle and late 1990s, the economic situation of people at the bottom of the socioeconomic ladder remained dismal and even worsened (Mishel, Bernstein, and Shierholz 2009). Economic and social policies, therefore, must be developed to address their needs. Here employment policy is crucial, as research documents the connection between extreme poverty and crime (see Chapter 7). According to Elliott Currie (1985:263), "a commitment to full and decent employment remains the keystone of any successful anticrime policy." Currie noted that Western nations with lower violent-crime rates than the United States all have much more effective employment policies than the United States does. Employment reduces poverty, especially among the economic underclass; it increases an individual's bond to society and sense of responsibility; and it reduces family stress and enhances family functioning. If the United States can reduce poverty by enabling more people to work at decent-paying jobs, crime will eventually decrease. Several specific

Unemployment lines indicate a social problem—the absence of a sufficient number of decent-paying jobs for the poor—that contributes to the crime rate.

policies to increase employment have been proposed elsewhere (Currie 1998). They include large public expenditures for job training and public works jobs and tax and other incentives for corporations to develop stable employment in urban areas.

2. *Provide government economic aid for people who cannot find work or who find work but still cannot lift themselves out of poverty.* Many of the poor are working poor. They have jobs at or close to the minimum wage, which still leaves them far below the poverty line. Other members of the poor are women with young children. They either cannot afford to work because of high day care costs or are unemployable because they lack a high school degree and/or job skills. If we do not provide for our poor, we are certain to increase the chances that their children will grow up to commit crime.

3. *End racial segregation in housing.* Douglas S. Massey and Nancy A. Denton (1993) documented the devastating effects that housing segregation, promoted in part by government public housing programs, had on African Americans during the last few decades of the past century. Housing segregation exacerbated their economic distress by trapping them in deteriorating neighborhoods with weakened social institutions and increasing crime rates.

4. *Restore the social integration and strengthen the social institutions of urban neighborhoods.* This proposal stems from social disorganization theory (see Chapter 7). Any measures to strengthen the urban neighborhoods in these respects should concentrate on children and adolescents. Examples here would include youth recreation programs, increased involvement of parents in school activities, increased involvement of youths in church-based religious and social activities, and adult–youth mentoring in job skills, hobbies, and other areas.

5. *Reduce housing and population density.* Crime is more likely when families live in apartment buildings, public housing projects, and other types of crowded housing than when they live more spread apart (Barkan 2000). New public housing for the poor should thus be larger and more dispersed geographically. If they desire, current residents of urban public housing projects and other dense housing should be able to move to such housing.

6. *Reduce urban neighborhood dilapidation.* Several scholars have discussed the physical incivilities of urban neighborhoods as a cause of their high crime rates (Skogan 1990; Stark 1987). These incivilities include graffiti, broken windows, abandoned buildings, and strewn trash. Such dilapidation may prompt nondeviant neighborhood residents to move elsewhere and makes those remaining feel stigmatized and less willing to report victimization to the police. It also encourages potential offenders to commit crime, because they feel the residents "are so indifferent to what goes on in their

Improving the physical conditions of urban neighborhoods should help to reduce street crime.

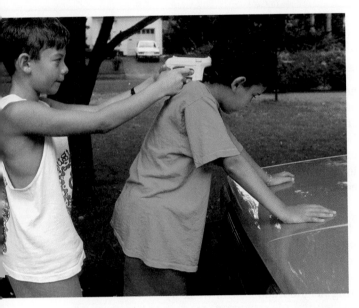

To help reduce violent crime, it is important that we begin to raise our boys away from the traditional masculine emphasis on violence.

neighborhood that they will not be motivated to confront strangers, intervene in a crime, or call the police" (Sampson 1995:208). Dilapidation also decreases the odds that children will come to respect the need to obey laws and other social norms. Although the actual incivilities–crime connection remains in dispute (see Chapter 7), efforts that successfully clean up neighborhoods might reduce crime.

7. *Change male socialization practices so that notions of masculinity move away from violence and other criminogenic attitudes and values.* Although we are not about to change masculinity overnight, it is possible for parents to begin to raise their boys according to a different value system. Parents who try to do this, of course, inevitably face the influences of violent-toy advertising, of violent TV shows and movies, and of their sons' friends raised according to traditional masculine values. Despite these influences, parents' socialization practices do make a difference, and to the extent they begin to raise their boys away from traditional masculine emphases on violence and economic success, crime will be reduced.

8. *Reduce social and economic inequality between women and men.* To the extent that rape and battering arise from women's economic and social subordination, reducing gender inequality should reduce these crimes. A complete discussion of policies addressing gender inequality is beyond our scope but would include, at a minimum, reducing the gender gap in wages and salaries and increasing career opportunities for women.

Review and Discuss

What are any three primary prevention measures that might reduce the crime rate?

DEVELOPMENTAL CRIME PREVENTION (SECONDARY PREVENTION)

A secondary prevention approach recognizes that serious crime is disproportionately committed by a small group of chronic offenders whose antisocial behavior began before adolescence. They tend to come from economically deprived, dysfunctional families characterized by parents whose relationships with each other and with their children are hostile rather than harmonious; by fathers (and stepfathers and boyfriends) who physically abuse mothers; by parents whose discipline of their children is either too permissive or too coercive; by parents who routinely spank and even physically and/or sexually abuse their children; and by parents with histories of criminality and of alcohol or other drug abuse (Welsh and Farrington 2007). These offenders likely attended run-down, dysfunctional schools with overcrowded classrooms and outmoded books and equipment, and more often than not they got poor grades in these schools and were uninvolved in school activities.

A secondary prevention approach thus recognizes that the seeds of juvenile delinquency and adult crime are planted long before delinquency and crime appear and that it is absolutely essential to focus prevention efforts on **developmental experiences** in early childhood that set the stage for later offending. As James Q. Wilson (1995:493) observed, "Prevention, if it can be made to work at all, must start very early in life, perhaps as early as the first two or three years, and given the odds it faces . . . be massive in scope."

If we could again wave a magic wand, we would reduce crime by immediately transforming dysfunctional families into the kind advocated by Dr. Benjamin Spock (1992) in his classic guide *Baby and Child Care.* We would have parents who treat each other and their children with loving respect; who do not abuse alcohol or other drugs; who supervise their children's behavior, and especially their sons' behavior, carefully without being overbearing; and who discipline their children firmly but fairly, and with little or no spanking and certainly no physical or sexual abuse. If we could wave a magic wand, we would also immediately transform our schools, especially those in poor, urban communities, into better places of learning.

Although once again we have no magic wand, there are still several practical policies that could help our parents and our schools do a better job of keeping our children from developing antisocial and then delinquent and criminal tendencies (Greenwood 2006; Welsh and Farrington 2007). These policies include the following:

9. *Establish well-funded early childhood intervention programs for high-risk children and their families.* These critical programs should target multiple risk factors and should involve, among other things, preschool education, home visits, and parenting training. A growing amount of evidence indicates that intensive early intervention programs of this nature can reduce later delinquency and other behavioral problems.

10. *Provide affordable, high-quality child day care for all parents who need it to work outside the home and flexible work schedules to allow parents to spend more time with children.* These two policies would enable parents to be employed and help ensure that their children have good caretaking. Currently, the United States lags behind many European nations that already provide government-sponsored day care and flexible work schedules. Adoption of these policies would reduce structural (unemployment and poverty) and developmental (poor child rearing) problems that create criminality.

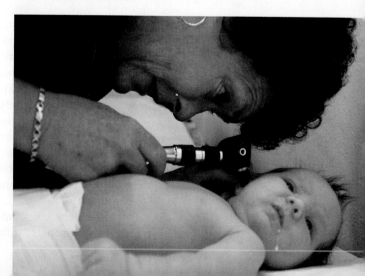

A developmental focus on early childhood risk factors will help reduce delinquency and adult crime. In this regard, it is essential that we expand prenatal and postnatal nutrition and other health services.

11. *Improve the nation's schools, especially in urban areas, where schools are beset by "savage inequalities" (Kozol 1991) that generate criminogenic conditions.* Dysfunctional schools should be thoroughly renovated and much better funded. In many areas, new schools should be built. New schools should be smaller than existing schools, and all schools should have small numbers of students in classes, with heavy involvement of community volunteers. Among other things, such measures will improve students' educational performance, strengthen their commitment to the educational process and their attachment

to their teachers, and encourage them to become more involved in school activities. All these achievements should in turn lower their risk for delinquency and later criminality.

12. *Provide prenatal and postnatal nutrition and other health-related services.* To the extent that poor prenatal and postnatal nutrition and other health problems impair children's neurological functioning, their chances for antisocial and thus later criminal behavior increase. United States prenatal and postnatal programs are currently inadequate, leaving many poor children at risk for neurological impairment.

13. *Expand the network of battered women's shelters and rape crisis centers.* These establishments have provided an invaluable service for women beaten and/or raped by husbands, boyfriends, and former husbands and boyfriends. However, their numbers and resources are currently inadequate to meet the need of the millions of women battered or raped each year. Expanding the network of shelters and centers would not only help protect these women from additional abuse, but would also reduce the likelihood that any children they might have will grow up in violent households.

Review and Discuss

What are any three secondary prevention measures that might reduce the crime rate?

CRIMINAL JUSTICE APPROACHES (TERTIARY PREVENTION)

A tertiary approach to crime prevention that is grounded in sociological criminology recognizes the "limits of the criminal sanction," to use Herbert Packer's (1968) famous term. It acknowledges that only very limited crime reduction can be achieved by relying on law and criminal justice and that any crime reduction that can be achieved comes only at a great cost of dollars and threats to civil liberties and civil rights. At the same time, it recognizes that crime is a serious problem and that the public must be kept safe from dangerous offenders. Several of the following criminal justice–based proposals would help make society safer at lower financial, social, and political costs than are true of current strategies. Others might not affect crime rates, but at least would raise public trust and confidence in criminal justice and have it operate more in line with democratic ideals.

14. *Reduce reliance on imprisonment and put more emphasis on community corrections.* This model is used by many western European nations. The surge in U.S. imprisonment since 1980 has accomplished little but cost us much. Reducing reliance on imprisonment would free up significant dollars for community corrections approaches. There is increasing evidence that these approaches save money, do not lead to more recidivism than imprisonment, and might even lead to less recidivism if they are properly funded (Petersilia 2008; Travis and Visher 2005). Greater use of these programs would save money and keep society at least as safe as, and perhaps a bit safer than, imprisonment would. Probation and parole officers should have much smaller caseloads to permit more intensive supervision of offenders released into the community.

    Offenders considered for community corrections should be nonviolent drug and property offenders. Nationally, about half of all state prisoners have been convicted either of a drug offense, property offense, or consensual offense such as commercialized vice. Without threatening public safety, most of these offenders could be placed into community corrections at a savings of several billion dollars per year, even after paying for their community corrections costs. The dollars saved could be used for employment, early family intervention, and other policies that would reduce crime. For example, the money saved for each offender going into community corrections could fund one preschool teacher who could be involved with five to ten children at high risk for developmental problems. Reducing reliance on imprisonment would also mean that new prison construction could stop, saving tens of billions of dollars in future construction and maintenance costs. These funds could also be reallocated to primary and secondary crime-prevention programs.

Efforts that improve prison conditions should help reduce crime by making it less likely that prisoners will commit new crimes after their release back into society.

15. *Make prisons and jails smaller, reduce overcrowding, and improve other decrepit prison and jail conditions.* Despite popular belief, conditions in many prisons and jails are substandard (Kappeler and Potter 2005). Current prison conditions do little to rehabilitate offenders and often make them worse. At a minimum, improving prisons would help reduce the extent to which offenders worsen because of their prison experience and thus lead to a safer society. This reform should include the establishment of much better educational, vocational, and other rehabilitation programs in prisons. These programs appear to reduce crime and would be even more effective were they adequately funded (Cullen 2007).

16. *Eliminate "three strikes and you're out" and mandatory imprisonment policies.* These policies have swelled our prison population without lowering the crime rate. Given that criminality declines sharply with advancing age, people sent to prison for life after a third felony stay in prison for many more years after they would have stopped committing crime. In general, many prison terms could be shortened, saving prison costs and reducing prison overcrowding, without endangering public safety (Tonry 2004).

17. *Consider repealing at least some of the present drug laws.* These laws might do more harm than good. They have unfairly targeted the African-American community, and they have cost billions of dollars in criminal justice expenses. The billions of dollars saved could be redirected to educational and treatment programs designed to prevent drug use from beginning and to halt drug use that has already started. Because of the very legitimate concerns raised by both proponents and opponents of drug decriminalization, a national debate must begin on what drug policies make the most sense.

18. *Eliminate the death penalty.* The death penalty has no general deterrent effect and costs at least twice as much as life imprisonment. It continues to be

arbitrary and discriminatory in its application and to put at least some innocent people at risk for death. In a nonsociological area, serious questions can be raised about the morality of capital punishment in a society that professes to be civilized.

19. *Expand community policing and consider expanding directed police activity in crime hot spots.* Some evidence indicates that community policing and directed police activity in crime hot spots may reduce crime and that community policing reduces fear of crime and may help lessen the incivilities of urban neighborhoods. Because directed patrol may overburden the courts, jails, and prisons and raise civil liberties questions, such activity should be considered carefully before being undertaken.

20. *Increase the hiring of minority and female police officers and develop a zero-tolerance policy for the hostility and discrimination they now experience from other officers.* This proposal would increase the respect of minority urban residents for the police and strengthen police–community relations. Although the crime-reduction benefit from this proposal may be minimal, a democratic society should not tolerate discrimination within its law enforcement community.

21. *Reduce police brutality and racial profiling.* Police departments should develop zero tolerance for such behaviors and take every step possible to identify and remove the officers responsible for them. Again, these measures might not reduce crime, but they would at least protect the public from police misconduct and reduce citizen disrespect for and hostility toward the police.

22. *Increase gun-control efforts.* The huge number of handguns in the United States is an important reason for our high number of homicides. If we could wave a magic wand and make all handguns disappear, our homicide rates would drop significantly. Without a magic wand, however, there are far too many handguns and far too many people who want handguns for these weapons to be eliminated entirely. Given these facts, the best we can do is to undertake policies that limit the supply of handguns for law-abiding citizens and offenders alike, especially youths, and that decrease the chances of gun accidents. Philip J. Cook and Mark H. Moore (1995) discussed several such policies, including (a) heavily taxing guns and ammunition to make them too expensive for at least some people, and especially adolescents, to buy; (b) substantially raising the licensing fee for gun dealers to reduce their number; (c) requiring that new guns include safety measures to reduce accidental use; (d) increasing community policing to reduce fear of crime and hence citizens' perceptions that they need handguns for protection; and (e) removing guns from homes where domestic violence occurs.

23. *Increase intolerance for white-collar crime and political corruption.* This will be no easy task. Even so, several policies might help limit white-collar crime and political corruption, including greater media attention to the harm of such crime; greater expenditure of resources on preventing, detecting, and enforcing current laws; and the development of new laws. More certain punishment, especially imprisonment, for white-collar and governmental offenders should also work. Although this "get tough" approach has not been shown to work with common criminals, it may have more of a deterrent effect on potential white-collar and governmental offenders (Friedrichs 2010).

Review and Discuss

What are any three tertiary prevention measures that might reduce the crime rate?

We now stand at a crossroads. Although crime rates are much lower now than in the early 1990s, conditions for the U.S. poor have been worsening over the past few decades, and the nation was in a serious recession at the time of this writing. States were realizing that they could no longer afford to pay for their great numbers of prisoners resulting from the nation's "get tough" policy on crime. They were also cutting back on various programs that aid the children most at risk for an eventual life of crime, namely, those growing up in poor, single-parent households. If we wanted to ensure that crime will increase, we would do exactly what we have been doing in regard to the poor among us.

Michael Tonry (2004:vii) observed, "The United States has a punishment system that no one would knowingly have built from the ground up. It is often unjust, it is unduly severe, it is wasteful, and it does enormous damage to the lives of black Americans." Taking this view one step further, Elliott Currie (1985:278) said that if we wanted for some reason to design a society that would be especially violent, it would look very much like what we now have. It would be a society with high rates of inequality and high rates of unemployment among the young, which deprives them of participation in community life. It would be a society that allows thousands of jobs to leave whole communities, disrupting their social organization and forcing people to migrate in search of new jobs. It would also be a society that promotes "a culture of intense interpersonal competition" and emphasizes material consumption to such a degree that many people violate the law to reach this level, while others experience anger and frustration over their inability to live up to this lofty standard.

In the same vein, Jeffrey Reiman and Paul Leighton (2010) note that if we wanted for some reason to design a criminal justice system that would certainly fail, it would also look very much like the one we now have. It would be a system that bans many consensual behaviors and forces people committed to those behaviors to engage in other types of crime. It would also be a system in which arrest, prosecution, and punishment are somewhat arbitrary and in which wealthy individuals and organizations committing very harmful behaviors generally avoid legal sanctions. Both sets of dynamics, Reiman and Leighton said, lead to resentment among the relative few who end up under the control of criminal justice officials. Next, it would be a system in which the prison experience is more likely to make inmates worse than better and a system in which prisoners learn no marketable skills in prison and have no jobs awaiting them when they leave prison. Finally, it would be a system in which ex-offenders are shunned by conventional society, lose their right to vote, cannot find work, and otherwise are prevented from reintegrating themselves into the conventional social order.

If we are honest, we would admit that we live in a society whose fundamental structural and cultural features contribute heavily to our high crime rates. We would also admit that we know that the criminal justice system is not working and cannot be made to work to reduce crime. If we are serious about reducing crime, we will undertake some or all of the preventive measures just listed. They may not all succeed, but we certainly cannot do much worse than we have been doing. Dickens, Dostoyevsky, and other great writers have reminded us that how we treat the poor and the criminals among us is a sign of what kind of a people we are. If we are to be true to our democratic, egalitarian ideals, we must attack the social roots of the crime and victimization that plague us so. Anything else would betray the noble principles on which our nation was founded.

Conclusion

This chapter has proposed several measures that hold at least some promise for reducing the rates of many types of criminal behaviors. The basis for all the proposals is a vast body of research, discussed in earlier chapters, on the structural and cultural causes of crime and victimization.

Chapter 1 mentioned that a key goal of this book was to develop your sociological imagination about crime. We hope we have succeeded. A sociological criminology tells us much about the society in which we live. As C. Wright Mills (1959) observed, the knowledge that the sociological imagination gives us is both terrible and magnificent. Your new sociological imagination about crime may be terrible for indicating the power of the social forces underlying crime and victimization. But it is also magnificent for pointing you to the possibility of changing these forces so that we can, at long last, have a safer society.

18

Summary

1. A public health approach emphasizes the need to prevent crime from occurring. The "get tough" approach underlying U.S. crime policy during the past few decades has not succeeded in doing this and has cost tens of billions of dollars.

2. The criminal justice funnel highlights the fact that only a very small percentage of all serious crimes lead to the incarceration of the offender. The huge drop throughout all stages of the funnel underscores the cost-ineffectiveness of reliance on the criminal justice system to reduce crime.

3. A public health approach to crime control involves primary, secondary, and tertiary prevention. A sociological prescription for crime reduction comprises several policies and actions to accomplish each kind of prevention.

Key Terms

criminal justice funnel 454

primary prevention 457

secondary prevention 457

tertiary prevention 457

developmental experiences 461

public health model 453

What Would You Do?

1. You are the mayor of a large city that has a limited budget. Your police chief has put in a request for an additional $1 million to hire and equip several more police officers. Meanwhile, the head of your Child Services Division has also put in a request for about $1 million to hire several more caseworkers to work with families in which children are at risk for neglect and/or abuse. You probably do have $1 million to allocate to one of these requests. Which one do you select, and why?

2. You are the warden of a medium-security state prison that was built to house 1,000 inmates but now is holding 1,600 inmates. Reflecting national statistics, about half of your inmates are behind bars for committing nonviolent property, drug, or consensual offenses. Most of them would not be a threat to public safety were they to be released from prison, but some of them would be a threat, and there is probably little way of predicting successfully the inmates who would fall into either group. Of course, you have no power to release any inmates, but you have been asked to testify before your state legislature's Criminal Justice Committee about the possible effects of releasing at least some of the inmates back into the community to relieve the crowding at your prison. What do you say in your testimony?

Glossary

abnormality   an abnormal biological or psychological condition said to be responsible for criminal behavior.

absolute deterrence   the effect of having some legal punishment versus the effect of having no legal punishment.

actus reus   the actual criminal act of which a defendant is accused.

adversary system   the idealized model of the criminal justice process in the United States in which the prosecutor and defense attorney vigorously contest the evidence concerning the defendant's guilt or innocence.

agents provocateurs   government agents who pretend to join a dissident group and then try to goad the group into committing violence or other illegal activity.

alien conspiracy model   the belief that a small number of Italian-American "families" control organized crime in the United States.

amateur theft   property crime committed by unskilled offenders who act when the opportunity arises.

anomie   as developed by Émile Durkheim, a state of normlessness in society in which aspirations that previously were controlled now become unlimited. Robert Merton adapted this term to refer to the gap between the institutionalized goal in the United States of financial success and the institutionalized means of working.

arbitrariness   the process occurring when legal outcomes are based on prejudice or other nonlegal criteria instead of legal factors, such as the seriousness of the crime and the strength of the evidence.

aspirations   strong desires or longings. As used in extensions of Merton's anomie theory, aspirations refer to economic and other goals of adolescents that result in frustration when they are not realized.

assault   an unlawful attack by one person on another to inflict bodily injury. Aggravated assault involves a serious injury or the use of a weapon. Simple assault involves only minor injuries and no use of a weapon.

atavism   the belief, popularized by Cesare Lombroso, that criminals are born as throwbacks to an earlier stage of evolution.

attachment   in Travis Hirschi's social control theory, the degree to which adolescents care about the opinions of conventional others, including parents and teachers, and feel close to them. The greater the attachment, the less the delinquency.

battering   physical assaults and other physical abuse committed against a woman by a male intimate.

booster   skilled, professional shoplifters who sell their stolen goods to fences or pawn shops.

bourgeoisie   as used by Karl Marx and Friedrich Engels, the class in capitalist society that controls the means of production.

bribery   the giving or accepting of money or other things of value in return for promises to grant favors to the party giving the bribe.

brothel   a house of prostitution.

brutality   a form of police misconduct involving the undue or excessive use of physical coercion to subdue a suspect or other citizen.

brutalization effect   the possibility that executions increase the homicide rate.

caseloads   the workload of prosecutors, defense attorneys, and judges.

casino   a building used for gambling.

causal order   the direction of the relationship between two variables.

certainty   the likelihood of being arrested.

child abuse   physical violence or sexual misconduct committed against children by their parents or other adults.

chronic offenders   a small number of offenders who commit a disproportionate amount of serious crime and delinquency and who persist in their criminality.

civil disobedience   the violation of criminal law for reasons of conscience.

classical school   a school of thought popular in the eighteenth century in Europe. Its main assumptions were that criminals act rationally and that the severity of legal punishment should be restricted to the degree necessary to deter crime.

climatological   as used in discussing the patterning of crime, refers to the variation of crime rates with climate and seasons of the year.

COINTELPRO   a secret FBI program, aimed at disrupting and discrediting dissident groups and individuals, that reached its zenith during the 1960s and early 1970s.

collective embezzlement   the stealing of company funds by top management. The term was first used to refer to one type of crime that characterized the U.S. savings and loan scandals of the 1980s.

common law   the system of law originating in medieval England and emphasizing court decisions and customs.

community policing   a style of policing in which police patrol neighborhoods on foot and try to help their residents solve community problems.

concentric zones   the division of cities into geographical sectors radiating out from the city's center.

concordance   a similarity of criminal behavior and other outcomes between identical twins.

conflict   as used in sociology and criminology, refers to a theory that assumes that people disagree on norms and act with self-interest because of their disparate socioeconomic positions.

consensus   as used in sociology and criminology, refers to a theory that people agree on norms despite their disparate socioeconomic positions.

constable   an official appointed by medieval English nobles to control poaching and otherwise monitor the behavior of people living on the nobles' land.

containment   as used in criminology, refers to a theory developed by Walter C. Reckless that stressed the inner and outer conditions that help prevent juvenile delinquency.

conventional social institutions   structured patterns of behavior and relationships, such as the family, the educational system, and religion.

corporate crime   an action by a corporation that violates the criminal law.

corporate violence   activities or neglect by corporations that lead to injury, illness, or death.

correctional supervision   placement in prison, jail, or on probation or parole.

corruption   dishonest practices, especially when committed by public or corporate officials.

courtroom work group   the "team" of prosecutor, defense attorney, and judge, all of whom are said to cooperate to expedite cases.

crackdown   the short-term concentration of police resources in a specific neighborhood, usually to control a specific activity, such as drug possession and trafficking.

crime   behavior that is considered so harmful that it is banned by a criminal law.

crime characteristics   aspects of a crime, such as its location and the typical victim–offender relationship.

crime control   the use of the criminal justice system to prevent and punish crime. The *crime-control model* refers to the belief that crime control is the primary goal of the criminal justice system.

crime myth   a widespread but inaccurate belief about crime.

crime victim   any person who unwillingly suffers a completed or attempted crime.

crime wave   a sudden and often distorted focus of the news media on one or more types of criminal behavior.

criminal careers   the continuation of criminal behavior past adolescence and young adulthood.

criminal intent   having the desire to commit a crime.

criminal justice funnel   the rapid drop from the number of actual crimes committed to the number of offenders incarcerated.

criminalization   the process by which lawful behaviors are turned into criminal ones because of the enactment of new laws.

criminogenic   crime causing.

criminology   the study of the making of laws, the breaking of laws, and society's reaction to the breaking of laws.

critical perspectives   views that challenge traditional understandings and theories of crime and criminal justice.

cultural myths   as used in criminology, refers to false beliefs in society that make crimes such as rape and battering more likely.

culture conflict   the clash of values and norms between different social groups, especially as it leads to the behavior of one group to be branded as criminal.

customs   norms that are unwritten and informal.

debunking motif   part of the sociological perspective; refers to the challenge sociology poses to conventional understandings of social institutions and social reality.

decision-making processes   the ways judges and prosecutors determine what happens at various stages of the criminal justice system.

delinquent peers   lawbreaking adolescents with whom a particular adolescent associates.

democratic society   a society in which the people freely elect officials to represent their views and interests and in which they are free from arbitrary government power.

democratic theory   the view that elected officials should represent the interests of all people in a democracy.

dependent variable   an attitude or behavior that changes because of the influence of an independent variable.

deterrence   in criminology, having a deterrent effect on crime.

deterrence theory   the belief that the threat or application of legal punishment prevents criminal behavior.

developmental experiences   aspects of childhood and adolescence that affect the likelihood of crime.

deviance   behavior that violates accepted norms and arouses negative social reactions.

deviance amplification   the process by which official labeling increases the likelihood of deviant behavior.

differential association   Edwin Sutherland's concept for the process by which adolescents become delinquent because they are exposed to more lawbreaking attitudes than to law-abiding attitudes.

differential opportunities   conditions or situations that are more or less favorable for the commission of crime.

discordance   a difference in criminal behavior and other outcomes between identical twins.

discretion   latitude in decision making.

double burden   the difficulties faced by minority female police officers because of their race and gender.

dowry deaths   murders of women in India and Pakistan because their families could not pay the expected dowry.

dramatization of evil   the process by which deviant labels affect self-images and promote continued deviance.

drift   the intermittent commission of delinquency.

due process   rights granted to criminal defendants by the U.S. Constitution and judicial rulings.

duress   threats or coercion on another to commit a crime.

economic deprivation   poverty and economic inequality.

ego   Sigmund Freud's term for the rational dimension of the personality that develops after the id.

embezzlement   the stealing or misappropriation of funds entrusted to an employee.

Enlightenment   an intellectual movement in the seventeenth and eighteenth centuries that challenged medieval religious beliefs.

erotica   written or visual materials dealing with sexual behavior and often intended to arouse sexual desire.

espionage   spying.

exclusionary rule   a rule that prohibits evidence from criminal trials that was gathered in violation of judicial rulings; also includes other procedural rules governing the gathering of evidence.

expressive offenses   crimes committed for emotional reasons and with little or no planning.

extralegal   refers to race, ethnicity, gender, social class, and other nonlegal factors that may affect arrest, sentencing, and other legal decision making.

family interaction   behavior and functioning within a family.

family structure   the nature and pattern of statuses in a family.

fear of crime   concern or worry over becoming a crime victim.

felony   a serious criminal offense punishable by a prison term of more than 1 year.

femicide   the murder of women and girls.

feminism   the belief that women deserve to be men's equals in economic, political, and social power.

fencing   the selling of stolen goods.

focal concerns   Walter Miller's term for beliefs and values said to be characteristic of lower-class males that increase their likelihood of delinquency.

general deterrence   deterrence that occurs when members of the public decide not to break the law because they fear legal punishment.

generalize   to apply knowledge of particular cases to other, similar cases.

genital mutilation   the excision of a clitoris.

genocide   the systematic extermination of a category of people because of their race, ethnicity, or religion.

goods   objects the public desires, several of which are provided by organized crime.

grass-eaters   police who engage in minor bribery and other corruption.

handgun control   efforts to restrict the supply and ownership of handguns.

harm reduction   a public policy strategy in which drug use is treated as a public health problem and not as a crime problem.

hate crime   violent or property crimes committed against the person or property of someone because of that person's race, ethnicity, religion, national origin, or sexual orientation.

heredity   the genetic transmission of physical characteristics, behavior, and other traits.

homicide   the unjustified killing of a human being.

hot spots   specific locations in neighborhoods in which crime is especially common.

id   Sigmund Freud's term for the instinctive, pleasure-seeking dimension of the personality that characterizes infancy.

incapacitation   physically preventing a convicted offender from committing a crime; usually refers to incarceration.

incarceration   the placing of a convicted offender in prison or jail.

incidence   the average number of offenses per person in the time period under examination.

independent variable   a sociodemographic characteristic or other trait that influences changes in a dependent variable.

individual characteristics   personal traits that influence the likelihood of committing an inequality crime or becoming a crime victim.

in/out decision   the determination of whether a convicted offender should be incarcerated.

instrumental offenses   crimes committed for material gain and with some degree of planning.

international comparisons   cross-national comparisons of crime rates.

interpersonal violence   physically injurious acts committed by one or more people against one or more others.

intraracial   within one race.

IQ   intelligence as measured by standardized tests.

Iran–Contra scandal   a scandal in the 1980s involving the illegal sale of weapons to Iran and the diverting of funds from that sale to Contra rebels in Nicaragua.

joyriding   the temporary stealing of a car or other motor vehicle in order to drive or ride in it for thrills.

kinds of people   the characteristics of individuals that generate criminality.

kinds of places   the structural and physical characteristics of neighborhoods and other locations that generate criminality.

labeling   defining a person or behavior as deviant.

laws   written, formal norms.

learning   acquiring attitudes, knowledge, and skills; in criminology, a process by which people become criminals.

learning theories   explanations that emphasize that criminal behavior is learned.

left realism   an approach to crime developed by radical criminologists in Great Britain that emphasizes the harm that crime causes and the need to take measures to reduce crime.

legalization   the elimination of laws prohibiting certain behaviors, especially consensual crimes.

liberation hypothesis   the view that racial discrimination in sentencing is more likely for defendants convicted of minor offenses than for those convicted of serious offenses.

life course   infancy, childhood, adolescence, young adulthood, and older stages of life.

lifestyle theory   the belief that certain leisure-time and other activities increase the chances of becoming a crime victim.

longitudinal studies   research in which the same people are studied over time.

mala in se   behaviors that are wrong in and of themselves.

mala prohibita   behaviors that are wrong only because they are prohibited by law.

male dominance   the supremacy of men in society.

manslaughter   an unjustified killing considered less serious or less blameworthy than murder.

marginal deterrence   the effect of increasing the severity, certainty, and/or swiftness of legal punishment.

Marxism   a set of beliefs derived from the work of Karl Marx and Friedrich Engels that emphasizes the conflict of interests between people based on whether they own the means of production.

mass media   modes of communication, such as television, radio, and newspapers.

measurement   in criminology, the determination of the frequency of criminal behavior and of the characteristics of offenders and victims.

meat-eaters   police who engage in serious forms of corruption.

mens rea   a guilty mind; refers to an individual having criminal intent.

misdemeanor   a relatively minor criminal offense punishable by less than 1 year in prison.

moral crusade   a concerted effort to prevent and punish behavior considered immoral.

moral development   the process by which children and adolescents develop their sense of morality.

more harm than good   in the drug legalization debate, refers to whether drug laws result in more disadvantages than advantages.

muckrakers   a group of early twentieth-century U.S. journalists and other social critics of political and corporate corruption and other misconduct.

National Crime Victimization Survey (NCVS)   an annual survey of criminal victimization sponsored by the U.S. Department of Justice.

neurotransmitters chemical substances that help neurons transmit impulses to each other across synapses.

news media the members of the mass media transmitting information about current events.

nonviolent pornography sexually explicit materials that do not involve violent acts.

norms standards of behavior.

objective deterrence the impact of actual legal punishment.

occupational crime crime committed in the course of one's occupation.

organizational crime crime committed on behalf of an organization.

overdramate to exaggerate for the news media the frequency and seriousness of violent crime.

patriarchy male supremacy.

patterning the social distribution of criminal behavior according to certain characteristics of locations and of individuals.

peacemaking criminology an approach that combines several humanistic strains of thought to view crime as just one of the many forms of suffering that characterize human existence.

personality aspects of an individual's character, behavior, and other qualities.

phrenology the belief that the size and shape of the skull indicate the propensity for criminal behavior.

pilferage employee theft of workplace items, usually of small value.

piracy robbery at sea.

plea bargaining negotiations between prosecution and defense over the sentence the prosecutor will request in return for a plea of guilty by the defendant.

police sexual violence (PSV) violence committed by police against female suspects or other female civilians.

political crime any illegal or socially harmful act aimed at preserving or changing the existing political and social order.

political violence interpersonal violence committed to achieve a political goal.

politics of victimization the ideological implications of government efforts to help victims of street crime.

positivism the view that human behavior and attitudes are influenced by forces both external and internal to the individual.

premenstrual syndrome symptoms such as severe tension and irritability occurring in the premenstrual phase.

prevalence the proportion of respondents who have committed a particular offense at least once in the time period under study.

price-fixing the practice whereby businesses conspire to fix prices on goods and services rather than let the free market operate.

primary deviance the first deviant act that someone commits; in labeling theory, primary deviance is said not to lead often to continued or secondary deviance unless labeling occurs.

primary prevention efforts to prevent problems such as disease, injury, or crime by focusing on aspects of the social or physical environment that contribute to these problems.

private troubles individual problems that many people have that they think stem from their own failings or particular circumstances.

professional fraud fraud committed by physicians, attorneys, and other professional workers.

professional theft property crime committed by skilled offenders who carefully plan their offenses.

proletariat as used by Karl Marx and Friedrich Engels, the class in capitalist society that does not control the means of production.

property crime theft and other crime committed against property.

psychoanalytic refers to explanations of human motivation and behavior that derive from the work of Sigmund Freud.

psychological consequences mental and emotional effects; in criminology, particularly from criminal victimization.

public health model   an approach to illness, injury, and other problems that emphasizes primary prevention.

public issues   social problems resulting from structural and other problems in the social environment.

public opinion   the views and attitudes of the public on important social, political, and economic issues.

public policy   government efforts to deal with public issues and societal needs.

punitiveness   public judgments of appropriate punishment for convicted criminals.

racial prejudice   unfavorable views toward a certain category of people because of their race.

rape   forced or nonconsensual sexual intercourse.

rational-choice theory   the view that people plan their actions and weigh the potential benefits and costs of their potential behavior.

rationalization   a justification or technique of neutralization that minimizes the guilt that criminal offenders may otherwise feel.

reinforcement   the rewarding of behavior; a key concept in differential reinforcement theory, which argues that criminal behavior and attitudes are more likely to be learned when they are reinforced by friends and/or family.

relative deprivation   the feeling that one is less well off than others.

relativist definition   labeling theory's view that deviance is not a property of a behavior, but is rather the result of how others regard that behavior.

religious fundamentalism   in Christianity and Judaism, the belief that the Bible is the actual word of God.

repression   government suppression of dissent through violent or legal means.

repressive law   Émile Durkheim's term for the punitive type of legal punishment that he thought characterizes traditional societies.

restitutive law   Émile Durkheim's term for the compensatory type of legal punishment that he thought characterizes modern societies.

restraint of trade   business practices that violate free market principles.

robbery   taking or attempting to take something from one or more people by force or threat of force.

routine-activities theory   the view that an individual's daily activities can affect his or her chances of becoming a crime victim.

ruling class   the capitalist class or bourgeoisie.

seasonal   of or relating to the seasons of the year; some crime rates vary from season to season and are thus said to be seasonal.

secondary deviance   continued deviance; said by labeling theory to result from the labeling of primary deviance.

secondary prevention   the identification of practices and situations that put certain individuals at risk for illness, injury, or criminality and efforts to address these risk factors.

self-control   the restraining of one's impulses and desires.

self-defense   violent or other actions committed to protect oneself or others.

self-referral   a physician's referral of patients to medical testing laboratories that the physician owns or in which the physician has invested.

self-report studies   surveys in which respondents are asked to report about criminal offenses they have committed.

sentencing preferences   public views of appropriate legal punishment for given crimes.

seriousness of crime   opinions regarding the importance or degree of harm associated with given crimes.

services   the performance of activities that the public desires, several of which are provided by organized crime.

sexual assault   nonconsensual or forced sexual contact that does not involve sexual intercourse.

severity   whether someone is incarcerated and, if so, for how long.

shaming   social disapproval.

sin   a morally improper act.

situational crime prevention   efforts in specific locations that aim to make it more difficult for offenders to commit crimes against potential victims.

sneaky thrill crimes   offenses committed for the excitement.

snitch   an amateur shoplifter.

social bond   the connection among individuals or between individuals and social institutions such as families and schools.

social control   society's restraint of norm-violating behavior.

social disorganization   the breakdown of social bonds and social control in a community or larger society.

social ecology   the relationship of people to their environment; in criminology, the study of the influence of community social and physical characteristics on community crime rates.

social inequality   the differential distribution of wealth, power, and other things of value in a given society.

social integration   the degree to which a community or society is characterized by strong or weak social bonds.

social learning   the view that individuals learn criminal attitudes and behaviors from others who already hold these attitudes and behaviors.

social organization   the pattern of relationships and roles in a society.

social pathology   the view that crime and deviance are symptoms of individual and societal sickness.

social structure   the pattern of social interaction and social relationships in a group or society; horizontal social structure refers to the social and physical characteristics of communities and the networks of social relationships to which an individual belongs, and vertical social structure refers to social inequality.

social ties   social bonds.

socialization   the learning of social norms, attitudes, and values.

sociological criminology   the sociological understanding of crime and criminal justice, stressing the importance of social structure and social inequality.

sociological imagination   the ability to attribute private troubles to problems in the larger social structure.

sociological perspective   the belief that social backgrounds influence individuals' attitudes and behaviors.

somatology   the belief that body size and shape influence criminality.

specific deterrence   deterrence that occurs when offenders already *punished* for lawbreaking decide not to commit another crime because they do not want to face legal consequences again.

spurious   a statistical relationship between two variables that exists only because the effects of a third variable have not been considered.

stalking state–corporate crime   cooperation between government agencies and corporations to commit illegal or socially injurious activities.

state terrorism   government rule by terror.

status frustration   disappointment and feelings of dissatisfaction resulting from the failure to do well in school; said by Albert Cohen to lead to delinquency among lower-class boys.

strain   anomie or frustration, stemming from the failure to achieve goals.

structural factors   aspects of the social structure.

subculture of violence   a set of attitudes, said to characterize poor urban communities, that approves the use of violence to deal with interpersonal problems and disputes.

subjective deterrence   the impact of people's perceptions of the likelihood of arrest and punishment.

superego   Sigmund Freud's term for the dimension of the personality that develops after the id and ego; this dimension represents society's moral code.

support system   the network of tipsters and fences that help burglars carry out their burglaries and dispose of their stolen goods.

survey   questionnaire administered to a set of respondents.

system capacity argument   the belief that areas with high crime rates have low arrest rates because the police have many more crimes to investigate and also realize that too many crimes would overburden the criminal justice system.

tabula rasa   blank slate; refers to the belief that human nature is neutral and can become good or bad because of society's influence.

target hardening   efforts to make homes, stores, and other buildings less vulnerable to burglary and other crimes.

technicalities   term, often pejorative, used for the rules governing the gathering of evidence against a criminal suspect.

temperament   personality.

terrorism   the indiscriminate use of violence to intimidate or coerce people to achieve social and political goals.

tertiary prevention   efforts to treat people already having a problem, such as illness or injury; in criminology, refers to efforts to deal with people who have already committed a crime.

testosterone   the so-called male hormone.

theoretical integration   the combining of two or more theories to present a more comprehensive explanation of crime.

treason   actions designed to overthrow one's government or otherwise weaken it severely.

underclass   the group of people living in persistent poverty and unemployment.

underreporting   the failure of crime victims to report crimes they have suffered or of respondents in self-report surveys to report crimes they have committed.

Uniform Crime Reports (UCR)   the FBI's annual compilation of crime statistics.

victim-impact statement   a written statement by a crime victim that discusses the effects of the victimization and sometimes makes recommendations for sentencing.

victim–offender relationship   refers to whether the victim and offender knew each other before the victimization occurred.

victim precipitation   activities by an eventual crime victim that initiate or further the events leading to the victim's victimization.

victimization   the suffering of a crime.

victimology   the study of victims and victimization.

violent crime   interpersonal violence, especially homicide, rape, assault, and robbery.

violent pornography   sexually explicit materials that depict violence.

Watergate scandal   the scandal in the early 1970s that involved illegal activity committed during the 1972 presidential campaign and the subsequent obstruction of justice; the scandal led to several criminal prosecutions and the resignation of President Richard Nixon.

white-collar crime   illegal or unethical acts committed by an individual or organization during the course of legitimate occupational activity.

working personality   the personality associated with a particular occupation.

wrongful execution   an execution of someone who in fact was innocent of the crime for which he or she was convicted.

zero-tolerance policing   a style of aggressive policing that encourages arrests for even minor infractions of the law.

References

Abadinsky, Howard. 2007. *Organized Crime.* Belmont, CA: Wadsworth.

Abagnale, Frank. 2005. "Check Fraud and Identity Theft." http://www.abagnale.com/pdf/AbagnaleFraudBulletinVol6.pdf.

Abelson, Reed. 2004. "How Schering Manipulated Drug Prices and Medicaid." *New York Times,* July 31:C1.

Abrahamson, Mark. 2010. *Classical Theory and Modern Studies: Introduction to Sociological Theory.* Upper Saddle River, NJ: Pearson.

Adams, James. 1995. *Sellout: Aldrich Ames and the Corruption of the CIA.* New York: Viking Press.

Adams, Kenneth, and Charles R. Cutshall. 1987. "Refusing to Prosecute Minor Offenses: The Relative Influence of Legal and Extralegal Factors." *Justice Quarterly* 4:595–609.

Adelstein, Jake. 2009. *Tokyo Vice: An American Reporter on the Police Beat in Japan.* New York: Pantheon.

Adler, Freda. 1975. *Sisters in Crime: The Rise of the New Female Criminal.* New York: McGraw-Hill.

———. 1983. *Nations Not Obsessed with Crime.* Littleton, CO: Fred B. Rothman & Co.

Adler, Freda, and William S. Laufer (eds.). 1995. *The Legacy of Anomie Theory.* New Brunswick, NJ: Transaction Publishers.

Adler, Jeffrey S. 1989. "A Historical Analysis of the Law of Vagrancy." *Criminology* 27:209–29.

Administration on Children, Youth, and Families. 2010. *Child Maltreatment 2008.* Washington, DC: U.S. Department of Health and Human Services, U.S. Government Printing Office.

AFL-CIO. 2007. *Death on the Job: The Toll of Neglect.* Washington, DC: AFL-CIO.

Agnew, Robert. 1992. "Foundation for a General Strain Theory of Crime and Delinquency." *Criminology* 30(1):47–87.

———. 1994. "The Techniques of Neutralization and Violence." *Criminology* 32:555–80.

———. 1999. "A General Strain Theory of Community Differences in Crime Rates." *Journal of Research in Crime and Delinquency* 36:123–55.

———. 2000. "Sources of Criminality: Strain and Subcultural Theories." Pp. 349–71 in *Criminology: A Contemporary Handbook,* edited by Joseph F. Sheley. Belmont, CA: Wadsworth.

———. 2002. "Experienced, Vicarious, and Anticipated Strain: An Exploratory Study on Physical Victimization and Delinquency." *Justice Quarterly* 19:603–32.

———. 2007. *Pressured into Crime: An Overview of General Strain Theory.* New York: Oxford University Press.

———. 2009. "The Contribution of 'Mainstream' Theories to the Explanation of Female Delinquency." Pp. 7–29 in *The Delinquent Girl,* edited by Margaret A. Zahn. Philadelphia: Temple University Press.

Agnew, Robert, Timothy Brezina, John Paul Wright, and Francis T. Cullen. 2002. "Strain, Personality Traits, and Delinquency: Extending General Strain Theory." *Criminology* 40:43–71.

Akers, Ronald L. 1977. *Deviant Behavior: A Social Learning Perspective.* Belmont, CA: Wadsworth.

———. 1989. "A Social Behavorist's Perspective on Integration of Theories of Crime and Deviance." Pp. 23–36 in *Theoretical Integration in the Study of Deviance and Crime: Problems and Prospects,* edited by Steven F. Messner, Marvin D. Krohn, and Allen E. Liska. Albany: State University of New York Press.

Akers, Ronald L., and Gary F. Jensen. 2006. "The Empirical Status of Social Learning Theory of Crime and Deviance: The Past, Present, and Future." Pp. 37–76 in *Taking Stock: The Status of Criminological Theory,* edited by Francis T. Cullen, John Paul Wright, and Kristie R. Blevins. New Brunswick, NJ: Transaction Publishers.

Akers, Ronald L., and Christine S. Sellers. 2009. *Criminological Theories: Introduction, Evaluation, and Application.* New York: Oxford University Press.

Akins, Scott. 2009. "Racial Segregation, Concentrated Disadvantage, and Violent Crime." *Journal of Ethnicity in Criminal Justice* 7(1):30–52.

Albanese, Jay S. 1982. "What Lockheed and La Costa Nostra Have in Common: The Effect of Ideology on Criminal Justice Policy." *Crime and Delinquency* 28:211–32.

———. 1996. "Looking for a New Approach to an Old Problem: The Future of Obscenity and Pornography." Pp. 60–72 in *Visions for Change: Crime and Justice in the Twenty-First Century,* edited by Roslyn Muraskin and Albert R. Roberts. Upper Saddle River, NJ: Prentice Hall.

Alpert, Geoffrey P., Roger G. Dunham, and Michael R. Smith. 2007. "Investigating Racial Profiling by the Miami-Dade Police Department: A Multimethod Approach." *Criminology & Public Policy* 6:25–56.

Alvarez, Alex, and Ronet Bachman. 2003. *Murder American Style.* Belmont, CA: Wadsworth/Thomson Learning.

Amir, Menachem. 1971. *Patterns in Forcible Rape.* Chicago: University of Chicago Press.

Amnesty International. 2004. *It's in Our Hands: Stop Violence Against Women. Summary.* London: Amnesty International.

———. 2007. *Maze of Injustice: The Failure to Protect Indigenous Women from Sexual Violence in the USA.* New York: Amnesty International USA.

———. 2010a. *Case Closed: Rape and Human Rights in the Nordic Countries: Summary Report.* London: Amnesty International.

———. 2010b. *"I Can't Afford Justice": Violence Against Women in Uganda Continues Unpunished and Unchecked.* London: Amnesty International.

Andersen, Travis. 2010. "City's Pastors Call on Fellow Clergy to Stem Youth Violence." *Boston Globe,* April 1:B6.

Anderson, Amy L., and Lorine A. Hughes. 2009. "Exposure to Situations Conducive to Delinquent Behavior: The Effects of Time Use, Income, and Transportation." *Journal of Research in Crime and Delinquency* 46(1):5–34.

Anderson, Elijah. 1999. *Code of the Street: Decency, Violence, and the Moral Life of the Inner City.* New York: W.W. Norton.

Andrews, D. A., and James Bonta. 2010. *The Psychology of Criminal Conduct.* Cincinnati: Anderson Publishing Company.

Andrews, D. A., and J. Stephen Wormith. 1989. "Personality and Crime: Knowledge Destruction and Construction in Criminology." *Justice Quarterly* 6:289–309.

Animal Legal & Historical Center. 2010. "Statutes/Laws: New York." http://www.animallaw.info/statutes/stusnyagri_mkts_121.htm.

Antonaccio, Olena, and Charles R. Tittle. 2007. "A Cross-National Test of Bonger's Theory of Criminality and Economic Conditions." *Criminology* 45(4):925–58.

Applegate, B. K., R. K. Davis, and F. T. Cullen. 2009. "Reconsidering Child Saving: The Extent and Correlates of Public Support for Excluding Youths from the Juvenile Court." *Crime & Delinquency* 55(1):51–77.

Applegate, Brandon K., Francis T. Cullen, Bonnie S. Fisher, and Thomas Vander Ven. 2000. "Forgiveness and Fundamentalism: Reconsidering the Relationship Between Correctional Attitudes and Religion." *Criminology* 38(3):71954.

Ardanlani, Sarah. 2010. "Homicide Report: 19 Killings Last Week in L.A. County, At Least Seven Gang-Related." *Los Angeles Times,* May 19: http://latimesblogs.latimes.com/lanow/2010/05/homicide-report-19-killings-last-week-in-la-county-at-least-6-gangrelated.html.

Arehart-Treichel, Joan. 2006. "Gene Variant in Abused Boys Linked to Antisocial Behavior." *Psychiatric News* 41(23):26.

Armstrong, David. 1999. "U.S. Lagging on Prosecutions." *Boston Globe,* November 16:A1.

Armstrong, Elizabeth A., Laura Hamilton, and Brian Sweeney. 2006. "Sexual Assault on Campus: A Multilevel, Integrative Approach to Party Rape." *Social Problems* 53:483–99.

Arnold, Laurence. 1999. "Survey Finds Gambling Woes Could Affect 20 Million in US." *Boston Globe, March 19:* A3.

Arnson, Cynthia. 1989. *Crossroads: Congress, the Reagan Administration, and Central America.* New York: Pantheon Books.

Arrigo, Bruce A., and Christopher R. Williams. 2010. "Conflict Criminology: Developments, Directions, and Destinations Past and Present." Pp. 401–12 in *Criminological Theory: Readings and Retrospectives,* edited by Heith Copes and Volkan Topalli. New York: McGraw-Hill.

Arseneault, Louise, Terrie E. Moffitt, Avshalom Caspi, Alan Taylor, Fruhling V. Rijsdijk, Sara R. Jaffee, Jennifer C. Ablow, and Jeffrey R. Measelle. 2003. "Strong Genetic Effects on Cross-situational Antisocial Behaviour Among 5-year-old Children According to Mothers, Teachers, Examiner-observers, and Twins' Self-Reports." *Journal of Child Psychology & Psychiatry & Allied Disciplines* 44(6):832–48.

Arvanites, Thomas M., and Robert H. Defina. 2006. "Business Cycles and Street Crime." *Criminology* 44:139–64.

Ashley, Bob. 2007. "To Name or Not Name the Accuser?" *Herald–Sun* (Durham, NC), April 15:A11.

Associated Press. 1995. "Fraud on Auto Insurers Targeted." *Boston Globe,* May 25:15.

———. 2004. "Knoller, Convicted in Dog Mauling, Released from Prison." http://www.sfgate.com/cgi–bin/article.cgi?f=/news/archive/2004/01/01/state0155EST0133.DTL.

———. 2007. "Authorities in U.S. Border Cities Say May Shootout Shows Danger of Drug Wars Crossing Over." *Dallas Morning News,* June 10: http://www.dallasnews.com/sharedcontent/dws/news/nation/stories/DN-borderviolence_10tex.ART.State.Edition1.43308b9.html.

Auerhahn, Kathleen. 2006. "Conceptual and Methodological Issues in the Prediction of Dangerous Behavior." *Criminology & Public Policy* 4:771–78.

Bachman, Jerald G., Lloyd D. Johnston, and Patrick M. O'Malley. 2009. *Monitoring the Future: Questionnaire Responses from the Nation's High School Seniors 2008.* Ann Arbor, MI: Survey Research Center, Institute for Social Research, University of Michigan.

Bachman, Ronet, and Linda E. Saltzman. 1995. *Violence Against Women: Estimates from the Redesigned Survey.* Washington, DC: Bureau of Justice Statistics, U.S. Department of Justice.

Bailey, William C. 1998. "Deterrence, Brutalization, and the Death Penalty: Another Examination of Oklahoma's Return to Capital Punishment." *Criminology* 36:711–33.

Baker, Al. 2010a. "Bias Seen in 'Police-on-Police' Shootings." *New York Times,* May 27:A30.

————. 2010b. "New York Minorities More Likely to Be Frisked." *New York Times,* May 13:A1.

Balakian, Peter. 2003. *The Burning Tigris: The Armenian Genocide and America's Response.* New York: HarperCollins.

Baldassare, Mark (ed.). 1994. *The Los Angeles Riots: Lessons for the Urban Future.* Boulder, CO: Westview Press.

Baldus, David C., George Woodworth, and Charles A. Pulaski. 1990. *Equal Justice and the Death Penalty: A Legal and Empirical Analysis.* Boston: Northeastern University Press.

Ball-Rokeach, Sandra J. 1972. "The Legitimation of Violence." Pp. 100–11 in *Collective Violence,* edited by Jr. James F. Short and Marvin E. Wolfgang. Chicago: Aldine.

Bandura, Albert. 1973. *Aggression: A Social Learning Analysis.* Englewood Cliffs, NJ: Prentice Hall.

Bannan, John R., and Rosemary S. Bannan. 1974. *Law, Morality, and Vietnam: The Peace Militants and the Courts.* Bloomington: Indiana University Press.

Barbassa, Juliana. 2004. "Farm Workers Seek Aid After Pesticides Hit." *Boston Globe,* May 30:A9.

Barkan, Steven E. 1985. *Protesters on Trial: Criminal Prosecutions in the Southern Civil Rights and Vietnam Antiwar Movements.* New Brunswick, NJ: Rutgers University Press.

————. 1986. "Interorganizational Conflict in the Southern Civil Rights Movement." *Sociological Inquiry* 56:190–209.

————. 2000. "Household Crowding and Aggregate Crime Rates." *Journal of Crime and Justice* 23:47–64.

————. 2006. "Religiosity and Premarital Sex During Adulthood." *Journal for the Scientific Study of Religion* 45:407–17.

Barkan, Steven E., and Steven F. Cohn. 2005. "Why Whites Favor Spending More Money to Fight Crime: The Role of Racial Prejudice." *Social Problems* 52:300–14.

Barlow, Hugh D., and Scott H. Decker (eds.). 2010. *Criminology and Public Policy: Putting Theory to Work.* Philadelphia: Temple University Press.

Baron, Larry, and Murray A. Straus. 1987. "Four Theories of Rape: A Macrosociological Analysis." *Social Problems* 34:467–89.

Baron, Stephen W. 2009. "Differential Coercion, Street Youth, and Violent Crime." *Criminology* 47(1):239–68.

Baron, Stephen W., and David R. Forde. 2007. "Street Youth Crime: A Test of Control Balance Theory." *JQ: Justice Quarterly* 24(2):335–55.

Baron, Stephen W., Leslie W. Kennedy, and David R. Forde. 2001. "Male Street Youths' Conflict: The Role of Background, Subcultural and Situational Factors." *Justice Quarterly* 18:759–89.

Barrows, Sydney Biddle, and William Novak. 1986. *Mayflower Madam: The Secret Life of Sydney Biddle Barrows.* New York: Arbor House.

Barry, Kathleen L. 1988. *Susan B. Anthony: Biography of a Singular Feminist.* New York: New York University Press.

Barstow, David. 2003. "U.S. Rarely Seeks Charges for Death in Workplace." *New York Times,* December 22:A1.

Bartol, Curt R., and Anne Bartol. 2011. *Criminal Behavior: A Psychological Approach.* Upper Saddle River, NJ: Prentice Hall.

Bartusch, Dawn Jeglum, and Ross L. Matsueda. 1996. "Gender, Reflected Appraisals, and Labeling: A Cross Group Test of an Interactionist Theory of Delinquency." *Social Forces* 75:145–77.

Baskin, Deborah R., and Ira B. Sommers. 1998. *Casualties of Community Disorder: Women's Careers in Violent Crime.* Boulder, CO: Westview Press.

Bauder, Julia (ed.). 2007. *Censorship.* Detroit: Greenhaven Press.

Baum, Katrina. 2007. *Identity Theft, 2005.* Washington, DC: Bureau of Justice Statistics, U.S. Department of Justice.

Baum, Katrina, and Patsy Klaus. 2005. *Violent Victimization of College Students, 1995–2002.* Washington, DC: Bureau of Justice Statistics, U.S. Department of Justice.

Baumer, Eric, Steven F. Messner, and Richard Rosenfeld. 2003. "Explaining Spatial Variation in Support for Capital Punishment: A Multilevel Analysis." *American Journal of Sociology* 108:844–75.

Baumer, Eric P., and Janet L. Lauritsen. 2010. "Reporting Crime to the Police, 1973–2005: A Multivariate Analysis of Long-Term Trends in the National Crime Survey (NCS) and National Crime Victimization Survey (NCVS)." *Criminology* 48:131–85.

Baumer, Eric P., Steven F. Messner, and Richard B. Felson. 2000. "The Role of Victim Characteristics in the Disposition of Murder Cases." *Justice Quarterly* 17:281–307.

Bayley, David H. 1996. "Lessons in Order." Pp. 3–14 in *Criminology: A Cross-Cultural Perspective,* edited by Robert Heiner. Minneapolis/St. Paul: West Publishing Company.

BBC News. 2005. "Air Pollution Causes Early Deaths." February 21: http://news.bbc.co.uk/2/hi/health/4283295.stm.

Beaver, Kevin M. 2009. *Biosocial Criminology: A Primer.* Dubuque, IA: Kendall/Hunt Publishing Company.

Beaver, Kevin M., Matt DeLisi, Daniel P. Mears, and Eric Stewart. 2009a. "Low Self-Control and Contact with the Criminal Justice System in a Nationally Representative Sample of Males." *JQ: Justice Quarterly* 26(4):695–715.

Beaver, Kevin M., Matt DeLisi, Michael G. Vaughn, and J. C. Barnes. 2009b. "Monoamine Oxidase A Genotype Is Associated with Gang Membership and Weapon Use." *Comprehensive Psychiatry* 51(2):130–34.

Beccaria, Cesare. 1819 (1764). *On Crimes and Punishment.* Philadelphia: Philip H. Nicklin.

———. 2006 (1764). "An Essay on Crimes and Punishments." Pp. 23–25 in *Criminological Theory: Past to Present: Essential Readings,* edited by Francis T. Cullen and Robert Agnew. Los Angeles: Roxbury Publishing Company.

Beck, Allen J., Thomas P. Bonczar, Paula M. Ditton, Darrell K. Gilliard, Lauren E. Glaze, Caroline Wolf Harlow, Christopher J. Mumola, Tracy L. Snell, James J. Stephan, and Doris James Wilson. 2000. *Correctional Populations in the United States, 1997.* Washington, DC: Bureau of Justice Statistics, U.S. Department of Justice.

Becker, Berneie. 2010. "West Virginia Coal Town Mourns the Miners Lost." *New York Times,* April 11:A20.

Becker, Gary S. 1968. "Crime and Punishment: An Economic Approach." *Journal of Political Economy* 76:169–217.

Becker, Howard S. 1963. *Outsiders: Studies in the Sociology of Deviance.* New York: Free Press.

Beckett, Katherine. 1997. *Making Crime Pay: Law and Order in Contemporary American Politics.* New York: Oxford University Press.

Beckett, Katherine, and Theodore Sasson. 2004. *The Politics of Injustice: Crime and Punishment in America.* Thousand Oaks, CA: Sage Publications.

Begley, Sharon. 2007. "The Anatomy of Violence." *Newsweek,* April 30:40–44.

———. 2009. "Don't Blame the Caveman." *Newsweek,* June 29:52–62.

Behr, Peter, and April Whitt. 2002. "Visionary's Dream Led to Risky Business." *Washington Post,* July 28:A1.

Belknap, Joanne. 2007. *The Invisible Woman: Gender, Crime, and Justice.* Belmont, CA: Wadsworth Publishing Company.

Bellair, Paul, and Thomas L. McNulty. 2005. "Beyond the Bell Curve: Community Disadvantage and the Explanation of Black–White Differences in Adolescent Violence." *Criminology* 43:1135–68.

Bellair, Paul E., and Thomas L. McNulty. 2009. "Gang Membership, Drug Selling, and Violence in Neighborhood Context." *JQ: Justice Quarterly* 26(4):644–69.

Beneke, Tim. 1995. "Men on Rape." Pp. 312–17 in *Men's Lives,* edited by Michael S. Kimmel and Michael A. Messner. Boston: Allyn and Bacon.

Bennett, Richard R. 2009. "Comparative Criminological and Criminal Justice Research and the Data That Drive Them." *International Journal of Comparative and Applied Criminal Justice* 33:171–92.

Bensinger, Ken, and Ralph Vartabedian. 2010. "Toyota Faces New Reports of Sudden-Acceleration Deaths." *Los Angeles Times,* February 15:A1.

Benson, Michael, John Wooldredge, Amy B. Thistlethwaite, and Greer Litton Fox. 2004. "The Correlation Between Race and Domestic Violence Is Confounded with Community Context." *Social Problems* 51:326–42.

Benson, Michael L., and Sally S. Simpson. 2009. *White-Collar Crime: An Opportunity Perspective.* New York: Routledge.

Bergen, Raquel Kennedy. 2006. *Marital Rape: New Research and Directions.* Harrisburg, PA: National Resource Center on Domestic Violence.

Berger, Peter L. 1963. *Invitation to Sociology: A Humanistic Perspective.* Garden City, NY: Anchor Books.

Berk, Richard, Azusa Li, and Laura J. Hickman. 2005. "Statistical Difficulties in Determining the Role of Race in Capital Cases: A Re-analysis of Data from the State of Maryland." *Journal of Quantitative Criminology* 21:365–90.

Berk, Richard A., Susan B. Sorenson, Douglas J. Wiebe, and Dawn M. Upchurch. 2003. "The Legalization of Abortion and Subsequent Youth Homicide: A Time Series Analysis." *Analyses of Social Issues & Public Policy* 3:45–64.

Berlow, Alan. 1999. "The Wrong Man." *Atlantic Monthly, November:66–91.*

Bernard, Thomas J. 1990. "Angry Aggression Among the 'Truly Disadvantaged'," *Criminology* 28:73–96.

Bernard, Thomas J., Jeffrey B. Snipes, and Alexander L. Gerould. 2009. *Vold's Theoretical Criminology.* New York: Oxford University Press.

Bernasco, Wim. 2009. "Burglary." Pp. 165–90 in *The Oxford Handbook of Crime and Public Policy,* edited by Michael Tonry. New York: Oxford Univeristy Press.

Bernasco, Wim, and Richard Block. 2009. "Where Offenders Choose to Attack: A Discrete Choice Model of Robberies in Chicago." *Criminology* 47(1):93–130.

Bernasco, Wim, and Floor Luykx. 2003. "Effects of Attractiveness, Opportunity and Accessibility to Burglars on Residential Burglary Rates of Urban Neighborhoods." *Criminology* 41:981–1001.

Bernburg, Jön Gunnar. 2010. "Labeling and Secondary Deviance." Pp. 340–50 in *Criminological Theory: Readings and Retrospectives,* edited by Heith Copes and Volkan Topalli. New York: McGraw-Hill.

Bernburg, Jön Gunnar, and Marvin D. Krohn. 2003. "Labeling, Life Chances, and Adult Crime: The Direct and Indirect Effects of Official Intervention in Adolescence on Crime in Early Adulthood." *Criminology* 41:1287–318.

Berner, Robert, and Adrienne Carter. 2005. "Swiping Back at Credit-Card Fraud." *Business Week,* July 11: http://www.businessweek.com/magazine/content/05_28/b3942095_mz020.htm.

Bernstein, Carl, and Bob Woodward. 1974. *All the President's Men.* New York: Simon and Schuster.

Bersani, Bianca, John Laub, and Paul Nieuwbeerta. 2009. "Marriage and Desistance from Crime in the Netherlands: Do Gender and Socio-Historical Context Matter?" *Journal of Quantitative Criminology* 25(1):3–24.

Best Wire. 2003. "Farmers Insurance: Right Tools, Research Can Catch Auto-Shop Schemes." April 1: http://prxy4.ursus.maine.edu:2223/universe/document?_m=bd941aa7ae738640113bc97166449bc2&_docnum=3&wchp=dGLbVtb-zSkVA&_md5=d7b6c7176e2518b4da7f87d45589fa44.

Biderman, Albert D., and Albert J. Reiss Jr. 1967. "On Exploring the 'Dark Figure' of Crime." *Annals of the American Academy of Political and Social Science* 374:1–15.

Bijleveld, Catrien C. J. H., and Paul R. Smit. 2005. "Crime and Punishment in the Netherlands, 1980–1999." *Crime and Justice: A Review of Research* 33:161–211.

Binagman, Jeff. 2010. "Bingaman Urges Administration to Crack Down on Vehicle Smuggling Across US-Mexico Border" (press release). http://bingaman.senate.gov/news/20100202-02.cfm.

Birch, James W. 1984. "Reflections on Police Corruption." Pp. 116–22 in *"Order Under Law": Readings in Criminal Justice,* edited by Roberg G. Culbertson. Prospect Heights, IL: Waveland Press.

Bishop, Donna M. 2006. "Public Opinion and Juvenile Justice Policy: Myths and Misconceptions." *Criminology & Public Policy* 5:653–64.

Bishop, Katy. 2004. "Rationalizations Aside, It's Still Called Stealing." *Albany Times-Union,* July 19: http://www.timesunion.com/AspStories/story.asp?storyID=267201&category=LIFE&BCCode=HOME&newsdate=7/19/2004.

Bjerk, David. 2007. "Measuring the Relationship Between Youth Criminal Participation and Household Economic Resources." *Journal of Quantitative Criminology* 23:23–39.

Bjornstrom, Eileen E. S., Robert L. Kaufman, Ruth D. Peterson, and Michael D. Slater. 2010. "Race and Ethnic Representations of Lawbreakers and Victims in Crime News: A National Study of Television Coverage." *Social Problems* 57:269–93.

Black, Dan, and Daniel Nagin. 1998. "Do 'Right to Carry' Laws Reduce Violent Crime?" *Journal of Legal Studies* 27:209–19.

Black, Donald. 1980. "The Social Organization of Arrest." Pp. 151–62 in *Police Behavior: A Sociological Perspective,* edited by Richard J. Lundman. New York: Oxford University Press.

Blackwell, Brenda Sims. 2000. "Perceived Sanction Threats, Gender, and Crime: A Test and Elaboration of Power-Control Theory." *Criminology* 38:439–88.

Blalock, Hubert. 1967. *Toward a Theory of Minority-Group Relations.* New York: John Wiley & Sons.

Blee, Kathleen. 2002. *Inside Organized Racism: Women in the Hate Movement.* Berkeley: University of California Press.

Block, Alan A., and Frank R. Scarpitti. 1985. *Poisoning for Profit: The Mafia and Toxic Waste in America.* New York: William Morrow.

Blumberg, Abraham S. 1967. "The Practice of Law as a Confidence Game: Organizational Cooptation of a Profession." *Law & Society Review* 1:15–39.

Blumberg, Mark. 1994. "Police Use of Excessive Force: Exploring Various Control Mechanisms." Pp. 110–26 in *Critical Issues in Crime and Justice,* edited by Albert R. Roberts. Thousand Oaks, CA: Sage Publications.

Blumberg, Rae Lesser. 1979. "A Paradigm for Predicting the Position of Women: Policy Implications and Problems." Pp. 113–143 in *Sex Roles and Social Policy,* edited by Jean Lipman-Blumen and Jessie Bernard. London: Sage Publications.

Blumstein, Alfred. 1993. "Making Rationality Relevant—The American Society of Criminology 1992 Presidential Address." *Criminology* 31(1):1–16.

———. 1995. *Youth Violence, Guns, and Illicit Drug Markets.* Washington, DC: National Institute of Justice, U.S. Department of Justice.

———. 2009. "Race and the Criminal Justice System." *Race and Social Problems* 1:183–86.

Blumstein, Alfred, and Jacqueline Cohen. 1980. "Sentencing of Convicted Offenders: An Analysis of the Public's View." *Law and Society Review* 14:223–61.

Blumstein, Alfred, and Joel Wallman (eds.). 2006. *The Crime Drop in America.* New York: Cambridge University Press.

Bohm, Robert M. 2007. *Deathquest: An Introduction to the Theory and Practice of Capital Punishment in the United States.* Cincinnati: Anderson Publishing Company.

Bohm, Robert M., and Brenda Vogel. 2011. *A Primer on Crime and Delinquency Theory.* Belmont, CA: Wadsworth Publishing Company.

Bonger, Willem. 1916. *Criminality and Economic Conditions.* Boston: Little, Brown.

Booth, Alan, Douglas A. Granger, Allan Mazur, and Katie T. Kivlighan. 2006. "Testosterone and Social Behavior." *Social Forces* 85:167–91.

Booth, Alan, and D. Wayne Osgood. 1993. "The Influence of Testosterone on Deviance in Adulthood: Assessing and Explaining the Relationship." *Criminology* 31(1):93–117.

Botchkovar, Ekaterina V., Charles R. Tittle, and Olena Antonaccio. 2009. "General Strain Theory: Additional Evidence Using Cross-Cultural Data." *Criminology* 47(1):131–76.

Boutwell, Brian B., and Kevin M. Beaver. 2010. "The Intergenerational Transmission of Low Self-Control." *Journal of Research in Crime & Delinquency* 47:174–209.

Bowers, William J., and Glenn Pierce. 1980. "Deterrence or Brutalization: What Is the Effect of Executions?" *Crime and Delinquency* 26:453–84.

Brabeck, K. M., and M. R. Guzmán. 1274. "Frequency and Perceived Effectiveness of Strategies to Survive Abuse Employed by Battered Mexican-Origin Women." *Violence Against Women* 14(11):1274–94.

Braga, Anthony A., and Brenda J. Bond. 2008. "Policing Crime and Disorder Hot Spots: A Randomized Controlled Trial." *Criminology* 46(3):577–607.

Braga, Anthony A., Glenn L. Pierce, Jack McDevitt, Brenda J. Bond, and Shea Cronin. 2008. "The Strategic Prevention of Gun Violence Among Gang-Involved Offenders." *JQ: Justice Quarterly* 25(1):132–62.

Braithwaite, John. 1981. "The Myth of Social Class and Crime Reconsidered." *American Sociological Review* 46:36–47.

———. 1989. "Criminological Theory and Organizational Crime." *Justice Quarterly* 6:333–58.

———. 1995. "White Collar Crime." Pp. 116–42 in *White-Collar Crime: Classic and Contemporary Views,* edited by Gilbert Geis, Robert F. Meier, and Lawrence M. Salinger. New York: Free Press.

———. 1997. "Charles Tittle's *Control Balance* and Criminological Theory." *Theoretical Criminology* 1:77–97.

———. 2001. "Reintegrative Shaming." Pp. 242–51 in *Explaining Criminals and Crime: Essays in Contemporary Criminological Theory,* edited by Raymond Paternoster and Ronet Bachman. Los Angeles: Roxbury Publishing Company.

———. 2007. "Encourage Restorative Justice." *Criminology & Public Policy* 6(4):689–96.

Braithwaite, Valerie. 2009. "Tax Evasion." Pp. 381–405 in *The Oxford Handbook of Crime and Public Policy,* edited by Michael Tonry. New York: Oxford University Press.

Branch, Taylor. 1998. *Pillar of Fire: America in the King Years, 1963–65.* New York: Simon and Schuster.

Branfman, Fred. 1972. *Voices from the Plain of Jars: Life Under an Air War.* New York: Harper and Row.

Brazy, David. 2010. "Students Rally to 'Take Back the Night.'" *Badger Herald,* April 30: http://badgerherald.com/news/2010/04/30/students_rally_to_ta.php.

Brennan, Patricia A., Sarnoff A. Mednick, and Jan Volavka. 1995. "Biomedical Factors in Crime." Pp. 65–90 in *Crime,* edited by James Q. Wilson and Joan Petersilia. San Francisco: Institute for Contemporary Studies Press.

Brennan, Pauline K., and Cassia Spohn. 2009. "The Joint Effects of Offender Race/Ethnicity and Sex on Sentence Length Decisions in Federal Courts." *Race and Social Problems* 1:200–17.

Brenner, Susan W. 2010. *Cybercrime: Criminal Threats from Cyberspace.* Westport, CT: Praeger.

Brewer, Devon D., John J. Potterat, Sharon B. Garrett, Stephen Q. Muth Jr., John M. Roberts, Danuta Kasprzyk, Daniel E. Montano, and William W. Darrow. 2000. "Prostitution and the Sex Discrepancy in Reported Number of Sexual Partners." *Proceedings of the National Academy of Sciences* 97:12385–88.

Bridges, George S., and Robert D. Crutchfield. 1988. "Law, Social Standing and Racial Disparities in Imprisonment." *Social Forces* 66:699–724.

Bridges, George S., Robert D. Crutchfield, and Edith E. Simpson. 1987. "Crime, Social Structure and Criminal Punishment: White and Nonwhite Rates of Imprisonment." *Social Problems* 34:345–61.

Briere, John, and Neil Malamuth. 1983. "Self-Reported Likelihood of Sexually Aggressive Behavior: Attitudinal Versus Sexual Explanations." *Journal of Research in Personality* 17:315–23.

Brinton, Howard H. 1952. *Friends for 300 Years.* New York: Harper and Row.

Brock, Peter. 1968. *Pacifism in the United States, from the Colonial Era to the First World War.* Princeton, NJ: Princeton University Press.

Brodeur, Paul. 1985. *Outrageous Misconduct: The Asbestos Industry on Trial.* New York: Pantheon Books.

Broehl, Wayne G. Jr. 1964. *The Molly Maguires.* Cambridge, MA: Harvard University Press.

Broidy, Lisa M. 2001. "A Test of General Strain Theory." *Criminology* 39:9–35.

Brown, Amy L., Maria Testa, and Terri L. Messman-Moore. 2009. "Psychological Consequences of Sexual Victimization Resulting from Force, Incapacitation, or Verbal Coercion." *Violence Against Women* 15(8):898–919.

Brown, Richard Maxwell. 1989. "Historical Patterns of Violence." Pp. 23–61 in *Violence in America: Protest, Rebellion, Reform,* edited by Ted Robert Gurr. Newbury Park, CA: Sage.

———. 1990. "Historical Patterns of American Violence." Pp. 4–15 in *Violence: Patterns, Causes, Public Policy,* edited by Neil Alan Weiner, Margaret A. Zahn, and Rita J. Sagi. San Diego: Harcourt Brace Jovanovich.

Browne, Angela. 1995. "Fear and the Perception of Alternatives: Asking 'Why Battered Women Don't Leave' Is the Wrong Question." Pp. 228–45 in *The Criminal Justice System and Women: Offenders, Victims, and Workers,* edited by Barbara Raffel Price and Natalie J. Sokoloff. New York: McGraw-Hill.

———. 2004. "Fear and the Perception of Alternatives: Asking 'Why Battered Women Don't Leave' Is the Wrong Question." Pp. 343–59 in *The Criminal Justice System and Women: Offenders, Prisoners, Victims, and Workers,* edited by Barbara Raffel Price and Natalie J. Sokoloff. New York: McGraw-Hill.

Brownmiller, Susan. 1975. *Against Our Will: Men, Women, and Rape.* New York: Simon and Schuster.

Brunson, Rod K. 2007. "'Police Don't Like Black People': African-American Young Men's Accumulated Police Experiences." *Criminology & Public Policy* 6:71–102.

Brunson, Rod K., and Ronald Weitzer. 2009. "Police Relations with Black and White Youths in Different Urban Neighborhoods." *Urban Affairs Review* 44(6):858–85.

Brush, Lisa D., Angela Hattery, and Earl Smith. 2007. "On Violence Against Women" (letters to the editor). *Contexts* 6(1):6–7.

Bryden, D. P., and S. Lengnick. 1997. "Rape in the Criminal Justice System." *Journal of Criminal Law and Criminology* 87:1194–384.

Brydensholt, H. H. 1992. "Crime Policy in Denmark: How We Managed to Reduce the Prison Population." In *Prisons Around the World: Studies in International Penology,* edited by Michael K. Carlie and Kevin I. Minor. Dubuque, IA: William C. Brown.

Bullough, Vern L., and Bonnie Bullough. 1977. *Sin, Sickness, and Sanity: A History of Sexual Attitudes.* New York: New American Library.

———. 1987. *Women and Prostitution: A Social History.* Buffalo, NY: Prometheus.

Burgess, Robert L., and Ronald L. Akers. 1966. "A Differential Association-Reinforcement Theory of Criminal Behavior." *Social Problems* 14:128–47.

Burgess-Proctor, Amanda. 2006. "Intersections of Race, Class, Gender, and Crime: Future Directions for Feminist Criminology." *Feminist Criminology* 1:27–47.

Burke, Garance. 2007. "Pesticide Drift from Nearby Farms Endangers Pupils, Calif. Data Show." *Boston Globe,* May 27: http://www.boston.com/news/nation/articles/2007/05/27/pesticide_drift_from_nearby_farms_endangers_pupils_calif_data_show/.

Bursik, Robert J. Jr. 1988. "Social Disorganization and Theories of Crime and Delinquency: Problems and Prospects." *Criminology* 26:519–51.

———. 2000. "Property Crime Trends." Pp. 215–31 in *Criminology: A Contemporary Handbook,* edited by Joseph F. Sheley. Belmont, CA: Wadsworth.

Burt, Martha R., and Bonnie L. Katz. 1984. "Rape, Robbery, and Burglary: Responses to Actual and Feared Victimization with Special Focus on Women and the Elderly." *Victimology* 10:325–58.

Burton, Austin. 2004. "Rape Shield Laws Outdated." *The Spectator* (Seattle University student newspaper), January 26: http://www.spectator-online.com/vnews/display.v/ART/2004/01/26/4015ed67e3bbe.

Bushnell, Rebecca W. 1988. *Prophesying Tragedy: Sign and Voice in Sophocles' Theban Plays.* Ithaca, NY: Cornell University Press.

Butterfield, Fox. 1994. "A History of Homicide Surprises the Experts: Decline in U.S. Before Recent Increase." *New York Times,* October 23:16.

———. 2000. "Cities Reduce Crime and Conflict Without New York-Style Hardball." *New York Times,* March 4:A1.

Button, James. 1989. "The Outcomes of Contemporary Black Protest and Violence." Pp. 286–306 in *Violence in America: Protest, Rebellion, Reform,* edited by Ted Robert Gurr. Newbury Park, CA: Sage Publications.

Cain, Maureen, and Alan Hunt (eds.). 1979. *Marx and Engels on Law.* New York: Academic Press.

Calavita, Kitty, Robert Tillman, and Henry N. Pontell. 1997. "The Savings and Loan Debacle, Financial Crime, and the State." In *Annual Review of Sociology,* edited by John Hagan. Palo Alto, CA: Annual Reviews.

Californians for Pesticide Reform. 2010. *Pesticide Protection Zones: Keeping Kids Safe at School.* San Francisco: Californians for Pesticide Reform.

Callahan, Trish. 2010. "Federal Safety Regulator Pledges to Ban Drop-Side Cribs." *Los Angeles Times,* May 8: http://www.latimes.com/news/nationworld/nation/la-na-crib-20100508,0,3553984.story.

Cameron, Mary Owen. 1964. *The Booster and the Snitch: Department Store Shoplifting.* New York: Free Press.

Campbell, R., A. E. Adams, and S. M. Wasco. 2009. "Training Interviewers for Research on Sexual Violence: A Qualitative Study of Rape Survivors' Recommendations for Interview Practice." *Violence Against Women* 15(5):595–617.

Cancino, Jeffrey M., Ramiro Martinez, and Jacob I. Stowell. 2009. "The Impact of Neighborhood Context on Intragroup and Intergroup Robbery: The San Antonio Experience." *Annals of the American Academy of Political and Social Science* 623:12–24.

Cao, Liqun, Anthony Adams, and Vickie J. Jensen. 1997. "A Test of the Black Subculture of Violence Thesis: A Research Note." *Criminology* 35:367–79.

Caputi, Jane, and Diana E. H. Russell. 1992. "Femicide: Sexist Terrorism Against Women." Pp. 13–21 in *Femicide: The Politics of Woman Killing,* edited by Jill Radford and Diana E. H. Russell. New York: Twayne Publishers.

Carey, Gregory. 1994. "Genetics and Violence." Pp. 21–58 in *Understanding and Preventing Violence: Biobehavioral Influences,* edited by Albert J. Reiss Jr., Klaus A. Miczek, and Jeffrey A. Roth. Washington, DC: National Academy Press.

Carvalho, Irene, and Dan A. Lewis. 2003. "Beyond Community: Reactions to Crime and Disorder Among Inner-City Residents." *Criminology* 41:779–812.

Caspi, Avshalom. 2000. "The Child Is Father of the Man: Personalities Continuities from Childhood to Adulthood." *Journal of Personality and Social Psychology* 78:158–72.

Caspi, Avshalom, Terrie E. Moffitt, Phil A. Silva, Magda Stouthamer-Loeber, Robert F. Krueger, and Pamela S. Schmutte. 1994. "Are Some People Crime-Prone? Replications of the Personality-Crime Relationship Across Countries, Genders, Races, and Methods." *Criminology* 32(2):163–95.

Catalano, Shannan. 2007. *Intimate Partner Violence in the United States.* Washington, DC: Bureau of Justice Statistics, U.S. Department of Justice.

Catalano, Shannan M. 2006a. *Criminal Victimization, 2005.* Washington, DC: Bureau of Justice Statistics, U.S. Department of Justice.

———. 2006b. *The Measurement of Crime: Victim Reporting and Police Recording.* New York: LFB Scholarly Publishing.

Cernkovich, Stephen A. 1978. "Value Orientations and Delinquency Involvement." *Criminology* 15:443–58.

Chacon, Richard. 1998. "Questions Raised on Campus Crime." *Boston Globe,* February 8:A1.

Chaiken, Jan M., Michael W. Lawless, and Keith A. Stevenson. 1975. "The Impact of Police Activity on Subway Crime." *Urban Analysis* 3:173–205.

Challenger, James. 2004. "Frustrated Employers Looking Closer to Find Good Hires." *California Job Journal,* July 25: http://www.jobjournal.com/thisweek.asp?artid=1198.

Chambliss, William J. 1964. "A Sociological Analysis of the Law of Vagrancy." *Social Problems* 12:67–77.

———. 1967. "Types of Deviance and the Effectiveness of Legal Sanctions." *Wisconsin Law Review* (Summer):703–19.

———. 1988. *On the Take: From Petty Crooks to Presidents.* Indianapolis: Indiana University Press.

Chambliss, William, and Robert Seidman. 1982. *Law, Order, and Powers.* Reading, MA: Addison-Wesley Publishing Company.

Chambliss, William J., Ronald C. Kramer, and Raymond Michalowski. 2010. *State Crime in the Global Age.* Devon, England: Willan.

Chamlin, M. B., A. J. Myer, and B. A. Sanders. 2008. "Abortion as Crime Control: A Cautionary Tale." *Criminal Justice Policy Review* 19(2):135–52.

Chamlin, Mitchell B. 1991. "A Longitudinal Analysis of the Arrest–Crime Relationship: A Further Examination of the Tipping Effect." *Justice Quarterly* 8(2):187–99.

Chamlin, Mitchell B., and John K. Cochran. 2006. "Economic Inequality, Legitimacy, and Cross-National Homicide Rates." *Homicide Studies* 10:231–52.

Chapple, Constance L. 2005. "Self-Control, Peer Relations, and Delinquency." *Justice Quarterly* 22:89–106.

Chen, Elsa Y. 2008. "The Liberation Hypothesis and Racial and Ethnic Disparities in the Application of California's Three Strikes Law." *Journal of Ethnicity in Criminal Justice* 6(2):83–102.

Cherbonneau, Michael, and Richard Wright. 2009. "Auto Theft." Pp. 191–222 in *The Oxford Handbook of Crime and Public Policy,* edited by Michael Tonry. New York: Oxford University Press.

Cherlin, Andrew J., Linda M. Burton, Tera R. Hurt, and Diane M. Purvin. 2004. "The Influence of Physical and Sexual Abuse on Marriage and Cohabitation." *American Sociological Review* 69:768–89.

Chesney-Lind, Meda. 2002. "Criminalizing Victimization: The Unintended Consequences of Pro-Arrest Policies for Girls and Women." *Journal of Research in Crime and Delinquency* 2:81–90.

———. 2004. "Beyond Bad Girls: Feminist Perspectives on Female Offending." Pp. 255–67 in *The Blackwell Companion to Criminology,* edited by Colin Sumner. Oxford: Blackwell Publishing.

Chesney-Lind, Meda, and Karlene Faith. 2001. "What About Feminism? Engendering Theory-Making in Criminology." Pp. 287–302 in *Explaining Criminals and Crime: Essays in Contemporary Criminological Theory,* edited by Raymond Paternoster and Ronet Bachman. Los Angeles: Roxbury Publishing Company.

Chesney-Lind, Meda, and Nikki Jones (eds.). 2010. *Fighting for Girls: New Perspectives on Gender and Violence.* Albany: State University of New York Press.

Chesney-Lind, Meda, and Lisa Pasko. 2004. *The Female Offender: Girls, Women, and Crime.* Thousand Oaks, CA: Sage Publications.

Chesney-Lind, Meda, and Randall G. Sheldon. 1992. *Girls, Delinquency, and Juvenile Justice.* Pacific Grove, CA: Brooks/Cole Publishing Company.

Chiang, Harriet. 2004. "Ex-UCSF Employee Gets 7-Year Sentence." *San Francisco Chronicle,* July 2: http://www.sfgate.com/cgi-bin/article.cgi?f=/chronicle/archive/2004/07/02/BAG4S7EU921.DTL.

Chiricos, Ted, Kelle Barrick, William Bales, and Stephanie Bontrager. 2007. "The Labeling of Convicted Felons and Its Consequences for Recidivism." *Criminology* 45:547–82.

Chiricos, Ted, Ranee McEntire, and Marc Gertz. 2001. "Perceived Racial and Ethnic Composition of Neighborhood and Perceived Risk of Crime." *Social Problems* 48:322–40.

Chiricos, Theodore G., and Miriam A. Delone. 1992. "Labor Surplus and Punishment: A Review and Assessment of Theory and Evidence." *Social Problems* 39(4):421–46.

Chiricos, Theodore G., and Gordon P. Waldo. 1975. "Socioeconomic Status and Criminal Sentencing: An Assessment of a Conflict Proposition." *American Sociological Review* 40:753–72.

Chomsky, Noam, and Edward S. Herman. 1979. *The Washington Connection and Third World Facism.* Boston: South End Press.

Clarke, Ronald V., and Rick Brown. 2003. "International Trafficking in Stolen Vehicles." *Crime and Justice: A Review of Research* 30:197–227.

Clarke, Ronald V., and Derek B. Cornish. 1985. "Modeling Offenders' Decisions: A Framework for Research and Policy." *Crime and Justice: A Review of Research* 6:147–85.

———. 2001. "Rational Choice." Pp. 23–42 in *Explaining Criminals and Crime,* edited by Raymond Paternoster and Ronet Bachman. Los Angeles: Roxbury Publishing Company.

Clarke, Ronald V., and Patricia M. Harris. 1992. "Auto Theft and Its Prevention." Pp. 1–54 in *Crime and Justice: A Review of Research,* edited by Michael Tonry. Chicago: University of Chicago Press.

Clear, Todd R. 2008. "The Effects of High Imprisonment Rates on Communities." *Crime and Justice: A Review of Research* 37:97–132.

———. 2010. "Policy and Evidence: The Challenge to the American Society of Criminology: 2009 Presidential Address to the American Society of Criminology." *Criminology* 48:1–25.

Clinard, Marshall. 1978. *Cities with Little Crime: The Case of Switzerland.* New York: Cambridge University Press.

Clinard, Marshall B., and Richard Quinney. 1973. *Criminal Behavior Systems.* New York: Holt, Rinehart and Winston.

Cloward, Richard A., and Lloyd E. Ohlin. 1960. *Delinquency and Opportunity: A Theory of Delinquent Gangs.* New York: Free Press.

Cochran, John K., and Mitchell B. Chamlin. 2000. "Deterrence and Brutalization: The Dual Effects of Executions." *Justice Quarterly* 17:685–706.

Cochran, John K., Mitchell B. Chamlin, and Mark Seth. 1994. "Deterrence or Brutalization? An Impact Assessment of Oklahoma's Return to Capital Punishment." *Criminology* 32(1):107–34.

Cochran, John K., Peter B. Wood, and Bruce J. Arneklev. 1994. "Is the Religiosity Delinquency Relationship Spurious? A Test of Arousal and Social Control Theories." *Journal of Research in Crime and Delinquency* 31(1):92–123.

Cohan, William D. 2010. "Will Wall Street Go Free?" *New York Times,* May 27: http://opinionator.blogs.nytimes.com/2010/05/27/will-wall-street-go-free/?emc=eta1.

Cohen, David B., and John W. Wells (eds.). 2004. *American National Security and Civil Liberties in an Era of Terrorism.* New York: Palgrave Macmillan.

Cohen, Lawrence E., and Marcus Felson. 1979. "Social Change and Crime Rate Trends: A Routine Activity Approach." *American Sociological Review* 44:588–607.

Cohen, Mark A., Alex R. Piquero, and Wesley G. Jennings. 2010. "Studying the Costs of Crime Across Offender Trajectories." *Criminology & Public Policy* 9(2):279–305.

Cohen, Richard M., and Jules Witcover. 1974. *A Heartbeat Away: The Investigation and Resignation of Spiro T. Agnew.* New York: Viking Press.

Cohen, Sharon. 2007. "Katrina Fraud Stretches Far Beyond Gulf." *Washington Post,* April 2: http://www.washingtonpost.com/wp-dyn/content/article/2007/04/02/AR2007040200379.html.

Cohen, William S. 1994. "Gaming the Health Care System: Billions of Dollars Lost to Fraud & Abuse Each Year." Washington, DC: Senate Special Committee on Aging.

Cohn, Steven F., and Steven E. Barkan. 2004. "Racial Prejudice and Public Attitudes About the Punishment of Criminals." In *For the Common Good: A Critical Examination of Law and Social Control,* edited by R. Robin Miller and Sandra Lee Browning. Durham, NC: Carolina Academic Press.

Cole, David. 1999. "Doing Time-In Rehab: Drug Courts Keep Addicts Out of Jail." *The Nation*:30.

———(ed.). 2009. *The Torture Memos: Rationalizing the Unthinkable.* New York: New Press.

Cole, David, and Jules Lobel. 2007. *Less Safe, Less Free: Why America Is Losing the War on Terror.* New York: New Press.

Coleman, James William. 2006. *The Criminal Elite: Understanding White-Collar Crime.* New York: Worth Publishers.

Collier, Richard. 2004. "Masculinities and Crime: Rethinking the 'Man Question'?" Pp. 285–308 in *The Blackwell Companion to Criminology,* edited by Colin Sumner. Oxford: Blackwell Publishing.

Collins, Randall. 1994. *Four Sociological Traditions.* New York: Oxford University Press.

Colvin, Mark, Francis T. Cullen, and Thomas Vander Ven. 2002. "Coercion, Social Support, and Crime: An Emerging Theoretical Consensus." *Criminology* 40:19–42.

Conklin, John. 1972. *Robbery and the Criminal Justice System.* Philadelphia: Lippincott.

Connell, Robert W. 1995. *Masculinities.* Berkeley: University of California Press.

Consumer Product Safety Commission. 2009. *2009 Annual Report to the President and the Congress.* Washington, DC: U.S. Consumer Product Safety Commission.

Consumer Reports. 1985. "Fords in Reverse." *Consumer Reports,* August:520–23.

———. 2010. "Social Insecurity: What Millions of Online Users Don't Know Can Hurt Them." *Consumer Reports,* June(6):24–27.

Conte, Andrew. 2007. "DeLay Says Top Dems Close to Treason." *Pittsburgh Tribune-Review,* April 24: http://www.pittsburghlive.com/x/pittsburghtrib/news/multimedia/s_504197.html.

Cook, Philip J., and Mark H. Moore. 1995. "Gun Control." Pp. 267–94 in *Crime,* edited by James Q. Wilson and Joan Petersilia. San Francisco: Institute for Contemporary Studies Press.

Copes, Heith, Kent R. Kerley, Karen A. Mason, and Judy Van Wyk. 2001. "Reporting Behavior of Fraud Victims and Black's Theory of Law: An Empirical Assessment." *Justice Quarterly* 18:343–63.

Copes, Heith, and Lynne Vieraitis. 2009a. "Identity Theft." Pp. 247–69 in *The Oxford Handbook of Crime and Public Policy*, edited by Michael Tonry. New York: Oxford University Press.

Copes, Heith, and Lynne M. Vieraitis. 2009b. "Bounded Rationality of Identity Thieves: Using Offender-Based Research to Inform Policy." *Criminology & Public Policy* 8(2):237–62.

———. 2009c. "Understanding Identity Theft: Offenders, Accounts of Their Lives and Crimes." *Criminal Justice Review* 34(3):329–49.

Cornell, Drucilla (ed.). 2000. *Feminism and Pornography*. New York: Oxford University Press.

Cornish, Derek B., and Ronald V. Clarke (eds.). 1986. *The Reasoning Criminal: Rational Choice Perspectives on Offending*. New York: Springer-Verlag.

"Corporate Tax Cheating Seen." 1991. *New York Times,* April 18:C6.

Cose, Ellis. 1990. "Turning Victims into Saints: Journalists Cannot Resist Recasting Crime into a Shopworn Morality Tale." *Time,* January 22:19.

Coston, Charisse Tia Maria. 1992. "The Influence of Race in Urban Homeless Females' Fear of Crime." *Justice Quarterly* 9(4):721–29.

Coughlin, Ellen K. 1994. "Mean Streets Are a Scholar's Lab." *Chronicle of Higher Education* September 21:A8–A9, A14.

Coupe, Timothy, and Laurence Blake. 2006. "Daylight and Darkness Targeting Strategies and the Risks of Being Seen at Residential Burglaries." *Criminology* 44:431–64.

Cressey, Donald R. 1971 (1953). *Other People's Money: A Study in the Social Psychology of Embezzlement*. Belmont, CA: Wadsworth Publishing Company.

Critchley, Thomas A. 1972. *A History of Police in England and Wales*. Montclair, NJ: Patterson Smith.

Cromwell, Paul. 1994. "Burglary: The Burglar's Perspective." Pp. 35–50 in *Critical Issues in Crime and Justice,* edited by Albert R. Roberts. Thousand Oaks, CA: Sage Publications.

Cromwell, Paul, and Karen McElrath. 1994. "Buying Stolen Property: An Opportunity Perspective." *Journal of Research in Crime and Delinquency* 31(3):295–310.

Crosnoe, Robert, Chandra Muller, and Kenneth Frank. 2004. "Peer Context and the Consequences of Adolescent Drinking." *Social Problems* 51:288–304.

Cullen, Francis T. 2007a. "Make Rehabilitation Corrections' Guiding Paradigm." *Criminology & Public Policy* 6(4):717–27.

———. 2007b. "Make Rehabilitation Corrections' Guiding Paradigm." *Criminology & Public Policy* 6:717–28.

Cullen, Francis T., and Robert Agnew (eds.). 2006. *Criminological Theory: Past to Present: Essential Readings*. Los Angeles: Roxbury Publishing Company.

——— (eds.). 2011. *Criminological Theory: Past to Present: Essential Readings*. New York: Oxford University Press.

Cullen, Francis T., Bonnie S. Fisher, and Brandon K. Applegate. 2000. "Public Opinion About Punishment and Corrections." *Crime and Justice: A Review of Research* 27:1–79.

Cullen, Francis T., P. Gendreau, G. R. Jarjoura, and J. P. Wright. 1997. "Crime and the Bell Curve: Lessons from Intelligent Criminology." *Crime & Delinquency* 43:387–411.

Cullen, Francis T., William J. Maakestad, and Gray Cavender. 2006. *Corporate Crime Under Attack: The Fight to Criminalize Business Violence*. Cincinnati, OH: Anderson Publishing Company.

Curran, Daniel J., and Claire M. Renzetti. 2001. *Theories of Crime*. Boston: Allyn and Bacon.

Currie, Elliott. 1985. *Confronting Crime: An American Challenge.* New York: Pantheon Books.

———. 1994. *Reckoning: Drugs, the Cities, and the American Future.* New York: Hill and Wang.

———. 1998. *Crime and Punishment in America.* New York: Henry Holt.

———. 2010. "On Being Right, But Unhappy." *Criminology & Public Policy* 9(1):1–10.

Dabney, Dean A., Richard C. Hollinger, and Laura Dugan. 2004. "Who Actually Steals? A Study of Covertly Observed Shoplifters." *Justice Quarterly* 21:693–728.

D'Alessio, Stewart J., and Lisa Stolzenberg. 1998. "Crime, Arrests, and Pretrial Jail Incarceration: An Examination of the Deterrence Thesis." *Criminology* 36:735–61.

Dalton, Katharina. 1961. "Menstruation and Crime." *British Medical Journal* 2:1752–53.

Daly, Kathleen. 1994. *Gender, Crime, and Punishment.* New Haven, CT: Yale University Press.

Daly, Kathleen, and Meda Chesney-Lind. 1988. "Feminism and Criminology." *Justice Quarterly* 5:497–538.

Danner, Mona J. E., and Dianne Cyr Carmody. 2001. "Missing Gender in Cases of Infamous School Violence: Investigating Research and Media Explanations." *Justice Quarterly* 18:87–114.

Daragahi, Borzou. 2007. "Iran Tightens Screws on Internal Dissent." *Los Angeles Times,* June 10:A1.

Darmon, Muriel. 2009. "The Fifth Element: Social Class and the Sociology of Anorexia." *Sociology* 43(4):717–33.

Darymple, Mary. 2006. "Treasury Auditors Find Taxpayers May Owe More Than IRS Thinks." *Associated Press,* April 25: http://web.lexis–nexis.com.prxy4.ursus.maine.edu/universe/document?_m=05bf7b6f4934432793a03efd74277afa&_docnum=20&wchp=dGLzVlz-zSkVb&_md5=28f2f23282a8c813c44df5dd9cad2a98.

Davies, Peter. 1973. *The Truth About Kent State: A Challenge to the American Conscience.* New York: Farrar, Straus, Giroux.

Davis, Joanne L., and Patricia A. Petretic-Jackson. 2000. "The Impact of Child Sexual Abuse on Adult Interpersonal Functioning: A Review and Synthesis of the Empirical Literature." *Aggression and Violent Behavior* 5:291–328.

Davis, Kingsley. 1937. "The Sociology of Prostitution." *American Sociological Review* 2:744–55.

Davis, Robert C., Barbara E. Smith, and Bruce Taylor. 2003. "Increasing the Proportion of Domestic Violence Arrests That Are Prosecuted: A Natural Experiment in Milwaukee." *Criminology & Public Policy* 2:263–82.

DeBenedetti, Charles, and Charles Chatfield. 1990. *An American Ordeal: The Antiwar Movement of the Vietnam Era.* Syracuse, NY: Syracuse University Press.

Decker, Scott, and Carol Kohfeld. 1985. "Crimes, Crime Rates, Arrests, and Arrest Ratios: Implications for Deterrence Theory." *Criminology* 23:437–50.

Decker, Scott, Richard Wright, Allison Redfern, and Dietrich Smith. 1993. "A Woman's Place Is in the Home: Females and Residential Burglary." *Justice Quarterly* 10(1):143–62.

DeFleur, Lois B. 1975. "Biasing Influences on Drug Arrest Records: Implications for Deviance Research." *American Sociological Review* 40:88–103.

DeFronzo, James, Ashley Ditta, Lance Hannon, and Jane Prochnow. 2007. "Male Serial Homicide: The Influence of Cultural and Structural Variables." *Homicide Studies* 11:3–14.

Deitch, Michele, Amanda Barstow, Leslie Lukens, and Ryan Reyna. 2009. *From Time Out to Hard Time: Young Children in the Adult Criminal Justice System.* Austin: LBJ School of Public Affairs, University of Texas at Austin.

DeKeseredy, Walter S. 2006. "Future Directions." *Violence Against Women* 12:1078–85.

DeKeseredy, Walter S., Martin D. Schwartz, Danielle Fagen, and Mandy Hall. 2006. "Separation/Divorce Sexual Assault: The Contribution of Male Support." *Feminist Criminology* 1:228–50.

DeLisi, Matt, Kevin M. Beaver, Michael G. Vaughn, and John Paul Wright. 2010. "Contemporary Perspectives on Biological and Biosocial Theories of Crime." Pp. 74–83 in *Criminological Theory: Readings and Retrospectives,* edited by Heith Copes and Volkan Topalli. New York: McGraw-Hill.

DeMaris, Alfred, and Catherine Kaukines. 2005. "Violent Victimization and Women's Mental and Physical Health: Evidence from a National Sample." *Journal of Research in Crime and Delinquency* 42:384–411.

Deming, Richard. 1977. *Women: The New Criminals.* Nashville, TN: Thomas Nelson.

Demos, John. 2008. *The Enemy Within: 2,000 Years of Witch-Hunting in the Western World.* New York: Viking.

Demuth, Stephen, and Susan L. Brown. 2004. "Family Structure, Family Processes, and Adolescent Delinquency: The Significance of Parental Absence Versus Parental Gender." *Journal of Research in Crime and Delinquency* 41:58–81.

Dieter, Richard C. 2009. *Smart on Crime: Reconsidering the Death Pealty in a Time of Economic Crisis.* Washington, DC: Death Penalty Information Center.

Dillon, Nancy. 2010. "Erin Andrews Alleged Stalker Michael Barrett Ordered to Serve Sentence in Atlanta Jail Near Her Home." *New York Daily News,* May 3: http://www .nydailynews.com/gossip/2010/05/03/10-05-03_erin_andrews_alleged_stalker _michael_barrett_ordered_to_serve_sentence_in_atlant.html.

Dobash, Rebecca Emerson. 2003. "Domestic Violence: Arrest, Prosecution, and Reducing Violence." *Criminology & Public Policy* 2:313–18.

Dobash, Russell P., R. Emerson Dobash, Margo Wilson, and Martin Daly. 1992. "The Myth of Sexual Symmetry in Marital Violence." *Social Problems* 39(1):71–91.

Dobrin, Adam. 2001. "The Risk of Offending on Homicide Victimization: A Case Control Study." *Journal of Research in Crime and Delinquency* 38:154–73.

Doerner, Jill K., and Stephen Demuth. 2010. "The Independent and Joint Effects of Race/Ethnicity, Gender, and Age on Sentencing Outcomes in U.S. Federal Courts." *JQ: Justice Quarterly* 27(1):1–27.

Doherty, Elaine Eggleston. 2006. "Self-Control, Social Bonds, and Desistance: A Test of Life-Course Interdependence." *Criminology* 44:807–33.

Dombrink, John. 2009. "Gambling." Pp. 599–618 in *The Oxford Handbook of Crime and Public Policy,* edited by Michael Tonry. New York: Oxford University Press.

Domhoff, G. William. 2010. *Who Rules America: Challenges to Corporate and Class Dominance.* New York: McGraw-Hill.

Donnerstein, Edward, Daniel Linz, and Steven Penrod. 1987. *The Question of Pornography: Research Findings and Policy Implications.* New York: Free Press.

Donohue, John J., and S. D. Levitt. 2001. "The Impact of Legalized Abortion on Crime." *Quarterly Journal of Economics* 116:379–420.

Doob, Anthony N., and Cheryl Marie Webster. 2003. "Sentence Severity and Crime: Accepting the Null Hypothesis." *Crime and Justice: A Review of Research* 30:143–95.

Dorfman, Lori, and Vincent Schiraldi. 2001. *Off Balance: Youth, Race and Crime in the News.* Washington, DC: Building Blocks for Youth.

Dorne, Clifford K. 2008. *Restorative Justice in the United States.* Upper Saddle River, NJ: Prentice Hall.

Doty, C. Stewart. 1994. "The KKK in Maine Was Not OK." *Bangor Daily News,* June 11–12:A11.

Downes, David. 2007. "Visions of Penal Control in the Netherlands." *Crime and Justice: A Review of Research* 36:93–125.

Downie, Leonard Jr. 1972. *Justice Denied: The Case for Reform of the Courts.* Baltimore, MD: Penguin Books.

Drug Policy Alliance. 2010. "Drug Policy Around the World: The Netherlands." http://www.drugpolicy.org/global/drugpolicyby/westerneurop/thenetherlan/.

DuBois, W. E. B. 1899. *The Philadelphia Negro: A Social Study.* Philadelphia: Publications of the University of Pennsylvania.

Dugan, Laura. 2009. "Terrorism." Pp. 428–54 in *The Oxford Handbook of Crime and Public Policy,* edited by Michael Tonry. New York: Oxford University Press.

Dugdale, Richard. 1877. *The Jukes: A Study in Crime, Pauperism, Disease, and Heredity.* New York: G.P. Putnam's Sons.

Duhart, Detis T. 2001. *Violence in the Workplace, 1993–99.* Washington, DC: Bureau of Justice Statistics, U.S. Department of Justice.

Durkheim, Émile. 1947 (1915). *The Elementary Forms of Religious Life.* Glencoe, IL: Free Press.

———. 1952 (1897). *Suicide.* New York: Free Press.

———. 1962 (1895). *The Rules of Sociological Method.* New York: Free Press.

———. 1983 (1901). "Two Laws of Penal Evolution." Pp. 102–32 in *Durkheim and the Law,* edited by Steven Lukes and Andrew Scull. New York: St. Martin's Press.

Durose, Matthew R., Donald Farole, and Sean P. Rosenmerkel. 2009. *Felony Sentences in State Courts, 2006—Statistical Tables.* Washington, DC: Bureau of Justice Statistics, U.S. Department of Justice.

Durose, Matthew R., Erica L. Smith, and Patrick A. Langan. 2007. *Contacts Between Police and the Public, 2005.* Washington, DC: Bureau of Justice Statistics, U.S. Department of Justice.

Dworkin, Andrea. 1989. *Pornography: Men Possessing Women.* New York: Norton.

Dye, Thomas R. 2010. *Understanding Public Policy.* Upper Saddle River, NJ: Prentice Hall.

Eckenrode, Vicky. 2007. "Increase in Gamblng Addiction Likely." *Topeka Capital Journal,* June 18: http://cjonline.com/stories/061807/kan_178268253.shtml.

Egelko, Bob. 2002. "Public Opinion Had Role in Court Ruling on Retarded." *San Francisco Chronicle,* June 30:A6.

Ehlers, Scott, Vincent Schiraldi, and Jason Ziedenberg. 2004. *Still Striking Out: Ten Years of California's Three Strikes Laws.* Washington, DC: Justice Policy Institute.

Ehrenreich, Barbara, and Deirdre English. 2005. *For Her Own Good: Two Centuries of the Experts' Advice to Women.* New York: Anchor Books.

Eichenwald, Kurt. 2002. "The Criminal-less Crime." *New York Times,* March 3:A1.

Eisenstein, James, and Hebert Jacob. 1977. *Felony Justice: An Organizational Analysis of Criminal Courts.* Boston: Little, Brown and Company.

Eiserer, Tanya, and Steve Thompson. 2009. "Are Dallas Police Correctly Counting All Burglaries?" *Dallas Morning News,* October 25: http://www.dallasnews.com/sharedcontent/dws/dn/latestnews/stories/102509dnmetundercount.3f5a19b.html.

Eisler, Peter. 2010. "'Growing Concern' over Marketing Tainted Beef." *USA Today,* April 15:A1.

Eisner, Manuel. 2003. "Long-Term Historical Trends in Violent Crime." *Crime and Justice: A Review of Research* 30:83–142.

Elias, Marilyn. 1994. "A Third of Women Hit by Male Partner." *USA Today,* July 7:10.

Elias, Norbert. 1978 (1939). *The Civilizing Process: The History of Manners.* New York: Urizen.

Elliott, Delbert S. 1994. "Serious Violent Offenders: Onset, Developmental Course, and Termination—The American Society of Criminology 1993 Presidential Address." *Criminology* 32(1):1–21.

Elliott, Delbert S., Suzanne S. Ageton, and Rachelle J. Canter. 1979. "An Integrated Theoretical Perspective on Delinquent Behavior." *Journal of Research in Crime and Delinquency* 16:3–27.

Elliott, Delbert S., David Huizinga, and Suzanne S. Ageton. 1985. *Explaining Delinquency and Drug Use.* Beverly Hills, CA: Sage Publications.

Engel, Robin Shepard, James J. Sobol, and Robert E. Worden. 2000. "Further Exploration of the Demeanor Hypothesis: The Interaction Effects of Suspects' Characteristics and Demeanor on Police Behavior." *Justice Quarterly* 17:235–58.

English, Diana J. 1998. "The Extent and Consequences of Child Maltreatment." *The Future of Children* 8:39–53.

Erlanger, Howard S. 1974. "The Empirical Status of the Subculture of Violence Thesis." *Social Problems* 22:280–92.

Eschholz, Sarah. 2002. "Racial Composition of Television Offenders and Viewers' Fear of Crime." *Critical Criminology* 11:41–60.

Eschholz, Sarah, Ted Chiricos, and Marc Gertz. 2003. "Television and Fear of Crime: Program Types, Audience Traits, and the Mediating Effect of Perceived Neighborhood Racial Composition." *Social Problems* 50:395–415.

Estrich, Susan. 2003. "Rape Shield Laws Aren't Foolproof." *USA Today,* July 27: http://www.usatoday.com/news/opinion/editorials/2003-07-27-estrich_x.htm.

Evans, T. David, Francis T. Cullen, R. Gregory Dunaway, and Velmer S. Burton Jr. 1995. "Religion and Crime Reexamined: The Impact of Religion, Secular Controls, and Social Ecology on Adult Criminality." *Criminology* 33:195–224.

Fackler, Martin. 2007. "Mayor's Death Forces Japan's Crime Rings into the Light." *New York Times,* April 21:A1.

Fagan, Jeffrey. 1994. "Women and Drugs Revisited: Female Participation in the Cocaine Economy." *Journal of Drug Issues* 24:179–226.

Faludi, Susan. 1991. *Backlash: The Undeclared War Against American Women.* New York: Crown.

Farnworth, Margaret, and Michael J. Leiber. 1989. "Strain Theory Revisited: Economic Goals, Educational Means, and Delinquency." *American Sociological Review* 54:263–74.

Farnworth, Margaret, Terence P. Thornberry, Marvin D. Krohn, and Alan J. Lizotte. 1994. "Measurement in the Study of Class and Delinquency: Integrating Theory and Research." *Journal of Research in Crime and Delinquency* 31(1):33–61.

Farrell, Greg. 2004. "Pfizer Settles Fraud Case for $430M." *USA Today,* May 14:1B.

Farrington, David P. 2003. "Developmental and Life-Course Criminology: Key Theoretical and Empirical Issues—The 2002 Sutherland Award Address." *Criminology* 41:221–55.

———. 2006. "Building Developmental and Life-Course Theories of Offending." Pp. 335–64 in *Taking Stock: The Status of Criminological Theory,* edited by Francis T. Cullen, John Paul Wright, and Kristie R. Blevins. New Brunswick, NJ: Transaction Publishers.

Farrington, David P., Rolf Loeber, and Magda Stouthamer-Loeber. 2003. "How Can the Relationship Between Race and Violence Be Explained?" Pp. 213–37 in *Violent Crime: Assessing Race and Ethnic Differences,* edited by Darnell F. Hawkins. New York: Cambridge University Press.

Faupel, Charles E., Alan M. Horowitz, and Greg S. Weaver. 2010. *The Sociology of American Drug Use.* New York: Oxford University Press.

Fazlollah, Mark. 1997. "11 More Cleared Due to Scandal." *The Philadelphia Inquirer,* March 25:A1.

Fazlollah, Mark, Michael Matza, Craig R. McCoy, and Clea Benson. 1999. "Women Victimized Twice in Police Game of Numbers." *Philadelphia Inquirer,* October 17:A1.

Federal Bureau of Investigation. 2009. *Crime in the United States: 2008.* Washington, DC: Federal Bureau of Investigation.

———. 2010. *Crime in the United States, 2009.* Washington, DC: Federal Bureau of Investigation.

Feeley, Jef, and Dawn McCarty. 2004. "Wyeth Wins One Case, Loses Another." *Daily Record* (Morris County, NJ), July 29: http://www.dailyrecord.com/business/business 1-wyethsuits.htm.

Feeley, Malcolm M. 1979. "Perspectives on Plea Bargaining." *Law and Society Review* 13:199–209.

Feld, Barry C. 2003. "The Politics of Race and Juvenile Justice: The 'Due Process Revolution' and the Conservative Reaction." *Justice Quarterly* 20:765–800.

Feldberg, Michael. 1980. *The Turbulent Era: Riot and Disorder in Jacksonian America.* New York: Oxford University Press.

———. 1998. "Urbanization as a Cause of Violence: Philadelphia as a Test Case." Pp. 53–69 in *The Peoples of Philadelphia: A History of Ethnic Groups and Lower-Class Life, 1790–1940,* edited by Allen F. Davis and Mark H. Haller. Philadelphia: University of Pennsylvania Press.

Felson, Marcus, and Rachel Boba. 2010. *Crime and Everyday Life.* Thousand Oaks, CA: Sage Publications.

Felson, Marcus, and Ronald V. Clarke. 2010. "Routine Precautions, Criminology, and Crime Prevention." Pp. 106–20 in *Criminology and Public Policy: Putting Theory to Work,* edited by Hugh D. Barlow and Scott H. Decker. Philadelphia: Temple University Press.

Felson, Richard B. 2006. "Is Violence Against Women About Women or About Violence?" *Contexts* 5(2):21–25.

Felson, Richard B., Jeffrey M. Ackerman, and Catherine A. Gallagher. 2005. "Police Intervention and the Repeat of Domestic Assault." *Criminology* 43:563–88.

Felson, Richard B., and Keri B. Burchfield. 2004. "Alcohol and the Risk of Physical and Sexual Assault Victimization." *Criminology* 42:837–59.

Felson, Richard B., and Dana L. Haynie. 2002. "Pubertal Development, Social Factors, and Delinquency Among Adolescent Boys." *Criminology* 40:967–88.

Felson, Richard B., and Marvin Krohn. 1990. "Motives for Rape." *Journal of Research in Crime and Delinquency* 27(3):222–42.

Felson, Richard B., and Kelsea Jo Lane. 2010. "Does Violence Involving Women and Intimate Partners Have a Special Etiology?" *Criminology* 48:321–38.

Felson, Richard B., and Henry J. Steadman. 1983. "Situational Factors in Disputes Leading to Criminal Violence." *Criminology* 21:59–74.

Felson, Richard B., Brent Teasdale, and Keri B. Burchfield. 2008. "The Influence of Being Under the Influence." *Journal of Research in Crime & Delinquency* 45(2):119–41.

Fenster, Jim. 1994. "Nation of Gamblers." *American Heritage* 45:34–45.

Ferdinand, Theodore. 1970. "Demographic Shifts and Criminality: An Inquiry." *British Journal of Criminology* 10:169–75.

Ferguson, Christopher J., and Richard D. Hartley. 2009. "The Pleasure Is Momentary . . . The Expense Damnable? The Influence of Pornography on Rape and Sexual Assault." *Aggression & Violent Behavior* 14(5):323–29.

Ferraro, Kathleen J. 1995. "Cops, Courts, and Woman Battering." Pp. 262–71 in *The Criminal Justice System and Women: Offenders, Victims, and Workers,* edited by Barbara Raffel Price and Natalie J. Sokoloff. New York: McGraw-Hill.

Few, Jenel. 2010. "Awards of Excellence Honor Students Who Beat the Odds." *Savannah Morning News,* May 12: http://savannahnow.com/news/2010-05-12/awards-excellence-honor-students-who-beat-odds-0.

Finan, Christopher M. 2007. *From the Palmer Raids to the Patriot Act: A History of the Fight for Free Speech in America.* Boston: Beacon Press.

Fisher, Bonnie S., Francis T. Cullen, and Michael G. Turner. 2000. *The Sexual Victimization of College Women.* Washington, DC: National Institute of Justice and Bureau of Justce Statistics, U.S. Department of Justice.

———. 2002. "Being Pursued: Stalking Victimization in a National Study of College Women." *Criminology & Social Policy* 1:257–308.

Fisher, Bonnie S., Leah E. Daigle, and Francis T. Cullen. 2010. "What Distinguishes Single from Recurrent Sexual Victims? The Role of Lifestyle-Routine Activities and First-Incident Characteristics." *Justice Quarterly* 27(1):102–29.

Fishman, Mark. 1978. "Crime Waves as Ideology." *Social Problems* 25:531–43.

Fitzpatrick, Kevin M., Mark E. La Gory, and Ferris J. Ritchey. 1993. "Criminal Victimization Among the Homeless." *Justice Quarterly* 10(3):353–68.

Fleck, Carole. 2002. "Avoid Car Repair Rip-Offs." *AARP Bulletin Online* July/August: http://www.aarp.org/bulletin/consumer/Articles/a2003-06-30-carrepair.html.

Fomby, Paula, and Andrew J. Cherlin. 2007. "Family Instability and Child Well-Being." *American Sociological Review* 72:181–204.

Ford, J. A. 2009. "Nonmedical Prescription Drug Use Among Adolescents: The Influence of Bonds to Family and School." *Youth & Society* 40(3):336–52.

Foster, Holly, and John Hagan. 2009. "The Mass Incarceration of Parents in America: Issues of Race/ Ethnicity, Collateral Damage to Children, and Prisoner Reentry." *Annals of the American Academy of Political and Social Science* 623:179–94.

Fox, James Alan, Jack Levin, and Kenna Quinet. 2008. *The Will to Kill: Making Sense of Senseless Murder.* Boston: Allyn Bacon.

Fox, James Alan, and Marianne W. Zawitz. 1998. *Homicide Trends in the United States.* Washington, DC: Bureau of Justice Statistics, U.S. Department of Justice.

Franiuk, Renae, Jennifer Seefelt, and Joseph Vandello. 2008. "Prevalence of Rape Myths in Headlines and Their Effects on Attitudes Toward Rape." *Sex Roles* 58(11/12):790–801.

Frank, Nancy K., and Michael J. Lynch. 1992. *Corporate Crime, Corporate Violence: A Primer.* New York: Harrow and Heston.

Frankfurter, Felix, and Roscoe Pound. 1922. *Criminal Justice in Cleveland.* Cleveland, OH: The Cleveland Foundation.

Freud, Sigmund. 1935 (1920). *A General Introduction to Psycho-Analysis.* New York: Liveright.

———. 1961 (1930). *Civilization and Its Discontents.* New York: Norton.

Friedman, Lauri S., and Jennifer L. Stancke (eds.). 2009. *Eating Disorders.* Farmington Hills, MI: Greenhaven Press.

Friedman, Leon. 1971. *The Wise Minority.* New York: Dial Press.

Friedman, Lucy N. 1994. "Adopting the Health Care Model to Prevent Victimization." *National Institute of Justice Journal* (228, November):16–19.

Friedrichs, David O. 2010. *Trusted Criminals: White Collar Crime in Contemporary Society.* Belmont, CA: Wadsworth Publishing Company.

Frost, Natasha A., Joshua D. Freilich, and Todd R. Clear (eds.). 2010. *Contemporary Issues in Criminal Justice Policy: Policy Proposals from the American Society of Criminology Conference.* Belmont, CA: Wadsworth.

Fyfe, James J. 1983. "The NIJ Study of the Exclusionary Rule." *Criminal Law Bulletin* 19:253–60.

———. 1993. "Police Use of Deadly Force: Research and Reform." Pp. 128–42 in *Criminal Justice: Law and Politics,* edited by George F. Cole. Belmont, CA: Wadsworth Publishing Company.

———. 2002. "Too Many Missing Cases: Holes in Our Knowledge About Police Use of Force." *Justice Research and Policy* 4:87–102.

Fyfe, James J., David A. Klinger, and Jeanne M. Flavin. 1997. "Differential Police Treatment of Male-on-Female Spousal Violence." *Criminology* 35:455–73.

Gabbidon, Shaun L. 2007. *W.E.B. DuBois on Crime and Justice: Laying the Foundations of Sociological Criminology.* Brookfield, VT: Ashgate Publishing Company.

Gabbidon, Shaun L., and Helen Taylor Greene. 2009. *Race and Crime.* Thousand Oaks, CA: Sage Publications.

Gabbidon, Shaun L., and George E. Higgins. 2009. "The Role of Race/Ethnicity and Race Relations on Public Opinion Related to the Treatment of Blacks by the Police." *Police Quarterly* 12(1):102–15.

Gammage, Jeff. 1997. "Baltimore Forges a Different Course on Drug Abuse." *Philadelphia Inquirer,* December 24:A1.

Garbarino, James. 2006. *See Jane Hit: Why Girls Are Growing More Violent and What We Can Do About It.* New York: Penguin.

Garcia, Venessa, and Janice Clifford (eds.). 2010. *Female Victims of Crime: Reality Reconsidered.* Upper Saddle River, NJ: Prentice Hall.

Gardner, Saundra. 1994. "Real Domestic Tragedy Continues." *Bangor Daily News,* June 29:A9.

Garland, David. 1990. *Punishment and Modern Society: A Study in Social Theory.* Chicago: University of Chicago Press.

Garrow, David J. 1981. *The FBI and Martin Luther King, Jr.* New York: Penguin Press.

Gau, Jacinta M., and Rod K. Brunson. 2010. "Procedural Justice and Order Maintenance Policing: A Study of Inner-City Young Men's Perceptions of Police Legitimacy." *JQ: Justice Quarterly* 27(2):255–79.

Gau, Jacinta M., and Travis C. Pratt. 2008. "Broken Windows or Window Dressing? Citizens' (in)Ability to Tell the Difference Between Disorder and Crime." *Criminology & Public Policy* 7(2):163–94.

Geis, Gilbert. 1987. "The Heavy Electrical Equipment Antitrust Cases of 1961." Pp. 124–44 in *Corporate and Governmental Deviance: Problems of Organizational Behavior in Contemporary Society,* edited by M. David Ermann and Richard J. Lundman. New York: Oxford University Press.

———. 1992. "White-Collar Crime: What Is It?" Pp. 31–52 in *White-Collar Crime Reconsidered,* edited by Kip Schlegel and David Weisburd. Boston: Northeastern University Press.

———. 1995. "White-Collar Crime." Pp. 213–21 in *Readings in Deviant Behavior,* edited by Alex Thio and Thomas Calhoun. New York: HarperCollins College Publishers.

———. 2000. "On the Absence of Self-Control as the Basis for a General Theory of Crime: A Critique." *Theoretical Criminology* 4:35–53.

Gerth, Hans, and C. Wright Mills (eds.). 1946. *From Max Weber: Essays in Sociology.* New York: Oxford University Press.

Gibbs, Jack P. 1968. "Crime, Punishment, and Deterrence." *Southwestern Social Science Quarterly* 48:515–30.

Gibbs, Nancy. 2010. "Sexual Assaults on Female Soliders: Don't Ask, Don't Tell." *Times-News* (Hendersonville, NC), March 8: http://www.time.com/time/magazine/article/0,9171,1968110,00.html.

Giblin, Matthew J., and Amber D. Dillon. 2009. "Public Perceptions in the Last Frontier: Alaska Native Satisfaction with the Police." *Journal of Ethnicity in Criminal Justice* 7(2):107–20.

Gibson, Chris L., J. Mitchell Miller, Wesley G. Jennings, Marc Swatt, and Angela Gover. 2009. "Using Propensity Score Matching to Understand the Relationship Between Gang Membership and Violent Victimization: A Research Note." *JQ: Justice Quarterly* 26(4):625–43.

Gibson, Chris L., Alex R. Piquero, and Stephen G. Tibbetts. 2000. "Assessing the Relationship Between Maternal Cigarette Smoking During Pregnancy and Age at First Police Conact." *Justice Quarterly* 17:519–42.

Gibson, Chris L., Christopher J. Sullivan, Shayne Jones, and Alex R. Piquero. 2010. "'Does It Take a Village?' Assessing Neighborhood Influences on Children's Self-Control." *Journal of Research in Crime and Delinquency* 47(1):31–62.

Gibson, Chris L., Jihong Zhao, Nicholas P. Lovrich, and Michael J. Gaffney. 2002. "Social Integration, Individual Perceptions of Collective Efficacy, and Fear of Crime in Three Cities." *Justice Quarterly* 19:537–64.

Gil, David G. 1979. *Violence Against Children.* Cambridge, MA: Cambridge University Press.

Gilbert, Martin. 1987. *The Holocaust: A History of the Jews of Europe During the Second World War.* New York: Henry Holt and Company.

Gilliam, F. D., and S. Iyengar. 2000. "Prime Suspects: The Influence of Local Television News on the Viewing Public." *American Journal of Political Science* 44:560–73.

Gilpin, Kenneth N. 2003. "Millions Are Victimized by Identity Theft, Survey Shows." *New York Times,* September 3:C2.

Giordano, Peggy. 2009. "Peer Influences on Girls' Delinquency." Pp. 127–45 in *The Delinquent Girl,* edited by Margaret A. Zahn. Philadelphia: Temple University Press.

Glaser, Daniel. 1956. "Criminality Theories and Behavioral Images." *American Journal of Sociology* 61:433–44.

Glassner, Barry. 2010. *The Culture of Fear: Why Americans Are Afraid of the Wrong Things.* New York: Basic Books.

Glover, Scott, and Matt Lait. 2000a. "Beatings Alleged to Be Routine at Rampart." *Los Angeles Times,* February 14:A1.

———. 2000b. "Police in Secret Group Broke Law Routinely, Transcripts Say." *Los Angeles Times,* February 14:A1.

Glymour, Bruce, Clark Glymour, and Maria Glymour. 2008. "Watching Social Science: The Debate About the Effects of Exposure to Televised Violence on Aggressive Behavior." *American Behavioral Scientist* 51(8):1231–59.

Goddard, Henry H. 1912. *The Kallikak Family: A Study in the Heredity of Feeblemindedness.* New York: Macmillan.

Goffman, Alice. 2009. "On the Run: Wanted Men in a Philadelphia Ghetto." *American Sociological Review* 74(3):339–57.

Goldstein, Scott, and Richard Abshire. 2008. "Teen Boys' Curiosity Started Deadly Chain of Events." *Dallas Morning News,* March 4:A1.

Goldston, James. 1990. *A Year of Reckoning: El Salvador a Decade After the Assassination of Archbishop Romero.* New York: Americas Watch Committee.

Golub, Andrew, Bruce D. Johnson, and Eloise Dunlap. 2007. "The Race/Ethnicity Disparity in Misdemeanor Marijuana Arrests in New York City." *Criminology & Public Policy* 6:131–64.

Gomez-Preston, Cheryl, and Jacqueline Trescott. 1995. "Over the Edge: One Police Woman's Story of Emotional and Sexual Harassment." Pp. 398–403 in *The Criminal Justice System and Women: Offenders, Victims, and Workers,* edited by Barbara Raffel Price and Natalie J. Sokoloff. New York: McGraw-Hill.

Goode, Erich. 2008a. *Deviant Behavior.* Upper Saddle River, NJ: Prentice Hall.

———. 2008b. *Drugs in American Society.* New York: McGraw-Hill.

Gotsch, Kara. 2007. "It's Right to Grant Former Felons the Right to Vote." *Washington Post,* May 13:B8.

Gottfredson, Michael, and Travis Hirschi. 1990. *A General Theory of Crime.* Stanford, CA: Stanford University Press.

Grann, David. 2009. "Trial by Fire: Did Texas Execute an Innocent Man?" *New Yorker,* September 7: http://www.newyorker.com/reporting/2009/09/07/090907fa_fact_grann.

Grannis, Kathy. 2009. "Troubled Economy Increases Shoplifting Rates, According to National Retail Security Survey (press release)." *National Retail Federation,* June 16: http://www.nrf.com/modules.php?name=News&op=viewlive&sp_id=746.

Greenberg, David F. 1993. "Introduction." Pp. 1–35 in *Crime and Capitalism: Readings in Marxist Criminology,* edited by David F. Greenberg. Philadelphia: Temple University Press.

Greenfeld, Lawrence A., and Tracy L. Snell. 1999. *Women Offenders.* Washington, DC: Bureau of Justice Statistics, U.S. Department of Justice.

Greenwood, Peter W. 2006. *Changing Lives: Delinquency Prevention as Crime-Control Policy.* Chicago: University of Chicago Press.

Griffin, Marie. 2010. "Feminist Criminology: Beyond the Slaying of Demons." Pp. 215–32 in *Criminology and Public Policy: Putting Theory to Work,* edited by Hugh D. Barlow and Scott H. Decker. Philadelphia: Temple University Press.

Griffin, Susan. 1971. "Rape: The All-American Crime." *Ramparts,* September:26–35.

Griffin, Timothy, and John Wooldredge. 2006. "Sex-Based Disparities in Felony Dispositions Before Versus After Sentencing Reform in Ohio." *Criminology* 44:893–923.

Gross, Alan M., Andrea Winslett, Miguel Roberts, and Carol L. Gohm. 2006. "An Examination of Sexual Violence Against College Women." *Violence Against Women* 12:288–300.

Groth, A. Nicholas. 1979. *Men Who Rape: The Psychology of the Offender.* New York: Plenum Press.

Guerette, Rob T., and Kate J. Bowers. 2009. "Assessing the Extent of Crime Displacement and Diffusion of Benefits: A Review of Situational Crime Prevention Evaluations." *Criminology* 47(4):1331–68.

Guo, Guang. 2005. "Twin Studies: What Can They Tell Us About Nature and Nurture?" *Contexts* 4(3):43–47.

Guo, Guang, Michael E. Roettger, and Tianji Cai. 2008. "The Integration of Genetic Propensities into Social-Control Models of Delinquency and Violence Among Male Youths." *American Sociological Review* 73(4):543–68.

Gurr, Ted Robert. 1989a. "Historical Trends in Violent Crime: Europe and the United States." Pp. 21–54 in *Violence in America: The History of Crime,* edited by Ted Robert Gurr. Newbury Park, CA: Sage Publications.

———. 1989b. "Political Terrorism: Historical Antecedents and Contemporary Trends." Pp. 201–30 in *Violence in America: Protest, Rebellion, Reform,* edited by Ted Robert Gurr. Newbury Park, CA: Sage Publications.

Gusfield, Joseph R. 1963. *Symbolic Crusade: Status Politics and the American Temperance Movement.* Urbana: University of Illinois Press.

Guzik, Keith. 2008. "The Agencies of Abuse: Intimate Abusers' Experience of Presumptive Arrest and Prosecution." *Law & Society Review* 42(1):111–44.

Hagan, Frank E. 1989. "Espionage as Political Crime? A Typology of Spies." *Journal of Security Administration* 12:19–36.

Hagan, John. 1990. "The Pleasures of Predation and Disrepute." *Law & Society Review* 24:165–77.

———. 1992. "The Poverty of a Classless Criminology—The American Society of Criminology 1991 Presidential Address." *Criminology* 30(1):1–19.

———. 1993. "The Social Embeddedness of Crime and Unemployment." *Criminology* 31(4):465–91.

———. 1994. *Crime and Disrepute.* Thousand Oaks, CA: Pine Forge Press.

Hagan, John, and Ruth Peterson (eds.). 1995. *Crime and Inequality.* Stanford, CA: Stanford University Press.

Hagan, John, and Wenona Rymond-Richmond. 2008. "The Collective Dynamics of Racial Dehumanization and Genocidal Victimization in Darfur." *American Sociological Review* 73(6):875–902.

Hagan, John, John Simpson, and A. R. Gillis. 1987. "Class in the Household: A Power-Control Theory of Gender and Delinquency." *American Journal of Sociology* 92:788–816.

Hagan, John, and Marjorie S. Zatz. 1985. "The Social Organization of Criminal Justice Processing Activities." *Social Science Research* 14:103–25.

Hall, Jerome. 1952. *Theft, Law, and Society.* Indianapolis, IN: Bobbs-Merrill.

Hamm, Mark S. 1995. *American Skinheads: The Criminology and Control of Hate Crime.* Westport, Ct: Praeger Publishers.

Harcourt, Bernard E., and Jens Ludwig. 2007a. "Reefer Madness: Broken Windows Policing and Misdemeanor Marijuana Arrests in New York City, 1989–2000." *Criminology & Public Policy* 6:165–82.

———. 2007b. "Reefer Madness: Broken Windows Policing and Misdemeanor Marijuana Arrests in New York City, 1989–2000." *Criminology & Public Policy* 6(1):165–81.

Harding, David J. 2010. *Living the Drama: Community, Conflict, and Culture among Inner-City Boys.* Chicago: University of Chicago Press.

Harlow, Caroline Wolf. 2005. *Hate Crime Reported by Victims and Police.* Washington, DC: Bureau of Justice Statistics, U.S. Department of Justice.

Harring, Sidney L. 1993. "Policing a Class Society: The Expansion of the Urban Police in the Late Nineteenth and Early Twentieth Centuries." Pp. 546–67 in *Crime and Capitalism: Readings in Marxist Criminology,* edited by David F. Greenberg. Philadelphia: Temple University Press.

Harrington, Penny, and Kimberly A. Lonsway. 2004. "Current Barriers and Future Promise for Women in Policing." Pp. 495–510 in *The Criminal Justice System and Women: Offenders, Prisoners, Victims, and Workers,* edited by Barbara Raffel Price and Natalie J. Sokoloff. New York: McGraw-Hill.

Harris, Anthony R., S. H. Thomas, G. A. Fisher, and D. J. Hirsch. 2002. "Murder and Medicine: The Lethality of Criminal Assault, 1960–1999." *Homicide Studies* 6:128–66.

Harris, Casey T., Darrell Steffensmeier, Jeffrey T. Ulmer, and Noah Painter-Davis. 2009. "Are Blacks and Hispanics Disproportionately Incarcerated Relative to Their Arrests? Racial and Ethnic Disproportionality Between Arrest and Incarceration." *Race and Social Problems* 1:187–99.

Harris, Gardiner. 1998. "Despite Laws, Hundreds Are Killed by Black Lung." *Courier-Journal* (Louisville, KY), April 19:A1.

———. 2009. "Pfizer Pays $2.3 Billion to Settle Marketing Case." *New York Times,* September 3:B4.

Harris, Ron. 2007. "They Fear Ambush, Snipers—and an Enemy Within." *St. Louis Post-Dispatch,* June 4:A1.

Hart, Ariel. 2004. "Report Finds Atlanta Police Cut Figures on Crimes." *New York Times,* February 21:A1.

Hartley, Richard D., Sean Maddan, and Cassia C. Spohn. 2007. "Prosecutorial Discretion: An Examination of Substantial Assistance Departures in Federal Crack-Cocaine and Powder-Cocaine Cases." *JQ: Justice Quarterly* 24(3):382–407.

Hawkins, Darnell F. 1994. "The Analysis of Racial Disparities in Crime and Justice: A Double-Edged Sword." Pp. 48–50 in *Enhancing Capacities and Confronting Controversies in Criminal Justice,* edited by Tom Hester, Yvonne Boston, Linda N. Ruder, Helen A. Graziadel, and Benjamin H. Renshaw III. Washington, DC: U.S. Department of Justice, Bureau of Justice Statistics.

———. 2003. "Editor's Introduction." Pp. xiii–xxv in *Violent Crime: Assessing Race and Ethnic Differences,* edited by Darnell F. Hawkins. Cambridge, MA: Cambridge University Press.

Hay, Carter, and Michelle M. Evans. 2006. "Has *Roe v. Wade* Reduced U.S. Crime Rates? Examining the Link Between Mothers' Pregnancy Intentions and Children's Later Involvement in Law-Violating Behavior." *Journal of Research in Crime and Delinquency* 43:36–66.

Hay, Carter, Edward N. Fortson, Dusten R. Hollist, Irshad Altheimer, and Lonnie M. Schaible. 2006. "The Impact of Community Disadvantage on the Relationship Between the Family and Juvenile Crime." *Journal of Research in Crime and Delinquency* 43:326–56.

Hayes International. 2009. "Theft Surveys: Shoplifting." http://www.hayesinternational .com/thft_srvys.html.

Hayes-Smith, Justin, and Rebecca Hayes-Smith. 2009. "Race, Racial Context, and Withholding Adjudication in Drug Cases: A Multilevel Examination of Juvenile Justice." *Journal of Ethnicity in Criminal Justice* 7(3):163–85.

Haynie, Dana L. 2003. "Contexts of Risk? Explaining the Link Between Girls' Pubertal Development and Their Delinquency Involvement." *Social Forces* 82:355–97.

Haynie, Dana L., and Danielle C. Payne. 2006. "Race, Friendship Networks, and Violent Delinquency." *Criminology* 44:775–805.

Haynie, Dana L., and Alex R. Piquero. 2006. "Pubertal Development and Physical Victimization in Adolescence." *Journal of Research in Crime and Delinquency* 43:3–35.

Haynie, Dana L., Eric Silver, and Brent Teasdale. 2006. "Neighborhood Characteristics, Peer Networks, and Adolescent Violence." *Journal of Quantitative Criminology* 22:147–69.

Haynie, Dana L., Harald E. Weiss, and Alex Piquero. 2008. "Race, the Economic Maturity Gap, and Criminal Offending in Young Adulthood." *JQ: Justice Quarterly* 25(4):595–622.

Heise, Lori, Mary Ellseberg, and Megan Gottemoeller. 1999. "Ending Violence Against Women." In *Population Reports, Series L. No. 11*. Baltimore, MD: Johns Hopkins University School of Public Health.

Helderman, Rosalind S. 2010. "Va. Senate Votes to Allow Guns in Restaurants." *Washington Post,* February 16: http://voices.washingtonpost.com/virginiapolitics/ 2010/02/va_senate_votes_to_allow_guns.html.

Hemenway, David. 2004. *Private Guns, Public Health.* Ann Arbor: University of Michigan Press.

Henderson, Wade. 1991. "Police Brutality IIs a National Crisis." Pp. 23–29 in *Police Brutality,* edited by William Dudley. San Diego, CA: Greenhaven Press.

Henriques, Diana B., and Jack Healy. 2009. "Madoff Goes to Jail After Guilty Pleas." *New York Times,* March 13:A1.

Hepburn, John. 1984. "Occasional Criminals." Pp. 73–94 in *Major Forms of Crime,* edited by Robert Meier. Beverly Hills, CA: Sage.

Herbert, Bob. 2000. "At the Heart of the Diallo Case." *New York Times,* February 28:A23.

———. 2007. "A Volatile Young Man, Humiliation and a Gun." *New York Times,* April 19:A27.

Herdy, Amy, and Miles Moffeit. 2004. "Betrayal in the Ranks." *Denver Post*: http:// www.denverpost.com/Stories/0,0,36%257E30137%257E,00.html.

Herrnstein, Richard J., and Charles Murray. 1994. *The Bell Curve: Intelligence and Class Structure in American Life.* New York: Free Press.

Hershkowitz, Leo. 1977. *Tweed's New York: Another Look.* Garden City, NY: Anchor Books.

Hester, Marianne. 1992. "The Witch-craze in Sixteenth- and Seventeenth-Century England as Social Control of Women." Pp. 27–39 in *Femicide: The Politics of Woman Killing,* edited by Jill Radford and Diana E. H. Russell. New York: Twayne.

Hicks, Karen M. 1994. *Surviving the Dalkon Shield IUD: Women v. the Pharmaceutical Industry.* New York: Teachers College Press (Columbia University).

Higgins, George E., Scott E. Wolfe, Margaret Mahoney, and Nelseta M. Walters. 2009. "Race, Ethnicity, and Experience: Modeling the Public's Perceptions of Justice, Satisfaction, and Attitude Toward the Courts." *Journal of Ethnicity in Criminal Justice* 7(4):293–310.

Hilinski, C. M. 2009. "Fear of Crime Among College Students: A Test of the Shadow of Sexual Assault Hypothesis." *American Journal of Criminal Justice* 34(1):84–102.

Hindelang, Michael J., Travis Hirschi, and Joseph Weis. 1979. "Correlates of Delinquency: The Illusion of Discrepancy Between Self-Report and Official Measures." *American Sociological Review* 44:995–1014.

Hipp, John R. 2007. "Income Inequality, Race, and Place: Does the Distribution of Race and Class Within Neighborhoods Affect Crime Rates?" *Criminology* 45(3):665–97.

———. 2010. "A Dynamic View of Neighborhoods: The Reciprocal Relationship Between Crime and Neighborhood Structural Characteristics." *Social Problems* 57:205–30.

Hipp, John R., Daniel J. Bauer, Patrick J. Curran, and Kenneth A. Bollen. 2004. "Crimes of Opportunity or Crimes of Emotion? Testing Two Explanations of Seasonal Change in Crime." *Social Forces* 82:1333–72.

Hipp, John R., and Daniel K. Yates. 2009. "Do Returning Parolees Affect Neighborhood Crime?: A Case Study of Sacramento." *Criminology* 47(3):619–56.

Hirschfield, Paul J. 2008. "The Declining Significance of Delinquent Labels in Disadvantaged Urban Communities." *Sociological Forum* 23:575–601.

Hirschi, Travis. 1969. *Causes of Delinquency.* Berkeley: University of California Press.

———. 1989. "Exploring Alternatives to Integrated Theory." Pp. 37–49 in *Theoretical Integration in the Study of Deviance and Crime: Problems and Prospects,* edited by Steven F. Messner, Marvin D. Krohn, and Allen E. Liska. Albany: State University of New York Press.

Hirschi, Travis, and Michael J. Hindelang. 1977. "Intelligence and Delinquency: A Revisionist Review." *American Sociological Review* 42:571–87.

Hobbs, Dick. 1994. "Mannish Boys: Danny, Chris, Crime, Masculinity and Business." Pp. 118–34 in *Just Boys Doing Business? Men, Masculinities and Crime,* edited by Tim Newburn and Elizabeth A. Stanko. London: Routledge.

Hobson, Barbara Meil. 1987. *Uneasy Virtue: The Politics of Prostitution and the American Reform Tradition.* New York: Basic Books.

Hochstetler, Andy, and Jeffrey A. Bouffard. 2010. "Classical and Rational Choice Perspectives." Pp. 19–35 in *Criminological Theory: Readings and Retrospectives,* edited by Heith Copes and Volkan Topalli. New York: McGraw-Hill.

Hoffman, Jan. 1998. "As Miranda Rights Erode, Police Get Confessions from Innocent People." *New York Times,* March 30:A1.

Holmes, Ronald M., and Stephen T. Holmes. 1994. *Murder in America.* Thousand Oaks, CA: Sage Publications.

Holtfreter, Kristy, Michael D. Reisig, and Travis C. Pratt. 2008. "Low Self-Control, Routine Activities, and Fraud Victimization." *Criminology* 46(1):189–220.

Hood, Jane C. 1995. "'Let's Get a Girl': Male Bonding Rituals in America." Pp. 307–11 in *Men's Lives,* edited by Michael S. Kimmel and Michael A. Messner. Boston: Allyn and Bacon.

Hooton, Earnest A. 1939a. *The American Criminal: An Anthropological Study.* Cambridge, MA: Harvard University Press.

———. 1939b. *Crime and the Man.* Cambridge, MA: Harvard University Press.

Horney, Karen. 1973. "The Problem of Feminine Masochism." In *Psychoanalysis and Women,* edited by J. Miller. New York: Brunner/Mazel.

Hoskin, Anthony W. 2001. "Armed Americans: The Impact of Firearm Availability on National Homicide Rates." *Justice Quarterly* 18:569–92.

Huddy, Leonie, and Stanley Feldman. 2009. "On Assessing the Political Effects of Racial Prejudice." *Annual Review of Political Science* 12(1):423–47.

Huff, C. Ronald. 2002. "Wrongful Conviction and Public Policy: The American Society of Criminology 2001 Presidential Address." *Criminology* 40:1–18.

Hughes, Donna M. 1999. "Legalizing Prostitution Will Not Stop the Harm." http://www .uri.edu/artsci/wms/hughes/mhvlegal.htm.

Hughes, Patricia Paulsen, David Marshall, and Claudine Sherrill. 2003. "Multidimensional Analysis of Fear and Confidence of University Women Relating to Crimes and Dangerous Situations." *Journal of Interpersonal Violence* 18(1):33–49.

Huisman, Kimberly A. 1996. "Wife Battering in Asian American Communities: Identifying the Service Needs of an Overlooked Segment of the U.S. Population." *Violence Against Women* 2:260–83.

Humphreys, Laud. 1975. *Teamroom Trade: Impersonal Sex in Public Places.* Chicago: Aldine.

Humphries, Drew. 2002. "No Easy Answers: Public Policy, Criminal Justice, and Domestic Violence." *Criminology & Public Policy* 2:91–96.

Humphries, Drew, John Dawson, Valerie Cronin, Phyllis Keating, Chris Wisniewski, and Jennine Eichfeld. 1995. "Mothers and Children, Drugs and Crack: Reactions to Maternal Drug Dependency." Pp. 167–79 in *The Criminal Justice System and Women: Offenders, Victims, and Workers,* edited by Barbara Raffel Price and Natalie J. Sokoloff. New York: McGraw-Hill, Inc.

Hunnicutt, Gwen, and Lisa M. Broidy. 2004. "Liberation and Economic Marginalization: A Reformulation and Test of (Formerly?) Competing Models." *Journal of Research in Crime and Delinquency* 41:130–55.

Inciardi, James A., Dorothy Lockwood, and Anne E. Pottieger. 1993. *Women and Crack-Cocaine.* New York: Macmillan.

Israel, Jonathan. 2010. *A Revolution of the Mind: Radical Enlightenment and the Intellectual Origins of Modern Democracy.* Princeton, NJ: Princeton University Press.

Jackman, Tom. 2004. "Guns Worn in Open Legal, But Alarm Va." *Washington Post,* July 15:A1.

Jackson, Brooks, and Kathleen Hall Jamieson. 2007. *UnSpun: Finding Facts in a World of Disinformation.* New York: Random House.

Jackson, Derrick Z. 1994. "Politicans' Crime Rhetoric." *Boston Globe,* October 24:15.

———. 1997. "No Wonder We're Afraid of Youths." *Boston Globe,* September 10:A15.

———. 1999. "From New Mexico's Governor, Rare Candor on Drugs." *Boston Globe,* October 13:A19.

Jackson, Pamela I. 1989. *Minority Group Threat, Crime, and Policing.* New York: Praeger.

Jackson, Sharon Boyd. 2010. "Domestic Violence: Overview of Theoretical Etiology, Psychological Impact and Interventions." In *Female Victims of Crime: Reality Reconsidered,* edited by Venessa Garcia and Janice Clifford. Upper Saddle River, NJ: Prentice Hall.

Jacob, Herbert. 1978. *Justice in America: Courts, Lawyers, and the Judicial Process.* Boston: Little, Brown and Company.

Jacobs, Bruce A., and Richard Wright. 1999. "Stick-Up, Street Culture, and Offender Motivation." *Criminology* 37:149–73.

———. 2006. *Street Justice: Retaliation in the Criminal Underworld.* New York: Cambridge University Press.

Jacobs, David, Jason T. Carmichael, and Stephanie L. Kent. 2005. "Vigilantism, Current Racial Threat, and Death Sentences." *American Sociological Review* 70:656–77.

Jacobs, David, and Stephanie L. Kent. 2007. "The Determinants of Executions Since 1951: How Politics, Protests, Public Opinion, and Social Divisions Shape Capital Punishment." *Social Problems* 54(3):297–318.

Jacobs, David, and Robert M. O'Brien. 1998. "The Determinants of Deadly Force: A Structural Analysis of Police Violence." *American Journal of Sociology* 103:837–62.

Jang, Sung Joon. 2002. "The Effects of Family, School, Peers, and Attitudes on Adolescents' Drug Use: Do They Vary with Age?" *Justice Quarterly* 19:97–126.

Janus, Samuel S., and Cynthia L. Janus. 1993. *The Janus Report on Sexual Behavior.* New York: Wiley.

Jarjoura, G. Roger. 1993. "Does Dropping Out of School Enhance Delinquent Involvement? Results from a Large-Scale National Probability Sample." *Criminology* 31:149–71.

Jenkins, Philip. 1988. "Myth and Murder: The Serial Killer Panic of 1983–85." *Criminal Justice Research Bulletin* 3:1–7.

Jensen, Gary F. 2000. "Prohibition, Alcohol, and Murder: Untangling Countervailing Mechanisms." *Homicide Studies* 4:18–36.

Johansen, Bruce E. 2005. *The Native Peoples of North America: A History.* Westport, CT: Praeger.

Johnson, Byron R., Sung Joon Jang, David B. Larson, and Spencer De Li. 2001. "Does Adolescent Religious Commitment Matter? A Reexamination of the Effects of Religiosity on Delinquency." *Journal of Research in Crime and Delinquency* 38:22–44.

Johnson, Carrie. 2004a. "Former Rite Aid Chairman Gets 8 Years." *Washington Post,* May 28:E3.

Johnson, David T. 2007. "Crime and Punishment in Contemporary Japan." *Crime and Justice: A Review of Research* 36:371–423.

Johnson, Devon. 2008. "Racial Prejudice, Perceived Injustice, and the Black-White Gap in Punitive Attitudes." *Journal of Criminal Justice* 36:198–206.

Johnson, Devon, and Joseph B. Kuhns. 2009. "Striking Out: Race and Support for Police Use of Force." *JQ: Justice Quarterly* 26(3):592–623.

Johnson, Dirk. 2000a. "Illinois Governor Hopes to Fix a 'Broken Justice.'" *New York Times,* February 19:A7.

———. 2000b. "Poor Legal Work Common for Innocents on Death Row." *New York Times,* February 5:A1.

Johnson, Kirk. 2004b. "Judge Limiting Sex-Life Shield at Bryant Trial." *New York Times,* July 24:A1.

Johnson, Michael P. 2006. "Conflict and Control: Gender Symmetry and Asymmetry in Domestic Violence." *Violence Against Women* 12:1003–18.

Johnston, Lloyd D., Patrick M. O'Malley, Jerold G. Bachman, and J. E. Schulenberg. 2008. *Monitoring the Future. National Survey Results on Drug Use, 1975–2008. Volume II. College Students and Adults Ages 19–50.* Bethesda, MD: National Institute on Drug Abuse.

Josephson, Matthew. 1962. *The Robber Barons: The Great American Capitalists, 1861–1901.* New York: Harcourt, Brace, & World.

Joutsen, Matti, and Norman Bishop. 1994. "Noncustodial Sanctions in Europe: Regional Overview." Pp. 279–92 in *Alternatives to Imprisonment in Comparative Perspective,* edited by Ugljesa Zvekic. Chicago: Nelson-Hall Publishers.

Kahane, L. H., D. Paton, and R. Simmons. 2008. "The Abortion–Crime Link: Evidence from England and Wales." *Economica* 75(1):1–21.

Kahn, Helen. 1986. "GAO Study Lists Remedies for Ford Park-Reverse Problem." *Automotive News,* June 23:39.

Kammeyer, Kenneth C. W. 2008. *A Hypersexual Society: Sexual Discourse, Erotica, and Pornography in America Today.* New York: Palgrave Macmillan.

Kanarek, Robin B. 1994. "Nutrition and Violent Behavior." Pp. 515–39 in *Understanding and Preventing Violence: Biobehavioral Influences,* edited by Albert J. Reiss Jr., Klaus A. Miczek, and Jeffrey A. Roth. Washington, DC: National Academy Press.

Kanin, Eugene J. 1970. "Sex Aggression by College Men." *Medical Aspects of Human Sexuality,* September:28ff.

Kappeler, Victor E., and Gary W. Potter. 2005. *The Mythology of Crime and Criminal Justice.* Prospect Heights, IL: Waveland Press.

Karmen, Andrew. 1990. *Crime Victims: An Introduction to Victimology.* Belmont, CA: Wadsworth.

———. 2010. *Crime Victims: An Introduction to Victimology,* 7th edition. Belmont, CA: Wadsworth Publishing Company.

Katz, Jack. 1988. *Seductions of Crime: Moral and Sensual Attractions of Doing Evil.* New York: Basic Books.

———. 1991. "The Motivation of the Persistent Robber." Pp. 277–306 in *Crime and Justice: A Review of Research,* edited by Michael Tonry. Chicago: University of Chicago Press.

Katz, Janet, and William J. Chambliss. 1995. "Biology and Crime." Pp. 275–303 in *Criminology: A Contemporary Handbook,* edited by Joseph F. Sheley. Belmont, CA: Wadsworth Publishing Company.

Kaufman, Joanne M. 2005. "Explaining the Race/Ethnicity–Violence Relationship: Neighborhood Context and Social Psychological Processes." *Justice Quarterly* 22:224–51.

———. 2009. "Gendered Responses to Serious Strain: The Argument for a General Strain Theory of Deviance." *JQ: Justice Quarterly* 26(3):410–44.

Kaufman, Peter Ives. 2007. *Incorrectly Political: Augustine and Thomas More.* Notre Dame, IN: University of Notre Dame Press.

Kay, Barbara. 2008. "On Domestic Violence, No One Wants to Hear the Truth." http://www.mensconfraternity.org.au/?page=p80.

Keating, Raymond J. 2004. "Get Government Out of Gambling Business." *Newsday,* August 10: http://www.newsday.com/news/columnists/ny-vpkea103924657aug10,0,5349844.column?coll=ny-news-columnists.

Kellerman, Arthur. 1996. *Understanding and Preventing Violence: A Public Health Perspective.* Washington, DC: Office of Justice Programs, National Institute of Justice.

Kellerman, Arthur L., et al. 1993. "Gun Ownership as a Risk Factor for Homicide in the Home." *New England Journal of Medicine* 329:1084–92.

Kelling, George L., and Catherine M. Coles. 1998. *Fixing Broken Windows: Restoring Order and Reducing Crime in Our Communities.* New York: Free Press.

Kelling, George L., Tony Pate, Duane Dieckman, and Charles Brown. 1974. *The Kansas City Preventive Patrol Experiment.* Washington, DC: The Police Foundation.

Kendrick, Walter M. 1987. *The Secret Museum: Pornography in Modern Culture.* New York: Viking Press.

Kennedy, John W. 2004. "The New Gambling Goliath." *Christianity Today,* August:50+.

Kenney, Dennis J., and James O. Finckenauer. 1995. *Organized Crime in America.* Belmont, CA: Wadsworth Publishing Company.

Kent, Stephanie L., and David Jacobs. 2005. "Minority Threat and Police Strength from 1980 to 2000: A Fixed-Effects Analysis of Nonlinear and Interactive Effects in Large U.S. Cities." *Criminology* 43:731–60.

Kerber, Ross. 2007. "TJX Credit Data Stolen." *Boston Globe,* January 18:A1.

Kerner Commission. 1968. *Report of the National Adivsory Commission on Civil Disorders.* New York: Bantam Books.

Kershaw, Sarah. 2004. "Suffering Effects of 50's A-Bomb Tests." *New York Times,* September 5:A1.

Kessler, Ronald. 1988. *Spy Versus Spy: Stalking Soviet Spies in America.* New York: Charles Scribner's.

Kethineni, Sesha, and Murugesan Srinivasan. 2009. "Police Handling of Domestic Violence Cases in Tamil Nadu, India." *Journal of Contemporary Criminal Justice* 25:202–13.

Khokha, Sasha. 2010. "'Pesticide Drift Eluding Efforts to Combat It." *National Public Radio,* February 28: http://www.npr.org/templates/story/story.php?storyId=123817702.

Kilmer, Beau. 2008. "Does Parolee Drug Testing Influence Employment and Education Outcomes? Evidence from a Randomized Experiment with Noncompliance." *Journal of Quantitative Criminology* 24(1):93–123.

Kim, Jinseok, and Karen A. Gray. 2008. "Leave or Stay? Battered Women's Decision After Intimate Partner Violence." *Journal of Interpersonal Violence* 23(10):1465–82.

Kimmel, Michael S. 2002. "'Gender Symmetry' in Domestic Violence: A Substantive and Methodological Research Review." *Violence Against Women* 8:1332–63.

Kimmel, Michael S., and Michael A. Messner (eds.). 2010. *Men's Lives.* Boston: Allyn and Bacon.

King, Martin Luther, Jr. 1969. "Letter from Birmingham City Jail." Pp. 72–89 in *Civil Disobedience: Theory and Practice,* edited by Hugo Adam Bedau. New York: Pegasus.

King, Ryan D., Michael Massoglia, and Ross MacMillan. 2007. "The Context of Marriage and Crime: Gender, the Propensity to Marry, and Offending in Early Adulthood." *Criminology* 45:33–65.

Kirk, David S. 2009a. "A Natural Experiment on Residential Change and Recidivism: Lessons from Hurricane Katrina." *American Sociological Review* 74(3):484–504.

———. 2009b. "Unraveling the Contextual Effects on Student Suspension and Juvenile Arrest: The Independent and Interdependent Influences of School, Neighborhood, and Family Social Controls." *Criminology* 47(2):479–520.

Kirkham, George L. 1984. "A Professor's 'Street Lessons,'" Pp. 77–89 in *"Order Under Law": Readings in Criminal Justice,* edited by Robert G. Culbertson. Prospect Heights, IL: Waveland Press.

Kitman, Jamie Lincoln. 2000. "The Secret History of Lead." *The Nation,* March 20:11–44.

Klaus, Patsy. 2007. *Crime and the Nation's Households, 2005.* Washington, DC: Bureau of Justice Statistics, U.S. Department of Justice.

Kleck, Gary, and M. Gertz. 1995. "Armed Resistance to Crime: The Prevalence and Nature of Self-Defense with a Gun." *Journal of Criminal Law and Criminology* 85:150–87.

Klein, Dorie. 1973. "The Etiology of Female Crime." *Issues in Criminology* 8:3–30.

———. 1995. "The Etiology of Female Crime: A Review of the Literature." Pp. 30–53 in *The Criminal Justice System and Women: Offenders, Victims, and Workers,* edited by Barbara Raffel Price and Natlie J. Sokoloff. New York: McGraw-Hill.

Klevens, Joanne, Gene Shelley, Carmen Clavel-Arcas, David D. Barney, Cynthia Tobar, Elisabeth S. Duran, Ruth Barajas-Mazaheri, and Janys Esparza. 2007. "Latinos' Perspectives and Experiences with Intimate Partner Violence." *Violence Against Women* 13:141–58.

Klier, John, and Shlomo Lambroza. 1992. *Pogroms: Anti-Jewish Violence in Modern Russian History.* New York: Cambridge University Press.

Klockars, Carl B. 1979. "The Contemporary Crises of Marxist Criminology." *Criminology* 16:477–515.

Knapp Commission. 1973. *Knapp Commission Report on Police Corruption.* New York: George Braziller.

Knepper, Paul. 2009. "How Situational Crime Prevention Contributes to Social Welfare." *Liverpool Law Review* 30:57–75.

Knightley, Phillip. 1987. *The Second Oldest Profession: Spies and Spying in the Twentieth Century.* New York: Norton.

Kohlberg, Lawrence. 1969. *States in the Development of Moral Thought and Action.* New York: Holt, Rinehart and Winston.

Komiya, Nobuo. 1999. "A Cultural Study of the Low Crime Rate in Japan." *British Journal of Criminology* 39:369–90.

Koppel, Herbert. 1987. *Lifetime Likelihood of Victimization.* Washington, DC: U.S. Department of Justice, Bureau of Justice Statistics.

Kornhauser, Ruth. 1978. *Social Sources of Delinquency.* Chicago: University of Chicago Press.

Koss, Mary P., Christine A. Gidycz, and Nadine Wisniewski. 1987. "The Scope of Rape: Incidence and Prevalence of Sexual Aggression and Victimization in a National Sample of Higher Education Students." *Journal of Consulting and Clinical Psychology* 52:162–70.

Kovandzic, Tomislav V., John J. Sloan, and Lynne M. Vieraitis. 2004. "'Striking Out' as Crime Reduction Policy: The Impact of 'Three Strikes' Laws on Crime Rates in U.S. Cities." *Justice Quarterly* 21:207–39.

Kovandzic, Tomislav V., and Thomas B. Marvell. 2003. "Right-to-Carry Concealed Handguns and Violent Crime: Crime Control Through Gun Decontrol?" *Criminology & Public Policy* 2:363–96.

Kovandzic, Tomislav V., and Lynne M. Vieraitis. 2006. "The Effect of County-Level Prison Population Growth on Crime Rates." *Criminology & Public Policy* 5:213–44.

Kovandzic, Tomislav V., Lynne M. Vieraitis, and Denise Paquette Boots. 2009. "Does the Death Penalty Save Lives? New Evidence from State Panel Data, 1977 to 2006." *Criminology & Public Policy* 8(4):803–43.

Kozol, Jonathan. 1991. *Savage Inequalities: Children in America's Schools.* New York: Crown.

Kramer, Ronald C. 1992. "The Space Shuttle *Challenger* Explosion: A Case Study of State-Corporate Crime." Pp. 214–43 in *White-Collar Crime Reconsidered,* edited by Kip Schlegel and David Weisburd. Boston: Northeastern University Press.

Kraska, Peter B., and Victor E. Kappeler. 1995. "To Serve and Pursue: Exploring Police Sexual Violence Against Women." *Justice Quarterly* 12:85–111.

Kreager, Derek A., Ross L. Matsueda, and Elena A. Erosheva. 2010. "Motherhood and Criminal Desistance in Disadvantaged Neighborhoods." *Criminology* 48:221–57.

Kristof, Nicholas D. 2010. "Is It Ever OK to Name Rape Victims?" *New York Times,* February 4: http://kristof.blogs.nytimes.com/2010/02/04/is-it-ever-ok-to-name-rape-victims/?scp=1&sq=naming%20rape%20victims&st=cse.

Krohn, Marvin. 2000. "Sources of Criminality: Control and Deterrence Theories." Pp. 373–99 in *Criminology: A Contemporary Handbook,* edited by Joseph F. Sheley. Belmont, CA: Wadsworth.

Krugman, Paul. 2010. "Looters in Loafers." *New York Times,* April 19:A23.

Kruttschnitt, Candace, and Kristin Carbone-Lopez. 2006. "Moving Beyond the Stereotypes: Women's Subjective Accounts of Their Violent Crime." *Criminology* 44:321–51.

KTLA-TV. 2010. "Wrongly Convicted L.A. Man Is Released from Prison." May 16: http://www.ktla.com/news/landing/ktla-wrongly-convicted,0,1246663.story.

Kubrin, Charis E., Steven F. Messner, Glenn Deane, Kelly McGeever, and Thomas D. Stucky. 2010. "Proactive Policing and Robbery Rates Across U.S. Cities." *Criminology* 48:57–97.

Kubrin, Charis E., and Eric A. Stewart. 2006. "Predicting Who Reoffends: The Neglected Role of Neighborhood Context in Recidivism Studies." *Criminology* 44:165–97.

Kubrin, Charis E., and Ronald Weitzer. 2003a. "New Directions in Social Disorganization Theory." *Journal of Research in Crime and Delinquency* 40:374–402.

Kubrin, Charis E., and Ronald E. Weitzer. 2003b. "Retaliatory Homicide: Concentrated Disadvantage and Neighorhood Culture." *Social Problems* 50:157–80.

Kuhl, Stefan. 1994. *The Nazi Connection: Eugenics, American Racism, and German National Socialism.* New York: Oxford University Press.

Kurtz, Howard. 1997. "The Crime Spree on Network News." *Washington Post,* August 12:01.

Lab, Steven P. 2010. *Crime Prevention: Approaches, Practices and Evaluations.* Cincinnati, OH: Anderson Publishing.

Labaton, Stephen. 1993. "Surgeon General Suggests Study of Legalizing Drugs." *New York Times,* August 12:A23.

Labaton, Stephen, and Lowell Bergman. 2000. "Documents Indicate Ford Knew of Defect But Failed to Report It." *New York Times,* September 12:A1.

Lacey, Marc, and Ginger Thompson. 2010. "Two Drug Slayings in Mexico Rock U.S. Consulate." *New York Times,* March 15:A1.

Lacey, Marck. 2010. "Mexican Leader to Visit U.S. as Woes Mount." *New York Times,* May 18:A12.

LaFree, Gary, and Laura Dugan. 2009. "Research on Terrorism and Countering Terrorism." *Crime and Justice: A Review of Research* 39:413–77.

LaFree, Gary, and Katheryn K. Russell. 1993. "The Argument for Studying Race and Crime." *Journal of Criminal Justice Education* 4(2):273–89.

Lalumière, Martin L., Grant T. Harris, Vernon L. Quinsey, and Marnie E. Rice. 2005. *The Causes of Rape: Understanding Individual Differences in Male Propensity for Sexual Aggression.* Washington, DC: American Psychological Association.

Land, Kenneth C., Raymond H. C. Teske Jr., and Hui Zheng. 2009. "The Short-Term Effects of Executions on Homicides: Deterrence, Displacement, or Both?" *Criminology* 47(4):1009–43.

Lane, Roger. 1986. *Roots of Violence in Black Philadelphia, 1860–1900.* Cambridge, MA: Harvard University Press.

———. 1989. "On the Social Meaning of Homicide Trends in America." Pp. 55–79 in *Violence in America: The History of Crime,* edited by Ted Robert Gurr. Newbury Park, CA: Sage Publications.

Lange, Mark. 2007. "The Gambling Scam on America's Poor." *Christian Science Monitor,* May 2: http://www.csmonitor.com/2007/0502/p09s01-coop.html?s=hns.

Langton, Lynn, Nicole Leeper Piquero, and Richard C. Hollinger. 2006. "An Empirical Test of the Relationship Between Employee Theft and Low Self-Control." *Deviant Behavior* 27:537–65.

Lanier, Christina, and Lin Huff-Corzine. 2006. "American Indian Homicide: A County-Level Analysis Utilizing Social Disorganization Theory." *Homicide Studies* 10:181–94.

Lanza-Kaduce, L., J. Lane, and D. M. Bishop. 2005. "Juvenile Offenders and Adult Felony Recidivism: The Impact of Transfer." *Journal of Crime & Justice* 28(1):59–78.

Larson, Richard C. 1975. "What Happened to Patrol Operations in Kansas City? A Review of the Kansas City Preventive Patrol Experiment." *Journal of Criminal Justice* 3:267–97.

Laub, John H., and Robert J. Sampson. 2003. *Shared Beginnings, Divergent Lives: Delinquent Boys to Age 70.* Cambridge, MA: Harvard University Press.

Laub, John H., Robert J. Sampson, and Gary A. Sweeten. 2006. "Assessing Sampson and Laub's Life-Course Theory of Crime." Pp. 313–33 in *Taking Stock: The Status of Criminological Theory,* edited by Francis T. Cullen. New Brunswick, NJ: Transaction Publishers.

Lauritsen, Janet L., and Karen Heimer. 2008. "The Gender Gap in Violent Victimization, 1973–2004." *Journal of Quantitative Criminology* 24(2):125–47.

Lauritsen, Janet L., Karen Heimer, and James P. Lynch. 2009. "Trends in the Gender Gap in Violent Offending: New Evidence from the National Crime Victimization Survey." *Criminology* 47(2):361–99.

Lauritsen, Janet L., and Robin J. Schaum. 2004. "The Social Ecology of Violence Against Women." *Criminology* 42:323–57.

Lea, John, and Jock Young. 1984. *What Is to Be Done About Law and Order?* New York: Penguin.

Leaf, Clifton. 2002. "Enough is Enough." *Fortune,* March 18:60–68.

Ledger, Kate. 2009. "Sociology and the Gene." *Contexts* 8(3):16–20.

Lee, Gary A. 1995. "U.S. Energy Agency Radiation Tests Involved 9,000, Study Says." *Washington Post,* February 10:A13.

Lee, Matthew R. 2006. "The Religious Institutional Base and Violent Crime in Rural Areas." *Journal for the Scientific Study of Religion* 45:309–24.

Lee, Matthew R., William B. Bankston, Timothy C. Hayes, and Shaun A. Thomas. 2007. "Revisiting the Southern Subculture of Violence." *Sociological Quarterly* 48:253–75.

Lee, Matthew R., and Terri L. Earnest. 2003. "Perceived Community Cohesion and Perceived Risk of Victimization: A Cross-National Analysis." *Justice Quarterly* 20:131–57.

Lee, Matthew R., and Shaun A. Thomas. 2010. "Civic Community, Population Change, and Violent Crime in Rural Communities." *Journal of Research in Crime and Delinquency* 47(1):118–47.

Lee, Min Sik, and Jeffery T. Ulmer. 2000. "Fear of Crime Among Korean Americans in Chicago Communities." *Criminology* 38:1173–206.

Lefcourt, Robert (ed.). 1971. *Law Against the People.* New York: Vintage Books.

Leigh, Paul, James P. Marcin, and Ted R. Miller. 2004. "An Estimate of the U.S. Government's Undercount of Nonfatal Occupational Injuries." *Journal of Occupational and Environmental Medicine* 46(1):10–18.

Lemert, Edwin M. 1953. "An Isolation and Closure Theory of Naive Check Forgery." *Journal of Criminal Law, Criminology and Police Science* 44:301–04.

Leonard, Eileen. 1995. "Theoretical Criminology and Gender." Pp. 54–70 in *The Criminal Justice System and Women: Offenders, Victims, and Workers,* edited by Barbara Raffel Price and Natalie J. Sokoloff. New York: McGraw-Hill.

Lerner, Michael A. 2007. *Dry Manhattan: Prohibition in New York City.* Cambridge, MA: Harvard University Press.

Levine, Adeline. 1982. *Love Canal: Science, Politics, and People.* Lexington, MA: Lexington Books.

Lewontin, Richard C., Steven P. R. Rose, and Leon J. Kamin. 1984. *Not in Our Genes: Biology, Ideology, and Human Nature.* New York: Pantheon.

Liazos, Alexander. 1972. "The Poverty of the Sociology of Deviance: Nuts, Sluts, and Perverts." *Social Problems* 20:103–20.

Lichtblau, Eric. 2000. "Older Americans Less Likely to Be Victims of Violent Crime." *Los Angeles Times* January 10:A1.

Liebow, Elliot. 1993. *Tell Them Who I Am: The Lives of Homeless Women.* New York: Free Press.

Liebow, Elliott. 1967. *Tally's Corner.* Boston: Little, Brown.

Lilienfeld, David E. 1991. "The Silence: The Asbestos Industry and Early Occupational Cancer Research—A Case Study." *American Journal of Public Health* 81:791–800.

Lilly, J. Robert, Francis T. Cullen, and Richard A. Ball. 2011. *Criminological Theory: Context and Consequences.* Thousand Oaks, CA: Sage Publications.

Lindsey, Linda L. 2011. *Gender Roles: A Sociological Perspective.* Upper Saddle River, NJ: Prentice Hall.

Lindsey, Robert. 1984. "Officials Cite a Rise in Killers Who Roam US for Victims." *New York Times,* January 22:1.

Linthicum, Kathie. 2010. "Orange County Woman Shoots, Wounds Dog After It Attacks Her 6-Year-Old Daughter." *Los Angeles Times,* May 19: http://mobile.latimes .com/inf/infomo?view=page7&feed:a=latimes_1min&feed:c=localnews&feed:i=5382 9257.

Liska, Allen E., and Mark D. Reed. 1985. "Ties to Conventional Institutions and Delinquency: Estimating Reciprocal Effects." *American Sociological Review* 50:547–60.

Littner, Ner. 1973. "Psychology of the Sex Offender: Causes, Treatment, Prognosis." *Police Law Quarterly* 3:5–31.

Loeber, Rolf, David P. Farrington, Magda Stouthamer-Loeber, Helene Raskin White, and Evelyn Wei (eds.). 2008. *Violence and Serious Theft: Development and Prediction from Childhood to Adulthood.* New York: Routledge.

Loeber, Rolf, and Magda Stouthamer-Loeber. 1986. "Family Factors as Correlates and Predictors of Juvenile Conduct Problems and Delinquency." Pp. 29–149 in *Crime and Justice: An Annual Review of Research,* edited by Michael Tonry and Norval Morris. Chicago: University of Chicago Press.

Logan, T. K., Jennifer Cole, Lisa Shannon, and Robert Walker. 2006. *Partner Stalking: How Women Respond, Cope, and Survive.* New York: Springer Publishing.

Lombroso, Cesare. 1876. *The Criminal Man (L'uomo Delinquente).* Milan: Hoepli.

———. 1920 (1903). *The Female Offender.* New York: Appleton.

Long, Ray, and Rick Pearson. 2009. "Impeached Illinois Gov. Rod Blagojevich Has Been Removed from Office." *Chicago Tribune,* January 30:A1.

Longshore, Douglas, Eunice Chang, and Nena Messina. 2005. "Self-Control and Social Bonds: A Combined Control Perspective on Juvenile Offending." *Journal of Quantitative Criminology* 21:419–37.

Lord, Vivian B., and Kenneth J. Peak. 2005. *Women in Law Enforcement Careers: A Guide for Preparing and Succeeding.* Upper Saddle River, NJ: Prentice Hall.

Lott, John R., Jr. 2000. *More Guns, Less Crime.* Chicago: University of Chicago Press.

Lovell, Jarret. 2009. *Crimes of Dissent: Civil Disobedience, Criminal Justice, and the Politics of Conscience.* New York: NYU Press.

Lowry, Brian. 2000. "More Experts Than Facts on Kids, Media Violence." *Los Angeles Times,* October 24:F1.

Lundman, Richard J. 2003. "The Newsworthiness and Selection Bias in News About Murder: Comparative and Relative Effects of Novelty and Race and Gender Typifications on Newspaper Coverage of Homicide." *Sociological Forum* 18:357–86.

Lundman, Richard J., and Robert L. Kaufman. 2003. "Driving While Black: Effects of Race, Ethnicity, and Gender on Citizen Self-Reports of Traffic Stops and Police Actions." *Criminology* 41:195–220.

Lundman, Richard J., and Brian R. Kowalski. 2009. "Speeding While Black? Assessing the Generalizability of Lange et al.'s (2001, 2005) New Jersey Turnpike Speeding Survey Findings." *JQ: Justice Quarterly* 26(3):504–27.

Lurigio, Arthur J., and Patricia A. Resick. 1990. "Healing the Psychological Wounds of Criminal Victimization: Predicting Postcrime Distress and Recovery." Pp. 50–68 in *Victims of Crime: Problems, Policies, and Programs,* edited by Arthur L. Lurigio, Wesley G. Skogan, and Robert C. Davis. Newbury Park, CA: Sage Publications.

Lyman, Michael D. 2010. *The Police: An Introduction.* Upper Saddle River, NJ: Prentice Hall.

Lyman, Michael D., and Gary W. Potter. 2011. *Organized Crime.* Upper Saddle River, NJ: Prentice Hall.

Lynam, Donald, Terrie E. Moffitt, and Magda Stouthamer-Loeber. 1993. "Explaining the Relation Between IQ and Delinquency: Class, Race, Test Motivation, School Failure, or Self-Control?" *Journal of Abnormal Psychology* 102:187–96.

Lynch, Colum. 1995. "Amnesty International Faults Rwanda War Crimes Tribunal." *Boston Globe,* April 6:14.

Lynch, James P., and Lynn A. Addington (eds.). 2007. *Understanding Crime Statistics: Revisiting the Divergence of the NCVS and the UCR.* New York: Cambridge University Press.

Lynch, Michael J., and Raymond J. Michalowski. 2006. *Primer in Radical Criminology: Critical Perspectives on Crime, Power and Identity.* Monsey, NY: Criminal Justice Press.

Lynch, Michael J., E. Britt Patterson, and Kristina K. Childs (eds.). 2008. *Racial Divide: Racial and Ethnic Bias in the Criminal Justice System.* Monsey, NY: Criminal Justice Press.

MacCoun, Robert M., and Karin D. Martin. 2009. "Drugs." Pp. 501–23 in *The Oxford Handbook of Crime and Punishment,* edited by Michael Tonry. New York: Oxford University Press.

MacFarquhar, Neil. 2007. "Iran Cracks Down on Dissent, Parading Examples in Streets." *New York Times,* June 24:A1.

Mack, Alison, and Janet Joy. 2000. *Marijuana as Medicine? The Science Beyond the Controversy.* Washington, DC: National Academies Press.

MacKenzie, Doris Layton, and Spencer De Li. 2002. "The Impact of Formal and Informal Social Controls on the Criminal Activities of Probationers." *Journal of Research in Crime and Delinquency* 39:243–76.

Macmillan, Ross. 2000. "Adolescent Victimization and Income Deficits in Adulthood: Rethinking the Costs of Criminal Violence from a Life-Course Perspective." *Criminology* 38:553–87.

Macur, Julie. 2010. "Lacrosse Player Admitted Shaking Woman." *New York Times,* May 4:A19.

Maguire, Mike. 1982. *Burglary in a Dwelling.* London: Heinemann.

Maher, Lisa, and Richard Curtis. 1995. "In Search of the Female 'Gangsta': Change, Culture, and Crack Cocaine." Pp. 147–66 in *The Criminal Justice System and Women: Offenders, Victims, and Workers,* edited by Barbara Raffel Price and Natalie J. Sokoloff. New York: McGraw-Hill.

Makarios, Matthew D. 2007. "Race, Abuse, and Female Criminal Violence." *Feminist Criminology* 2:100–16.

Males, Mike, and Meda Chesney-Lind. 2010. "The Myth of Mean Girls." *New York Times,* April 1:A23.

Mann, Coramae Richey. 1990. "Black Female Homicide in the United States." *Journal of Interpersonal Violence* 5:176–201.

Manza, Jeff, and Christopher Uggen. 2006. *Locked Out: Felon Disenfranchisement and American Democracy.* New York: Oxford University Press.

Marcum, Catherine D. 2010. "Routine Activity Theory: An Assessment of a Classical Theory." Pp. 43–55 in *Criminological Theory: Readings and Retrospectives,* edited by Heith Copes and Volkan Topalli. New York: McGraw-Hill.

Markowitz, Fred E., Paul E. Bellair, Allen E. Liska, and Jianhong Liu. 2001. "Extending Social Disorganization Theory: Modeling the Relationships Between Cohension, Disorder, and Fear." *Criminology* 39:293–320.

Marsh, Clifton E. 1993. "Sexual Assault and Domestic Violence in the African-American Community." *Western Journal of Black Studies* 17:149–55.

Marshall, Linda L., and Patricia Rose. 1990. "Premarital Violence: The Impact of Family of Origin Violence, Stress, and Reciprocity." *Violence and Victims* 5:51–64.

Martin, Kimberly, Lynne M. Vieraitis, and Sarah Britto. 2006. "Gender Equality and Women's Absolute Status: A Test of the Feminist Models of Rape." *Violence Against Women* 12:321–39.

Martin, Marie Alexandrine. 1994. *Cambodia: A Shattered Society.* Berkeley: University of California Press.

Martin, Sandra L., Amy Ong Tsui, Kuhu Maitra, and Ruth Marinshaw. 1999. "Domestic Violence in Northern India." *American Journal of Epidemiology* 150 (August 15):417–26.

Martin, Susan E. 2004. "The Interactive Effects of Race and Sex on Women Police Officers." Pp. 527–41 in *The Criminal Justice System and Women: Offenders, Prisoners, Victims, and Workers,* edited by Barbara Raffel Price and Natlie J. Sokoloff. New York: McGraw-Hill.

Martinez, Ramiro, Jr. 2002. *Latino Homicide: Immigration, Violence, and Community.* New York: Routledge.

Martinez, Ramiro, Jr., and Abel Valenzuela (eds.). 2006. *Immigration and Crime; Race, Ethnicity, and Violence.* New York: New York University Press.

Marvell, Thomas B., and Carlisle E. Moody Jr. 2001. "The Lethal Effects of Three Strikes Laws." *Journal of Legal Studies* 30:89–106.

Marvell, Thomas B., and Carlisle E. Moody. 1995. "The Impact of Enhanced Prison Terms for Felonies Committed with Guns." *Criminology* 33:247–81.

———. 1996. "Specification Problems, Police Levels, and Crime Rates." *Criminology* 34:609–46.

Marx, Karl, and Friedrich Engels. 1962 (1848). "The Communist Manifesto." Pp. 21–65 in *Marx and Engels: Selected Works.* Moscow: Foreign Language Publishing House.

Massey, Douglas S., and Nancy A. Denton. 1993. *American Apartheid: Segregation and the Making of the Underclass.* Cambridge, MA: Harvard University Press.

Maston, Cathy T., and Patsy Klaus. 2010. *Criminal Victimization in the United States, 2007—Statistical Tables.* Washington, DC: Bureau of Justice Statistics, U.S. Department of Justice.

Mastrofski, Stephen D., David Weisburd, and Anthony A. Braga. 2010. "Rethinking Policing: The Policy Implications of Hot Spots of Crime." Pp. 251–64 in *Contemporary Issues in Criminal Justice Policy,* edited by Natasha A. Frost, Joshua D. Freilich, and Todd R. Clear. Belmont, CA: Wadsworth.

Mather, Lynn M. 1973. "Some Determinants of the Method of Case Disposition: Decisionmaking by Public Defenders in Los Angeles." *Law and Society Review* 8:187–215.

Matsueda, Ross L. 1988. "The Current State of Differential Association Theory." *Crime and Delinquency* 34:277–306.

———. 2001. "Labeling Theory: Historical Roots, Implications, and Recent Developments." Pp. 223–41 in *Explaining Criminals and Crime: Essays in Contemporary Criminological Theory,* edited by Raymond Paternoster and Ronet Bachman. Los Angeles: Roxbury Publishing Company.

Matsueda, Ross L., and Kevin Drakulich. 2009. "Perceptions of Criminal Injustice, Symbolic Racism, and Racial Politics." *Annals of the American Academy of Political and Social Science* 623:163–78.

Matsueda, Ross L., Derek A. Kreager, and David Huizinga. 2006. "Deterring Delinquents: A Rational Choice Model of Theft and Violence." *American Sociological Review* 71:95–122.

Matthews, Roger, and Jock Young (eds.). 1992. *Issues in Realist Criminology.* London: Sage.

Matza, David. 1964. *Delinquency and Drift.* New York: Wiley.

Matza, Michael, Craig R. McCoy, and Mark Fazlollah. 1998. "Panel to Overhaul Crime Reporting." *Philadelphia Inquirer,* December 9:A1.

Mauer, Marc. 2006. *Race to Incarcerate.* New York: New Press.

———. 2009. "Racial Disparities in the Criminal Justice System." Testimony prepared for the House Judiciary Subcommittee on Crime, Terrorism, and Homeland Security (October 29).

Maynard, Micheline. 2010. "U.S. Is Seeking a Fine of $16.4 Million Against Toyota." *New York Times,* April 6:A1.

MayoClinic.com. 2004. "Compulsive Gambling." http://www.mayoclinic.com/invoke .cfm?objectid=74AD9859-7FCC-46D0-851BEB27EE5CC91B.

Mazerolle, Lorraine, Rebecca Wickes, and James McBroom. 2010. "Community Variations in Violence: The Role of Social Ties and Collective Efficacy in Comparative Context." *Journal of Research in Crime and Delinquency* 47(1):3–30.

Mazur, Allan. 2009. "Testosterone and Violence Among Young Men." Pp. 190–204 in *Biosocial Criminology: New Directions in Theory and Research,* edited by Anthony Walsh and Kevin M. Beaver. New York: Routledge.

McCaghy, Charles H., Timothy A. Capron, J. D. Jamieson, and Sandra Harley Carey. 2008. *Deviant Behavior: Crime, Conflict, and Interest Groups.* Boston: Allyn & Bacon.

McCarthy, Bill. 1995. "Not Just 'For the Thrill of It': An Instrumentalist Elaboration of Katz's Explanation of Sneaky Thrill Property Crimes." *Criminology* 33:519–38.

———. 2002. "New Economics of Sociological Criminology." *Annual Review of Sociology* 28:417–42.

McCarthy, Bill, and Teresa Casey. 2008. "Love, Sex, and Crime: Adolescent Romantic Relationships and Offending." *American Sociological Review* 73(6):944–69.

McCarthy, Bill, Diane Felmlee, and John Hagan. 2004. "Girl Friends Are Better: Gender, Friends, and Crime Among School and Street Youth." *Criminology* 42:805–35.

McCarthy, Bill, and John Hagan. 2003. "Sanction Effects, Violence, and Native North American Street Youth." Pp. 117–37 in *Violent Crime: Assessing Race and Ethnic Differences,* edited by Darnell F. Hawkins. New York: Cambridge University Press.

———. 2005. "Danger and the Decision to Offend." *Social Forces* 83:1065–96.

McCarthy, Bill, John Hagan, and Todd S. Woodward. 1999. "In the Company of Women: Structure and Agency in a Revised Power-Control Theory of Gender and Delinquency." *Criminology* 37:761–88.

McDowall, David, Alan J. Lizotte, and Brian Wiersema. 1991. "General Deterrence Through Civilian Gun Ownership: An Evaluation of the Quasi-Experimental Evidence." *Criminology* 29(4):541–59.

McDowall, David, and Brian Wiersema. 1994. "The Incidence of Defensive Firearm Use by U.S. Crime Victims, 1987 Through 1990." *American Journal of Public Health* 84:1982–84.

McGarrell, Edmund F., and Natalie Kroovand Hipple. 2007. "Family Group Conferencing and Re-Offending Among First-Time Juvenile Offenders: The Indianapolis Experiment." *JQ: Justice Quarterly* 24(2):221–46.

McGee, Jim. 1995. "Drug Smuggling Industry Is Built on Franchises." *Washington Post,* March 26:A1.

McGloin, Jean Marie. 2009. "Delinquency Balance: Revisiting Peer Influence." *Criminology* 47(2):439–77.

McGloin, Jean Marie, and Alex R. Piquero. 2010. "On the Relationship Between Co-Offending Network Redundancy and Offending Versatility." *Journal of Research in Crime and Delinquency* 47(1):63–90.

McGloin, Jean Marie, Travis C. Pratt, and Alex R. Piquero. 2006. "A Life-Course Analysis of the Criminogenic Effects of Maternal Cigarette Smoking During Pregnancy." *Journal of Research in Crime and Delinquency* 43:412–26.

McGovern, George S., and Leonard F. Guttridge. 1972. *The Great Coalfield War.* Boston: Houghton Mifflin.

McGrory, Brian. 1994. "Easy-Going Image, Violent Acts." *Boston Globe,* June 19:12.

McIntire, Nathan. 2010. "Three People Found Dead in Alhambra Home in Apparent Muder-Suicide." *Pasadena Star-News,* April 8: http://www.pasadenastarnews.com/news/ci_14847577.

McKinley, James C. Jr. 2010. "Fleeing Drug Violence, Mexicans Pour into U.S." *New York Times,* April 18:A1.

McNulty, Thomas L., and Paul E. Bellair. 2003a. "Explaining Racial and Ethnic Differences in Adolescent Violence: Structural Disadvantage, Family Well-Being, and Social Capital." *Justice Quarterly* 20:1–31.

———. 2003b. "Explaining Racial and Ethnic Differences in Serious Adolescent Violent Behavior." *Criminology* 41:709–48.

McQuade, Samuel C. III. 2009. "Cybercrime." Pp. 475–98 in *The Oxford Handbook of Crime and Public Policy,* edited by Michael Tonry. New York: Oxford University Press.

McVay, Douglas A. 2010. *Drug War Facts.* http://www.drugwarfacts.org/cms/.

Meadows, Robert J. 2010. *Understanding Violence and Victimization.* Upper Saddle River, NJ: Prentice Hall.

Mears, Daniel P., and Avinash S. Bhati. 2006. "No Community Is an Island: The Effects of Resource Deprivation on Urban Violence in Spatially and Socially Proximate Communities." *Criminology* 44:509–47.

Mears, Daniel P., Xia Wang, Carter Hay, and William D. Bales. 2008. "Social Ecology and Recidivism: Implications for Prisoner Reentry." *Criminology* 46:301–40.

Mednick, Sarnoff A., William F. Gabrielli Jr., and Barry Hutchings. 1987. "Genetic Factors in the Etiology of Criminal Behavior." Pp. 74–91 in *The Causes of Crime: New Biological Approaches,* edited by Sarnoff A. Mednick, Terrie E. Moffitt, and Susan Stack. New York: Cambridge University Press.

Meier, Robert F., and Gilbert Geis. 2007. *Criminal Justice and Moral Issues.* New York: Oxford University Press.

Meier, Robert F., and Terance D. Miethe. 1993. "Understanding Theories of Criminal Victimization." Pp. 459–99 in *Crime and Justice: A Review of Research,* edited by Michael Tonry. Chicago: University of Chicago Press.

Mel, Jianming, and Mu Wang. 2007. "Social Change, Crime, and Criminology in China." *Crime & Justice International* 23 (March/April):14–21.

Melde, Chris. 2009. "Lifestyle, Rational Choice, and Adolescent Fear: A Test of a Risk-Assessment Framework." *Criminology* 47(3):781–812.

Meldrum, Ryan C., Jacob T. N. Young, and Frank M. Weerman. 2009. "Reconsidering the Effect of Self-Control and Delinquent Peers: Implications of Measurement for Theoretical Significance." *Journal of Research in Crime and Delinquency* 46(3):353–76.

Melton, Heather. 2010. "Rape Myths: Impacts on Victims of Rape." In *Female Victims of Crime: Reality Reconsidered,* edited by Venessa Garcia and Janice Clifford. Upper Saddle River, NJ: Prentice Hall.

Melton, Heather C. 2007. "Predicting the Occurrence of Stalking in Relationships Characterized by Domestic Violence." *Journal of Interpersonal Violence* 22(1):3–25.

Meltz, Barbara F. 1995. "The Unsparing Rod." *Boston Globe,* April 27:A1.

Menard, Scott. 2000. "The 'Normality' of Repeat Victimization from Adolescence Through Early Adulthood." *Justice Quarterly* 17:543–74.

———. 2002. *Short- and Long-Term Consequences of Adolescent Victimization* Washington, DC: Office of Juvenile Justice and Delinquency Prevention.

Menard, Scott, Sharon Mihalic, and David Huizinga. 2001. "Drugs and Crime Revisited." *Justice Quarterly* 18:269–99.

Menard, Scott, and Barbara J. Morse. 1984. "A Structuralist Critique of the IQ-Delinquency Hypothesis." *American Journal of Sociology* 89:1347–78.

Menzies, Robert. 1992. "Beyond Realist Criminology." Pp. 139–56 in *Realist Criminology: Crime Control and Policing in the 1990s,* edited by John Lowman and Brian D. MacLean. Toronto: University of Toronto Press.

Merton, Robert K. 1938. "Social Structure and Anomie." *American Sociological Review* 3:672–82.

Messerschmidt, James W. 1986. *Capitalism, Patriarchy, and Crime: Toward a Socialist Feminist Criminology.* Totowa, NJ: Rowman and Littlefield.

———. 1993. *Masculinities and Crime: Critique and Reconceptualization of Theory.* Lanham, MD: Rowman and Littlefield.

———. 1997. *Crime as Structured Action: Gender, Race, Class, and Crime in the Making.* Thousand Oaks, CA: Sage.

Messner, Steven F., Robert D. Baller, and Matthew P. Zevenbergen. 2005. "The Legacy of Lynching and Southern Homicide." *American Sociological Review* 70:633–55.

Messner, Steven F., Glenn Deane, and Mark Beaulieu. 2002. "A Log-Multiplicative Association Model for Allocating Homicides with Unknown Victim-Offender Relationships." *Criminology* 40:457–79.

Messner, Steven F., Sandro Galea, Kenneth J. Tardiff, Melissa Tracy, Angela Bucciarelli, Tinka Markham Piper, Victoria Frye, and David Vlahov. 2007. "Policing, Drugs, and the Homicide Decline in New York City in the 1990s." *Criminology* 45(2):385–414.

Messner, Steven F., and Richard Rosenfeld. 2007. *Crime and the American Dream.* Belmont, CA: Wadsworth.

Meyers, Marian. 1996. *News Coverage of Violence Against Women.* Newbury Park, CA: Sage.

Meyrowitz, Elliott L., and Kenneth J. Campbell. 1992. "Vietnam Veterans and War Crimes Hearings." Pp. 129–40 in *Give Peace a Chance: Exploring the Vietnam Antiwar Movement,* edited by Melvin Small and William D. Hoover. Syracuse, NY: Syracuse University Press.

Michalowski, Raymond J., and Susan M. Carlson. 1999. "Unemployment, Imprisonment, and Social Structures of Accumulation: Historical Contingency in the Rusche-Kirchheimer Hypothesis." *Criminology* 37:217–49.

Miczek, Klaus A., Margaret Haney, Jennifer Tidey, Jeffrey Vivian, and Elise Weerts. 1994. "Neurochemistry and Pharmacotherapeutic Management of Aggression and Violence." Pp. 245–514 in *Understanding and Preventing Violence: Biobehavioral Influences,* edited by Albert J. Reiss Jr., Klaus A. Miczek, and Jeffrey A. Roth. Washington, DC: National Academy Press.

Miethe, Terance D., and Robert F. Meier. 1990. "Opportunity, Choice, and Criminal Victimization: A Test of a Theoretical Model." *Journal of Research in Crime and Delinquency* 27(3):243–66.

Miethe, Terance D., Mark C. Stafford, and J. Scott Long. 1987. "Social Differentiation in Criminal Victimization: A Test of Routine Activities/Lifestyle Theories." *American Sociological Review* 52:184–94.

Miles, Steven H. 2009. *Oath Betrayed: America's Torture Doctors.* Berkeley: University of California Press.

Milgram, Stanley. 1974. *Obedience to Authority.* New York: Harper and Row.

Miller, D.W. 2001a. "Poking Holes in the Theory of 'Broken Windows.'" *Chronicle of Higher Education,* February 9:A14.

Miller, H. V., W. G. Jennings, and L. L. Alvarez-Rivera. 2009. "Self-Control, Attachment, and Deviance Among Hispanic Adolescents." *Journal of Criminal Justice* 37(1):77–84.

Miller, J. Mitchell, J. Eagle Shutt, and J. C. Barnes. 2010. "Learning Theory: From Seminal Statements to Hybridization." In *Criminological Theory: Readings and Retrospectives,* edited by Heith Copes and Volkan Topalli. New York: McGraw-Hill.

Miller, Jody. 2000a. "Feminist Theories of Women's Crime: Robbery as a Case Study." Pp. 25–46 in *Of Crime and Criminality: The Use of Theory in Everyday Life,* edited by Sally S. Simpson. Thousand Oaks, CA: Pine Forge Press.

———. 2001b. *One of the Guys: Girls, Gangs, and Gender.* New York: Oxford University Press.

———. 2009. "Prostitution." Pp. 547–77 in *The Oxford Handbook of Crime and Public Policy,* edited by Michael Tonry. New York: Oxford University Press.

Miller, Jody, and Scott H. Decker. 2001. "Young Women and Gang Violence: Gender, Street Offending, and Violent Victimization in Gangs." *Justice Quarterly* 18:115–40.

Miller, Jody, and Christopher W. Mullins. 2009. "Feminist Theories of Girls' Delinquency." Pp. 30-49 in *The Delinquent Girl,* edited by Margaret A. Zahn. Philadelphia: Temple University Press.

Miller, Joshua D., and Donald Lynam. 2001. "Structural Models of Personality and Their Relation to Antisocial Behavior: A Meta-Analytic Review." *Criminology* 39:765–98.

Miller, Mark. 2000b. "A War over Witnesses." *Newsweek,* June 26:55.

Miller, Matthew, David Hemenway, and Deborah Azrael. 2007. "State-Level Homicide Victimization Rates in the US in Relation to Survey Measures of Household Firearm Ownership, 2001–2003." *Social Science and Medicine* 64:656–64.

Miller, Ted, Marc Cohen, and Brian Wiersema. 1996. *Victim Costs and Consequences: A New Look.* Washington, DC: National Institute of Justice, U.S. Department of Justice.

Miller, Walter B. 1958. "Lower Class Culture as a Generating Milieu of Gang Delinquency." *Journal of Social Issues* 14:5–19.

Mills, C. Wright. 1959. *The Sociological Imagination.* London: Oxford University Press.

Mills, Steve, Maurice Possley, and Ken Armstrong. 2000. "Shadows of Doubt Haunt Executions." *Chicago Tribune,* December 17(A1).

Mintz, Morton. 1985. *At Any Cost: Corporate Greed, Women, and the Dalkon Shield.* New York: Pantheon Books.

———. 1992. "Why the Media Cover up Corporate Crime: A Reporter Looks Back in Anger." *Trial* 28:72–77.

Mishel, Lawrence, Jared Bernstein, and Heidi Shierholz. 2009. *The State of Working America 2008/2009.* Ithaca, NY: ILR Press, an imprint of Cornell University Press.

Mitton, Roger. 2007. "Rise in Violent Crime Rattles Vietnam." *Straits Times* (Singapore), January 9:1.

Moffitt, Terrie, and Avshalom Caspi. 2006. "Evidence from Behavioral Genetics for Environmental Contributions to Antisocial Conduct." Pp. 108–52 in *The Explanation of Crime: Context, Mechanisms, and Development,* edited by Per-Olof H. Wikström and Robert J. Sampson. New York: Cambridge University Press.

Moffitt, Terrie E. 1993. "Adolescence-Limited and Life-Course-Persistent Antisocial Behavior: A Developmental Taxonomy." *Psychological Review* 100:674–701.

———. 2003. "Life-Course-Persistent and Adolescence-Limited Antisocial Behavior: A Ten-Year Research Review and a Research Agenda." In *Causes of Conduct Disorder and Juvenile Delinquency,* edited by Benjamin B. Lahey, Terrie E. Moffitt, and Avshalom Caspi. New York: Guilford Press.

———. 2006. "A Review of Research on the Taxonomy of Life-Course Persistent Versus Adolescence-Limited Antisocial Behavior." Pp. 277–311 in *Taking Stock: The Status of Criminological Theory,* edited by Francis T. Cullen, John Paul Wright, and Kristie R. Blevins. New Brunswick, NJ: Transaction Publishers.

Moffitt, Terrie E., G. L. Brammer, Avshalom Caspi, J. P. Fawcett, M. Raleigh, A. Yuwiler, and Phil A. Silva. 1998. "Whole Blood Serotonin Relates to Violence in an Epidemiological Study." *Biological Psychiatry* 43:446–57.

Mokdad, Ali H., James S. Marks, Donna F. Stroup, and Julie L. Gerberding. 2004. "Actual Causes of Death in the United States, 2000." *Journal of the American Medical Association* 291(10, March 10):1238–45.

Mokhiber, Russell, and Robert Weissman. 1999. "Top 100 Corporate Criminals of the 1990s." *Mother Jones,* September 7: http://www.motherjones.com/news/feature/1999/09/fotc1.html.

Monkkonen, Eric. 1981. *Police in Urban America, 1860–1920.* New York: Cambridge University Press.

Moon, Byongook, Merry Morash, Cynthia Perez McCluskey, and Hye-Won Hwang. 2009. "A Comprehensive Test of General Strain Theory: Key Strains, Situational- and Trait-Based Negative Emotions, Conditioning Factors, and Delinquency." *Journal of Research in Crime and Delinquency* 46(2):182–212.

Moore, Mark H. 1995. "Public Health and Criminal Justice Approaches to Prevention." Pp. 237–62 in *Building a Safer Society: Strategic Approaches to Crime Prevention,* edited by Michael Tonry and David P. Farrington. Chicago: University of Chicago Press.

Moore, Molly. 2007. "Report Gives Details on CIA Prisons." *Washington Post,* June 9:A1.

Morales, Julio. 2010. "Education Rally Near CSUN Leads to Several Arrests." *KPCC,* March 4: http://www.scpr.org/news/2010/03/04/education-rally-near-csun-leads-several-arrests/.

Morgan, Kathryn. 2005. "Victims, Punishment, and Parole: The Effect of Victim Participation on Parole Hearings." *Criminology & Public Policy* 4:333–60.

Morgan, Robin. 1977. *Going Too Far.* New York: Random House.

Morris, Allison. 2002. "Critiquing the Critics: A Brief Response to Critics of Restorative Justice." *British Journal of Criminology* 42:596–615.

Morris, Gregory D., Peter B. Wood, and R. Gregory Dunaway. 2006. "Self-Control, Native Traditionalism, and Native American Substance Abuse: Testing the Cultural Invariance of a General Theory of Crime." *Crime & Delinquency* 52:572–98.

Morris, Nancy A., and Lee Ann Slocum. 2010. "The Validity of Self-Reported Prevalence, Frequency, and Timing of Arrest: An Evaluation of Data Using a Life Event Calendar." *Journal of Research in Crime & Delinquency* 47:210–40.

Morris, Nigel. 2008. "The Big Question: Does Fear of Crime Reflect the Reality of Life on Britain's Streets?" *The Independent,* January 222:30.

Morselli, Carlo, Pierre Tremblay, and Bill McCarthy. 2006. "Mentors and Criminal Achievement." *Criminology* 44:17–43.

Mosse, George L. 1975. *Police Forces in History.* Beverly Hills, CA: Sage.

Moyers, Bill. 1988. *The Secret Government: The Constitution in Crisis.* Cabin John, MD: Seven Locks Press.

Moynihan, Daniel P. 1965. *The Negro Family: The Case for National Action.* Washington, DC: U.S. Department of Labor.

Mullen, Paul E., and Michele Pathé. 2002. "Stalking." *Crime and Justice: A Review of Research* 29:273–318.

Mullins, Christopher W., Richard Wright, and Bruce A. Jacobs. 2004. "Gender, Streetlife and Criminal Retaliation." *Criminology* 42:911–40.

Murray, Don. 2005. "After the Rampage." *CBC News, November 15*: http://www .cbc.ca/news/reportsfromabroad/murray/20051115.html.

Murray, John P. 2008. "Media Violence: The Effects Are Both Real and Strong." *American Behavioral Scientist* 51(8):1212–30.

Musto, David F. (ed.). 2002. *Drugs in America: A Documentary History.* New York: New York University Press.

Myers, Martha A. 1990. "Economic Threat and Racial Disparities in Incarceration: The Case of Postbellum Georgia." *Criminology* 28:627–56.

———. 1995. "The New South's 'New' Black Criminal: Rape and Punishment in Georgia, 1870–1940." Pp. 145–66 in *Ethnicity, Race, and Crime: Perspectives Across Time and Place,* edited by Darnell F. Hawkins. Albany: State University of New York Press.

———. 2000. "The Social World of America's Courts." Pp. 447–71 in *Criminology: A Contemporary Handbook,* edited by Joseph F. Sheley. Belmont, CA: Wadsworth.

Myrstol, B. 2005. "Making the Grade? Public Evaluation of Police Performance in Alaska." *Alaska Justice Forum* 22:5–10.

Nadelmann, Ethan A. 1992. "Drug Prohibition in the United States: Costs, Consequences, and Alternatives." Pp. 299–322 in *Drugs, Crime, and Social Policy: Research, Issues, and Concerns,* edited by Thomas Mieczkowski. Boston: Allyn and Bacon.

———. 2008. "Let's End Drug Prohibition." *Wall Street Journal—Eastern Edition,* December 5:A21.

Naffine, Ngaire (ed.). 1995. *Gender, Crime and Feminism.* Brookfield, VT: Dartmouth Publishing Company.

Nagin, Daniel S. 2007. "Moving Choice to Center Stage in Criminological Research and Theory: The American Society of Criminology 2006 Sutherland Address." *Criminology* 45(2):259–72.

Nagin, Daniel S., Francis T. Cullen, and Cheryl Lero Jonson. 2009. "Imprisonment and Reoffending." *Crime and Justice: A Review of Research* 38:115–200.

Nagin, Daniel S., and Greg Pogarsky. 2001. "Integrating Celerity, Impulsivity, and Extralegal Sanction Threats into a Model of General Deterrence: Theory and Evidence." *Criminology* 39:865–91.

Naik, Gautam. 2009. "What's on Jim Fallon's Mind? A Family Secret That Has Been Murder to Figure Out." *Wall Street Journal,* November 30:A37.

Nakamura, David, Christian Swezey, and Daniel de Vise. 2010. "Accused U-Va. Player George Huguely Attacked Sleeping Student, Teammates Say." *Washington Post,* May 8: http://www.washingtonpost.com/wp-dyn/content/article/2010/05/07/AR2010050704056.html?hpid=topnews.

National Retail Federation. 2007. "Retail Losses Hit $41.6 Billion Last Year, According to National Retail Security Survey (press release)." June 11: http://www.nrf.com/modules.php?name=News&op=viewlive&sp_id=318.

Netherlands Ministry of Foreign Affairs. 2008. "FAQ Drugs: A Guide to Drug Policy." http://www.minbuza.nl/dsresource?objectid=buzabeheer:58788&type=pdf.

Newman, Graeme, and Pietro Marongiu. 1994. "Penological Reform and the Myth of Beccaria." In *The Origins and Growth of Criminology: Essays on Intellectual History, 1760–1945,* edited by Piers Beirne. Brookfield, VT: Dartmouth Publishing Company.

Nieuwbeerta, Paul, Daniel Nagin, and Arjan Blokland. 2009. "Assessing the Impact of First-Time Imprisonment on Offenders' Subsequent Criminal Career Development: A Matched Samples Comparison." *Journal of Quantitative Criminology* 25(3):227–57.

Nisbett, Richard E. 2009. *Intelligence and How to Get It: Why Schools and Cultures Count.* New York: W.W. Norton.

Nobiling, Tracy, Cassia Spohn, and Miriam DeLone. 1998. "A Tale of Two Counties: Unemployment and Sentence Severity." *Justice Quarterly* 15:459–85.

Nobles, Matt R., Kathleen A. Fox, Nicole Piquero, and Alex R. Piquero. 2009. "Career Dimensions of Stalking Victimization and Perpetration." *JQ: Justice Quarterly* 26(3):476–503.

Noggle, Burl. 1965. *Teapot Dome: Oil and Politics in the 1920s.* New York: Norton.

O'Kane, James M. 1992. *The Crooked Ladder: Gangsters, Ethnicity, and the American Dream.* New Brunswick, NJ: Transaction Books.

Oates, Stphen B. 1983. *The Fires of Jubilee: Nat Turner's Fierce Rebellion.* New York: New American Library.

O'Donnell, Jayne. 2000. "Suffering in Silence." *USA Today,* April 3:1A.

O'Donoghue, T., and M. Rabin. 2001. "Risky Behavior Among Youths: Some Issues from Behavioral Economics." Pp. 29–67 in *Risky Behavior Among Youths: An Economic Analysis,* edited by J. Gruber. Chicago: University of Chicago Press.

Office of National Drug Control Policy. 2001. *What America's Users Spend on Illegal Drugs 1988–2000.* Washington, DC: Office of National Drug Control Policy.

Ogle, Robbin S., Daniel Maier-Katkin, and Thomas J. Bernard. 1995. "A Theory of Homicidal Behavior Among Women." *Criminology* 33:173–93.

Okrent, Daniel. 2010. *Last Call: The Rise and Fall of Prohibition.* New York: Scribner.

Ormsby, Avril. 2010. "UK Crime Down But Rising Fears Benefit Opposition." *Reuters,* March 17: http://www.reuters.com/article/idUSLDE62A16J.

Ornstein, Charles. 2004. "Sale of Body Parts at UCLA Alleged." *Los Angeles Times,* March 6:A1.

Orwell, George. 1949. *Nineteen Eighty-Four: A Novel.* New York: Harcourt, Brace & World.

Osgood, D. Wayne, and Amy L. Anderson. 2004. "Unstructured Socializing and Rates of Delinquency." *Criminology* 42:519–49.

Osgood, D. Wayne, Janet K. Wilson, Patrick M. O'Malley, Jerald G. Bachman, and Lloyd D. Johnston. 1996. "Routine Activities and Individual Deviant Behavior." *American Sociological Review* 61:635–55.

Ousey, Graham C., and Charis E. Kubrin. 2009. "Exploring the Connection Between Immigration and Violent Crime Rates in U.S. Cities, 1980–2000." *Social Problems* 56(3):447–73.

Ousey, Graham C., and Matthew R. Lee. 2007. "Homicide Trends and Illicit Drug Markets: Exploring Differences Across Time." *Justice Quarterly* 24:48–79.

Packer, Herbert L. 1968. *The Limits of the Criminal Sanction.* Stanford, CA: Stanford University Press.

Pager, Devah. 2009. *Marked: Race, Crime, and Finding Work in an Era of Mass Incarceration.* Chicago: University of Chicago Press.

Park, Robert E., Ernest W. Burgess, and Roderick McKenzie. 1925. *The City.* Chicago: University of Chicago Press.

Parker, L. Craig. 2001. *The Japanese Police System Today: A Comparative Study.* Armonk, NY: M.E. Sharpe.

Parker, Robert Nash. 1989. "Poverty, Subculture of Violence, and Type of Homicide." *Social Forces* 67:983–1007.

Paschall, Mallie J., Miriam L. Ornstein, and Robert L. Flewelling. 2001. "African American Male Adolescents' Involvement in the Criminal Justice System: The Criterion Validity of Self-Report Measures in a Prospective Study." *Journal of Research in Crime and Delinquency* 38:174–87.

Passas, Nikos. 1990. "Anomie and Corporate Deviance." *Contemporary Crises* 14:157–78.

Passmann, Florenz, and John Whitley. 2003. "Confirming More Guns, Less Crime." *Stanford Law Review* 55:1315–70.

Pastore, Ann L., and Kathleen Maguire (eds.). 2010. *Sourcebook of Criminal Justice Statistics.* http://www.albany.edu/sourcebook/index.html.

Paternoster, Raymond. 1984. "Prosecutorial Discretion in Requesting the Death Penalty: A Case of Victim-Based Racial Discrimination." *Law and Society Review* 18:437–78.

———. 1991. *Capital Punishment in America.* New York: Lexington Books.

Paternoster, Raymond, and Ronet Bachman (eds.). 2001. *Explaining Criminals and Crime: Essays in Contemporary Criminological Theory.* Los Angeles: Roxbury Publishing Company.

Paternoster, Raymond, and Robert Brame. 2008. "Reassessing Race Disparities in Maryland Capital Cases." *Criminology* 46:971–1007.

Payne, Allison Ann. 2009. "Girls, Boys, and Schools: Gender Differences in the Relationships Between School-Related Factors and Student Deviance." *Criminology* 47(4):1167–200.

Peak, Kenneth J., and Ronald W. Glensor. 2008. *Community Policing and Problem Solving: Strategies and Practices.* Upper Saddle River, NJ: Prentice Hall.

Pepinsky, Hal. 2006. *Peacemaking: Reflections of a Radical Criminologist.* Ottawa: University of Ottawa Press.

Pepinsky, Harold E., and Paul Jesilow. 1984. *Myths That Cause Crime.* Cabin John, MD: Seven Locks Press.

Perez-Pena, Richard. 2000. "The Death Penalty: When There's No Room for Error." *New York Times,* February 13:WK3.

Perry, Barbara. 2008. *Silent Victims: Hate Crimes Against Native Americans.* Tucson: University of Arizona Press.

Petersen, Melody, and Christopher Drew. 2003. "New Safety Rules Fail to Stop Tainted Meat." *New York Times,* October 9:A1.

Petersilia, Joan. 1983. *Racial Disparities in the Criminal Justice System.* Santa Monica, CA: Rand Corporation.

———. 2008. "California's Correctional Paradox of Excess and Deprivation." *Crime and Justice: A Review of Research* 37:207–78.

Peterson, Ruth D., and William C. Bailey. 1991. "Felony Murder and Capital Punishment: An Examination of the Deterrence Question." *Criminology* 29(3):367–95.

Peterson, Ruth D., and Lauren J. Krivo. 2005. "Macrostructural Analyses of Race, Ethnicity, and Violent Crime: Recent Lessons and New Directions for Research." *Annual Review of Sociology* 31:331–56.

———. 2009. "Segregated Spatial Locations, Race-Ethnic Composition, and Neighborhood Violent Crime." *Annals of the American Academy of Political and Social Science* 93–107.

Peterson, Ruth D., Lauren J. Krivo, and Mark A. Harris. 2000. "Disadvantage and Neighborhood Violent Crime: Do Local Institutions Matter?" *Journal of Research in Crime and Delinquency* 37:31–63.

Petrik, Norman D., Rebecca E. Petrik Olson, and Leah S. Subotnik. 1994. "Powerlessness and the Need to Control." *Journal of Interpersonal Violence* 9:278–85.

Petts, Richard J. 2009. "Family and Religious Characteristics' Influence on Delinquency Trajectories from Adolescence to Young Adulthood." *American Sociological Review* 74(3):465–83.

Phillips, Julie A. 2002. "White, Black, and Latino Homicide Rates: Why the Difference?" *Social Problems* 49:349–74.

Phillips, Scott. 2009. "Status Disparities in the Capital of Capital Punishment." *Law & Society Review* 43(4):807–38.

Phillips, Scott, Jacqueline Matusko, and Elizabeth Tomasovic. 2007. "Reconsidering the Relationship Between Alcohol and Lethal Violence." *Journal of Interpersonal Violence* 22:66–84.

Piquero, Alex R., and Jeff A. Bouffard. 2007. "Something Old, Something New: A Preliminary Investigation of Hirschi's Redefined Self-Control." *Justice Quarterly* 24:1–27.

Piquero, Alex R., and Matthew Hickman. 1999. "An Empirical Test of Tittle's Control Balance Theory." *Criminology* 37:319–41.

Piquero, Nicole Leeper, M. Lyn Exum, and Sally S. Simpson. 2005. "Integrating the Desire-for-Control and Rational Choice in a Corporate Crime Context." *Justice Quarterly* 22:252–80.

Piquero, Nicole Leeper, and Alex R. Piquero. 2006. "Control Balance and Exploitative Corporate Crime." *Criminology* 44:397–430.

———. 2010. "Overview of Self-Control Theory." Pp. 299–307 in *Criminological Theory: Readings and Retrospectives,* edited by Heith Copes and Volkan Topalli. New York: McGraw-Hill.

Piquero, Nicole Leeper, and Andrea Schoepfer. 2010. "Theories of White-Collar Crime and Public Policy." Pp. 188–200 in *Criminology and Public Policy,* edited by Hugh D. Barlow and Scott H. Decker. Philadelphia: Temple University Press.

Piquero, Nicole Leeper, and Miriam D. Sealock. 2004. "Gender and General Strain Theory: A Preliminary Test of Broidy and Agnew's Gender/GST Hypotheses." *Justice Quarterly* 21:125–88.

Pogarsky, Greg, and Alex R. Piquero. 2003. "Can Punishment Encourage Offending: Investigating the 'Resetting' Effect." *Journal of Research in Crime and Delinquency* 40:95–120.

Polk, Kenneth. 1994. *When Men Kill: Scenarios of Masculine Violence.* New York: Cambridge University Press.

Pollak, Otto. 1950. *The Criminality of Women.* Philadelphia: University of Pennsylvania Press.

Pomfret, John. 1999. "Chinese Crime Rate Soars as Economic Problems Grow." *Washington Post,* January 21:A19.

Pontell, Henry N. 1984. *A Capacity to Punish: The Ecology of Crime and Punishment.* Bloomington: Indiana University Press.

———. 2010. "Wall St. Fraud and Fiduciary Responsibilities: Can Jail Time Serve as an Adequate Deterrent for Willful Violations?" Testimony to Subcommittee on Crime and Drugs, Committee on the Judiciary, United States Senate, May 4.

Pontell, Henry N., and Kitty Calavita. 1993. "The Savings and Loan Industry." Pp. 203–46 in *Beyond the Law: Crime in Complex Organizations,* edited by Michael Tonry and Albert J. Reiss Jr. Chicago: University of Chicago Press.

Pope, C. Arden III, R. T. Burnett, G. D. Thurston, M .J. Thun, E. E. Calle, D. Krewski, and J. J. Godleski. 2004. "Cardiovascular Mortality and Long-term Exposure to Particulate Air Pollution: Epidemiological Evidence of General Pathophysiological Pathways of Disease." *Circulation* 109 (January 6):71–77.

Pope, Carl E., and Howard N. Snyder. 2003. *Race as a Factor in Juvenile Arrests.* Washington, DC: Office of Juvenile Justice and Delinquency Prevention, U.S. Department of Justice.

Post, Tim. 1994. "Blood Bath." *Newsweek,* February 14:20–23.

Potter, Gary W. 1994. *Criminal Organizations: Vice, Racketeering, and Politics in an American City.* Prospect Heights, IL: Waveland Press.

Potter, Hillary. 2006. "An Argument for Black Feminist Criminology: Understanding African American Women's Experiences with Intimate Partner Abuse Using an Integrated Approach." *Feminist Criminology* 1:106–24.

Pratt, Travis C., and Francis T. Cullen. 2000. "The Empirical Status of Gottfredson and Hirschi's General Theory of Crime: A Meta-Analysis." *Criminology* 38:931–64.

———. 2005. "Assessing Macro-Level Predictors and Theories of Crime: A Meta-Analysis." *Crime and Justice: A Review of Research* 32:373–450.

Pratt, Travis C., Francis T. Cullen, Kristie R. Blevins, Leah E. Daigle, and Tamara D. Madensen. 2006. "The Empirical Status of Deterrence Theory: A Meta-Analysis." *Advances in Criminological Theory* 15:367-95.

Pratt, Travis C., and Jacinta M. Gau. 2010. "Social Disorganization Theory." Pp. 104–12 in *Criminological Theory: Readings and Retrospectives,* edited by Heith Copes and Volkan Topalli. New York: McGraw-Hill.

Press, Eyal. 2006. "Do Immigrants Make Us Safer?" *New York Times Magazine,* December 3:20+.

Pridemore, William Alex. 2007. "Socioeconomic Change and Homicide in a Transitional Society." *Sociological Quarterly* 48:229–51.

———. 2008. "A Methodological Addition to the Cross-National Empirical Literature on Social Structure and Homicide: A First Test of the Poverty-Homicide Thesis." *Criminology* 46(1):133–54.

Pritchard, David, and Dan Berkowitz. 1993. "The Limits of Agenda-Setting: The Press and Political Responses to Crime in the United States, 1950–1980." *International Journal of Public Opinion Research* 5:86–91.

Public Health Reports. 1998. "Health Ranks Fifth on Local TV News." *Public Health Reports* 113:296–97.

Quinney, Richard. 1974. *Critique of Legal Order: Crime Control in Capitalist Society.* Boston: Little, Brown.

Radelet, Michael L., Hugo Adam Bedau, and Constance E. Putnam. 1992. *In Spite of Innocence: Erroneous Convictions in Capital Cases.* Boston: Northeastern University Press.

Rafter, Nicole. 2004. "Earnest A. Hooton and the Biological Tradition in American Criminology." *Criminology* 42:735–71.

———. 2008. *The Criminal Brain: Understanding Biological Theories of Crime.* New York: New York University Press.

Rand, Michael R. 2009. *Criminal Victimization, 2008.* Washington, DC: Bureau of Justice Statistics, U.S. Department of Justice.

Randall, Melanie, and Lori Haskell. 1995. "Sexual Violence in Women's Lives: Findings from the Women's Safety Project, a Community-Based Survey." *Violence Against Women* 1:6–31.

Random House *Webster's College Dictionary.* 2000. New York: Random House.

Rankin, Joseph H., and Roger Kern. 1994. "Parental Attachments and Delinquency." *Criminology* 32:495–515.

Rankin, Joseph H., and L. Edward Wells. 1990. "The Effect of Parental Attachments and Direct Controls on Delinquency." *Journal of Research in Crime and Delinquency* 27(2):140–65.

Rasche, Christine E. 1988. "Minority Women and Domestic Violence: The Unique Dilemmas of Battered Women of Color." *Journal of Contemporary Criminal Justice* 4:150–71.

Rastogi, Mudita, and Paul Therly. 2006. "Dowry and Its Link to Violence Against Women in India: Feminist Psychological Perspectives." *Trauma, Violence & Abuse* 7:66–77.

Rebellon, Cesar J. 2005. "Can Control Theory Explain the Link Between Parental Physical Abuse and Delinquency? A Longitudinal Analysis." *Journal of Research in Crime and Delinquency* 42:247–74.

Rebovich, D., and J. Layne. 2000. *The National Public Survey on White Collar Crime.* Morgantown, WV: Natinal White Collar Crime Center.

Reckless, Walter C. 1961. "A New Theory of Delinquency and Crime." *Federal Probation* 25:42–46.

Reckless, Walter C., Simon Dinitz, and Ellen Murray. 1956. "Self-Concept as an Insulator Against Delinquency." *American Sociological Review* 21:744–56.

Reeves, Margaret, Anne Katten, and Marthua Guzmán. 2003. *Fields of Poison 2002: California Farmworkers and Pesticides.* San Francisco: Californians for Pesticide Reform.

Reiman, Jeffrey, and Paul Leighton. 2010. *The Rich Get Richer and the Poor Get Prison: Ideology, Class, and Criminal Justice.* Upper Saddle River, NJ: Prentice Hall.

Reinarman, Craig, Peter D. A. Cohen, and Kaal L. Hendrien. 2004. "The Limited Relevance of Drug Policy: Cannabis in Amsterdam and in San Francisco." *American Journal of Public Health* 94:836–42.

Reisig, Michael D., and Roger B. Parks. 2000. "Experience, Quality of Life, and Neighborhood Context: A Hierarchical Analysis of Satisfaction with Police." *Justice Quarterly* 17:607–30.

Reiss, Albert J., Jr. 1980a. "Officer Violations of the Law." Pp. 253–72 in *Police Behavior: A Sociological Perspective,* edited by Richard J. Lundman. New York: Oxford University Press.

———. 1980b. "Police Brutality." Pp. 274–96 in *Police Behavior: A Sociological Perspective,* edited by Richard J. Lundman. New York: Oxford University Press.

Renzetti, Claire. 2011. *Feminist Criminology.* New York: Routledge.

Reynolds, Pam. 1987. "Thousands are Locked in with the Danger." *Boston Globe,* March 29:A18.

Rhodes, Richard. 2000. "The Media Violence Myth." *Rolling Stone,* November 23:6.

Richlin, Amy (ed.). 1992. *Pornography and Representation in Greece and Rome.* New York: Oxford University Press.

Riggs, David S., and Dean G. Kilpatrick. 1990. "Families and Friends: Indirect Victimization by Crime." Pp. 120–38 in *Victims of Crime: Problems, Policies, and Programs,* edited by Arthur J. Lurigio, Wesley G. Skogan, and Robert C. Davis. Newbury Park, CA: Sage Publications.

Riksheim, Eric, and Steven M. Chermak. 1993. "Causes of Police Behavior Revisited." *Journal of Criminal Justice* 21:353–82.

Rios, Victor M. 2009. "The Consequences of the Criminal Justice Pipeline on Black and Latino Masculinity." *Annals of the American Academy of Political and Social Science* 623:150–62.

Risen, Tom. 2010. "Critics Say Drug Control Policy Should Focus on Demand." *National Journal,* May 13: http://burnafterreading.nationaljournal.com/2010/05/obama-targets-cartel-supply-mu.php.

Ritter, Alison, and Jacqui Cameron. 2006. "A Review of the Efficacy and Effectiveness of Harm Reduction Strategies for Alcohol, Tobacco, and Illicit Drugs." *Drug & Alcohol Review* 25:611–24.

Ritzer, George. 2008. *Modern Sociological Theory.* Belmont, CA: Wadsworth.

Roberts, Julian V. 2009. "Listening to the Crime Victim: Evaluating Victim Input at Sentencing and Parole." *Crime and Justice: A Review of Research* 39:347–412.

Robinson, Amanda, and Christopher Maxwell. 2008. "The Challenge of Responding Effectively to Violence Against Women in a Global Context." *International Journal of Comparative and Applied Criminal Justice* 32:133–47.

Robinson, Matthew Barnett. 2009. *Justice Blind? Ideals and Realities of American Criminal Justice.* Upper Saddle River, NJ: Prentice Hall.

Rodrigo, Jessica. 2010. "Students Overcome Great Odds." *Rio Rancho Observer,* May 9: http://www.observer-online.com/articles/2010/05/09/news/doc4be4a3f33702c000071151.txt.

Rodriguez, Nancy. 2007. "Juvenile Court Context and Detention Decisions: Reconsidering the Role of Race, Ethnicity, and Community Characteristics in Juvenile Court Processes." *JQ: Justice Quarterly* 24(4):629–56.

Rojek, Dean G., James E. Coverdill, and Stuart W. Fors. 2003. "The Effect of Victim Impact Panels on DUI Rearrest Rates: A Five-Year Follow-Up." *Criminology* 41:1319–40.

Roncek, Dennis W., and Pamela A. Maier. 1991. "Bars, Blocks, and Crimes Revisited: Linking the Theory of Routine Activities to the Empiricism of 'Hot Spots.'" *Criminology* 29(4):725–53.

Rorabaugh, W.J. 1995. "Alcohol in America." Pp. 16–18 in *Drugs, Society, and Behavior,* edited by Erich Goode. Guilford, CT: Dushkin Publishing Group.

Rose, Harold M., and Paula D. McClain. 2003. "Homicide Risk and Level of Victimization in Two Concentrated Poverty Enclaves: A Black/Hispanic Comparison." Pp. 3–21 in *Violent Crime: Asssessing Race and Ethnic Differences,* edited by Darnell F. Hawkins. New York: Cambridge University Press.

Rosecrance, John D. 1988. *Gambling Without Guilt: The Legitimation of an American Pastime.* Pacific Grove, CA: Brooks/Cole Publishing Company.

Rosen, Marie Simonetti. 1995. "A LEN Interview with Prof. Carl Klockars of the University of Delaware." Pp. 107–14 in *Annual Editions: Criminal Justice 95/96,* edited by John J. Sullivan and Joseph L. Victor. Guilford, CT: Dushkin Publishing Group.

Rosenfeld, Richard. 2006. "Patterns in Adult Homicide: 1980–1995." Pp. 130–63 in *The Crime Drop in America,* edited by Alfred Blumstein and Joel Wallman. New York: Cambridge University Press.

———. 2009. "Crime Is the Problem: Homicide, Acquisitive Crime, and Economic Conditions." *Journal of Quantitative Criminology* 25(3):287–306.

Rosenfeld, Richard, and Robert Fornango. 2007. "The Impact of Economic Conditions on Robbery and Property Crime: The Role of Consumer Sentiment." *Criminology* 45(4):735–69.

Rosenfeld, Richard, Robert Fornango, and Andres F. Rengifo. 2007. "The Impact of Order-Maintenance Policing on New York City Homicide and Robbery Rates: 1988–2001." *Criminology* 45(2):355–84.

Rosenzweig, Daniel. 2004. "4 Companies Are Charged with Food Safety Violations." *Los Angeles Times,* July 16: http://www.latimes.com/news/local/orange/ la-me-taint16jul16,1,61136.story?coll=la-editions-orange.

Rosoff, Stephen M., Henry N. Pontell, and Robert Tillman. 2010. *Profit Without Honor: White Collar Crime and the Looting of America.* Upper Saddle River, NJ: Prentice Hall.

Ross, Edward A. 1965 (1907). *Sin and Society: An Analysis of Latter-Day Iniquity.* Gloucester, MA: P. Smith.

Ross, Jeffrey Ian. 2003. *The Dynamics of Political Crime.* Newbury Park, CA: Sage Publications.

Roth, Jeffrey A. 1994. *Psychoactive Substances and Violence.* Washingtion, DC: National Institute of Justice, U.S. Department of Justice.

Roth, Michael P. 2011. *Crime and Punishment: A History of the Criminal Justice System.* Belmont, CA: Wadsworth.

Rothe, Dawn L., and David Kauzlarich. 2010. "State Crime Theory and Control." In *Criminology and Public Policy: Putting Theory to Work,* edited by Hugh D. Barlow and Scott H. Decker. Philadelphia: Temple University Press.

Rowan, Edward L. 2006. *Understanding Child Sexual Abuse.* Jackson: University of Mississippi Press.

Rubenstein, Richard E. 1970. *Rebels in Eden: Mass Political Violence in the United States.* Boston: Little, Brown and Company.

———. 1987. *Alchemists of Revolution: Terrorism in the Modern World.* New York: Basic Books.

Rumbaut, Rubén G., and Walter A. Ewing. 2007. *The Myth of Immigrant Criminality and the Paradox of Assimilation: Incarceration Rates Among Native and Foreign-born Men.* Washington, DC: American Immigration Law Foundation.

Rusche, George S., and Otto Kirchheimer. 1939. *Punishment and Social Structure.* New York: Columbia University Press.

Russell, Diana. 1984. *Sexual Exploitation: Rape, Child Sexual Abuse, and Harassment.* Beverly Hills, CA: Sage Publications.

Russell, Katheryn. 2009. *The Color of Crime.* New York: New York University Press.

Sabol, William J., Heather C. West, and Matthew Cooper. 2009. *Prisoners in 2008.* Washington, DC: Bureau of Justice Statistics, U.S. Department of Justice.

Sadovi, Carlos. 2010. "Homes of Two Officers Burglarized: Gun, Badge, Armor Vest Stolen." *WGN News,* May 22: http://www.chicagobreakingnews.com/2010/05/homes-of-two-officers-burglarized-gun-badge-armor-vest-stolen.html.

Safrian, Hans. 2010. *Eichmann's Men.* New York: Cambridge University Press.

Sampson, Robert J. 1995. "The Community." Pp. 193–216 in *Crime,* edited by James Q. Wilson and Joan Petersilia. San Francisco: Institute for Contemporary Studies Press.

———. 2006a. "How Does Community Context Matter? Social Mechanisms and the Explanation of Crime Rates." Pp. 31–60 in *The Explanation of Crime: Context, Mechanisms, and Development,* edited by Per-Olof H. Wikström and Robert J. Sampson. New York: Cambridge Univeristy Press.

———. 2006b. "Open Doors Don't Invite Criminals." *New York Times,* March 11:A15.

———. 2008. "Rethinking Crime and Immigration." *Contexts* 7(2):28–33.

Sampson, Robert J., and Dawn Jeglum Bartusch. 1999. *Attitudes Toward Crime, Police, and the Law: Individual and Neighborhood Differences.* Washington, DC: National Institute of Justice, U.S. Department of Justice.

Sampson, Robert J., and John H. Laub. 1993. *Crime in the Making: Pathways and Turning Points Through Life.* Cambridge, MA: Harvard University Press.

———. 2005. "A General Age-Graded Theory of Crime: Lessons Learned and the Future of Life-Course Criminology." Pp. 165–81 in *Integrated Developmental and Life-Course Theories of Offending,* edited by David P. Farrington. New Brunswick, NJ: Transaction Publishers.

Sampson, Robert J., Jeffrey D. Morenoff, and Stephen W. Raudenbush. 2005. "Social Anatomy of Racial and Ethnic Disparities in Violence." *American Journal of Public Health* 95:224–32.

Sampson, Robert J., and Steve Raudenbush. 2001. *Disorder in Urban Neighborhoods: Does It Lead to Crime?* Washington, DC: National Institute of Justice, U.S. Department of Justice.

Sampson, Robert J., and William Julius Wilson. 1995. "Toward a Theory of Race, Crime, and Urban Inequality." Pp. 37–54 in *Crime and Inequality,* edited by John Hagan and Ruth D. Peterson. Stanford, CA: Stanford University Press.

Sanday, Peggy Reeves. 1981. "The Socio-Cultural Context of Rape: A Cross-Cultural Study." *Journal of Social Issues* 37:5–27.

Sapolsky, Robert M. 1998. *The Trouble with Testosterone: And Other Essays on the Biology of the Human Predicament.* New York: Scribner.

Saunders, Daniel G. 2002. "Are Physical Assaults by Wives and Girlfriends a Major Social Problem? A Review of the Literature." *Violence Against Women* 8:1424–48.

Schafer, Stephen. 1974. *The Political Criminal.* New York: Free Press.

Schmitt, Eric. 2004. "Military Women Reporting Rapes by U.S. Soldiers." *New York Times,* February 25:A1.

Schnebly, Stephen M. 2002. "An Examination of the Impact of Victim, Offender, and Situational Attributes on the Deterrent Effect of Defensive Gun Use: A Research Note." *Justice Quarterly* 19:377–98.

Schneider, Elizabeth M., Cheryl Hanna, Judith G. Greenberg, and Claire Dalton. 2008. *Domestic Violence and the Law: Theory and Practice.* New York: Foundation Press.

Schneider, Keith. 1993. "Nuclear Scientists Irradiated People in Secret Research." *New York Times,* December 17:A1.

Schneider, Linda, and Arnold Silverman. 2010. *Global Sociology: Introducing Five Contemporary Societies.* New York: McGraw-Hill.

Schreck, Christopher J., Melissa W. Burek, Eric A. Stewart, and J. Mitchell Miller. 2007. "Distress and Violent Victimization Among Young Adolescents." *Journal of Research in Crime & Delinquency* 44(4):381–405.

Schreck, Christopher J., and Bonnie S. Fisher. 2004. "Specifying the Influence of the Family and Peers on Violent Victimization: Extending Routine Activities and Lifestyles Theories." *Journal of Interpersonal Violence* 19:1021–41.

Schreck, Christopher J., Jean Marie McGloin, and David S. Kirk. 2009. "On the Origins of the Violent Neighborhood: A Study of the Nature and Predictors of Crime-Type Differentiation Across Chicago Neighborhoods." *JQ: Justice Quarterly* 26(4):771–94.

Schreck, Christopher J., Eric A. Stewart, and Bonnie S. Fisher. 2006. "Self-Control, Victimization, and Their Influence on Risky Lifestyles: A Longitudinal Analysis Using Panel Data." *Journal of Quantitative Criminology* 22:319–40.

Schreck, Christopher J., Richard A. Wright, and J. Mitchell Miller. 2002. "A Study of Individual and Situational Antecedents of Violent Victimization." *Justice Quarterly* 19:159–80.

Schwartz, Jennifer, Darrell J. Steffensmeier, and Ben Feldmeyer. 2009. "Assessing Trends in Women's Violence via Data Triangulation: Arrests, Convictions, Incarcerations, and Victim Reports." *Social Problems* 56(3):494–525.

Schwartz, Martin, Walter S. DeKeseredy, David Tait, and Shahid Alvi. 2001. "Male Peer Support and a Feminist Routine Activities Theory: Understanding Sexual Assault on the College Campus." *Justice Quarterly* 18:623–49.

Schwendinger, Julia R., and Herman Schwendinger. 1983. *Rape and Inequality.* Newbury Park, CA: Sage Publications.

Scott, Donald W. 1989. "Policing Corporate Collusion." *Criminology* 27:559–87.

Scully, Diana. 1995. "Rape Is the Problem." Pp. 197–215 in *The Criminal Justice System and Women: Offenders, Victims, and Workers,* edited by Barbara Raffel Price and Natalie J. Sokoloff. New York: McGraw-Hill.

Seffrin, Patrick M., Peggy C. Giordano, Wendy D. Manning, and Monica A. Longmore. 2009. "The Influence of Dating Relationships on Friendship Networks, Identity Development, and Delinquency." *JQ: Justice Quarterly* 26(2):238–67.

Sellin, Thorsten. 1938. "Culture Conflict and Crime." New York: Social Science Research Council.

Sellin, Thorsten, and Marvin E. Wolfgang. 1964. *The Measurement of Delinquency.* New York: Wiley.

Sennott, Charles M. 1995. "Rights Groups Battle Burning of Women in Pakistan." *Boston Globe,* May 18:1.

Serrano, Richard A. 1998. *One of Ours: Timothy McVeigh and the Oklahoma City Bombing.* New York: Norton.

Shapiro, Joseph. 2010. "Campus Rape Victims: A Struggle for Justice." *National Public Radio,* February 24.

Sharp, Elaine B., and Paul E. Johnson. 2009. "Accounting for Variation in Distrust of Local Police." *JQ: Justice Quarterly* 26(1):157–82.

Sharp, Susan F., Meghan K. McGhee, Trinia L. Hope, and Randall Coyne. 2007. "Predictors of Support of Legislation Banning Juvenile Executions in Oklahoma: An Examination by Race and Sex." *Justice Quarterly* 24:133–55.

Shaw, Clifford R., and Henry D. McKay. 1942. *Juvenile Delinquency and Urban Areas.* Chicago: University of Chicago Press.

Shelden, Randall G. 1982. *Criminal Justice in America: A Sociological Approach.* Boston: Little, Brown.

———. 2008. *Controlling the Dangerous Classes: A Critical Introduction to the History of Criminal Justice.* Boston: Allyn and Bacon.

———. 2010. *Our Punitive Society: Race, Class, Gender and Punishment in America.* Long Grove, IL: Waveland Press.

Sheldon, William. 1949. *Varieties of Delinquent Youth.* New York: Harper and Row.

Sheley, Joseph F., and C. D. Ashkins. 1981. "Crime, Crime News, and Crime Views." *Public Opinion Quarterly* 45:492–506.

Sherman, Lawrence W. 1980. "Causes of Police Behavior: The Current State of Quantitative Research." *Journal of Research in Crime and Delinquency* 17:69–100.

———. 1992. *Policing Domestic Violence: Experiments and Dilemmas.* New York: Free Press.

———. 1993. "Defiance, Deterrence, and Irrelevance: A Theory of the Criminal Sanction." *Journal of Research in Crime and Delinquency* 30(4):445–73.

———. 2011. *Experimental Criminology.* London: Sage.

Sherman, Lawrence W., and Richard A. Berk. 1984. "The Specific Deterrent Effects of Arrest for Domestic Assault." American Sociological Review 49:261–72.

Sherman, Lawrence W., and Ellen G. Cohn. 1989. "The Impact of Research on Legal Policy: The Minneapolis Domestic Violence Experiment." *Law and Society Review* 23:117–44.

Sherman, Lawrence W., Patrick R. Gartin, and Michael E. Buerger. 1989. "Hot Spots of Predatory Crime: Routine Activities and the Criminology of Place." *Criminology* 27:27–55.

Sherman, Lawrence W., Denise C. Gottfredson, Doris L. MacKenzie, John Eck, Peter Reuter, and Shawn D. Bushway. 1998. *Preventing Crime: What Works, What Doesn't, What's Promising.* Washington, DC: Office of Justice Programs, National Institute of Justice.

Sherman, Lawrence W., and Dennis P. Rogan. 1995. "Effects of Gun Seizures on Gun Violence: 'Hot Spots' Patrol in Kansas City." *Justice Quarterly* 12:673–93.

Shermer, Lauren O'Neill, and Brian D. Johnson. 2010. "Criminal Prosecutions: Examining Prosecutorial Discretion and Charge Reductions in U.S. Federal District Courts." *JQ: Justice Quarterly* 27(3):394–430.

Shichor, David. 1985. "Male/Female Differences in Elderly Arrests." *Justice Quarterly* 2:399–414.

Shoemaker, Donald J. 2010. *Theories of Delinquency: An Examination of Explanations of Delinquent Behavior.* New York: Oxford University Press.

Shook, Jeffrey J., and Sara A. Goodkind. 2009. "Racial Disproportionality in Juvenile Justice: The Interaction of Race and Geography in Pretrial Detention for Violent and Serious Offenses." *Race and Social Problems* 1:257–66.

Short, James F. Jr. 2007. "Criminology, Criminologists, and the Sociological Enterprise." Pp. 605–38 in *Sociology in America: A History,* edited by Craig Calhoun. Chicago: University of Chicago Press.

Short, James F. Jr., and F. Ivan Nye. 1957. "Reported Behavior as a Criterion of Deviant Behavior." *Social Problems* 5:207–13.

Shover, Neal. 1973. "The Social Organization of Burglary." *Social Problems* 20:499–514.

———. 1991. "Burglary." Pp. 73–113 in *Crime and Justice: A Review of Research,* edited by Michael Tonry. Chicago: University of Chicago Press.

Shover, Neal, and Heith Copes. 2010. "Decision Making by Persistent Thieves and Crime Control Policy." Pp. 128–49 in *Criminology and Public Policy: Putting Theory to Work,* edited by Hugh D. Barlow and Scott H. Decker. Philadelphia: Temple University Press.

Shover, Neal, Greer Litton Fox, and Michael Mills. 1994. "Long-Term Consequences of Victimization by White-Collar Crime." *Justice Quarterly* 11(1):75–98.

Shover, Neal, and Andrew L. Hochstetler. 2000. "Crimes of Privilege." In *Criminology: A Contemporary Handbook,* edited by Joseph F. Sheley. Belmont, CA: Wadsworth.

Shover, Neal, and Jennifer Scroggins. 2009. "Organizational Crime." Pp. 273–303 in *The Oxford Handbook of Crime and Public Policy,* edited by Michael Tonry. New York: Oxford University Press.

Siegel, Jane A., and Linda M. Williams. 2003. "The Relationship Between Child Sexual Abuse and Female Delinquency and Crime: A Prospective Study." *Journal of Research in Crime and Delinquency* 40:71–94.

Silver, Eric. 2002. "Mental Disorder and Violent Victimization: The Mediating Role of Involvement in Conflicted Relationships." *Criminology* 40:191–212.

Silver, Eric, and Brent Teasdale. 2005. "Mental Disorder and Violence: An Examination of Stressful Life Events and Impaired Social Support." *Social Problems* 52:62–78.

Simon, David R. 2008. *Elite Deviance.* Boston: Allyn and Bacon.

Simon, Rita James. 1975. *Women and Crime.* Lexington, MA: Lexington Books.

Simons, Ronald L., Leslie Gordon Simons, Callie Harbin Burt, Gene H. Brody, and Carolyn Cutrona. 2005. "Collective Efficacy, Authoritative Parenting and Delinquency: A Longitudinal Test of a Model Integrating Community- and Family-Level Processes." *Criminology* 43:989–1029.

Simons, Ronald L., Leslie Gordon Simons, Yi-fu Chen, Gene H. Brody, and Kuei-hsiu Lin. 2007. "Identifying the Psychological Factors That Mediate The Association Between Parenting Practices and Delinquency." *Criminology* 45(3):481–517.

Simonsen, Clifford E., and Jeremy R. Spindlove. 2007. *Terrorism Today: The Past, the Players, the Future.* Upper Saddle River, NJ: Prentice Hall.

Sinclair, Upton. 1990 (1906). *The Jungle.* New York: New American Library.

Singer, Dorothy G., and Tracey A. Revenson. 1997. *A Piaget Primer: How a Child Thinks.* Madison, CT: International Universities Press.

Skogan, Wesley. 1990. *Disorder and Decline: Crime and the Spiral of Decay in American Neighborhoods.* New York: The Free Press.

Skolnick, Jerome H. 1994. *Justice Without Trial: Law Enforcement in Democratic Society.* New York: Macmillan.

Skorneck, Carolyn. 1992. "683,000 Women Raped in 1990, New Government Study Finds." *Boston Globe,* April 24:1.

Smith, Bruce W., Zsuzsanna Z. Papp, Erin M. Tooley, Erica Q. Montague, Amanda E. Robinson, and Cynthia J. Cosper. 2010. "Traumatic Events, Perceived Stress and Health in Women with Fibromyalgia and Healthy Controls." *Stress & Health: Journal of the International Society for the Investigation of Stress* 26(1):83–93.

Smith, Craig S. 2005. "Riots and Violence Spread from Paris to Other Cities." *New York Times,* November 6:3.

———. 2007a. "Hundreds Are Arrested in Post-Election Riots Across France." *New York Times,* May 8:A8.

Smith, M. Dwayne. 2000. "Capital Punishment in America." Pp. 621–43 in *Criminology: A Contemporary Handbook,* edited by Joseph F. Sheley. Belmont, CA: Wadsworth.

Smith, Michael R., Matthew Makarios, and Geoffrey P. Alpert. 2006. "Differential Suspicion: Theory Specification and Gender Effects in the Traffic Stop Context." *Justice Quarterly* 23:271–95.

Smith, R. Jeffrey. 2007b. "FBI Violations May Number 3,000, Official Says." *Washington Post,* March 21:A7.

Snow, David A., and Sarah A. Soule. 2009. *A Primer on Social Movements.* New York: W.W. Norton.

Solis, Carmen, Edwardo L. Portillos, and Rod K. Brunson. 2009. "Latino Youths' Experiences with and Perceptions of Involuntary Police Encounters." *Annals of the American Academy of Political and Social Science* 623:39–51.

Sorensen, Jon, and Donald H. Wallace. 1999. "Prosectuorial Discretion in Seeking Death: An Analysis of Racial Disparity in the Pretial Stages of Case Processing in a Midwestern County." *Justice Quarterly* 16:559–78.

Sorensen, Jonathan R., James W. Marquart, and Deon E. Brock. 1993. "Factors Related to Killings of Felons by Police Officers: A Test of the Community Violence and Conflict Hypotheses." *Justice Quarterly* 10(3):417–40.

Soss, Joe, Laura Langbein, and Alan R. Metelko. 2003. "Why Do White Americans Support the Death Penalty?" *Journal of Politics* 65:397–421.

South Carolina Attorney General's Office. 2005. "Insurance Fraud." http://www.scattorneygeneral.com/public/insurance/AttnyGenFraudBro_comp.pdf.

Spangler, Todd. 2000. "Pa. Gunman Kills 2, Wounds 3 Seriously." *Boston Globe,* March 2:A9.

Spano, Richard, Joshua D. Freilich, and John Bolland. 2008. "Gang Membership, Gun Carrying, and Employment: Applying Routine Activities Theory to Explain Violent Victimization Among Inner City, Minority Youth Living in Extreme Poverty." *JQ: Justice Quarterly* 25(2):381–410.

Spelman, William. 2006. "The Limited Importance of Prison Expansion." Pp. 97–129 in *The Crime Drop in America,* edited by Alfred Blumstein and Joel Wallman. New York: Cambridge University Press.

Spock, Benjamin. 1992. *Dr. Spock's Baby and Child Care.* New York: Pocket Books.

Spofford, Tim. 1988. *Lynch Street: The May 1970 Slayings at Jackson State College.* Kent, OH: Kent State University Press.

Spohn, Cassia, John Gruhl, and Susan Welch. 1987. "The Impact of Ethnicity and Gender of Defendants on the Decision to Reject or Dismiss Felony Charges." *Criminology* 25:175–92.

Spohn, Cassia, and David Holleran. 2000. "The Imprisonment Penalty Paid by Young, Unemployed Black and Hispanic Male Offenders." *Criminology* 38:281–306.

———. 2001. "Prosecuting Sexual Assault: A Comparison of Charging Decisions in Sexual Assault Cases Involving Strangers, Acquaintances, and Intimate Partners." *Justice Quarterly* 18:651–88.

Stack, Steven. 1987. "Publicized Executions and Homicide, 1950–1980." *American Sociological Review* 52:532–40.

Stanford, Sally. 1966. *The Lady of the House.* New York: G.P. Putnam.

Stark, Evan. 2004. "Race, Gender, and Woman Battering." Pp. 171–97 in *Violent Crime: Assessing Race and Ethnic Differences,* edited by Darnell F. Hawkins. New York: Cambridge University Press.

Stark, Rodney. 1987. "Deviant Places: A Theory of the Ecology of Crime." *Criminology* 25:893–911.

Steen, Sara, Rodney L. Engen, and Randy R. Gainey. 2005. "Images of Danger and Culpability: Racial Stereotyping, Case Processing, and Criminal Sentencing." *Criminology* 43:435–68.

Steffens, Lincoln. 1904. *The Shame of the Cities.* New York: McClure, Phillips.

Steffensmeier, Darrell, and Emilie Allan. 2000. "Looking for Patterns: Gender, Age, and Crime." Pp. 85–127 in *Criminology: A Contemporary Handbook,* edited by Joseph F. Sheley. Belmont, CA: Wadsworth.

Steffensmeier, Darrell, and Stephen Demuth. 2006. "Does Gender Modify the Effects of Race-Ethnicity on Criminal Sanctioning? Sentences for Male and Female White, Black, and Hispanic Defendants." *Journal of Quantitative Criminology* 22:241–61.

Steffensmeier, Darrell, and Dana Haynie. 2000. "Gender, Structural Disadvantage, and Urban Crime: Do Macrosocial Variables also Explain Female Offending Rates?" *Criminology* 38:403–38.

Steffensmeier, Darrell, Jeffery Ulmer, and John Kramer. 1998. "The Interaction of Race, Gender, and Age in Criminal Sentencing: The Punishment Cost of Being Young, Black, and Male." *Criminology* 36:763–97.

Steffensmeier, Darrell, Hua Zhong, Jeff Ackerman, Jennifer Schwartz, and Suzanne Agha. 2006. "Gender Gap Trends for Violent Crime, 1980 to 2003: A UCR-NCVS Comparison." *Feminist Criminology* 1:72–98.

Steffensmeier, Darrell J. 1986. *The Fence: In the Shadow of Two Worlds.* Totowa, NJ: Rowman & Littlefield.

Steffensmeier, Darrell J., and Jeffery T. Ulmer. 2005. *Confessions of a Dying Thief: Understanding Criminal Careers and Illegal Enterprise.* New York: Transaction Publishers.

Stewart, Eric A. 2007. "Either They Don't Know or They Don't Care: Black Males and Negative Police Experiences." *Criminology & Public Policy* 6:123–30.

Stewart, Eric A., Kirk W. Elifson, and Claire E. Sterk. 2004. "Integrating the General Theory of Crime into an Explanation of Violent Victimization Among Female Offenders." *Justice Quarterly* 21:159–81.

Stewart, Eric A., Christopher J. Schreck, and Ronald L. Simons. 2006. "'I Ain't Gonna Let No One Disrespect Me': Does the Code of the Street Reduce or Increase Violent Victimization Among African American Adolescents?" *Journal of Research in Crime and Delinquency* 43:427–58.

Stewart, Eric A., and Ronald L. Simons. 2006. "Structure and Culture in African American Adolescent Violence: A Partial Test of the 'Code of the Street' Thesis." *Justice Quarterly* 23:1–33.

Stewart, Eric A., Ronald L. Simons, Rand D. Conger, and Laura V. Scaramella. 2002. "Beyond the Interactional Relationship Between Delinquency and Parenting Practices: The Contribution of Legal Sanctions." *Journal of Research in Crime and Delinquency* 39:36–59.

Stiles, Beverly L., Xiaoru Liu, and Howard B. Kaplan. 2000. "Relative Deprivation and Deviant Adaptations: The Mediating Effects of Negative Self-Feelings." *Journal of Research in Crime and Delinquency* 37:64–90.

Stimson, Gerry V., and Pat O'Hare. 2010. "Harm Reduction: Moving Through the Third Decade." *International Journal of Drug Policy* 21:91–93.

Stinchcomb, Jeanne B. 2010. "Drug Courts: Conceptual Foundation, Empirical Findings, and Policy Implications." *Drugs: Education, Prevention & Policy* 17(2):148–67.

Stolzenberg, Lisa, and Stewart J. D'Alessio. 2008. "Co-Offending and the Age-Crime Curve." *Journal of Research in Crime & Delinquency* 45(1):65–86.

Stone, Isidor F. 1989. *The Trial of Socrates.* New York: Anchor Books.

Straus, Murray A. 1980. "Victims and Aggressors in Marital Violence." *American Behavioral Scientist* 23:681–704.

———. 1993. "Physical Assaults by Wives: A Major Social Problem." Pp. 67–87 in *Current Controversies on Family Violence,* edited by Richard J. Gelles and Donileen R. Loseke. Newbury Park, CA: Sage Publications.

———. 2006. "Future Research on Gender Symmetry in Physical Assaults on Partners." *Violence Against Women* 12:1086–97.

Straus, Murray A., and Richard J. Gelles. 1986. "Societal Change and Change in Family Violence from 1975 to 1985 as Revealed by Two National Surveys." *Journal of Marriage and the Family* 48:465–79.

Strom, Kevin J., and John M. MacDonald. 2007. "The Influence of Social and Economic Disadvantage on Racial Patterns in Youth Homicide over Time." *Homicide Studies* 11:50–69.

Stucky, Thomas D., and John R. Ottensmann. 2009. "Land Use and Violent Crime." *Criminology* 47(4):1223–64.

Substance Abuse and Mental Health Services Administration. 2009. *Results from the 2008 National Survey on Drug Use and Health: National Findings.* Rockville, MD: Substance Abuse and Mental Health Services Administration, U.S. Department of Health and Human Services.

Sudnow, David. 1965. "Normal Crimes: Sociological Features of the Penal Code in a Public Defender's Office." *Social Problems* 12:255–76.

Surette, Ray. 2011. *Media, Crime, and Criminal Justice: Images, Realities, and Policies.* Belmont, CA: Wadsworth Publishing Co.

Sutherland, Edwin. 1940. "White-Collar Criminality." *American Sociological Review* 5:1–12.

Sutherland, Edwin H. 1937. *The Professional Thief.* Chicago: University of Chicago Press.

———. 1939. *Principles of Criminology.* Philadelphia: Lippincott.

———. 1947. *Principles of Criminology.* Philadelphia: J.P. Lippincott.

———. 1949. *White Collar Crime.* New York: Holt, Rinehart, and Winston.

Suttles, Gerald. 1968. *The Social Order of the Slum.* Chicago: University of Chicago Press.

Sutton, John R. 2004. "The Political Economy of Imprisonment in Affluent Western Democracies, 1960–1990." *American Sociological Review* 69:170–89.

Sweeten, Gary. 2006. "Who Will Graduate? Disruption of High School Education by Arrest and Court Involvement." *Justice Quarterly* 23:462–80.

Sweeten, Gary, Shawn D. Bushway, and Raymond Paternoster. 2009. "Does Dropping Out of School Mean Dropping into Delinquency?" *Criminology* 47(1):47–91.

Swigonski, Mary E., Robin S. Mama, and Kelly Ward. 2001. *From Hate Crimes to Human Rights: A Tribute to Matthew Shepard.* New York: Harrington Park Press.

Sykes, Gresham M., and David Matza. 1957. "Techniques of Neutralization: A Theory of Delinquency." *American Sociological Review* 22:664–70.

Takagi, Paul. 1974. "A Garrison State in a 'Democratic Society,'" *Crime and Social Justice* 1:27–33.

Tannenbaum, Frank. 1938. *Crime and the Community.* Boston: Ginn.

Tarbell, Ida M. 1904. *The History of the Standard Oil Company.* New York: McClure, Phillips.

Taylor, Ian, Paul Walton, and Jock Young. 1973. *The New Criminology: For a Social Theory of Deviance.* London: Routledge and Kegan Paul.

Taylor, Terrance J., David Holleran, and Volkan Topalli. 2009. "Racial Bias in Case Processing: Does Victim Race Affect Police Clearance of Violent Crime Incidents?" *Justice Quarterly* 26(3):562–91.

Teague, Rosie, Paul Mazerolle, Margot Legosz, and Jennifer Sanderson. 2008. "Linking Childhood Exposure to Physical Abuse and Adult Offending: Examining Mediating Factors and Gendered Relationships." *JQ: Justice Quarterly* 25(2):313–48.

Teasdale, Brent, and Eric Silver. 2009. "Neighborhoods and Self-Control: Toward an Expanded View of Socialization." *Social Problems* 56(1):205–22.

Teehan, Sean. 2010. "In Growing Numbers, the Bereaved Again Walk for Peace." *Boston Globe,* May 11:A1.

Terrill, William, Eugene A. Paoline III, and Peter K. Manning. 2003. "Police Culture and Coercion." *Criminology* 41:1003–34.

The Sentencing Project. 2010. *Felony Disenfranchisement Laws in the United States.* Washington, DC: The Sentencing Project.

Thomas, Charles W., and Donna M. Bishop. 1984. "The Effect of Formal and Informal Sanctions on Delinquency: A Longitudinal Comparison of Labeling and Deterrence Theories." *Journal of Criminal Law and Criminology* 75:1222–45.

Thomas, Charles W., Robin J. Cage, and Samuel C. Foster. 1976. "Public Opinion on Criminal Law and Legal Sanctions: An Examination of Two Conceptual Models." *Journal of Criminal Law and Criminology* 67:110–16.

Thomas, Gordon. 1989. *Journey into Madness: The True Story of Secret CIA Mind Control and Medical Abuse.* New York: Bantam Books.

Thomas, Ken. 2010. "89 Deaths May Be Linked to Toyota Recalls." *Boston Globe,* May 26:B11.

Thomas, William I., and Dorothy Swaine Thomas. 1928. *The Child in America: Behavior Problems and Programs.* New York: Knopf.

Thomas, William I., and Florian Znaniecki. 1927. *The Polish Peasant in Europe and America.* New York: Knopf.

Thompson, Melissa, and Milena Petrovic. 2009. "Gendered Transitions: Within-Person Changes in Employment, Family, and Illicit Drug Use." *Journal of Research in Crime and Delinquency* 46(3):377–408.

Thompson, Steve. 2010. "Dallas Police Department." *Dallas Morning News,* April 27: http://www.dallasnews.com/sharedcontent/dws/news/localnews/stories/DN-crimes tats_27met.ART.State.Edition2.3e2bd3.html.

Thoreau, Henry D. 1969. "Civil Disboedience." Pp. 27–48 in *Civil Disobedience: Theory and Practice,* edited by Hugo Adam Bedau. New York: Pegasus.

Thornberry, Terence P. 1987. "Toward an Interactional Theory of Delinquency." *Criminology* 25:863–91.

———. 1989. "Reflections on the Advantages and Disadvantages of Theoretical Integration." Pp. 51–60 in *Theoretical Integration in the Study of Crime and Deviance: Problems and Prospects,* edited by Steven F. Messner, Marvin D. Krohn, and Allen E. Liska. Albany: State University of New York Press.

———. 2009. "The Apple Doesn't Fall Far from the Tree (or Does It?): Intergenerational Patterns of Antisocial Behavior—The American Society of Criminology 2008 Sutherland Address." *Criminology* 47(2):297–325.

Thornberry, Terence P., and Marvin D. Krohn. 2005. "Applying Interactional Theory to the Explanation of Continuity and Change in Antisocial Behavior." Pp. 183–209 in *Integrated Developmental and Life-Course Theories of Offending,* edited by David P. Farrington. New Brunswick, NJ: Transaction Publishers.

Thornberry, Terence P., Alan J. Lizotte, Marvin D. Krohn, Margaret Farnworth, and Sung Joon Jang. 1994. "Delinquent Peers, Beliefs, and Delinquent Behavior: A Longitudinal Test of Interactional Theory." *Criminology* 32(1):47–83.

Thornhill, Randy, and Craig T. Palmer. 2000. *A Natural History of Rape: Biological Bases of Sexual Coercion*. Cambridge, MA: MIT Press.

Tieger, Todd. 1981. "Self-Rated Likelihood of Raping and Social Perception of Rape." *Journal of Research in Personality* 15:147–58.

Tillman, Robert, and Henry N. Pontell. 1992. "Is Justice 'Collar-Blind'?: Punishing Medicaid Provider Fraud." *Criminology* 30(4):547–73.

Tilly, Charles. 1989. "Collective Violence in European Perspective." Pp. 62–100 in *Violence in America: Protest, Rebellion, Reform*, edited by Ted Robert Gurr. Newbury Park, CA: Sage Publications.

Tittle, Charles R. 1969. "Crime Rates and Legal Sanctions." *Social Problems* 16:409–23.

———. 2004. "Refining Control Balance Theory." *Theoretical Criminology* 8:395–428.

Tittle, Charles R., Lisa M. Broidy, and Marc G. Gertz. 2008. "Strain, Crime, and Contingencies." *JQ: Justice Quarterly* 25(2):283–312.

Tittle, Charles R., Wayne J. Villemez, and Douglas A. Smith. 1978. "The Myth of Social Class and Criminality: An Empirical Assessment of the Empirical Evidence." *American Sociological Review* 43:643–56.

Tjaden, Patricia, and Nancy Thoennes. 1998. *Prevalence, Incidence, and Consequences of Violence Against Women: Findings from the National Violence Against Women Survey*. Washington, DC: U.S. Department of Justice.

———. 2000. *Full Report of the Prevalence, Incidence, and Consequences of Violence Against Women*. Washington, DC: National Institute of Justice and the Centers for Disease Control and Prevention.

Toby, Jackson. 1980. "The New Criminology Is the Old Baloney." Pp. 124–32 in *Radical Criminology: The Coming Crises*, edited by James A. Inciardi. Beverly Hills, CA: Sage Publications.

Tolnay, Stewart E., and E. M. Beck. 1995. *A Festival of Violence: An Analysis of Southern Lynchings, 1882–1930*. Urbana: University of Illinois Press.

Tomaskovic-Devey, Donald, and Patricia Warren. 2009. "Explaining and Eliminating Racial Profiling." *Contexts* 8(2):34–39.

Tonry, Michael. 1994. *Malign Neglect: Race, Crime, and Punishment in America*. New York: Oxford University Press.

———. 2004. *Thinking About Crime: Sense and Sensibility in American Penal Culture*. New York: Oxford University Press.

———. 2008. "Learning from the Limitations of Deterrence Research." *Crime and Justice: A Review of Research* 37:279–311.

———. 2009a. "Crime and Public Policy." Pp. 3–21 in *The Oxford Handbook of Crime and Public Policy*, edited by Michael Tonry. New York: Oxford University Press.

———. 2009b. "The Mostly Unintended Effects of Mandatory Penalties: Two Centuries of Consistent Findings." *Crime and Justice: A Review of Research* 38:65–114.

Tonry, Michael, and Matthew Melewski. 2008. "The Malign Effects of Drug and Crime Control Policies on Black Americans." *Crime and Justice: A Review of Research* 37:1–44.

Topalli, Volkan. 2005. "When Being Good Is Bad: An Expansion of Neutralization Theory." *Criminology* 43:797–835.

Topalli, Volkan, Richard Wright, and Robert Fornango. 2002. "Drug Dealers, Robbery and Retaliation: Vulnerability, Deterrence and the Contagion of Violence." *British Journal of Criminology* 42:337–51.

Travis, Cheryl B. (ed.). 2003. *Evolution, Gender, and Rape*. Cambridge, MA: MIT Press.

Travis, Jeremy, and Christy Visher (eds.). 2005. *Prisoner Reentry and Crime in America*. New York: Cambridge University Press.

Travis, Jordan. 2010. "Worried Neighbors Speak Out About Shootings." *Muskegon News,* April 8: http://www.mlive.com/news/muskegon/index.ssf/2010/04/worried_neighbors_speak_out_ab.html.

Tunnell, Kenneth D. 1990. "Choosing Crime: Close Your Eyes and Take Your Chances." *Justice Quarterly* 7:673–90.

———. 1996. "Let's Do It: Deciding to Commit a Crime." Pp. 246–58 in *New Perspectives in Criminology,* edited by John E. Conklin. Boston: Allyn and Bacon.

———. 2006. *Living Off Crime.* Lanham, MD: Rowman & Littlefield.

Turk, Austin T. 1969. *Criminality and Legal Order.* Chicago: Rand McNally.

———. 1991. "Seductions of Criminology: Katz on Magical Meanness and Other Distractions." *Law and Social Inquiry* 16:181–94.

———. 1993. "Back on Track: Asking and Answering the Right Questions." *Law & Society Review* 27(2):355–59.

Tynan, Trudy. 2002. "Medical Improvements Lower Homicide Rate." *Washington Post,* August 12:A2.

Tzouliadis, Tim. 2008. *The Forsaken: An American Tragedy in Stalin's Russia.* New York: Penguin Press.

U.S. News & World Report. 1982. "Corporate Crime: The Untold Story." 1982 *U.S. News & World Report,* September 6:25.

Ueno, H. 1994. "Police in Japan." In *Police Practices: An International Review,* edited by D.K. Das. Metuchen, NJ: Scarecrow Press.

Unnever, James D. 2008. "Two Worlds Far Apart: Black-White Differences in Beliefs About Why African-American Men Are Disproportionately Imprisoned." *Criminology* 46(2):511–38.

Unnever, James D., Mark Colvin, and Francis T. Cullen. 2004. "Crime and Coercion: A Test of Core Theoretical Propositions." *Journal of Research in Crime and Delinquency* 41:244–68.

Unnever, James D., and Francis T. Cullen. 2006. "Christian Fundamentalism and Support for Capital Punishment." *Journal of Research in Crime and Delinquency* 43:169–97.

———. 2010. "The Social Sources of Americans' Punitiveness: A Test of Three Competing Models." *Criminology* 48:99–129.

Unnever, James D., Francis T. Cullen, and Bonnie S. Fisher. 2007. "'A Liberal Is Someone Who Has Not Been Mugged': Criminal Victimization and Political Beliefs." *JQ: Justice Quarterly* 24(2):309–34.

Unnever, James D., Francis T. Cullen, and Cheryl L. Jonson. 2008. "Race, Racism, and Support for Capital Punishment." Pp. 45–96 in *Crime and Justice: A Review of Research,* edited by Michael Tonry. Chicago: University of Chicago Press.

Unnever, James D., Francis T. Cullen, Scott A. Mathers, Timothy E. McClure, and Marisa C. Allison. 2009. "Racial Discrimination and Hirschi's Criminological Classic: A Chapter in the Sociology of Knowledge." *JQ: Justice Quarterly* 26(3):377–409.

Urbina, Ian. 2010. "BP Used Riskier Method to Seal Well Before Blast." *New York Times,* May 27:A1.

Urbina, Ian, and Michael Cooper. 2010. "Deaths at West Virginia Mine Raise Issues About Safety." *New York Times,* April 7:A1.

U.S. Census Bureau. 2010. *Statistical Abstract of the United States: 2010.* http://www.census.gov/compendia/statab/. Washington, DC: U.S. Government Printing Office.

U.S. Department of the Treasury. 2009. "Update on Reducing the Federal Tax Gap and Improving Voluntary Compliance U.S." Washington, DC: Author

Vaden, Ted. 2007. "Tricky Issue: Naming Sex Case Accusers." *News & Observer* (Raleigh, NC), January 28:A25.

Valdez, Avelardo, and Stephen J. Sifaneck. 2004. "'Getting High and Getting By': Dimensions of Drug Selling Behaviors Among American Mexican Gang Members in South Texas." *Journal of Research in Crime and Delinquency* 41:82–105.

van Dijk, Jan. 2008. *The World of Crime: Breaking the Silence on Problems of Security, Justice and Development Across the World.* Thousand Oaks, CA: Sage Publications.

van Dijk, Jan, John van Kesteren, and Paul Smit. 2008. *Criminal Victimisation in International Perspective: Key Findings from the 2004–2005 ICVS and EU ICS.* Devon, England: Willan Publishing.

Van Wormer, Katherine Stuart, and Clemens F. Bartollas. 2011. *Women and the Criminal Justice System.* Upper Saddle River, NJ: Prentice Hall.

Vaughn, Jason. 2010. "Police Identify One of Two Shooting Victims Killed Tuesday Evening in KCMO." *WDAF-TV,* April 7: http://www.fox4kc.com/wdaf-story-kcmo-shootings-fatal-040610,0,4226549.story.

Vazsonyi, Alexander T., and Rudi Klanjšek. 2008. "A Test of Self-Control Theory Across Different Socioeconomic Strata." *JQ: Justice Quarterly* 25(1):101–31.

Vélez, María B. 2006. "Toward an Understanding of the Lower Rates of Homicide in Latino Versus Black Neighborhoods: A Look at Chicago." Pp. 91–107 in *The Many Colors of Crime: Inequalities of Race, Ethnicity, and Crime in America,* edited by Ruth D. Peterson, Lauren J. Krivo, and John Hagan. New York: New York University Press.

Vieraitis, Lynne M., Sarah Britto, and Tomislav V. Kovandzic. 2007. "The Impact of Women's Status and Gender Inequality on Female Homicide Victimization Rates: Evidence from U.S. Counties." *Feminist Criminology* 2:57–73.

Visher, Christy A. 1983. "Gender, Police Arrest Decisions, and Notions of Chivalry." *Criminology* 21:5–28.

———. 2000. "Career Offenders and Crime Control." Pp. 601–19 in *Criminology: A Contemporary Handbook,* edited by Joseph F. Sheley. Belmont, CA: Wadsworth.

Visher, Christy A., Adele Harrell, Lisa Newmark, and Jennifer Yahner. 2008. "Reducing Intimate Partner Violence: An Evaluation of a Comprehensive Justice System-Community Collaboration." *Criminology & Public Policy* 7(4):495–523.

Vogel, Brenda L., and James W. Meeker. 2001. "Perceptions of Crime Seriousness in Eight African-American Communities: The Influence of Individual, Environmental, and Crime-Based Factors." *Justice Quarterly* 18:301–21.

Vold, George. 1958. *Theoretical Criminology.* New York: Oxford University Press.

Volz, Matt. 2010. "Legalized Medical Marijuana Faces Backlash in Several States." *Bangor Daily News,* May 22–23:A1.

Wadsworth, Tim. 2010. "Is Immigration Responsible for the Crime Drop? An Assessment of the Influence of Immigration on Changes in Violent Crime Between 1990 and 2000." *Social Science Quarterly* 91:531–53.

Wagner, John. 2004. "Ehrlich Advocates Drug Treatment over Jail." *Washington Post,* July 21:B3.

Walberg, Matt, and Carlos Sadovi. 2009. "2 Inmates Convicted of '88 Slayings to Go Free." *WGN News,* July 7: http://www.chicagobreakingnews.com/2009/07/2-inmates-convicted-of-88-slayings-to-go-free-burge-kitchen-reeves.html.

Walberg, Matthew. 2009. "Burge Linked Cases: 2 Men Freed for Five 1988 Murders as Prosecutors Find Insufficient Evidence for Retrial." *Chicago Tribune,* July 8: http://articles.chicagotribune.com/2009-07-08/news/0907080057_1_prosecutors-find-insufficient-evidence-jon-burge-freed.

Walker, Lenore E. 1984. *The Battered Woman Syndrome.* New York: Springer Publishers.

Walker, Lenore E., and Angela Browne. 1985. "Gender and Victimization by Intimates." *Journal of Personality* 53:179–95.

Walker, Samuel. 1998. *Popular Justice: A History of American Criminal Justice.* New York: Oxford University Press.

——. 2011. *Sense and Nonsense About Crime, Drugs, and Communities: A Policy Guide.* Belmont, CA: Wadsworth Publishing Company.

Walker, Samuel, Cassia Spohn, and Miriam DeLone. 2007. *The Color of Justice: Race, Ethnicity, and Crime in America.* Belmont, CA: Wadsworth Publishing Company.

Wallace, John M. Jr., Ryoko Yamaguchi, Jerald G. Bachman, Patrick M. O'Malley, John E. Schulenberg, and Lloyd D. Johnston. 2007. "Religiosity and Adolescent Substance Use: The Role of Individual and Contextual Influences." *Social Problems* 54:308–27.

Wallman, Joel. 1999. "Serotonin and Impulsive Aggression: Not So Fast." *HFG Review* 3(Spring):21–24.

Walsh, Anthony, and Kevin M. Beaver (eds.). 2009. *Biosocial Criminology: New Directions in Theory and Research.* New York: Routledge.

Walsh, Jeffrey A., and Ralph B. Taylor. 2007. "Predicting Decade-Long Changes in Community Motor Vehicle Theft Rates: Impacts of Structure and Surround." *Journal of Research in Crime and Delinquency* 44:64–90.

Ward, Dick. 1995. "Vietnam: The Criminal Justice Challenge of Moving Toward a Market Economy." *CJ International* 11(3) (May–June).

Warner, Barbara D. 2003. "The Role of Attenuated Culture in Social Disorganization Theory." *Criminology* 41:73–97.

——. 2007. "Directly Intervene or Call the Authorities? A Study of Forms of Neighborhood Social Control Within a Social Disorganization Framework." *Criminology* 45:99–129.

Warner, Barbara D., and Brandi Wilson Coomer. 2003. "Neighborhood Drug Arrest Rates: Are They a Meaningful Indicator of Drug Activity? A Research Note." *Journal of Research in Crime and Delinquency* 40:123–38.

Warner, Barbara D., and Glenn L. Pierce. 1993. "Reexamining Social Disorganization Theory Using Calls to the Police as a Measure of Crime." *Criminology* 31(4):493–517.

Warr, Mark. 1993. "Age, Peers, and Delinquency." *Criminology* 31(1):17–40.

——. 2000. "Public Perceptions of and Reactions to Crime." Pp. 13–31 in *Criminology: A Contemporary Handbook,* edited by Joseph F. Sheley. Belmont, CA: Wadsworth Publishing Company.

——. 2002. *Companions in Crime: The Social Aspects of Criminal Conduct.* New York: Cambridge University Press.

——. 2009. "Safe at Home." *Contexts* 8(3):46–51.

Warren, Jennifer. 2009. *One in 31: The Long Reach of American Corrections.* Washington, DC: Pew Center on the States.

Washington, Harriet A. 2006. *Medical Apartheid: The Dark History of Medical Experimentation on Black Americans from Colonial Times to the Present.* New York: Doubleday.

Wauchope, Barbara, and Murray A. Straus. 1990. "Physical Punishment and Physical Abuse of American Children: Incidence Rates by Age, Gender, and Occupational Class." Pp. 133–48 in *Physical Violence in American Families: Risk Factors and Adapatations to Violence in 8,145 Families,* edited by Murray A. Straus and Richard J. Gelles. New Brunswick, NJ: Transaction Books.

Wax, Emily. 2003. "Thousands in Congo Suffer Scars of Violent Wartime Rapes." *Boston Globe,* November 3:A8.

Webber, Craig. 2007. "Reevaluating Relative Deprivation Theory." *Theoretical Criminology* 11:97–120.

Websdale, Neil, and Meda Chesney-Lind. 2004. "Doing Violence to Women: Research Synthesis on the Victimization of Women." Pp. 303–22 in *The Criminal Justice*

System and Women: Offenders, Prisoners, Victims, and Workers, edited by Barbara Raffel Price and Natalie J. Sokoloff. New York: McGraw-Hill.

Weidner, Robert R., and William Terrill. 2005. "A Test of Turk's Theory of Norm Resistance Using Observational Data on Police-Suspect Encounters." *Journal of Research in Crime and Delinquency* 42:84–109.

Weiner, Neil Alan, Margaret A. Zahn, and Rita J. Sagi. 1990. "Introduction: What Is Violence?" Pp. xi–xvii in *Violence: Patterns, Causes, Public Policy,* edited by Neil Alan Weiner, Margaret A. Zahn, and Rita J. Sagi. San Diego, CA: Harcourt Brace Jovanovich.

Weisburd, David, Shawn Bushway, Cynthia Lum, and Sue-Ming Yang. 2004. "Trajectories of Crime at Places: A Longitudinal Study of Street Segments in the City of Seattle." *Criminology* 42:283–321.

Weisburd, David, Cody W. Telep, Joshua C. Hinkle, and John E. Eck. 2010. "Is Problem-Oriented Policing Effective in Reducing Crime and Disorder? Findings from a Campbell Systematic Review." *Criminology & Public Policy* 9(1):139–72.

Weisburd, David, Laura A. Wyckoff, Justin Ready, John E. Eck, Joshua C. Hinkle, and Frank Gajewski. 2006. "Does Crime Just Move Around the Corner? A Controlled Study of Spatial Displacement and Diffusion of Crime Control Benefits." *Criminology* 44:549–91.

Weiss, Mike. 1984. *Double Play: The San Francisco City Hall Killings.* Reading, MA: Addison-Wesley Publishing Co.

Weitzer, Ronald, Steven A. Tuch, and Wesley G. Skogan. 2008. "Police-Community Relations in a Majority-Black City." *Journal of Research in Crime and Delinquency* 45(4):398–428.

Welles, Chris. 1989. "America's Gambling Fever." *Business Week,* April 24: 112–17.

Wellford, Charles F., John V. Pepper, and Carol V. Petrie (eds.). 2004. *Firearms and Violence: A Critical Review.* Washington, DC: National Academies Press.

Wells, William. 2002. "The Nature and Circumstances of Defensive Gun Use: A Content Analysis of Interpersonal Conflict Situations Involving Criminal Offenders." *Justice Quarterly* 19:127–57.

Wells-Barnett, Ida B. 2002. "Southern Horrors: Lynch Law in All Its Phases." Pp. 23–38 in *African American Classics in Criminology & Criminal Justice,* edited by Shaun L. Gabbidon, Helen Taylor Greene, and Vernetta D. Young. Thousand Oaks, CA: Sage Publications.

Welsh, Brandon C., and David P. Farrington (eds.). 2007a. *Preventing Crime: What Works for Children, Offenders, Victims and Places.* New York: Springer.

———. 2007b. "Save Children from a Life of Crime." *Criminology & Public Policy* 6(4):871–79.

———. 2009. "Public Area CCTV and Crime Prevention: An Updated Systematic Review and Meta-Analysis." *JQ: Justice Quarterly* 26(4):716–45.

Wenzel, Suzanne L., Barbara D. Leake, and Lillian Gelberg. 2001. "Risk Factors for Major Violence Among Homeless Women." *Journal of Interpersonal Violence* 16:739–52.

West, Candace, and Don H. Zimmerman. 1987. "Doing Gender." *Gender and Society* 1:125–51.

Westermann, Ted D., and James W. Burfeind. 1991. *Crime and Justice in Two Societies: Japan and the United States.* Pacific Grove, CA: Brooks/Cole Publishing Company.

Western, Bruce. 2006. *Punishment and Inequality in America.* New York: Russell Sage Foundation Publications.

Western, Bruce, and Christopher Wildeman. 2009. "The Black Family and Mass Incarceration." *Annals of the American Academy of Political and Social Science* 621:221–42.

Westley, William A. 1970. *Violence and the Police.* Cambridge, MA: MIT Press.

White, Ben. 2003. "ImClone's Waksal Gets Maximum Jail Sentence." *Washington Post,* June 11:A1.

White, Jacquelyn W., and John A. Humphrey. 1995. "Young People's Attitudes Toward Acquaintance Rape." Pp. 161–68 in *Readings in Deviant Behavior,* edited by Alex Theo and Thomas Calhoun. New York: HarperCollins.

Whyte, William Foote. 1943. *Street Corner Society: The Social Structure of an Italian Slum.* Chicago: University of Chicago Press.

Widom, Cathy S., and Michael G. Maxfield. 2001. *An Update on the "Cycle of Violence."* Washington, DC: National Institute of Justice, U.S. Department of Justice.

Widom, Cathy Spatz, and Hans Toch. 1993. "The Contribution of Psychology to Criminal Justice Education." *Journal of Criminal Justice Education* 4(2):251–72.

Wiesner, Margit, Hyoun K. Kim, and Deborah M. Capaldi. 2010. "History of Juvenile Arrests and Vocational Career Outcomes for At-Risk Young Men." *Journal of Research in Crime and Delinquency* 47(1):91–117.

Wikström, Per-Olof H., and Rolf Loeber. 2000. "Do Disadvantaged Neighborhoods Cause Well-Adjusted Children to Become Adolescent Delinquents? A Study of Male Juvenile Serious Offending, Individual Risk and Protective Factors, and Neighborhood Context." *Criminology* 38:1109–42.

Wilgoren, Jodi. 2003. "Governor Assails System's Errors as He Empties Illinois Death Row." *New York Times,* January 12:A1.

Wilkinson, Deanna L., Chauncey C. Beaty, and Regina M. Lurry. 2009. "Youth Violence Crime or Self-Help? Marginalized Urban Males' Perspectives on the Limited Efficacy of the Criminal Justice System to Stop Youth Violence." *Annals of the American Academy of Political and Social Science* 623:25–38.

Williams, Marian R., Stephen Demuth, and Jefferson E. Holcomb. 2007. "Understanding the Influence of Victim Gender in Death Penalty Cases: The Importance of Victim Race, Sex-Related Victimization, and Jury Decision Making." *Criminology* 45(4):865–91.

Williams, Scott. 1994. "ABC Special Takes the Scare Out of Life." *Boston Globe,* April 20:72.

Wilson, James Q. 1995. "Crime and Public Policy." Pp. 489–507 in *Crime,* edited by James Q. Wilson and Joan Petersilia. San Francisco: Institute for Contemporary Studies Press.

———. 2009. "Looking for Crime's Smoking Gun." *Los Angeles Times,* January 8:A17.

Wilson, James Q., and George L. Kelling. 1982. "Broken Windows: The Police and Neighborhood Safety." *Atlantic Monthly,* March: 29–38.

Wilson, Mark. 2010. "Kentucky Mine Where Two Died Had Roof Support Problems." *Evansville Courier & Press,* April 30: http://www.courierpress.com/news/2010/apr/30/two-killed-in-roof-collapse-many-violations-to/.

Winkler, Cathy. 2002. *One Night: Realities of Rape.* Walnut Creek, CA: AltaMira Press.

Wisotsky, Steven. 1995. "A Society of Suspects: The War on Drugs and Civil Liberties." Pp. 129–34 in *Drugs, Society, and Behavior,* edited by Erich Goode. Guilford, CT: Dushkin Publishing Group.

Wittebrood, Karin, and Paul Nieuwbeerta. 2000. "Criminal Victimization During One's Life Course: The Effects of Previous Victimization and Patterns of Routine Activities." *Journal of Research in Crime and Delinquency* 37:91–122.

Wolfgang, Marvin E. 1958. *Patterns in Criminal Homicide.* Philadelphia: University of Pennsylvania Press.

Wolfgang, Marvin E., and Franco Ferracuti. 1967. *The Subculture of Violence.* London: Social Science Paperbacks.

Wolfgang, Marvin E., Robert M. Figlio, Paul E. Tracy, and Simon I. Singer. 1985. *The National Survey of Crime Severity.* Washington, DC: U.S. Department of Justice.

Wood, Daniel B. 2008. "California Pays Rising Price for Prison Growth." *Christian Science Monitor,* April 22: http://www.csmonitor.com/2008/0422/p03s03-usju.html.

Wooldredge, John. 2007. "Neighborhood Effects on Felony Sentencing." *Journal of Research on Crime and Delinquency* 44:238–63.

Worrall, John L., and Tomislav V. Kovandzic. 2007. "COPS Grants and Crime Revisited." *Criminology* 45:159–90.

Wright, Bradley R. Entner, and C. Wesley Younts. 2009. "Reconsidering the Relationship Between Race and Crime: Positive and Negative Predictors of Crime Among African American Youth." *Journal of Research in Crime and Delinquency* 46(3):327–52.

Wright, John P., Kevin M. Beaver, Matt DeLisi, Michael G. Vaughn, Danielle Boisvert, and Jamie Vaske. 2008. "Lombroso's Legacy: The Miseducation of Criminologists." *Journal of Criminal Justice Education* 19(3):325–38.

Wright, John Paul, and Kevin M. Beaver. 2005. "Do Parents Matter in Creating Self-Control in Their Children? A Genetically Informed Test of Gottfredson and Hirschi's Theory of Low Self-Control." *Criminology* 43:1169–202.

Wright, John Paul, David E. Carter, and Francis T. Cullen. 2005. "A Life-Course Analysis of Military Service in Vietnam." *Journal of Research in Crime and Delinquency* 42:55–83.

Wright, John Paul, Stephen G. Tibbetts, and Leah E. Daigle. 2008. *Criminals in the Making: Criminality Across the Life Course.* Thousand Oaks, CA: Sage Publications.

Wright, Kevin N. 1985. *The Great American Crime Myth.* Westport, CT: Greenwood Press.

Wright, Richard, Robert H. Logie, and Scott H. Decker. 1995. "Criminal Expertise and Offender Decision Making: An Experimental Study of the Target Selection Process in Residential Burglary." *Journal of Research in Crime and Delinquency* 32:39–53.

Wright, Richard T., and Scott Decker. 1994. *Burglars on the Job: Streetlife and Residential Break-ins.* Boston: Northeastern University Press.

Wright, Richard T., and Scott H. Decker. 1998. *Armed Robbers in Action: Stickups and Street Culture.* Boston: Northeastern University Press.

Wu, Yuning, Ivan Y. Sun, and Ruth A. Triplett. 2009. "Race, Class or Neighborhood Context: Which Matters More in Measuring Satisfaction with Police?" *JQ: Justice Quarterly* 26(1):125–56.

Xie, Min, and David McDowall. 2008a. "The Effects of Residential Turnover on Household Victimization." *Criminology* 46(3):539–75.

———. 2008b. "Escaping Crime: The Effects of Direct and Indirect Victimization on Moving." *Criminology* 46(4):809–40.

Xu, Yili, Mora L. Fiedler, and Karl H. Flaming. 2005. "Discovering the Impact of Community Policing: The Broken Windows Thesis, Collective Efficacy, and Citizens' Judgment." *Journal of Research in Crime and Delinquency* 42:147–86.

Yanda, Steve, Jenna Johnson, and Daniel de Vise. 2010. "Mourners Gather for Funeral of U-Va. Student Yeardley Love." *Washington Post,* May 8: http://www.washingtonpost.com/wp-dyn/content/article/2010/05/08/AR2010050802136.html?hpid=topnews.

Yang, Sue-Ming. 2010. "Assessing the Spatial-Temporal Relationship Between Disorder and Violence." *Journal of Quantitative Criminology* 26:139–63.

Young, Cathy. 2006a. "Family Violence Strikes Men, Too." *Boston Globe,* January 9: http://www.boston.com/news/globe/editorial_opinion/oped/articles/2006/01/09/family_violence_strikes_men_too/.

Young, Jock. 1986. "The Failure of Criminology: The Need for a Radical Realism." Pp. 4–30 in *Confronting Crime,* edited by Roger Matthews and Jock Young. Beverly Hills, CA: Sage Publications.

Young, Saundra. 2010. "E. Coli Cases Down in 2009, CDC Says." CNN, April 15: http://www.cnn.com/2010/HEALTH/04/15/foodborne.illness.cdc/index.html.

Young, Vernetta. 2006b. "Demythologizing the 'Criminalblackman': The Carnival Mirror." Pp. 54–66 in *The Many Colors of Crime; Inequalities of Race, Ethnicity, and Crime in America,* edited by Ruth D. Peterson, Lauren J. Krivo, and John Hagan. New York: New York University Press.

Zahn, Margaret A., and Angela Browne. 2009. "Gender Differences in Neighborhood Effects and Delinquency." Pp. 164–81 in *The Delinquent Girl,* edited by Margaret A. Zahn. Philadelphia: Temple University Press.

Zalman, Marvin, Brad Smith, and Angie Kiger. 2008. "Officials' Estimates of the Incidence of 'Actual Innocence' Convictions." *JQ: Justice Quarterly* 25(1):72–100.

Zatz, Marjorie S., and Nancy Rodriguez. 2006. "Conceptualizing Race and Ethnicity in Studies of Crime and Criminal Justice." pp. 39–53 in *The Many Colors of Crime: Inequalities of Race, Ethnicity, and Crime in America,* edited by Ruth D. Peterson, Lauren J. Krivo, and John Hagan. New York: New York University Press.

Zilney, Lisa Anne. 2011. *Drugs: Policy, Social Costs, Crime, and Justice.* Upper Saddle River, NJ: Prentice Hall.

Zimbardo, Philip G. 1972. "Pathology of Imprisonment." *Society* 9:4–8.

Zimring, Franklin E. 2006. *The Great American Crime Decline.* New York: Oxford University Press.

Zimring, Franklin E., and Gordon Hawkins. 1997. *Crime Is Not the Problem: Lethal Violence in America.* New York: Oxford University Press.

Name Index

Schaum, R.J., 96
Schiraldi, V., 30, 33
Schmitt, E., 274
Schnebly, S.M., 262
Schneider, E.M., 14
Schneider, K., 355
Schoepfer, A., 319, 337
Schreck, C.J., 98, 129, 178, 249
Schultz, G., 381
Schwartz, J., 69
Schwartz, M., 276
Schwendinger, H., 227
Schwendinger, J.R., 227
Scott, D.W., 337
Scroggins, J., 320
Scully, D., 276, 278
Sealock, M.D., 180, 229
Seefelt, J., 31
Seffrin, P.M., 190
Seidman, R., 225
Sellers, C.S., 127, 129, 145, 152, 164, 201, 206, 216, 217, 225, 226, 231
Sellin, T., 40, 213, 221
Sennott, C.M., 269
Serpico, F., 409
Serrano, R.A., 360
Seth, M., 445
Shapiro, J., 54
Sharp, E.B., 43
Sharp, S., 42
Shaw, C.R., 162–167, 174, 188
Shelden, R.G., 33, 318, 402, 433
Sheldon, R.G., 304
Sheldon, W., 134, 137
Sheley, J.F., 31
Shepard, M., 257
Sherman, L.W., 17, 96, 218, 286, 287, 288, 306, 413, 417, 418
Shermer, L., 435
Sherrill, C., 34
Shichor, D., 416
Shierholz, H., 458
Shoemaker, D.J., 163, 189, 193
Shook, J.J., 437
Short, J. F., 4, 6, 7, 8, 58
Shover, N., 106, 121, 124, 127, 297, 298, 299, 305, 306, 320, 334
Shutt, J.E., 190
Siegel, J.A., 104
Sifaneck, S.J., 18
Sigler, J.L., 113
Silver, E., 154, 202, 206
Simmons, R., 146
Simon, D.R., 325, 327
Simon, R.J., 68
Simons, R.L., 154, 206, 247, 249
Simonsen, C.E., 366
Simpson, E.E., 436
Simpson, J., 231
Simpson, N.B., 276, 281
Simpson, O.J., 28, 276, 281, 433, 446
Simpson, S.S., 213, 335
Sinclair, U., 319, 331
Singer, D.G., 150
Skogan, W., 459
Skolnick, J.H., 400, 403, 407
Skorneck, C., 273
Sloan, J.J., 440
Slocum, L.A., 59
Smit, P., 64, 87
Smit, P.R., 441
Smith, B., 281, 448
Smith, B.E., 287

Smith, C.S., 173
Smith, D.A., 74
Smith, E., 282
Smith, E.L., 405, 414
Smith, M.D., 446, 447
Smith, M.R., 414, 417
Snell, T.L., 67
Snipes, J.B., 116, 118, 135, 138, 149, 154, 170, 175, 177, 189, 191
Snow, D.A., 364
Snyder, H.N., 437
Sobol, J.J., 410
Socrates, 359
Solis, C., 43
Sommers, I.B., 249
Sorensen, J., 436, 446
Sorensen, J.R., 408
Soss, J., 42
Soule, S.A., 364
Spangler, T., 256
Spano, R., 96
Spelman, W., 442
Spindlove, J.R., 366
Spock, B., 461
Spofford, T., 352
Spohn, C., 71, 106, 214, 232, 411, 412, 413, 422, 431, 435, 436, 437, 439
Spohn, C.C., 435
Srinivasan, M., 269
Stack, S., 445
Stafford, M.L., 253
Stanford, L., 318
Stark, E., 277, 459
Stark, R., 74, 162, 167, 168
Steadman, H.J., 243
Steen, S., 436
Steffens, L., 319, 323, 357
Steffensmeier, D., 69, 75, 76, 232, 249, 298, 302, 437, 439
Steffensmeier, D.J., 18, 416
Sterk, C.E., 98
Stevenson, K.A., 418, 421
Stewart, E.A., 98, 165, 200, 247, 249, 412
Stewart, M., 323
Stiles, B.L., 167
Stimson, G.V., 384
Stinchcomb, J.B., 387
Stolzenberg, L., 55, 420
Stone, I.F., 362
Stouthamer-Loeber, M., 71, 151, 231
Stowell, J.I., 19, 252
Straus, M.A., 259, 273, 279, 283
Strom, K.J., 166
Stucky, T.D., 168
Subotnik, L.S., 279
Sudnow, D., 429
Sun, I.Y., 42
Surette, R., 27, 30, 32, 260
Sutherland, E., 8–9, 187–190, 296, 319, 320, 335, 343
Suttles, G., 164
Sutton, J.R., 431
Sweeney, B., 282
Sweeten, G.A., 76, 202, 204, 216
Swezey, C., 111
Swigonski, M.E., 257
Sykes, G.M., 187, 194, 195

T

Takagi, P., 408
Tannenbaum, F., 215
Tarbell, I.M., 319

Taylor, B., 287
Taylor, R.B., 302
Taylor, T., 217
Taylor, T.J., 55
Teague, R., 198
Teasdale, B., 154, 202, 206, 378
Teehan, S., 159
Terrill, W., 17, 406
Teske, R.H.C., 444
Testa, M., 103
Tewksbury, 306
Therly, P., 269
Thoennes, N., 271, 273, 283, 284
Thomas, C.W., 41, 216
Thomas, D.S., 39
Thomas, G., 355
Thomas, K., 329
Thomas, S.A., 165
Thomas, W.I., 39, 163
Thompson, M., 204
Thompson, S., 49
Thoreau, H.D., 362
Thornberry, T.P., 18, 153, 187, 204, 205, 207
Thornhill, R., 140
Tibbets, S.G., 145, 203
Tieger, T., 276
Tillman, R., 27, 75, 106, 318, 320, 321, 322, 326, 331, 332, 336, 337, 434
Tilly, C., 359
Tittle, C.R., 74, 125, 172, 187, 202, 223
Tjaden, P., 271, 273, 283, 284
Toby, J., 225
Toch, H., 186
Tolnay, S.E., 432
Tolstoy, L., 362
Tomaskovic-Devey, D., 414
Tomasovic, E., 243
Tonry, M., 122, 125, 305, 306, 413, 437, 439, 457, 463, 465
Topalli, V., 55, 95
Tory, M., 439
Travis, C.B., 140
Travis, J., 23, 462
Tremblay, P., 190
Trescott, J., 423
Triplett, R.A., 42
Truman, 85, 89, 90, 91, 245, 252, 268, 272
Tuch, S.A., 43
Tunnell, K.D., 121, 298
Turk, A.T., 165, 213, 221, 303
Turner, M.G., 100, 276, 284, 285
Turner, N., 360
Tweed, W.M., 357
Tynan, T., 245
Tzouliadis, T., 351

U

Ueno, H., 411
Uggen, C., 432
Ulmer, J., 232
Ulmer, J.T., 18, 38, 302
Unnever, J.D., 41, 42, 72, 203
Urbina, I., 317, 332

V

Vaden, T., 32
Valdez, A., 18
Valenzuela, A., 73
Vandello, J., 31
Vanderbilt, C., 318
van Dijk, J., 61, 64, 87

Subject Index

Photo Credits

CHAPTER 17

p. 426: PhotoEdit Inc.
p. 428: PhotoEdit Inc.
p. 429: AP Wide World Photos
p. 433: Culver Pictures, Inc.
p. 434: AP Wide World Photos
p. 436: PhotoEdit Inc.
p. 437: CORBIS- NY
p. 438: PhotoEdit Inc.
p. 444: Bob Daemmrich/PhotoEdit

CHAPTER 18

p. 452: Courtesy: NYPD Photo Unit
p. 455: PhotoEdit Inc.
p. 458: PhotoEdit Inc.
p. 459: Omni-Photo
    Communications, Inc.
p. 460: PhotoEdit Inc.
p. 461: AP Wide World Photos
p. 463: Getty Images, Inc.
    Getty News